Handbook of Contemporary Urban Life

An Examination of Urbanization,
Social Organization,
and Metropolitan Politics

David Street
and Associates

Handbook of Contemporary Urban Life

Jossey-Bass   Publishers
San Francisco • Washington • London • 1978

HANDBOOK OF CONTEMPORARY URBAN LIFE
An Examination of Urbanization, Social Organization, and Metropolitan Politics
        by David Street and Associates

Copyright © 1978 by: Jossey-Bass, Inc., Publishers
                      433 California Street
                      San Francisco, California 94104
                              &
                      Jossey-Bass Limited
                      28 Banner Street
                      London EC1Y 8QE

Library of Congress Catalogue Card Number LC 78-1155

International Standard Book Number ISBN 0-87589-372-4

Manufactured in the United States of America

JACKET DESIGN BY WILLI BAUM

FIRST EDITION

Code 7813

*The Jossey-Bass Social
and Behavioral Science Series*

Preface

Handbook of Contemporary Urban Life provides a series of interrelated critical formulations of our current knowledge of life in a highly urbanized America. It seeks to understand and explain how Americans and their social order have been affected by and have adapted to the pervasive processes of urbanization in the twentieth century. Processes that concern us in this volume range broadly from massive shifts of population and resources within and between metropolitan areas to alterations in family and sex roles and political behavior as influenced by urban change.

    Urban does not equal *city* or *problems*, although these terms are among the important objects of analysis for several contributors. Nor is it to be assumed that, because society has become highly urbanized, the study of urban life is therefore equivalent to the study of society as a whole. Instead, the contributors to the *Handbook* generally seek to analyze changes and continuities in those aspects of social organization and patterns of living that are directly affected by processes of urbanization and that continue to vary by location even in the highly urbanized society. We are concerned with both the specific forms that processes of urbanization take and the limits, the cultural lags, and the adaptations to urbanization. In particular, we seek to explore the tensions that exist between modernism and traditionalism, between the mass society and the persistence of local ties, and between center and periphery—and the outcomes of these tensions, such as the character and quality of life and the capacity of local and other subnational units for governance.

The principal motive for compiling this book is to reassert the importance and to specify the character of linkages between such theoretical interests as those just mentioned and the wealth of empirical findings on urban life that have continued to accumulate. We are now past a decade in which "urban studies" frequently became a shorthand for the troubles of race and poverty and in which the sheer amount of research far outweighed the degree of discipline in its pursuit. The substance and aspirations of urban sociology once again require concerted and coherent attention to survive the recurrent tendencies to define this field as whatever about cities is presently frightening, topical, or esoteric. Another important motive for compiling the volume is the judgment that the nation is presently reaching the limits of some of the important processes of urbanization, thus making a systematic stock-taking especially propitious.

The handbook format provides a worthy vehicle for pursuing these tasks; it allows the publication of chapters that are highly sophisticated, both theoretically and empirically, that are intellectually critical, and that are appropriately provocative. Our intended audience consists of professionals, both in sociology and related disciplines, as well as graduate students and advanced undergraduates with interests in urban matters.

The materials in the *Handbook* are organized into five parts. The first deals with ecological and other theoretical approaches to understanding urbanization and social organization. The second considers change and persistence in local and traditional ties, including those to family, sex roles, race, ethnicity, and religion. The third part presents chapters analyzing social control in urban society through the criminal justice system, education, the welfare system, and the impersonal controls of the "built" or physical environment. The fourth part, on communications and politics, looks at television, print media, politics in city and suburb, social planning and metropolitan sprawl, and the situation and prospects of cities in the "urban heartland" of the nation. The final part places the concept of urbanization in a broader perspective, first by an explicit analysis of changes in rural life and second by an historical and comparative essay on urbanization in Western nations. In the concluding chapter I partially synthesize research to date and look ahead to the potentials for the further study of urban life.

Several of the *Handbook's* authors made suggestions that helped to shape the character of the volume as a whole. These included Steven T. Bossert, Jeffrey L. Davidson, Paul M. Hirsch, Morris Janowitz, and Gerald D. Suttles. Debbee Rebolloso of the Department of Sociology, University of Illinois at Chicago Circle, has been invaluable in her assistance.

Chicago, Illinois   David Street
March 1978

Contents

Contents

The Authors

David Street is professor of sociology and head of the Department of Sociology at the University of Illinois at Chicago Circle. Prior to 1976 he served on the faculties of the University of Chicago, the State University of New York at Stony Brook, and the University of Michigan. He earned his B.S. degree (1957) in education at Northern Illinois University and his M.A. and Ph.D. degrees (1958, 1962) in sociology at the University of Michigan. As a graduate student he was awarded fellowships by the Ford Foundation (1957-58) and the National Institute of Mental Health (1960-61).

Street is the author of numerous articles concerned with race relations, juvenile corrections, and welfare; his books include *Poverty and Social Change* (with K. A. Grønbjerg and G. D. Suttles, in press), *Race and Education in the City: Findings on Chicago* (1969), *Innovation in Mass Education* (Ed., 1969), and *Organization for Treatment* (with R. D. Vinter and C. Perrow, 1966). He was coeditor of the series *Process and*

Change in American Society (1970-1973) and editor of *Series on Studies of Urban Society* (1968-1971). An active member of the American Sociological Association, Street has also served as president of the Illinois Sociological Association (1969-1970). Presently he is completing a monograph on public assistance with George Martin and Laura Gordon.

Street and his wife Jane, an administrator and editor, live in Chicago; they have one son, a student at Northern Illinois University.

Steven T. Bossert is assistant professor of sociology at the University of Michigan and was on leave during 1977 to serve as an Associate of the National Institute of Education. He is currently working on publications derived from his 1975 Ph.D. dissertation from the University of Chicago, "Tasks and Social Relationships in Classrooms." His research interests include school and classroom organization and socialization outcomes, organizational change, and qualitative methods in evaluation research.

Harvey M. Choldin is associate professor of sociology at the University of Illinois at Urbana-Champaign, where he is also affiliated with the Center for Asian Studies. He is the author of publications on such topics as density and crowding, kinship and migration, and economic development and fertility. Currently he is studying households and family life in the urban environment and the development of an "urban information system" to make community statistics available to citizens and students.

Jeffrey L. Davidson is assistant professor of sociology at the University of Delaware. He is presently rewriting his 1977 Ph.D. dissertation from the University of Michigan, "The Social Construction of Political Communities," as a research monograph. His research interests include community organization (especially the relations between human service organizations and communities), urban political behavior, neighborhood differentiation, and suburban social organization.

Theodore N. Ferdinand is professor of sociology at Northern Illinois University. He is the author of *Typologies of Delinquency* (1966) and *Juvenile Delinquency: Big*

Brother Grows Up (1977). He is presently continuing a
series of historical studies of police or courts in Boston,
Salem, New Haven, and Rockford (Illinois), together
with an analysis of effects of a juvenile correctional
institution upon adjustment during and after incarcera-
tion.

Mark D. Gottdiener is assistant professor of sociology at Brooklyn College of the City University of New York. He is the
author of *Planned Sprawl: Private and Public Interests in
Suburbia* (1977) and is presently pursuing research on the
impact of fiscal change on central city communities, regional metropolitan growth and its social planning implications, and the sociology of fashion and its relationship
to urban culture.

Shirley Harkess is associate professor of sociology at the University of Kansas. Her publications include *Women and
Their Work* (with A. Stromberg, eds., 1977) and articles
on migration, class, women's roles, elites, and politics in
Colombia; she is continuing her writing on women's roles
in Colombia and is developing a general formulation on
sex roles.

Amos H. Hawley is Kenan Professor Emeritus in the Department of Sociology at the University of North Carolina,
Chapel Hill. His publications include *Human Society*
(1950), *The Changing Shape of Metropolitan America*
(1955), *The Metropolitan Community: Its People and
Government* (with B. Zimmer, 1970), and *Urban Society:
An Ecological Approach* (1971). He is currently
(1977-1978) president of the American Sociological
Association.

Paul M. Hirsch is a sociologist and assistant professor in the
Graduate School of Business at the University of Chicago.
He is principal editor of *Strategies for Communication
Research: The 1977-78 Sage Annual Review of Communication Research* and has published widely in journals
and magazines. In 1975 he received a Rockefeller Foundation Humanities Fellowship, and he served as a consul-
tant to the Social Science Research Council's Committee
on Television and Social Behavior in 1976 and 1977.

Albert Hunter is associate professor of sociology at the Center
for Urban Affairs at Northwestern University. He is the
author of *Symbolic Communities* (1974) and of articles
on neighborhood change and the ecological structure and
change of cities. His current research concerns national
federations of community organizations and crime in urban communities.

Morris Janowitz is Distinguished Service Professor of Sociology
and the College at the University of Chicago. His publications include *Public Administration and the Public*
(1958), *The Community Press in an Urban Setting* (rev.
ed., 1967), *Institution Building and Urban Education*
(1969), and *Political Conflict: Essays in Political Sociology* (1970). He has just completed a book on the macrosociology of America (in press).

Harry M. Johnson is professor of sociology at the University of
Illinois at Urbana-Champaign. He is the author of *Sociology: A Systematic Introduction* (1960) and has contributed to several edited collections and to numerous journals. Currently he is editor of *Sociological Inquiry*, the
quarterly journal of Alpha Kappa Delta, the national sociology honor society. His interests include sociological
theory, ethnic-group relations, and religion.

John D. Kasarda is associate professor of sociology at the University of North Carolina, Chapel Hill. He is the coauthor
of *Contemporary Urban Ecology* (with B. J. L. Berry,
1977) and has written articles dealing with ecology, fertility, community attachment, and research methodology.
He is also continuing collaborative work with Charles Bidwell on the organization of school districts and student
achievement.

William Kornblum is associate professor of sociology at the
Graduate School of the City University of New York. He
is the author of *Blue Collar Community* (1974). Since
1974, Kornblum has been working on a study of the ecology and politics of beaches and barrier islands. He is also
conducting research and planning studies for the National
Park Service.

Sidney Kronus is associate professor of sociology at the University of Illinois at Urbana-Champaign. His publications include *The Black Middle Class* (1971), *Discrimination Without Violence: Miscegenation and Racial Conflict in Latin America* (with M. Solaun, 1973), and a series of articles on modernization, race, ethnicity, and housing in Latin America. He is currently working on an updated analysis of the black middle class in the United States.

Diana Pearce is assistant professor of sociology at the University of Illinois at Chicago Circle. She is presently developing publications from her 1976 Ph.D. dissertation from the University of Michigan, "Black, White, and Many Shades of Gray: Real Estate Brokers and Their Racial Practices." Her research interests include housing segregation, school segregation, race and poverty, and women and poverty.

Robert O. Richards is associate professor in the Department of Sociology and Anthropology at Iowa State University. He has published articles on regional transportation, race relations, and citizen participation. He is interested in urban sociology, conflict and accommodation, minority groups, and the sociology of knowledge.

Bryan R. Roberts is reader in sociology at the University of Manchester, England. He has conducted important research on urbanization in Latin America, and his books include *Organizing Strangers: Poor Families in Guatemala City* (1973). Recently he has been directing a comparative study of urbanization in Manchester and in Barcelona, Spain.

W. Paul Street is a retired professor of education at the University of Kentucky, having earlier taught English and journalism at what is now Northern Illinois University and directed the centennial celebration of the National Education Association. While in Kentucky he was director of the Bureau of School Services, which completed a series of school surveys and an evaluation of the impact of community-action programs. He presently lives in DeKalb, Illinois.

Gerald D. Suttles is professor of sociology at the University of
Chicago. His publications include *The Social Order of the
Slum* (1968), *The Social Construction of Communities*
(1972), and *Poverty and Social Change* (forthcoming,
with K. A. Grønbjerg and D. Street). His work has been
recognized with a C. Wright Mills Award and a Laing
Award. Presently he is studying the effects of urban fragmentation on political participation.

Terry Williams is a Ph.D. candidate in sociology at the Graduate School of the City University of New York. He is
especially interested in the leisure cultures of central-city
communities and has conducted research for numerous
agencies, including the National Park Service and the
Black Theater Alliance.

Handbook of Contemporary Urban Life

*An Examination of Urbanization,
Social Organization,
and Metropolitan Politics*

Part One

Urbanization and
Social Organization

*Urbanization in twentieth-century America has involved changes
that deeply alter social organization. Each of the chapters in
this section deals with these changes. Amos H. Hawley's Chapter One, "Urbanization as Process," distinguishes and analyzes
three phases of urbanization, a city-building phase, a metropolitan phase, and a diffuse phase involving substantial dispersion.
John D. Kasarda's Chapter Two, "Urbanization, Community,
and the Metropolitan Problem," focuses on both centrifugal and
centripetal trends in metropolitan areas, which have increasingly
mismatched residence and employment, produced strains on resources, and diminished the capacity of central cities to serve as
true centers of their metropolitan areas.*

    *The social changes that Hawley and Kasarda discuss are
within the purview of the traditional ecological approach. In
Chapter Three, "Life-Style, Leisure, and Community Life,"
William Kornblum and Terry Williams seek to broaden that per-*

1

spective substantively by analyzing changes in leisure life-styles and proposing that these have come to have a major influence on the physical and social characteristics of both metropolitan regions and city neighborhoods. Chapter Four, "Changing Social Order of the Metropolitan Area" by Morris Janowitz and David Street, seeks to combine an ecological approach with a concern for social integration and politics. While seeing patterns of metropolitan change as producing a critical disarticulation of community of residence and community of work, the authors assert that these changes do not destroy the local community and indeed suggest that the result may be a strengthening of community organization.

1

Urbanization as Process

Amos H. Hawley

The term *urbanization* is used in this chapter to refer to the growing organization of specialists who manufacture goods and provide services that are exchanged for products of surrounding regions. Such an organization depends on the transportation and communication facilities at its disposal. It takes form at an intersection of routes and lives on the traffic that travels over those routes. Viewed internally it is a communication system, a relatively dense network of interactions among producing organizations, administrative and service agencies, and leisure time arrangements. Thus the techniques for movement over space are of vital importance. By the same token, changes in those techniques are the most critical of all urbanization processes, because they enable all other growth processes to operate. Our examination of urbanization processes will be based on these assumptions. But first a further word about growth is necessary.

An organization cannot grow without increasing the need for communication and exchanges. For if the growing organization is to retain its coherence, there must be specialization of

3

functions and centralization of administration. And these, obviously enough, imply pathways for exchanges of information, materials, and products. Movement of any kind over the pathways requires time and energy, the so-called frictions of space (Haig, 1926). Without technological advancement, the possibilities of organizational growth are soon exhausted, for the costs of sustaining necessary flows among an enlarging mass of interdependent units become prohibitively high. There is, in effect, an asymptotic property inherent in any organizational technology. In contrast, improvements in the techniques for movement reduce the friction and thus relax the restraints on growth. Preexisting activities may be further subdivided and allocated to separate units while formerly external activities may be incorporated into the growing system. The interplay between changes in organization and in the instruments for interaction is cumulative. A change in one raises the probability of a change in the other (see Hawley, 1971, and Kasarda, 1974). The growth process might be expected to continue as long as new technical advancements occur or until extrinsic limits are encountered.

An important circumstance attending urbanization is that it is often unfolding from not one but several places. Thus, the growth trend in any one organization is eventually affected by the growth trend in others. Eventually the several processes, if carried far enough, will converge and coalesce, thereby creating a single, overarching urban organization. But, with or without multiple points of unfolding, urbanization tends to approach a limit fixed by the boundaries of the area over which society exercises control or by the efficiency of the technology for movement. The upper limit encountered is determined by both the population involved and the territory encompassed. As a result, urbanization processes may differ as growth approaches its limit.

It follows from the theoretical position adopted here that an appropriate way of subdividing a long-term growth trend is in terms of periods in the progress of transportation and communication technology. The modern history of the conquest of distance may be regarded as consisting of three major stages. The first, which lasted from the 1830s to the first quarter of the twentieth century, was an era of steam-powered transportation. It was responsible for the city-building phase of urbanization. A second stage began around 1920 and has not yet faded from view; it is marked by petroleum and electrically powered methods of bridging distances. During this period the expanded, or metropolitan, phase of urbanization developed. A third stage, which started early in the present century, became more noticeable after 1950 and is still in its formative period. In this stage transportation is guided by electronic instrumentation and may be powered by atomic reactions, hydrogen fuels, and other unconventional energy sources. These innovations are leading to a phase of diffuse urbanization. Our attention here will be occupied mainly with the metropolitan phase. But the city-building phase must be understood because it laid down a set of conditions with which subsequent urbanization has had to contend. About the phase of diffuse urbanization we shall have relatively little to say, since it belongs to the future rather than to the present.

The City-Building Phase

Transportation and Communication Technology. This phase was characterized by the rise of long-distance, bulk-haul carriers and the steam-powered ship and railway. Developed initially for coastal and river use, the steam-powered ship appeared on the high seas in the 1840s and within three decades had virtually replaced the sailing vessel. In the meantime, the steam railway, having begun as a feeder to deep-water ports, was spreading a web of rail lines overland. By the end of the third quarter of the nineteenth century, railway route systems were nearing completion. Countless improvements were made in trains and steam-powered ships throughout the nineteenth century. One of special note, however, was the telegraph. Initially introduced for traffic-control purposes, the telegraph was employed later in general communication, though its use was confined primarily to long-distance exchanges. The telegraph inaugurated a subtle revolution in humankind's relation to space, by separating communication from transportation for the first time. Thus, news and information could move independently of people and materials.

The nineteenth-century advances in transportation and communication technology accelerated the industrial revolution in America. Ideas were transported across oceans and inland regions and mingled with local experiences to create new inventions and improve earlier ones. Productivity increased rapidly, first in manufacturing and then in agriculture. New resources were discovered in distant locations and linked to production centers. A continent-wide domestic market for agricultural as well as industrial products developed. Institutions were able to extend their influence across regions, because the telegraph had added a new dimension to the centralization of administration. Ultimately a pattern of urban settlements developed, comprised of major entrepôt cities at port locations, manufacturing and market centers at interregional transportation nodes, and local distributing and shipping points at intraregional sites (Duncan and Lieberson, 1970).

Population Redistribution. The general trend in population redistribution in the United States is shown in Table 1. In

Table 1. United States Population, by Area of Residence, 1790-1970.

Census Year	Number (in thousands)				Percentage			
	Total	Rural Farm	Rural Non-farm	Urban	Total	Rural Farm	Rural Non-farm	Urban
1970[a]	203,212	9,712	44,679	148,821	100.0	4.8	22.0	73.2
1960	178,464	15,635	50,297	112,532	100.0	8.7	28.3	63.0
1950	150,697	23,048	39,900	89,749	100.0	15.3	25.1	59.6
1940	131,669	30,547	26,698	74,424	100.0	23.2	20.3	56.5
1930	122,775	30,529	23,291	68,955	100.0	24.9	18.9	56.2
1920	105,710	31,974	19,578	54,158	100.0	30.1	18.7	51.2
1910[b]	91,972	49,973		41,999	100.0	54.4		45.6
1900	75,995	45,835		30,160	100.0	60.3		39.7
1880	50,155	36,026		14,129	100.0	71.8		28.2
1860	31,443	25,227		6,216	100.0	80.2		19.8
1840	17,069	15,224		1,845	100.0	89.2		10.8
1820	9,638	8,945		693	100.0	92.8		7.2
1800	5,308	4,986		322	100.0	93.9		6.1
1790	3,929	3,729		202	100.0	94.9		5.1

[a]A new definition of *urban,* introduced in 1950, eliminated the incorporation requirement. Urban data for both old and new definitions were published for 1950 and 1960, then for the new definition only in 1970. The large increase in the 1970 urban figures is due to the inclusion of many places formerly defined as rural nonfarm. The figures given for 1950 and 1960 are for the old definition.

[b]The Census Bureau did not distinguish rural farm from rural nonfarm populations before 1920.

Source: U.S. Bureau of the Census. *Number of Inhabitants.* U.S. Summary, 1970. Table 7.

that table urban population is defined, for every year but 1970, as the residents of incorporated places of 2,500 or more people. It will be observed that by 1920 urban population had increased from about one twentieth to over one half of the total. From 1830 to 1870 was a period of particularly rapid urban growth; the increase averaged 4 percent per year, almost twice the rate of growth of the rural population. During the next fifty years the average annual rate of urban growth subsided to 3 percent, but that was still three times the growth rate of the rural population.

Through the nineteenth century, the growth of urban areas derived mainly from foreign immigration and natural increase; part of this growth was also supplied from the farm population by rural to urban migration. As Table 2 shows, prior

Table 2. Farm Output in the United States, 1890-1963.

Year	Output	Output per Working Hour	Output per Unit Input	Working Hours
1963	303	659	188	46
1960	285	559	178	51
1950	236	291	147	81
1940	190	173	125	110
1930	170	146	111	116
1920	150	125	104	120
1910	138	118	107	117
1900	130	118	112	110
1890	100	100	100	100

Note: 1890 = 100.

Source: National Commission on Technology, Automation, and Economic Progress, 1966, pp. 142-143.

to 1920, increases in farm output exceeded increases in farm output per working hour; thus agriculture was a growing industry. But that opportunities in agriculture were approaching a ceiling is apparent in the last column of Table 2, which shows an end to the growth of working hours devoted to agriculture after 1920. Unfortunately, the farm population was not reported separately in the census until 1920. When these data did appear (see Table 1), they revealed that the farm population reached a plateau by 1920, which tilted slightly downward in the years immediately following.

Through the nineteenth century, large urban places grew at the expense of small cities, a tendency carried over into the first two decades of the twentieth century. While the total number of urban places increased, the number of small places decreased; those that grew into larger-size categories were not replaced by new towns. The patterns are reflected in Table 3. The drift of growth toward larger places is more pronounced in

Table 3. Cumulative Percentage Distributions of Urban Places and Urban Population, by Size of Place, United States, 1840-1960.

Size of Place	1960	1940	1920	1900	1880	1860	1840
	Number of Places						
1,000,000 and over	0.1	0.1	0.1	0.1	0.1	—	—
500,000 and over	0.4	0.4	0.4	0.3	0.4	0.5	—
250,000 and over	1.0	1.1	0.9	0.8	0.8	0.7	0.7
100,000 and over	2.6	2.8	2.5	2.1	2.1	2.2	2.2
50,000 and over	6.7	5.9	5.3	4.6	3.8	4.0	3.7
25,000 and over	15.2	12.0	10.6	9.3	8.6	8.8	9.0
10,000 and over	38.1	31.2	27.7	25.5	23.4	23.6	28.1
5,000 and over	64.5	59.1	54.4	52.5	58.3	58.3	64.8
2,500 and over	100.0	100.0	100.0	100.0	100.0	100.0	100.0
Number of places	4996	3464	2722	1737	939	392	131
	Population						
1,000,000 and over	15.5	21.2	18.7	21.4	8.5	—	—
500,000 and over	25.4	29.9	30.2	26.8	22.1	22.1	—
100,000 and over	34.7	40.3	38.5	35.3	31.3	26.4	17.0
50,000 and over	45.0	50.9	50.6	47.1	43.9	42.4	28.1
25,000 and over	57.4	60.7	60.3	56.2	50.5	49.7	38.1
10,000 and over	70.4	70.7	69.7	65.5	60.9	60.5	50.9
5,000 and over	86.1	84.0	82.7	79.5	76.4	74.7	72.9
2,500 and over	94.4	93.2	91.9	90.1	88.6	90.4	90.7
Population (in thousands)	100.0	100.0	100.0	100.0	100.0	100.0	100.0

Source: U.S. Bureau of the Census, 1961, pp. 16-17.

respect to population. In 1840 about 50 percent of the total urban population were in places of less than 10,000 people. In 1920 the proportion in places of that size had declined to about 30 percent, while places of 50,000 or more people held over 50 percent of the urban population. The drift of concentration in later years has been toward urban places of moderate size, that is, from 10,000 to 100,000 people. Of that we shall have more to say in a later section.

The movement toward the cities operated selectively, thereby leaving its imprint on the composition of the populations at both the origins and destinations. Persons eighteen to thirty years of age were disproportionately numerous in the migration streams. So were single people. Thus, cities acquired low dependency ratios, while the places of origin had relatively high ratios. The attraction of youth together with the delayed expansion of educational opportunities into rural areas resulted in the better educated favoring urban destinations. The size of place affected selectivity: The proportion of young adults, well-educated adults, and unmarried adults until recently varied directly with the size of city, while the dependency ratio was inversely related (Duncan and Reiss, 1956, pp. 32-37). These correlations were quite probably due to the tendency for migration to move gradually up the size hierarchy; migrants from farms moved to small cities, small cities lost migrants to medium-sized cities, and medium-sized cities lost population to large cities (Taeuber, 1965). The principal exceptions to that pattern of movement have been the recruited migrations, in which people, notably the blacks during World War I, were induced to move long distances from farms to large cities.

There are, of course, significant differences between urban places of different sizes that are due to functional differences associated with size rather than to migration selectivity. Institutional specialization, the proportion of the labor force in administrative employment, the volume of retail sales, the frequency of innovations—these and many other characteristics vary with size of place (Ogburn and Duncan, 1964). More recently, the studies of Fischer (1975) and Willets, Bealer, and Crider (1974) have revealed a persistence of differences in social values among residents of different-sized cities and of rural areas of varying distances from a city. Whether such differences are due to differences traceable to migration selectivity or resulting from peculiar socialization effects in different types of places has not been ascertained.

The Urban Pattern. The centripetal effect of steam power was manifested in the physical pattern of the city. With rail and water transportation, the high cost of terminal facilities and of starting and stopping the heavy carriers prohibited their use for short-distance transportation. Hence, while encouraging regional specialization in agriculture and mining, steam-powered transportation necessarily led manufacturing activities to gravitate to points where raw materials could be deposited easily and with a minimum of reshipment, that is, at transportation nodes where rail and water routes intersected. Furthermore, steam generated in the stationary power plants of industry could not be transported far before it cooled and condensed. Industries and their ancillary services, therefore, clustered closely about terminal facilities (Lampard, 1955).

Reliance on steam power left local transportation in a primitive state, dependent on pedestrian and animal-powered locomotion. Accordingly, population and service agencies huddled closely about employing institutions; thus, industrial, commercial, and residential land uses were intermingled in a seemingly random distribution. A very small proportion of a city's population could afford the time and cost of retreating to exclusively residential areas. For the most part, however, the city's buildings were erected on narrow lots fronting on narrow streets, which were laid out in a grid pattern. The introduction of the electric street railway began to break up the compactness of the nineteenth-century city by allowing wider separation of residential and nonresidential uses of space and greater land use specialization in districts, although the linearity of the street railway routes restricted this influence. The compactness of physical patterns persisted and presented a powerful inertia to all subsequent forces of change (Hawley, 1971, chap. 5).

The circumstances that shaped the compact city supplied the basis for the well-known concentric zonal theory of urban growth and form (Hurd, 1903; Burgess, 1923). This states that the necessarily close juxtaposition of interregional transportation terminal facilities establishes a single point of entry for virtually all new populations and facilities. Accordingly, growth concentrates at that point and spreads outward in an essentially symmetrical fashion as available land is used up. The centrifugal spread is accompanied by a redistribution of activities, with the intensity of land use declining on a gradient with distance from the transportation node. The gradient declines quickly because the time required for and cost of local movements are great; it stops abruptly because locations beyond a sixty-minute walking radius are all but inaccessible. Adaptations of rail transportation to local travel did extend the radius somewhat, but they did not alter the strategic importance of the central point of entry. By marking off class intervals of land-use intensities on a plotted gradient, it is possible to chart a series of concentric zones describing the urban land-use pattern. In doing so, of course, one incurs the risk of implying a greater degree of homogeneity of land use within each zone than is actually the case. Nevertheless, the concentric zone concept proved to be a useful approximation so long as there was a single major point of entry. It cannot, however, be applied when there are several points of entry into urban space, such as occurred in the next transportation stage.

The Metropolitan Phase

Transportation and Communication Technology. The decade of 1910 to 1920 may be regarded as a milestone in the course of urbanization in the United States. In the census of 1920, the proportion of the total population living in urban places passed the 50 percent mark (see Table 1). It thus was made clear that the industrial and service sectors had become dominant in the national economy. Soon afterwards, as will be seen, the relative decline in the agricultural labor force became an absolute decline. That a reorganization in the pattern of local life was taking place was also made unmistakably clear in that decade. For it was then that a new scale of local distance was imposed on the compact city inherited from the nineteenth century. Also, the decade ending in 1920 was the first in which the average growth rate in territory surrounding major cities exceeded the average growth rate within the cities (Hawley, 1956). Furthermore, if adjustments are made for changes in central city boundaries, it appears that deconcentration had begun at least a decade earlier (Kasarda and Redfearn, 1975).

Of central importance to this new era of urbanization was a series of dramatic improvements in short-distance transportation and communication. An adaptation of rail transportation to intracity use, in the form of the electric street railway, was demonstrated feasible in 1887, but not until the decade of 1910 to 1920 was it widely applied. Passenger traffic on street railways peaked in 1929, declined rapidly, and by 1950 had all but disappeared.

The nemesis of the street railway was the motor vehicle. That, too, had been shown to be practicable around the turn of the century, but it was not until there was a reduction in production costs that it could be afforded by substantial numbers of people. Adoption came quickly after 1910. Automobile registration increased fifteenfold between 1910 and 1920 and tripled in the next decade. By 1930 there was nearly one motor vehicle in use per household. So rapid had been the spread of the automobile that hard-surfaced street and road construction lagged far behind. That was felt acutely in the land surrounding the cities, where rural roads were without all-weather surfaces until the late 1920s. Street surfacing underwent a series of technical advances during the 1920s, and all-weather street and road systems extended beyond cities into the countryside. The two decades following 1914 were periods of doubling of the mileage of hard-surfaced roads. As city street networks were linked more directly to rural road systems and to intercity highways, the central business districts of cities were in increasing competition with outlying service locations.

In the meantime, a significant improvement in short-distance communication was taking shape. The telephone, introduced in the 1880s, spread rapidly after 1900 with the reduction of the costs of electric power transmission. But not until after 1920 were more than half of all households equipped with telephones. Yet another improvement in the early part of the century was the extension of sanitary sewer and water pipelines to all incorporated territories of cities and to some outlying localities.

As might be expected, the new technology for short-distance movement spawned innovations in the acquisition of the new products and innovations to facilitate their use. Among the former were retail and service agencies and an expansion of credit, especially for installment buying. The latter included traffic controls, such as laws and police and court procedures, licensing regulations, special insurance arrangements, and planning services. As the application of the new technology became broader, the division of labor grew in complexity, for numerous new manual and nonmanual specializations evolved. Thus the urban social structure received direct as well as indirect elaboration from the new instrumentalities for movement.

Enhanced Mobility. The immediate effect of the improvements in short-distance transportation was to enlarge the space over which interrelated activities could occur without reducing the frequency of interaction. The sixty-minute radius was potentially increased from three or four miles to forty or fifty miles, though the actual distance was approximately half the potential because of the time lost in the traffic congestion that soon developed. Urban residents quickly took advantage of the opportunities to roam widely over urban space. Consumers engaged in comparative shopping in scattered locations, workers sought employment in a much extended labor market, and people chose avocations and associations far beyond their immediate vicinity. The penetration of rural areas by networks of all-weather roads and telephone lines enabled farm people to break out of their relative isolation to enjoy frequent visits to distant points, to travel beyond villages having limited facilities, and to extend their activities to urban centers (Aronson, 1971). As a result, life-style differences between urban and rural populations steadily diminished (Fuguitt, 1963).

It seems entirely probable that the heightened mobility has partially substituted for residence changes. Every year since 1947 the Current Population Survey has obtained information on residence changes in the preceding year in a national sample of households (U.S. Bureau of the Census, 1971a, pp. 7-8). The proportion annually reporting residence changes has remained constant for twenty-eight years at near 19 percent. Meanwhile, the number of automobiles registered has increased from 37.3 million to 103.6 million, or by 177 percent, and the number of households with telephone lines has increased from two of every three households to one in virtually every household. Evidently the lengthening commuting distances and the quickening flow of goods and information of all kinds have held in check the relative frequency of household relocations.

The cultural counterpart of the greater mobility is a standardization of the terms of communication and exchange. Standardization has eliminated differences of language and weights and measures, and has progressively reduced the remaining sectional, ethnic, and socioeconomic peculiarities of idiom, frames of reference, and institutional procedures. Mass production and distribution of clothing, food, reading matter, music, entertainment, and consumer goods of all kinds have obscured superficial distinctions and have minimized inequalities of access. Although to the casual observer the trend might have imposed a sameness over society, it has enormously facilitated movement and communication. And in so doing it has opened wide the range of opportunities for individual expression and the cultivation of special interests.

Elaboration of Structure. The increased ease of local

movement joined with advances in production technology to stimulate further specialization. Diversification spread through manufacturing, retailing, servicing, and governmental institutions, while occupations became increasingly specialized. Every advance in specialization led to a further elaboration of organization. To the costs of the more refined technology were added the costs of maintaining communications in the more complex organizations; ultimately economies had to be sought in the enlargements of the scale of activities.

For much the same reasons, organizations serving personal interests ranging from hobbies to political action had to be developed. Thus, the structure of producing and servicing institutions was overlaid with voluntary groups addressed to every conceivable vocational and avocational interest. These, as with producing organizations, have tended to grow, through federation of local groups, to enable them to maintain communications with the parent system. There would appear to be few aspects of urban collective life not addressed by organizations of some form.

The reorganization resulting from urban transformation is observable in the changing structure of the labor force shown in Table 4. Thus, while the proportion of people in the manual occupations has changed little since 1910, the composition of

Table 4. Percent Distribution of the U.S. Labor Force
by Occupation, 1910-1970.

Occupation	1970	1960	1950	1940	1930	1920	1910
Nonagricultural	97.9	93.9	88.0	82.8	79.0	75.1	69.0
White collar	47.4	41.3	38.1	31.3	29.9	25.6	21.1
Professional	14.5	11.2	7.6	6.5	6.1	5.0	4.4
Proprietors, managers, and officials	8.1	8.4	10.9	7.6	7.5	6.8	6.5
Clerical and sales	24.8	21.7	19.7	17.2	16.3	13.8	10.2
Manual	50.5	52.6	49.9	51.5	49.1	49.5	47.9
Skilled	13.9	13.5	12.8	11.0	12.9	13.5	11.7
Semiskilled	29.2	26.8	37.1[a]	21.0	16.4	16.0	14.7
Unskilled	7.4	12.3		18.8	19.8	20.0	21.5
Agricultural	3.1	6.1	12.0	17.0	21.0	24.9	31.0
Farmers and managers	1.8	3.9	7.9	10.0	12.4	15.5	16.5
Farm laborers	1.3	2.2	4.1	7.1	8.6	9.4	14.5

[a]Includes semiskilled and unskilled.

Sources: U.S. Bureau of the Census. Occupational Trends in the United States, 1900 to 1950. Working Paper No. 5. Also, U.S. Bureau of the Census. Detailed Characteristics. U.S. Summary, 1960, 1970.

that broad category has changed significantly. Labor-intensive employment, represented by the unskilled class, has declined to about a third of what it had been in 1910. Most of that loss has been absorbed by machine-tending or capital-intensive occupations, that is, the semiskilled class, though some gain occurred in the skilled class. But the most substantial changes took place in the white collar category. The professional category and the clerical and sales category grew continuously through the period, the former by a threefold and the latter by a twofold increase. Proprietors, managers, and officials, however, reached their numerical peak in 1950 and have since declined. That has been due in part, no doubt, to the growth in the scale of enterprises. A more detailed analysis would show an absolute decline of proprietors and a compensating increase in managers and officials.

With the growth in scale of organizations came an increase in the number of levels of administration and supervision (Meyer, 1972), which, in turn, made further growth possible. Furthermore, as organizations grew vertically, they also grew horizontally. The establishment of branches at widely scattered locations or the merging and federating of preexisting enterprises and associations created a thickening web of intercity relations. Those, too, fell into a hierarchical pattern, with central offices administrating through echelons of regional and district offices. Thus, increasing numbers of people found themselves employed as workers in multilevel corporations, as members of nationally organized labor unions or professional associations, as purchasers of retirement annuities from corporately organized firms, or as buyers of consumer goods from chain organizations, many administrated from distant central offices. After observing that corporate organizations number somewhere close to one million, Hacker (1965, p. 26) estimated the average individual is involved with as many as 150 corporations. Moreover, hierarchical structures with central offices in strategic locations have developed around virtually all avocational interests (Gale Research Company, 1975). Large-scale organizations have also absorbed much of the creative energy of people. Whereas in 1920 over 70 percent of all patents were issued to individuals, that proportion is now issued to corporations (U.S. Bureau of the Census, 1960, p. 603).

It is not surprising that in the process of organizational proliferation and specialization, the most persistent general-purpose institution, the family, was subjected to the functional attrition experienced by other general-purpose institutions

before it. One task after another has tended to leave the domain
of the family and to reappear in specialized agencies serving the
community. Such tasks include socialization to work roles, arrangements for dating and marriage, and emotional support in
crises; these and other tasks are addressed by a range of direct
services to individuals and residences currently offered by the
commercial, professional, or public sectors of an urban place.
Not the least important of the many consequences of this trend
is the mobility imperative imposed upon the family. Its members must be prepared and equipped to move to and from
numerous destinations each week. Average daily travel distances
per household have increased fivefold since 1915 and now
amount to approximately fifty miles (Automobile Manufacturers Association, 1971; Smith, 1961). As a result, multiple-car
ownership has become commonplace.

   Centripetal and Centrifugal Movements. The concentration phase of population redistribution in the United States did
not end in 1920. By that year the increase in agricultural productivity passed population growth; thus, agricultural output
exceeded demand for agricultural products. Inevitably, therefore, growing numbers of workers were displaced from agriculture. The onset of absolute decline in the farm labor force happened to coincide with the end of large-scale foreign immigration, thereby lending a further impetus to the farm-to-city
migration. Net migration from farms averaged 500 thousand per
year between 1920 and 1930, subsided to less than 400 thousand per year in the depression decade of the 1930s, then rose
to over one million per year after 1946 through 1960, and then
fell off somewhat as the size of the base population was reduced
(Economic Research Service, 1966, pp. 8-9). The shrinkage of
the farm population became all too evident after 1940, as seen
in Table 1. In 1950, the farm population's proportion of the
total was half what it had been in 1920, and it declined again by
about 50 percent in each of the decades following 1950. Consequently, population densities in cities continued to increase
until 1950 in the larger places and until later dates in smaller
places (Kasarda and Redfearn, 1975). However, it is apparent
from the small proportion remaining in the farm residence category that the era of farm-to-city migration is nearing its end.

   Noteworthy in Table 1 is the rapid growth of the rural
nonfarm population, which is urban in all respects but name
(Campbell, 1975). Some of that growth resulted simply from
reclassification as residents gave up farming their lands and

turned to nonfarm employment. But some of it came from emigration from the cities. That is, before the concentration phase of population redistribution had spent itself, a localized deconcentration movement of city populations had begun.

A centrifugal drift of urban population was not entirely new. In the years preceding the introduction of the new developments in short-distance transportation and communication, an outward movement was generated from the displacement by high-intensity land uses of low-intensity land uses in the zones surrounding the nodal points of interregional routes. Population declines in the innermost zones of large urban places began as early as the 1870s and became more general at the end of the nineteenth century. But this centrifugal movement occurred within short distances of urban cores, for as we noted, intramural transport made daily travel distances of more than a few miles impractical.

As the frequency and range of daily movement and communication grew, the compact city was placed under increasingly severe strain. The centrifugal drift of urban components accelerated. Whereas this previously was primarily a response to competitive pressures for space in the core of cities, this outward movement became more a matter of choice, abetted on the one hand by traffic densities and the growing obsolescence of property in the inner city and on the other hand by the availability of low-cost lands at the peripheries of built-up areas. As high residential growth rates moved outward from one distance interval to the next, there was left in the wake a widening zone of declining population growth. The area of high growth rates moved past municipal boundaries into adjacent territory from which urban centers formerly drew much of their growth. Residential invasions of outlying territory began early along rail routes where commuter train services were provided, shifted later to radial highways, and subsequently filled in the intervening spaces between radial routes.

By 1920, growth rates in outlying or suburban territories exceeded growth rates of central cities with populations of 50,000 or more. As can be seen in Table 5, the disparity in growth rates widened through 1960. A departure from that trend appeared for the first time in the most recent census decade. We will consider that change in a later section.

In the meantime, the pattern of population movement in the nation at large was changing. With the rapid decline in the farm population and the rise in the urban proportion of the

Table 5. Increase of Metropolitan Population, 1900-1970.

	Percent Increase		
Census Decade	Central City (A)	Remainder of Area (B)	Ratio (B ÷ A)
1960-1970	4.2	21.7	5.17
1950-1960	7.0	48.3	6.90
1940-1950	12.9	34.4	2.67
1930-1940	5.3	13.3	2.51
1920-1930	22.6	34.8	1.57
1910-1920	25.6	21.5	.84
1900-1910	41.9	39.7	.73

Note: Based on area boundaries adjusted to 1950 Standard Metropolitan Statistical Area (SMSA) definition.

Source: U.S. Bureau of the Census. Number of Inhabitants. U.S. Summary, 1970.

population, the volume of rural to urban migration diminished and was replaced by a compensating interurban migration. The shift in sources brought a change of destinations. Urbanward movements formerly terminated in the innermost zones of the central city if the migrants were inexperienced in urban life and in outer sections of the city if the newcomers were experienced. But as interurban moves became increasingly numerous, they tended to terminate in suburban territory with ever greater frequency.

The spillover of urban growth into suburban areas engulfed and transformed the settlements already there. Formerly self-contained villages and towns lost their general stores, weekly newspapers, general medical practitioners, and locally centered interests, and received in exchange modern specialties offered from a distance or from recently constructed shopping centers. Roadway improvements were followed by influxes of commuters to and from the central city. Adjacent farmlands were converted to real estate subdivisions upon which were constructed new towns. Side roads in the intervening space were soon lined with mobile home colonies and other nonfarm residences. With the dispersion of urban populations came a development on previously open country of a full set of urban services—a network of paved streets, street lighting, sanitary sewer and water lines, fire and police protection, schools, churches, and shopping centers. That in turn led to an acceleration of the centrifugal movement.

Industrial relocation soon followed the outward drift of population. Although an explanation of the industrial movement is somewhat more complex than that of population, much of the movement resulted from improvements in local transportation and communication. For one thing, the separation of the central office from production functions became feasible. In fact, centralization of administration and the deconcentration of production proved to be concurrent processes. With a mobile labor force, industrial plants gained a wide range of locational choice. Nor did deconcentration involve losing the economies that had made inner-city industrial locations attractive; the telephone and motor-vehicle delivery services extended the availability of such economies over a broad area. Many of the services to industry actually followed their customers to outlying locations (Hoover, 1959). Such locations, moreover, enabled industry to take full advantage of the flexibility of the motor truck. Its adaptability to small-lot cargoes, ability to deliver door-to-door, and freedom from fixed schedules could not be matched by the rail or waterway. The motor truck was as responsible as anything else for the breakup of the single point of entry into urban space. Finally, assembly-line production methods called for new building designs using much greater amounts of space. The cheaper lands on the edges of built-up areas were thus attractive. Given these and other considerations, the centrifugal drift of industrial establishments gathered momentum.

The dispersion of employing institutions over outlying territory added another incentive to live in the suburbs, namely, to shorten the commuting time. A substantial proportion of the people who moved from the central cities to the suburbs in six areas studied were employed in suburban establishments (Hawley and Zimmer, 1970). Morgan (1967) reported that in the twelve largest urbanized areas work trips were shorter for suburban than for central city residents, though in smaller areas suburban trips were longer. Many suburban residents, however, have found themselves spending more time traveling to work than they had anticipated before they moved as a result of the increased traffic densities on lateral and circumferential roads (Lansing, 1966).

Unlike the past, in which lands in the inner areas of cities that had been vacated by residential users were taken up by high-intensity, nonresidential users, the cycling of land uses has been occurring with diminishing frequency since 1950. The result in many of the old urban centers is a spreading zone of property abandonment. Obsolescence, rising costs of maintenance, and delayed tax-assessment write-downs (Rybeck, 1970; Center for Community Change and the National Urban League, 1971) have all contributed to the new phenomenon. But lying beneath such fiscal matters is the widened range of locational options available to all urban activities.

Unfortunately for the fiscal welfare of the core city, in most instances the city has been unable to extend its boundaries and thus contain the widening distribution of its components. Opposition to annexation has arisen from incorporated villages and cities on the periphery and from rural nonfarm residents willing to accept low-quality services in lieu of central city taxes. The opposition grew more entrenched as the demand for additional services gave rise to additional governmental units in the suburban area. In the end, many of the larger central cities found themselves surrounded by semiautonomous units of government while continuing to serve as the principal source of administrative, professional, and shopping services. The consequent fragmentation of the fiscal resource, that is, the tax base, of the expanded urban unit has resulted in numerous inequities not only between the central city and its suburbs, but also among suburban governments (Campbell and Dollenmayer, 1975; Zimmerman, 1975). The problems of the suburbs have been aggravated by the increasing volume of traffic going through their jurisdictions to other destinations. Many of the central city's maintenance problems are also descending on suburban areas.

Selectivity in Deconcentration. A closer examination of the centrifugal movements of urban populations in the period since 1920 reveals several tendencies that have altered the urban settlement pattern. Prominent among these is the selectivity that has been at work. In the vanguard of the outward movement have been young families seeking more suitable environments for family life at reasonable costs. They have been accommodated by the construction of new housing at the moving edge of the built-up area. Thus, the median age of the population and of housing declines as one moves from the inner core of a city. Although there is usually a trade-off of building costs with land costs, newer residential properties are usually more expensive than older residential properties. That, together with the increased time and cost of daily travel to the inner core and other destinations, has meant selectivity by income as well as social group in the outward movement. And income, of course, is associated with level of educational attainment and with occupation. The residential properties vacated by the higher socioeconomic classes have often been filled, after having been subdivided for denser occupancy, by broken families, recent migrants from rural areas, and people of lower socioeconomic status generally.

There are, however, a number of differentials in the selectivity of the centrifugal movement. In the first place, the improved mobility has permitted residential land users to withdraw from areas of varied land uses. The urban land-use pattern thus has evidenced an increasing homogenization within zones and districts. Consequently segregation has increased. Nevertheless, although the socioeconomic status of residents has generally increased with distance from the core, at any given distance there has been considerable diversity. The diversity has been comprised of several homogeneous localities, primarily in terms of property values but also to a lesser degree in terms of socioeconomic characteristics. Quite often the internal uniformity of residential areas has been secured by restrictive regulations and subdivision specifications. But even without such deliberate tactics, a de facto segregation has arisen from the similarity of location requirements of like kinds of people as well as from their ability to pay the costs of given residential sites.

The two processes of selectivity and segregation have been carried into the suburban movement. That is to be expected, of course, for the suburban movement is simply a continuation of the movement that has operated within the central city. Still, suburban territory has become distinguished from the central city by the prevalence of complete family units from the middle and upper socioeconomic levels. The suburbs have been comprised of relatively homogeneous residential colonies, though these differed among themselves in the cost of properties and in the extent of nonresidential activities. Poorer communities have often included industrial establishments and usually been adjacent to central city boundaries. Most affluent communities have often been exclusively residential and situated farther afield (Schnore, 1963).

In recent years, however, the selective process has changed significantly. Whereas prior to 1940 suburban territory was poorly equipped with urban services, had very little rental housing, and contained few employing institutions, these deficiencies were remedied rapidly after World War II. Consequently, the outward movement of population became less selective, representing a greater cross-section of population.

Blue collar workers and nonfamily households increasingly participated in the centrifugal movement. How people in the lower socioeconomic classes have distributed themselves in suburban territory has not been fully investigated. But it is probable that the older suburban cities adjoining central city boundaries and rural nonfarm areas have absorbed many of these people.

One aspect of selectivity has lingered on after others have all but disappeared: selection by income. The suburban drift continues to draw from the top of the income range in virtually every occupational and educational category (Hawley and Zimmer, 1970). Evidently, moving to the suburbs still requires considerable means for a down payment on housing, multiple-car ownership, and other substantial outlays.

Just as the history of population trends records the transformation of America from an agrarian to a highly mobile, industrial society, it also illustrates the changing position of the large black minority. The intersectoral concentration of blacks in cities, while not new, has accelerated noticeably in the last three decades; this has been accompanied by a rapid evacuation by white residents. The resulting majorities of blacks in a number of cities have brought about de facto segregation on an unprecedented scale. The situation is not stable, however. A growing movement of blacks to the suburbs, mostly to older suburban cities and rural nonfarm areas, has been reported in recent Current Population Surveys. This has been due partly to the rapid rise of a black middle class with resources to devote to more costly residences and partly to the efforts of black industrial workers to reduce travel time to work. As socioeconomic differences between black and white populations are reduced, their residential distribution should become more similar.

Two seemingly contradictory tendencies have been mentioned in the preceding discussion. On the one hand, proximity has lost much of its significance as a determinant of the location of activities. As noted earlier, heightened mobility has enabled individuals to travel long distances for their work, shopping, and leisure time interests (Scaff, 1952), a fact that is reported in various traffic surveys and special studies. Average daily travel distances have been shown to vary directly with economic status and to be subject to family life-cycle stage restraints (Foley, 1952). Thus, the neighborhood seems to have declined as a social unit for all but the poorest members of a community (Caplovitz, 1967). Although what is considered to be the scope of the neighborhood varies considerably, however it is defined,

one study showed that more friends of respondents lived outside of the respondents' own neighborhoods than within them
(Smith, Form, and Stone, 1954). Information on this particular
trend is scarce, and it may well be that the imperfectly known
present is being contrasted with an illusory view of the past. It
is of interest, however, that a follow-up study of James West's
Plainville, U.S.A. (1945) found that proximity had ceased to be
a factor in the choice of interpersonal association in a rural village and in the surrounding farm areas (Gallagher, 1961).

On the other hand, despite the widening area within
which routine activities are pursued, urban residents have been
regrouping themselves in relatively homogeneous clusters. The
tendency is manifested in central cities (Uyeki, 1964) and even
more conspicuously in suburban areas. How is one to reconcile
that fact with the indications of neighborhood decline? It may
be that the clustering is simply an attempt by each family to
assure the resale value of its residential property. Or it may be
common location requirements that draw households of a given
type into close proximity without generating social interactions.
But Suttles (1975) argued that the neighborhood, though much
attenuated, has not disappeared. He regarded the households in
a particular locality as sharing "presumed good-will" that can be
mobilized, for example, for mutual protection. In other words,
the neighborhood is capable of responding as a unit in crisis
situations, but at all other times it exists as so many discrete
entities.

The Metropolitan Concept. The expanded urban pattern
created by the centrifugal movement has been designated as a
metropolitan area, or, in U.S. Census Bureau language, a Standard Metropolitan Statistical Area (SMSA). The SMSA is defined as an urban aggregation of 50,000 or more people in one
or two closely situated municipalities, the county containing
the urban core, and adjacent counties whose residents are believed to be functionally integrated with the central county.
The distinction, of course, between a center and a noncenter is
in large part a product of the inability of the center to extend
its boundaries. Moreover, the size specification for the center
seems arbitrary. Virtually all sizes of urban places have residential developments beyond their legal boundaries whose occupants commute to and from the centers. How the population
size of 50,000 marks a significant difference from smaller places
and a significant similarity among all places that are larger has
not been made clear.

There is another, more venerable use of the term *metropolitan*. It describes a broadly defined area that includes a major center—a metropolis—and the lesser cities, villages, and intervening areas whose diverse activities are administered and coordinated through the institutions located in the major center. Although not precise, this definition can apply to only a small number of metropolitan areas per region or country. Boundary delimitation, however, is a serious problem, especially in view of the extensive interpenetration of metropolitan influences that has occurred in recent times (Pappenfort, 1959). For that reason the use by an official statistical agency of simple, easily determined criteria is understandable. Nevertheless, it is unfortunate that the criteria employed by the U.S. Bureau of the Census are not more discriminating. It seems highly unlikely that there are as many as 265 bona fide metropolitan areas in the nation. In any case, the question may soon become a matter of historic interest, for it seems that the metropolitan concept itself is already becoming obsolete.

Diffuse Urbanization Phase

Transportation and Communication Technology. A third stage in the reduction of the frictions of space began with another set of revolutionary advances in long-distance transportation and communication, particularly the latter.

Radio, which appeared shortly after the telephone, underwent many improvements in military usage during World War I and spread rapidly through the civilian population in the 1920s as a news, entertainment, and advertising medium. Similarly, television, demonstrated to be feasible in the 1930s, was held in abeyance by World War II and then became ubiquitous after 1950. Commercial air travel was in its infancy before 1940, but in the postwar period it quickly displaced railways and ships as the principal mode of long-distance passenger transportation. With these improvements came many others, such as the reduction of long-distance telephone tolls, the radiotelephone, satellite communications, and supersonic aircraft, to name but a few. Furthermore, new sources of transportation power are now being developed. It is not unlikely that modern society is on the threshold of extraordinary advances in the technology of transportation.

Deconcentration. These developments have added impetus to the deconcentration trend begun by the earlier improvements in short-distance transportation and communication. By the 1960s, the outward movement of population from cities had reached far into fringe counties of metropolitan areas and had begun to affect adjacent, nonmetropolitan counties. Signalling events still to come, net losses from migration in these nonmetropolitan counties decreased to less than half of what such losses had been in earlier decades. Since 1970 the outward movement of growth has invaded nonadjacent non-metropolitan counties, reversing a trend of loss extending over at least two decades. Moreover, growth in these outlying counties exceeded growth in metropolitan counties for the first time. The most impressive such turnaround occurred in counties in which there are no villages or towns with more than 2,500 people (Beale and Fuguitt, 1975a). This is surprising, since a study conducted in 1972 using a national sample reported that most respondents preferred to live outside of but within easy commuting distance of a city of 50,000 or more people (Fuguitt and Zuiches, 1975). It is quite possible that a number of people either misrepresented their preferences or chose residential locations far from metropolitan centers because of more compelling factors.

There is no reason to believe that these data indicate anything other than a broadening of the zone of dispersion of urban population. A full explanation, however, is still lacking. Beale and Fuguitt (1975a) showed that in 1970 the rapidly growing nonmetropolitan counties had high proportions of persons sixty years of age and over, four-year state-supported institutions of higher education, and low proportions of blacks. Thus, it seems probable that there may be a tendency to escape the problems of large cities in search of conditions suitable to new and different life-styles. Shifts in the economy might also be contributing to such locational decisions. Many of the rapid-growth industries, notably electronics and chemicals, in which transportation costs for raw materials and for shipment to markets are a relatively small part of the cost of production, are almost unrestricted in their choices of location. Hence, they can be persuaded by considerations of worker amenities, as heavy industries cannot be, to locate in areas of mild climates and abundant leisure time opportunities. It is also true, of course, that the monopoly that cities once had on access to information, art, the theater, and opportunity to associate with others of specialized interests has all but disappeared. Individuals can now live almost anywhere in a modern society without being deprived of cultural opportunities.

Decline of Proximity. There are some writers, notably

Webber (1963), who foresee the possibility of a "community without propinquity." Intellectual and managerial elites have already attained that independence of space in some of their roles, says Webber, and may be expected to extend that freedom to their other activities in the future. Since what is urban is essentially a communication system, it is no more bound by space than the existing technology requires. Thus as Friedmann (1961-62, p. 103) has said: "With their success in organizing the life of a society, both as a pattern of activities and as a pattern in space, the traditional notion of a city as a place having definite geographic limits will tend gradually to disappear."

But the elimination of boundaries assumes a progressive decrease in the costs of transportation and communication. How far that can be carried is a matter for speculation. To date the savings have been most clearly in time. Whether there have also been savings in resource costs might depend on the accounting methods used. It is clear that an increasing share of the household budget is being devoted to mobility and access to sources of information. It is also true that many other costs have been paid indirectly by the consumer through taxes for the construction and maintenance of roads and for traffic controls and administration, and through advertising and delivery costs absorbed in the prices of products. For such costs to have no limiting and patterning effects on the future distribution of human settlement requires the continuance, if not a raising of, the present level of affluence. The level will need to be high enough to cover rising costs of raw materials and environmental preservation as well as of mobility and communication.

Yet there are demographic changes in process that may offset the budgetary limitations on household travel distances. The growing prevalence of the two-child family not only promises a rise in per capita income in households but also an earlier conclusion of the family-rearing stage of the life cycle. Residence changes and far-ranging daily movements will therefore be made easier. That the smaller family will be inclined to return to central city residence, as has been suggested (Hoover, 1972), seems unlikely. An unresolvable energy shortage would, of course, alter matters drastically. Without that, it is doubtful that the distance scale of the 1950s and 1960s will be a reliable gauge for the future.

2

Urbanization, Community, and the Metropolitan Problem

John D. Kasarda

Although analytically distinct, the concepts of industry and community have become so interwoven in urban society that one concept is frequently defined in terms of the other. We talk about mining communities, manufacturing communities, college towns, administrative cities, and other functional types of territorial localities. At the same time, the increasing scale of urban units and growing mobility of their inhabitants have fostered numerous nonterritorial networks ("communities without propinquity"), where bonds of common identity and patterns of social interaction are determined more by professional or industrial affiliation than by residential locale (Webber, 1963).

In this chapter, our focus is on communities as territorial

27

entities with particular emphasis given to the dominant urban unit of today—the metropolitan community. We shall begin with an overview of the now classic ecological model of the industrial metropolis as formulated by Chicago sociologists Robert E. Park and Ernest W. Burgess. The expansion of the American metropolis will then be examined first in terms of its technological stimuli and then from the vantage of the redistribution of population and industrial activity. Next the economic strains resulting from the expansion process will be reviewed and their implications for employment opportunities and fiscal problems in central cities and suburbs discussed. We will conclude with a documentation of the post-World War II expansion of the industrial metropolis and assess its impact on the financial welfare of our central cities and their inhabitants.

Classic Ecological Model of the Metropolis

The classic ecological model of the industrial metropolis evolved during an era of massive concentrative migration in the United States. As industrialization and urbanization operated concurrently, waves of foreign-born and rural immigrants converged on northern and midwestern cities in search of improved social conditions and economic opportunities. At the peak of this period (circa 1893 to 1898), a young newspaper reporter, Robert E. Park, was writing human interest stories for metropolitan dailies in New York, Chicago, Detroit, Denver, and Minneapolis about the problems facing the newly arriving immigrant groups. Park, who had an engaging mind and was well read in the biological sciences, was struck with the amazing similarity between the immigrants' "struggle for survival" in the expanding metropolis and Darwin's (1860) ecological-evolutionary model. He was particularly impressed with the adaptation process (including conflicts, adjustments, accommodations, and assimilation) in the local immigrant communities and how urban order seemed to emerge naturally through unplanned processes of competition, invasion, succession, segregation, and dominance. Park later became a member of the faculty of the department of sociology at the University of Chicago, where along with his colleague, Ernest Burgess, he formulated an ecological model of the industrial metropolis.

In essence, the Park-Burgess theory views the industrial metropolis as a dynamic adaptive system that relates various population groups, commercial institutions, and local industries to each other and to the outside world (Park and Burgess, 1921, 1925; Park, 1952). Its internal structure (that is, its physical and social subareas, nodes, networks, and gradients of change with distance from the center) is seen as evolving not through any form of planning or design but through competition and the spontaneous operation of the marketplace. The effect is territorial differentiation and segregation of various ethnic groups, industrial facilities, and activity patterns into relatively homogeneous subareas, which Park and Burgess labeled "natural areas" because of their unplanned evolution. Such natural areas in the metropolis include the central business district, the rooming house area, the slum, the ethnic ghetto, the "bright lights" area, and the industrial zone.

The underlying premise of the ecological model is that the overall spatial pattern of the urbanized area, including the location of specific natural areas, is also regulated by competition (Alihan, 1938). This premise reflects the sociopolitical and economic milieu of nineteenth- and early twentieth-century America, where the dynamics of privatism and laissez-faire enterprise prevailed. Relatively unfettered by public intervention, industries and commercial institutions compete for strategic locations, which, once established, provide them with economic advantages (externalities) through which they can exercise control (dominance) over the functional use of land in other parts of the community (McKenzie, 1933). This strategic location, or area of dominance, is found at the point of highest accessibility, the community's geographic center. It is at the center where the largest number of people converge daily to work, shop, and conduct their business. Consequently, land values are substantially higher in the central business district than in the surrounding area. Expecting to reap profits when the central business districts expand, speculators frequently acquire the land and buildings immediately adjacent to the central business districts. Since speculators are concerned primarily with the future value of the land per se rather than the buildings on it, the area surrounding the central business district deteriorates into a slum (the "zone-in-transition").

The zone-in-transition, including its slums and immigrant ghettos, performs an important function for the metropolitan community, however. Its relatively inexpensive (albeit crowded and deteriorating) housing and propinquity to expanding industries provide a convenient and affordable locus of settlement for newly arriving immigrants. Park, Burgess, and their students at the University of Chicago lucidly described how each migrant group initially concentrates in a highly segregated ethnic enclave within the deteriorating zone where they face suspicion, distrust, and discrimination from earlier ethnic arrivals; yet, with the passage of time, how each group is able to adjust and assimilate into city life, slowly climb the socioeconomic ladder, and escape to better residences further removed from the ethnic ghettos and slums. They are then replaced by another wave of arriving immigrants, who replicate the spatial and temporal process of mobility and assimilation (Burgess and Bogue, 1964; Cressey, 1938; Freedman, 1948; Hauser, 1961; McKenzie, 1929). It is these successive movements, first-generation settlement in the core followed by residential progression outward toward the periphery over time, that are responsible for the correspondence between length of residence of the immigrant group in the city, the group's socioeconomic status, and the distance that the group resides from the central business district. This interpretation constitutes the classic concentric zonal model of the expanding metropolis (Burgess, 1925).

Transportation and the Evolution of Metropolitan Form

Of course, the expansion of the industrial metropolis into territorially differentiated residential, commercial, and industrial subareas would not have occurred to the extent that it did had it not been for revolutionary improvements in short-distance transportation and communication. Where transportation is primitive, inhabitants and their employing and service institutions must be in relatively close proximity (the distance in the local community typically determined by pedestrian movement). Territorial differentiation of urban areas is thereby limited, with each local community or neighborhood providing residence, employment, and sustenance goods and services. The urbanized area as an aggregate may grow, but it does so in a fissionlike manner, characteristic of early preindustrial cities, where there was limited functional interdependence among the various cellular subareas (Sjoberg, 1955, 1960).

Such was the situation in the United States before 1870, when walking was the predominant mode of urban movement. Then came a sequence of public transportation innovations that completely restructured the metropolis. The first was the introduction of the horse-drawn streetcar (circa 1870), which enabled substantial numbers of urban residents to live as far as five miles from their place of work and commute on a daily basis. The electric trolley lines and streetcars of the 1880s and 1890s extended the commuting radius to ten miles, and when rapid transit electric trains arrived at the turn of the century, the urban population was able to expand outward as far as twenty miles from the center of the city (Hawley, 1950; Tobin, 1976; Ward, 1971). Radial strings of new suburban developments sprouted along these commuter rail lines, giving the city a star-shaped population pattern.

The commuter railways signified the beginning of widespread suburbanization and territorial differentiation in the metropolis. Places of residence and places of work became increasingly separated and segregated, as did the distances between the lowest- and highest-income neighborhoods. The poorest groups, who, as noted above, were typically first-generation migrants, simply could not afford commuting costs on a daily basis and therefore remained concentrated in the older, deteriorating residential units near inner-city industrial zones. The wealthier third- and fourth-generation inhabitants, on the other hand, pushed outward to superior residential suburbs far removed from the dense city smoke, congestion, and decaying urban neighborhoods. With spatial mobility matching social mobility, a crystallized sociospatial residential distribution emerged attuning the income and status of residents to the exclusiveness and desirability of the neighborhood.

Commercial institutions likewise began a selective redistribution process, with convenience goods and service establishments following the middle- and upper-income groups outward, while administrative, communications, financial, and professional services increased in the city center to serve the entire metropolitan population. The central business district took on the form of a specialized financial and administrative hub, and as the population dispersed along the rail lines, the entire metropolis began to acquire a new physical structure.

The electric commuter trains were inflexible, however. They operated on fixed time schedules and tended to constrain urban expansion to those areas located near the rail arteries. It was the development of the motor vehicle in the late nineteenth century that overcame these limitations and substantially accelerated the expansion process. Between 1900 and 1930, motor vehicle registration increased from 8,000 to 26,352,000, or from an average of one automobile for every ten thousand persons to an average of one for every household (U.S. Bureau of the Census, 1960). During the same period, extensive peripheral highway systems evolved, weaving a tight web of hard-surfaced roads throughout the suburban hinterland. The speed and convenience of the automobile, together with the hard-surfaced roads, brought many previously isolated towns and villages into routinized contact with the central city. Some of those towns and villages were as far as fifty miles away.

Throughout this period, significant advances and improvements in short-distance communications technology occurred. Household and business telephones became ubiquitous; regularly scheduled radio broadcasts began from urban centers; and central-city newspapers were distributed daily to virtually all outlying communities. Such communications developments contributed immensely to the social and economic integration of the expanding urban complex (McKenzie, 1933).

There was a price paid, however, by the outlying communities after they were absorbed into the expanding metropolis. Because of their semiindependent nature, these communities had previously provided and supported their own sustenance organizations, consumer services, and local institutions. After they were brought into daily contact with the urban centers, their small shops, stores, food producers, and semiprofessional service units could not compete effectively with their larger and more diversified counterparts in the central cities. Many of their movie theaters, newspapers, and banks closed entirely. A large number of their basic goods and service establishments, especially grocery stores and restaurants, were replaced by standardized services, distributed through chain outlets and branch offices of units headquartered in the urban centers (Hawley, 1971, p. 148). Some of these outlying communities were functionally transformed, becoming residential suburbs primarily housing a commuting population who worked either in the city or suburban ring. Others became retail centers, distributing convenience goods to nearby residential developments. Still others were transformed into industrial suburbs when manufacturers found that they could decentralize their production facilities from the congested core yet easily maintain daily contact with central-city institutions and draw on the new automobile-owning labor force.

In sum, late nineteenth- and early twentieth-century advances in transportation and communication not only were responsible for the spatial expansion of the metropolis but also eliminated the semiautonomy and heterogeneous work-residence-service structure of many outlying towns and villages. These communities were absorbed and integrated into a single diffuse community composed of territorially specialized subunits, linked together by a routinized system of daily social and economic interactions. This altogether new type of community became known as the metropolitan community (Gras, 1922; McKenzie, 1933; Bogue, 1949).

Metropolitan Growth and Deconcentration

Not until 1910, however, did the Bureau of the Census recognize the inadequacy of the political boundaries of the city as a territorial unit for measuring urban population. At that time, the bureau introduced the category "metropolitan districts" to take into account the spread of the urban complex well beyond the city limits. Since then the United States has become increasingly metropolitan in scope. Despite recent population increases in many nonmetropolitan counties (see Beale, 1975; Tucker, 1976; Berry and Dahmann, 1977), metropolitan areas as a whole have continually absorbed larger shares of the national population increase. In 1900, less than one third of the U.S. population resided in urban areas that met present metropolitan criteria. By 1975, over 150 million people, or nearly three quarters of the U.S. population, resided within 270 metropolitan units designated as Standard Metropolitan Statistical Areas (SMSAs); over 95 percent resided within the labor shed, the zone of reasonable commutation, of their central cities (Hawley and Rock, 1975, p. 14).

Population growth was only one demographic manifestation of metropolitan expansion, however. Another was deconcentration, or movement outward from the central cities. Deconcentration, commonly known as suburbanization, is a multifaceted phenomenon that has been measured for metropolitan areas as a whole in three ways: (1) relative decennial growth rates (percent change) of suburban ring population compared to central city population; (2) absolute decennial growth in the suburban ring population, compared to absolute decennial growth in the central cities; and (3) comparative decennial changes in the population density of the central cities and suburban rings. Deconcentration begins using the first measure when the suburban ring of a metropolitan community grows at a faster rate than the central city. The 1920s have traditionally been considered a transitional decade for the deconcentration of the metropolitan population using the relative growth rate method (see Bogue, 1953; Hawley, 1956). However, such studies did not consider the fact that substantial annexation of suburban territory by central cities inflated central-city growth rates and artificially deflated suburban growth rates. When adjustments for annexation are made, the suburban rings of metropolitan areas are seen to have been growing at faster rates than the central cities in all regions of the country since at least 1900 (Kasarda and Redfearn, 1975). As a result, by 1970 more people resided in the suburban rings of SMSAs (76 million) than in the central cities (64 million).

The second indicator of deconcentration measures the extent to which raw population increases in the suburban rings exceed increases in the central cities. This indicator measures the share of metropolitan growth accounted for by growth in the suburban rings. Adjusting for annexation, suburban rings as a whole exhibited larger absolute increases in population than did the central cities in every decade since 1930, with many individual suburban rings assuming a larger share of metropolitan growth a decade or so earlier. By the 1960s, essentially all metropolitan growth was accounted for by suburbanization, as absolute population declines in numerous central cities offset gains in others.

The third indicator of deconcentration measures the degree to which metropolitan centers have declined in population density while density in peripheries has increased. Most studies of urban population densities document successively lower density levels for those cities that evolved during periods of faster, more efficient local transportation (Duncan and others, 1961a; Guest, 1973; Mills, 1970; Winsborough, 1963). Nonetheless, with the exception of some of our oldest central cities, deconcentration, as measured by decennial density declines within constant city boundaries, is largely a post-World War II phenomenon. Even after 1950, real central-city density declines (those not masked by annexation) were highly selective, occurring mostly in the larger, older central cities in the Northeast and North Central regions of the nation (Kasarda and Redfearn, 1975). This finding calls into question the conventional wisdom that suburban commuter trains and the increase in mass automobile usage (from 1920 to 1950) were responsible for depopulating the cities—or even decreasing density patterns within existing central-city boundaries. Without doubt, the automobile and commuter trains, along with rising real incomes, federally

insured home mortgages, and state and federally funded suburban highways, encouraged and facilitated the suburbanization
of the middle and upper-middle class in metropolitan America.
However, as fast as these groups moved beyond central-city
boundaries, they were replaced by lower-income groups in the
typical Burgess concentric growth pattern. The outcome, of
course, has been growing numbers of metropolitan poor concentrated in the central cities, while the suburban rings serve as the
residential locus of the upwardly mobile social groups.

Commercial and Industrial Redistribution

The growth and selective deconcentration of metropolitan population were matched with a significant alteration in the
commercial and industrial structure of both the central cities
and the suburban rings. The dispersion of retail establishments
and consumer services closely followed the suburbanization of
middle- and upper-income groups. Between 1954 and 1977,
over 15,000 suburban shopping centers and regional malls were
constructed to serve the expanding metropolitan population. By
1978 these shopping centers and malls accounted for more than
one-half the annual retail sales in the United States, and the
trend shows no signs of abating. In documenting the suburban
shopping center boom, *Fortune* magazine reported:

> The shopping center has become the piazza of
> America. In big metropolitan areas and smaller cities alike
> ... indoor piazzas are reshaping much of American life.
> Giant regional shopping centers have risen by the hun-
> dreds across the nation and are still going up by the score.
> To an amazing degree, they are seizing the role once held
> by the central business district, not only in retailing but
> as the social, cultural, and recreational focal point of the
> entire community. Grim, formal, unwelcoming, old cities
> scarcely fit the more relaxed lifestyle of the newly affluent
> middle class with considerable leisure. . . . In many cities
> middle class white shoppers are beginning to abandon the
> downtown to the poor and blacks except from nine to five,
> Monday through Friday [Breckenfeld, 1972, p. 86].

Many commercial and service establishments that are
located in suburban shopping centers and malls are outlets or
branches of headquarter units remaining in the central business

districts. Other headquarters migrated directly to the suburbs, closing their inner-city establishments entirely when middle-class clientele no longer resided in the vicinity. Their proprietors found that opening new stores in the suburban rings not only brought them closer to their traditional patrons but also enabled them to design their establishments much more compatibly with modern transportation, storage, and distribution technologies than was possible in the older inner-city sectors (Meyer, Kain, and Wohl, 1965).

The shift of manufacturing industries to the suburbs paralleled the deconcentration of retail trade. Prior to the era of the automobile and truck, central cities provided distinct locational advantages to large manufacturing establishments. These advantages included superior rail and water transportation facilities, suited for receiving raw material and distributing finished products to regional and national markets; a large, diverse, and relatively cheap labor supply; and external economies, including complementary businesses and industries and the full range of public services (electricity, water, police and fire protection, and so on) that were more effectively provided there than in outlying communities.

During the past fifty years, changing modes of transportation and production technology altered the central cities' locational advantages. Industries soon discovered that early urban street patterns were not designed to handle the automobile and truck. Traffic congestion, lack of employee parking space, and problems of freight transfer greatly increased direct and indirect costs, particularly for those manufacturers located in the old, densely settled sections of the cities. On the other hand, the development of suburban highway systems, extensive automobile ownership, and increased dependence by manufacturers on trucking for receiving raw materials and supplies and shipping finished products made uncongested suburban sites more attractive. Manufacturers recognized that by locating on or near suburban expressways they could reduce their transportation costs, tap an adequate automobile-owning labor supply, and solve problems of employee parking and freight transfer.

A second factor that encouraged suburbanization of large industry was the changing mode of manufacturing technology from unit processing to mass production and assembly-line methods. Old central-city manufacturing facilities had been constructed as multistory, loftlike structures that are not adaptable to much of today's mass production technology. The assembly line, in particular, has large horizontal space requirements that are more difficult and more costly to obtain in the central city than in the suburban rings. Just as in retail and wholesale sectors, large manufacturers realized that it was more practical to build newly designed facilities on relatively inexpensive suburban ring land than to convert their obsolete inner-city structures. New metropolitan industries with large space requirements would rarely ever consider a central-city site, usually locating their production facilities directly in the suburban rings.

A third, equally important factor stimulating the suburbanization of industry was the widespread development of suburban public services and external economies, which as noted above had previously been concentrated in the central cities and their adjacent, built-up areas. The spread of electricity and gas lines, water utilities, sanitary waste systems, police and fire protection, and highway services throughout the suburban rings released manufacturers from their dependency on the central cities. Moreover, rapid suburban development after World War II also brought housing, local suppliers, subcontractors, and other complementary services to nearby areas, which provided manufacturers with additional suburban externalities.

With the push factors of obsolete inner-city structures, lack of inexpensive space for expansion, increasing taxes, deteriorating public services, rising city crime rates, and vandalism operating concurrently with the suburban pull factors noted above, manufacturing industry fled to the suburban rings en masse. Between 1947 and 1972 metropolitan central cities in this country lost a net total of 1,146,845 manufacturing jobs while their suburban rings gained 4,178,230. Had it not been for substantial increases in post-World War II manufacturing employment in younger, smaller SMSA central cities and cities in the South and West, the net employment decline in metropolitan central-city manufacturing would have been more than double the above figure.

In contrast to the deconcentration of the manufacture of standard goods and services, the number of establishments offering specialized goods and services has actually increased in the central business districts. The nature of these establishments still makes it advantageous for them to have a central location that maximizes their accessibility to the largest number of people and firms in the metropolis. Such establishments as airline ticket agencies, advertising firms, brokerage houses, consulting

firms, financial institutions, and legal, government, and professional complexes have been accumulating in the central business
districts, replacing many of the standardized goods and services
establishments that were unable to afford the increasing land
values of a central location.

The 1960s and 1970s also witnessed a remarkable growth
of administrative office buildings in the central business districts
of our biggest SMSAs. Administrative headquarters rely on large
pools of clerical workers and the complement of legal, financial,
communications, and specialized business services that are most
readily available in central business districts. In downtown Manhattan, for example, over 75 million square feet of office space
was added between 1965 and 1972—an increase of more than
50 percent. In other large central cities, the picture is much the
same. Between 1960 and 1972, central office space increased by
52 percent in Chicago, 79 percent in San Francisco, 82 percent
in Atlanta, and 100 percent in Houston (Manners, 1974). However, many central-city office structures are now experiencing
high vacancy rates, and given the deteriorating externalities of
an inner-city location, one must wonder whether the central
business districts can continue to attract and hold administrative, professional, and financial functions while the rest of the
U.S. economy suburbanizes. Almost weekly another corporation leaves a large central city for a suburban location. Thus,
while white collar employment has increased in the central
cities, it has grown in the suburban rings at a rate four times
faster (Kasarda, 1976). There seems little reason to doubt that
the central cities will capture smaller and smaller shares of
metropolitan white collar employment in the future. Moreover,
as we shall document shortly, since white collar employment
growth in the administrative and professional services sectors in
central cities is not nearly offsetting the huge losses of central-
city jobs in other sectors, the overall employment base of the
cities continues to decay.

Thus, the growth of administrative and professional office structures in the central business districts, together with the
suburbanization in heavy industry, middle-income population,
and establishments providing consumer goods and services, has
spatially reorganized the modern metropolis. Population groups,
land use, and activity patterns have been systematically redistributed, increasing both the degree of territorial specialization
and functional interdependence of localized areas within the
metropolis. In the expanded metropolitan community, residen-

tial suburbs rely on other sectors of the metropolitan area for their daily supplies of food, clothing, news, entertainment, and other recurrent household needs. They also depend on other portions of the expanded community, some as far as sixty miles distant, for their employment opportunities. It is precisely this dependence on other portions of the metropolitan community that enables these suburbs to specialize in residential development (Bollens and Schmandt, 1970, p. 9).

Conversely, central-city institutions depend on the residential suburbs to provide a large proportion of employees, particularly professionals, clerical staff, and managers. And central business district department stores, speciality shops, and business and professional services draw their patrons and clientele from throughout the metropolitan community. Bollens and Schmandt (1970, p. 9) comment on the great interdependence between the center and periphery of the expanded metropolis: In New York City, several million persons daily pour into Manhattan to work, man the executive suites, conduct business, shop, or to be entertained. In other SMSAs across the nation, the pattern is the same; only the scale is smaller. The people of the metropolis, in short, share a common spatial area for their daily activities. Within this area, although its limits may be imprecisely defined, an intricate web of business and social interrelationships exists and a high degree of communication and interchange among residents, groups, and firms continually takes place.

Strains of Metropolitan Expansion

We see then that the centripetal and centrifugal movements of metropolitan expansion have absorbed all segments of the metropolitan community into a single, diffuse social and economic organization. However, in reshaping the metropolis these movements have also introduced problems for its functioning as a coherent entity. Such problems have impinged most heavily on the economic viability of the central cities.

One fundamental problem is that the political reorganization of the metropolitan community has not adjusted to its socioeconomic reorganization. Absorbed into the metropolitan community is the myriad of originally autonomous villages, townships, small cities, special districts, and other administrative jurisdictions that have remained politically discrete. Metropolitan expansion itself produced additional governmental frag-

mentation as populations spreading into unincorporated sub-
urban-ring territory inexorably sought some form of local rule.
In 1972, nearly 23,000 local government units were operating
within 264 metropolitan communities designated as SMSAs.
The thirty-three largest SMSAs alone contained 8,847 local governments, or an average of 268.1 governmental units per SMSA
(U.S. Bureau of the Census, 1973a). This maze of heterogeneous and overlapping governments has resulted in fragmented taxing powers, public service inefficiencies, conflicting
public policies, and administrative impotence in dealing with
many of today's urban problems that have become metropolitan in scope.

Absence of political reorganization within the metropolitan community has placed particularly severe strains on the central cities' ability to finance adequate municipal services. Essentially, two factors lie behind these fiscal strains. First, the
exodus of higher-income population, retail trade, and large
industrial establishments to the politically autonomous suburban rings has substantially diminished central-city tax bases.
Wealthy commercial, industrial, and residential suburbs are
commonly found today adjacent to bankrupt central cities,
with only an invisible administrative boundary separating the
two.

The second factor is that much of the responsibility for
financing municipal services, many of which are used by central-
city and suburban residents alike, has fallen on central-city governments. In the expanded metropolitan community, suburban
residents regularly use central-city streets, parks, zoos, museums, and other public facilities at no or nominal charges; the
daily presence of large numbers of suburbanites in the central
city creates problems for the sanitation and public health departments and poses additional fire risks, which are reflected in
the allocation of funds for fire protection; and the routine
movement into and out of the central city by the large and
growing commuting population leads to traffic congestion on
city arteries, which requires a major component in the budget
for funding both the police and highway maintenance departments. These are only some of the costs that result from the
services central-city governments provide to their suburban
neighbors. The suburbanites, however, by residing in separate
political jurisdictions are often sheltered from the fiscal burden
of these municipal service costs.

Furthermore, numerous suburban jurisdictions have established zoning regulations, covenants, and extravagant hous-

ing quality standards to maintain their upper-income residential composition, while financial institutions, real estate agencies, and residents of middle-class white suburbs frequently practice overt housing discrimination against those perceived to be of lower social standing (Berry and Kasarda, 1977; Mueller, 1976). By these widespread practices, middle- and upper-income suburban communities ensure that the vast majority of minorities and urban poor are confined to the central cities, and they thus avoid the costs of public housing, public health, and social, rehabilitative, and other welfare services that impose a heavy burden on the operating budgets of many central cities.

Because of this combination of factors, public service demands on the central cities have dramatically increased while their fiscal ability to support additional public services is diminishing. The problem, it appears, is not that metropolitan resources are insufficient to support municipal services but that the largest portion of those resources has been redistributed to the politically autonomous suburban rings. In short, metropolitan expansion in the absence of political reorganization has created an unfair distribution of economic resources and service costs between the cities and suburbs and is a major cause of the financial crises facing our central cities today.

Residential-Employment Mismatches

Exacerbating the economic malady of the central cities is the growing mismatch between employment opportunities in the central cities and the skills of the resident labor force. Prior to 1950, central cities were the locus of large, diverse quantities of blue collar jobs that required little education or training. These jobs provided ready employment opportunities for unskilled and semiskilled migrant groups, and because of their proximity to lower-income neighborhoods, they were easily accessible by either pedestrian movement or public transportation. With the expansion of the metropolitan community, lower-income groups continued to flow into the urban centers, while job opportunities appropriate to their education levels and skills were dispersed. Conversely, as middle- and upper-income white collar workers moved to the suburban rings, central city white collar jobs increased substantially. Between 1960 and 1970, for example, central cities of 101 longitudinally comparable SMSAs lost a total of 828,257 blue collar jobs while actually gaining 485,447 white collar positions (Kasarda, 1976). The growth of administrative, financial, clerical, professional, and other specialized white collar jobs in and around the central business districts, along with the suburbanization of blue collar jobs, has had a major impact on the occupational structure of the central cities. The central cities have become increasingly specialized in jobs that have high educational prerequisites just at the time that their resident populations are increasingly composed of those with poor educational backgrounds (Chinitz, 1964; Gold, 1972; Kain, 1970; Wilburn, 1964). As a result, inner-city unemployment rates are more than twice the national average and even higher among inner-city residents who have traditionally found employment in blue collar industries that have migrated to suburban locations (Downs, 1973; Friedlander, 1972; Harrison, 1972, 1974; Hoskin, 1973).

Another consequence of the mismatch between residence groups and employment opportunities is increased commuting between the suburbs and the central business districts of our larger SMSAs. In the mornings one observes large streams of white collar workers commuting into the central business districts from their residential suburbs, while in the opposite lanes large streams of inner-city residents commute to their blue collar jobs in industrial suburbs. In the evening the flows are reversed. One must contemplate the energy savings alone that would be obtained if the residences of these groups were adjacent to their workplaces.

The commuting necessitated by metropolitan expansion has been especially costly for minorities and blue collar ethnic whites residing in the inner city. As blue collar industries have deconcentrated, they have relocated on scattered sites along suburban beltways and expressways. Their dispersed nature makes public transportation from central-city neighborhoods to suburban industrial complexes impractical, requiring almost all city residents who work in the rings to commute by private automobile. The high and increasing costs of inner-city automobile ownership (including insurance and maintenance) imposes a heavy financial burden on these people. Moreover, a large portion of inner-city residents, particularly low-income minorities, cannot afford automobile ownership. In the Chicago metropolitan area, for example, four out of five inner-city adult blacks do not own automobiles (Zimmer, 1975). One outcome is growing frictional as well as structural unemployment among city residents who lack access to cars (Foley, 1975). (*Frictional* unemployment refers to the minimum unemployment that would exist even under conditions of "full employment," as workers move between jobs; *structural* unemployment refers to the lack of mobility in some sectors of the labor force and in- sufficient demand for some types of labor.) A second outcome, as indicated above, is that larger and larger portions of the take- home pay of many inner-city residents are consumed by the costs of commuting to suburban employment by automobile.

Hard pressed (and often overlooked) too are inner-city white ethnics who historically have been employed in the indus- tries that are suburbanizing the fastest. Many of these people originally purchased their inner-city residences near their indus- trial jobs for relatively small sums of money. Because of racial transition in nearby neighborhoods, high crime rates, the decon- centration of industry, and an oversupply of inner-city housing created by the flight to the suburbs, housing values have risen much slower in their neighborhoods than in the suburbs. As their jobs have suburbanized, numerous inner-city white ethnics find themselves not only physically removed from employment opportunities but also residentially trapped by the high cost of suburban housing.* One solution that white ethnics have em- ployed is to purchase mobile homes. As a result, thousands of mobile home communities have sprouted in unincorporated peripheral areas of SMSAs during the past decade. No doubt, the mobile home community binge will accelerate as suburban housing prices further exceed suburban workers' financial abil- ity.

The deleterious effects of the residence-workplace mis- match have not been nearly so great for middle- and upper- income suburban residents who commute to the cities. Because of their higher incomes, automobile ownership and commuting costs do not absorb as large a portion of their income as do the same costs for the inner-city commuter. Moreover, because their jobs are concentrated at a central location, where public trans- portation lines converge, they may take advantage of this option and often reduce their real costs of transportation. In some of our largest SMSAs (New York City and San Francisco are the prime examples) suburban commuters who use public transportation are actually subsidized by the city, since the per- rider cost to the cities is greater than the purchase price of the transportation token. The general problem that suburban resi-

*This idea was stimulated by William Yancey of Temple Univer- sity, who is conducting research on the effects of industrial deconcen- tration on inner-city white ethnics.

dents, through their routine use of central-city services and facilities, contribute to greater marginal service costs for the city than the marginal revenue they generate has become known as the "suburban exploitation thesis" (Neenan, 1970; Kasarda, 1972).

Drawing the foregoing sections together, we are arguing that the centrifugal and centripetal movements inherent in metropolitan expansion are at the root of the current economic and fiscal problems plaguing our large central cities. These movements, which are analytically distinct but interrelated, include (1) the exodus to the suburbs of middle- and upper-income families; (2) the huge influx into the central cities of poor minority groups, the chronically unemployed, the aged, social misfits, and others who tend to be more of a fiscal liability than an asset to central-city budgets; (3) the drift of commerce and industry beyond the taxing jurisdiction of the cities, which has eroded municipal tax bases and made needed blue collar jobs physically inaccessible to many inner-city residents; (4) the buildup in central cities of administrative office structures, financial institutions, specialized professional and technical services, and other white collar business complexes whose jobs require substantial education and training, and hence are inappropriate to the growing concentrations of unskilled and poorly educated inner-city residents; and (5) the daily flow into the central city of large numbers of suburbanites, who regularly use central-city public services and facilities as part of their working, shopping, and recreational activities. The combined effect of these movements is increased debt service for the central cities as their fiscal base contracts and their public service needs increase.

Some Illustrative Data

Let us now document some of the basic migrations that have occurred in metropolitan America since World War II and assess their impact on demographic, employment, and fiscal problems of the central cities. We will present and discuss briefly eight tables to highlight major demographic and industrial transformations in the metropolitan community that have fiscally strained the central cities.

Considering first the suburbanization of metropolitan population, Table 1 shows population change (adjusted for annexation) in central cities from 1950 to 1960 and from 1960 to

Table 1. Metropolitan Central-City Population (Adjusted for
Annexation), by Region and Age.

Metropolitan Characteristic	Number of SMSAs	Mean Size		Mean Change
		1950	1960[a]	
Region				
Northeast	35	490,012	473,391	−16,621
South	57	193,748	200,181	6,433
North Central	56	282,315	276,827	− 5,488
West	17	371,321	422,868	51,547
Inception Date[b]				
Before 1900	47	742,833	728,542	−14,291
1900-1920	63	170,716	181,520	10,804
1920-1950	55	84,503	90,776	6,273
Total	165	304,946	307,091	2,145
		1960	1970[c]	
Region				
Northeast	36	481,925	471,029	−10,898
South	77	200,393	205,984	5,591
North Central	59	283,276	268,551	−14,725
West	28	321,172	350,421	29,259
Inception Date[b]				
Before 1900	47	748,198	724,665	−23,533
1900-1920	63	216,511	221,966	5,455
1920-1950	55	118,812	125,241	6,429
After 1950	35	78,334	90,338	12,004
Total	200	291,475	291,473	2

Note: To make them comparable with other regions, metropolitan areas in New
England were evaluated as county-based equivalents rather than town units. This
slightly reduced the number of metropolitan areas in that region.

[a]In 1950 area.

[b]Date when city met present metropolitan criteria.

[c]In 1960 area.

1970 by region and age of the SMSA. These data clearly demonstrate that population deconcentration (in terms of real central-
city declines) has indeed been selective, with cities located in
the traditional industrial heartland (the Northeast and North
Central regions) losing population each decade, while those in
the South and West have continued to grow. The selective deconcentration pattern is also reflected by metropolitan age,
with the oldest metropolitan central cities losing substantial
population, while newer central cities maintain their growth.

These data, of course, only indicate total population changes and therefore do not illustrate the racial and socioeconomic components that have made deconcentration highly selective internally. Most of the older central cities and those located in the Northeast and North Central regions, while exhibiting absolute population losses, registered large absolute gains in minority and lower-income population during each decade. As a case in point, between 1960 and 1970, just under 500,000 white, middle-class residents left New York City and were replaced by 579,000 blacks, most with education backgrounds and skills suited primarily for blue collar employment.

Table 2, which documents central-city and suburban manufacturing job changes between 1947 and 1972, illustrates

Table 2. Changes in Manufacturing Employment for Central Cities
and Suburban Rings (Adjusted for Annexation), 1947-1972.

Metropolitan Characteristic	Number of SMSAs	Central City		Suburbs	
		Mean	Absolute	Mean	Absolute
Size					
Under 250,000	113	244	27,572	3,566	402,958
250,000-500,000	63	−1,079	−67,977	9,094	572,922
500,000-1 million	36	−6,289	−226,404	18,872	679,392
Over 1 million	33	−26,669	−880,077	76,450	2,522,850
Inception Date[a]					
Before 1900	49	−27,977	−1,370,873	47,104	2,308,096
1900-1920	63	563	35,469	12,242	771,246
1920-1950	53	2,058	109,074	11,162	591,586
After 1950	80	992	79,360	6,341	507,280
Region					
Northeast	42	−18,346	−770,532	16,252	682,584
South	98	3,221	315,658	11,896	1,165,808
North Central	68	−13,327	−906,236	21,057	1,431,876
West	37	5,789	214,193	24,268	897,916
Total	245	−4,681	−1,146,845	17,054	4,178,230

[a]Date when city met present metropolitan criteria.

clearly, however, what is happening to blue collar jobs in our large, old central cities and central cities in the Northeast and North Central regions. One can observe an extremely strong relationship between metropolitan area size and suburbanization of manufacturing jobs. The larger the metropolitan area, the greater the central-city manufacturing job loss and the greater the employment gain in the suburbs. The thirty-three largest central cities in this country alone suffered a net loss of over 880,000 manufacturing jobs, while their suburbs gained more than 2.5 million jobs in this industrial sector.

Examining suburbanization of manufacturing employment by age of the metropolitan area, Table 2 shows that the oldest metropolitan central cities have experienced devastating losses in manufacturing jobs. In the forty-nine SMSAs that met metropolitan criteria before 1900, 1,370,873 manufacturing jobs were lost in the central cities, while their suburbs gained 2,308,096 positions. Newer SMSAs likewise exhibited substantial suburban growth in manufacturing employment, but their central cities did not suffer the crippling employment losses that the oldest SMSA central cities experienced.

Finally, Table 2 shows that manufacturing employment deconcentration is also highly selective by region. Central cities of SMSAs in the Northeast and North Central regions lost 770,532 and 906,236 manufacturing jobs, respectively. Yet central cities of SMSAs in the South and West regions of the nation exhibited large absolute employment gains. The regional breakdown further illustrates the shift of national industrial growth from the northern states to the South and West, with central cities in the Northeast and North Central regions suffering most of the manufacturing employment loss.

Table 3 presents data on the change between 1947 and 1972 in retail trade employment in the central cities and suburban rings of 247 SMSAs for which these data were available. Notice again that metropolitan size, age, and region describe quite well employment deconcentration in retailing, with the older, larger Northeast and North Central cities suffering the heaviest retail employment losses. The thirty-three central cities of SMSAs over 1 million population lost 565,125 retail jobs; the forty-nine SMSA central cities that attained metropolitan status before 1900 lost 757,491 retail jobs; the forty-two Northeast and 68 North Central SMSA central cities lost a total of 702,940 retail jobs. Conversely, the central cities of smaller, younger SMSAs and central cities of SMSAs in the South and West all showed retail employment gains.

Metropolitan employment deconcentration in the wholesale sector mirrors that of the retail sector. Table 4 indicates that the same types of cities (old, large, Northeast and North Central) are suffering the greatest job attrition in wholesale trade. When one combines the total central-city job losses in manufacturing, retail trade, and wholesale trade within the

Table 3. Changes in Retail Employment for Central Cities and
Suburban Rings (Adjusted for Annexation), 1947-1972.

Metropolitan Characteristics	Number of SMSAs	Central City		Suburbs	
		Mean	Absolute	Mean	Absolute
Size					
Under 250,000	115	550	63,250	3,144	361,560
250,000-500,000	63	87	5,481	8,624	543,312
500,000-1 million	36	−2,225	−80,100	17,961	646,596
Over 1 million	33	−17,125	−565,125	71,528	2,360,424
Inception Date[a]					
Before 1900	49	−15,459	−757,491	45,131	2,211,419
1900-1920	63	449	28,287	11,813	744,219
1920-1950	53	984	52,152	9,074	480,922
After 1950	82	1,227	100,614	5,796	475,272
Region					
Northeast	42	−9,098	−382,116	17,522	735,924
South	99	626	61,974	12,014	1,189,386
North Central	68	−4,718	−320,824	17,591	1,196,188
West	38	1,698	64,524	20,798	790,324
Total	247	−2,334	−576,498	15,837	3,911,739

[a]Date when city met present metropolitan criteria.

largest and oldest central cities and those central cities in the
Northeast and North Central regions, the figures are boggling.
The thirty-three central cities of SMSAs with greater than a
million population lost a total of 1,747,218 jobs in the manufacturing, retail, and wholesale sectors between 1947 and 1972,
while their suburbs gained 5,681,313 jobs. The forty-nine
SMSA central cities that attained metropolitan status prior to
1900 lost a total of 2,495,129 manufacturing, retail, and wholesale jobs between 1947 and 1972, while their suburbs gained
5,324,487 jobs; the 110 SMSA central cities in the Northeast
and North Central regions lost a total of 2,696,384 manufacturing, retail, and wholesale jobs, while their suburbs gained a total
of 4,709,742 jobs in the same three industrial sectors. These
figures provide striking testimony to the massive deconcentration of economic activity since World War II in the larger,
older metropolitan areas of the North. As we have argued, this
extensive deconcentration has meant not only major tax revenue loss for the affected central cities but also an acute deterioration of employment opportunities for inner-city residents,
who generally cannot fill white collar administrative and professional service jobs, which we noted are actually accumulating in
these metropolitan centers.

Table 4. Changes in Wholesale Employment for Central Cities and
Suburban Rings (Adjusted for Annexation), 1947-1972.

Metropolitan Characteristics	Number of SMSAs	Central City		Suburbs	
		Mean	Absolute	Mean	Absolute
Size					
Under 250,000	114	257	29,298	860	98,040
250,000-500,000	63	488	30,744	2,616	164,808
500,000-1 million	36	184	6,624	6,970	250,920
Over 1 million	33	−9,152	−302,016	24,183	798,039
Inception Date[a]					
Before 1900	49	−7,485	−366,765	16,428	804,972
1900-1920	63	1,118	70,434	3,848	242,424
1920-1950	53	663	35,139	3,076	163,028
After 1950	81	320	25,920	1,251	101,331
Region					
Northeast	42	−5,236	−219,912	8,007	336,294
South	98	679	66,524	4,178	409,444
North Central	68	−1,423	−96,764	4,807	326,876
West	38	390	14,820	6,294	239,172
Total	246	−956	−235,176	5,332	1,311,672

[a]Date when city met present metropolitan criteria.

Illustrating the extent to which blue collar job opportunities are being replaced by white collar professional, technical, and administrative jobs in old northern central cities, Table 5 presents changes in the number of central-city jobs for five selected occupational categories in eighteen northern cities that attained 50,000 population before 1900. It is clear that these eighteen central cities registered substantial losses in employment in each of the three occupations categorized as blue collar

Table 5. Number of Jobs in Five Occupational Categories
in Eighteen Northern Cities, 1960-1970.

Occupation	1960	1970	Change
Professional and technical	1,018,663	1,222,650	203,987
Clerical	1,833,483	1,920,551	87,068
Craftsmen	1,099,584	904,231	−195,353
Operatives	1,673,811	1,188,200	−485,611
Laborers	320,074	251,264	−68,810

Note: Figures are for eighteen SMSA central cities in the Northeast and North Central regions that had populations of at least 50,000 each before 1900 and did not annex more than 5 percent of their population between 1960 and 1970. The data were computed from metropolitan place-of-work reports from the 1960 and 1970 censuses.

—craftsmen, operatives, and laborers—yet large gains in white collar professional, technical, and clerical employment. The total number of blue collar jobs in the eighteen cities declined by 749,774 positions in just a ten-year period, while white collar professional, technical, and clerical employment expanded by 291,055 positions.

With many blue collar workers still residing in central cities while blue collar jobs disperse to the suburban rings, and with many white collar workers having moved to the suburbs while white collar jobs continued to expand in the center, we should expect not only large declines in the number of people who live in the city and work there, but also substantial increases in the number of commuters from central-city residences to suburban jobs and from suburban residences to central-city jobs. Table 6, which provides data for 101 longitu-

Table 6. Journey-to-Work Streams Within 101 Longitudinally
Comparable SMSAs.

Residence/Workplace	1960	1970	Change
City/City	10,108,888	8,798,312	−1,310,576
City/Suburb	945,158	1,608,627	663,496
Suburb/City	3,118,779	3,994,045	880,316
Suburb/Suburb	5,967,787	8,549,448	2,581,661

dinally comparable SMSAs (that is, adjusted for annexation), shows that between 1960 and 1970 this was indeed the case. The number of central-city residents who also worked in the city declined by 1,310,576 between 1960 and 1970—1,098,577 of whom held blue collar jobs. During the same period, commuters from the suburbs to the cities increased by 880,316— 641,552 of whom were suburbanites holding white collar jobs in the central cities.

The deconcentration of metropolitan population since 1950 and large increases in the absolute number of suburban residents who commute to the central cities has placed additional public service burdens on the central cities. For example, the suburban rings of all SMSAs in the Northeast and North Central regions of the nation increased in size by an average of slightly over 100,000 residents per decade between 1950 and 1970, while the central cities population in these regions was unchanged (Kasarda and Redfearn, 1975). If only one out of every ten of these new suburban residents maintained regular contact with the central cities, this would have increased the average number of suburban residents regularly using the city by 10,000 persons during each decade. Thus, it seems likely that although some of these central cities experienced absolute declines in resident population, the total number of people using the city on a daily basis actually increased.

Beginning with the working assumption that central-city public services develop to accommodate the total amount of activity conducted in the central city, much of which stems from the suburban population, let us examine the proposition that suburban growth and numbers of suburban commuters have a substantial impact on the operating costs for central-city services (Kasarda, 1972). Tables 7 and 8 highlight the findings.

The path coefficients (standardized partial-regression coefficients) presented in Table 7 describe the direct effects of

Table 7. Path Coefficients Between Changes in Operating Expenditures (in Constant Dollars) for Central-City Service Functions and Changes in Central-City and Suburban Populations.

Service Function	1950-1960		1960-1970	
	Central City	Suburban Ring[a]	Central City	Suburban Ring[a]
Police	−0.12	0.74	0.13	0.56
Fire prevention	0.01	0.79	0.17	0.54
Highway	−0.13	0.61	0.17	0.51
Sanitation	−0.03	0.72	0.18	0.62
Recreation	−0.10	0.80	0.23[b]	0.54
General control	−0.10	0.51	0.20[b]	0.58

Note: The data pertain to 168 SMSAs defined as of 1950. Police service includes police patrols and communications, crime-prevention activities, detention and custody of persons awaiting trial, traffic safety, vehicular inspection, and the like. Fire prevention services include inspection for fire hazards; maintaining fire-fighting facilities, such as fire hydrants; and other fire prevention activities. Highway services include maintenance of streets, highways, and related structures; snow and ice removal; toll highways and bridge facilities; and ferries. Sanitation services include street cleaning, collection and disposal of garbage and other waste, sanitary engineering, smoke regulation, and other health activities. Recreation services include maintenance of museums and art galleries, playgrounds, play fields, stadiums, swimming pools and bathing beaches, municipal parks, auditoriums, auto camps, recreation piers, and boat harbors. General control includes central staff services and agencies concerned with tax assessment and collection, accounting, auditing, budgeting, purchasing, and other finance activities (U.S. Bureau of the Census, 1970, pp. 64-67).

[a]$p < 0.001$.

[b]$p < 0.01$.

Source: Kasarda, 1972.

central-city population change and suburban population change during the two decades from 1950 to 1970 on change in operating expenditures (in constant dollars) for six common central-city service functions. It is clear that change in operating expenditures for common public services in the central cities has been very sensitive to changes in the size of the suburban population since 1950. In fact, change in operating expenditures for each of the public service functions has been far more closely related to change in the suburban population than to change in the central-city population itself. Note, however, that with the exception of general control, the impact of suburban growth was greater on each central service expenditure between 1950 and 1960 than between 1960 and 1970. I expect that the impact of suburban population growth on city services will decline much further between 1970 and 1980, since the continuing suburbanization of white collar jobs, prestigious department stores, professional services, and many cultural and recreational complexes will substantially reduce the use of the central cities by suburbanites. Nevertheless, the measured impact of suburban population growth on city operating expenditures to date remains substantial.

One of the reasons that the suburban impact has remained strong is that the absolute number of suburban commuters to central-city jobs is a linear function of suburban population size $(r = 0.94)$. Moreover, regarding degree of non-

Table 8. Path Coefficients Between Per Capita Operating Expenditures for Central-City Public Services and Selected Variables in 1960.

Service Function	Central City Population (log)	Suburban Commuters (log)[a]	Central City Age	Central City Income (Per Capita)	Percent Nonwhite Central City
Police	−0.02	0.52	0.06	0.17	0.16
Fire prevention	−0.52[a]	0.44	0.32[a]	0.21[b]	−0.04
Highway	−0.40[a]	0.28	0.14	0.18	−0.08
Sanitation	0.02	0.31	−0.18	0.14	0.26[a]
Recreation	−0.18	0.24	0.03	0.11	0.12
General control	−0.21[b]	0.28	0.25[a]	0.20[b]	0.22[b]

Note: Data based on 157 SMSAs.

[a] $p < 0.001$.

[b] $p < 0.01$.

Source: Kasarda, 1972.

resident use of the central city, the same study showed that the ratio of suburban residents working in the central city to the resident central-city population increased disproportionately with the size of the suburban population. A zero-order correlation coefficient of 0.46 was found between suburban population size and the ratio of suburban residents working in the central city to the central-city resident population. On the average, there were 132 suburban commuters per 1,000 central-city residents (Kasarda, 1972).

Table 8 documents the relative effect of size of the suburban commuting population on operating expenditures of central-city service functions. Controlling for central-city size, central-city age, per capita income of central-city residents, and the percentage of nonwhite residents in the city, the number of suburban commuters exhibits highly significant direct effects on all measured per capita public service expenditures in the central cities. It is interesting to point out that, controlling for the number of suburban commuters, metropolitan age, and resident composition, there is a substantial economy of scale in providing fire and highway services in central cities. That is, *ceteris paribus*, as the population size of a central city increases, per capita expenditures for fire and highway services rise less than proportionately.

The important result for our purpose, though, is that neither the size nor the population composition of central cities inflates per capita operating costs nearly as much as does the number of suburbanites who commute to work in the central city. Together, Tables 7 and 8 empirically support the thesis that the huge growth of the suburban population since World War II and concurrent increases in the absolute numbers of suburban commuters making routine use of the central city has substantially raised the demand and hence increased the costs of providing common central-city public services.

The question of whether suburban populations are exploiting the central cities by imposing marginal costs on the central cities without full repayment of the additional service costs remains debatable. Many suburban residents who regularly use the city pay city income taxes, user charges (such as bridge tolls), and sales taxes, and they indirectly raise the tax value of private buildings where they work or shop. However, limited research has indicated that these sources do not generate the necessary revenue to cover the additional city service costs that suburbanites create. Neenan (1970), for example, in a detailed

econometric analysis of benefit and revenue flows between
Detroit and six of its suburban municipalities, representing both
residential and industrial suburbs, concluded that the suburban
communities enjoy a considerable net gain from the public service sector of Detroit. Neenan's analysis showed that the net subsidy to the suburban communities from Detroit ranges from
$1.73 per capita to the low-income industrial suburb of High-
land Park to $12.58 per capita to the high-income residential
and commercial suburb of Birmingham. Moreover, these figures
do not include the indirect subsidy that Detroit provides to
many of its suburban communities by bearing a disproportionate share of the metropolitan welfare burden. If racial and
income exclusionary practices of many suburban communities
are considered, the measured subsidy they receive from the central cities would no doubt increase.

Summary and Comment

To reiterate, the argument developed in this chapter is
that the two-way movements of metropolitan expansion are the
source of the employment and fiscal problems faced by large
metropolitan central cities in the United States. The basic movements have involved the drift of middle- and upper-income
population to the suburban rings and their replacement in the
cities by much lower income groups, the suburbanization of
commerce and blue collar industries beyond the taxing jurisdictions of the central cities and beyond the reach of the urban
poor, and the daily flow into and out of the central city of large
numbers of suburbanites, who thus add to the costs of city public services. The specific consequences of these interrelated
movements include eroding city tax bases, exceptionally high
rates of inner-city unemployment, rising urban welfare rolls,
and increased debt service.

The data presented dramatically illustrate that the old,
large central cities in the northern industrial belt are rapidly losing their employment base to the suburbs and to the newer
regions of the South and West. Jobs that are increasing in the
large, older northern cities, such as in administration and professional services, are inappropriate for the educational backgrounds and skills of the majority of their residents. Commuting
both into and out of the cities has, therefore, greatly increased
since World War II and placed additional strains on the operating budgets of city governments and the personal budgets of

inner-city residents who must drive to blue collar jobs dispersed throughout the suburban rings.

What can we say about the future of the metropolitan community? While our statements here are necessarily specula- tive, the trends appear well established. We should anticipate a continuing larger absolute movement of whites compared with blacks and other minorities from the central cities, which will eventually lead the overall central-city residential composition to minority dominance. We should also anticipate a continued deterioration of blue collar employment opportunities in the central cities and concurrent growth of those opportunities in the suburban rings, leading to expanding pockets of unemploy- ment and poverty in the inner cities and the evolution of larger numbers of lower-income (working class) suburban enclaves near industrial parks and other suburban blue collar job com- plexes. Mobile home communities will proliferate in suburban ring areas, especially in the rural fringe portions.

The long-term process of lower-income populations mi- grating to the central cities and then moving outward to better residential zones as their socioeconomic status improves will remain strong, however. For example, the median family in- come of central-city blacks who migrated from nonmetropoli- tan areas between 1970 and 1975 was only $5,037—about one- half that of black families already residing in the central cities. The average family income of all those entering the central cities between 1970 and 1974 was $10,300, compared with $12,500 for those leaving the central cities (Berry and Dah- mann, 1977; U.S. Bureau of the Census, 1975a, 1975b). The aggregate income in 1973 of families and unrelated individuals who moved out of the central cities between 1970 and 1974 was $55.3 billion, whereas that for families and unrelated indi- viduals who moved into the cities during this period was $25.7 billion. As a whole, central cities suffered a net loss of $29.6 billion in aggregate annual personal income between 1970 and 1974, resulting from differential migration and the wide gap in income levels between immigrants to and emigrants out of the central cities (U.S. Bureau of the Census, 1975b). Thus, while family income levels in the suburbs increased (in constant dol- lars) an average of 4.6 percent between 1970 and 1974, central- city income levels actually declined an average of 0.3 percent (Berry and Dahmann, 1977). These ominous declines in the aggregate personal income and in the average family and un- related individual income of central-city residents are a response to the basic structural transformations described in this chapter.

Some point to encouraging signs for the cities, such as the restoration and revival of inner-city high-income neighborhoods (for example, Georgetown in the District of Columbia and New Town on Chicago's north side) and the growth of luxury apartments and condominiums at prime locations in and around the central business districts of our large cities. However these enclaves of inner-city residential wealth have attracted small numbers compared with the overall emigration to suburbia of middle- and upper-income families that has occurred since World War II. Poor public schools and high crime rates in the inner cities remain powerful repelling forces, which have tended to dissuade all but a unique set of middle- and upper-income persons from returning from suburbia to city residences. Most of those returning are not middle- and upper-income families with school-age children but adult singles, young professionals, newly married couples, and older, wealthier couples whose children have left the household. Many are semitransient, moving after short periods of time, while others are only part-time city residents who maintain vacation or recreational homes elsewhere. In almost all cases, they reside in highly segregated complexes (by age as well as by race and class), fortified by electric door locks, security guards, closed-circuit television, and what otherwise has come to be known as the "architecture of defense."

From a sociological perspective, racial, ethnic, and class polarization has replaced the old notion of the urban melting pot. Segregation rather than assimilation is the pervasive sociospatial feature in both city and suburb. What the White House Commission on Crimes of Violence predicted in 1969 is now approaching reality:

> We can expect further social fragmentation of the urban environment, formation of excessively parochial communities, greater segregation of different racial groups and economic classes . . . and polarization of attitudes on a variety of issues. It is logical to expect the establishment of the "defensive city," the modern counterpart of the fortified medieval city, consisting of an economically declining central business district in the inner city protected by people shopping or working in buildings during daylight hours and "sealed off" by po-

lice during nighttime hours. Highrise apartment buildings and residential "compounds" will be fortified "cells" for upper-, middle- and high-income populations living at prime locations in the inner city. Suburban neighborhoods, geographically removed from the central city, will be "safe areas," protected mainly by racial and economic homogeneity and by distance from population groups with the highest propensities to commit crime. Many parts of central cities will witness frequent and widespread crime, perhaps out of police control [Mulvihill, Tumin, and Curtis, 1969].

These polarization patterns and consequent economic disparities between the central cities and suburban rings will likely grow as the deconcentration of white collar jobs, professional and financial services, prestigious retail establishments, and cultural and entertainment facilities makes central-city services and facilities superfluous to the suburban masses. With core domination on the wane, even in the administrative and professional service sectors, central business districts are becoming just one specialized node in a multinodal, multiconnective metropolitan system of suburban office building complexes, industrial parks, and regional shopping centers and malls. Fueled by the interaction of social, economic, and technological forces, the reverse thrust of counterurbanization has transformed the fried-egg pattern of the old industrial metropolis into a pattern that now looks more like a scrambled egg. In the process, the bulk of this nation's urban wealth and tax resources has shifted from the cities to the suburbs and exurbs.

The outcome of all the above will likely be a new form of geopolitical welfare, as federal and state governments increasingly transfer funds on an areal basis from more economically viable suburban and exurban communities to the less viable central cities. Postindustrial counterurbanization forces are so strong that only through growing infusions of intergovernmental transfers and subsidies, such as revenue sharing, block grants, and jobs programs, will large central-city governments be able to pay their bills and provide employment for their poor.

3

Life-Style, Leisure, and Community Life

William Kornblum
Terry Williams

The physical and social characteristics of metropolitan regions are now influenced as much by the leisure life-styles of American culture as by any other social force. This observation, which will be developed as the general theme of this chapter, appears to be true for the microecological level of the neighborhood as well as for the present development of entire metropolitan regions. In the previous century, the location of business districts and industrial production centers played the dominant role in

The research and writing for this chapter were made possible, in part, by a summer stipend from the National Endowment for the Humanities in 1977. The authors wish to thank Professor Rolf Meyersohn for his most generous assistance in the research and his insightful comments on the text.

Life-Style, Leisure, and Community Life 59

shaping the physical and temporal features of the cities. Pleasure grounds for the work-worn urban masses were usually "river ward" honky-tonks or the "beaux arts" parks and promenades designed with the tastes of a more elite public in mind.

Today, entire geographic regions like the coast of Florida, the foothills of Arizona, the major national parks of the Pacific Northwest and the Rockies, much of southern California, and the barrier islands of the East Coast may be regarded as "recreationscapes" (Carter, 1975; Thomas, 1956). These vast areas of land and supporting access systems serve populations for whom the primary attractions are resources of fresh air, open space, and water. This is particularly true for the "Sun Belt" region, which is experiencing the greatest population and economic growth. On a national scale these demographic shifts are explained in large part by the competitive advantage of warmer climates in an era of rising energy costs, as well as by the previously uneven distribution of industry between the North and South. But in many areas of the southern rim, the migration of relatively affluent and leisured populations is a major population stream as well.

Even within the oldest cities of the North American continent, in the interior of New York, Boston, Montreal, Philadelphia, and San Francisco, for example, the loss of industrial capacity is offset somewhat by the role that these central cities play as entertainment zones and centers for the production of popular culture. Some cities are purveyors of fun and intellectual stimulation mainly for their own metropolitan populations. Cities like New York, Boston, and Los Angeles, however, are important producers of culture and entertainment on national and even global levels (Hall, 1966).

In many respects these are highly problematic trends. The resources of the rapidly developing, recreation-centered areas of the continent are continually threatened with overuse. Dilemmas of planning for public use and future preservation severely tax the capabilities of public agencies at all levels of government (Jarrett, 1966). Nor is it clear that the older cities will succeed in maintaining their dominance as centers for the production and consumption of culture. Physical blight, segregation of the poor in ghetto neighborhoods, the suburbanites' fear of the central city, and the immense influence of television and the auto are only a few of the counter tendencies that account for the growth of entertainment zones in suburbia and the continued drain of population and resources from the central city.

If leisure behavior is becoming an increasingly important influence on the shape and quality of life of metropolitan regions, it is also true that changes in this behavior are notoriously difficult to predict. One must examine a variety of currents and crosscurrents in order to make even the roughest estimates of future directions of change in American tastes in entertainment, relaxation, and recreation (Zuzanek, 1976). And above all, differences in class and socioeconomic status still account for major differences in how people organize their lives outside the workplace. Although television, the automobile, and mass education are mighty contributors to the formation of a national culture, these powerful institutions have not eliminated the growth of subcultures that find their expression in the diverse leisure life-styles of the population. Just as television has helped to create national audiences for political campaigns and sporting events, it has also introduced the population to a multitude of new ways to spend leisure time. Surfing, karate, crafts fairs, soccer, hang gliding, meditation, encounter groups, organic gardening, sexual innovation, and cross country skiing are all examples of leisure behavior that create their own social worlds. There are many others one could mention, but these are some examples whose popularity has grown significantly within the past ten years (Cheek and Burch, 1976).

Study of the spread and the ecology of leisure cultures is of immense importance in attempts to plan for the future of the nation's natural resources of land, water, air, and energy. For example, there are millions of Americans who enjoy camping and fishing in their leisure time. But there are many more millions who prefer to watch paid performers play games and take risks. While one might wish that more people would engage in participatory recreation like fishing and camping, it is also true that any drastic shift in the demands placed on the nation's sport fisheries could have quite dangerous consequences for the balance of food resources. Unfortunately, the all too frequent response to this problem is to perpetuate inequities based on socioeconomic status. Neglect of the poor, elderly, and handicapped in the delivery of recreational services remains the most serious problem of the field. We shall show later in this chapter that the policies of public agencies in the field of recreation and leisure services too often amount to nothing less than socialism for the well-off.

The ecological perspective of this analysis represents something of a shift from the concerns for the future of leisure and recreation that were being expressed during the 1950s and most of the 1960s. Once the people of North America had developed their own approaches to play and recreation, a topic that is perhaps best treated in Dulles's masterful *America Learns to Play* (1965), cast aside puritanical restraints, and fought for free time from the occupational routine, sociologists began to question what people would do with their newfound freedom. Throughout DeGrazia's *Of Time, Work, and Leisure* (1962) and Larrabee and Meyersohn's *Mass Leisure* (1958), the theme of adjustment to increasing leisure is the main concern. Summing up the issue, Riesman noted, "For many people today, the sudden onrush of leisure is a version of technological unemployment; their education has not prepared them for it and the creation of new wants at their expense moves faster than the ability to order and assimilate these wants" (1958, p. 366).

For various reasons that will be outlined shortly, the "leisure explosion" that was feared in the middle of the century never occurred. At the same time, however, in the work of Riesman, Berger, Meyersohn, and other founders of the field of leisure study in sociology, there is a keen awareness of the equity problem and the environmental stress that accompanies the rapid escalation of wants. Thus in the same essay cited above, Riesman (1958, p. 382) wrote a prophetic warning to those who would gloat over the affluence of their society: "By concentrating all energies in preserving freedom from want and pressing for consumer satiation at ever more opulent levels, we jeopardize this achievement in a world where there are many more poor nations than rich ones and in which there are many more desires, even among ourselves, for things other than abundance."

Today this warning is commonplace, but three decades ago a much smaller number of social scientists like Lewis Mumford, Harrison Brown, and David Riesman were applying ecological principles and concerns about resources to problems of the urban environment. In 1938, for example, Mumford (p. 251) wrote:

> Since 1910 or thereabouts, the highways of motor traffic have begun to spread out from every metropolis in ever thickening and multiplying streams; these highways carry with them the environment of the metropolis: the paved highway, the filling station, the roadside slum, the ribbon development of houses, the roadhouses and caba-

ret. The farther and faster one travels, the more the life that accompanies one remains like that one has left behind. The same standardization of ugliness; the same mechanical substitutes; the same cockney indifference to nature; the same flippant attitude; the same celluloid pleasures and canned noise. A row of bungalows in the open country alongside an express highway is a "metropolitan fact"; so are the little heaps of week-end cabins by lake or stream or oceanside. Their density and concentration may not be greater than that of a rural village, but in their mode of life, their amusements, their frame of social reference, they are entirely metropolitan, hardly better or worse for being fifty miles away from the center.

Mumford and his mentor Patrick Geddes, the British urban sociologist, viewed metropolitan growth from a perspective that owed much to the influence of nineteenth-century upper-class radicals and reformists like Ruskin, William Morris, and the Fabian socialists (Mumford, 1938). Today this perspective is quite alive in the work of regional planners and ecologists like Ian McHarg, whose book *Design with Nature* (1969) is an advanced statement of the environmental tradition in planning and in critical urban thought. The perspective on leisure, and especially outdoor recreation resources, that is developed here owes a great deal to this tradition. But the planners' condemnation of mass leisure frequently exhibits quite overt elitism. The stress given in these pages to the problem of equity in the allocation of recreation and leisure resources is a necessary counterpoise to the values of "pure" environmentalists (Sills, 1975).

The overall influence that leisure and recreation choices exert over the ecology of metropolitan regions is only now becoming a field of empirical research in urban studies. Pioneering work on the subject such as Clawson and Knetsch's *The Economics of Outdoor Recreation* (1967), Whyte's *The Last Landscape* (1970), and DeGrazia's *Of Time, Work, and Leisure* (1962) are now joined by the excellent political analysis offered by Robert Caro in *The Power Broker* (1974) and the extensive time-budget research of economists and sociologists. These sources and others that will be reviewed provide the foundation of an understanding of the economic, cultural, and political forces that form the population's leisure choices. These choices, in turn, play a major role in bringing about patterns of metropolitan land use and transportation. In developing this theme, therefore, it is necessary to turn first to the subject of participation rates and the use of scarce leisure time by the residents of metropolitan North America.

Stratification and Use of Leisure Time

Sociologists who have reviewed available quantitative studies of time use since the early decades of the twentieth century are in general agreement that the predictions of rapidly increasing leisure time were rather hasty. Continuing occupational time pressures have prevented the rise of a leisure class as a widespread phenomenon except in the most negative forms of unemployment and underemployment. It is true that the transformation from an agrarian to an industrial society did create the conditions for mass leisure. But the actual distribution of free time in the form of leisure for wage workers had to await hard-won reforms like the child labor laws and the forty-hour week (Veblen, 1953; DeGrazia, 1962; Anderson, 1961). These changes were generally resisted by the owners of capital and thus took longer to penetrate throughout the industrial order than did changes in the nature of production itself. For this reason the average length of time spent at work for industrial workers did not begin diminishing steadily until the middle decades of this century. These reductions tended to level off for most groups in the 1960s. Due to overtime work, salaried employment, and second jobs, the mean time spent at work today is 46.0 hours per week, even though significant proportions of workers in the labor force hold part-time jobs. This is particularly true of women, who have been entering the labor force in record numbers since the 1950s. The decades since 1950 have been marked by a very low (2 percent per decade) decrease in working hours. This almost imperceptible decline promises to hold despite the increasing prevalence of longer vacations, earlier retirement, and experiments with altered work schedules and four-day work weeks (Kando, 1975).

The phrase "less work, less leisure" remains a good summary of the current situation in most industrial societies, and especially so in the United States and Canada (Swados, 1958). Scarcity of work and rapid technological change leave high proportions of the potential labor force out of work or in school. The unemployed and students are populations with relatively large amounts of free time but with limited expendable income

for leisure pursuits (Kreps, 1968). At the other extreme, at least
8 percent of nonagricultural workers in the United States work
60 hours per week or more as opposed to the 4 percent who did
so in 1940 (Henle, 1966). Only about 2 percent of this rise is
accounted for by people with extra jobs. A somewhat greater
proportion are scientists, corporate executives, professors, lawyers, and other professionals who strive for professional prestige
and tend to invest their free time in work and work-related
activities like education (Wilensky, 1963). The paradoxical consequence of this trend is that the households with the greatest
education, training, and motivation for a diversity of leisure experiences have the least time to pursue them. For this segment
of the population, which Linder aptly calls the "harried leisure
class," the hectic pace of work is carried over to family and
leisure life (Linder, 1970).

Americans tend to choose blocks of leisure rather than
additions to their daily discretionary hours (Zuzanek, 1976).
An indication of this fact is the rapid increase in paid vacations
in recent years. In 1965 only 7 percent of all plant workers received nine or more holidays per year. By 1973 that had increased to 46 percent of the blue collar labor force. Of course
this increase in official holidays does not imply that hourly
workers actually enjoy them as free time, since a common pattern for workers is to actively seek work on holidays because
they are "premium" wage-rate days. Vacations are less easily
converted into wage equivalents, but workers with young families or heavy financial burdens do frequently "cash in" their
vacations as well, a pattern that extends the harried quality of
work and leisure life in many blue collar communities. The
length of vacations in major industries is increasing, nevertheless, especially now that steel workers are eligible for thirteen-
week vacations after fifteen years of service. In general, it
appears that vacation and holiday leisure time is preferred over
reductions in weekly hours because it allows for a larger range
of choices in activities and less loss due to commuting (Kreps
and Spengler, 1966). On the other hand, this leisure time use
tends to encourage more investment in recreation goods and
property and more centrifugal movement from cities and suburbs to exurban or rural recreation areas.

Studies in which respondents record daily time budgets
reveal that work, commuting, and personal care (including
sleep) leave North Americans with somewhat less than an average of five hours of nonobligatory time per day. On a weekly

basis, employed, married men work an average of 51.3 hours (including commuting) and have an average of 34.6 hours weekly of free time. Employed, married women averaged about 39 hours at work, performed an average of 33 hours of household work (against an average of 11.5 hours for their husbands), and had about 26 hours per week for leisure pursuits. In general, working women have approximately 10 hours less free time than do their husbands (Robinson, 1976; Vanek, 1974). Surprisingly, the pattern does not vary on weekends, due especially to the longer hours devoted to shopping, household chores, and personal care on those days.

Even the most aggregated distribution of actual free time, as presented in Table 1, shows that most leisure hours are spent in the home or automobile. Clearly television, leisure travel (mainly in automobiles), socializing with friends and kin, and reading the paper consume far more of the average American's

Table 1. Percentage of Free-Time Use, by Sex and Employment Status.

Leisure Activity	Employed Men (N = 520)	Employed Women (N = 342)	Housewives (N = 355)
Leisure travel	7	6	6
Study	4	3	1
Religion	3	4	4
Organizations	2	1	3
Radio	2	2	1
TV (home)	35	26	28
TV (away)	—	1	—
Read paper	9	6	6
Read magazines	2	3	2
Read books	1	2	2
Movies	1	1	1
Social (home)	7	12	10
Social (away)	12	12	12
Conversation	4	7	8
Active sports	3	2	1
Outdoors	1	—	1
Entertainment	2	3	1
Cultural events	—	—	—
Rest	2	4	4
Other leisure	3	7	10
Total	100	100	100

Note: A dash indicates less than 0.5 percent. Totals do not add to exactly 100 percent due to rounding.

Source: Robinson, 1976, p. 92.

leisure time than does participation in the civic culture of the community or in outdoor recreation outside the home. Indeed, in this culture television, the personal auto, and the circle of kin and friends are the pillars of everyday life outside the workplace.

This observation is confirmed in the work of other sociologists, who find that well over 70 percent of all visits to public recreation places are made by kin or friendship groups (Cheek, Field, and Burch, 1976). Chapin's study of the leisure and travel behavior of a sample of residents of Washington, D.C., also confirms the home-centered aspect of most personal free time. His sample of white and black respondents traveled an average of 9.00 and 11.24 miles, respectively, to their main jobs, while recreation mean trip lengths were within a 2.32 and 2.64 mile radius of the home, respectively (Chapin, 1974, p. 138).

While the average time-budget profile of American leisure shows the extreme dominance of the news media, of relaxation around the home, and of socialization with kin and friends, neither the great diversity of leisure pursuits nor the varied extremes of leisure behavior appear directly in the figures. Neither the deadening burden of excess free time among the unemployed nor the much more merry pace of fun among the affluent is shown in the overall figures. For an understanding of these patterns, it is necessary to look at what occurs in specific kinds of social settings within the nation's metropolitan regions. Analysis of daily life data are inadequate for this purpose, and quick judgments about the future of mass culture and leisure are extremely risky. In the 1950s and early 1960s, the rise of television and new professional sports led to the fashionable claim that the United States was becoming a sedentary society, that mass leisure pursuits led to the dangers of "spectatoritis" (Collins, 1954). More recently, authors like Scitovsky (1976) and MacCannell (1976) have pointed to the failure of American culture to stimulate consumer satisfaction, especially in leisure. consumption. Theirs are critical studies of the modern consumer economy and what appears to be its various forms of alienated leisure. While the writers personally share their bias against sedentary and consumerist activities, their critical viewpoint ignores the behavior of millions of energetic and creative Americans. As Dulles (1965, p. 396) observed about the leisure explosion following World War II:

> Every manufactured entertainment, for all its drawbacks, represented for the common man something

he had never before known, while the successive crazes for sports and games gave his life unprecedented scope. The broad pattern of mid-twentieth century recreation looked quite different to those who had the opportunity to enjoy it for the first time than it did to the sophisticated students of mass culture. Moreover, in addition to participant sports, the steadily growing range of hobbies and other individual forms of amusement once again suggested that commercial entertainment could never wholly monopolize popular recreation.

The range of interests of the American public is so broad as to defy description. Fads, crazes, and trends broaden the diversity of free-time use each year as the democratization of leisure and recreation continues. Some of the most important forms of recreation and their changes in popularity have tremendous impact on the ecology and social life of metropolitan regions.

Leisure Institutions and the Metropolitan Ecology

Recreation is a $70 billion a year business in the United States. The annual ebb and flow of vacationers to the continent's recreation grounds is a migration pattern unparalleled in its volume and complexity. The economic base of entire cities like Miami, San Diego, Las Vegas, San Juan, and Honolulu are dependent on this traffic, and even in New York, with its more diverse economy, tourism is the second most important industry. A complete inventory of leisure's influences on metropolitan growth is impossible here. But if one considers the influence of parks and open spaces, organized sports, and music and cultural institutions, many of the major contemporary influences are revealed.

Study of the role played by parks and open spaces in creating a metropolitan ecology is gaining emphasis in urban sociology and regional planning. Recognition of the relationship between parks and the quality of urban life is essential to this perspective. As August Heckscher (1977, p. 2) observed: "The future of cities will, it is clear, be largely determined by the degrees to which people develop a positive desire to live in them. Compactness is no longer a necessity (except as energy shortages may ultimately make it so). If people continue to gather in tightly knit agglomerations, it will be because they enjoy the stimulation and benefits which city life provides. Among the benefits, agreeable open space should not be underestimated."

The spatial organization of most North American cities is quite dependent on the physical and social influence of major parks. The Burnham plan for Chicago and Olmsted's great parks in New York, Philadelphia, and San Francisco were designed to preserve the outstanding features of the original topography of cities and to enhance the mental health of city people. Although in recent years the latter function of parks has come under question (Gans, 1968), the great city parks should be thought of as more than playgrounds or shady oases from the pace of daily urban life. They are one of the only common meeting grounds for the city's diverse populations. They offer a glimpse at a city's civic culture and its level of civilization. It should also be recalled that Washington, D.C., Indianapolis, Cleveland, Philadelphia, Boston, San Antonio, New York, Toronto, Montreal, Kansas City, San Francisco, and Cincinnati all maintain major park systems within the central city, which were planned in the early period of each city's rapid settlement. Thenceforth these parks established the limits and the contours of future urban growth. The history of park systems in cities often reveals the basic conflicts over land use that continue to influence metropolitan patterns of growth.

The history of struggles by the political and economic leaders of Kansas City to achieve a city plan based on a skeletal system of parks and boulevards is a fine example of the central role that parks have played in urban growth dynamics. Heckscher (1977, p. 202) describes the Kansas City conflict as follows:

> The achievement of a coherent park system was not without its dramatic moments and its eccentric characters. The 1890 battle for the establishment of a park and boulevard authority was at the bottom of the age-old fight between two concepts of the city. On the one hand were land speculators—those who put growth above all other goals and set as a foremost value their capacity and that of their brethren to enrich themselves. On the other side were those with an image of what a decent city for living might be.
>
> In the course of rhetorical exchanges the speculators declared parks to be places "where scented dudes smoke cigarettes and play croquet with girls as silly as

themselves." They spoke of boulevards as "streets decorated for the wives and daughters of millionaires to drive
on." But they met their match in the park forces. A crucial amendment to the city charter was carried in 1895.
"Kansas City is going to move on" cried the park leaders
of the day. "The new age dates from the election of yesterday, when the mossbacks went down before the forces
of progress."

Not every city had an elite that welcomed the ideas of
the city planners or so readily opened their purses to pay the
fees for resource preservation and park landscaping. Not every
vote ended happily, nor do they today, for the cause of greenery and outdoor life. San Francisco lost its park building momentum after the earthquake of 1906. New York's metropolitan park system grew enormously under the reign of Robert
Moses, but total surrender to the automobile now effectively
deprives the 35 percent of New York City households that do
not have cars from gaining equal access to the great parks and
beaches of Long Island and the Hudson Valley (Caro, 1974).
And in Los Angeles, the failure to develop a strong parks constituency at all levels of the city polity permitted the encroachment of sprawling tract housing on invaluable mountainsides
and ocean frontage.

The historical conditions and conflicts that characterize
park development may produce lasting differences in the physical and social ecology of metropolitan regions. These conflicts
also may indicate the relative importance of what Banfield
(1961) has called "public regarding" versus "private regarding"
political segments of a city's elite. In general, park issues frequently continue to command the time and attention of metropolitan elites who otherwise pay relatively little attention to the
day-to-day trials of city politics and political party organization.
Along with other cultural institutions of American cities, parks
continue to excite the civic participation of families who represent "old wealth" and who frequently find themselves aligned
against those who wish to diminish open space and park lands in
favor of more intense uses, such as freeways and sports stadiums. Indeed, the steady rise of participatory and spectator
sports since the turn of the century has produced some of the
most controversial issues between park and sports advocates.

The social forces that account for public participation in
sports grow more complex each decade. Here the striking facts

are those regarding the enormous numbers of participants and spectators. Youth and adolescent sports alone account for a great deal of public investment of time and money, especially in suburban communities and medium-sized cities. This is a relatively new development. Before World War II, the typical youth sports field was not the well-organized and manicured little league stadium but the dusty sandlot. Today, high school and little league sports are a major pastime in communities like Reading, Pennsylvania; Canton, Ohio; Hamtramck, Michigan; Everett, Washington; and hundreds of nonuniversity, blue collar towns in which the dreams of parents for social mobility for their children are intensely focused on the competitive sports field. This aspect of sports alone is worthy of a major study, but we shall necessarily limit this discussion to the influence of sports institutions on the metropolitan ecology.

In 1976 Americans owned about 50 million pleasure boats, from small rowboats to yachts. In the same year 10 million Americans, primarily adolescents, used skateboards. Sixteen million played tennis and about 14 million played golf. For golfers, this was an increase from about 8 million twenty years ago when golf, like tennis, was an elite pastime. Since 1955, the number of tennis courts increased from 13,188 to well over 20,000. The number of softball diamonds rose from 12,000 in 1955 to more than 19,000 in 1976. On the more sedentary side of sports consumption, it may be noted that major league baseball attendance in 1976 was 31 million, an increase of 1.2 million above 1973. There are now twenty-six major league baseball teams and thirteen cities with over a million ticket sales annually. Professional basketball hosted 9.8 million fans in the 1976-77 season, about 2 million more than in the previous year. For the purposes of this paper, it is noteworthy that in American cities there are 118 sports arenas with seating capacities of over 4,000.

The politics of league franchises and of the financing and location of major sports complexes is one of the most revealing issues in the nation's metropolitan regions. The growth proponents of any metropolitan region can be expected to line up solidly behind proposals to build major new sports facilities. New stadiums are symbolic of an aggressive booster concept of urban achievement, just as electric interurban trains and skyscrapers were in earlier periods of urban development. This is especially true when, as in the cases of Houston and Seattle, the new stadium promises to elevate the city to major league status.

Competition between the New Jersey Meadowlands and the stadiums of New York City is another good example of the major role professional sports now play in metropolitan growth. In the vast New York and New Jersey metropolitan region, the issues about how many teams will play particular sports and where they will be located go well beyond the apparent bickering between the team owners themselves. At the heart of the matter is competition for the attention of millions of people, whom the media salesmen term *prime demographics,* that is, the mobile adults in the family-forming years who are the key spenders for most consumer goods. With its concentration of a wide variety of sports and gambling opportunities and its convenience for auto travel from all points in the region, the Meadowlands represents the new generation of sports and spectator "cities," which, unlike the typical baseball and football stadiums of earlier decades, is no longer tied to the pedestrian and mass transit arteries of the city. Even more significant, the influence of the Meadowlands sports complex may tip the balance of media coverage sufficiently toward New Jersey to produce the necessary power alignments that will result in a new TV station for that media-poor side of the metropolitan region. In other words—and this is a proposition for further research— the ecology of sports complexes is intimately tied to the growth of TV markets, and both are dependent on negotiations among economic and political elites at metropolitan and national levels of the society. Big sports can shape the growth of television institutions just as the reverse has been true for the spectacular rise of professional athletics in general.

Another instance in which the growth of sports institutions alters the overall culture of the society is found in the rise of sports betting. Race track and other sports betting areas are related to the larger issue of gambling, a feature of the changing national culture that may have a lasting influence on urban life in America. It is difficult to determine now where the trend toward liberalization of gambling laws will lead individual metropolitan areas. It is quite certain, however, that the coming decade of metropolitan growth and social change will be much influenced by the spread of all forms of legalized gambling.

It is estimated that some 69 million Americans (about 48 percent of the adult population) patronize some form of legal or illegal commercial gambling each year (Commission on the Review of the National Policy Toward Gambling, 1976, p. 3). Of respondents in a national sample, 80 percent favored some form of legalized gambling, and in New York City alone

200,000 people place daily bets with Off Track Betting. With the legislation of casino gambling in Atlantic City, New Jersey, and the rapid spread of state lotteries since New Hampshire voters authorized the first state lottery in the twentieth century, legitimate gambling has seriously begun to compete with illegal games and betting.

The consequences of these trends are immense. The economics of entire communities may rise and fall with the legalization and control of gambling. More to the point of this essay, it is quite certain that gambling can generate the quantities of capital required to rebuild some of the declining inner-city and waterfront entertainment districts that declined with the rise of television, the spread of shoreline pollution, and the lure of warmer climates. The business community in places like the hotel district of the Catskill Mountains, the older beach communities of Los Angeles, Times Square in New York, Miami Beach, and the French Quarter of New Orleans views legalized gambling as perhaps the only means, given present money markets, to generate sufficient capital and patronage for the economic revitalization of formerly great bright-light districts. With the rebirth of these entertainment zones can come increased jobs for thousands of service workers, entertainers, and the entire range of occupations and leisure organizations that make city life fun.

The very unfortunate aspect of gambling as a means to revitalize decaying entertainment zones is that expenditures for gambling are regressive. A 1975 survey for the Commission on the Review of the National Policy Toward Gambling revealed that although the average amount spent on gambling increased as a function of income, the lower-income groups tended to spend a larger proportion of their income on gambling. Among respondents reporting household incomes less than $5,000, the percent spent on gambling amounted to 0.6 percent as opposed to 0.18 percent for those in the $30,000 or over bracket. These figures indicate that gambling is as regressive as the sales tax. Although it is estimated that legalization and adoption of the major forms of gambling throughout the country would generate some $8.2 billion annually, which might generate sorely needed jobs and investment in older central cities and metropolitan entertainment zones (Atlantic City is the most notable example), the burden of this increased economic growth would be borne by those least able to afford it (Commission on the Review of the National Policy Toward Gambling, 1976, pp. 65-67).

National and state investments in cultural institutions also tend to be regressive. In 1976 the National Endowment for the Arts allocated $98 million for the arts, including grants to museums, opera houses, art galleries, symphony orchestras, and dance companies. Biased toward the tastes of the educated middle and upper-middle class citizen, the publicly supported cultural institutions of North American cities tend to draw audiences of the same strata. Still, as Suttles has indicated elsewhere in this volume, investment in the great cultural institutions of central cities are an important incentive for continued middle class residence in inner cities. The role of cultural institutions in forming the character of metropolitan regions should never be neglected.

As an example of the importance of cultural institutions, consider the situation of amateur and professional orchestras. In the United States there are now over 1,400 orchestras, which cost about $40 million annually to operate and include at least thirty major symphony orchestras. Like sports teams, these organizations are community-forming institutions. They bring people with resources of talent, time, and money together for an activity that not only makes music but also provides a focus for identification and community pride. The same may be said frequently for smaller musical ensembles, including jazz and rock bands, choirs, ethnic music groups, and chamber music groups. According to a Harris Poll conducted in 1977, these and other musical activities draw from a musical talent pool estimated at 36 million Americans.

Museum attendance is another indicator of the relative importance of cultural institutions in the metropolitan ecology. The Smithsonian in Washington is the nation's most popular museum with about 15 million annual visitors. New York's Metropolitan Museum of Art may host as many as 5 million visitors, while the Statue of Liberty receives about 1.2 million. Chicago's Field Museum has about 1.5 million visitors annually; the Los Angeles County Museum of Natural History has about 1.2 million; the Boston Museum of Fine Arts has about 0.5 million; and the Denver Museum of Natural History about 0.8 million visitors each year. Thus while museum attendance is less important demographically than many other forms of recreation, it ranks well with even such mighty attractions as professional sports (Weaver, 1973).

From an ecological viewpoint, an important characteristic of museums in metropolitan regions is their centralizing influence. Aside from the historical facts of museum growth in cities, especially their place as monuments to the great elite collectors of Europe and America, museums have definite advantages in maintaining their central location in cities.' The New York Metropolitan Museum of Art, for example, each year hosts about 22 percent of visitors who are not residents of the metropolitan region, a fact that might suggest that its location in the interior of Manhattan is no longer necessary. But another 55 percent of the museum's visitors come from Manhattan or adjacent communities. Indeed, a full 23 percent of the visitors walk there from their apartments. This audience uses a great international art institution as its local resource and provides it with an enormous base of public support.

The same general pattern holds for lesser museums in metropolitan regions. The Newark Museum does not attract the large national and international audience that the Metropolitan Museum does, but it draws very heavily from both local and surrounding metropolitan New Jersey and New York communities. Significantly, it draws a rather high proportion of blue collar visitors, who tend to visit museums in much greater frequency when they are located adjacent to their communities (Johnson, 1969).

Of course not all cultural institutions have an advantage in central location, nor are they at all limited to the few examples treated here. Indeed the rapid growth of amateur theater and professional repertory theater in suburban communities deserves an analysis of its own. For the communities in which these institutions are found, their role as cultural centers and identity-forming symbols also cannot be overlooked.

A number of cities in the United States and Canada have created very successful entertainment districts close to the downtown commercial centers by recycling public fairgrounds. San Diego's restored Balboa Park is near museums and exhibitions on fairgrounds from the Panama-California Exposition of 1915; Seattle used its former World's Fair grounds for the site of its sports center and its major opera house; and Montreal's planners adapted the Expo fairgrounds in the St. Lawrence River adjacent to the central city. These are all outstanding examples of how the centralization of cultural facilities can contribute to revitalization of downtown areas, but the success of these attempts requires much more than the mere construction of impressive public edifices. The mobilization of thousands of the inner city's residents is required to ensure that once constructed, the cultural facilities will have the patrons and operating funds necessary to present high-quality entertainment. In this regard, the Tyrone Guthrie Theater in Minneapolis and the Seattle Opera are outstanding examples of how active participation by thousands of local citizens can maintain the operation of cultural institutions that have achieved national significance. But the maintenance of public enthusiasm and support is quite difficult and requires leadership that has skills in community organization as well as the requisite artistic ability (Salem, 1974; Baumol and Bowen, 1966).

In summary, analysis of trends in three leisure institutions—parks, sports, and cultural organizations—touches many of the important areas of leisure's influence on metropolitan regions. Park systems have an obvious although too often neglected impact on a region's physical ecology and its overall civic culture. The organization of professional sports leagues is quite dependent both on the size and the demographics of metropolitan regions, but controversies about sports facilities are indicators of more fundamental political cleavages. Finally, major cultural institutions can often remain as critical centralizing forces. Orchestras, museums, and theaters often engender their own occupational communities and unique constituencies. What is lacking in the analysis, however, is an indication of how specific subcultures influence entertainment zones and leisure areas of metropolitan regions.

Leisure Areas and Life-Styles in the Central Cities

The central cities of North America are witnessing a variety of changes in their specialized entertainment zones. Unfortunately, most tend to be for the worse. Faltering budgets for public parks, museums, and other cultural institutions; unchecked blight in the entertainment districts; the spread of pornography and commercial sex; closure of movie theaters and the ancillary businesses that thrived next to them—this, with many exceptions throughout urban America, is the familiar litany of the ills of the central-city leisure market.

These trends, and some of the forces that produce them, are by now rather well understood. Suburbanization and the suburbanite's fear of most central-city areas, as well as the impact of television and the automobile, have severely diminished the importance of central location in leisure behavior outside the home. This was apparent to urban scholars well before World War II. Still, the combined impact of these forces was not felt in full force until the late 1960s. For example, from 1954 to 1970 the number of movie theaters declined by 31 percent. With the decrease in central theaters came the concomitant growth of movies in suburban shopping centers and drive-in theaters. Nevertheless, the decline of the central movie theater meant the decline of nighttime leisure life in thousands of central-city neighborhoods throughout North America. With the movie house went the ice cream parlor or local restaurant that depended on the theater trade and that together with the theater created the nucleus of an entertainment zone in the most modest community or neighborhood.

The decline of bright-light districts and amusement parks is an even more striking example of changing ecological patterns in metropolitan North America after the 1940s. In the early and middle decades of the century every city emulated the great entertainment districts of New York City, Chicago, and Los Angeles. For good waterside entertainment there were few leisure centers that could rival Coney Island, Atlantic City, Chicago's Riverview, and St. Louis's Busch Gardens. All of these areas and hundreds of others modeled after them in smaller cities fell on harder times in recent years. The most devastating effects have been felt in medium-sized and small cities whose entertainment districts were developing in the 1940s and 1950s. Towns like Akron, Youngstown, Gary, Newark, and many others suffered most in the competition with the major metropolitan centers for the diminishing cosmopolitan clientele.

The major entertainment districts in the metropolitan centers have suffered, but they retain a good deal of vitality even as their monopoly on entertainment beyond the home has been lost to suburban competition. Broadway continues to be the mecca for commercial theater in the New York and New Jersey metropolitan region, just as downtown Seattle is for its region. An important determinant of the relative viability of urban entertainment zones is, of course, their accessibility. Too many central-city districts cannot compete with suburban locations due to lack of space for parking, while at the same time these districts lack adequate mass transit access. The older major cities of the United States have not had this problem quite so severely. They tend to have both a cosmopolitan population who seeks the cultural outlets that are best located centrally and a working class ethnic population that requires centralization to support specialized ethnic tastes. For this reason one finds ethnic commercial districts in Chicago and St.

Louis, for example, long after the majority of the ethnic group has moved into the suburbs. Since the central cities retain the commercial center for most ethnic groups, the older centers are once again the location of first settlement whenever there are new waves of immigration. New York has become the capital of major streams of migration from Latin America and Asia and has a new cultural transfusion that has rejuvenated many declining neighborhoods and commercial districts within the central city.

Nor is it necessary that these be nationality groups, as the experiences of San Francisco and Seattle demonstrate. Both these central cities have homosexual communities that have made tremendous contributions to the civic and leisure life available to the metropolitan population in general. What has been described as San Francisco's "culture of civility" owes a great deal to the cosmopolitan influence of the city's gay communities (Levine, 1977). It is doubtful that the great diversity of restaurants, theaters, musical groups, and other cultural institutions in these cities would flourish as they do without the efforts of gay entrepreneurs and the support of gay clients. Indeed the same can be said for most major American central cities. Here again, because their sexual preferences set them apart from the familistic suburbanites and because of the emphasis on artistic and cultural achievements in gay community life, the central location of the inner city offers a great many attractions to male and female homosexuals.

The central location of commercial sex and sexually deviant groups is not regarded as a blessing by the guardians of civic virtue. Writing in 1938, Mumford (pp. 265-266) noted:

> Every step in relaxation from spontaneous horse-play to drunkenness, from flirtation with music to a sexual orgy, is conducted with a view toward producing a maximum profit for the enterpriser. Saturnalia charges what the traffic will bear. Bawdiness . . . becomes itself a jaded, night-in-night-out part of metropolitan routine: it measures its titillations and charges accordingly. And since the overt code of Western society has no place for such compensatory outbursts or moral holidays, an additional air of furtiveness hangs over these enterprises, even when they have official sanctions. Thus is formed a tie-up with the underworld of racketeers and criminals which introduces new elements of degradation into gambling

and promiscuous sexual intercourse: connections between "respectable classes" and the underworld, by way
of pleasure, amusement and sexual release, that tend to
undermine the morale of the body politic.

Mumford's moralistic tone does not prevent an accurate
explanation of why pleasure seekers and the entrepreneurs who
serve them are a convenient target for criminals and corrupt
officials. The passage is also a good counterpoise to the writing
of journalists who often make it appear that the proliferation of
sex shops and pornography outlets is a new phenomenon in central entertainment zones. What is new, however, is the decline
of diversity in these areas. The closing of movie theaters, restaurants, and other retail establishments leaves vacancies in high-
rent entertainment zone properties. These can only be filled by
"adult use" tenants who can afford the extremely high rents.
This in turn leads to the emergence of red light districts that
specialize in a variety of commercialized sex. Again, these are
not new trends. They have been typical ecological processes in
American cities since the Gilded Age. Higher-status residents
have moved out of declining neighborhoods and many of their
diverse forms of entertainment have followed them.
    Where there are attractive residential areas adjacent to
such districts, the trend may be prevented, as in San Francisco's
North Beach, New York's Greenwich Village, Chicago's Old
Town, and Vancouver's Gastown. But where the entertainment
zone and its patrons account for the majority of non-work-hour
uses, it is much more difficult to alter the spread of commercialized sex.
    Detroit and Boston are two cities that have experimented
with the creation of legalized red light districts or "combat
zones," as they are called by the local press and police. These
districts are modeled after the European cities like Amsterdam
that have had legalized zones of prostitution for most of the
century. In principle, the creation of legal red light districts permits the city to strenuously enforce bans on the same behavior
elsewhere in the city. So far the zones have had very mixed
results, since it has proved quite difficult to maintain the safety
of visitors to them and it has been extremely difficult for the
cities to close similar establishments located elsewhere in the
central city. New York has so far rejected the idea of creating a
specific legal red light zone in the Times Square area and instead
has attempted to limit the spread of commercial sex establish-

ments through zoning limitations. All attempts at intervention in this central-city leisure life are fraught with legal and political hazards, and most city governments are extremely wary of experimentation.

Zoning and tax incentives are two of the most powerful policy strategies that cities have at their disposal in attempting to alter the downward spiral of entertainment zones. Here again, experiences in New York are a good example. In the late 1960s the future of the city's legitimate theater district in the Broadway area and elsewhere seemed threatened by the problems of a frightened middle class clientele, decaying physical structures in many older theaters, and of course the competition from television. Under the leadership of Mayor Lindsay and City Planner Donald Elliot, the city passed a new zoning ordinance that gave very lucrative exemptions from height and other restrictions to builders who would renovate or construct new theater facilities in the Broadway district. In consequence of this strategy and other quite tangible support to live theater, New York's legitimate theater audiences have grown in the 1970s, and the city is enjoying a renewal of its commercial theater (Moore, 1976; Barnett, 1974).

The vitality of entertainment zones is quite directly linked to the social history of particular life-styles in the city. The influence of ethnic enclaves and homosexuals in arts and leisure institutions has already been noted. In general it is clear that the voluntary segregation of single people, sophisticated upper-middle class urbanites, and art-related occupational groups can be both the product and the further cause of vitality in central-city leisure areas. The French Quarter in New Orleans, for example, has traditionally been a neighborhood for a felicitous mixture of Cajuns, bohemians, entertainers, gays, racially mixed marriages, and conventional apartment dwellers. This population base and that of the surrounding central city supports the weekday nightlife of the area, which in turn allows the weekend and tourist trade to spawn an even greater selection of restaurants and night spots. A similar example is the Capital Hill district of Seattle, home to a steadily growing number of communes and alternative community institutions. Collective action allows the communal groups to establish a great variety of small shops, restaurants, musical groups, and local associations in the neighborhood and also catalyzes similar activities elsewhere in the city.

The Hollywood district of Los Angeles in its prime was

also an example of how the centralization of a particular cultural group can lead to the growth of additional leisure institutions. Before the breakup of the big studios in the 1960s, the centralization of movie production created a residential base of movie celebrities and leaders of the motion picture industry. This population naturally attracted a larger number of tourists and hopefuls, whose patronage of commercial establishments in the area allowed Hollywood to become a major entertainment zone for the Los Angeles region (Powdermaker, 1972). Technological change and the emigration of celebrities has caused a decline in the relative importance of Hollywood as an entertainment zone of national significance. Nevertheless, its reputation, like that of Times Square, continues to sustain a seedy but flourishing nightlife. At the same time, the tremendous growth of a relatively affluent and highly mobile population throughout southern California has produced an incredible range of far-flung entertainment districts and specialized leisure cultures. The Los Angeles-San Diego corridor sustains numerous liberty zones for military personnel (for example, San Diego and Long Beach downtowns); bohemians (for example, Venice Beach); satellite city entertainment zones like Pasadena; older movie and vice districts of which Hollywood is the best example; university-based entertainment zones in Westwood, La Jolla, and elsewhere; suburban-family fun cities like Newport Beach; retirement havens in Palm Springs and La Jolla; and honky-tonk border towns like Tijuana.

For metropolitan regions that retain a central core, the problems of poverty and unemployment pose the most severe challenge to the vitality of leisure areas. Surveys that compare black and white central-city populations show very little difference in leisure preferences when income is held constant (Yancey, 1971). But with unemployment rates among inner-city blacks persisting at a level of about 15 percent for adults and more than 30 percent for young people throughout most of the 1970s, it is impossible for the vast majority of black households to join in the worlds of leisure beyond the neighborhood. Like generations of impoverished urban underclass people who came before them, today's inner-city poor develop their own highly local forms of association. These center around street corner peer groups, card parties, bars, pool halls, and the ubiquitous television set. But men and women without work or hope for satisfying jobs in the future can hardly be said to have leisure either. Instead their lives tend to be ruled by a desperate round of confrontations with impersonal bureaucracies and by efforts to establish shreds of self-respect (Liebow, 1967). A common product of ghetto despair was well described by James Baldwin in the 1950s. This passage from *Nobody Knows My Name* (1961) has, tragically, not become in the least dated:

> Many have given up. They stay home and watch the TV screen, living on the earnings of their parents, cousins, brothers, or uncles and only leave the house to go to the movies or to the nearest bar. "How're you making it?" one may ask, running into them along the block, or in the bar. "Oh, I'm TV-ing it," with the saddest, sweetest, most shamefaced of smiles, and from a great distance. This distance one is compelled to respect; anyone who has travelled so far will not easily be dragged again into the world. There are further retreats, of course, than the TV screen or the bar. There are those who are simply sitting on their stoops, "stoned," animated for a moment only, and hideously, by the approach of someone who may lend them the money for a "fix." Or by the approach of someone from whom they can purchase it, one of the shrewd ones, on the way to prison or just coming out.

While it is an accurate description of a withdrawal state, Baldwin's description obviously does not apply to all levels of black society, nor is the phenomenon limited to one racial group. On the other hand, one cannot underestimate the tremendous influence of television and radio in America's black communities. Typically the TV, purchased on the installment plan, becomes a substitute for travel, vacation homes, theater tickets, magazine subscriptions, hobbies, and cars (Caplovitz, 1963). TV dependence, it must be said, also produces high levels of consumer demands among blacks, who ironically become one of the most captive markets in the population. In 1972 black America earned $51.8 billion and faithfully spent an estimated $46 billion in the American economy.

Despite the plagues of poverty, crime, and discrimination, black central-city audiences are becoming an increasingly important source of support for the arts and other leisure institutions in the urban centers. The black middle class is smaller than it should be—in 1972 only 2.1 percent of black families had incomes of $25,000 or more against 8 percent of white families with that income—but blacks are disproportionate supporters and producers of the lively arts. Thus, in New York in 1975, there were no less than twelve major Broadway productions with all-black casts. These productions were commercially successful and drew white audiences. Of course, New York does not have a monopoly on good theater for this audience. Philadelphia, Boston, Atlanta, San Francisco, and Los Angeles, to name only the major centers, all have thriving black theater. Unfortunately, government support has been less than fair, a situation that the Black Theatre Alliance and other organizations are attempting to remedy (Williams and Goering, 1977).

While examples could be given from additional spheres of central-city leisure life, the important point here is that black America appears to be verging on a cultural renaissance that could have a lasting influence on American urban life. It is already clear through the history of jazz and theater what a vigorous and confident black artistic and intellectual stratum can contribute to the culture of American cities. What is not at all certain now, however, is whether the larger society has the determination to assist in doing what is necessary to prevent a desperate lumpen proletariat from destroying central-city life. In the long run, the viability of American culture may hinge on the outcome of this issue. Even this schematic review of control of city leisure life suggests that the ecology of entire metropolitan regions can fall around the social devastation of collapsing black cities. Nor will the vaunted "escape to suburbia" have meaning if the choices offered by central-city life are lost.

Suburban Leisure Life-Styles and the Metropolitan Ecology

In the sprawling postindustrial environment of North America, the urban-suburban dichotomy loses most of its significance. Time-budget studies of leisure choices show little variation between urban and suburban residents when socioeconomic variables were held constant (Robinson, 1976). What does matter in explaining differences in how Americans use their scarce resources of time and money is socioeconomic status and family life cycle. A blue collar family with strong ethnic identifications behaves much the same way in an industrial neighborhood of Chicago as it does in one of the Levittowns (Gans, 1967; Berger, 1960; Kornblum, 1974). Similarly, an upper–middle class family in Westport, Connecticut, spends its time in roughly the same style as an equivalent family living in a renovated townhouse in Brooklyn's Park Slope or in Cambridge, Massachusetts. The amount of space each has to use may differ and so will the amount of energy each family uses to pursue its pleasures, but the essential differences in behavior are determined by a complex set of class, cultural, and idiosyncratic variables, which contribute to each group's leisure preferences. Major differences in leisure life-styles do persist in North American society, and these are especially shaped by occupation and class status. But as a label for the middle masses of American society, the term *suburbia* is inadequate. Private homes and backyards (or equivalents), automobiles, vacations, television viewing, family picnics, do-it-yourself projects, and participation in voluntary associations are ubiquitous both inside and outside the central city. As categories of activities they are too broad to reveal differences in the leisure life-style of class-status groups in the population.

During the period of rapid suburban growth in the United States, from roughly 1945 to 1965 (and continuing now in the southern and southwestern states), sociologists and journalists commonly warned of the dangers of homogeneity and standardization of life-styles. Their criticism applied the "mass society" critique to the great explosion of a commercialized life-style, the second auto, the fast food franchise, the shopping center, and other features of the suburban ecology. These came to be symbols of the presumed extreme pressures for conformity that suburban environments and cultures exerted on newcomers. But even in the 1950s, perceptive observers like Herbert Gans, David Riesman, and Bennett Berger saw that suburban life-styles could be highly diverse and that suburban opinion leaders could tolerate quite divergent life-styles as long as the life-styles did not disturb the leaders' expensive peace. Of greater alarm to many authors was what Riesman called the "Suburban Dislocation," the flight to suburbia as a rejection of the city and industrialism, a revolt guided by images of the homestead with space and greenery, "an omnipresent dream, carrying overtones of the Bible, peasant life and folk imagery" (Riesman, 1958, p. 184). But what was especially problematic in this shift in the cultural center of American society was the lack of positive models for creative and personally satisfying life-styles:

> No, what is missing in suburbia, even where the quality of life has not deteriorated, is not the result of claustrophobic conformity to others' sanctions. Rather,

there would seem to be an aimlessness, a pervasive low-keyed unpleasure. This cannot be described in terms of traditional sorrow but is one on which many observers of the American visage have commented, notably Erich Fromm in *The Sane Society* and Goodman in *Communitas*. For millions of people work no longer provides a central focus in life and the breadwinner is no longer the chief protagonist in the family saga—just as Saturday night no longer provides a central focus for festivity. In fact, the decentralization of leisure in the suburbs is not only spatial but temporal, as evenings from Thursday through Sunday are oriented to play rather than work and are not individually accented or collectively celebrated.

At the same time, leisure has not picked up the slack—as, in earlier writings, I was too sanguine that it might. Whatever balances of work and play might have been possible for preindustrial man, postindustrial man is keyed, as I remarked earlier, to greater expectations. He has learned more "needs" and cannot in any case reconstitute the institutions industrialism destroyed. It is almost inconceivable, for example, to imagine a reconstitution of the folk arts which everywhere—in Nigeria as in New Orleans, in Damascus as in Tennessee—prove fragile in the face of mass-produced music and imagery [Riesman, 1958, p. 184].

This passage captures and almost predicts the main dimensions of insightful protest against suburban life that emerged so strongly in the late 1960s. The women's liberation movement, the human potential movement, and the counterculture in its various manifestations are all essentially middle class rejections of suburban stereotypes (Rozak, 1969). In the 1950s it appeared that women returned to the labor market, which was only beginning to regain pre-Depression levels, because of the needs of families to earn enough to maintain costly suburban life-styles. While this may be true, the contemporary ideology of both the women's movement and human potential groups reflects a deep dissatisfaction among women, particularly from the middle class and upper-middle class strata, with the traditional home-centered complex of feminine roles. The mother as chauffeur, shopper, housekeeper, keeper of the kids, and skilled bridge player is replaced by the demand by women that they be coequals and coproviders in a more symmetrical family power structure (Young and Willmott, 1977). The earlier impetus for this ideological movement came perhaps from central-city areas, where the concentration of career women and politically astute leaders caused the movement to take hold more quickly. But the spread of liberation ideologies to "typical" middle class suburban areas did not lag far behind. Membership in the National Organization for Women and other groups as well as the spread of "consciousness raising" groups as a free-time activity came to be as much a feature of suburban communities in the early 1970s as it had been in university and intellectual neighborhoods earlier.

The emergence of symmetrical family role patterns is far from complete in the American middle class. As noted earlier, the rising participation of women in the labor force is also accompanied by inequalities in leisure for working women, especially those with young children. Older suburban life-styles do not disappear simply because new ones develop. Consciousness raising and active political participation exist along with tennis, the ritual of shopping, and the weekly round of housework, lessons, socializing, and simple relaxation. Working middle class mothers are today's leaders of the harried leisure class (Young and Willmott, 1977; Vanek, 1974).

If these changes in suburban culture create the basis for a greater diversity in life-styles, they also have inescapable ecological implications. First, the larger number of roles that suburban women occupy increases the family dependence on two or more automobiles; poor mass transit in the suburbs contributes to this trend. Thus the space reserved for cars and other motor vehicles increases. As Seeley, Sims, and Loosly (1956, p. 127) observed:

> While the house is an expensive device to permit and enforce privacy, it is also true that the superior purchasing power of the Crestwood resident is used to secure more and more mechanical devices that constantly invade this privacy: radio, television, and the telephone are almost universal. The telephone, which the more affluent place beside their beds, and even occasionally in the bathroom, allows the invasion at any hour by a casual caller of the private areas that are regularly denied the nearest kin and the dearest friends. The automobile, which continues to grow steadily in size and cost, seems to be only

slightly less successful in gaining access to the home. The older houses in Crestwood Heights kept their garages (like the old coach houses) discreetly out of sight. In the newer houses, however, the garage has entered into the essential design and rationale. The immense slab which serves as a single door for the two-car garage dominates the smaller, less pretentious door used by human beings. The space devoted to the car is often greater than that occupied by the living room.

This description of the encroachment on personal space by the technology and objects of suburban life was written about an affluent suburban community in the mid 1950s. Perhaps it is dated by the energy crisis and the trend toward smaller autos, but this is questionable. The much-heralded decline of the auto-industrial age remains more of a wishful myth than a reality. After all, this passage was also written before the recreational vehicle boom and the mania for citizen's band radio (Rothschild, 1973). Although each of these innovations remains a key object in a minority life-style, each can be viewed as representing the further extension of suburbia on the road and beyond the metropolitan region itself.

Second Homes and Regional Parks

A vitally important result of the increasing diversity of suburban life-styles is that once on the road, the relatively affluent North American population requires an elaborate series of facilities for recreation away from home. Preferably this is a spacious place, like a resort area or a national park, where the various family members can "do their thing." Both the rapid rise in second-home ownership and the often contradictory demands placed on regional and national recreation locales are two important consequences of these demands.

Second-home ownership, as Mumford observed in the 1930s, represents universal suburbanization. In 1970 the U.S. Census Bureau reported that 2.89 million households, or 4.6 percent of the total, owned second homes. This is still a relatively small proportion of the population, but in 1967 only 2.9 percent of the total, representing 1.2 million fewer households, owned second homes. This 25 percent per year increase most certainly was not maintained in the recession of the early 1970s, but it has nevertheless already brought major demographic changes in what were once isolated rural villages. In some of the very picturesque villages of Vermont, for example, ratios of permanent to second-home residents of 1.9:1 are common. Nor is there any indication that this trend will cease. The National Tourism Resources Review Commission estimated that "by 1980, vacation home construction could account for almost 8 percent of projected 1980 housing starts" (Meyersohn, 1976).

In proportion to available space beyond the metropolitan regions, the second home demand is relatively insignificant. But 67 percent of vacation cottages were located within a 100-mile radius of the permanent dwelling. For the major metropolitan regions of the continent, which tend to be located on the coasts or in the Great Lakes region, second-home ownership is not evenly distributed over the available open space. Instead, wherever land speculators and builders are not checked, the little homes crowd the regions' most desirable places as on Fire Island, the Hamptons, the shores of Lake Michigan, the bluffs of the Mississippi, the Gulf Coast, the beaches and promontories of California, and equivalent, priceless natural areas in metropolitan regions throughout the United States and Canada. As a vacation-home settlement becomes more established and densely populated, it eventually becomes a retirement community or suburban development that expands the radius of metropolitan growth.

Attempts to save remaining desirable open space or, even more ambitiously, to convert it to park land for public use prove extremely difficult despite the concerted efforts of groups like the Conservation Foundation, the Regional Planning Association, the Nature Conservancy, and the National Resources Defense Council. These voluntary associations attempt to persuade state and national agencies to purchase vital natural areas within and outside the metropolitan regions. Since 1965, when the U.S. Department of the Interior began its large-scale investments in national seashores and national recreation areas, they have met with considerable success. Since that same year Congress has created National Park Service-administered facilities at Cape Cod, Fire Island, Indiana Dunes, Assateague Island, Cape Hatteras, Cape Lookout, and Padre Island. These and other barrier islands that are being planned for inclusion in the federal park system are well within a day's trip from major metropolitan regions. On a more depressing note, the public seashores owned and operated by all levels of government comprise only

2 percent of the total U.S. coastline. To further complicate the
situation, planning for the development of public use of these
hard-won concessions from private ownership has proved to be
extremely difficult. Public access to Indiana Dunes, Fire Island
on Long Island, and Cape Cod, to name only three examples,
has been rendered very difficult. Public transit access is fought
by residents of second-home communities, whose residences on
the shore are private enclaves protected by federal ownership of
surrounding lands from further commercial development (Kornblum, 1975).

A Final Note on Urban National Parks

The national parks in the United States receive some
120 million visitors each year. Of this number, the overwhelming proportion are white, middle class residents of home-owning
families. For example, the results of a 1968 survey of visitors to
national parks shows that only 4.4 percent of the visitors were
nonwhite (Cheek, Field, and Burch, 1976). Creation of the national seashores and national recreation areas at Lake Mead
(where thousands of vacationers with recreational vehicles and
fatigued gamblers from Las Vegas enjoy federally subsidized
recreation in flooded canyons) has done very little to narrow
the income gap in access to the continent's great natural pleasure grounds. In consequence of this, in 1972 Congress passed
additional legislation, at the urging of urban delegations, for the
creation of new urban national recreation areas in the Cleve-
land-Akron area, the New York and northern New Jersey
metropolitan region, and the San Francisco Bay Area. Gateway
National Recreation Area in New York and New Jersey and
Golden Gate National Recreation Area in San Francisco were to
be prototypes of a string of new urban federal parks such as had
been proposed by the Outdoor Recreation Resources Review
Commission in 1962. Equivalent new federal urban parks have
been proposed for the Chicago-Milwaukee region, the Detroit
area, the Atlanta region, for Los Angeles' Santa Monica Mountains, the Mississippi Delta, and numerous other locations in the
immediate vicinity of urban regions.

But resistance to this urban parks movement is also building in the fiscally conservative quarters of the federal government. A 1976 study by the Office of Management and Budget
argued that since most poor and blue collar Americans, who admittedly are badly served by the existing national parks and

recreation areas, prefer their relaxation and recreation in neighborhoods or around the home, it is wasteful to invest in new and ambitious regional park systems. In consequence of this attack and the general reluctance of park and recreation professionals in the federal government to press for urban park programs, the urban recreation areas projects continue to be stalled in bureaucratic and fiscal mires.

That inner-city households do not generally travel to regional parks is clearly no argument not to build them. First, the data on leisure time use are based on the availability of resources and alternatives. If regional parks, and especially the high-quality federal facilities for which urbanites are taxed, are not accessible, naturally urbanites will continue not to visit them. The difficulties of providing mass transit to metropolitan region parks may not prove insurmountable in the future as energy shortages produce new transportation priorities. Gateway in New York City already hosts some 8 million annual visitors, making it the most heavily used of the nation's federal park facilities. On a hot summer Sunday there are more black people on Gateway's Riis beach than would be found in all the national parks of the nation combined. Despite this fact, it will have been at least seven years since this old city beach was transferred to federal ownership and yet not a cent of capital development funds has been spent on improving its decaying physical plant. This situation is typical of federal urban park projects throughout America. Perhaps the pragmatism of the late 1970s will produce new policies and programs of employment to transform these doldrums. One sincerely hopes so, since all available evidence demonstrates that current use of the national park system represents yet another case of public subsidy of middle and upper-middle class leisure preferences.

4

Changing Social Order of the Metropolitan Area

Morris Janowitz
David Street

The Basis of Community

In contemporary society, the territorial distribution of human settlements is complex and ambiguous. The residential patterns of the social bloc, the neighborhood, and the community—the constituent elements of the metropolis—cannot be summarized by a neat and simplified map with easily discernible boundaries.[1] The separation of work and residence enlarges the tendency of catchment areas—areas circumscribed by political, administrative, or service agencies—to vary widely in their stability, diffuseness of boundaries, and internal cohesion; similarly, in any given residential settlement there is a wide variation

90

in the members' involvement and sense of attachment. The persistent forecast of the disappearance of the local community with the development of industrialism in Western Europe and the United States has not been realized. This prediction foresaw a trend toward the atomization of interpersonal relations. The anticipated result was that the durable social units would be linked to occupation and the attendant social classes, the residential community becoming an epiphenomenon.

Yet the community retains significance; the highly industrialized society, with its defects, strains, and dilemmas, cannot be reduced to the consequences of its division of labor. The content and effectiveness of its moral values are crucially conditioned by the social organization of the familial and residential community. Indeed, in a democratic parliamentary system, the advent of advanced industrialism and urbanization increases the centrality of family-residential communities as a basis for political participation.

The pattern of human settlement under advanced industrialism responds to the impact of technology and economic trends—to population growth, deconcentration of population density, an increase in the magnitude of the scale of organization, and the emergence of powerful and more flexible modes of transportation—although each of these trends has its limitations (Davis, 1955; Gibbs and Davis, 1961; Hawley, 1971; Timms, 1971). The processes of societal change are not adequately described by a model of unilinear gemeinschaft versus gesellschaft. It would be a distortion of intellectual history to assume that since 1950 sociologists have rediscovered the local community and the primary group within modern urban settlements. From the beginning of sociology as an academic discipline, there has been a stream of sociologists who have asserted that the spatial organization of the household-residence was not a residue from earlier societies. On the contrary, the residential community in the urban metropolis is an adaptation to social change; it is a social construction and a political one as well (Park and Burgess, 1921, p. 162; Park, 1925; Hillery, 1968; Keller, 1968; Konig, 1968; Warren, 1972). None of the early students of the community in modern society implied that the local neighborhood-community structures were strong, viable, or effectively articulated into the larger society. Rather, the tradition of local community research emphasized both the powerful solidarities that could develop in communal settlements and their institutional weakness, especially in linking the local area to the political process and the larger society. In particular, they recognized that localistic sentiments could stand as barriers to participation in the larger metropolis.

Community

Community is not to be thought of as the convergence of social interests and moral values, a usage emphasized by Robert MacIver (1936) and his disciples that has validity for some purposes but obscures the contemporary analysis of the separation of work and residence. Community can be thought of as a geographically based form of social organization that directly supplies its members with the major portion of their sustenance needs. The daily transactions of goods and services offer a basis for delimiting the structure of the community. Sustenance is broadly defined and is best understood when associated with socialization and the transition through the stages of the life cycle. Of course, a person's sustenance needs are met by institutions that diffuse throughout the entire nation-state and can involve the world economy, but the household-residential community incorporates the scope of the daily transactions. In the metropolis, local territorially based social systems emerge out of these transactions, and these patterns are what is meant by the local urban community.[2] As a result, the social reality of the residential community reflects a series of service and socialization institutions and the symbolic definitions imposed on the locality in order to create a social order in which households seek to survive. In its most apparent manifestation, the local urban community is a set of symbols that are internalized by the residents to varying degrees—for without the symbolic identifications there is no reference to an underlying local community. Sociologists stress the "institution building" by governmental agencies, political groups, and voluntary associations, which are required if a local urban community is to exist over time (Suttles, 1972).

Obviously the notion of local urban community in the context of advanced industrialism is not the same as the historical notions of community associated with a peasant, feudal, or even rural society (Shils, 1957). We are not dealing with a social system giving little opportunity for individuation or partial withdrawal. Community in the metropolitan setting is not the coercive format of the "ideal type" small town as portrayed by the novelist of the 1920s, nor does the notion of community refer to some futuristic form in which local relations are completely bureaucratized and impersonalized. Residential community in Western Europe and the United States in the latter half of the twentieth century involves important elements of voluntarism, self-interest, and contractual relations designed to benefit the well-being of the person and his or her household.

A variety of formulations have been utilized to highlight the realities and specializations of a residential community in a society with an industrial order based on rational considerations of self-interest, including the notion of a community of "limited liability" (Janowitz, 1967). Persons responding to the existing cultural norms are likely to demand more from their community than they will invest. But more significantly, their relation to the community—their social investment—is such that when the community fails to serve their needs, they will withdraw. Withdrawal implies either actual departure from the local community or merely a decline in or lack of involvement. Some degree of withdrawal is inherent in the process of social change, and withdrawal accompanies the aging of the householders. We are dealing with both the life cycles of the person and the community, but older communities can renew their population and their institutional networks. Withdrawal accompanies changes in the ethnic, racial, and occupational composition of a community. However, persons develop a "psychic" commitment to a local area, which can persist after the community fails to serve their needs. Moreover, the extent of withdrawal varies from community to community and from social group to social group. But for most persons there is a point at which they cut their losses, and there is a point of social disorganization at which a locality can revive its social organization only by means of extensive external assistance.

The service functions that take place in the local community have undergone drastic change since World War I. The reliance on locally based service institutions has sharply declined, but the local community has specific functions that are not easily transferred to other groups. The residential social organization is the locus within which the stages of the life cycle are given moral and symbolic meaning. Each generation seeks— although it does not necessarily succeed—in investing in the next generation through the schools and the agencies of socialization that persist as the central institutions of the locality. Even the consumption-oriented localities with few children, the areas of single people and older couples without children that adjoin the central business district, are replete with a variety of formal and informal "schools" that indoctrinate each new generation of adult newcomers in the values and practices of the locality. These community schools teach such subjects as baking bread, basket weaving, karate, muscle control, and transcendental meditation.

The socialization process is not merely the outcome of nurturing and sustaining the person through the life cycle, however. The local residential organization is the catchment area for fashioning accountability and developing links to political institutions. This is especially the case in a society in which responsibility is widely diffused and readily avoided. Within the social space of family residence, persons have the opportunity and, in varying degrees, the necessity of aggregating their competing self-interests. Obviously, the mechanisms for strengthening a sense of accountability are imperfect. However, we wish to explore the articulation of communal life with the larger political process. The emergence of more complex and more differentiated institutions does not necessarily mean the elimination of older arrangements, although it implies their adaptation and specialization. In particular, the growth in the size, scale of organization, and complexity of the human settlement does not mean that personalized relations are being replaced by impersonalized ones. On the contrary, our underlying assertion is that the separation of work and residence multiplies the number, range, and content of personal attachments, which form the base of the culture of the metropolis (Simmel, 1903).

The sum total of the emergent patterns of interaction can be pervasive and powerful for the individual who is a member of the "literary set," a religious cult, a political sect, and the like. They can even be as binding as the patterns of interaction generated under the conditions of peasant or so-called folk society. No person has argued and demonstrated this assertion as effectively as Schmalenbach (1922) in his analysis of modern youth movements and his concern with "communion." Alternatively, for some the modern community provides a paucity of interpersonal interaction and support, thus failing psychic needs. Thus a wide range of interactions and attachments emerges within the metropolis. The existence of an increased number of impersonal, weak, and even "agonized" contacts is not necessarily detrimental, for they can contribute to the autonomy, personal freedom, and creativity required for the community of limited liability. The inability of a person to solve the dilemmas created by the enlargement of his social space can be disastrous, but at the same time without these voluntaristic aspects of urban culture there can be no resolution of the separation of work and residence.

Since the end of World War II, the local community in the United States has served as the locus of intense group conflict along communal dimensions, especially with regard to racial and ethnic lines. The accumulated research on the metropolis underlines the continuing sequence of competition, conflict, and partial accommodation (or organization, disorganization, and reorganization). Yet the residential community has not served as the locus of revolutionary confrontation. Community tensions reflect socioeconomic position, but they have distinct and separate histories. In fact, as there has been a long-term decline of purposive violence in the industrial sector (Janowitz, in press), the observation can also be offered that during the period 1920 to 1977 there has been a parallel transformation of community-based and communally organized violence. The race riots of the 1960s were a short-term deviation in this downward trend. The deconcentration of population in the central city, the social decay of older neighborhoods, and the suburban economic dominance over the central city have resulted in a persistent and increased pattern of criminality, both individual and organized. The intensity, persistence, and scope of diffuse violence and criminality in the inner city have seriously weakened and distorted the local political institutions. Nevertheless, regardless of their socioeconomic status, residential areas throughout metropolitan centers have become more and more important loci for political participation. Occupational interest groups and the symbolism of social class self-interest have been fundamentally augmented and enlarged with a sharper definition and stronger emphasis on local community political power.

A sheer increase in expenditures for public education and for the welfare state associated with a broadened definition of citizenship is at work (see Janowitz, 1976; Marshall, 1950; Wilensky, 1975). The citizenry is increasingly aware and sensitive to the relevance of the local community as a source of life chances. The demands for local control or local participation reflect the desire for a larger share of public expenditures, but these demands also reflect the increased pressure to ensure an element of supervision and accountability in the performance of

the agencies of the welfare state, particularly those that penetrate the residential community (Suttles, 1975). In short, the
symbolism of social class has been the vehicle for the effective
enlargement of political participation during the emergence of
industrialism in Western Europe and the United States. With the
advent of the welfare state, the dimension of territoriality—the
residential community—moves into the forefront of political
rhetoric and political conflict. Under advanced industrialism,
political leaders find it necessary to augment the appeals of
social class with those of community participation. As a result,
our analysis must deal with the increased ecological and institutional differentiation between the social organization of work
and that of family residence and with the resulting disarticulations. It also must deal with the difficulties of aggregating and
balancing the increasing demands of family-residence interests
and of integrating them effectively into the structure of the
larger society.

Hypotheses

Our task is to examine the format of local social organization. The following observations will guide this effort. Our
underlying assumption is that the importance of the local family residential social organization has increased since 1920 as a
basis for integrating the person and the household into the
political process and for balancing self-interest with larger social
responsibilities. We can formulate four specific hypotheses
about the internal organization of the residential community;
they are designed to throw some light on the linkages between
the local community and the larger metropolis.

Hypothesis One. As a result of advanced industrialism,
the increase in population, the growth in the scale of service
organizations, and the flexibility of the system of motorized
transportation, there has been a deconcentration of human settlement and a decline in the use of local service facilities, both
public and private. However, the decline in the use of local facilities has not been accompanied by a significant long-term decline in local social bonds or in community satisfaction, sentiments, and participation in the period since 1920. This is in part
because the strength of community settlements and attachments is not a function of urban density or distance from the
center of the metropolis.

Hypothesis Two. The location of employment, variations

in household income, the territorial distribution of socio-economic groupings, and the length of the journey to work have produced the recognized social disarticulation between the central city and the suburbs of the metropolitan areas. As a result of these trends, it is appropriate to speak of the social disarticulation between the locus of work and the residential community. Further, as judged by measures of income and family structure, the increased magnitude of scale of the metropolitan community has been accompanied by greater social differentiation among local community areas.

Hypothesis Three. Consistent with the above hypotheses, the strength of community sentiments, attachments, and participation derives more and more from the specialized household and socialization processes that remain located in the residential district. Rather than the notion of the loss of community, we are dealing with the social construction of specialized communities in which the agencies of government and voluntary associations are decisive. Because of the powerful disruptive factors that impinge on the residential locality, Gerald Suttles's term "defended community" is highly appropriate (Suttles, 1972, pp. 21-44).

Hypothesis Four. Because the political system emphasizes territorial representation, and because the expansion of the governmental functions includes many welfare state functions that are geographically based, local residential political participation and local residential political decision making have grown in importance since the end of World War II. The local family-residential social organization remains the catchment area in which the metropolitan-wide and societal-wide constituencies are mobilized. However, at the same time, it is the arena—actual and potential—for balancing competing interests and conflicting aspirations.

This last hypothesis must be seen in the context of the long historical changes in urban settlement, local and metropolitan, since the Civil War. The emergence of a national industrial system and the associated financial and service enterprises has been accompanied by a decline in the ability of the business elites to dominate patterns of local politics and local political decision making directly. Likewise, the ability of the trade union movement to influence local political patterns directly has also declined, both as a result of the decline in integrated working-class communities linked to specific industrial establishments and the attenuation of ethnic-religious solidarities. As

a result, the local residential community became the locus of a
network of voluntary associations linking the local residents to
highly fragmented and decentralized political parties. The study
of the local community requires the exploration of these local
voluntary associations and their effectiveness and ineffective-
ness as institutions.

Residential Settlement and Resource Distribution

The long-term trends since the turn of the century have
involved growth in population, an increased concentration of
population in metropolitan areas, and at the same time a suburbanization of metropolitan populations. (See Chapters One
and Two by Hawley and Kasarda, respectively, in this volume
for discussions of these trends and accompanying processes.)
The history of urbanization in the United States describes the
operation of a self-propelling system of growth outward from
urban centers, a process little affected by the central government until after World War II. The growth has been markedly
without grand design and subject particularly to great urban
sprawl. The resulting stark decay of the central city became
politically visible in the decade of the 1960s, but the ecologists
had been plotting the patterns of deconcentration extending
back before 1900.

Analysis of population trends since 1920 clarifies our
hypothesis concerning the increased disarticulation between the
locus of occupation and residential community. This is especially true if one compares the pattern of population growth
during the period of 1920 to 1945 with the period between
1945 and 1976, since in the latter period the population dynamics tended to strain local and metropolitan social organization much more than in the former. Three observations are in
order. First, the birth rate and total population growth during
the period 1920 to 1940 was low to medium and relatively constant as compared with the period after 1940, when it was high
and markedly variable. Second, the pattern of population
growth in the second period changed and distorted the structure
of the population pyramid to a much greater extent. In particular, the ratio of young persons and old persons to middle-aged
people increased. In other words, the ratio of dependent persons to active wage earners grew. Both of these trends strained
communal institutions, in particular the educational and welfare
institutions that had to adapt to the rapidly increased popula-

tion. This was especially the case for the mass educational system, which by 1970 was facing further disruption because of a reverse trend yielding a drastic reduction in the size of the primary grade population. Third, the social composition of the population increase changed markedly between these two periods. In the first the percentage of population growth due to foreign-born immigrants was low and relatively stable, while in the second the ratio of foreign-born immigrants to native births was much higher. To speak of the social demography of the United States as an advanced industrial society is to make special reference to the uniquely high inflow of permanent foreign immigrants. This trend is similar to the previous two in that it also strains community institutions of socialization and welfare. A proportion of the immigrants are highly trained professionals who rapidly become socially integrated, but the bulk is unskilled.

City-Suburban Differentiation. The metropolitan patterns of residential settlement that result from population growth reflect the location of economic enterprise and of employment opportunities as well as the residence of wage earners. The basic trend in resource distribution is greater overall socioeconomic differentiation and a resulting disarticulation between the central city and suburban ring. First, the limited element of convergence between the central city and the ring rests on two trends. In the centrifugal direction, it is well recognized that the longer-term trend is not only loss of white collar residents but also blue collar jobs in the central city (see Chapter Two). In the centripetal direction, there is an increase in white collar employment in the central cities, although the increase in these kinds of jobs is even greater in the suburban ring. In other words, the growth of white collar jobs has prevented a greater decline of employment in the central city. To a considerable degree this is the result of the concentration of particular types of professional, financial, and governmental services in the core of the metropolis.

As a result, the profiles of occupations of the labor force between central cities and suburban rings appear to have converged. However, in terms of human settlement—that is, in the residential location of different occupational groups and the distribution of household resources—the central city and the suburban ring have in fact increased in divergence with a resultant increase in disarticulation. The apparent convergence of occupational profiles by place of work is the result of the increased frequency and extended length of the journey to work (Morgan, 1967; Kain, 1967; Hawley, 1971; Kain, 1970). What is crucial, as has been repeatedly and extensively documented, is that the socioeconomic gap in the residential population of the central city and the suburban ring has increased for the second period of our analysis. By the second decade of this century the average distance from home to workplace was 1.5 miles in the Chicago area, which does not appear atypical (Duncan, 1965). By 1960 the trip to work averaged 4.7 miles. On the basis of a sample of 101 SMSAs adjusted for annexation, a further increase in the journey to work across the boundaries of the central city has been documented for the period of 1960 to 1970 for both blue collar and white collar workers (see Chapter Two). This increase is augmented by the increase in the number of employees who cross the end of the suburban ring to work outside of the SMSA. These data hardly reflect the full scope of the long-term process of deconcentration of employment locations, for we are dealing not only with the increased length of time in the journey to work but also with an enlargement in the diversity of direction. The centrifugal and centripetal flows result in an increased diversity in the direction of the flow of traffic to work. The increased diversity is accompanied by a similarly diverse pattern of traffic flow in the utilization of urban services and leisure time activities, basically reflecting the decline in dominance of the central business district and the rise of service centers throughout the metropolitan area.

Beneath the web of daily transportation, the distribution of the population reveals a continued increase in the differences in social composition between the central city and the suburb, reflecting the concentration in the core of the metropolis of low-income, less educated, and minority group people. These people include the greatest numbers suffering social disabilities —poverty-stricken pensioners, broken and incomplete families, medically and mentally ill or physically handicapped persons. The gap between the central city and the suburban ring is in effect greater than that revealed by the measures of central tendency. Within the central city there is an important but very limited segment of high-income households who reside in high-rise apartment houses constructed since 1960 to hold and attract persons seeking the life-style of the central city. In short, while the idea of a middle majority has relevance for the suburban ring, the central city is more and more the focus of a highly segmented population.

The economic consequences of this pattern of human settlement, employment location, and family resources has been to
exacerbate the economic strain confronting the welfare state.
As examined elsewhere (Janowitz, 1976), the United States as
an advanced industrial society has had, on the basis of existing
economic practices, to face a chronic public deficit to accommodate welfare state expenditures. As is well recognized, the
management of this deficit is complicated by the unequal distribution of household incomes between the suburban rings and
the central city and the requirements for social welfare expenditures. The existing mechanisms of taxation and revenue allocation persistently obstruct the creation of metropolitan-wide
fiscal systems. But the pattern of disarticulation also involves
the services and burdens the central city shoulders for the suburbs. Without providing adequate social or economic supports
to the central city or the metropolitan area as a whole, the suburbs have been able to export or resist the incorporation of
undesirable land uses and populations. One of the most dramatic examples is the enforced territorial confinement of commercialized vice to the central city, while the clients are overwhelmingly suburban residents. The irony is that during the
process of deconcentration of population, there were a variety
of declining neighborhoods near the central business district
that could serve as the centers of vice and prostitution without
high public visibility. However, the efforts to preserve and
renew selected local communities in the central city brought
local residents into direct confrontation with organized vice and
prostitution. The rapid emergence of a municipal fiscal crisis
after 1970, especially in New York City, has served as a dramatic indicator of the consequences of the differentiation of
the suburbs from the central city (Congressional Budget Office,
1975). As a result, the ecology of employment opportunities
and the distribution of economic resources in each metropolitan
center sets the parameters for the social segregation of the
population that takes place in each local urban community and/
or neighborhood.

Differentiating Variables. The pattern of population distribution is more than the result of economic competition and
available income. Three basic variables are operative: income,
family structure, and ethnic or racial composition—each partly
reflecting prestige considerations. These variables supply the
basis for the ecological analyses developed by Ernest W.
Burgess, Eshrev Shevky, and Albert Hunter and are applicable

for the entire period of 1920 to 1970 (Hunter, 1974). There is good reason to believe that they have been operative over a longer period of time, but data on small areas of cities necessary to analyze these variables have been collected by the U.S. Census only since 1920. The findings for the Chicago area indicate the extent to which these variables account for the social organization of the local community and in particular for the balance between change and stability. In Chicago the analysis has been performed for the period 1930 to 1970 in terms of the seventy-five well-known local community areas delineated by Burgess. For this period the three factors of income, family structure, and ethnic or racial composition persist as basic parameters. However, over time there is increasing differentiation among the seventy-five areas; this conclusion can be inferred from the observation that from 1930 to 1970 these three factors account for less of the variance among communities. As would be expected, economic status since 1930 remains the dominant factor by which persons locate themselves, whereas the significance of family status has declined. On the other hand, the importance of ethnic-racial status has increased.

What overall patterns emerge from these data on the population composition of the local community areas? No single set of categories will suffice, but in varying degrees the ideas of zones, sectors, and multinucleation are applicable. In fact, it is striking that the classic pattern of Burgess's zones linking distance from the center of the metropolis to increasing income and "familism" persists to a considerable degree over time (Hunter, 1974, pp. 19-66; Guest, 1971; Haggerty, 1971). One line of modification is that some zones have been altered into elongated and enlarged sectors as conceptualized by Hoyt (1939). This shift is the result of the fact that the corridors of transportation that have been created have attenuated and elongated the concentric character of urban growth. In addition, there has been a trend toward multinucleation reflecting the rise of service centers outside the downtown central business district (Harris and Ullman, 1945).

Related is the question of the changing territorial dimension of ethnic-racial distributions. The full meaning of "ethnic enclave" must await the discussion below concerning the scope and strength of ethnic identification in the United States, which despite the long-term pressures to maintain such identification, particularly through new immigration, continues to decline and attenuate overall. However, in terms of geographic location alone, with ethnicity measured in terms of percent foreign born, it is indeed striking that ecological research demonstrates the considerable persistence of ethnic segregation. The degree of ethnic residential segregation is strongly influenced by income level and status in that higher income leads to more rapid dispersal. But foreign-born groups and their second-generation descendants, despite their movement into the suburbs, display a noteworthy degree of residential segregation (Kantrowitz, 1969). The quantitative measures of ethnic segregation hardly reveal overwhelming concentration that produces ideal "enclaves," but they do show a significant tendency to aggregate. However, the new patterns of the journey to work alter the ecology of the ethnic community and make it markedly less self-contained, and this is even more the case when one examines the decline in the use of local service facilities.

The crux of ethnic segregation is the continuous expansion of the black ghetto since 1920, and since 1950 of the Spanish-speaking ghetto. In particular, ecological segregation occurs throughout almost all of the black social structure. Even in the case of the black ghetto, however, its self-containedness has weakened. First, the trend in the journey to work implies that a larger and larger proportion of blacks will work outside the ghetto. Second, there has been a fundamental shift in the housing market for black residents in the central city. Since 1965 the "dual housing market" enforced by prejudice and informal sanctions has weakened. The differential pricing in housing—both in rental property and in owner-occupied residences—has declined, and in some areas by 1976 the cost of comparable housing for blacks was lower than for whites. The increase in the supply of housing for blacks has been in part the result of the suburbanization of whites following the long-term relocation of job opportunities.[3] Third, the emergence of racially integrated residential communities has served to alter the social definition of the territorial distribution of the black population. (The definition of racial integration is not a numerical balance, since at any given percentage level the reality might well be a transitional phase from an all-white community to an all-black community. The definition of residential integration is economically based; it occurs when whites sell or rent to blacks and blacks in turn rent or sell to whites.) Likewise, the opening of the suburbs for blacks has had an impact even though the number involved has been limited. At times the supply of housing for blacks in the suburbs has exceeded economic demand, since the reluctance of blacks to suburbanize is in part a personal and group preference for central-city locations as well as relatively subtle processes of racial "steering" in the real estate industry (Pearce, 1976). Nevertheless, the central black ghetto found in each of the U.S. metropolises is a contiguous enclave in which the full range of income and occupational groupings—each of the ordered segments of the black community—is to be found.

As a basis for a partial synthesis of these trends, we must emphasize that the local urban community in its various forms has a distinctive meaning not because it connotes a dense concentration of human settlement or a pattern of social segregation, but because of the particular consequences that locality has for the social organization and the cultural values of the residents. We return to our earlier assertion that even the largest metropolis has a measure of internal organization and order because there is a network of social relations generated by the daily journey to work and the daily transactions of each household. The impact of community institutions on the overall social order is complicated and weakened because since 1920 metropolitan growth and deconcentration and increased flexibility of transportation have caused a decline in the use of local service facilities (Chapin, 1974). At the macro level this decline can be measured by the increase in decentralized shopping centers and complexes for rendering professional services. In the twenty-year period from 1954 to 1974, over 14,000 shopping centers have been constructed, most serving suburban populations.

Increases in locating selected service functions in central business districts also contributed to this trend. At the micro level, we have available Hunter's (1975) restudy of a local urban community in Rochester, New York, which in 1940 had 13,030 residents, a number that declined to 11,890 by 1970. In the period from 1949 to 1974 the percentage who made use of local facilities—within five blocks of their homes—declined for grocery shopping, small purchases, church, movies, and doctor visits; only local banking increased. In general the decline in the use of local facilities increases faster and more extensively among higher-income groups, but the trend penetrates deeply throughout the ordered segments of the metropolis. The decline is present in the suburban developments more than in the central city, and it is also to be found among the black and Spanish-speaking enclaves in varying degrees as well.

The trends in population settlement, the ecology, and the social composition of the urban locality set the stage for examination of the hypothesis that the deconcentration of population and the decline in the use of facilities do not necessarily produce a weakening of community identification and community participation. There is no reason to assume that social changes that produce new forms eliminate all the older structures. The transformation in the journey to work and the decline in the use of local facilities mean that the local urban community and the neighborhood have specialized their functions. The argument to be pursued in the next section is that, in particular, the atrophy of local sustenance institutions has been accompanied by an intensification in the importance of the local socialization function throughout the life cycle and of new ingredients of the socialization cycle. Instead of the classical gemeinschaft-gesellschaft perspective, with its inherent empirical limitations, we speak of a socialization perspective that applies to the entire household, including the children, as it locates and relocates from one human settlement to another and demonstrates over time in varying degree its capacity to internalize the norms of the new locality.

Local Community and Socialization

The transitory character of social relations in the metropolis does not prevent the proliferation of intricate and elaborate social patterns rooted in community organization. Men and women and their offspring exert themselves energetically to move their residential life-styles toward some ideal, and higher standards of living make this aspiration reasonable. In order to have an effective social order in the urbanized society, however, the territorial attachments must be articulated into the larger political structure of each metropolitan center—a state of affairs that is yet to be achieved and that remains problematic.

Classic community studies such as the two monographs on Middletown by Robert and Helen Lynd (1929, 1937) and the multivolume investigation of Newburyport by W. Lloyd Warner and his associates (Warner and Lunt, 1941; Warner and Srole, 1945; and Warner and others, 1949) were based on the premise that community research supplies the locus of the study of the total society. In this view, the community study affords the opportunity for the investigator or small research team to undertake an intensive and comprehensive investigation in depth and to proceed on the basis of a holistic approach. However, one does not confront the total society when one investigates a community, especially the relatively small and separate town or city that is the object of much community research. On the contrary, the power of the community study tradition is that it *does* make use of a specialized perspective. It highlights the distinctive consequences of territoriality on social structure, societal organization, and especially the socialization of successive generations. Community research requires the sociologist to identify the boundaries—real and symbolic—and the social space in which a person and members of his or her household exist and proceed through the life cycle. To speak of an occupational or industrial order without reference to the variety of community settings in which occupational groups reside is to distort fundamentally the analysis of the social organization of an advanced industrial society (Beshers, 1962).

Community research has been enriched by those investigators schooled in the traditions and methods of social anthropology who have worked in small population centers; the Lynds and Warner reflect the benefits of this perspective. But from the very origins of urban sociology, sociologists have sought to explore the local communities that exist in the ever expanding massive centers of the population. This tradition, as practiced by Charles Booth in England; Georg Simmel in Germany; and W. L. Thomas, W. E. B. DuBois, Robert E. Park, and Ernest W. Burgess in the United States, has stimulated a continuous stream of research that focuses on the consequences of territoriality in the metropolis (for example, McKenzie, 1923; Clena, 1929; Sweetser, 1941). This intellectual tradition encompasses not only rich institutional and interpersonal analysis based on participant observation, as epitomized in the continuity of studies from *The Gold Coast and the Slum* by Harvey Zorbaugh (1929) to *Blue Collar Community* by William Kornblum (1974), but also includes the efforts to develop statistical social indicators of local community life.

It can be argued that few succinct and conclusive hypotheses or precise statistical models derive from the accumulated efforts to study the social format of the residential community, and that the weight of scholarship has produced a detailed and trenchant portrayal of social reality and a concern with style, language, and expression. The sociology of the urban locality in this view is essentially ethnographical. Clearly, urban sociology is one of the all too few links between sociology and humanistic analysis; in particular, the community study is the vehicle for approaching the existential dilemmas of everyday life. However, the richness of detail should not divert attention from the observations these studies make about long-term trends concerning the format and symbolic character of residential localities. The community studies of the 1920s can be compared with those of the 1960s and 1970s, and their similarities and contrasts supply revealing if not necessarily completely representative findings. Since 1945 there have been a limited number of surveys of particular areas that supply relevant social indicators, and in particular indicators of the growth and impact of the community press have been increasingly revealing (Janowitz, 1967; Larsen and Edelstein, 1960; Greer, 1962a; Greer and Kube, 1959; Greer, 1962c; Greer, 1963, chap. 5).

Salience of the Local Community. The point of departure is the observation that, in the United States, geographical, territorial, and institutional place names—precise or vague, but not ethnic—serve as the basis for community images and boundaries. The social organization of the metropolis is, of course, fundamentally molded by the pattern of racial and ethnic segregation. However, as of 1976 ethnicity did not operate as an explicit or primary basis of the cognitive maps and designation held by the citizenry of their residential localities. Even the grim realities of segregation of races and of Spanish-speaking populations operate in a complex fashion: The racial and ethnic characteristics contribute to the larger boundaries of the black and Spanish enclaves, but these ghettos have become differentiated into small localities described by territorial place names that reflect geography, institutions, and social status—the constituent elements of ordered social segmentation.

As Robert E. Park and Ernest W. Burgess emphasized, "It is evidently important that the people who compose a community and share in the common life should have a sufficient body of common memories to understand one another" (1921, p. 765). In the context of an advanced industrial society, with its continuous pattern of residential mobility, it takes but a short history, which is passed on by word of mouth.[4] But the group memory of the history of a locality can be quickly forgotten. A two-dimensional map with fixed boundaries presents an oversimplified picture of the territorial images in the minds of men and women.[5] The social space of a resident is not only diffuse but multiple, reflecting various household needs and practices and indicating the resident's sentiments, attachments, and actual local participation. Moreover, an important minority of residents hold more than one kind of identification: They see themselves as members of a particular locality and at the same time residents of a larger sector of the city. These images are not part of a zero-sum game. The distinction between community and society can best be noted in the hierarchy of images that the resident holds of his daily social space in contrast to the strength and weakness of his feelings of national identification as a citizen. Elements of political nationalism are also to be found in the local community.

Albert Hunter in 1967 and 1968 undertook a massive effort to chart the perceptions of social space through study of the symbolic communities of the central city of Chicago, building on the work of the 1920s by Ernest W. Burgess. Presumably his findings are not fundamentally different from those one would encounter in other major metropolitan centers except that Chicago has been more extensively researched. In the 1920s Burgess defined 75 "exhaustive and mutually exclusive" community areas in Chicago. He was aware of many smaller neighborhoods and of the complexity of the symbolic boundaries of local areas, but he sought to construct a simplified map both for research and administrative purposes. Hunter's map of localities, as presented in *Symbolic Communities* (1974), offers a much more complex and variegated pattern. While Burgess focused on 75 community areas, Hunter charted both neighborhood and community areas and emerged with a much larger number of operative localities—over 200. We believe that the central city of Chicago has experienced some increase in residential nucleation, but it is difficult to be certain; it is impossible to know whether the number of localities has increased or more refined methods of research have led to more elaborated categories and more detailed findings.

But a powerful element of continuity can be seen by the fact that 43 percent of the persons surveyed by Hunter made use of the same place names encountered by Burgess a half century earlier. In essence, territorial community in the metropolis rests on some element of tradition even if it is encompassed only by geographical continuity. Moreover, Hunter found that an overwhelming 86 percent of the residents were able to offer specific place names for the localities in which they resided; these were essentially devoid of ethnic symbolism. It is striking the extent to which the residents' images of the locality contained both a center and a periphery (Shils, 1961). Peripheries were defined as parks, vacant land, railroads and elevated lines, expressways, and city limits, in that descending order. The center was generally a shopping area, a major traffic intersection, or a configuration of community facilities. But the choice was a symbolic definition, for there were frequently alternative physical or geographical possibilities.

Historical reconstruction of the images of the local community is a difficult task. However by 1920, despite the massive influx of ethnic groups, cognitive definitions of the local community seldom emphasized ethnicity. In fact, the historical accounts of local communities based on the reports of old settlers, which go back as far as the Civil War period, reveal that the ethnic concentrations seldom produced ethnic place names for local communities. Most ethnic enclaves were composed of various nationalities—this mixture produced the essential preconditions for both acculturation and assimilation. The occasional designation of Greektown, Little Italy, and Polonia referred to the persistence of ethnic service centers for local residents, suburbanized ethnics, and a broader clientele from the larger metropolis. It was as if the cognitive definitions and labels of residential localities indicated the aspiration to link the ethnic residents to the larger metropolis. It was, of course, in the black ghetto that ascription persisted the longest as the sole basis for naming local communities. For example, in Chicago up to the outbreak of World War II, the residents of the black ghetto thought of themselves as residents of Bronzeville (Drake and Cayton, 1945). As the ghetto expanded into existing white neighborhoods and local communities, the older names were taken over by the new black citizenry.

We are interested in the correlates that explain different degrees of community cohesion and account for a person's identification with his or her locality. Even the crude measure of whether a person makes use of a place name to identify his or her residence reveals community social organization. As would be expected, persons from upper-status backgrounds are more likely to hold clear cognitions and more elaborate conceptions of the social space in which they reside than are lower-status persons. Perceptions are more elaborate also among persons who have extensive voluntary association membership. However, these variables cannot be considered powerful; instead, the single variable that does have a strong influence is the measure of community socialization—the length of residence. This central finding anticipates a variety of characteristics of community social organizations. Thus, of those who lived in the local community less than one year, 27.5 percent did not know the name for the local community; while for those who lived in the community twenty years or more, this percentage dropped to 9.6. Controlling length of residence attenuated the difference between whites and blacks on this measure of community identification.

Cognitive definitions and images of one's residential community are related to local sentiments—to the existence and strength of positive and negative attitudes. The data collected by Hunter confirm a series of findings of other studies that underline the existence of a relatively high degree of satisfaction with community throughout the various social segments, both in the central city and the suburb. These attitudes are an aspect of the syndrome of the community of limited liability. A high degree of satisfaction is frequently compatible with a willingness and even proclivity to move to a "better" community. Even more striking, the long-term trend in satisfaction with one's local community is one of consistent and almost unvarying positive sentiments, in contrast to rapidly fluctuating attitude patterns of satisfaction with one's financial position, and in particular in contrast to increased negativism toward the central institutions of society. It is as if the local community served as a "defended" refuge from the tensions of the larger society, as a social space for partial retreat (Suttles, 1968).

Thus, the sample of 600 respondents in the Chicago area interviewed in 1950 for the study of *The Community Press in an Urban Setting,* revealed that only 12.5 percent were dissatisfied with their local community (Janowitz, 1967, p. 128). This is comparable to the percentage (12.4) encountered by Hunter in his survey almost two decades later on an equivalent population (Hunter, 1974, p. 118). The findings of Scott Greer for metropolitan St. Louis, which included suburban areas, produced similar results in the mid 1950s. The findings of these metropolitan surveys also appear to be nationally representative. This can be seen by the fact that the Hunter sample revealed that 47 percent were clearly positive about "the city or place you live in," and this percentage is comparable for national samples collected in 1973 and 1974 (Smith, 1975a). Relevant national trend data derive from a surrogate question about "your housing situation" (Smith, 1975b). From 1963 to 1971, the percentage who responded that they were satisfied varied only slightly from 74.6 percent (1963) to 79.2 percent

(1969) to 77.4 percent (1971). This is particularly striking given the large variation in feelings of relative deprivation concerning one's financial condition. As was to be expected, there was a limited positive association between satisfaction with one's residential locality and membership in the more privileged social segments of the metropolis. But again, this association was not very strong; very high levels of satisfaction could be found in low-income neighborhoods, while particular middle class suburban residents expressed only average levels of satisfaction.

Importantly, these data indicate that since 1920 the decline in the use of local facilities has had a very limited impact on the cognitive definitions and images that the residents hold of their locality. Even more importantly, the diversity of patterns of journey to work and to service and leisure time facilities is unrelated to the continuity of positive sentiment and attitudes as well as actual informal and formal participation in the local environment. Positive attachments have not been attenuated; instead, the basis for attachment to the local community has adapted to changes in the industrial order. In essence, the idea of loss of community fails to capture the realities of the network of interpersonal relations and primary group ties that are constantly being fashioned and refashioned.

Local Socialization. Support for the perspective of the neighborhood and local community as a system of local socialization rests on both cross-sectional national survey data and on longitudinal comparisons of particular community studies over the past half century. The most impressive data derive from a national British survey on patterns of social bonds, the findings of which were reanalyzed by Kasarda and Janowitz (1974). The central findings converge with and explicate the findings of earlier and more limited analyses completed in the United States. They are that community size and density have very limited consequences on a person's social bonds to his locality and very limited effects on his community participation or community sentiments. That is, persons who live in large and dense urban settlements have no weaker or more limited informal and kinship ties than do the residents of smaller and less densely populated areas. By contrast, the single most important variable leading to stronger social bonds is length of residence. Social class and life cycle have a positive impact on stronger social bonds, but much less than length of residence. The importance of family cycle and the presence of children in strengthening local social bonds has been emphasized by authors of various community surveys, and this process operates by means of the social relations generated by the school and associated institutions. The findings also underline the relative importance of voluntaristic efforts in the social construction of local communities.[6] As has been frequently emphasized, persons with more education have a strong interest in their local community and are more likely to be directly involved in local voluntary association. Moreover, it is of crucial importance that membership in local voluntary associations strengthens social bonds, community sentiments, and attachments regardless of social position. Thus the integration of a person in a local area reflects less his "societal-wide social status" (occupation and race) than his local "social position" (in particular length of residence, number of children, and patterns of daily behavior) (Hunter, 1974, p. xiii).

These findings can be restated to highlight the consequences of size and density—the key variables of the gemeinschaft-gesellschaft perspective. Residence in communities of increased size and density does not result in a substitution of secondary organizational for primary and informal contacts. Rather, organizational ties foster more extensive primary contacts in the local community. None of these conclusions deny the relevance of the concept of loss of community as a basis for social criticism and for creating new social goals. However, the available cross-sectional data hardly support the simplistic conception of the growth of atomization or alienation of the person and his household. The variable of residential mobility moves the analysis into the longitudinal mode. The development of urbanization and advanced industrialism in the United States has not been accompanied by an increase in the amount of residential mobility. Hawley (1971) reports, for example, that in every census since 1850 the proportion of the population (adjusted for age difference) reported living in the state of their birth has varied between 66 and 70 percent; he concludes that very little change has occurred. Moreover, most household moves take place during the ages of 25 to 35. After that age there is a marked increase in residential stability, and we are not faced with a "social doomsday machine," with ever increasing rates of geographical mobility.

An explicit longitudinal study of the social organization of a local residential community comes from research on one locality in Rochester, New York, first conducted in 1949 by Donald L. Foley and repeated by Albert Hunter in 1974

(Hunter, 1975). The study has the drawback that it deals with a university-related local area in which the residents have displayed a powerful commitment to central-city values and racial integration. It is therefore a rather special case, but this type of community can be found in one form or another in each of the major metropolitan areas. The data collected at the two points in time over a quarter of a century on "informal neighboring" and on the residents' "sense of community" clearly reveal a strengthening of the community of limited liability. While there was a decline in the use of local service facilities, the level of informal neighboring remained the same or increased and the expressed sense of community increased significantly. Placed in historical context, community studies based on the participant observation approach of the Chicago school also aid in longitudinal comparisons. Two such studies are of particular relevance. One is *The Gold Coast and the Slum,* the classic monograph by Harvey Zorbaugh published in 1929 dealing with a locality characterized by high residential mobility, a very wide range of social segments, and the presence of strong resistance to collective community organization. The other is *Blue Collar Community* by William Kornblum (1974), a historical-sociological analysis of the neighborhood of South Chicago from the turn of the century to the early years of 1970. This is a community study of a steel mill concentration and surrounding ethnic neighborhoods, a locality characterized by high residential stability and a gradual process of ethnic transformation. The culture of the factory and the plant-based trade unions penetrated into the residential community and vice versa.

One-half century after the publication of *The Gold Coast and the Slum,* the boundaries of the area have not changed; the locality is still delimited by North Avenue on the north, Lake Michigan on the east, and the Chicago River on the south and west; however, the name has changed from the "Lower Northside" to the "Near Northside." The local area has been transformed more by the pouring of concrete than by social changes. Rooming houses have been replaced by four-story apartments, while near Lake Michigan the older brownstone mansions have given way to luxury high-rise apartments. Adjoining the Chicago River, the area of Little Italy, once the site of blighted single-family units, has been recast into a massive high-rise public housing project. The social extremes in the populations remain and population density is high. Blacks have replaced the ethnics. While the socialites have declined, they have not vanished. They have been augmented by hardworking business and banking executives plus "big time" professionals. The former flow of native immigrants from rural areas with high school education seeking to penetrate the cultural and social life of the area has been replaced by college graduates from suburban enclaves having similar aspirations.

Despite social heterogeneity, high residential mobility, and institutional fragmentation, Zorbaugh found a strong sense of local identity. A striking portion of the residents worked in the area or nearby. But the atmosphere of the area reflected not its work habits but its relatively self-contained informal social contacts and local institutions, which catered to the consumer, aesthetic, and cultural tastes of the residents. It was and remains an area in which adults socialize and develop differentiated tastes. Zorbaugh emphasized the weakness of the central voluntary association—the Lower North Community Council—which started as an all-purpose organization during World War I and survived as a defensive community maintenance group. One of the sharpest changes over the decades was the growth in number and vitality of local community organizations still strongly oriented toward a defensive posture. Presently these voluntary associations, although having specific purposes and goals, express a generalized concern for the fate of the area. The local party organization and especially the alderman have become closely linked to these voluntary associations, and the alderman serves as an intermediary between these voluntary associations and the municipal government.

South Chicago presents a profound contrast to the Near Northside in the social organization of a residential locality, not only because the area is dominated by its industrial establishments but also because ethnic groups supply the basis for the ordered segmentation of the locality. The most significant contrast is that the socialization process focuses on the young people and the next generation; the well-being of the adults is taken for granted and is not an issue. Industrial relations have been violent and remain conflictive, and local politics are outrightly belligerent. But with the passage of time, and especially since the end of World War II, the local educational system and associated youth-serving institutions have had to face marked social changes. With its limited educational capacity, the public school system long operated with some effectiveness because it was taken for granted that preparation for a career in the steel mills was the effective goal. This goal supplied an operating logic even though more and more young men sought other types of employment. Since 1945, however, fewer men have chosen to enter the mills, and there has been increasing pressure to educate the young females for active employment rather than for household duties only. An influx of Mexican and black minorities has only compounded the educational problems. The voluntary associations and the political organs are highly active and closely linked to the ethnic structure of the locality. However, over time there has been a fragmentation and weakening sense of community, since these organizations have limited impact on the social tensions created by ethnic succession and by the dilemmas and limitations family and educational institutions encounter in seeking to socialize the next generation.

Family and School. There is a long and rich tradition of sociological writings that focus on the presumably increasing strain resulting from the gap between family socialization and the realities of the industrial and occupational setting (Firth and others, 1970; Bott, 1971; Burgess and Locke, 1953). Each particular community study highlights the wide variation in patterns of transition by which young people move from the residential community to the world of work. One aspect of this literature has been to examine long-term trends in the social organization of the family under the hypothesis that a weakening of the family under advanced industrialism increases the complexities and strain in this process of socialization and transition. Although the post-World War II period has witnessed a short-term increase in "familism," the long-term trends have been toward smaller families, more employed wives, an increase in the number of divorces, and a larger proportion of the population living in incomplete or reconstituted families (Glick, 1957; Davis, 1972b; Glick, 1975). The argument is that each of these trends increases the difficulties of local socialization. While the research findings are hardly conclusive, the argument has strong plausibility. According to Census Bureau data in 1976, only 65 percent of U.S. households had both a husband and wife living together; this was a decline from 71 percent in 1970. In that six-year period, the number of families headed by women rose 33 percent and the number of men living as "primary individuals"—either alone or with nonrelatives—jumped 61 percent. Similarly the increase in illegitimate children has been substantial both for whites and blacks; in 1969 it was estimated that over 50 percent of the first children born to black mothers were illegitimate.

However, an adequate analysis of the relationship between the residential community and the world of work requires a supplementary line of reasoning. With the increased separation of the locus of work from the residence, the family finds it harder to handle the children's transition to adulthood, and the burden increasingly shifts onto the educational system. Thus it has become commonplace for social critics and sociologists to point to the limitations of the educational institutions in supplying an appropriate system of transition from the family to adult occupation. The comprehensive high school has served as the regulating and bridging institutional mechanism, which has sought a balance between preparation for an increasingly complex division of labor and the development of a sense of collective identity loosely linked to residential locality. During the period 1920 to 1940, the comprehensive high school operated as a device to overcome barriers to higher education that were based on geographical and community segregation. It was not the goal of the comprehensive high school to increase social and economic equality, but to extend the potential basis of access to higher education. Moreover, until the outbreak of World War II, the comprehensive high school was at least compatible with the needs of youngsters who were to enter blue collar occupations. The administrative procedures ensured a steady exodus from the comprehensive high school into the world of work through flexible attendance requirements. More importantly, the size, location, and values of the comprehensive high school were not antithetical to the realities of occupational life in the industrial sector.

Extensive research literature on the post-World War II transformation of the comprehensive high school underlines the strain on its capacity to serve as a local institution of socialization (Gordon, 1957; Gottlieb and Reeves, 1963; Coleman, 1966; Bachman and others, 1971). This transformation has had varying consequences for all social segments but particularly for the children of low-income families. The comprehensive high school has found itself operating in a changed labor market in which the age of entrance into the industrial and service sector has been raised by legislative and administrative decree, the increase in minimum wages, and employer-union negotiations. The removal of youngsters from the labor market has been a humanitarian, welfare, and economic goal. However, the long-term changes in the comprehensive high school have exacerbated the tasks of youth socialization and the transition from community to occupation, especially in a period when the age of entrance into the labor market has been rising. Since 1945 the size of the high school unit has increased under the stimulation of educational policies claiming that larger high schools are required to effect an adequate comprehensive school. The result has been a weakening of local community ties and increased difficulty in maintaining an internal discipline and sense of purpose in many high schools. Paradoxically, the increase in the size of the comprehensive high school has not meant that individual schools are able to maintain a relatively representative student body. In fact, there has been a growth in the homogeneity of the student body, thereby limiting the high school's ability to serve as a bridging institution to the larger society. This increased homogeneity is the result of the increase in the scale of social segregation in local areas, particularly in the central city with its black ghetto. Moreover, the loss of industry in the central city has meant that the distance between the factory and the comprehensive high school has increased, especially for the central city high school.

The increased requirements of school attendance have been accompanied by a growth in the value of a college preparatory curriculum. This trend has been strongly enforced by the values emphasized in the mass media. These long-term transformations have increased the difficulties that important segments of the youth population have in making the transition to adult occupations. In particular, the impact has been most painful for youngsters from low-income households, which lack a tradition of family involvement in the industrial setting, and for selected elements of the middle strata, who have found prolonged participation in an educational setting particularly difficult to sustain. The expansion of the mass education system has increased the emphasis on age grading and limited the range of contact youngsters have with a wide variety of adults. Since it is both impossible and undesirable to revert to earlier forms, there have been many recommendations for experiments to modify secondary education toward goals of a new mixture between work experience and classroom experience (Janowitz, 1969; Coleman and others, 1974). With the end of the draft, even the armed forces have weakened in their capacity to serve as a bridge between school and adult occupational life (Villemez and Kasarda, 1976). These trends help account for the increase in deviant and criminal behavior among youth groups as well as the persistent strength of the counterculture, fundamentalist youth religions, and parapolitical youth movements. With the role of the schools weakened, the process of transition from family to occupation is more and more mediated by nonlocal institutions of socialization, particularly the mass media, the legal and criminal justice system, and the bureaucratized social welfare services.

But the pressure and pace of the life cycle are overriding. The disruption and tension associated with the transition into an occupation outside of one's residential community hardly stand as permanent and immovable barriers to the subsequent development of local residential attachments that come with marriage and the passage of time. The life cycle generates the basis for communal attachments for each new and successive generation. We are dealing not with a middle class phenomenon but one that permeates the entire social structure. The most powerful indicator of the intersection of the hierarchy of the industrial order and the geography of the locality is that deviant and criminal behavior declines markedly after the age of twenty-five, regardless of social and legal policy. Aspiring to a stable household implies that the bulk of the next generation will seek to enter the labor market and at the same time develop their own communal network in a fashion compatible with the norms of the larger metropolis. The social costs of the process of transition are high. The incidence of temporary disruption grows as the rate of persistent youth unemployment under "stagflation" has increased, and there are those who are permanently affected. The tensions and strain of incorporating new cohorts into a relatively stable communal life not only fall on the younger generation but also increase the discontent of the older generation and widen the disarticulation between age groupings. The obverse of the strain on the comprehensive high school as a local institution is the disarticulation of the diffuse institutions designed to handle the socialization and support of the cohorts entering later maturity, for constructing one's own household does not include care of one's aging parents in the welfare state.

We are not dealing merely with interpersonal processes by which a person and his household struggle to make the transition through the stages of the life cycle. We are dealing with institutional structure and the issues of "institution building," by which the residential locality supplies or fails to supply a setting for collective problem solving and an effective social order.

Voluntary Associations and the Local Community

Local socialization throughout the life cycle not only relates the person and his or her household to the industrial and occupational order but also fashions political orientations and behavior. It is a classic theme that the political process in the United States has traditionally rested on a network of voluntary associations, especially local ones. We will briefly assess the consequences of an increased separation of work and residence on this structure and network of community-based voluntary associations over the half century since the end of World War I. A question arises as to the extent to which participation in community-based voluntary associations serves to adjudicate conflicts of group interest and to mold stable and effective political orientations. It is not sensible to accept the simple notion that local community participation inevitably promotes the resolution of group conflicts. Intensification of participation often reflects a disarticulation between local groups and the more encompassing levels of administration and politics; it can push the resolution of differences upward toward the national level, where it may contribute to stalemate.

Our hypothesis, however, is that on balance the operations of local community associations tend to result in the resolution of conflicts of interest and the development of effective modes of political participation. This occurs as the increased separation of work and residence diminishes the influence of occupational, professional, and economic groupings over decisions made in a decentralized political system within locally organized political and administrative units. The separation of work and residence creates a political vacuum that only the elaboration of local association activities can fill.

The importance of local groupings also derives from the fact that by its very nature participation involves more than self-interest. The reality that these groupings compete for public resources should not obscure their underlying ideology, which seeks to give content to the idea of collective responsibility among neighbors. A collective defense of the community flows from the task of socializing the new residents and the next generation of offspring. Because members of different households share a single territory, the special interests of each are brought into interaction so that their relative merit and importance can be considered and even debated—so that a working definition of or at least aspiration for a larger or public interest may emerge (Janowitz and Suttles, 1977). In the local community, a person and his or her household have the opportunity—by no means generally realized—both to internalize and aggregate the cost and benefits of alternative political policies. All citizens are forced to consider their definitions of the "good society" and the "good community" and to confront the costs they will have to bear for such a social order. If they wish to call the police to complain about a rowdy house party nearby, they will have to bear the ultimate cost of so doing; the burden cannot be shifted to impersonal third parties.

At an endless number of interaction points, the neighborhood and community are loci where the appetites for economic self-interest encounter an element of face-to-face reality testing. The family across the hall that will water the plants and take in the mail is participating in mutual self-help and not an economic exchange. If they have any vitality, these patterns of interpersonal assistance influence both the goals and tactics of local voluntary associations. In turn, the accomplishments—and more often the lack of accomplishment—of local community initiative serve to socialize one to participation in the larger political process. It is painfully obvious, as shown at points throughout this volume, that the geographical scope of community organizations does not articulate with the jurisdictions of the political and administrative units of metropolitan government. Yet one of the essential characteristics of political parties in a parliamentary system is that they are organized on a geographical basis—not in terms of institutional or group interests —and that the contests for political power are waged in the smallest territorial units. Except in the worst wards, dominated by absentee or criminal leaders, the political parties must penetrate the locality and present themselves as legitimate to the social organization of the residential community. As a result, the broadest issues of collective responsibility at the national level must resonate in the residential locality.

Ethnicity and Race. The high levels of local voluntary association activity on the contemporary scene are misunderstood if they are seen as expressions of a rising tide of ethnicity. Place of residence and the operations of local associations are of course related to trends in ethnicity and the strength of ethnic identifications, including, of course, racial identifications. However, the long-term trend since World War I has been a weakening of ethnic solidarity and a specialization of its scope.

In any given period it is necessary to separate the new immigrants who enlarge the ethnic social base from the older elements for whom the issues of persistence of ethnic identity are problematic. Immigration restrictions in 1920 brought a long-term interruption in the flow of ethnic immigrants. However, after World War II, the flow increased unexpectedly. While the relative magnitude has never reached the pre-World War I concentrations, the postwar figure is that about 20 percent of the population growth is due to immigration (U.S. Bureau of the Census, 1975e). Moreover, the new immigration has included many trained professionals, university professors, journalists, and political leaders, resulting in highly visible new immigrants.

Patterns of both residence and language supply important indicators of ethnic cohesion and solidarity and serve to correct the image of a rapid melting pot. Ecological research highlights the relatively high persistence of residential segregation (or concentration) of ethnic groupings (Kantrowitz, 1969, 1972, 1973; Guest and Weed, 1976). These studies measure ethnicity by descent—namely, foreign born versus native born, and by the means of the national heritage of the first generation. In particular, these studies emphasize that residential segregation persists despite suburbanization. Higher socioeconomic status reduces the degree of residential segregation of ethnicity, but from an overall point of view ethnicity has an independent effect. However, the ecological studies do not address the consequences of lower density and increased mobility. Geographic concentration is only an indirect indicator of ethnic solidarity and self-conceptions, especially of the changes in the social basis of ethnic identification. Therefore, language has become a more crucial quantitative measure. On the basis of the extensive documentation collected by Joshua A. Fishman, the decline in "language loyalty" can be taken as a powerful indicator of the overall weakening of ethnic attachments. By 1960, the non-English-language resources of the United States were "undoubtedly smaller than they had been a decade or two previously" (Fishman, 1966, p. 382). As of 1960 it was estimated that 19 million persons, or 11 percent of the entire U.S. population, possessed a non-English mother tongue. The flow of new immigrants—legal and illegal—from Spanish-speaking countries injected an important new component of foreign-language speakers. But given the long-term history of U.S. immigration, to point to one tenth of the population as foreign-language speakers does not warrant describing this percentage as high. Moreover, the key measure would be the degree to which households of foreign-language speakers transmit the mother tongue to their children, and there is very little data on this point. The continuing decline of the foreign-language press despite the inflow of new immigrants is another indicator of the long-term decline in language loyalty.

More direct measures of ethnic solidarity and self-conceptions are required, particularly measures that highlight the difference between assimilation and acculturation (Rosenthal, 1960). Acculturation refers to incorporation into the occupational structure and the acceptance of key values of the larger society; assimilation implies loss of a sense of consciousness of descent and particularistic group identity. In the absence of adequate national survey data on long-term trends in ethnic identification, we can estimate that more than half the adult population of the United States as of 1976 did not have a meaningful or relatively clear or discernible ethnic sentiment (including racial identifications). Some indication of the waning of ethnic identification can be drawn from those community studies—past and present—that reveal the changing meaning and scope of ethnic identification in the United States. From the community studies of the 1920s one is struck by the pervasive and almost coercive character of ethnicity and ethnic solidarity. Ethnicity and associated religious sentiments were central themes in the sense of personal consciousness.

The comparison with the literature generated after 1950 is striking, although only a few of the empirical researches are directly relevant. The documentation that has been collected brings into focus the importance of voluntary associations and of conscious efforts—particularly of political groups—to maintain and strengthen ethnic symbolism. This conclusion emerges in the range of literature from the reportage in *Beyond the Melting Pot,* by Nathan Glazer and Daniel P. Moynihan (1963), to the historically based community research on the ethnic groups of South Chicago by William Kornblum (1974). In the recent period ethnicity has its meaning principally through politics. It erupts from its subdued form in the moments of heavy political pressure and political conflict, and in this regard operates as a very important element of cleavage.

Thus revival of ethnicity and ethnic identity needs to be placed in a historical framework. Important to the visibility of ethnic sentiments is that they tend to be concentrated in the central city. In part this reflects the settlement pattern of the stream of new immigrants and the persistence of older lower-income social elements. However, the increased political involvement and participation of blacks and Spanish-speaking groups has contributed to the apparent revival—while in effect we are dealing with the entrance into the political arena of formerly excluded groups. It seems reasonable to conclude that while the process of acculturation continues, the rate of assimilation has slowed but hardly stopped. Further, the increase in deconcentration of human settlement and the increased range of daily and residential mobility have weakened the territorial basis of ethnic solidarities. Ethnic groupings still retain a discernible element of geographical social organization, but they have come to reflect the increasing disarticulation of the residential community from the occupational system. In turn, the ethnic basis of local community organization has declined, while geographical and territorial affiliation per se becomes more relevant. Ethnic groupings emerge more and more as a specialized type of "interest group," which involves an important emphasis on self-respect. Ethnic leaders remain aware of their geographical base, but ethnic politics is increasingly managed by metropolitan and national mass media and organizational specialists. The last step in the transformation is that presidential candidates cannot operate without special staff advisers on ethnic affairs, whose task is to mobilize the ethnic consistency as much as to transmit the perspectives and demands of the groups involved.

Voluntary Associations in the Community of Limited Liability. Thus one should not overemphasize the ethnic factor even in local politics. As a result, the local community of limited liability emerges more and more as "pure" territorial social organization. We return to the very definition of the residential community as the community of limited liability. The vitality of the residential community and its contribution to the larger political structure rest on and are strongly conditioned by the voluntary associations that link the citizen to the administrative and political agencies of the state. The conflicts of interest that concern locally based voluntary associations are frequently pushed upward in the political structure, but local territorial attachments of voluntary associations and their leaders significantly modulate and even resolve conflicts which present issues that can be tested against local realities. This is hardly to deny that particular local issues such as racial integration by means of school busing have produced explosive conflict. However, even

these conflicts in the context of the community of limited liability tend to be resolved or transformed by the redistribution
of the population. In the United States, communal conflict has
not resulted in the development of paramilitary voluntary associations with persistent destructive consequences as it has in
other nations.

The system of local community-based voluntary associations is a particular manifestation of the elaborate network of
associational membership in the United States. The level of participation in the United States in voluntary associations is higher
than that of most Western European parliamentary nations
(Almond and Verba, 1965, chap. 5). Moreover, the network is
heavily based in the localities, in part reflecting the great separation of local and national government in the United States. It is
erroneous to accept the conclusions of those writers who emphasize that even this extensive network of voluntary associations encompasses only a minority citizenry. The long-term
trend appears to be one of increasing levels of such participation
(Hyman and Wright, 1971; Curtis, 1971). Further, persons become involved in a voluntary association at times when specific
needs and controversies arise, so that membership during one's
lifetime tends to be high; the network of voluntary associations
is extended by a person's access through family members, relatives, and friends; and although participation tends to be correlated with social rank, segments of the blue collar workers with
strong trade union and church affiliations have more effective
voluntary association anchors than do elements of the white
collar population. Of overriding importance is that more extensive involvement in voluntary associations is positively linked to
both stronger local social bonds and communal identifications
and also to higher levels of political participation in elections,
both local and national (Olsen, 1972; Almond and Verba,
1965).

As stressed above, we are dealing with a local socialization process in which length of residence is a key variable associated with increased voluntary association membership. It is of
course essential to avoid simple cause-and-effect explanations.
Instead, two observations can be made that throw light on the
impact of voluntary associations on aggregating and balancing
local community interests and influencing local political institutions. First, if one analyzes the available quantitative survey
data on political behavior, one encounters a local political context or local political culture that has a strong and independent

impact. In this regard, *local* has a multiple meaning; it refers to metropolitan as opposed to national and to community as opposed to metropolitan. In simple terms, the same background characteristics produce different community and political perspectives depending on the concentration of these characteristics in a given community. Thus, for example, if one proceeds on a community-by-community basis, those persons who have social background characteristics likely to produce Republican perspectives are less likely to behave politically as Republicans if they find themselves in mainly Democratic communities (Segal and Meyer, 1969; Segal and Wildstrom, 1970). The concentration of political partisans can be taken as a rough indicator of the political setting of the locality. In this sense, the political context is more important than, for example, the ethnic context.

Second, along with the existing political context, "civic leadership" operates as an important set of variables accounting for the character of local community perspectives and participation. Robert C. Angell's (1951) classic study of the moral integration of major cities emphasized the key importance of three social stratification variables—residential mobility, cultural heterogeneity, and socioeconomic differentiation—in accounting for lower levels of moral integration among the cities in his sample. He found that the character of community leadership and of local civic participation—although difficult to measure —had to be taken into account for an adequate explanation of those cities that displayed higher than anticipated levels of moral integration. Moreover, in comparing the moral integration of these cities in 1970 with their situation in 1940 (Angell, 1974), he found that the socioeconomic variables declined in importance, and by inference, the variables of civic leadership increased in importance. This is essentially the conclusion that most local community power studies have reached.

If one examines the operation of local voluntary associations and assumes an increase in their impact, it becomes necessary to distinguish different organizational styles and outcomes. One can ask under what conditions do their enlarged activities operate merely as a veto pressure, and thereby contribute to political stalemate? Under what conditions do they aggregate their influence and balance competing pressures so as to contribute to a more effective political balance, especially by balancing the interests between the workplace and the residential community? One must initially note a negative trend, the result of the increase in electoral redistricting that has become more frequent since 1950. It has weakened the links between voluntary associations and local political agencies by constantly changing the cognitive perception of the locality. "South Shore is not much of a community anymore since they broke up the sixth ward" is a typical reaction to altered electoral boundaries. Changes in election districts mean that the resulting enclaves bear even less relationship to the local natural area or to the format of administrative areas.

On the other hand, by conscious effort local community organizations have sought to adapt themselves to the shifting basis of electoral representation and to the reality that boundaries of the administrative agencies of government are much more inclusive than the natural areas of neighborhoods and local communities. Because of the increased nucleation and fragmentation of the urban environment, the number of local community organizations has grown since the end of World War II, reflecting smaller-size localities. For the city of Chicago, the number of neighborhood and local community organizations had grown to over 250 by 1968 (Hunter, 1974). At the same time, this proliferation of separate units has been accompanied by a strong movement toward hierarchical federation. In fact, one-half of the neighborhood and local community organizations were affiliated with a "roof organization" representing wide sectors of the central city. The roof organizations varied from loose federations to complex, multitiered organizations with complex constitutions, staffs, and extensive financial resources. Even the Gold Coast area of Chicago has witnessed this development; the increased number of local organizations in the Near Northside community area has produced a Committee on Community Organization to coordinate the various groups. The effectiveness and durability of these roof associations vary widely. The organizations reflect the aspiration of individual organizations to relate to the broader scope of political institutions and administrative agencies but to do so without the loss of a local base. The success of these coordinating agencies rests on the ability of the competing local leaders to develop a measure of internal accommodation and self-regulation, which implies an element of compromise. This trend toward hierarchical federation has increased the actual and potential capacity of community organizations to operate as more than veto groups. Of course, the division between central-city and suburban organizations remains, although basic issues of mass transportation and the management of the environment supply the initial basis for new political coalitions.

Conclusion

This analysis of social organization in the urban metropolis has often juxtaposed the hierarchical dimension of industrial and occupational institutions against the territorial dimension of residential communities. The four hypotheses that were explored reflect the argument that the increased disarticulation between occupational institutions and the residential-household communities strains the social and political orders. The increase in the scale of bureaucratic organization and the enlargement of the means of transportation are the proximate causes of strain, but there is no reason to accept the notions of a simple evolutionary model in the division of labor or a loss of community in the residential sector. Indeed, we have suggested that social changes have enlarged the importance of socialization and political functions in the local community.

Thus the increase in scale does not result in increased uniformity. On the contrary, the outcome is greater differentiation and greater interdependence. Fortunately, these trends do not confirm those classic theories that anticipate impersonality and atomization of social relations. Unfortunately, however, interdependence does not produce and insure integration and coordination within the metropolis or between the population concentrations and the total society. The local residential community has come more and more explicitly to serve as a political arena for balancing competing group interests, although it is hardly able to fill this role effectively.

Notes

1. The analysis of the metropolitan community presented here will be elaborated and placed into a macrosociological theoretical framework involving social control in advanced industrial society in Janowitz, forthcoming.

2. The term *neighborhood* is often used to refer to local urban community, but it more often refers to smaller social blocs reflecting local social solidarities, patterns of interpersonal attraction, and self-help.

3. The decline of the dual housing market may well have had a strong impact on the process of racial succession in residential neighborhoods. From the period 1920 to 1960, the research literature placed a strong emphasis on the "tipping point." In the process of competition, invasion, and succession, population change was described as following a

definite pattern. First, the rate of change was low as the initial blacks entered a white community and remained relatively low until a tipping point was reached of between 20 and 40 percent. In this range, the character of the neighborhood or community underwent rapid change. There is reason to believe that the increase in housing available to blacks and the greater difficulty of low-income white families in suburbanizing has changed this pattern into a more continuous and gradual process. Data collected and analyzed for the period 1963 to 1967 point in this direction (see Piccagli, 1975).

4. The construction of community boundaries can become the explicit task of governmental agencies. In New York City, the City Planning Commission has consciously sought to develop community planning areas that articulate with the natural settings of localities. Local planning boards were established in 1949 by Mayor Robert F. Wagner, then borough president of Manhattan, and were mandated in all boroughs by the City Charter. In June 1966 the commission announced twenty-four criteria for marking the boundaries and sought community comment on these criteria. In addition to corresponding with health, school, welfare policy, and urban renewal districts, these criteria included physical factors and lines of the original villages of the city and historical areas, such as Yorkville in Manhattan or Riverdale in the Bronx.

5. For a discussion of the statistical perceptual measures of community boundaries, see Form and others (1974), Shevky and Bell (1955), Shevky and Williams (1949), Lynch (1960), Duncan and others (1961b), Theodorson (1961), and Downs and Stea (1973).

6. The survey, of 2199 citizens, was designed to assist the Royal Commission on Local Government in England in making recommendations to restructure the size and format of governmental units. Random samples were drawn in 100 local authority areas throughout England (excluding London). No comparable body of data exists for the United States, but there is little reason to believe that the patterns of relationships among variables would be significantly different for this country. Residential mobility is higher in the United States than in Great Britain, which could affect the overall level of integration. That there are strong similarities between the United States and Britain in the internal organization and patterns of social behavior of neighborhoods is a conclusion reinforced by the findings of a comparative study of Bristol, England, and Columbus, Ohio (Bracey, 1964).

Part Two

Local and
Traditional Ties

In urban sociology, a recurrent conclusion is that—in contrast to what Louis Wirth might have meant in his 1938 classic "Urbanism as a Way of Life"—life under urbanization goes on much as before. True enough, but the point of empirical inquiry must be to move beyond the recognition that we live neither wholly gemeinschaft nor wholly gesellschaft lives to specify the complications and ambiguities that result from urban social change. The first entry in this section, Chapter Five, "Persistence of Local Sentiments in Mass Society" by Albert Hunter, approaches this problem most pointedly in terms of its theoretical dimensions. Seeking to develop a model of community development and local sentiments, Hunter stands the traditional problem of mass society versus local ties on its head, asking ultimately if the rise of mass society may not facilitate local involvement and attachment.

The other chapters in the section are more concerned with empirical developments. In Chapter Six, "Family and Sex Roles in Urban Society," Shirley Harkess looks at community type as one of a cluster of factors, including changes in the occupational order and variations in rates of marriage and child-bearing, that may affect family and sex roles. Of special interest to her is the question of whether some types of communities provide a broadened acceptance of a pluralism of family or sex role forms. Chapter Seven, "Race, Ethnicity, and Community," by Sidney Kronus, examines the urbanization of blacks and the degree of change and persistence in ethnicity and the survival of ethnic communities. Harry M. Johnson's Chapter Eight, "Religion in Urban Society," addresses the questions of whether urbanization of the society is accompanied by a decline in the importance of religion and what role religious institutions play in addressing urban problems.

5

Persistence of Local Sentiments in Mass Society

Albert Hunter

As advances are made in history, the organization which has territorial groups as its base (village or city, district, province, etc.) steadily becomes effaced. . . . These geographical divisions are, for the most part, artificial and no longer awaken in us profound sentiments. . . .

They persist, not only through sheer force of survival, but because there still persists something of the needs they once answered. The material neighborhood will always constitute a bond between men; consequently, political and social organization with a territorial base will certainly exist [Emile Durkheim, *The Division of Labor in Society,* 1964, pp. 27-28].

> Among well-disposed people the necessity or con-
> veniency of mutual accommodation very frequently pro-
> duces a friendship not unlike that which takes place
> among those who are born to live in the same family. . . .
> Even the trifling circumstance of living in the same neigh-
> bourhood has some effect of the same kind. We respect
> the face of a man whom we see every day, provided he
> has never offended us. . . . There are certain small good
> offices, accordingly, which are universally allowed to be
> due to a neighbour in preference to any other person who
> has no such connection [Adam Smith, *The Theory of
> Moral Sentiments*, 1971, p. 329].

A specter is haunting the rise of modern mass society, the specter of the isolated, alienated urbanite, uprooted, roaming unattached through the streets of the city, a perpetual stranger, fearful but free. The purpose of this chapter is to trace this illusion and to assess its validity in the light of recent research. In the process we will see that the specter may be likened to a cloud: in part it is a wispy light entity full of holes through which rays of sunlight and blue sky pour through, while in part it is what the observer chooses to make of it, an imaginary beast of a benevolent or malevolent mein. We must be careful in observing and interpreting this specter, however, for it carries some of the more emotional concepts in the sociological literature—sentiment and attachment, community and kinship, neighbor and friend. We will have to be careful to maintain the eye of the sociological skeptic, being as neutral as possible, so that we more clearly understand and predict its fate.

Therefore, we must first establish the value positions that too often underlie discussions of this topic. The first centers around a nostalgic yearning for the small community that many feel has been lost in today's world. Intertwined with this yearning is a nostalgia not only of place but also of time, as Kevin Lynch has noted in his book *What Time Is This Place?* (1972). The positive sentiments of past time and place are often juxtaposed with negative sentiments toward the present, and polarities around contrasting the simple with the complex, the innocent with the worldly, and the known with the unknown. The filtered past comes to us as a known pattern, but the raw present presents daily confusions that seem to defy understanding.

A second bias centers around the connotations of the word *community*. There exists an inherent bias not only in the lay conception but more nefariously within social science itself toward viewing community as an unqualified good. The positive connotations of friendliness, warmth, and support are seldom countered with the accompanying characteristics of constraint and conformity, and the loss of privacy, individualism, and freedom. We will not debate these points except insofar as they have assumed a central position in sociological theories or have been explored empirically as variables in sociological research. Instead, we will attempt to describe and define community and to understand more clearly the sentiments associated with it.

Finally, we must not confuse sentiment with sentimentalism. I will paint no romantic or romanticized pictures but rather will treat sentiments as legitimate individual and collective variables in the study of communal life. In short, to study sentiments, we must take care not to be sentimental ourselves.

Theoretical Legacy

The initial visions of the specter I have just alluded to are to be found in the major writings of the classical social theorists, such as Marx, Weber, Durkheim, and Simmel. Their theories have been propagated elsewhere, as in Stein's *The Eclipse of Community* (1960), Nisbet's *The Quest for Community* (1953), and most trenchantly in the often cited article "Urbanism as a Way of Life" by Wirth (1938). To use Stein's categories, the argument simply put is that the major social transformations of the eighteenth and nineteenth centuries, urbanization, industrialization, and bureaucratization, produced a social structure that destroyed the previous local affinities such as kinship and community. It is as if these parochial sentiments and attachments were lost in the sheer size and density of cities, clouded over by the smog and smoke from factories and crushed lifeless under the bulk of the bureaucratic forms.

Although each of the classical statements may vary slightly in the specific characteristics emphasized in the emerging "mass society," the effect on local sentiments and attachments is generally interpreted in the same way—they will either be destroyed or lost. However, as the opening quotations in this chapter suggest, the eclipse is partial, the destruction incomplete, and the loss limited.

The opening quotations notwithstanding, we will begin our discussion with the nineteenth-century social theorists who described the transformation of Western society. To Stein's three global processes of urbanization, industrialization, and bureaucratization, we should add the massive immigrations that accompanied these, and the rise of nationalism and the modern nation-state.

For Marx (1956), the rise of capitalism out of and in opposition to the feudal order, based on tradition, land, the estates, and subinfeudation, presented a new social order based on a growing distinction between social classes. The bonds of community were being replaced by market relations just as the market itself became the organizing unit replacing the feudal estate. The growing density of the factors of production in cities during the later stages of industrial capitalism was seen to be a critical factor in the emergence of a new social bond, the bond of the working class with class consciousness that would replace the social bond of the traditional community. The community of land, epitomized in the agricultural peasantry, was seen to be at best a conservative, if not reactionary, force.

For Durkheim (1964), the increasing division of labor in society was seen to be an outcome of the increasing ecological density that in turn arose from the human propensity to aggregate. Out of the ecological density arose a dynamic "moral density," resulting in a diversity of interests and an organic social order based on difference and interdependence. The old mechanical order of similarity and shared interest gave way to diversity exemplified in the increasing division of labor. As in Marx's interpretation, however, the fall of the local community as a basis of social order would not long leave a vacuum, for in its stead one would find the rapid rise of work-related associations of interest. Defining these in occupational rather than in class terms, Durkheim emphasized the job-related homogeneity of interest, which implied a greater number and diversity of social solidarities than did Marx's classes. However, this new solidarity was not totally devoid of communal sentiments, for underlying the diversity of interests expressed in the organic social order would always remain some communal sentiments. However, these would be directed not toward parochial places as in the past but toward the overarching, emerging nation-state, which laid claim to monopolizing (among other things) personal allegiance and collective sentiments. The old local community was replaced by the new community of the nation-state.

For Weber (1958), the central process was one of an increasing rationalization or "demystification" of modern life. Rationality became formally embodied in the bureaucratic

structure of organized social life. Like Marx's industrial, capital-
istic classes and Durkheim's urbanized, occupational groups, the
ideal bureaucracy for Weber became the object of new allegiance that would supersede parochial sentiments. Efficiency
and rationality became central values within the new social
organization, which viewed the irrationality of sentiments in
general and sentiments of community in particular as anathema.

Where Durkheim stressed the *nation* as the communal
underpinning of the new nation-state, Weber stressed the *state*
as the efficient structure that would maintain social order
through its exclusive right to use violence.

A more vivid description of the developing specter of
modern urban life was presented by Simmel (1950) in his essay
"The Metropolis and Mental Life." Considering the market, the
money economy, and the division of labor from the previous
theories as key structural characteristics of the modern metropolis, Simmel then spelled out their sociopsychological consequences for individuals. The size, density, and heterogeneity
that Wirth (1938) was later to emphasize were seen to lead to a
cognitive and psychic overload that required the urbanite to
blur distinctions and to become more categorical and less discriminating as well as more objective and less subjective—in
short, to develop the aloof, blasé urban attitude. What some
might have seen as tolerance for diversity, others saw as indifference. The demands for efficiency, punctuality, and specialization occasioned by the division of labor resulted in a narrowing
of personality, a uniqueness that was rightly linked to individualism and freedom but that was objectively and not subjec-
tively defined. People were different, given the diversity and
division of labor, but at the price of not developing full personalities or interacting with and experiencing others as full personalities. People become things as their relationships become
defined through the money economy and the market: "By
being the equivalent to all the manifold things in one and the
same way, money becomes the most frightful leveler. . . . All
things float with equal specific gravity in the constantly moving
stream of money" (Simmel, 1950, p. 414). The result, according to Simmel, is that "the individual has become a mere cog in
an enormous organization of things and powers which tear from
his hands all progress, spirituality and value" (p. 422).

In summary, the historical legacy presented a picture in
which the rise of modern mass society destroyed more parochial
communal forms of association. Community was superseded by

the overarching, industrial, bureaucratized nation-state, propelling every person toward individualism and freedom with the accompanying isolation, alienation, and anomie. New forms of association developed but did not rest on the broad-based, personal, and territorial sentiments of community; rather, they resulted from the narrow, specific, rational interests of individuals. The world was no longer one of people in communities but rather one of people against society.

Community Lost—The Empirical Legacy

The study of the loss of local community sentiments in mass society is most clearly exemplified by two general empirical traditions: the research of the Chicago School of the 1920s and 1930s, which focused on the disorganization of primary kinship and ethnic bases of solidarity within Chicago's neighborhoods; and research on the transformation of small-town life as a result of the increasing scale of social organization at both the metropolitan and national levels. Exemplary studies of this transformation include Warner's *Yankee City* (1963), the Lynds' *Middletown* (1929) and *Middletown in Transition* (1937), and Vidich and Bensman's *Small Town in Mass Society* (1968).

The Chicago School. The research of the Chicago School has often been interpreted, somewhat inaccurately, as positing a ubiquitous disorganization of urban primary ties of neighbors and kin. This misreading stems largely from the emphasis placed on Wirth's "Urbanism as a Way of Life" (1938), which was considered to be a summary statement of the empirical research of the Chicago School. To be sure, much of the Chicago research did focus on the social problems of the day, such as family disorganization (Mowrer, 1927), mental illness (Faris and Dunham, 1939), crime and delinquency (Thrasher, 1926), transient marginal populations like *The Hobo* (Anderson, 1923) and *The Unadjusted Girl* (Thomas, 1927), and institutions that catered to these populations, such as *The Taxi Dance Hall* (Cressey, 1932). However, one must remember that these researchers had a specific social problem orientation often coupled with an ameliorative policy perspective. These studies were, in fact, deviant case analyses and are often inaccurately interpreted as representing the full picture of urban life during this period.

A second series of studies on the ethnic groups that migrated to Chicago and settled in segregated "natural areas" also resulted in declining ethnic and neighborhood sentiments. The invasion-competition-succession sequence that resulted as wave after wave of ethnic groups passed through Chicago's neighborhoods was seen to lead to a decline of such sentiments, either positively as a result of the processes of acculturation and assimilation (Thomas and Znaniecki, 1958; Wirth, 1938) or negatively as a result of the previously mentioned social problems.

Wirth's (1938) essay, which drew on the related theoretical essay by Simmel (1950), failed to document persisting bases of social order and local sentiment that were also a part of the Chicago findings. Especially in the work of Burgess and his students (Burgess, 1972), one finds a careful documenting of the "natural areas" of the city that persist as "symbolic communities" to the present day (Hunter, 1974). Also, the "melting pot" hypothesis of acculturation and assimilation that was largely the basis for the expected decline of ethnic neighborhoods has proven to be questionable, as Glazer and Moynihan (1963) have shown in *Beyond the Melting Pot.* The need to maintain local ethnic and neighborhood sentiments was seen to be critical, for example, to the political processes of aggregating demands and establishing power bases (Gosnell, 1939) and to the governmental process of providing a manageable delivery of urban services (Lineberry, 1977).

Thus, although many of the Chicago School's empirical findings did focus on personal and social disorganization that were linked to a demise of local sentiments toward neighbor, kin, and fellow ethnic, the overemphasis on this perspective was partly a function of a social problem orientation and a selective summary and one-sided interpretation of the Chicago School's empirical work.

Transformation of Small Town Life. The second empirical tradition documenting the decline of local community sentiments focused not on the urban neighborhood but rather on the small towns of America as they were increasingly absorbed by the emerging metropolitan and national scale of modern social organization. Greer, in *The Emerging City* (1962a), described a process that explained this transformation: Technological changes in transportation and communication resulted in a shrinking space/time ratio that increased the geographical mobility of goods, people, and ideas. Socially, this resulted in the rise of nonspatial, large-scale organizations of interest, which replaced the parochial, spatially and temporally bounded social world of the local community. In short, modern man, as Webber (1963) suggested, was able to have "community without propinquity." This general thesis of an "increase in scale" may be seen to summarize the three studies we will briefly examine below.

Warner, in his *Yankee City* study (1963), pointed to the loss of local community sentiments as a function of the increasing metropolitan scale of industrial organization, which turned local, family-owned firms into branch plants of regional and national corporations. Power and control over industry shifted to ever larger corporations located in metropolitan centers, while management of local plants shifted to transient, professional managers. The new managers' interests lay with careers in the corporations. This was in contrast to the previous old family owner/managers who maintained a major interest in the well-being of the social and political life of the community and its residents. This produced a distinction that Merton (1968) described as "locals" versus "cosmopolitans" and that a number of writers documented as a major shift in the nature of political power and control in local communities (Schulze, 1969; Dahl, 1961). As a result of this transformation of industry and shift in power, class interests, both of workers and managers, crosscut and undermined the existing common interests found within the community. Community died, according to Warner, in the violent strikes that ultimately erupted; class conflict replaced common community sentiments.

In their Middletown studies, the Lynds (1929, 1937) also documented a similar loss of local community sentiment and solidarity. The earlier Middletown study documented the degree to which a single extended family dominated the economic, political, and social life of their community, which was relatively stable, parochial, and seemingly self-sufficient and which maintained a set of institutions to satisfy its routine needs. This stability and self-sufficiency were shattered by the Depression, prompting the Lynds to return for their second study. As in Warner's *Yankee City,* Middletown was now comprised of fighting factions of workers versus the commercial and industrial elite. The communal harmony and complacency of the earlier period were replaced by class conflict. However, in contrast to Yankee City, this transformation was brought about not by the displacement of locally owned industry by national corporations but rather by the growing recognition of different groups and classes that the fate of Middletown was inextricably linked to national economic and governmental structures. Middletown, in short, had discovered that it was not an isolated, autonomous, self-sufficient community; the Depression had destroyed this illusion. Rather, it was a community that was a small part of a much larger whole over which Middletowners had relatively little influence. Collective interests assumed a class rather than a community base, and the new scale was national, not local.

A similar loss of small-town autonomy in the face of the large-scale institutions of mass society was studied by Vidich and Bensman (1968) in "Springdale," a farming community in upstate New York. In contrast to the harsh reality thrust upon Middletowners by the Depression, these authors documented the way in which Springdalers clung to the persisting myths about small-town life, which masked the prevailing and at times oppressive reality. For example, the myth of local autonomy was maintained in spite of the fact that farmers' complaints about crop prices did not acknowledge that these prices were set hundreds of miles away in the trading pits of the Chicago Board of Trade. Also, their myth of self-sufficiency prevented them from clearly seeing that for many services, such as highways and schools, they were dependent on the resources and expertise of higher levels of government. Although Springdale, like Middletown and Yankee City, had lost functions and lost control over its own destiny, its residents clung to a set of anachronistic beliefs about the friendly virtues of small-town life in contrast to the wicked ways of the big city. At times the reality crept through and the big city was seen to be awesome as well as awful, which resulted in a debilitating and profound ambivalence on the part of the Springdale residents. As the Whites noted in their little volume *The Intellectual Versus the City* (1962), such attitudes have long been a central part of American social thought. It is ironic, as Vidich and Bensman note, that one of the major sources for perpetuating these contrasting images of rural virtue and urban immorality is the mass media, itself emanating from the metropolitan centers of the mass society.

Thus, the studies of small-town life tended to reinforce the picture of a looming specter that was painted by the Chicago School, namely, that throughout America—in big-city neighborhoods and in small rural towns—the social structure and sentiments of local community were dissolving.

Community Found: Urban Residues and Suburban Selectivity

The rediscovery of local community sentiments in mass society occurred in a series of case studies that have become minor classics within contemporary American sociology. It is noteworthy that most of these were either case studies of ethnic communities in older urban areas or of the emerging post-World War II suburbs. These two empirical traditions were critical in causing a rethinking of the hypothesized loss of local community sentiments. These traditions differed not so much in their findings as in their interpretations. The urban ethnic studies tended to find isolated pockets of residual local sentiments, which were considered carryovers from a previous era. The suburban studies tended to emphasize a more conscious search for community that was a selective merger of the small-town life of the past with the modern requirements of metropolitan America.

Urban Residues. Whyte's *Street Corner Society* (1943) was significant precisely because it documented the degree of social organization and social solidarity that existed in what followers of the Chicago School were more apt to refer to as the disorganized "slum." Although Whyte gave relatively little documentation for a full understanding of the institutional structure of Boston's North End, he presented a very clear picture of the strength of primary ties that existed in Doc's gang "the Nortons" and in Chick's club of upwardly mobile college men. The sentiments and loyalties engendered in these groups served to organize the routine day-to-day life of the community's residents. The one institution that Whyte analyzed in some detail for its linkage to these primary ties was the political machine. Doc's ill-fated political campaign for a local office allowed Whyte to study the almost feudal aggregation of personal loyalty that existed in the ethnic neighborhoods and that constituted the power base of local politicians.

A more comprehensive study by Gans (1962b) in another of Boston's Italian communities, the West End, came to essentially the same conclusions as Whyte's. The persistence of local community sentiments was rooted in the existence of a pervasive "peer group culture." The "urban villagers" were able to exist in this seemingly contradictory role because the primary groups (exemplified by the extended family and such male peer groups as childhood gangs and adult social athletic clubs) served to isolate the "villagers" from the larger urban world. Ironically, it was this insularity that rendered the West Enders incapable of dealing with the larger political and economic forces that threatened the destruction of their community through urban renewal.

A more recent study by Suttles (1968) in Chicago's multiethnic Taylor Street neighborhood also emphasized how the sentiments and loyalties of primary relationships formed a basis of social order. Going beyond Whyte and Gans, however, Suttles showed how the primary ties based on the status distinctions of age, sex, and ethnicity, coupled with territorial segregation of specific groups, provided a "segmental social order." This was a social order in which groups that otherwise would have been in frequent conflict instead negotiated a spatial and social ordering that provided a degree of tolerance and acceptance in a generally hostile and untrustworthy environment. By extending primary ties across these age, sex, and ethnic divisions, a network of knowledge about other persons provided a system of personal accountability, acceptance, and social control.

These are but a few of the studies that have attested to the persistence of residual elements of primary ties and local sentiments in urban neighborhoods within mass society. For the most part, these studies analyzed lower class, ethnic communities in older urban neighborhoods.

These studies emphasized the strength of primary and peer relationships—often linked to extended kin and ethnic loyalties—as the basis for local community sentiments. It should be noted that just as the Chicago School had concentrated its efforts on the social problem area and discovered social disorganization, so too may these studies be criticized as having focused on a somewhat unusual collection of communities. Their representativeness was questioned, and indeed the authors themselves seem not to have fully recognized that the areas they studied were more than anachronistic residues from an earlier era. Local community sentiments, in short, were seen to exhibit a selective persistence—they were surprisingly alive in a world that had earlier considered them extinct.

Suburban Selectivity. At the same time that the researchers were busy discovering the urban residues of local community sentiments, other researchers were leaving the central city to follow their fellow urbanites to the emerging communities of single-family homes and green lawns in suburbia. The size, density, and heterogeneity of the city, with its negative personal and social consequences, were being replaced by this new merger of what was hoped would be the best of both urban and rural worlds. A central motivation in this movement was seen by some to be a conscious search for the personal relations and sentiments of local communities. However, as Rossi (1955) and Abu-Lughod and Foley (1970) have noted, the primary motive for the suburban movement was the linkage of family and child-centered interests with the single-family home.

Whyte (1956), in his study of the new suburban community of Park Forest, a suburb of Chicago; Gans (1967), in his study of Levittown, a suburb of Philadelphia; and Seeley, Sims, and Loosly (1956), in their study of Crestwood Heights, a suburb of Toronto, all documented the emergence of informal and formal associations of neighbors, which often centered on the joint interests of children and home. This family and child centeredness led Whyte to describe the suburban setting as a "filiarchy."

These writers saw the suburban community as a consumption unit, a homogeneous, residential, "bedroom" community linked to the larger metropolitan world primarily through the careers of commuting husbands and fathers. In contrast, then, to the effects of bureaucratization, urbanization, and industrialization that Warner and the Lynds had described earlier, the suburban setting was seen as a partial solution to the maintenance of selective sentiments of local community through a spatial segregation of home and work. As later writers such as Farley (1976) and Wirt and others (1972) began to show, suburbia did not constitute a new spatial and political phenomenon; rather, it was a selective migration—an extension of family- and locality-centered interests that had simply spilled beyond the city's rim as metropolitan areas increased in size and scale. These analysts of the suburban scene were careful to note that this social world did not represent a return to the idyllic small-town life of the past. The relationships with neighbors were more transient and less binding than those of friends and kin, and as Keller (1968) noted, echoing our beginning quotation from Adam Smith, the neighbor emerged as a differentiated role. What Gans called the "quasi-primary" relationships of suburbia were still significant, however, in generating local sentiments of community.

In summary, both the older urban villagers and the newer suburbanites represented an important corrective to the earlier empirical studies of the loss of local community sentiments in mass society. In both, the family and the primary relationships existing in the residential neighborhood formed the basis for the persisting residues and selective sentiments of community.

Minimal Versus Emergent Perspectives

In the previous section we saw that in the 1950s American sociologists rediscovered the sentiments of community in urban residues and selective suburban developments. Ensuing research has generally accepted the presence of local sentiments but diverged into two perspectives. The first, or *minimal,* perspective sees local sentiments as persisting residuals that are real but of limited significance in modern social life. By contrast, the second, or *emergent,* perspective sees local sentiments as new social constructions of reality that are not simply holdovers from a previous era. It also sees the significance of local sentiments as varying across space and time.

The Minimal View. The minimal perspective is exemplified in Keller's summary book *The Urban Neighborhood* (1968). The role of neighbor is seen as a limited and sharply circumscribed relationship providing a few residual functions, for example, mutual assistance and emergency aid in times of need. Similarly, the work of Wellman (1976) on "urban networks" suggests that for the most part urbanites engage in social relationships based on interests that transcend the limited scope of the local urban community; instead, contemporary urbanites are seen to operate on a broader metropolitan-wide scale. However, Wellman found that certain functions, such as "helping relationships," are maintained at the scale of the local neighborhood. These include borrowing the proverbial "cup of sugar," watching a neighboring home while the family is on vacation, and providing emergency aid when needed.

A similar minimal argument is presented by Fischer (1976) when he distinguishes between "just neighbors" (people who live nearby) and "real neighbors" (an intimate personal group). The conversion of the former into the latter occurs, according to Fischer, under conditions of functional necessity (such as mutual assistance), prior relationships (as with the ethnic enclaves studied by Whyte, Gans, and Suttles), or lack of alternatives (especially for those with limited mobility, such as carless housewives, children, and the elderly). He concludes that in modern mass society these three factors are of decreasing significance and therefore the neighborhood is reduced from a meaningful social group to a mere happenstance of physical proximity.

The Emergent View. Researchers taking the emergent perspective either see local community sentiments as the product of new and emerging reconstructions or see neighborhoods as occasionally playing a critical role in the organization of modern urban life. It is as if Adam Smith's "small good offices" were small in number but loomed large in their import, or as if Emile Durkheim's persisting neighborly needs were not trivial matters.

One of the earlier versions of this emergent perspective was the "community of limited liability" first proposed by Janowitz (1967) and more fully elaborated in Greer's *The Emerging City* (1962a). The community of limited liability holds that individuals' orientations and attachments to their communities are limited and variable across individuals, communities, and time. Communities, or more specifically local community sentiments, are variables that differ according to a resident's age, sex, social class, family characteristics, and, perhaps most importantly, length of residency. The question becomes not simply whether local sentiments are still significant, but for whom and for what reasons. This limited, variable orientation to community is seen in a sense to be an exchange relationship (Blau, 1967). An individual's investments in the community (emotional, social, and, economic) depend on the degree to which the community provides commensurate rewards. When the local community fails to meet an individual's needs, because of changes in either the individual or the community, the individual will withdraw—if not physically, then socially and emotionally. Conversely, if the local community is seen as an important social unit from which an individual feels he or she derives benefits, then the individual is likely to become involved socially, emotionally, and economically. Community organizers are acutely aware that such involvement may lead to a positive spiral of community development. The effectiveness of the local community in meeting residents' needs will attract new residents and entice fellow residents to become involved, thereby leading to increased resources and increased effectiveness.

Other examples of emergent community sentiments are outlined by Suttles (1972) in his volume *The Social Construction of Communities.* One of the communities that he identifies is the "defended neighborhood," which is basically a local area threatened by external social or ecological change. Such communities tend to become mobilized over issues that threaten the central values of the residents. It is because proximity means a shared or common fate that such mobilization of action and sentiment occurs. The often hostile response to urban renewal programs by local residents (Wilson, 1966) exemplifies the defended community's spontaneous quality, while the Alinsky (1946) "conflict model" of community organizing represents a more conscious manifestation.

A more persistent and stable example of an emergent community is defined by Suttles as the "contrived community." However, this term has a pejorative connotation of being more artificial and more manipulative than what are often assumed to be unplanned, natural, grass roots communities. Therefore, I suggest an alternative, more neutral category of "conscious community" that highlights several critical distinctions. First, conscious communities are positively assertive rather than negatively reactive; second, they are consciously defined and articulated in belief systems that may range from being relatively vague "images" (Lynch, 1960) to highly integrated, utopian world views (Kanter, 1972); and third, conscious communities exhibit a greater temporal/spatial stability.

The primary structural ingredient of the conscious community is the development of a more formal community organization that provides critical internal and external functions for maintaining local solidarity and sentiments. Internally, such groups provide a structure within which primary bonds of neighboring may be developed and within which the common community interests may become expressed and translated into specific organizational goals. Externally, the organization becomes the "legitimate" representative of the community, an identifiable vehicle or corporate body that may more easily interact with outside agencies and institutions (Hunter, 1974). It may even be that such organized local groups are fostered by external agencies and institutions that find it difficult to interact or deal with such a diffuse entity as a community (Taub and others, 1977). An example of the development of a conscious community is seen in the study of an urban neighborhood in Rochester, New York (Hunter, 1975). Responding first as a conflict community to external threats from the local airport and to the "blockbusting" tactics of local realtors, the residents developed a local organization that survived by broadening the scope of its activities and developing a conscious ideological position on the community's central values (specifically, commitment to urban living in a racially integrated community). This ideological community may be seen to lie between communities with a vague self-image and utopian communities with a totally encompassing belief system.

A final category of emergent communities that has been identified is what I will call "vicarious communities." Above all others, these exemplify the degree to which people, individually and collectively, may develop parochial sentiments and attachments independently of what are usually considered to be the functional and social bases of such sentiments. In a study of shopping behavior, Stone (1954) found that residents who lacked objective social ties to their local communities, such as formal and informal relationships with local residents, were more likely than those with such ties to transform typical shopping encounters into more personalized relationships. This vicarious primary tie is exemplified by the elderly person holding up the checkout line at the grocery store by engaging in friendly, personal gossip with the cashier. This may occur much to the consternation of those waiting in line, who may feel that this should be nothing more than an efficient market transaction so that they may return to their families and friends more quickly. In short, what Weber (1958) and Simmel (1950) saw as the epitome of the rational urban relationship, the market encounter, is transformed into a more intimate personal relationship. In another study, Stone (1968) found that subjective identification with a community by being a fan at spectator sports was more likely to occur among those people who had the fewest objective social ties to the community. Janowitz (1967) found that avid readers of the local community press in Chicago were often using it as a substitute for personal, firsthand involvement in the local social world.

Finally, in *Symbolic Communities* (Hunter, 1974), I documented the way in which people quite often maintain symbolic attachments to places in which they formerly lived or to the place in which they presently live but as it existed at a previous time in their lives. It should be noted that these vicarious communities are not simply individual aberrations. They may exist within a collective local culture often referring back to a significant historical event or period in the life of the community. This historical symbolism was precisely what Firey (1945) found to be a critical factor in preserving Beacon Hill and the Commons as distinct areas of collective sentiment in downtown Boston. In short, the vicarious community epitomizes the fact that local sentiments are emergent and socially constructed realities—at times existing without any clear referent to current objective reality.

In summary, the minimal and the emergent perspectives begin from the same point—local neighborhoods continue to exist, almost by definition, as social units based on physical proximity. These views differ most profoundly, however, in the significance attributed to local sentiments in the conduct of social life in modern mass society.

A Dynamic Model of Emergent Community Sentiments

The preceding discussion of different approaches and interpretations to parochial sentiments in modern mass society may be used to organize a set of sequential stages in their development. It should be noted that I am referring to the process of community development in a broader sense than that currently in vogue. The current attempts at conscious institution building in urban neighborhoods represent but one possible stage in the general sequence that I am proposing. Furthermore, this model may be likened to Smelser's (1963) "value added" model of collective behavior, in that a community will not necessarily pass from one stage to the next unless critical structural preconditions exist.

The first stage is that of *residual neighborhoods*— Fischer's (1976) "just neighbors" and Wellman's (1976) "networks of necessity"—in short, minimal local collective sentiments based primarily on physical proximity. All successive stages presume the residual neighborhood of proximity. The second stage, which I term *emergent communities,* involves a more conscious and variable conception of parochial sentiments. Communities in this stage are often conflict communities that are responding to a real or perceived external threat to the existing state of the neighborhood that mobilizes an attempt to conserve or preserve threatened values. Such external threats may come from a population transition, such as blacks moving into previously all-white neighborhoods, but increasingly such opposition arises in response to governmentally planned actions, such as school busing or the building of expressways. This stage represents an inherently conservative force geared to preservation. The homogeneity of interest that arises in conflict communities is specific to the external threat, which may be seen as the galvanizing vehicle or catalyst for transforming residual communities into reactive communities. The discussion by Suttles of defended neighborhoods constitutes an excellent example.

The third stage is what I refer to as *conscious communities*. The critical distinction between these and emergent communities is the development of a rather clearly articulated set of central values that are positively advanced as defining characteristics of the community and their embodiment in a more formally structured community organization. Represented here are the wide range of activities usually included within the concept of community development. Such positive assertions may involve outside support such as federal funds for model cities or community action programs; but as a general principle, the transition from the second to the third stage requires at least a partial solution to external threats such that the community is not simply defending itself but instead has taken the offensive in promoting central values within the community. The transition also requires the ability to mobilize resources, internally and externally, to generate an enduring structure that becomes a legitimate representation of the community's interests in relationships with larger external institutions of mass society. The general range we are proposing here runs the continuum from partial "ideological communities" (Hunter, 1975) to the more extreme and encompassing "utopian communities" (Kanter, 1972).

The final and fourth stage I refer to as *vicarious* or *symbolic communities*. This stage epitomizes the notion of the consciously constructed community, for it may in fact be found even among those who do not overtly and behaviorally participate in the local organized social life of an area but nonetheless symbolically transform their local world into a meaningful unit of personal identification. Examples of this type of community are to be found in the research of Stone (1954) and Janowitz (1967), who found that individuals objectively unintegrated into the social life of a community maintained a vicarious identification through other symbolic activities. Another example is the many elderly residents symbolically identifying with an area because their past was spent within the locale and its institutions. This is perhaps most poignantly noted in Fried's (1969) study of "Grieving for a Lost Home." Such symbolic identification may extend beyond the individual's memory into the "cultural memory" of an area. Vicarious and symbolic identification with an area may stem from historical events and meanings. The sentiments and symbolism of Beacon Hill in Boston as studied by Firey (1945) exemplify this form of vicarious community. This stage of community sentiment requires at a minimum that some supporting institutions from the third stage either currently operate or at one time have operated in the area to provide an objective basis for this symbolic transformation.

In summary, the above stages of residual community, conflict community, conscious community, and vicarious community exemplify a progression in local sentiments that depend primarily on the external structural preconditions existing within the mass society and the relationship of the local community to that mass society, rather than simply the inherent characteristics and composition of the local community itself. Such propositions require that we rethink the nature of mass society and its linkage to local community sentiments.

Rethinking Mass Society and Local Sentiments

Mass society is usually viewed negatively. Kornhauser (1959) has summarized these negative conceptions under two general categories: the aristocratic critique and the democratic critique. The former sees the debasement of central values and institutions to the lowest common denominator; the latter sees a centralization of power and prestige that renders the isolated individual powerless and alienated. Kornhauser sees each of these as partial truths, with the true mass society represented by both high accessibility of elites to the masses (aristocratic critique) and high manipulation of masses by the elite (democratic critique).

Most negative conceptions of mass society have been revised or qualified in the light of subsequent research. For example, the "two-step flow of communication" documented by Katz and Lazarsfeld (1955) in their study of the mass media emphasized the degree to which the media did not impinge directly on isolated individuals but rather was filtered both through "opinion leaders" and the natural social groups to which individuals belonged. In a similar vein, one may view much of the research that has "rediscovered" the existence of local community solidarities within urban society as representing a revision of mass society theories as they apply to urban life. In an important article, "Community Attachments in Mass Society," Kasarda and Janowitz (1974) have shown the degree to which what they call the "linear perspective" (derived from

Wirth)—that size, density, and heterogeneity will lead to a disappearance of local attachments in mass society—is not supported. Instead, they found that local attachments are likely to persist as a function of such variables as family status, personal ties, and length of residence in the local community. This "systemic perspective," they argue, requires a reconception of mass society and local attachments that does not necessarily see the two as antithetical, but as coexisting in a more complex structure of institutions and interests than the previous simplified theories hypothesized. However, little has been done in developing a more systemic revision of mass society and local sentiments that incorporates these new findings. In this section, we will attempt this task, and in the next section we will present some exemplary data.

     We will begin by rethinking mass society from the perspective of Shils (1975), one of the few theorists to give a positive interpretation to the social changes covered by the general rubric "mass society." Taking a comparative approach in contrasting modern society with traditional society and using the metaphor of "center and periphery," Shils maintained that "the novelty of 'mass society' lies in the relationship of the mass of the population to the center of the society. The relationship is a closer integration into the central institutional and value systems of the society" (p. 93). Echoing Marx, Durkheim, and Weber, he added that mass society "is vertically integrated in a hierarchy of power and authority and a status order" (p. 93). A society-wide, shared set of values that defines a status order are exemplified empirically in contemporary American society by the two status variables of occupation, or more generally class, and race. A generally shared value system of status ranking implies that within mass society a relatively common set of evaluations will be applied to the social positions and communal contexts within which individuals are located. Shared values, however, do not imply similarity in the outcome of evaluations, especially when comparisons are made between commonly shared standards and the more varied objective realities of given situations. Objective inequalities exist, and evaluations of situations will vary directly as the inequality varies. As Shils said, "Inequalities exist in mass society and they call forth at least as much resentment, if not more, than they ever did. Indeed, there is perhaps more awareness of the diversity of situation and the conflict of sectional aspirations in this society than in most societies of the past" (p. 96).

The "diversity of situation" when applied to the arena of local communities in modern urban societies has been one of the major research concerns of human ecology since its inception. The study of the spatial segregation of populations into different neighborhoods and local communities stems from the early Chicago School through research by the Duncans (1955) and Schnore (1965a) and more recent work by Guest (1971), Hunter (1974), and Berry and Rees (1969). As recent research in "social area analysis" (Shevky and Bell, 1955), or "factorial ecology," has shown, socioeconomic status, racial-ethnic status, and family or life cycle status have repeatedly emerged as the three most important dimensions of social differentiation and spatial segregation within modern industrial cities. It appears that these dimensions selectively distribute the population among homogeneous local communities. Viewing this as a "locational decision process" in which individuals attempt to maximize a complex set of values, Berry and Rees (1969, pp. 460-461) said:

> The inhabitants of the city are faced with a fundamental decision: where to live. The principal determinants of such a housing choice are three in number—the price of the dwelling unit (either in rental or in purchase value terms); its type; and its location both within a neighborhood environment and relative to place of work. These determinants have parallels in the attributes of the individual making the housing choice: the amount he is prepared to pay for housing, which depends on his income; his housing needs, which depend on his marital status and family size, that is, his stage-in-life cycle; his life-style preferences, which will affect the type of neighbor he will want; and, finally, the location of his job. When the values of the two sets of characteristics match, a decision to purchase housing will be made.

In short, as Form (1954) and more recently Harvey (1973) have suggested, the various economic, governmental, and status-ranking institutions of mass society operate to determine the spatial distribution of scarce values in local residential communities. The result is a differentiated territorial matrix into which individuals will locate, by choice and by constraint, and which they will differentially evaluate. Mass society, then, has produced a constellation of local communities that exhibits *relative* homogeneity internally. However, externally among communities there is relative heterogeneity and diversity. The result, in Durkheim's terms, is to produce a micro local scale of mechanical solidarity based on similarity and a macro metropolitan-wide scale of organic solidarity based on diversity and interdependence. Given the presence of the mass media and the mobility of the population that are characteristic of mass society, it is likely that individuals, as Shils (1975) suggested, will be very aware of these differential evaluations of local areas and be able to make such judgments independently of actual residence.

As we have seen, many theorists and contemporary investigators of local community sentiments see them minimally as persisting residues of limited significance in modern mass society. However, contrasted with this view is what I refer to as the emergent perspective, which sees such local sentiments not only as a persistent and variable *condition* of mass society, but also in important ways as a unique *product* of mass society.

One may see local sentiments as a condition of mass society from the revisionist research and theories, which suggest that all social action requires some motivational element, some cathexis or sentiment that is rooted in personal relationships. For example, the importance of primary groups in the urban social structure has its parallel in the study of formal organizations (what to Weber constituted the epitome of rationality in mass society). From the research of Mayo (1945), Blau (1955), and Dalton (1959), one sees that formal organizations work not in spite of such primary relationships and sentiments but because of them. Similarly, as Stouffer and others (1949), Janowitz and Shils (1948), and more recently Moskos (1969) have shown, nationalism and patriotism, although significant realities of mass society, are insufficient to explain the behavior and motivations of soldiers in combat. Instead, one must look to the informal relationships and sentiments that inhere within primary groups as they operate within the larger structure.

In countering the view of the alienated individual in mass society, Shils (1975) said that personal attachment and sentiment were not simply residues or conditions of mass society, and more significantly that in mass society "there has been a transcendence of the primordially and authoritatively given, a movement outward toward . . . the experience of other minds and personalities. It gives rise to and lives in personal attachment" (p. 101). From this perspective, mass society has unfettered the growth of volitional personal attachments. Therefore, once located within the ecological matrix of mass society (that is, the *relatively* homogeneous local communities that are differentiated from one another by the central values of mass society), personal primary relationships will then emerge as a *product* of mass society. These in turn will foster personal sentiments that will be generalized to the setting in which they occur, the collective unit of the local community. It is not simply that local sentiment based on shared space is a residue, but rather, that mass society has permitted propinquity itself to become an important basis for defining relationships. Within mass society the relatively autonomous, functionally and institutionally integrated local community may be lost, but the local sentiments of neighborhood persist and flourish. It is as if in Homans' (1950) model of the human group mass society provides the external *evaluative* system within which the internal *affective* system will emerge.

Thus, I am suggesting not only that local sentiments persist within mass society but that there are unique structural characteristics of mass society that when translated onto the urban landscape permit local community sentiments to develop. They emerge not simply as partial and archaic residues, but in new forms and with new functions that mass society has permitted and perhaps requires. These new forms are only hinted at above, but to be significant such sentiments must be translated into collective social action. The middle class, suburban movement of the 1950s, the inner-city riots of the 1960s, and the ethnic, working class neighborhood movement of the 1970s, along with various ideological and utopian communities that emerged throughout this period, attest to the uneven, faltering, but inexorable attempts to translate local community sentiments into collective political action. The emergence of metropolitan and national federations of local community groups throughout urban America (such as National Neighbors, National Alliance of Neighborhoods, and National People's Action) suggests a new social and political structure based on local community sentiments.

Furthermore, it should be noted that such federations imply that a zero-sum conception of community sentiments often assumed implicitly is questionable. Echoing Durkheim, Martindale (1958), for example, suggested that in modern mass society the community of the nation-state grows at the expense of the local community. I would suggest rather an additive or multiplicative system in which collective sentiments and attachments, up and down the vertical scale of integration (Warren, 1971; Walton, 1971), serve to reinforce one another. In Shils's (1975) words, mass society is characterized by a closer integration of the periphery with the center, and it appears that local community sentiments may operate as a new critical link in that integration.

Finally, I would caution against a simplification that would see local community sentiments persisting only as the territorial manifestation of class interests. To be sure, these are often of primary importance, but to ignore the other critical dimensions of race, ethnicity, religion, life-style, and life cycle would underrepresent the varied forms that community-based interests may take. It is at the level of the local community that mass society uniquely converges in its myriad forms and from which rises, in the shared fate of propinquity, the multiple and varying forms of community interests and local sentiments.

Empirical Example of Local Sentiments in Mass Society

The following data are presented not as a test but as an example of the intersection of the concepts of mass society and local sentiments that were developed in the previous section. Parsons and Shils (1951) in their theory of social action distinguished between the sentiments of evaluation and attachment as two of the "pattern variables" by which people orient themselves to their situations. That is, in defining a situation in which goal-directed action is to occur, people must first develop a cognitive image or be able to know or define the situation and its elements. Second, they must make evaluations of the situation and its elements using a general set of values. Third, people's emotions, sentiments, or attachments must be linked to the situation because they provide the "motive force" or motivation from which social action emerges. Finally, the normative constraints of social structure provide a set of more specific expectations that guide social action within the specific situation defined.

If we consider local communities as situations that are subject to these variable orientations by residents, then the two sentiments of evaluation and attachment should be distinguished from one another, especially in the light of our previous discussion of mass society. Evaluations of local areas should reflect the application of the central values of mass society to the variable but objective situations—the local communities—in which people reside. That is, how people objectively evaluate their local communities will depend on how well their communities measure up against a general, society-wide set of values. Our previous discussion suggests that social class and race exemplify two central values of mass society that are significant in creating the variable physical matrix of the modern metropolis. If this is so, then we would expect the sentiment of local evaluations to be highly variable depending on the objective social class and racial composition of residents in their local community. However, in contrast to evaluation, the local sentiment of attachment is more specific to the particular situations of people. Therefore, we should expect local attachments to vary not by such general social values as class and race, but rather by the degree of personal social integration in the local community. That is, in Homans' (1950) terms, the development of the internal affective system should depend on the degree of personal integration and primary interaction that develops in the more objectively defined external system of mass society. In short, we should expect local evaluation to vary by the more general values of mass society, and local attachments to vary by the more local social statuses such as friendship patterns and social integration into the local community.

The data are taken from a survey of over 800 residents of Chicago drawn from local communities throughout the city. The data and research methods are presented in detail elsewhere (Hunter, 1974), but of interest here are two open-ended items that were coded in terms of the two sentiments of local evaluation and local attachment. The former was coded in terms of whether residents expressed positive, negative, or ambivalent evaluations of their local communities. The latter was coded in terms of whether people expressed attachment to their local community of residence versus some other area or expressed no feelings of local attachment whatsoever. The principal independent variables focused on people's class and race and their degree of social participation in primary relationships within the local area, as well as their length of residence.

As we see in Tables 1 and 2, evaluation of the local community varies by both occupation and race. The higher socioeconomic status of the occupation, the more positive the evaluation of the local community; in addition, whites are more likely to evaluate their local community positively than blacks. However, in contrast to evaluation of their local areas, we see

Table 1. Percentage of Respondents Indicating Positive Evaluation of
Local Community and Percentage Indicating Attachment to Local
Community, by Occupational Category.

| | Occupational Category | | | |
Local Sentiment	Professional-Managerial	Other White Collar	Blue Collar	Service Worker
Evaluation "Positive"	47.2	44.0	42.1	30.4
	(36)	(282)	(297)	(56)
Attachment "Here"	33.6	44.9	40.1	35.7
	(36)	(283)	(297)	(56)

Table 2. Percentage of Respondents Indicating Positive Evaluation of
Local Community and Percentage Indicating Attachment to Local
Community, by Race.

| | Race | |
Local Sentiment	White	Black
Evaluation "Positive"	47.5	28.8
	(570)	(198)
Attachment "Here"	43.6	35.7
	(571)	(199)

that attachment to the area shows relatively little variation by
class or race. In Tables 3 and 4 a different picture emerges.
Using the length of residence and the location of friends as measures of local social integration, we see that evaluation of the
local area varies little. However, attachment to the local area
varies remarkably: Longer-term residents and those having most
friends in the area are much more likely to express attachment
to the local community than are newcomers or those who have
most friends living outside the area.

Table 3. Percentage of Respondents Indicating Positive Evaluation of
Local Community and Percentage Indicating Attachment to Local
Community, by Length of Residence.

| | Years of Residence | | | | |
Local Sentiment	Less Than 1	1 to 4	5 to 9	10 to 19	More Than 20
Evaluation "Positive"	40.0	40.0	38.5	46.1	45.6
	(40)	(130)	(135)	(191)	(237)
Attachment "Here"	12.5	25.4	34.8	40.3	62.0
	(40)	(130)	(135)	(191)	(237)

Table 4. Percentage of Respondents Indicating Positive Evaluation of
Local Community and Percentage Indicating Attachment to Local
Community, by Location of Friends.

| | Location of Friends | |
Local Sentiment	Inside Area	Outside Area
Evaluation "Positive"	42.9	41.7
	(177)	(396)
Attachment "Here"	52.5	34.1
	(177)	(396)

In summary, these data exemplify the degree to which
the central values of mass society, reflected ecologically in the
general statuses of class and race, provide the external objective
differentiation that results in variable evaluations of local communities by their residents. However, once located within the
local communities of this differentiated territorial matrix, the
positive sentiments of local attachments emerge as a function of
primary relationships that get established within the relatively
homogeneous and proximate local communities.

Conclusion

The specter with which we began this chapter has not disappeared magically within the words of these pages. No chants
or spells will dispel its looming presence. However, it is hoped
that this brief review and recasting of thought about local sentiments in mass society has provided an outline of the various
shapes and forms the specter may assume. It is hoped as well
that the exaggerated claims of those who see local communities
collapsing before the efficient juggernaut of rational large-scale
mass society and of those more positively oriented "neighborhood utopians" are equally tempered. I have no desire to discourage thinking of either vein—neither that which sees individual freedoms emerging out of the demise of such "false
conscious" anachronistic attachments nor that which harkens to
a reconstituted social order within which individuals in their
local communities reassert control over the institutions that
affect their daily lives (Altshuler, 1970). However, I would suggest that policy and planning objectives with a more immediate
and limited time scale should recognize the upper and lower
limits that local communities may play within modern mass
society. Therefore in these concluding comments I will attempt

to relate our previous discussion to some of the broader policy issues.

Lower Limits of Community. Those who see local communities collapsing assume what I previously referred to as the minimal perspective, and they err by underestimating the degree to which local communities and the sentiments that inhere within them remain as viable bases of collective social action. This limited vision has several interrelated components.

The first of these is an overemphasis on production as opposed to consumption, and as Choldin (1977) has noted, local communities are primarily units of collective consumption. Therefore, in theoretical and empirical studies that emphasize a production orientation—for example, classical human ecology and more recent work in urban political economy—local communities are often slighted as significant units of social organization. At most they are simply seen to be the repositories of differentially distributed economic and class values (Molotch, 1976; Castells, 1977). This, as we have seen, is in fact one of the significant points of intersection between mass society and local communities. However, the consumption and credit markets are significant bases of mobilization of economic and class interests independent of production class relationships. Furthermore, these consumption interests are uniquely centered in local communities in contrast to production interests. For example, the urban riots of the 1960s were defined by some analysts as communal and commodity riots (Kerner and others, 1968). Furthermore, in the 1970s the issue of "redlining" (the denial of mortgage money for housing in older urban neighborhoods) has exemplified the degree to which important political action may arise out of the local neighborhood as an economic unit of commodity and capital consumption. In short, the local neighborhood continues to play a significant economic role in the intersection of mass society and local interests.

Local community sentiments, however, extend beyond the limited sphere of economic and class interests. Life-style and race, though highly correlated with class, continue to operate as powerful and independent bases of collective social action. For example, the life-style dimension exemplifies the degree to which institutions and agencies geared to the family and to child rearing—such as schools, churches, day care centers, and parks and leisure activities—continue to operate at the local level. It is impossible to ignore these local interests, to expect them to disappear, or to translate them solely into class terms.

In short, from a policy perspective it becomes imperative to ascertain which among the numerous institutions of modern mass society now operate or will effectively operate in the future at the scale of the local community. Where they now persist or at best emerge sporadically, policies and programs must be developed that recognize the diversity of these interests, their need for a more structured and organized form, and a response to residents' desires for participating in the decision making and control over their functioning.

Upper Limits of Community. Just as the minimalists err by underestimating the significance of local communities, so the neighborhood utopians err by seeing a "community revival" or "neighborhood movement" as answering most if not all of society's contemporary problems. As has been noted elsewhere (Hunter and Suttles, 1972), their exaggerated expectations are rooted in a misconception of local communities as isolated, relatively self-sufficient, and self-directed units of social organization. Mass society is seen as having usurped functions and activities that local units can and should control. In short, there is in their rhetoric relatively little recognition given to the *limits* of local communities—not simply spatially, but functionally. Certain social problems, such as national defense, perhaps cannot be solved at the local level but are in fact societal problems within the contemporary "world system" (Wallerstein, 1974a). It is ironic, as Barbera (1977) has noted in a parallel argument with respect to the family, that the responsibility for solutions to some social problems is often placed directly on the units of social organization, such as families or communities, that are also seen to be collapsing, or losing functions, as a result of broader and more general social changes. A more limited perspective would suggest that only certain functions and certain problems can be solved by the local community. Again, a central policy question becomes one of ascertaining which problems and which functions.

The idea of an upper limit to local communities points to the direction that future policies and programs should take, namely, providing the links between the sentiments and interests of local communities and the overarching economic and status distributive systems of mass society. This is basically a political problem of providing avenues of collective representation that allow local community interests to affect the larger-scale distributive systems. Linking local community interests with the larger-scale organizations of production directly addresses the older question of home/work separation. This is not simply a spatial separation that is answered by transportation engineers planning routes with shorter commuting times; rather, it is a political and social problem that addresses the divergent interests between geopolitical centers of production and local centers of consumption. The organization of economic interests of production long ago extended beyond the parochial limits of local communities. For example, taxes, corporate interests, capital, and people themselves gravitate to the centers of society, as Shils (1975) would suggest; but it is important that links be maintained so that local community interests may flow in the same direction and so that the central values may as easily flow back to the local communities.

Mass society will not disappear and, as I have suggested throughout this chapter, neither will the local sentiments of community. There must be a concerted effort from both the top and the bottom to establish a working relationship that is realistically within the upper and the lower limits of community. In this way Adam Smith's "small good offices" may continue to be performed within Emile Durkheim's "material neighborhood," and these may in turn continue to humanize modern mass society.

6

Family and Sex Roles in Urban Society

Shirley Harkess

The relationship of family and sex roles to urbanization seems obvious: If documentation is called for, research is easily available. However, this impression is superficial. The traditional fields of urban sociology and the sociology of the family have yet to be systematically articulated with one another (see Fischer, 1976), and their intersection with the emerging sociology of sex roles is unclear. Fortunately, reviews of each of these areas have appeared recently (Fischer, 1972, 1975a, 1975b, 1976; Farber, 1975, 1976; Lipman-Blumen and Tickmayer, 1975), which assess the present state of each field and suggest lines of future inquiry and conceptualization. We will discuss these reviews and then indicate the direction of this chapter.

Note: For their help in the preparation of this chapter, I would like to thank Jonathan Reader, Terry Rosenberg, and Ann Stromberg. Responsibility for any errors remains my own.

One impetus for the sociological study of the family has been the problematic relationship between urbanization and industrialization on the one hand and the family on the other. Reduction in the number of societal purposes that the family serves is one possibly negative effect frequently attributed to industrialization and urbanization. Despite Goode's (1963) conceptualization of the conjugal family and Sussman and Burchinal's (1962) introduction of the "modified extended family," which allow for ties to family members outside of the household, the focus has been on the change from the extended to the nuclear family, especially in the context of migration to the city.

The dichotomization of the family into extended and nuclear forms is subsumed in Farber's (1975, 1976) conceptualization of kinship institutions in bilateral societies as centripetal and centrifugal. Not only the form of household composition but also other aspects of residence, such as location, migration, and kin networks (as well as the "structural arrangements" of marriage, fertility, property rights, interaction between generations, ties to blood and affinal relatives, and the family's relationship to the community), are classified by Farber as internally consistent in "pulling inward and ... engaging the obligation and/or loyalty of members" or minimizing "property-based familial ties and expelling members outward" (Farber, 1976, p. 282). The centripetal kinship organization arises from factionalism in a society as families organize to promote their own special interests in a system of social stratification. Centrifugal kinship organization results from communalism in a society as "members of families and kin groups" are "dispersed throughout the society," scattering the "loyalties and obligations of any individual" to further the "common interests which weld a population into a coherent society" (Farber, 1976, p. 282). Farber (1975) based this conceptualization on the assumption that family and kinship institutions have dual but competing functions of differentiation and cohesion of various segments of society.

His analysis is relevant to this chapter for several reasons. First, we can conclude from it that the functions of differentiation and cohesion are mutually interactive; and we can connect levels of analysis, in that family cohesion creates differentiation in society while differentiation within the family creates societal cohesion. Second, we will use the perspective of family differentiation that Farber suggests, studying the family's internal workings, gender and generational relations, and deviant but family-related behavior. Finally, since centripetal and centrifugal kinship institutions are seen as ideal types toward which a society may gravitate, it is useful to consider how groups positioned differently in the social structure depart from these types.

Thus we will first take the contemporary United States to illustrate societal cohesion and familial differentiation. Second, we will see how the concept of differentiation is especially applicable not only to sex roles in U.S. cities but also to our decision to emphasize the different forms of the conjugal family and subnuclear variants rather than to rely on the extended versus nuclear dichotomy (see Greer, 1973, and Laslett, 1973, for further justification of this decision). Third, we will mention social class and ethnic variation where possible.

Due to their call for the "systematic exploration of sex as a stratification variable" in their review of sex role research, Lipman-Blumen and Tickmayer (1975, p. 324), like Farber in his consideration of the family, were drawn to an analysis of differentiation. Differentiation is the foundation of stratification in the sense that emergent units are rank-ordered according to societal values. Sex role differentiation is but one form of the division of tasks and the individuals who perform them. If we define *role* as the expectations and behavior associated with a position in the social structure, then our interest is in who occupies which roles. The distribution of differentiated roles and consequently the rewards of stratification may result from the achievement of motivated individuals or it may come from ascription to social categories, such as sex. Lipman-Blumen and Tickmayer (1975, p. 313) described sex differentiation as a "system whereby roles and tasks are distributed on the basis of the ascribed characteristics of sex." Only to the extent that certain tasks are generally assigned to one sex can we speak of a sex role. Our labelling of the concept as sex role differentiation instead of sex differentiation preserves the separation of role and occupant and thereby suggests that the integration of the two may be problematic, as it currently is. In the eyes of Parsons (1942), however, the integration of a role and its occupant of a particular sex was not always a problem.

Extrapolating from Durkheim (1933), Parsons (1942) early maintained that equilibrium in the conjugal family depended on sex stratification within it as well as within the labor market. While he recognized the strain inherent in the distinction, Parsons pointed out that men achieved status in society from their occupation, whereas women derived status from their husband's occupational achievement. For women in the family, therefore, ascription implied derived or vicarious achievement (see Lipman-Blumen, 1973). Outside the family, women's achievement—or ascription—has generally been ignored by students of society. With women entering the labor force comes the possibility of their achievement and the question of how to combine a woman's personally acquired status with her derived one, a consequence noted by Eichler (1973) and Safi-lios-Rothschild (1975). In fact, in one study of 566 employed wives, it was found that a woman's occupational status has an impact on her class identification that is nearly equal to the im-pact of her husband's occupational status (Ritter and Hargens, 1975). The differentiation and stratification of occupant and role may, therefore, be changing for women and men.

In the context of our analysis, we suggest that industriali-zation and urbanization in the United States contributed to dif-ferentiation among tasks and occupants. Occupant differentia-tion—the distribution of tasks—was increasingly based on the achievement of individual men. For women, however, occupant differentiation meant the continuation of sex-based ascription, since the family constituted a barrier to the physically separate place of employment (Oppenheimer, 1973). With the postindus-trial development of a white collar and service economy, a breakdown in sex role differentiation in the labor market began to take place. The question for us now is whether family and occupational roles will consequently merge, being redefined for both male and female occupants. In this chapter women's par-ticipation in the labor force and their occupational placement are taken as indicators of changing sex roles.

The articulation of the sociology of the family and of sex roles with urban sociology was introduced by Lofland (1975) in her criticism of the latter field for its sexist bias. Finding that in urban ethnographies women have been portrayed as "just there," she faulted urban sociologists for their reliance on the community model. Conceptualizing the community as "the relationships, social organization, culture, and commitments that can be *bounded* within a *spatially contiguous area*" (Lofland, 1975, p. 147, italics in original), urban sociologists, in Lofland's view, have concentrated their research efforts in ethnic and working-class areas in the city—precisely those areas of greatest sex role differentiation—and have ignored areas where women might be more active. As an antidote, Lofland proposed attending to space-specific, translocal as well as local relationships in addition to space-transcendent ones. She suggested studying women's settings, such as beauty parlors, parks, and coffee shops, instead of men's bars, and studying the urban environment of upper-middle class women, which may be more extensive and more complex than that of their male counterparts because of their attending meetings, chauffeuring, shopping, and volunteering. While our own approach is more demographic-ecological than microsociological, we will examine examples of space-transcendent and space-specific local and translocal relationships. When the emphasis is more macro than micro, investigations oriented toward the conjugal family and sex roles are found scattered throughout the recent urban literature.

Although Fischer (1975a) employed the community model with the consequence for women that Lofland predicted (women were mostly uninfluential, even in his analysis of the family; Fischer, 1976), he separated the ecological from the social aspects of the community concept in order to explore their interrelationship: "The proper central issue of urban sociology is that which initially concerned the entire discipline: the nature of the moral order (community) and of the individual within that order (personality). By assessing the consequences of variations in settlement patterns (community), urban sociology advances our general understanding of the structural determinants of community and personality" (Fischer, 1975a, p. 68). Elsewhere Fischer (1972, 1975b, 1976) elaborated a "subcultural theory of urbanism" to account for the consequences of population concentration in an area.

In Fischer's (1975b, 1976) formulation, the size and density of a community independently create rather than destroy diverse subcultures. New subcultures result from migration and structural differentiation, and existing ones flourish as a critical mass of members is reached and contacts with other subcultures take place, which promote diffusion of peripheral values as well (Fischer, 1972). The creation of diverse subcultures, therefore, is the process by which behaviors and beliefs in urban areas diverge from the norms of the society, although the direction of such urban unconventionality is not in one direction only (Fischer, 1975b). Subcultural theory synthesizes the two competing schools of thought in urban sociology: determinist or Wirthian theory, which posits that ecological factors ultimately result in social disorganization and anomie, and compositional or nonecological theory (Gans, 1962a, 1967), which asserts that the few existent and not necessarily negative urban-rural differences can be attributed to differences in age, ethnicity, life cycle, or social class rather than to ecological factors (Fischer, 1975b, 1976). As Fischer (1975b, p. 1337) says: "The real implication (of the subcultural model) is theoretical: a full understanding of life in cities requires incorporation of ecological factors, subcultural development, and diffusion in a dynamic model."

In addition to intercommunity variation, variation within an urban area is of concern to us. While the determinist, non-ecological, and subcultural arguments may be reproduced at the level of the neighborhood, there is, as Fischer (1975a) noted, no theory of intracommunity variation to connect the ecological with the social in order to determine what conditions make a neighborhood, spatially defined, a significant social unit. The answer to the question—and it is a question, not an assumption —seems to depend on the importance of the area to its residents (Fischer, 1975a), not just to outside observers.

Having set the stage for this chapter, we will briefly describe the present form of the conjugal family and the nature of sex roles. The analysis of role interchangeability in the conjugal family, variation in subnuclear living arrangements as an incidence of centrifugal kinship, and women's participation in the labor force as an illustration of the degree of sex role differentiation, forms the context in which the relationship to intercommunity differences in size and distance should be explored. Within the limits of the data it is our contention that these features of family and sex roles, heretofore regarded as unconventional, vary within and among urban areas and may become characteristic of them.

Contemporary Status of the Conjugal Family and Sex Roles: Space-Transcendent Change

With regard to the conjugal family, what is now a role triad may become a dyad or an individual unit, especially for those women born after 1934 (Uhlenberg, 1974). The conjugal family triad results from marriage and the birth of children. Alternatives to it represent permutations of these two processes. There may be marriage without children (in the case of the voluntarily childless couple) and children without marriage (in the case of the single parent) as two role dyads, and neither marriage nor children in the case of the individual unit. Logically between the childless couple and the individual, although closer in reality to the former than the latter, is the couple that is living together and presumably childless (see Bernard, 1975). These various relationships are apparent everywhere (less than half—42 percent—of all households conform to the husband-wife-child triad; Intercom, 1976), but they have not yet been institutionalized as alternatives to the conjugal family.

Among the dyadic arrangements, the incidence of the single parent is undeniably great, but there are only slight indications of the institutionalization of the single parent. At present, the dyad of single parent (usually the mother) and child is seen to result from divorce. Thirteen percent of all families (and one third of all black families) are headed by a woman, the proportion having grown by 73 percent since 1960 (U.S. Bureau of the Census, 1976). While divorce or separation accounted for half of these families headed by women in 1973, over a third resulted from the death of a spouse and 13 percent were unmarried mothers (U.S. Bureau of the Census, 1974). Typically women head a family only temporarily, usually not more than five or six years (Sawhill, 1976). Among the divorced or widowed, however, it appears from census data that in recent years there has been a slight reduction in the number of persons who remarry (Glick, 1975). This slight evidence for the institutionalization of this alternative to the conjugal family is exceeded somewhat by evidence for the institutionalization of the voluntarily childless couple.

The incidence of marriage without children is low, however. It is estimated to be 4 percent of Canadian couples (Veevers, 1972). Among the voluntarily childless, who from two small samples appear to be relatively young (about thirty years old), urban, at least middle class, and married five to seven years (Veevers, 1973, in London and Toronto; Gustavus and Henley, 1971, in the United States), the decision not to have children evolved over time (Veevers, 1973). It was a matter of recognizing something that had already happened rather than consciously bringing about their childlessness. In the process, wives relied on their husbands' support, and both relied on the at least symbolic option of adoption in the face of perceived societal criticism. At the time of Veevers's study, the ideology of the women's movement exerted little influence on these wives' decision making, causing Veevers (1973) to point out the appar-

ent pronatalism of the movement because of its support of policies favoring maternity leaves and day care, which would make
motherhood easier. The ambivalence of the women's movement
and of the couples themselves reflects the larger society, where
in 1973 only 1 percent of Gallup respondents considered the
childless family ideal (Hoffman, 1974).

Yet, as Blake (1974) warned us, public opinion is inconsistent. Pohlman (1974), for example, found a shift in attitude
toward acceptance of voluntary childlessness as an alternative
life-style emerging in the late 1960s, and demographer Bumpass
(1975) predicted that childless families will become more common in the next decade. Rather than viewing childlessness as a
liability, a perhaps unintended consequence of romanticism between husband and wife or of women's educational and occupational achievement as does Blake (1974), this alternative will
increasingly be consciously chosen—as it was for one third of
Veevers's (1973) respondents. Too, it is childless couples who
most often express happiness with their marriage (Institute for
Social Research, 1974).

Involving neither marriage nor children, the couple that
lives together may resemble the voluntarily childless marriage.
Both the incidence and the degree of institutionalization of this
alternative to the conjugal family triad are growing. During the
1960s there was an eightfold increase in the number of household heads who reported living not with relatives but with an
unrelated adult of the opposite sex. By 1970 a quarter of these
143,000 unmarried couples were composed of female household heads with a man living in. The greatest numerical increase
in couples living together has been among the elderly, while the
most rapid increase has been among the young (Glick, 1975);
for those under thirty-five, the number choosing to live with
one or more unrelated individuals of either sex doubled from
1970 to 1975 (Morrison and Wheeler, 1976). Favored by Mar-
garet Mead, among others, this form of relationship may be
institutionalized as a preliminary to marriage.

The individual unit is the final case among the set of
alternatives to the conjugal family. Kobrin (1976) found that
the incidence of the one-person household doubled from 1950
to 1973 to include 18.5 percent of all households in the United
States. The increase has come from specific age-sex groups:
older women, young men, and to some extent young women.
Among unmarried men and women aged twenty-five to thirty-
four, there was an increase in the proportion heading households from 33 percent in 1970 to 43 percent in 1975. In 1975

most of these household heads lived alone, men as often as women (U.S. Bureau of the Census, 1974; Kobrin, 1976). It should be noted that in 1973 fewer men and women over the age of thirty-five had never married than in 1960 (Kreps and Clark, 1975, p. 27). Younger men outnumber older men, but older women outnumber the younger ones who live alone, due, as Kobrin (1976) argues, to the aging of the female population. Using Levy's (1965) view that nonnuclear family residence norms are more easily maintained when high mortality means that few persons actually survive to become aged kin, Kobrin concluded that formerly older women could live with their kin and yet there was only a small proportion of such families. As mortality declined, residence norms changed so that now a large number of older women live alone. Residence norms among young men and women have changed too, as they move out earlier from their families of orientation to apartments or college dorms (Kobrin, 1976).

While we may be reluctant to accept her prediction, Kobrin (1976, p. 137) interpreted her findings as showing that the family is less central as a social institution:

> The great increase in persons living separately from families and the concentration of these people at the youngest and oldest stages of the adult life cycle, indicate two major changes: that a process of age-segregation is going on, and that there is a decreasing tolerance for family forms which include non-nuclear members. Family membership is becoming much less continuous over the life cycle, affecting the relationships between the generations (which are now much less visible to each other) and life cycle patterns of interaction generally. . . .
>
> As the age-sex structure of the population resembles less and less the age-sex composition of the nuclear family, and the population contains more and more adults who are dissociated from such families, the nuclear family as it is now constituted, and is now ordinarily studied, will become a less central social institution. Family membership will occur over a more restricted portion of the life cycle, and, at any given time, perhaps less than a majority of adults will be living in families. The rest, if current trends continue, will live alone.

Kobrin implicated demographic change as the cause of the single-person household. We add to this the factor of

women's occupational achievement accompanying industrialization and urbanization and conclude that the incidence and institutionalization of the single-person household as well as of the
voluntarily childless couple, the cohabiting one, and the single
parent will increase. Should public policies and private practices
now in effect be altered, however, women and men may be able
to integrate occupational achievement and family life in the
conjugal family triad by effecting a change in the internal dynamics of the conjugal family itself, leading from the role specializations of husband and wife to role interchangeability
(Scanzoni, 1975).

Role specialization in the conjugal family and role interchangeability are distinguishable only analytically, whereas
reality is a matter of degree. Role specialization has withstood
women's entrance into the labor force. Their employment has
been secondary to their primary role of wife and mother, so
that sex segregation occurs in the home just as it does in the
marketplace. As women achieve in occupations, desegregation
at home may increase. Role interchangeability in the conjugal
family will be attained only if both partners to the marriage
change the way that they combine occupation and family. Although role interchangeability is popular advice for dual-job
couples, it requires wives to suppress family involvement for
occupational achievement and husbands to redefine the way occupation and family have been articulated for them. Now a
man's occupational role subsumes his family role—to do well in
a job is to be a good husband and father. But more actual involvement in the work of the home—housekeeping and child
care—is necessary if his wife is to have a chance to achieve outside the home.

The participation of women in the labor force, an indicator of a breakdown in sex role differentiation, has greatly increased in recent years from a baseline of 23 percent in 1920.
Now 46 percent of all women over the age of sixteen are employed (U.S. Department of Labor, 1975). This doubling of
women's labor force rate represents the behavior of women who
are wives and mothers. With 58 percent of all employed women
now married (U.S. Department of Labor, 1975), there are fewer
differences in women's labor force participation related to their
marital status, although now the association of female labor
force participation with alternatives to the conjugal family also
needs closer scrutiny (see Kreps and Clark, 1975).

More significant are the changes experienced by women

who are mothers. Between 1940 and 1974 their labor force activity rate quintupled, causing the Department of Labor (1975, p. 26) to term this "probably the most significant labor force change the country experienced during this period." Nearly one half (46 percent) of all mothers in the nation have entered the labor force, comprising 38 percent of the women there. Over half (51 percent) of mothers with husbands present and children in school (aged six to seventeen) are economically active, somewhat more than those wives with no children under eighteen (43 percent), although at comparable ages childless wives have higher participation rates. The mothers of preschool children (under six) have increased their rate of participation from 29 percent in 1967 to 37 percent today (U.S. Department of Labor, 1975), suggesting continuous activity throughout the life cycle for some mothers, especially younger ones (see Kreps and Clark, 1975; Darian, 1976).

One group of women in particular already demonstrates such continuity—minority women. Although the labor force participation rate of minority women is now similar to that of all women (49 and 46 percent, respectively) the record of minority women has been relatively stable. Between 1948 and 1974 their rate increased only 2 percent. One of the largest rates (61 percent) occurs among minority women in the main childrearing period, ages twenty-five to thirty-four. In fact, when we turn to labor force participation rates according to marital status and present age of children, the greatest difference between minority and white women occurs for husband-present wives with children under six years of age: 52 and 32 percent, respectively (U.S. Department of Labor, 1975).

Despite some gains, the concentration of women workers in a narrow range of occupations proportionately and normatively sex-typed for women continues. The modal occupational category "clerical" represents 35 percent of the women in the labor force, and "service" 21 percent. Specifically, in 1973 more than two fifths of all women in the labor force could be found in ten occupations—secretary, retail trade salesworker, bookkeeper, private household worker, elementary schoolteacher, waitress, typist, cashier, sewer and stitcher, and registered nurse. Three fourths could be found in just fifty-seven occupations, and three fourths of the employees in thirty-one of these occupations were women. While minority women concentrate in service occupations (38 percent), by 1973 almost a fourth were clerical employees, up from 10 percent a decade before; 12 percent were private household workers (U.S. Department of Labor, 1975). Associated with this narrow range of occupations are women's median earnings, which in 1974 were only 57 percent of men's earnings derived from full-time, year-round employment (U.S. Bureau of the Census, 1976).

The change and stability in the conjugal family and sex roles indicated by these data are what we have labeled *space-transcendent*. While men and women throughout the United States are being affected by family and sex role changes, the distribution of these changes among and within urban areas varies with different consequences for local residents.

Interurban Variation in Family and Sex Roles

The emergence and possible institutionalization of several family forms and the related breakdown of sex role differentiation implied by women's entrance into the labor force are the phenomena whose variations among and within cities we wish to examine. At least to the extent that data are available, it may also be possible to draw on subcultural and nonecological theories in addition to the determinist view to begin explaining what is still seen by many as urban unconventionality. First, what do the data tell us about interurban variations in family forms and women's labor force participation for space-specific local and translocal relationships?

Space-Specific Local Relationships. Affecting family formation in urban areas is the ratio of men to women, which in 1970 ranged from a low of 93.2 men per 100 women in SMSAs of at least one million inhabitants to a high of 98.6 in totally rural, nonmetropolitan areas adjacent to SMSAs (Hines, Brown, and Zimmer, 1975, pp. 12, 69). The incidence of families that are not husband-wife units does not vary as dramatically according to size of metropolitan or nonmetropolitan areas (Hines, Brown, and Zimmer, 1975, p. 21), but fertility rates vary inversely, especially for the minority population (Hines, Brown, and Zimmer, 1975, pp. 16-17). In 1970, too, 24 percent of young married couples in metropolitan areas had no children under eighteen compared with 20 percent in nonmetropolitan areas (U.S. Bureau of the Census, 1971a, p. 20; Fischer, 1976, p. 143). While there was little variation in the proportion of children living with only one parent, female-headed households were more prevalent in metropolitan than nonmetropolitan areas (11.4 and 9.3 percent, respectively, in 1970; Hines,

Brown, and Zimmer, 1975, pp. 21, 22). Single adults living alone or in unrelated groups are more prevalent among metropolitan households (20 percent) than nonmetropolitan (17 percent) (U.S. Bureau of the Census, 1971a, p. 78; Fischer, 1976, p. 143). Finally, the participation of women in the labor force varies directly with the size of metropolitan and nonmetropolitan areas, from 41.4 percent in SMSAs of a million people to 31.1 percent in totally rural nonmetropolitan areas adjacent to SMSAs (Hines, Brown, and Zimmer, 1975, p. 30).

While interurban variation in living arrangements and sex integration in the labor market is indicated by the measures selected, the differences are small, and for those measures for which data are available (sex ratio, fertility, and women's labor force participation), differences have become less pronounced since 1960 (Hines, Brown, and Zimmer, 1975). Associated with the diminution of the effect of size are two trends in migration in the 1970s: Entire metropolitan areas, not just their central cities, are experiencing absolute population declines (Morrison, 1976), and for the first time in this century, nonmetropolitan areas are growing at a faster rate than metropolitan areas (Beale, 1975; Morrison, 1976). The family-related measures support determinist theory: The organization of kinship appears more centrifugal, but these demographic differences may only reflect the specialization of the conjugal family and its subnuclear variants in fewer functions than a subcultural theory might elucidate. And, as Fischer (1972) points out, kinship, as a central value, may be less subject to diffusion.

A 1970 replication of a 1940 study of the "moral integration" of sixty-three SMSAs of at least 100,000 people presents a similarly mixed picture for women's participation in the labor force (Angell, 1974). In 1940 the percentage of married women working was considered a significant negative correlate of urban integration, which was indeed borne out by the data. For the forty-three cities compared, the proportion of employed wives was correlated −0.54 with an index of integration combining welfare and crime data. By 1970, however, Pearson's r had dropped to −0.05 for the combined index for sixty-three cities (Angell, 1974, p. 615). That the measure no longer predicts urban disintegration suggests, perhaps, the extent to which a breakdown in sex role differentiation in the labor force has been institutionalized. On the basis of this study and the previous demographic data, we conclude that women's participation in the labor force has become more conventional than unconventional, prompting our reliance on either a nonecological or subcultural explanation of the interurban differences that remain in 1970. Of course, no explanation can be given until specific variables are controlled.

Findings of studies in which controls have been introduced into the association of marriage, fertility, and women's labor force participation yield some support for a subcultural explanation of the association. In the first study, Preston and Richards (1975) isolated the effect of urban work opportunities for women, as a structural variable, on the proportion ever married among those aged twenty-two to twenty-four in the 100 largest SMSAs in 1960 and 1970, a decade marked by a sharp decline in this proportion. These data show that the demand for female labor may raise the average marriage age for women. Preston and Richards operationalized women's economic opportunity with two significant measures: the "femaleness" of the industrial structure—the proportion of an SMSA's labor force that women would constitute if each industry in the area had the same proportion of women employees as that in the industry nationally (Bowen and Finegan, 1969, p. 744; Preston and Richards, 1975, p. 213)—and employed women's median earnings. Of similar significance as an indicator of women's economic opportunities was the ratio of men to women in the SMSAs: a lower sex ratio implied a lower proportion of young married women. Lastly, the size of the SMSA in 1960, the only year for which the data were prepared, had a significant negative influence on marriage.

The direction of the effect of city size on marriage bore out Preston and Richards' (1975) hypothesis that more alternatives to marriage are available in large cities rather than the counterhypothesis that a positive scale effect would result from the greater variety of people in larger cities and the possibly more extensive social circles from which a suitable partner could be selected.

Because there might also be a negative scale effect if *effective* social circles are smaller in large cities, as they might be if there are fewer men than women (Glick, 1975), the authors recommended further investigation of the size variable. The findings of this study support Preston and Richards' (1975) view that, in contrast to arguments that a woman's job may encourage a man to feel that he could afford to marry (Goode, 1963; Sklar, 1971; Davis, 1972a; Preston and Richards, 1975), having a job might encourage a woman to feel that she could afford not to marry (Preston and Richards, 1975, p. 210) or, in the case of a related study (Preston, 1973), not to have many children once married.

Preston and Richards (1975) suggested that fertility may also be low in those SMSAs where marriage is delayed. Yet a comparison of the subcultural and nonecological explanations of fertility (Slesinger, 1974) produces only weak support for this suggestion. In the 1965 National Fertility Study there were differences in the number of children born to married women under forty-five according to size of place, but when duration of marriage, religion, work experience, and education were controlled, only a little additional variance was explained by size of place. In Preston and Richards' analysis of urban context, the femaleness of the occupational structure and women's earnings had a negative effect on marital fertility. Although the indirect effects of urbanism through economic opportunities for women and the sex ratio were not assessed by Preston and Richards, since they would have had to have tested completely the subcultural model, the independent negative effect of metropolitan size on the proportion married among young women supports the model.

Some idea of how employment, homemaking, and family activities, among other pursuits, are integrated by individual metropolitan residents was given by Chapin's (1974) study of activity patterns in the city. Variations by city size in a national survey of a sample of SMSAs in 1969 put Chapin's analysis of data, collected in Washington, D.C., in 1968, in context. Although small, there were clear differences in the average number of hours individual household heads and their spouses spent on the job, doing housework, and with the family (Chapin, 1974, p. 102). The greatest variation among large (at least one million inhabitants in 1960), medium (250,000 to 1,000,000), and small (under 250,000) SMSAs occurred in time spent on the job, and the least in the time spent on family activities. On weekdays, the larger the metropolitan area the more time spent at work and on homemaking.

The model on which Chapin's analysis was based includes the propensity to engage in an activity and the opportunity to do so as influences on the overall activity pattern. Opportunity is seen to be affected by the perceived availability and quality of the facility or service, while propensity is produced by predisposing individual motivations and preconditioning role and person characteristics (Chapin, 1974, p. 33). In the Washington study, only factors preconditioning an activity were investigated: work status, sex, child-rearing responsibility, and whether any child under thirteen was present. Chapin's model grew from two assumptions: "activity patterns of the metropolitan community vary with the cultural makeup of the community" and "they vary with the social structural context of the community and its subcultural spheres of influence" (1974, p. 36).

Of the 1,667 Washington residents sampled, 59 percent were employed full-time, only 8 percent part-time, and 33 percent were not employed; 56 percent of the sample were women; and 22 percent were black. Outside of sleep, on weekdays most time was spent on work and homemaking, with little time spent on family activities compared with other discretionary uses (Chapin, 1974, p. 98). Differences by race were significant only for family activities, which were considerably more prevalent in white households (Chapin, 1974, p. 126). Within each of the racial categories, in comparison, no differences appeared in family activities that were correlated with income, occupation, or education, but there was significant variation in the amount of time spent at work and in homemaking (Chapin, 1974, pp. 128-129).

Sex differences were also significant: Men spent more time on the job (7.35 hours versus 3.26 hours per weekday), while women spent more time on homemaking and family activities (4.75 versus 1.33 hours). Influences on the allocation of time to family activities were then examined, with work status, sex role, and childrearing responsibility cumulatively controlled. Controlling for the last two characteristics reduced the effect of work status on family activities. For family activities, sex role and childrearing responsibility appeared to be a more important source of influence than work status. The substantial difference between white and black households noted above persists. We suggest that one reason for the importance of sex role and childrearing responsibility may well be the way investigators classified various activities as family ones and hence discretionary rather than obligatory homemaking ones: In collapsing 225 activity categories to 40 and then to 12, some activities like overseeing children's study or practice, most likely performed by women with children, were considered discretionary family activities, thereby heightening sex role differences (Chapin, 1974, pp. 115, 117-118, 252).

Given these differences in the time spent with the family

according to sex and childrearing responsibility, we would expect some variation in these patterns for metropolitan areas of different sizes if data were available. Although smaller than the influences of sex and child status, the existence of an independent effect of city size remains a substantively significant question as "it indicates a common pressure on an aggregated population with implications for serious effects at that aggregate level" (Fischer, 1975a, p. 70).

An individual's propensity to engage in an activity—whether employment, homemaking, or family activities—is also affected, in Chapin's (1974, p. 33) model, by the predisposing factors of motivation and thought. Light may be shed on such factors by findings from the study of another metropolitan area in the United States. Duncan, Schuman, and Duncan (1973) updated a 1955 opinion survey of the adult population of Detroit with a study of a representative cross-section in 1971. Predisposing factors were indicated by opinions about role interchangeability in the conjugal family, fertility, and women's participation in the labor force that prevailed during this period.

The sharing of roles by husbands and wives encompasses both making decisions about tasks and actually performing them. With regard to the former, it appears that sex role differentiation still obtained in Detroit: Husbands dominated three of the six decision areas examined and wives dominated two, and the influence of husbands increased rather than decreased. The only area in which egalitarianism is the dominant mode of decision making is which house or apartment to take, although here too wives ceded decision-making power to husbands between 1955 and 1971 (from a 23 percent to a 14 percent wife-dominant decision and from a 19 percent to a 23 percent husband-dominant).

In contrast to decision making, the performance of tasks like shopping seemed the domain of Detroit wives, a finding reflecting sex role differentiation between leadership and the division of labor. The wife carried out five of the six tasks investigated. Husbands tended to be the ones who repaired things around the house, and in no area was egalitarianism the dominant mode. Three areas evidenced change over the sixteen-year period: More wives shopped for groceries than shared the task equally with their husbands; more wives and husbands paid bills jointly; and more husbands fixed their own breakfast before going to work than had their wives fix it for them (Duncan, Schuman, and Duncan, 1973, pp. 12-17). Analyzing the division

of labor between husband and wife separately from decision
making, as we have done, illustrates the differentiation of sex
roles—husbands tended to make decisions while wives performed household tasks. This pattern, as the authors pointed
out, did not change dramatically in Detroit since 1955.

In contrast was the marked change in Detroit wives' ideal
number of children—from the three- and four-child family of
1955 to the two-child family of 1971 (mentioned by half the
women and by half of all adults). There was, however, only a
very slight increase in the proportion favoring less than two children, from one to four percent. Views about women's participation in the labor force in Detroit were as mixed as those about
role specification in the conjugal family and the ideal size of the
family. Money remained the main reason given by both men
and women for women's employment. In combination with
money, "the most frequently mentioned noneconomic reason
for women working is variously described as a desire to get out
of the house, boredom at home, or a dislike of housework or
married life" (Duncan, Schuman, and Duncan, 1973, p. 22). At
neither time did women or men mention very often (about 5
percent) that women worked to be independent or because of
the nature of the job. "Although a decisive majority of respondents continued to feel that women have special problems
working, the opinion was held less widely in 1971 than in
1955. . . . Women, whatever their view on the special problems
women encounter in working, opposed restrictions on the work
women can do more often than did their male counterparts"
(pp. 22-23).

Except for women's opposition to restricted work opportunities for their sex and wives' endorsement of a smaller ideal
family, the structural changes of household centrifugality and
women's entrance into the labor force (and, if more gradually,
into sex-atypical occupations in the labor market) were not reflected in the attitudinal responses elicited from Detroit residents. How might we explain this? One explanation lies in the
nature of the Detroit study itself. Queries about role relationships within the conjugal family were made only of those currently in such a relationship. It is not surprising, therefore, that
their views did not change radically. Perhaps this lack of change
in sex role differentiation both within and between husband-
wife decision making and the household division of labor is one
impetus for alternatives to this structure, such as the childless
couple or the single-person household. A second explanation of

the stability in men's and women's perspectives on the latter's participation in the labor force is the continued interpretation of employment as a secondary role for women rather than primary or equal to their family role. A third explanation, subsuming the first two, derives from the intricate relationship of micro to macro data.

Space-Specific Translocal Relationships. How micro-macro differences in the conjugal family and sex roles counter or reinforce one another is a topic worthy of future research. A case study of urban migration, a space-specific translocal relationship, may reveal the connection by explaining the apparent weakness of city effects compared with more direct individual influences.

In his study of the influence of urban context on individual men's occupational status attainment and income in fifteen of the largest cities in the United States, C. W. Mueller (1974) found that individual characteristics and not contextual differences (whatever they might be, since Mueller essentially controlled for city size) explained between-city differences in mean occupational attainment. Mueller extrapolated from this finding to conclude that a city's population came to match the occupational opportunity structure of that city by means of equilibratory processes, especially urban migration. In- and out-migration evidently operated to produce a fit between resident composition and occupational structure. Too, Mueller surmised, nonmigrants were likely socialized to fit the structure in which they would continue to reside, and business and industry might adjust to match the composition of the urban population.

Hendrix (1975) further probed the role of migration to discover "why the findings of most macro-level studies fit the intervening opportunities while micro-level studies often show concentrated streams based on ascriptive ties rather than a rational dispersion of migrants, especially among working-class people" (p. 536). In his analysis of census data on migration between 1955 and 1960 from one State Economic Area (SEA) comprised of eleven counties in the Ozark Mountains to 179 other SEAs within a 620-mile radius, and of survey data on 111 out-migrants from one small community, he found that:

> The micro-level data show an extensive tendency, especially among working-class migrants, to follow the paths of siblings and other kin predominantly because of the information they supply on working and living condi-

tions. Thus, at the micro-level, migration is a blend of rational concerns about work and reliance on kin in finding it. Numerous small kinship-based chain migration streams flow to a variety of destinations, producing a macro-level pattern of dispersion that appears rational and that meets the migration requisite of modern society [p. 536].

Although we might question the modernity of a society in which occupations are sex-typed, the applicability of the research of Mueller and Hendrix to women has potential.

For example, in the case of family formation by marriage, the direction of the effect of the in-migration of women on the proportion aged twenty-two to twenty-four and married was not anticipated (Preston and Richards, 1975). Introducing migration (indicated by the proportionate decade increase of women aged twenty to twenty-four) into the analysis did not diminish the significance of the variables of urban economic context, allowing the conclusion that natives rather than recent migrants were most affected by it. Instead of a negative effect, which would suggest the movement of single women who desire work, the significant effect of migration was positive. From the low correlations between the migration ratio and the femaleness of the industrial structure and women's median earnings, the authors determined that the pattern of women's migration was not efficient. On the contrary, Preston and Richards (1975, p. 218) cited census data showing that a young married woman was more likely to have made a long-distance move in the previous five years than a young single woman. The unexpected positive relationship between marriage and migration will be further buttressed by additional analyses of the geographic mobility of married women and their participation in the labor force. First, however, we will investigate the effect of migration on the other aspect of family formation—fertility.

In an attempt to disentangle this problematic relationship, Long (1970) contended that whether movers between high- and low-fertility areas, not just rural-to-urban migrants, have higher or lower fertility rates than urban natives depended on the reasons for moving and conditions at the destination. In an economically developed nation like the United States, where intermetropolitan migration is substantial, he further contended that migration did not necessarily represent exposure to different fertility norms; value differentials might thus be controlled to study the relationship between migration and fertility, the guiding hypothesis being that children inhibit migration (Long, 1970, p. 298). In comparing data on the fertility of women in interregional migration streams with data of noninterregional migrants in the region of birth (origin) and destination (Kiser, Grabill, and Campbell, 1968; Long, 1970), Long (1970, p. 302) found that the fertility of migrants was generally lower than that of nonmigrants in either region of origin or destination. In addition, interregional migrants had a smaller range of variation in their fertility. Long attributes this to migrants' more uniform socioeconomic profile than nonmigrants. Since these findings pertained to a rather special case, "more work needs to be done on the diffusion of norms (including those involving fertility) resulting from various types of migration under various circumstances," as Long (1970, p. 314) urged.

Following his own dictum, Long (1972) traced the effects of age of husband, ages of children, and number of children on the probability of long-distance movement of husband-wife families using census data from 1968 to 1970. Controlling for the age of the household head, which was the variable with the greatest effect, school-age children (six to seventeen years old) restricted long-distance mobility, presumably because parents did not wish to transfer their children from one school district to another (Long, 1972, p. 374). The number of children, in comparison, was inversely related to moving between counties. Having more than one child of school age intensified the effect.

For women who headed families, the depressant effect of fertility also appeared. In general, these single parents were more geographically mobile than men who headed husband-wife families at the same age and with the same number and ages of children. Women who headed families did not move as much as couples with no children. Childless couples were so mobile that the greatest difference in the percentage moving between counties occurred between such couples and those who had one child.

While age of children appeared as a major influence on between-county migration, the direction of causality may run either way, with families choosing a community for its child-raising possibilities or discovering that they like a community after their children's attendance at school has created ties for them. Pursuing this line of analysis, Long (1974) then turned to the relationship between wives' labor force participation and long-distance movement across county or state lines using

census data. He found that a wife's employment somewhat discouraged her husband's long-distance migration, regardless of
his occupational status, but only after the age when he was
likely to be established in his occupation. Husbands' long-
distance movement, however, interrupted wives' participation in
the labor force. It seems that by dropping out of the labor force
wives facilitated the movement of their husbands. From this
study it is possible to draw comparisons with the work of Preston and Richards (1975), as well as to understand how such
interruption of a wife's employment experience lowers her earnings and preserves the secondary status of her occupational role.
This effect is more apparent for a more select group—the dual-
career couples among a national sample of 1964-1968 college
graduates (Duncan and Perrucci, 1976). Characteristics of a husband's occupation such as its prestige and the location of occupational opportunities affected a family's interstate migration,
whereas those of the wife's occupation had no effect.

     Although the studies we have cited do not directly con-
cern urban migration, they provide evidence for Mueller's
(1974) suggestion that migration equilibrates resident population composition and occupational structure and Hendrix's
(1975) linking of ascription from family ties to achievement in
the aggregate for migrants. We find that migration is associated
with family formation in varying ways. Movement accompanies
the marriage of young women (Preston and Richards, 1975),
yet given the effect of a person's age on his or her mobility, it
limits the size of the conjugal family unit (Long, 1970, 1972).
The subnuclear households of childless couples and women who
are single parents are the most mobile over long distances
(Long, 1972). Regardless of the number of children, their
school attendance seems to inhibit family migration. That the
number and ages of children delimit sex role differentiation
appears in the equilibrating process.

     Quite simply, the long-distance movement of husbands is
usually in search of a job (Long, 1972, p. 375), while wives'
migration depends on their ascriptive family ties. Their employment at the point of destination, the particular occupation they
enter, and their possible achievement in it remain secondary in
every sense (Long, 1974; Duncan and Perrucci, 1976). What,
then, of those women who are not married? We know that their
rate of labor force participation is higher than that of their married counterparts and that their achievement in an occupation,
at least as indicated by their earnings, is greater (Havens, 1973).
Yet Mueller's (1974) opinion that nonmigrants were likely so-

cialized to fit the occupational structure in which they will reside seems to be borne out by Preston and Richards' (1975) discovery that it was the native female population that responded to the femaleness of the occupational structure and the local level of women's earnings by delaying marriage. In the lives of many women, married and unmarried or migrant and native, sex role differentiation is manifest in varying degrees.

This institutionalized pattern we may attribute, in accordance with Fischer's (1975b) view, not entirely to compositional effects but to the creation of a certain subculture in large cities—that of the role-specialized conjugal family. In particular, in our examination of space-specific local and translocal relationships, we have partially shown how the differentiation of the metropolitan occupational structure and migration maintains sex role differentiation. Despite family efforts at role interchangeability, the incidence of subnuclear variants in living arrangements, and the entrance of women into the labor force, the strength of the dominant family culture remains strong enough to embrace such changes that occur among metropolitan areas.

Intraurban Variation in Family and Sex Roles

Interest in the pattern of social life within the city has traditionally been translated into an examination of what makes a certain spatially delimited area a social unit: What relationships develop among residents? To this issue we, along with Lofland (1975), add the question of the relationship of local residents to other parts of the metropolis. Doing this, we can classify recent intraurban research as either emphasizing space-specific relationships or translocal ones. The answer to both questions, as Fischer (1975a) deduces, partially depends on the importance of the area to its residents.

Indispensable to an understanding of the pattern of urban life is a focus on family and sex roles. It is true that the relationships that knit the collection of people in a neighborhood into a social group reach beyond the family, especially when the family is seen as the conjugal unit, yet the form that the conjugal family or alternative living arrangements take brackets the establishment of additional ties. The roles ascribed to men and women further structure urban life. In this way some notion of the family and sex roles would illuminate how links among families and individuals are formed.

A theory explaining these or any other relationships is

presently underdeveloped. While determinist, nonecological, and subcultural perspectives may be drawn on to explain the intraurban case, their applicability to this level of analysis is less than immediate. There is a logical difficulty in applying the determinist view in that social differentiation becomes both what is to be explained as well as its cause, since differentiation accompanies greater size (Fischer, 1976, p. 273). The assertion that there is nothing to be explained after nonecological or compositional effects have been accounted for has been most forcefully articulated at the intraurban level of analysis (Gans, 1962a). The extension of subcultural theory has to date been the subject of few studies, especially of the family and sex roles. Its logic, however, makes it relevant for the contents of this volume: "The critical factor is the ability of specific sets of people to come together in numbers sufficient to support an active subculture and its institutions. Having those numbers in a community is only part of the process. The viability of a subculture also depends on the access (in terms of travel time and cost) that those people have to one another and their institutions" (Fischer, 1976, p. 231). We will therefore attempt to trace the association of the ecological and social in the lives of families and men and women, the absence of data necessitating that we simply keep in mind significant nonecological effects.

Our opinion that some knowledge of sex roles and the family is basic to an understanding of neighborhood local and translocal social life derives from the significance of family status as an independent variable in social area analysis, along with economic and racial-ethnic status (Shevky and Bell, 1955) and their association with neighborliness. Residents of primarily familistic social areas appear to neighbor more than residents of less familistic ones (Greer, 1956; Greer and Kube, 1959; McGahan, 1972). The origin of the conceptualization of family status as a major determinant of neighborhood relationships in the determinist perspective is apparent in the view that secondary contacts replace the primary ties of neighborhood and kinship in the metropolis. In fact, the dimension is often labeled "familism-urbanism" (Greer, 1962a).

In what has come to be known as factorial ecology, familism-urbanism is a factor on which the following variables load highly: percent married in the census tract, fertility, percentage of single-family dwelling units, and the participation of women in the labor force (see Hunter, 1974). The assumption underlying social area analysis is that in a highly urban area few are married, fertility is low, there are few single-family dwelling units, and many women are employed (see McGahan, 1972). McGahan (1972, pp. 398-399) summarizes Greer's (1956, 1962a; Greer and Kube, 1959; Greer and Orleans, 1968) theory of the opportunity structure for neighboring from the empirical generalizations of social area analysis:

(1) The ecological structure of the urban community in part consists of subareas differentiated along the familism-urbanism dimension.

(2) The structure of opportunities for interaction of the neighboring type varies directly according to the degree of familism of the subarea.

(3) The greater the opportunity for interaction, the greater the actual neighboring among those individuals so predisposed.

(4) Whereas the degree of familism of a neighborhood determines, to some extent, the structure of opportunities for neighboring, access to that structure may be determined by various individual characteristics.

This form of analysis emphasized social areas in contrast to natural or spatial areas (Hunter, 1974), but among the exceptions (Greer, 1956; Bell and Boat, 1957; Anderson and Egeland, 1961), the context of the neighborhood appears to be an influence on individuals. As Fischer (1975a) noted, whether these effects are the consequences of the social context or of local ecological factors remains an empirical question (see Fischer and Jackson, 1976).

Hunter (1974) examined the influence of neighborhood context in his study of local communities in Chicago from 1930 to 1960. Based on factor analyses of nine variables derived from census data, his research related the seventy-five natural areas mapped by the Chicago School to the social areas of factorial ecology. Hunter found that in 1930, 1940, 1950, and 1960, economic status, family status, and racial-ethnic status consistently emerged as principal factors of urban segregation; but family status, as defined, declined in importance as racial-ethnic status increased, and economic status persisted as the most important factor. The decline of family status as a basis of ecological segregation can be seen to support Abu-Lughod's (1969) theory that with metropolitan growth, economic status becomes dominant (Hunter, 1974, p. 34). The importance of family status decreased in part because housing type was not as closely associated with other characteristics of local communities and in part because fertility (the percentage of children under five) shifted its highest loading from the family status factor to the racial ethnic factor, thus reflecting the growing concentration of young black families in the central city as young white families moved to the suburbs (Hunter, 1974, pp. 30-35).

Based on Chicago, is Hunter's research generalizable to other urban areas? It may be if the trend in the family status factor is indicative of patterns in its components. For example, a pattern of declining importance of women's participation in the labor force may be analogous to its growing irrelevance to the moral integration of metropolitan areas (Angell, 1974), suggesting the conventionality of labor force activity if not the primacy of an occupational role for women. However, the decreasing significance of family status in Hunter's (1974) research was not attributed to changes in this component. Too, only a portion of one metropolitan area in the United States up to 1960 was under investigation. It could be said that the changes that have occurred in family and sex roles took place after this time and perhaps have not yet had a chance to be reflected in ecological patterns. As important as the replication of past studies is, it may be that other indicators of family status, such as stage in the life cycle (see Popenoe, 1974) and percent childless couples, single parents, and single individuals, would produce more variation. It is for this reason that the connection between family and sex roles and ecological patterns is the subject of this chapter.

If intraurban variation in family and sex roles is the concern, how should ecological areas in the city be defined? For analytical purposes, Fischer (1976, p. 273) parsimoniously recommended distance from the city center as the measure, rather than residential land use, density, housing type, commuting, recency, "familism," or political jurisdiction. To distance we would add time because of its particular significance on a day-to-day basis for women, regardless of their situation (see Palm and Pred, 1974, for a time-geographic analysis). Although we must rely on other definitions of areas within the city, our theoretical interest is in spatial and temporal correlates of urban variations in living arrangements and sex role differentiation.

In addition to continually increasing residential segregation by race and social class between the city proper and the suburb, especially when measured by income (see Farley,

1976), the data show continued differences between the two types of areas in metropolitan family form and sex role differentiation. Marked internal differentiation is what contributes to the interurban pattern, as suburbs more nearly resemble nonmetropolitan areas. City and suburban populations differ according to stage in the family life cycle, and mobility patterns reinforce these differences (Long and Glick, 1976). For greater metropolitan areas (those SMSAs of more than a million people), the sex ratio in the core (the counties containing the primary central city of the metropolitan area) is as low as 92.0, while that of fringe counties is 96.2 (Hines, Brown, and Zimmer, 1975, pp. 4, 12). Here, too, the proportion of families that are not husband-wife units varies more markedly (17.2 percent in the core versus 10.4 percent in the fringe) than among all metropolitan and nonmetropolitan comparisons (Hines, Brown, and Zimmer, 1975, p. 21). Fertility differentials between core and fringe, in contrast, are reduced, especially when measured by the number of children ever born to ever-married women aged thirty-five to forty-four (Hines, Brown, and Zimmer, 1975, pp. 16-17), thus verifying Hunter's findings for Chicago areas in 1960 (Hunter, 1974). For both the proportion of children living with only one parent and the proportion of female-headed households, sharp core-fringe differences prevail in the largest SMSAs (Hines, Brown, and Zimmer, 1975, pp. 21, 22). The gap is not as great for women's labor force participation rates (42.1 percent in the core versus 39.7 percent in the fringe; Hines, Brown, and Zimmer, 1975, p. 30). The indicators for which we have data show, then, that the core-fringe difference in the sex ratio remained the same from 1960 to 1970 (although the ratio for each area dropped; Hines, Brown, and Zimmer, 1975, p. 69), while fertility and female labor force participation differentials grew smaller during the decade. In fringe counties the proportion of women employed increased by 71.6 percent compared with an increase of 27.9 percent for the core (Hines, Brown, and Zimmer, 1975, p. 33). This is the suburban manifestation of mothers entering the labor force during the 1960s.

To what may we attribute such intraurban variation in measures closely related to the formation of families via marriage or alternative living arrangements? Fischer (1975b) indicated that the practical economics of housing in the United States, rather than cultural values, has been the major cause of the move to suburbia, basing his view on Guest's (1972, pp. 167-168) research finding that the concentration of married couples with children in areas distant from the center city is due to the existence there of low-density, new, and spacious housing (see Greer, 1973). These 1960 data from Cleveland and sixteen other metropolitan areas cannot reveal the possible ecological changes associated with the greater similarity in core-fringe fertility and women's participation in the labor force that we have indicated. It is possible that the entrance of suburban mothers into the labor force in the 1960s is one force contributing to the post-1970 growth of nonmetropolitan areas (including those with the least commuting to SMSAs; Morrison, 1976) as social influences dynamically interact with ecological patterns. Linking the two grows from what we know about space-specific local and translocal relationships within households and between the sexes.

Space-Specific Local Relationships. Hypothetically, this section could be the most extensive of the chapter if it incorporated the multitude of community-type studies carried out in suburban and central city neighborhoods. Many of these studies have commented on relationships within the conjugal family and, at least indirectly, on relationships between men and women. Such a review is bypassed for three reasons:

1. Although rich in insight, the ethnographic study of single neighborhoods cannot adequately test intracommunity variation in the socioecological interface. Just as the study of one urban community or even one neighborhood cannot prove or disprove determinist, nonecological, or subcultural theories of interurban patterns, the analysis of time and distance within the metropolis, like that of size among cities, requires more than one neighborhood (see Fischer, 1975a).

2. With regard to the conjugal family and sex roles specifically, the dearth of current sociological research is great (Schnore, 1972; Long and Glick, 1976), and most of the neighborhood studies manifest the normative or empirical bias against women that Lofland inveighs against. That is, when women are not ignored as social actors, they are frequently portrayed in highly differentiated sex roles, as are men, because those neighborhoods rich in community and kinship figures—generally ethnic and working class communities—are selected as research sites (Lofland, 1975). To these sites we would add suburban neighborhoods as sex-role-differentiated locales for women. Studies of these areas slight women's employment, denying the variation that is there (see those noted in Lofland, 1975, and Fischer, 1976). There are exceptions to this general

criticism—for example, Howell's (1973) study of a white work-ing class neighborhood in Washington, D.C., and Ladner's (1971) work on urban black women—but the pattern holds.

3. Of the research that does exist, we will emphasize translocal relationships, loosely defined here as long-term mobil-ity or daily movement, in response to Lofland's (1975) plea and our own belief in the importance of distance and time to the dynamics of intraurban variation. A more complete picture of intraurban variation in family and sex roles than that given by our overview of census data does emerge from the work of Long and Glick (1976), a comparison of activity patterns between black and white working class communities (Chapin, 1974), and various studies of dwelling type and household density as the most localized of settings.

Summarizing their review of census data on additional variables of conjugal family formation (marriage and child bear-ing) and women's employment in cities and suburbs, Long and Glick (1976) stated that "suburban areas became more hetero-geneous during the 1960s, with proportionately more persons in the 'singles' category, fewer married couples, more working mothers. But central cities also reflected such changes, and this tendency reduced the extent to which central cities and suburbs became more alike" (p. 52). Partially based on the greater vari-ety of employment and housing in the urban fringe areas of SMSAs, there is now a smaller proportion of people living as couples than in 1960 and substantially more who are separated, divorced, or never married (Long and Glick, 1976, pp. 41, 46). Although in both 1960 and 1970 wives in central cities had higher labor force participation rates than wives in the rest of the SMSAs, rates greatly increased in the suburbs.

Within metropolitan areas, variations were found in activ-ity patterns between black and white working class city neigh-borhoods in 1969 and 1971 (Chapin, 1974). In the predomi-nantly white neighborhood, significantly more time was spent on the main job on a weekday than in the black neighborhood, while there were no significant differences by neighborhood in the amount of time spent on homemaking and family activities (Chapin, 1974, p. 172). A key indication of continued role spe-cialization in the conjugal family was significant across-the-board differences by sex in the time allocated to the main job, homemaking, and family activities (the only exception was family activities in the black neighborhood; p. 176). Black and white men devoted more time to the job, while women allocated more of their time to homemaking and family activities, particularly white women employed only part-time (p. 180). Therefore, it seems that only in the black community did men and women spend about equal time with the family. Black and white women expended equal amounts of time on homemaking (pp. 174, 176), but white women had more time with their families. In addition to the differences in family and sex roles between city and suburb and between black and white working-class neighborhoods (Hines, Brown, and Zimmer, 1975; Long and Glick, 1976; Chapin, 1974), the question of even more space-specific local effects has been raised in investigations of type of dwelling and density within the household.

The association between type of dwelling and family and sex roles seems variable and interactive, as indicated by its relationship to both fertility and employed women's social contacts. In relating dwelling to fertility for a longitudinal sample of Anglo, Mexican-American, and black couples in Racine, Wisconsin, between 1960 and 1971, Curry and Scriven (1976) found that living in an apartment did not depress fertility, as we might have expected. The independent effect of apartment residence was negligible regardless of minority group status. Like Felson and Solaún (1975), they hypothesized that another ecological variable of city-wide import—the availability of housing as interpreted by future parents—intervened. In Racine, housing was available throughout the study period. Fertility, in turn, was found to have an independent positive effect on the number of rooms per dwelling, again regardless of ethnic category. That the subjective element was important is evident by the fact that, at least in Felson and Solaún's (1975) site, Bogota, Colombia, there were actually fewer persons per room in apartments than in houses.

The subjective is also important in Michelson's (1974) longitudinal study of the social contacts of employed wives moving to downtown high-rise apartments or houses in Toronto. There was little evidence that the apartment dwellers expected contact, but they were objectively no more isolated than wives in houses partially because 78 percent of the apartment-dwelling women were employed while only 30 percent of the wives moving to single-family houses were. There are, then, "different *paths* to friendship as a consequence of the wife's family-employment status, which in turn tends to coincide largely with the selection of housing and location—so much so that in practical terms these factors must all be considered

simultaneously" (Michelson, 1974, p. 169). Michelson concluded that this "community without propinquity" is "not distributed randomly among the population but appears within
particular social and physical contexts within the city" (p. 169).

In contrast to the effects of dwelling type in Toronto was
the lack of effect of household density (people per room) in
that same city on relationships within the conjugal family
(Booth and Edwards, 1976). Among the range of husband-wife
and parent-child and sibling interactions, modest effects appeared only for parents' striking their children and children's
quarreling. Coupled with this finding was the apparent decline
from 1940 to 1970 in density and the proportion of households
with more than one person per room in the United States, such
that now households in central cities and SMSAs are no more
crowded than the national average (Carnahan, Gove, and Galle,
1975). Again, however, the subjective enters: wives' feelings of
being crowded affected the husband-wife bond negatively. The
study by Booth and Edwards, like research on dwelling type,
indicates that the effect of the most space-specific, local ecological context depends on how it is evaluated and by whom.

As preliminary as these data are and despite their lack of
essential controls, they show changes in family form and sex
role differentiation in both city and suburb. Pluralism in family
form and women's employment now characterizes suburb as
well as city, but persistent differences remain. In a case study of
a black and a white working class city neighborhood, time was
found to be allocated among the job, homemaking, and the
family differently than it was for the whole metropolitan area
or the metropolitan racial reference group. Sex role differentiation obtained throughout except in one instance—the family life
of black men and women. The egalitarianism prevalent here—if
the equal expenditure of time is one measure of role interchangeability in the conjugal family—merits further examination. With what have distance from the city center and time
expenditure interacted to structure the social world of men and
women in and out of families?

The process of creating subcultures within the metropolis, alluded to by Fischer (1975b) in his subcultural theory of
urbanism, may lie in the interpretation of these ecological phenomena, as studies of dwelling type and density have suggested
(see Booth and Edwards, 1976). Women may see things differently than men.

Space-Specific Translocal Relationships. If we accept distance and time as the criteria defining the parts of a metropolis and how it affects individual residents, then our interest should be less in the static definition of those parts than in the dynamics of how people relate to them. The relationship is two-way. Movement through space and time affects men and women, especially those in families, by shaping their lives, while, in turn, their movement gives shape to the metropolis. Movement may be permanent or temporary. All else being constant, a person's sex role and marital and parental status greatly affect long-term mobility within the metropolitan area, while the patterns of daily movement continually constrain the expression of sex roles and conjugal family forms.

This seemingly innocuous phrase—long-term mobility in the metropolis—signifies the major experience of urban centers in the postwar United States: suburbanization, the movement from city center to outlying rural areas. Inextricably a part of this movement was the realization of a tenet of the American dream—the possession of a single-family dwelling with its own land. Although attributable not to individuals' intentions, at least not initially, but to the economics of housing, the fusing of the ecology of locale and the demography of the migration stream with the ideology of property of one type has been tight enough to resist, sequentially, the inefficiencies if not costs of location, changes in the social composition of the migrant stream, and perhaps the emergence of person- rather than family-centered beliefs. If these three forces of change begin to work together, will suburbs remain uniquely distinguishable as areas in which conjugal families live in their own homes?

Long and Glick (1976), noting the lesser role of migration to metropolitan areas from nonmetropolitan areas, examined the extent to which city centers were still the places "where people meet and marry before moving to suburbs to raise children" (p. 40). They set out to probe the opposite notion, that families may now be forming in the suburbs. Their data consisted of the infrequently analyzed figures for net migration by age for the white population in metropolitan counties between 1950 and 1970 (see Frey, 1975). From 1950 to 1960 and, contrary to their hypothesis, from 1960 to 1970, the net migration of central city and suburban counties was concentrated among persons of the age of parents and their children. It did not appear, therefore, that single, young adults were moving to the suburbs before forming families. Further support is offered by 1970-1973 data showing the movement of men and women under twenty-five to the central city from the rest of the SMSA. Young women who headed families also moved to the city center from the suburbs. Married couples, in contrast, continued to move out. While families moving from cities to suburbs averaged higher incomes than those moving into the city, they were less well-off than families who stayed in the suburbs. While movement between cities and suburbs was great, it was exceeded by movement within and between central cities and within and between the suburban parts of different SMSAs (Long and Glick, 1976). The findings of Long and Glick are replicated and elaborated by Frey (1975).

Part of the movement within central cities or suburbs is also within counties. An analysis of the relationship between moving within a county and the number and ages of children was included in Long's (1972) previously mentioned analysis of residential mobility. In line with earlier research and allowing for the husband's age, husband-wife families with children under six were more likely to move within counties than families also or exclusively having children between six and seventeen. The strength of the effect was similar to that for between-county migration. Moving a short distance (within a county) was usually associated with housing; specifically, young children usually necessitated moving from an apartment to a single-family dwelling or from a smaller to a larger house. Contrary to earlier views (for example, Sabagh, Van Arsdol, and Butler, 1969; Long, 1972) that a large number of children encourage local mobility, Long found an inverse relationship between family size and short-distance moving—at least for those households headed by men younger than forty-five with fewer than three children. For such men with three and four children, the relationship was positive.

This unexpected finding—that small families promoted local mobility—is supported by Powers and Thacker's (1975) microlevel research in a Puerto Rican and nonwhite Bronx neighborhood. Recently mobile wives had lower fertility than long-term residents, a response attributed by Powers and Thacker to a tight local housing market. Depending again on how environment is interpreted, those women with fewer children (or higher incomes) could move from neighborhoods that they perceived as being less desirable.

Further contributing to the movement to better local housing is the wife's participation in the labor force. In conjunction with his previously reported research, Long (1974) found that a wife's employment increased the local mobility of her family. He surmised that "the income earned by working wives appears to enable the family to upgrade its housing, and the fact that at each age men with working wives were more mobile within counties suggests repeated moving over the family life cycle to successively more desirable housing units" (p. 346).

Even local movement reduces a wife's labor force involvement, however, and by dropping out of the labor force she increases short-distance family mobility. Paradoxically, then, when the 1965-1970 interval is considered, either continuation or dropping out of the labor force is correlated with her family's local mobility. It may be that her dropping out compels a move to less desirable housing, but it seems more likely that her participation is closely tied to a specific consumption goal—the purchase of a home or the acquisition of better living quarters—and less likely that participation in itself represents a change in sex role differentiation.

Essentially permanent intraurban mobility is mainly related to stability in family form (after marrying and rearing children, young couples continue to move to suburbs) and sex role differentiation (women's involvement in the labor force is dispensable, indicating role specialization in the family). However, fewer rather than more children stimulate local movement, a factor bolstering women's contribution of their earnings to acquiring new housing. To the extent that the movement between city and suburb or within counties is a space-specific, translocal relationship, it is a means to the ends of the conjugal family and sex role differentiation (other than perhaps limiting family size). It is a way to realize the American dream, despite the consequences some of these locational decisions may have on daily lives.

Of the ecological dimensions we have considered—space-transcendent, space-specific, and local and long-term translocal—it is daily movement that traditionally most distinguishes men and women. It is thought that men suffer few restrictions on their almost daily movement while women suffer many because of the constraints of child care. Historically and cross-culturally, sex role differentiation in daily movement has been a matter of degree, depending on the nature of lactation, the society's economy, and women's role in it. The trend in the United States has not always been toward fewer restrictions on mobility for women—there have been periods of increasing restriction, especially for married women. One occurred in the nineteenth century, when in the course of industrialization workplace became separated from household. Sex role differentiation, a cultural universal, came to have an ecological analogue for many wives and their husbands, middle class and otherwise. In this respect, industrialization and urbanization in the United States had an effect on women contrary to the liberating one on men (see Laslett, 1973). A second period, more liberating, we would suggest, is that begun by suburbanization after World War II. This intraurban shift was accompanied by the postindustrialization of the economy, of which the employment of mothers and wives in growing white collar and service industries was a part. Household is increasingly separated from workplace as more metropolitan workers commute across city and suburban boundaries (Kasarda, 1976).

It is possible to discern the outlines of what the contemporary separation of household and job means for women's employment in various occupations. Rosenthal (1978) argues that almost regardless of where they live or of their socioeconomic status, older women workers, such as those who typified the trend toward women's greater participation in the labor force in the 1950s and early 1960s, may have entered sex-atypical occupations to realize not sex equality but the middle class, role-specialized conjugal family ideal. Rosenthal's prime example is school bus driving. A mature woman worker's willingness to pioneer in this regard is met by the willingness of employers to manipulate features of the job to attract middle-aged women when no other categories of workers are available. Rosenthal's speculations seem to be supported by research on a national sample of women in the 1960 U.S. population (Darian, 1975).

Darian (1975) compared the labor force participation rates of white, married women living with their husbands by the age of their youngest child and their occupation, classified according to its convenience. Although not a specifically urban variable, the convenience of an occupation was determined by the availability of work at home, walking to work (since women who do so evidently spend less time traveling to their jobs than those using other means of transportation; Shea and others, 1970; Darian, 1975), and working less than thirty hours a week. It was found that convenient working conditions reduced the constraint of children on wives' employment in 1960. Once more at the micro level, these results were strongly reinforced by Rosenberg's (1973) analysis of the 1968-1969 New York City Urban Employment Survey of Puerto Rican women in ghetto neighborhoods. First, women relied on informal methods of finding employment since "they operate within a very socially and spatially confined network" (Rosenberg, 1973, p. 5). Second, jobs for such women were available in their neighborhoods. Third, perhaps as a result of the first two factors, the number of years a young woman had lived in New York City positively correlated with her income. Rosenberg concluded that "the informal networks used so often by Puerto Rican women do successfully operate to place candidates in available nearby jobs" (p. 15). The work by Rosenthal, Darian, and Rosenberg shows how women's participation in the labor force, our indicator of sex role differentiation, and their occupational placement are affected by the contingencies of daily movement.

Variations in the constraints of space and time on women are systematically developed by Palm and Pred (1974); for example, "The married woman in a one-car household frequently finds herself in such a position because she willingly or unwillingly accepts the notion that her husband has the role of primary 'breadwinner' and is thereby entitled to a wider commuting range and greater freedom of movement, even if she has a much more tightly packed post-work activity schedule due to her housekeeping and childrearing roles" (p. 25).

It is no surprise, then, that the housewives Michelson (1973) studied were dissatisfied with the locational aspects of their neighborhood. Their husbands, in contrast, were quite satisfied. On the basis of their time-geographic perspective on temporary and spatial demands, Palm and Pred (1974) isolated two problems, availability of day care and access to transportation, which Coser (1975) utilized to construct a typology conceptualizing geographic displacement and social change for women.

Starting from the premise that geographic displacement threatens social stability, Coser (1975) maintained that women are restricted in their movement because the direction of any extension of their role set is not easily predictable. The restriction of women's geographic movement to the home, therefore, implies restriction on their upward social mobility. Public opposition to the establishment of child care centers represents one manifestation of this restriction. Yet "to remove this restriction from women would mean weakening their guardianship of the home. If women really had full equality of opportunity with men, the family as an institution, while probably not disappearing, would cease to be what it has been so far" (Coser, 1975, p. 477). While we may not entirely agree with Coser's conjecture, it is possible to see how the availability of child care would extend the role set of many women, although perhaps not always in predictable ways.

Space-specific translocal relationships, long-term or daily, epitomized by the family's search for a home and a woman's care for her children, have been analyzed in terms of family and sex roles, respectively; they reveal barriers to change rather than innovation or adjustment. A countersubculture has been discovered by Hunter in his 1975 replication of Foley's 1952 study of Rochester. The residents of one city neighborhood consciously selected the area for its middle class, racially integrated, and urban rather than suburban characteristics and attempted to create a community. Among the reasons residents gave for their decision was the neighborhood's proximity to their places of employment and education. The people of this neighborhood are "countering the home/work separation and commuting pattern of suburbia by reestablishing home/work proximity. Reduced reliance on the automobile and the capacity to 'walk to work' are seen as especially valuable by the increasing number of two-career families who live in the area" (Hunter, 1975, p. 456).

Conclusion

We have examined the changes in family and sex roles in urban society occurring within and among urban areas using Lofland's (1975) distinction between space-transcendence and space-specific localism or translocalism. In the belief that the institution of kinship in the United States tends to the centrifugal (Farber, 1975, 1976), we have focused on the conjugal family and alternative household compositions. The paucity of research on the male sex role led us to adopt women's employment as an indicator of sex role change, that is, a breakdown in the differentiation between women and men. The connection between these two issues has been provided by the question of role specialization in the conjugal family versus role interchangeability. Clearly, data are insufficient to document changes in family form and sex role differentiation taking place in urban environments. By presenting what data are available, this chapter can hopefully direct others into key areas.

After summarizing the current incidence of family forms in the United States and women's participation in the labor force as change—or stability—transcending space, we have en-

deavored to associate each with space-specific local and translocal relationships among cities and within them. Among cities
the indicators of at least hypothetical importance are population size and interurban migration. Within cities, the emphasis
has been on the city-suburban distinction and mobility, long-
term or daily. The ideas underlying our work involve the creation of a subculture in the interaction of a population and its
composition with its ecological context, and our analysis supports the viability of a subcultural rather than a strictly ecological or nonecological explanation.

It is our view that the conjugal family and role specialization within it constitute a subculture pervasive enough to incorporate the incipient breakdown of sex role differentiation (indicated by women's employment) and to prevent institutionalization of alternate family forms (the voluntarily childless couple,
the single parent, and the single individual). From our analysis,
how this subculture operates seems to depend at least partially
on the size of the metropolitan area as well as its occupational
structure. Large cities and occupations sex-typed for women inhibit the marriage of young women already residing in the area
and decrease their fertility (Preston and Richards, 1975). Migrant women are not affected by these variables; but after marriage has taken place, low fertility and the preschool age of children promote family migration (Long, 1970, 1972). Yet family
migration interrupts wives' participation in the labor force
(Long, 1974). The aggregate interurban effects, therefore, are
mixed. At the micro level, in comparison, the record is one of
role specialization in the conjugal family (Chapin, 1974; Duncan, Schuman, and Duncan, 1973). Within the metropolis, differences between the city and the suburb in family form and
women's employment persist, and the subjective interpretation
of the context of dwelling and its density helps to explain these
differences. It is intraurban mobility that provides the best picture of how the subculture of the role-specialized conjugal family is created through couples' search for housing and women's
care for children.

We cannot say whether the association between industrial
change and the separation of the individual from the family will
be experienced in the same way by women as it was by men.
With industrialization in the nineteenth century, a man was increasingly separated from his extended family. It is our working
hypothesis that women, with postindustrialization, will emerge
as individuals from the conjugal family. The process, however, is

a two-step one. It is through the experience of employment that women will come to have an occupation. Articulation with the family is yet to be effected, but several alternatives to the role specialization of the conjugal family seem likely. The meaning of the breakdown of sex role differentiation in the occupational sphere for greater inequality—not between men and women but among individuals and families or households—has yet to be understood.

7

Race, Ethnicity, and Community

Sidney Kronus

We are born into this world with the ascribed characteristics of
sex, family, religion, race, ethnicity, community, and sometimes
tribe. These characteristics exert powerful influences on our
lives, for they largely define who we are, where we are, whom
we interact with, and what we are—regardless of whether or not
we attempt to modify these characteristics. These characteristics are central to an individual's identity and are also of extreme importance in the identity or profile of a nation. In this
chapter I will address the question of how the primordial bonds
of race, ethnicity, and community have adapted to the rapid
process of urbanization in the United States. More specifically, I
will explore the impact of the urbanization of the black population and the suburbanization of industry and the white population on the racial and ethnic arrangements of community life
in America. People live in communities, black and white. We all

live and work in geographic areas with physical boundaries and certain facilities, areas that have emotional and symbolic meanings for us and areas where we have established a social network to some degree. What are the boundaries? What are the facilities? What symbolic meanings do they convey? What is the nature of the social networks, both in racial and ethnic terms, in urban and suburban America?

A Racial View

The black view of America shows historical patterns of white power and racism. It is a scene filled with violent confrontations between blacks and whites that will probably flare up again in the future as long as the social and economic differentials between the two groups remain high. Factors that continue to produce racial conflict include differential power, intergroup competition for scarce resources, and of course, racism.

Let us look first at the geographic distribution of the black population in the United States that has resulted from urbanization. In the nineteenth and early twentieth centuries, the rural South was the home of the large majority of blacks. Then masses of the black population poured out of the South and into the urban North and West. This period has drawn to a close. The black population, comprising 11 percent of our population, is today more metropolitan and urban than the white. In 1970 our metropolitan areas were home for over 70 percent of the black population compared with less than 65 percent of the white; the central cities of these areas were home for 55 percent of the nation's blacks and only 25 percent of the nation's whites (Taeuber, 1975). Yet does this mean that blacks and whites are living together in urban America? The answer is no.

Within the cities, four out of five of the households remain in segregated neighborhoods, and only 4 percent of the households are located in neighborhoods that are more than 10 percent black (Bradburn and others, 1971). With the exception of some decent neighborhoods recently abandoned by whites, the living conditions in segregated black areas of the central city are, for the most part, the worst in the city except for Skid Row, and a significant proportion of our metropolitan black population lives in the deplorable conditions of public housing projects (Moore, 1969; Rainwater, 1970). Also, the white flight to the suburbs has not been accompanied by a substantial black suburban migration (Schnore, André, and Sharp, 1976). Only about 5 percent of all suburbanites are black, and they live mostly in older areas typified not by large homes and spacious lots but by industry, old housing, and a large proportion of rental units. Between 1960 and 1970 the white suburban population increased by 15 million and the black by only 800 thousand, leading Taeuber (1975, p. 17) to conclude, "In the North the suburbs were in 1960 and remained in 1970 a white preserve" and that "patterns of residential segregation seem to be among the most tenacious of the many forms of racial segregation" (p. 14). Further, Berry and others (1976a, p. 262) concluded from their study of six varied community areas from the Chicago metropolitan area that "substantial residential integration by race is unlikely to emerge either in central city or suburb in years to come; segregation will continue to be a fundamental feature of the American scene as long as race remains a 'master status-determining trait.' " These patterns of residential segregation between central city and suburb and within central-city areas are not due solely to economic differences or lifestyle desires but rather to a restricted black housing market resulting from white racist practices, as we shall see.

Occupation. Differential power and black-white competition for scarce resources result from the relative imbalance in human resources—economic, social, and political—that exists between the two racial groups. We turn now to an analysis of the position of blacks in the United States with regard to their power base.

It has been some time since blacks were mostly found in the agricultural sector of our society. Both world wars, with their attendant urban migration and extensive civil rights and affirmative action legislation, have allowed blacks to accumulate more resources than they ever had in the past, although many discriminatory practices, both individual and institutional, continue to exist. The proof of their existence is the bleak portrait of low occupational status coupled with severe income disadvantages, high rates of unemployment, and the degrading specter of welfare dependency. One of the few glimmers of hope is found in the advancing educational attainment of blacks and their increasing political power, reflected by a rapid increase in elected black officials. Let us look more closely at these factors, detailed by the U.S. Bureau of the Census (1972).

In 1971, only 13 percent of employed blacks held professional, managerial, and technical positions compared with over one quarter of all employed whites (27 percent). In the field of law, for example, where it is extremely important for black people to have strong representation to protect their rights and further their interests, only 3,000, or 1 percent of the over 300,000 lawyers in the United States, are black. Whites outnumber blacks by more than two to one as managers and administrators and in sales work. Thus whites have a distinct advantage in holding desirable, well-paying positions in our society. Looking at the less desirable, low-paying positions, we find that black people hold a two-to-one advantage in private household, farm, and laboring jobs (over 40 percent black compared with 20 percent white). Thus, although the urbanization of the United States has liberated the black man and woman from the drudgery and toil of field labor in the rural South, it has not yet lifted them very far up the ladder of mobility in our cities. Census income data clearly reflect the occupational structure. The median income for black families is still less than two thirds that of whites: For blacks it is slightly less than $6,500 and for whites it is slightly over $10,500. Detailed analysis shows that a black worker is paid about $1,200 less for doing the same job as a white. The effects of affirmative action are not yet evident.

Employment. More bleak than occupation or income is unemployment. In his penetrating study of lower-class black life in the metropolis, Liebow (1967) rightly pointed out the ability to support one's self and family as the key feature in determining the relative success of the black man's life in the city. With the exception of the period during World War II, the unemployment rate for blacks has been about twice as high as that for whites, a pattern that continues into the 1970s. One out of ten blacks was jobless in 1971 compared with one out of twenty for whites. In addition, the jobless rate for black Vietnam veterans was over 15 percent, and fully one third of all black teenagers were unemployed, figures that again were almost twice those for whites. These persisting high rates of black unemployment determine the degree to which blacks must exist below poverty levels and the degree to which they will be forced to join the welfare rolls.

Poverty and Welfare. Of the over 25 million persons below the poverty level in 1970, approximately 8 million were black and 16 million white, but in terms of their respective populations, fully one third of the black population was living below the poverty line compared with one tenth of the white. In terms of welfare, half of all recipients were white and over 40

percent were black. These figures seem very high for blacks and
for an understandable reason. The mass migration of blacks
from the rural South transferred their poverty to the metropolis. As Piven and Cloward (1971) pointed out, blacks did not
appear in significant proportions on the Aid to Dependent Children rolls until 1948. The majority of blacks who migrated to
the metropolitan areas of the North brought with them the
legacy of the South. They were poorly educated, had few
marketable skills, often were in poor health, and had entered an
urban market where discrimination existed. It is little wonder
then that they were in a very poor position to compete successfully in the labor market, and as a consequence they ended up
on the welfare rolls. This lack of success can be seen to be the
root cause of what is either considered as the deterioration of
the black family (Frazier, 1939; Moynihan, 1965) or as urban
adaptation (Billingsley, 1968; Hill, 1972). Regardless of termi-
nology, a large proportion of urban blacks lived with desertion,
separation, divorce, illegitimacy, and delinquency. Nonmarital
sexual relations were casual, and there was a large proportion of
female-headed households. Whether one views the black family
situation as a "tangle of pathologies" or as an adapted differentiated role strength, the causes are to be found in the great
structural inequities between whites and blacks brought about
by racism and the consequent lack of resources of the black
urban immigrant. Now that this migration has ended and hopefully the legacy of the rural South has diminished, we can look
at some of the more positive effects of the urbanization of the
black population.

   Education. Perhaps the most notable gain of black people
during their transformation from rural to urban dwellers has
been the rise in their educational attainment. This is extremely
important because our labor market is ever increasing its emphasis on higher education and technical skills. Although the issues
in public education—desegregation, busing, and community
versus centralized control—have been and still are severe problems in urban America, black penetration into higher education
within the last few years has been truly impressive. Aided by
legal and financial efforts, both public (mainly federal) and private, the percentage of blacks between the ages of eighteen and
twenty-four enrolled in colleges jumped dramatically from 10
percent in 1965 to 18 percent in 1971 (U.S. Bureau of the
Census, 1972). During a six-year period, black college enrollment almost doubled, while during the same period white

enrollment increased only 1 percent (from 26 percent to 27 percent). The debate remains over the value of black colleges versus white colleges—black institutions being interested in the students and providing a congenial atmosphere versus the white institutions providing a quality education and the best facilities. Nevertheless, in recent years the pattern of enrollment has shifted in favor of white institutions. In 1960 more than half of all black students attended black colleges; ten years later the proportion was reduced to one third, and it is still decreasing rapidly. Thus, for increasing proportions of blacks, doubts about the quality of their education will no longer be a handicap when they seek employment. In the highest realm of higher education, however, the picture for blacks is not so improved. At a time when it is increasingly important to have a postgraduate degree, black graduate school enrollment is exceedingly low —less than 2 percent of all graduate students. In a country where there are less than 2,000 black Ph.D.s, blacks earned less than 1 percent of the doctorates granted in 1970. This is doubly sad, because at the present time a black with an advanced degree is the most desirable person in the market because of affirmative action pressures on government and business as well as academia.

Change in Class Structure. Despite the problems encountered by the majority of the black population that migrated to our cities, there has been an increase in the number of blacks entering the middle class. It is estimated that from the early 1950s to the late 1960s the black middle class increased from about 5 percent to 25 percent of the black population (Kronus, 1971; Pettigrew, 1971).

Most blacks reside in predominantly black neighborhoods; some do live in white neighborhoods but they usually have college educations, white collar positions, a comfortable life-style, and a stable family and social life. Some can even be called elites—not just entertainment and sports figures and a few successful entrepreneurs, but executives, administrators, educators, and officials who in terms of income, education, position, and daily interaction with the white community are integrated into the mainstream of American life. As I have stated elsewhere (Kronus, 1971, p. 136), "This movement may be considered by some as 'tokenism,' but if it is, it is a degree of tokenism never before witnessed, even during Reconstruction." The impact of urbanization on blacks in the United States has left its mark in the black ghettos of inner cities, but we must not

forget that by 1970 fully one fourth of all black families in the
United States earned $15,000 or more annually.

Business. One of the major reasons why blacks have not
done better economically is the failure of black entrepreneurship to develop jobs and training that would favor the black
man in his new urban environment. As of 1969, there were only
163,000 black-owned firms in the United States, a mere 2.2 percent of all firms. Even more dismaying is the fact that the gross
receipts of all black-owned enterprises accounted for only three
tenths of 1 percent, or less than half of 1 percent of the total: a
mere $4.5 billion out of $1.5 trillion (U.S. Bureau of the Census, 1972).

There are several reasons why there are so few black businesses. First, black businesses tend to be self-owned, small
businesses that employ at most a few individuals. Four out of
five black businesses do not have any paid employees, and in
nine out of ten a black is the sole proprietor. The ratio of paid
employees to the number of black businesses is less than one
per establishment, which indicates few job opportunities and a
high probability that if there are any employees at all, they are
unpaid family members. This is a picture of beginning businesses: the mom-and-pop operation where only two people
working long hours can eke out an existence for a family. Also,
despite the northern urban migration, over half of these businesses are located in the South.

Second, black businesses are small and relatively unprofit-
able because due to institutionalized segregation in both the
North and South, they cater almost exclusively to the black
community, where the main need has been for personal services.
Thus blacks started small retail establishments—restaurants,
food stores, clothing and cleaning establishments, and service
enterprises such as barber shops, beauty salons, cosmetic stores,
and funeral homes. Due to a lack of capital because the white
financial structure was unwilling to make loans, blacks have not
been able to develop large-scale production and manufacturing
enterprises. Thus, whites control the employment opportunities
for blacks in the city and dominate its economic life.

In addition to white control of employment opportunities in the city and its attendant racial discrimination, we now
have the white flight to the suburbs, where many employment
opportunities are located. In a recent study of six metropolitan
areas (Baltimore, Buffalo, Chicago, Detroit, Philadelphia, and
Pittsburgh), Christian (1975, pp. 244-245) concluded:

(1) Central cities are rapidly losing their preeminence as the place of location of industrial firms and production workers.

(2) Firms and employment opportunities lost from the central city are primarily those which are relocating to dispersed suburban locations.

(3) Although central cities have historically lost manufacturing firms and employment opportunities, the critical nature of recent losses is related to the continuing immigration of black and nonwhite populations seeking those job opportunities which are most rapidly relocating to suburban locations.

(4) Job relocations to dispersed suburban municipalities appear to produce insurmountable barriers as black and nonwhite central city residents are not relocating in large numbers to suburban locations to avail themselves of these relocated job opportunities.

(5) The majority of job opportunities relocating from the central city to suburban locations is increasingly being found farther and farther from the residences of black and nonwhite central city populations.

Christian went on to note that it was precisely in these black and nonwhite areas of the central city where people have the lowest rate of automobile ownership and difficult, expensive access to public transportation. Further analysis of these patterns is provided in Kasarda's Chapter Two of this volume.

In addition to the loss of industrial firms, there is also a loss of locally owned and operated small businesses as the ecological succession finds blacks moving into previously white residential areas of the city. Aldrich and Reiss (1976), in a study of small businesses in areas where racial succession has occurred in Boston, Chicago, and Washington, D.C., found that the number of businesses decreased as whites left because new white businessmen did not enter these areas of business and because not enough blacks had both the capital requirements and business experience to take over the businesses. This left the new black community in the area with a net loss of jobs and increased the cost of the goods and services no longer provided locally. Thus, despite the efforts of the Small Business Administration and other federal agencies, the failure of black capitalism in urban America is a fact of life.

Politics. Historically, black voter registration and voting behavior have left a great deal to be desired. But recent federal legislative changes that outlawed methods to keep blacks from voting in the South (grandfather clauses, white primaries, poll taxes, literacy tests, gerrymandered districts, and the use of physical restraint) and massive voter registration drives have succeeded in bringing blacks both in the North and South to the polls, where their influence has been felt. Blackwell (1975) noted that the black vote was instrumental in the elections of Roosevelt (in 1940), Truman, and Kennedy. He also noted that black voter registration in the South doubled from 1952 to 1964 and, following the Civil Rights Act of 1965, tripled by 1966. By 1968, fully two thirds of all blacks of voting age were registered to vote in the United States. Blackwell (1975, pp. 210-211) went on to document the rapid rise in the number of black elected officials from 1,185 in 1969 to 2,621 in 1974, a 121 percent increase:

> On the national level, for example, one black senator was elected in 1966 but largely from a white constituency in Massachusetts. However the number of blacks elected to the House of Representatives more than tripled between 1964 and 1973, rising from 5 to 16, including four black women. By 1974, there were more than 200 blacks in the state legislatures of the country, two lieutenant governors (Colorado and California), approximately 110 mayors and almost 3,000 other elected officials including, among others, vice-mayors, county officials, law enforcement officers, judges, and school superintendents. Blacks had indeed moved toward a politics of governance involving control over the decision-making apparatus in selected communities, though to a lesser degree at the national level.

Despite these gains, the political ascension of blacks is still in its infancy. Machine politics still survive in Chicago, where political patronage at low-level positions for blacks still controls the vote. The support for "backlash" candidates who take strong anticrime positions, like Mayor Rizzo of Philadelphia, has yet to be overcome. Also, because of the recency of black succession to political offices in such cities as Atlanta, Cleveland, Detroit, and Newark, it is premature to assess whether blacks can deal successfully with the physical blight of housing in our cities or the social blight of crime and drugs in the streets. Not only are blacks disadvantaged by not having political experience, but city governments (New York being a prime example) are caught in a web of poverty, unemployment, loss of tax base, and increasing costs for social services, public transportation, and housing. Also, the patronage that was available to elected officials in the past has been greatly reduced by the civil service system and federal controls over expenditures. How blacks can translate their political victories into increased benefits for the black community under such adverse conditions remains to be seen. Surely their task is more difficult than it was for the ethnic forces that gained political power before them.

Riots and Civil Disorders. A prominent feature of urban America, even before the massive urbanization of blacks, has been the race riot. Violence is a danger signal. Interpersonal and social violence has many implications. It may be used to arouse the public conscience or to dramatize deprivations and unrealized goals. It can also be a simple means for reducing individual social tensions. Combined with the death of Martin Luther King, Jr., and the development of the black power movement by Stokely Carmichael, Eldridge Cleaver, and H. Rap Brown, collective racial violence can be seen as an instrument for changing the black's position in the social structure.

The major question to be answered is what blacks have gained by the use of violence. Greenstone and Peterson (1973) indicated that the economic and political gains that could be attributed to the rioting of the 1960s were very limited, but they do agree that the rioting may have provided political leverage for black demands.

However, the magnitude of the changes necessary in public education, housing, and income to equalize the black position is immense. It is also clear that blacks are fed up with the rhetoric of opportunity and promises; they want results. It follows, then, that even with the measures that have been designed to prevent and curtail future outbreaks of urban violence, as long as the large differential exists between blacks and whites in the United States, some alternative to peaceful and legal means will yet issue from our cities. This alternative can only be more violence. Hopefully, our cities will receive the social and economic aid necessary to avert such recurrences, but this will occur only if the federal and state governments make a firm decision that our cities are worth saving.

Conclusions. Race is as culturally, economically, and politically salient in our urbanized society as it was when blacks lived in the rural South. It existed as a powerful bond among people during the times of a simple agrarian economy, and it persists today in our complex urban society, partly as a response to discrimination but also as a basic sentiment about who a person is. For some blacks, it is a very positive voluntaristic sentiment rooted in black pride, heritage, and accomplishment under the most severe of circumstances. For other blacks, it is a negative feeling that reflects the oppression felt at the hands of a white-dominated society. Blackwell (1975) noted that discrimination toward blacks up to the middle of this century was based on racist institutional norms that propounded the biological inferiority of blacks. He then argued that racists now cite black cultural inferiority, due to deficiencies in cultural and social background, as an alibi for educational neglect and as an explanation for the failures of blacks to rise in the social structure.

The forces of urbanization have not diminished the importance of race as a primordial sentiment; if anything, urbanization has aided in preserving and making more positive the bond. Before urbanization, most blacks were illiterate, landless, and destitute, living on isolated farms in the South. Today, most blacks are above the poverty level, few are left in agriculture, and educational levels are rising as is political power. The black power movement and the proliferation of black organizations, some militant and some moderate, have developed a greater sense of unity and a more positive image of black identity. The divisions between the middle class and the masses struggling in our urban ghettos are severe, but the common bond remains. With education and particularly civic participation increasing, more and more blacks will be making decisions that directly affect their struggle for structural parity. This may not take place for some time, but if and when it does, race will still remain a primary bond in the social affairs of our country.

An Ethnic View

Herberg (1955) concluded that ethnic identification in American life was declining, being absorbed by the three major religious identities of Protestantism, Catholicism, and Judaism. Yet not two decades later, Glazer and Moynihan (1970, p. ix), commenting on New York City, stated, "Religion as a major line of division in the city is for the moment in eclipse. Ethnicity and race dominate the city." In another statement they suggested, "It seems clear that ethnic identity has become more salient, ethnic self-assertion stronger, ethnic conflict more marked in the last twenty years" (Glazer and Moynihan, 1970, p. 39). These statements raise a very important question: Now that massive European immigration to the United States is over and many persons are second-, third-, or even fourth-generation Americans, what is the effect of ethnic identity today on our urban and suburban society?

A Definition of Ethnicity. Ethnicity is conceptually extremely complex. According to Williams (1975, p. 125), "In the cultural system, ethnicity may involve language, religious beliefs and practices, institutional norms and values, expressive styles, food preferences, and so on. Ethnic collectivities vary in size, interconnectedness, definiteness and strength of boundaries, degree of social closure, centralization, stratification, control of resources, relationships with allies and enemies, internal interdependence, degree and kind of social control of members." People do not choose to belong to an ethnic category; they are born into it. The maintenance of ethnic identity is, however, highly voluntaristic. Whether a person's sentiments are positive or negative, he relates to his ethnic identity through symbolic and emotional ties. Because of this relationship to the culture of one's ancestors, the individual must decide whether to retain all or selected aspects of his ethnic heritage in the face of competing demands by the larger society. Childhood socialization within the home and the school often places great stress and inner conflict on the individual. Yet, ethnicity is a sense of peoplehood based on shared and observable traits: physical characteristics, cultural patterns, historical experiences, religious convictions, and even language. Shils (1957) called these "primordial ties" and Geertz (1963) saw these ties as "of some unaccountable absolute import."

Ethnic Groupings in the United States. Ethnic locational patterns in the United States are not the result of a random process but are based on the immigrant group's time of arrival, route of travel, and ethnic cohesion. Port of entry and proximity to homeland account for the concentrations of French-Canadians in the Northeast, Mexicans and Chinese in the West and Southwest, Puerto Ricans in New York, and Cubans in Florida. Although ethnic concentration can be partly explained by the desire of people to live with their own kind, it is primarily related to how different the immigrant groups were from prevailing American society. If their physical characteristics, language, culture, and religion differ greatly from the dominant white Anglo-Saxon Protestant norms and they want to preserve these traits, then they must live together in order to maintain the institutions that will preserve their way of life. Once the initial concentrations have been established, there is a strong tendency for the pattern to be adhered to by subsequent migrants and thus to persist.

Hutchinson (1956), using both 1920 and 1950 census data, showed the persistence of ethnic concentrations through the second generation. It is interesting to note the correspondence of his findings with more recent research with regard to industrial employment. Hutchinson noted the concentration of Czechoslovakian and Yugoslavian immigrants in heavy metal industries in Pennsylvania, Ohio, and Illinois. In a recent monograph, Kornblum (1974) described the internal dynamics of the steel community of South Chicago, where Serbo-Croatian life still exists and is centered around community and industry. It is clear that the Serbs and the Croatians want to preserve their ways of life, but it is also very important to note the impact of their occupations and union participation on this process. Within the steel plants, getting and keeping a job are largely matters of family contacts, getting along well with other workers, and seniority; the ethnic dimension is of primary importance.

Further evidence of the preservation of ethnic identity is provided by Kantrowitz (1969) in his study of New York City. He found levels of ethnic segregation in the second generation that were as high as those found among racial groups. His study showed that over 50 percent of all people of southern European origin would have to be moved to areas inhabited by persons of northern European origin to achieve ethnic integration. Further, among two Scandinavian Protestant groups, the Norwegians and the Swedes, the segregation index is high; each group has its own newspapers, and although they partially intermarry, they are not highly integrated with each other. Gans (1968) estimated that two thirds to three quarters of the population of urban areas maintain contact with immediate and extended ethnic neighborhoods. In a recent survey (U.S. Bureau of the Census, 1969), 75 million Americans defined themselves as belonging to one of seven ethnic groups, and research on suburbs (Berger, 1960; Gans, 1962b, 1967) indicates the persistence of ethnicity and ethnic concentration in city and suburb.

Ethnic Allegiances. In their original study of ethnic groups in New York City, Glazer and Moynihan (1970) con-

cluded that the Germans had disappeared as a segregated, clearly discernible ethnic group and had become assimilated. This
was not true of Germans in other cities, such as Chicago. In the
introduction to the same study, they also talked of evidence of
the resurgence of ethnicity. How can ethnic groups disappear in
some places and not others, and how can there be a resurgence?

Ethnicity served a very positive function for the immigrants who came to America. The environment was foreign, hostile, and alienating to people who could not speak our language
or understand our institutions and culture. The preservation of
the ways of their national origins to make a comfortable atmosphere lessened the shock of complete change and overt personal alienation.

The role played by religion to preserve these bonds is best
described by Stout (1975, pp. 208-209), "At the center of the
ethnic group was the church, which supplied the cohesion and
insularity necessary for retaining a distinct ethnic community. . . . Group consciousness and activity flowed from the
church, which did not exist primarily to spread evangelical
Christianity to the World, but rather, to *preserve the ethnic solidarity of the group.*" This ethnic solidarity provided the basis
for identity and meaning for individuals within the group. As
ethnic groups learned the ways of America and as second and
third generations came into ever greater contact with our norms
and institutions, the possible choices multiplied. Second and
third generations could choose to keep their ethnic loyalties
and sympathies, to combine them with American sentiments, or
to reject them totally. These possibilities are linked internally to
socialization but are also linked externally to opportunities. Persons may choose not to be identified with the group of their
origin, but as long as others make that identification, individuals
can be constrained by them. In this sense ethnicity, unlike race
(where identification by physical traits is unavoidable), has both
a voluntary and involuntary aspect to it.

Arguments for the Decline of Ethnicity. There is no
doubt that ethnic identity has declined for second-, third-, and
fourth-generation Americans. The days of mass in-migration of
white populations are over, and many indicators reveal a decline
in ethnic identification. Perhaps the strongest indicator of cultural value retention (ethnicity) is language. Persons who retain
their native tongues and dialects can experience and communi-
cate the symbolic meanings of their socially constructed world
in their own unique manner. Dinnerstein and Reimers (1975, p.

143) summarized the rapid decline of foreign-language use as measured by the decline of foreign-language newspapers:

> Institutions depending upon foreign languages began to disappear as the immigrants' descendents could not use them. The German-language press was thriving at the eve of World War I and was the most important of the foreign-language presses; it accounted for about 40 percent of the circulation of the foreign-language press. The war shattered the German-American press and hurt the standing of the German language generally; it was driven off the news-stands and out of the schools. In 1910 there were 70 German dailies in America; in 1960 only 6 remained. Other major foreign-language newspapers also declined, especially the Yiddish, Italian, and Scandinavian ones. Italian dailies decreased in number from 12 earlier in the century to 5 in 1960; French dailies decreased in number from 9 to 1 during the same period. From a high of 142 dailies in 1910 the foreign-language press has less than half that number today, and the number and circulation of weeklies has dropped about 75 percent in the same time.

They went on to note that the only foreign-language press that has not declined rapidly is the press of the newest groups to arrive, that is, Spanish papers, which serve the Mexican, Puerto Rican, and Cuban-American populations.

Closely tied to the decline of foreign-language usage has been the decline of ethnic organizations, especially churches. As foreign languages were eliminated from church services, nationality parishes and denominations with strong nationality bonds disappeared. Along with the loss of ethnic identity in the church, the same process took place in other organizations, such as social clubs, benefit societies, and welfare organizations. The combination of the process of ecological succession that broke up homogeneous ethnic neighborhoods and the rise of governmental welfare programs destroyed the ethnic cohesion provided by these organizations (Dinnerstein and Reimers, 1975). Private ethnoreligious schools also declined but in recent years have made a resurgence.

Since the family is the primary unit of social life in any society, endogamous ethnic marriages signal the retention of ethnic identity and exogamous ethnic intermarriages indicate the ultimate form of ethnic assimilation (Gordon, 1964). For the immigrants, marriage outside the ethnic group was uncommon, but succeeding generations with their increased social contacts have eroded that pattern. Kennedy (1952) found that in New Haven, Connecticut, ethnic intermarriage increased greatly between 1860 and 1950 but within religious lines. Thus, Irish, Italians, and Poles intermarried but within Catholicism; Americans of English ancestry, Germans, and Scandinavians intermarried but within Protestantism; and she found a very low rate of intermarriage among Jews. This led to the conclusion that a "triple melting pot" was taking place in America, where ethnicity as a marriage boundary was rapidly declining but religion persisted. Similar results for ethnic intermarriage between Italians and Poles in Buffalo between 1930 and 1960 are provided by Bugelski (1961). In 1930 three out of four marriages for these two groups were intraethnic, and by 1960, approximately three out of four were interethnic, indicating a rapid decline of ethnic cohesion. Studies on Mexican-Americans in Los Angeles (Mittlebach and Moore, 1968) and Puerto Ricans in New York (Fitzpatrick, 1966) showed the same pattern. More recent data indicate that even religious boundaries are breaking down, as an ever increasing proportion of Jews marry out of their faith (Goldstein and Goldscheider, 1968; Dinnerstein and Reimers, 1975).

The proponents of the demise of ethnicity cite that the causes of this decline can be traced directly to the industrialization and urbanization of America. Public schools, which were needed to educate an industrial labor force, provided different values and contact with other groups. In the 1970s, with over half the college-age population in institutions of higher learning, it is not surprising that ethnic culture breaks down. The mass media, which bring the dominant American cultural values into all homes, as well as the ease of transportation, which allows coast-to-coast travel in a few hours, tend to homogenize our people. Upward social mobility, with its demands for a corporate or professional image, does not reward or even condone the retention of ethnic identity. Finally, the flight to suburbia, which a large proportion of our previously urban ethnic populations has followed, is accompanied more by class and racial issues than ethnic ones (Whyte, 1956; Winter, 1961; Dobriner, 1963; Sklare and Greenblum, 1967).

Persistence of Ethnicity in America. Nevertheless, ethnicity is still a factor in American society today. In a few areas of our nation it persists almost in its original form; in others it has attenuated but will still have implications for some time to come. We must not forget that it was the processes of industrial-ization and urbanization that brought immigrants to our shores and provided our nation with its powerful ethnic dimension in the beginning, and it is these same processes that now weaken the ethnic dimension in our society. The impulses for the pri-mordial bonds and the personal needs for survival, protection, comfort, and hope for the future are still as essential for the people of today as in the past. For some, whose ecological, occupational, and educational locations in the structure of American society are much the same as their parents' and grand-parents', the ethnic factor is extremely pervasive. Others who have moved to better sections of our cities or suburbs and have climbed up the social ladder through educational and occupa-tional achievement still retain elements of their cultural heri-tage. For them, ethnicity is a meaningful but minor departure from the values and life-style of the American dream. Finally, there are those for whom the poverty, ignorance, parochialism, and rigidity of existence within the ethnic community provided the impetus to leave by means of geographical mobility, social mobility, or both, and who now submerge their ethnic back-ground in the sea of Americans who have no ethnic identity other than that of American. These are people who have changed their names, speak without accents, subscribe to ecu-menical beliefs, and desire only the good-paying positions and beautiful homes that American society can provide for them and their children. They are people who when asked where they are from give their American birthplace rather than their nation-ality. Thus, when we speak of ethnicity in America today we are speaking about two groups of people: those who retain their culture as much as possible and those who retain only selected elements of the culture but still identify with the ethnic group.

There are two primary sources of ethnic retention and even resurgence in the 1970s. The first is the relative lack of residential and social mobility experienced by a substantial pro-portion of urban ethnic groups. The second is the rise of white ethnic consciousness in response to the actions and demands put forth by blacks during the 1960s, when black ethnic con-sciousness asserted itself more forcefully than it ever had before and was closely followed by a similar movement among Indians and Mexican-Americans.

Earlier we noted the relatively high degree of residential

segregation that exists in urban America. Glazer and Moynihan (1970, p. lvi) provided information on the relative lack of occupational mobility of white ethnic groups in New York City compared with that of blacks:

> One key fact that is often ignored is that most members of the white ethnic groups are *not* successful. . . . We do not know just how ethnic groups are distributed by income and occupation, since the census gives us little assistance and is, in any case, badly out of date. But a sample survey of New York adults taken in 1963 offers some ground for thought on this issue. Thus, if we consider professional employment alone, 9.5 percent of Negroes were so engaged, compared to 3 percent of Puerto Ricans, 5 percent of Italians (first and second generation), 9 percent of Irish (first and second generation), 11 percent of other Catholics (including third and higher generations of Italian and Irish), 10.5 percent of foreign-born Jews, 21.5 percent of native-born Jews and 22 percent of white Protestants. From the point of view of the Puerto Rican, using this measure alone, the Negro is doing quite well; from the point of view of the Italians, Negroes include a large number of professionals.

To a great extent, the lack of occupational mobility experienced by white ethnic groups in New York City and their inability to obtain professional and managerial positions are due to their lack of higher education. A 1960 study of native-born males, ages twenty-five to thirty-four, in New York City (Rosenwaike, 1973) showed that one quarter of native whites of native parentage had completed college and one third of the Jewish population with eastern European parents had completed college; in constrast, the figure for males of British, German, and Irish ancestry was one in five. For Italians and Puerto Ricans, the figure was less than 10 percent. It is not surprising, then, that occupational achievement is very low for these groups, and although there is no available data, it would not be hazardous to speculate that their income levels remain at very low levels as well.

Although the evidence is not comprehensive (Gans, 1962; Suttles, 1968; Kantrowitz, 1969; Glazer and Moynihan, 1970; Rosenwaike, 1973; Kornblum, 1974), we can assert that there is a continuing tendency for ethnic groups to occupy ecological locales in our cities and particular industrial and occupational niches in American society as a result of desire, habit, and the effects of discrimination and blocked opportunities. Throughout urban America we find pockets of Irish, Poles, Italians, and Asian-Americans, as well as the late-arriving Puerto Ricans, concentrated in ethnic communities undergoing ecological succession in varying degrees under conditions that Suttles (1968) termed "ordered segmentation." They choose to live in ghetto and nonghetto areas and have not made the transition to suburban, upper-middle class status. Their situation in life and their problems are accurately portrayed by Glazer and Moynihan (1970, p. xxvi):

> Whether we say "blue-collar" or "lower middle-class" or "homeowner" in New York City, or whether we say "Italian" or "Irish" is not unimportant, and yet we know we are talking about roughly the same people. So the mass media discourse about the "white ethnic groups" or the "white working- and lower-middle class" —the people are the same, and the issues are the same: their feelings that they have been ignored, have received little from government in recent years, and have born the brunt of costs involved in the economic and political rise of the Negroes.

In their final sentence, Glazer and Moynihan touched on the second major factor that has renewed ethnic identity in urban America—"the rise of the Negroes." During the 1960s, blacks and other racial groups experienced a rise in collective ethnic consciousness and made heavy demands on American society. They pressed for desegregated education, access to higher education, federal assistance for housing, welfare programs, job opportunities, and in general an affirmative action program that would increase their participation and advantage in all areas. These programs threatened the way of life of white, lower-middle class and blue collar ethnics in our cities. Neighborhood schools were broken up by redistricting and busing became a major issue. Higher educational institutions modified entrance requirements, developed black and Latino ethnic studies programs, and actively recruited racial minority students that white ethnics saw as diminishing their own children's chances at higher education. Racial minority members were given preferential treatment in hiring practices, and urban welfare rolls swelled. Militant blacks achieved prominence in the mass media, and white ethnic urban dwellers saw the black political and economic gains under these new, artificial standards as a real threat to their rights, opportunities, and lifestyles. Further, they felt that they were paying for these gains with their own tax dollars. As Dinnerstein and Reimers (1975, p. 216) stated, "Despite more than a decade of prosperity, these middle Americans lack economic affluence: they are still very close to layoff, strikes, plant reductions, tax squeezes, inflation, and now reverse discrimination."

To combat these threats, whites have rallied around the bond of ethnicity. Taking their cue from the blacks, they have started thinking about their own ethnicity, supported white ethnic organizations, and revived their heritage around slogans of "Irish Power," "Italian Power," and "Polish Power." This is not a return to ethnicity for its own sake but rather as a means to an end. If it is legitimate for blacks and other racial groups to press for their own interests—and with some success—then it is a legitimate means for whites as well.

In the realm of power and conflict, ethnicity has always been a factor. Politics in the United States, especially city politics, has always had to deal with ethnicity (Glazer and Moynihan, 1970; Dinnerstein and Reimers, 1975; Ornstein, 1974; Rossides, 1976). Slate making to provide representation for white ethnic groups has been and still is a fact of life. Parties must contend with the "Irish vote," "Polish vote," "Jewish vote," and so on. In New York City, to have an Irish, Italian, or Jewish name is an asset, as it is to have a Polish one in Buffalo, German in Milwaukee, or Hispanic in cities of the Southwest. Key appointments are made at all political levels with an eye to their ethnic effect. The ethnic dimension in politics has been heightened by recent pressure tactics to the point of polarization. Black candidates and liberal white candidates run on platforms of welfare and redistribution; the ethnics, such as Rizzo in Philadelphia, Stenvig in Minneapolis, and, until recently, Yorty in Los Angeles and "King Richard" Daley in Chicago, take anticrime, antibusing, and antiquota positions and favor limited taxation and domestic spending—all of which can be seen as being antiblack.

There are also other reasons for the preservation of ethnic identities. First, international events have had great import for ethnic migrants to the United States, although this factor has declined for all but a few groups. For the newcomers who live close to their native lands, such events still have significance and serve to maintain ethnic identity. French-Canadians in New England, Mexican-Americans in the Southwest, Cubans in the South, and Puerto Ricans still follow developments in their homelands. The only other group in our society whose ethnic identity is deeply influenced by events abroad are the Jews. Beyond the lavish financial and moral support given the state of Israel, there is a continued commitment and concern for its existence. This continual concern heightens the awareness of American Jews to their ancestry (Dinnerstein and Reimers, 1975, p. 156).

Second, Glazer and Moynihan (1970) point to the revolution in the Catholic church as a factor in heightening ethnic attachments. They argue that the liberalization that has taken place in this once very conservative institution has forced many Catholics of eastern and southern European heritage to rally around ethnicity to put forth their feelings toward integration and other black-white issues. Glazer and Moynihan (1970, p. xxv) also pointed out what may be a significant change in the perception of personal identity, with class and occupational status being supplanted by ethnicity: "Today it may be better to be an Italian than a worker. Twenty years ago, it was the other way around."

Third, ethnicity is fed by the efforts of intellectuals and writers to preserve and glorify the images of various cultural histories. Sklare (1974) focused on the preeminence of this mechanism among the Jews, but it serves other groups as well. Then, there is the effect of Hansen's Law (Hansen, 1937), which stipulates that the efforts of the second generation to cast off their ethnic background is followed by the efforts of the third generation to find out who they are and where they came from: "What the grandfather came with, the son tries to forget and the grandson tries to remember." What overall impact this has on our society is not known, but the proliferation of language and culture courses other than Spanish, French, and German and the multitude of ethnic history courses in modern universities serves the needs of a sizable number of students.

The role of private schools in preserving cultural heritage has always been great for Jews and Asian-Americans. Hebrew schools and Japanese-language and Chinese-language schools have always been a part of the American city. Catholic schools have always been important in maintaining ethnicity, especially for the Irish, and in the 1960s integration, busing, and loss of community control over neighborhood schools forced an upsurge in parochial school enrollments. In the public realm, the recent Supreme Court ruling in *Lau* v. *Nichols*, which requires public schools to teach children in a language that they understand, will certainly preserve the ethnic identity of Spanish-speaking Americans for a longer time than if the decision had been reversed. What effect bilingual education will have on the mobility chances of Spanish-speaking Americans has yet to be seen. The 1972 establishment by Congress of a National Advisory Council on Ethnic Heritage Studies and an Ethnic Heritage Program will also preserve the ethnic dimension for future generations if enough funds are allocated.

To conclude, mass education, social mobility, and American culture have eroded the saliency of ethnicity in American life and are continuing to do so today. Yet ethnicity still persists and is heavily retained in many urban residential and industrial niches in our society. In part ethnicity serves as a vehicle for collective action and social protest against the demands of the black community. Given the intensity of the conflict in our urban centers, the efficacy of ethnicity as an organizing principle that serves to focus power and mask racism, and the lack of peaceful alternatives available to whites who cannot flee to the suburbs, it is likely that ethnicity will continue to be important. The political dimension will also keep it important, as will the desire of many individuals to retain aspects of their cultural heritage.

Effect of Urbanization on Community Life

Definition of Community. Communities are composed of three main elements: common ties (including race and ethnicity), social interaction, and spatial location or locale (Suttles, 1972; Hunter, 1974). The community can be seen as a territorial basis for associational selection as well as an identity that distinguishes it from other territorial and nonterritorial populations. In most cases, it is also an object of administration. All of us live in some type of community, even though the range is great. Bernard (1973, p. 187) summed up the importance of community to the individual:

> At the local community level there is confrontation, visual if not tactile, emotional if not intellectual.

People still live next door to others, they eat, sleep, love, hate, avoid, or seek one another in a given locale. Whether or not they have much to do with their neighbors, they use the same grocery store or supermarket, attend the same movie houses, and patronize the same beauty parlors or barber shops. Owners or renters, they depend on the same community services such as, humble as they may be, garbage collection, street cleaning, and police protection. However, emancipated from spatial barriers and however independent of locale the elite may be, it is still on the community scene that for most human beings interaction takes place.

As Bernard indicates, most individuals do interact within a community setting, but the forces of urbanization have radically changed the nature of that interaction.

Earlier Urban Communities. In order to explore the changes that have taken place, especially with respect to race and ethnicity, we will look first at the factors and processes that shaped our earlier forms of urban community life.

The balkanization of America was nowhere more visible than in the cities of our country, where segregation by ethnicity, race, and class, aided by the designs of those who controlled the real estate market, produced a mosaic of distinct residential enclaves. Industry demanded a large blue collar labor force that was filled by masses of immigrants.

Primary groups played a central role in forming the social structure and moral order of urban neighborhoods. Families, adult peer groups, and adolescent gangs formed within spatial boundaries that included religious, ethnic, occupational, and class homogeneity to define a basic unit of social organization. Within these units were the elements of identity with place, loyalties, trust, and the bonds of common descent that made up the fabric of our urban society. These deep communal roots provided the basis for competition within cities for resources. Political organizations were based on these neighborhood and community organizations, and socialization and identity were deeply rooted in a multiplicity of heavily overlapping social bonds. Ecological succession took place as migration shifted from northern and western to southern and eastern Europe. Chicago witnessed the transformation of "Swedetown" to "Little Italy." Communities were strong but they were also permeable. As cities spread out and better housing became available to groups moving slowly up the stratification hierarchy, ecological succession took place. For others who remained in their traditional industrial and class niches, the community remained almost totally intact; the area was defended successfully. Newman (1973) used the term "segregated pluralism" to describe this situation. I prefer the term "shifting segregated pluralism," for although many communities remained intact, there was an orderly sociological shifting within the city. These patterns of community cohesion, development, and change were greatly influenced by the impact of further urbanization: the changing patterns of industrial needs, transportation, communication, and the black migration to our cities.

Forces of Industrialization and Urbanization. By the mid twentieth century, American industry was shifting to more and more automation, which demanded more and more white collar workers. The baby boom and returning servicemen forced the educational system to expand in a more efficient, centralized manner. The "cold war" motivated the federal government to provide funds to train a mushrooming army of space and high technology personnel. Planned communities spawned by rapid suburban expansion (the "contrived community") provided the bulk of residential growth. These events provided the opportunity for many members of ethnic communities to gain social mobility and leave their old neighborhoods.

Highway and commercial construction was always a threat to urban ethnic enclaves, but since the 1950s, with massive aid from the federal government and pressure from a thriving automotive industry, a construction boom has eliminated a large number of older neighborhoods in order to provide access to the city for suburban dwellers, thereby increasing the rate of suburbanization. This pace was quickened by the construction of new schools and federal housing projects. The rise of television, which coincided with the decline in foreign-language newspapers and radio stations, contributed greatly to cutting through the insularity of urban ethnic enclaves.

Mass consumption, mass production, and demands for equalitarianism emphasized class and status concerns at the expense of the primordial bonds of family, ethnicity, religion, and community. Kornhauser (1968) pointed out that mass equalitarianism is achieved at the expense of other social bases of inequality, such as ethnic and religious membership. We

would add community identification to such a list of social
bases.

The federal government's role in the administration of
equalitarianism must not be overlooked. Standards for schools
and hospitals and a multiplicity of welfare programs brought
forth federal requirements and agencies that impinged on existing community structures. Warren (1963) made the distinction
between the horizontal pattern in communities, where relationships are between local units, and the vertical pattern, which
tied communities and local units to larger political units. Increasingly over the last two decades, the actions of federal,
state, and municipal governments have forced communities to
deal more in vertical arrangements, thus depriving communities
of much of their autonomy and many of their efforts at self-
determination.

The mass black migration to our urban centers changed
the established pattern of ecological succession significantly.
With respect to earlier ethnic groups, communities were relatively permeable and group replacement occurred in an orderly
fashion. With blacks, however, the pattern changed to one of
organized defense, hostility and violence, and bitter conflict. In
working-class communities where social and geographical mobility is highly limited (Suttles, 1968; Kornblum, 1974) the
process of succession goes on; in other communities where
mobility is easier, racial succession is complete (Molotch, 1973).
Bernard (1973, p. 46) pointed out the reasons for the lack of
movement by blacks:

> Among whites, occupation, financial standing, and
> educational attainment were all positively related to verti-
> cal housing mobility; this was much less so in the case of
> nonwhites. Among them, education and occupation
> helped relatively little. This meant that even when educa-
> tion, occupation, and financial standing would normally
> have eventuated in upward residential mobility, such up-
> ward mobility was not occurring among black people.
> Those who could compete for good housing were not per-
> mitted to. Even if they could pay they were prevented
> from buying or renting the house or apartment they
> wanted.

The blacks find obstacles somewhat motivated by racism, but
much of their problem comes from the fact that our urban areas
present conditions different from when the white ethnic groups

achieved upward mobility. The earlier ethnic groups, in conjunction with the city's political machinery, provided their own welfare programs; good public schools did not carry the importance they do today; and although vigilance had to be maintained, the crime rate was low. Today, with welfare dependency so high among blacks, white communities—especially working-class ones—feel that they are being unfairly burdened with the expense. Community control of the schools and busing are two important issues that separate whites from blacks, for the incidence of disciplinary problems in public schools is highly correlated with black enrollment. Wilson (1968a), in a study of over one thousand Boston home owners, found that their major concerns were not with the physical environment (pollution, housing, or transportation) but with threats to the social environment such as violence, crime, rebellious youth, racial tension, and delinquency.

Community in Contemporary Society. These forces have indeed altered the nature of urban community life in America as well as added a new dimension: the suburb. The question we must now ask ourselves is what is the nature of community life in urban and suburban America and what is its future.

Communities in contemporary society contain the same elements as communities in the past, but in many instances these elements have changed significantly. We can distinguish four types of communities in urban and suburban America today: the black or nonwhite community; the ethnically and racially mixed "defended community"; the institutionally dominated, racially and class mixed "ideological community"; and the white community.

In the black community, the element of common ties is race alone. Lower class, working class, and middle class blacks are forced to live in densely populated areas that inhibit the spatial separation necessary to create and maintain their own communal life-styles. This condition, brought about by segregationist practices in the housing market perpetrated by community organizations, home owners, and realtors alike (Molotch, 1973), forces together different classes in the same locale. Although the different classes of blacks do have common interests in community services, such as police protection and physical maintenance, in many respects their interests clash, with the middle class concerned about status issues and the lower class about welfare. This is one of the primary reasons for the political weakness of many black communities.

The social interaction in black communities reflects the

mixing of class and status groups, where the middle class members feel the oppression of the lower class groups. Adolescents are pressured into joining gangs and following the life-style of the lower class members, for whom the legitimate routes of mobility, education, delayed gratification, and legal pursuits hold little promise. This causes problems in community interaction because the schools, streets, and parks are the territories of the organized gang and are therefore unsafe for all others. Identity with the locale is certainly present, but except for the gangs, who take pride in the protection of their territory, the identification is negative. Middle class members who can afford to live elsewhere are constrained by market practices, and when they do gain entry into neighborhoods of their choice by paying the "black tax" (Molotch, 1973), the area quickly fills up with the very same lower class elements they were trying to escape. The lower classes live in these areas quite simply because they can afford no better, and for both groups the interactional patterns are dominated by fear and hostility produced by the fact that the people who inhabit these all-black areas have no choice. Thus, for blacks particularly and for most other nonwhite groups (Mexican-Americans, Indians, and to an extent Asian-Americans and Puerto Ricans), segregation is not an attempt to preserve cultural values, to maintain in-group solidarity, or to provide interactional associational patterns with persons of common ancestry, but an effort by the white community to restrict the social roles of these racial groups and blunt their impact on the larger society.

In the defended communities, the primordial bonds of ethnicity, religion, and social interaction combine with identification with place to produce the purest sense of community in our urban areas. Although these communities are seen as the most stable, they are still a stage in the process of ecological succession. In the Addams area of West Chicago (Suttles, 1968), the Italians are being displaced by Mexicans, Blacks, and Puerto Ricans. In South Chicago (Kornblum 1974), Serbo-Croatians, Italians, and Poles are being displaced by Mexicans and Blacks. Yet the pace of this succession is much slower than that described for South Shore by Molotch (1973). Suttles used the concept of "ordered segmentation" to describe this process as having "two related features: (1) the orderly relationship between groups and (2) the sequential order in which groups combine in instances of conflict and opposition" (1968, p. 10). He noted that age, sex, territoriality, and personal reputation are used as distinctions in the Addams area more than the distinctions of occupation, education, or other attainments used in the wider society. Suttles went on to describe the differentiation: "Each ethnic section of the Addams area differs from the others in the extent to which it possesses a standardized routine for managing safe social relations" (1968, p. 225). Thus each neighborhood is a community in itself with territorial boundaries being very important, and these boundaries and identities are the foundation elements out of which neighborhoods and communities are socially constructed.

Kornblum (1974) observed a similar pattern of ordered segmentation in South Chicago, where kinship, ethnic affiliation, religion, and neighborhood were important aspects of life. The Serbs, Croatians, Poles, Italians, and even the Mexicans saw their ethnic networks and affiliations as descent groups. These groups competed organizationally in the realms of politics and union activities and especially in the steel mills. For these groups, community was a way of life, and the destruction of community raised the potential for loss of extended family organization and participation in a multiplicity of ethnic and neighborhood events. Every institution from the home and corner bar to the church and the steel mill reinforced the primordial bonds of ethnicity, community, and the whole interlocking web of traditional identities. It is not the loss of the community that is in doubt, but the time span that it will take. Hopefully a slow, orderly succession will not disrupt the situation beyond repair, for with less than one in five of the children of the mill workers going on to college, a classic example of what Wiley (1967) called the "ethnic mobility trap," their future will remain with the mills. Kornblum (1974, p. 213) described the situation of a Polish steelworker in the following way:

> During my years of residence in the community, this neighborhood area was the scene of continued racial and ethnic invasion. The church mentioned was increasingly visited by black and Mexican newcomers. On the other hand, the same steel worker three years later volunteered the opinion that although the blacks and the Mexicans were slowly becoming the dominant group in the neighborhood, his own patterns of neighborhood affiliation had not been appreciably affected. To his immense relief, the blacks seemed to prefer their own churches, and the Polish congregation was left largely unthreatened

by the newcomers. He expected that many of his younger
relatives would move out of the neighborhood, but his
kin of an equivalent age were maintaining their houses
and not making any sudden plans to leave unless "things
begin to get bad for us." Most of the younger families in
his Polish kinship network would probably move to
newer neighborhoods of second settlement where they
would be near enough to their parents to maintain the
solidarity of their kinship and ethnic attachments.

In analyzing the defended community, it is critical to
understand the vertical dimension in urban community life.
Change comes in from the outside through political, economic,
and extracommunity channels. The racial invasion and differential fertility of the newcomers drive the old settlers out. Segmented groups band together to fight the erosion of the community, but the erosion continues as these groups become fewer
in number and smaller in spatial terms. Nevertheless primary-
group bonds exist, as Suttles (1972, p. 251) concluded: "On the
West Side of Chicago, for example, ethnicity is a primordial distinction of great importance simply because there is not much
else by which to distinguish people."

An interesting development in the urbanization process
has been the birth of the ideological community. Hunter
(1975), repeating a study done twenty-five years earlier in the
nineteenth ward community near the University of Rochester,
found the persistence of a community of about 12,000. Although community use of local facilities had declined, the
social, interactional, and cultural—that is, the symbolic—dimensions of the community remained stable and in some areas had
even increased. He attributed this phenomenon to two major
factors: the dominance of a major institution committed to providing a close residential community (much like the University
of Chicago has done with the Hyde Park area) and the values of
the people, which are counter to those of most Americans. The
dominant institution can greatly influence the governmental
and real estate interests in an area to insure maintenance of residences and high quality urban services. The people that the
institution attracts reject suburbia and commuting, like the ability to be able to walk to work, desire a racially mixed area, and
consciously seek community. Hunter (1975, p. 550) had high
hopes for these communities: "The prevalence of 'ideological
communities' around major institutions located in older areas of

central cities—such as medical complexes and universities—
though relatively unique within a given metropolitan area may
be sufficiently general nationwide to provide a limited but persistent set of counter values to 'the loss of community' in urban
settings."

Hunter's thesis may be correct, but I feel it needs some
further thought. Requiring the support of a financially powerful
institution is not much solace for the majority of urban residents. South Shore had the largest, most financially powerful
community organization in the United States (Molotch, 1973),
but without the power of an institution such as a large university or hospital, it failed to prevent racial succession. Hunter
described the high socioeconomic character of the nineteenth
ward, but South Shore had the same characteristics. He cited
the people's conscious search for community, but this is true of
suburban migrants as well. Everyone would like to be able to
walk to work and not battle rush hour traffic, but given the spatial distribution of our cities, how feasible is this for most
Americans? Finally, concerning the desire to live in a racially
integrated neighborhood, an area that has moved from an all-
white population in 1940 to 4.5 percent black in 1970 would
not bother the bulk of middle and upper-middle class white
Americans. Those five or six hundred blacks have little influence on their schools, the safety of the streets, or the neighboring and associational networks within the community, and do
not threaten their occupational positions as blacks do in defended neighborhoods. In short, the ideological community is a
reversal of a trend toward suburbanization and loss of community, but its unique features do not retain the primordial and
sacred bonds for ethnic Americans and provide few opportunities for middle and upper-middle class Americans to develop an
identity with locale in the central city as opposed to the suburbs.

The suburban community is where more and more Americans reside. *Suburbanization* may be a misnomer since it refers
to urbanization over city limits and since within city limits
there are communities very similar to those we label "suburban"—communities and neighborhoods with large lots and
good modern homes or relatively expensive apartments (Kasarda, 1976). Suburban areas are typified by centralized shopping
plazas and malls, centralized schools where children are bussed
by necessity, class and status positions being determined by
associational and interactional patterns more than the more

sacred common-descent ties. Although primordial bonds have attenuated greatly in these areas, researchers have found that ethnicity, religion, extended family contacts, and even identity with locale have not totally disappeared (Berger, 1960; Gans, 1962b, 1967; Lenski, 1961; Sklare and Greenblum, 1967). The separation of work from residence and the concentration of daily activities outside the home and neighborhood have reduced the sense of belonging. Yet the demands are the same for defense and protection of children, their socialization, and general welfare. In many instances groups move to a suburb en masse and retain many of their cultural and associational elements. The image of the "gilded ghetto" is one of affluence overlaid on a historical tradition that did not include an affluent life-style. Needless to say, this disrupts the bonds of the past. One could speculate that if the factors associated with community identification and organizational participation in the city are length of residence, having children, and higher class status (Hunter, 1974), then these factors should carry over to the suburbs. However, the major influences of the attachment and evaluation on a community depend on individual social integration and primary interaction within the locale. These take much time as well as motivation. One in five families moves every year in America, and although most of them are middle and upper middle class, many are upwardly mobile working class. It follows that along with the decline in ethnic attachments, identification with the symbolic community of locale must decline also. The defended community, being almost a total institution, is reduced to the "community of limited liability" (Greer, 1962d; Janowitz, 1967), where local orientation and participation are found in suburban and urban settings but are attenuated, variable, and much less binding, giving the picture of a partial institution. Parenti (1967) argued that ethnic groups could maintain cohesion and identity without an ecological base, but to what extent is this too attenuated when compared with the strength of earlier forms of ecological and ethnic solidarity?

8

Religion in Urban Society

Harry M. Johnson

This chapter is chiefly concerned with three questions. First, does urbanization, together with other factors, tend to bring about a decline in the importance of religion for society? Second, what role does religion play in dealing with the social problems of the cities in the United States? Third, what are the differences among various types of churches? In addition, we shall speculate on future prospects.

    Making urbanization possible on a larger scale and giving suburban and rural populations characteristics once associated exclusively with cities are certain technological and social changes. In particular we might mention the increasing productivity of labor, the rise in literacy and average educational levels, the ubiquity of radio and television, and the extensive availability of transportation. Not only do people in rural areas get information about events in remote parts of the world as quickly as people in the cities, but they can also, at least in the United States, visit cities more frequently and see for themselves some of the diversity of modern life.

Continued Vitality of Religion

Broadly speaking, there are among sociologists two differing conceptions of religion in the United States. According to one view, religion is basically dying out, and what remains is either indifferent and even obstructive with regard to needed social change or essentially irrelevant to the main problems and developments of the modern world. This view maintains that among middle-class, educated people religion is no longer composed of deeply held meaningful beliefs about a supernatural order. Middle class churches are allegedly so transformed by secularization that they are really only loosely knit clubs in which essentially worldly people organize pleasant social activities and display their success in the competitive struggle. Furthermore, lower class churches, although they admittedly still take traditional beliefs about God and the afterlife seriously, are accused of rendering their members politically inactive because the attention and energies of these people are diverted from real problems—these churches reassure their low-status members that, despite appearances, they are really important people, indeed more important than the rich and powerful, and will be duly rewarded beyond the grave. An opinion held by some observers, notably Hadden (1971, pp. 1-14; see also Stark and Glock, 1971), is that religion in most denominations in the United States has become largely a matter of ethics ("Love thy neighbor") rather than supernatural beliefs, and on this basis these observers think it likely that the churches will slowly die out.

The other view of religion in America, with which I agree, is that religion is not dying out but is changing. Obviously, the observers who take this position have a broader definition of religion.

In Berger's book *A Rumor of Angels* (1969), a partial summary and a partial revision of his previous works, we find a theory designed to explain the decline and perhaps the eventual death of religion. The sociology of knowledge is said to show that any "world view," coherent "perspective," or "plausibility structure" is accepted because it is supported by other people in everyday social interaction, by mechanisms of social control, and by the process of socializing children. By destroying the religious consensus that had existed, the Reformation allegedly broke up this system. The theory further holds that urbanization aggravates the corrosive processes by bringing people of highly diverse backgrounds into interaction with one another. Bringing together people who have differing and often mutually inconsistent plausibility structures undermines the plausibility of each structure. Finally, the fragmented realities are made more precarious by the pervasive influence of education and the mass media. The sociology of knowledge, which makes us clearly aware of these processes, thus allegedly gives the final blow to all dogmatic conceptions of ultimate reality as it produces the extreme relativization of all knowledge and belief systems. The sheer existence of the sociology of knowledge presumably destroys belief in a supernatural order by showing the inescapable relativity of such belief.

As a result of all this, Berger, though reluctant, is almost ready to accept the eventual demise of belief in a supernatural order. Taking urbanization as a handy symbol for the whole complex of corrosive forces, he paraphrases Gabriel LeBras, the famous student of French Catholicism: "A certain railroad station in Paris appears to have a magical quality, for rural migrants seem to be changed from practicing to non-practicing Catholics the very moment they set foot in it" (Berger, 1969, p. 40). But Berger ultimately takes heart from the observation that the debunkers of tradition use a double standard. They relativize the past but treat the present as absolute. Why, Berger asks, should their disbelief in traditional religious verities be regarded as the last word? Perhaps we can "relativize the relativizers." Perhaps, he thinks, the supernatural will stage a comeback, after all.

Berger's account, however, is vulnerable to at least three criticisms:

1. Although social support is particularly important for the plausibility of religious ideas (since they are nonempirical if taken literally), unanimity of support is far from necessary for the viability of religious beliefs. Neither urbanization nor the confrontation of different religions is a new phenomenon. For example, once the covenant religion of the Jews came into contact with other religions in Canaan, its subsequent history was full of rivalry and conflict with both non-Jewish religions and sectarian movements within Judaism. One of these movements, Christianity, prospered and lived to shape many societies de-

spite its encounters with other religions and its internal schisms throughout its entire history.

2. It is an overstatement to say that ideas are accepted only because of social support for them. Properly understood, the sociology of knowledge does not relativize all knowledge to the same extent or in the same way. Science is not a passing fad or, indeed, anything radically new; something like systematized, tested empirical knowledge is part of every culture. The knowledge of modern science, in any case, is not the same sort of thing as doctrines of reincarnation, predestination, or free will. Although some scientific ideas are of course tentative, science as a whole consists of relatively certified, cumulative knowledge, and its impact on some of the ideas of traditional theology is certainly great. In particular, the plausibility of the idea of free will and thus of responsibility, which made acceptable the idea of enduring hell as punishment for sinners, is greatly weakened (Glock and Stark, 1965a, pp. 289-306; Parsons, 1967).

3. Although he in effect agrees with Durkheim's ideas concerning the sociocultural construction of reality, Berger mostly ignores other Durkheimian ideas that are just as important. Religion has roots in the human situation far too deep to be destroyed by the progress of science and the interaction of mutually inconsistent formulations of ultimate reality. Durkheim suggested, and subsequent research has strongly confirmed, that religious symbols found in myth and ritual stand at least in part for an actual reality, namely, the ideal society, which is immanent in empirically observable societies yet at the same time transcends them; indeed, these religious symbols are part of the very constitution of societies (Swanson, 1964). Myth and ritual express and renew moral commitment and cohesive participation in the body of believers. Thus, as Durkheim stressed, "constitutive symbolism" (Parsons, 1966) creates and maintains a moral community that transcends the life and reach of any single individual and confers on the community as a whole and on its individuals powers that are supernatural in the sense that they transcend the kind of empirical reality studied in physics, chemistry, and biology (Fallding, 1974). Further, as Fallding emphasized, all religions, since they do in fact create some degree of social solidarity, must be in touch with objective ultimate reality. However, since no religion formulates or creates perfectly all the necessary and sufficient conditions for the highest possible degree of solidarity, no religion can be said to encompass ultimate reality; we therefore must distinguish

sharply between religion and the objective ultimate reality that it imperfectly symbolizes. As Fallding noted, this distinction is often symbolized in religion itself in the formulation that God is known but imperfectly.

To the possible objection that a society can have a shared morality without supernatural beliefs, the best answer seems to be that value systems are more consensual, more stable, and more meaningful if they are grounded in quasi-cognitive definitions of the human situation; these in turn cannot rely solely on empirical science. The need for religion is related to the biological nature of man. The human species is gregarious; interdependence, the starting point of community, is implied in the helplessness of the human infant and the relatively continuous (as opposed to periodic) strength of the sexual drive. Yet genetically determined instincts, in the sense of detailed patterns of response adapted to stable features of the environment and to biological needs, are relatively lacking. To compensate for this lack, however, there is the capacity to develop symbolic systems, which some people regard as the principal characteristic of the human species. These symbolic systems (cultures) constitute the basis for a significant degree of solidarity and cooperation. Universally, a subsystem of human cultural systems is religion (constitutive symbolism).

Thus, biologically determined (or, better, conditioned) social interaction perpetually gives rise to culture, including religion or constitutive symbolism; and culture in turn makes possible a relatively stable community, with continuity lasting over many generations. The cultural pattern is subject to change, however, brought about by and expressed in sectarian protest and the religious aspect of revolutionary movements. As Fallding (1974) noted, particular religions come and go, but religion, as part of human culture and the highest level of direction and control of human societies, will exist as long as the human situation exists.

What is sometimes taken for the *decline* of religion can better be viewed as a process of cultural differentiation. It is scientifically desirable to distinguish between an assertion of a total loss of function (for example, of the family or of religion) and an observation of a reduction in the *diffuseness* of function, a special kind of loss resulting from a process of differentiation. From a primordial, diffuse "religious" matrix, philosophy, science, and religion proper have gradually separated, although they are not absolutely independent of one another. Religion, shorn of authority in the other fields, retains certain pattern maintenance and integrative functions for society and personality partly because science and philosophy are quite inadequate to perform those functions. It can be argued that once the essential character of religion has been released from its earlier embeddedness in a diffuse culture, religion can contribute uniquely and more flexibly to social systems and personalities. From our present vantage point, we can now see that the earlier diffuseness involved a certain amount of confusion. Partly as a result of religious legitimization of secular change, one might say that the cultural sphere of competence of religion has been progressively narrowed, but it is still possible for religious commitment to express itself in every sphere of life, however differentiated that sphere itself may be from *directly* and *specifically* religious culture and social organization. For example, a person may question or guide the uses of science or secular law from a religious perspective. The view of religious evolution that has been sketched here has grown mainly from the insights of Durkheim and Weber (see Parsons, 1966, 1968, 1971, 1974).

What have been the results for religion of the processes touched on by Berger: the growth of science, including the sociology of knowledge; the proliferation and contact of incompatible conceptions of ultimate reality; and the effects of urbanization, education, and the mass media? At least three fairly general results can be discerned.

First, religion must be distinguished not only from ultimate reality itself but from the truth about ultimate reality. Writing of so-called liberal Protestant theology, the University of Chicago theologian Langdon Gilkey said:

> Under [the influence of science], recent Protestant theology has generally agreed or, better, conceded (with the early liberals, this was voluntary, but with many conservatives involuntary) that matters of fact within the space-time continuum are to be determined by scientific inquiry. . . . This vast shift forced by modern science in turn led to a complete reinterpretation of what religious truth is. . . . Modern theologians . . . have regarded theology as reflection on religion, and thus as the very human and fallible *result* of religious faith or experience rather than as the sacred *object* of religious faith, that is, as an authoritative exposition of divinely revealed truth. . . . Clearly the burning question of the status, meaningful-

ness, and verifiability of [systems of religious symbols],
referent in some sense to reality and yet establishing no
matters of fact, was bound sooner or later to arise, as it
has uncomfortably in the most recent theology of the last
decade [1968, p. 138].

An aspect of the development described by Gilkey
(1968) is the decline of dogmatism. Dogmatism is the insistence
that certain beliefs are right and others wrong. But it is possible
to take religious symbols seriously without being dogmatic
about them. Thus, liberal Protestants (or Catholics or Jews or
Muslims) can be open and tentative about their theology (their
attempts to give intellectual coherence to their religious faith)
and yet have a religious faith to which they are committed. The
disturbing and potentially fruitful tension between the ideal or
transcendent and the visible world of actual experience remains.

Second, the native conception of free will is no longer
plausible to people who know anything about psychology and
the other social sciences.

Third, the impact of science, of urbanization, of the mass
media, and of swift global communication has not been felt
evenly in all segments of the population. Investigations of Christian laymen by Glock and Stark (1965a, 1965b) and of the
clergy by Hadden (1969) show that (1) all denominations are
divided between theological conservatives and liberals, (2) some
denominations are more liberal than others, (3) within each
denomination both clergy and laity are divided, (4) the clergy
and laity in each denomination tend to agree, and (5) on the
whole, younger and better-educated clergymen and laymen are
more likely to be theologically liberal.

We can give a few examples to illustrate these findings.
Given a choice among several statements about God, 99 percent
of the Southern Baptist laity chose the statement "I know God
really exists and I have no doubts about it." Ninety-six percent
of sect members (the Assemblies of God, the Church of God,
the Church of Christ, the Church of the Nazarene, the Four-
square Gospel Church, and one independent tabernacle studied)
also chose that statement. Only 71 percent of all Protestants
and 81 percent of all Catholics did so, and at the liberal extreme, only 41 percent of the Congregationalists. Very similar
divisions were found on questions about the divinity of Jesus,
miracles, the afterlife, the Devil, and being born sinful.

It should be noted, however, that religious symbols can

perform their functions whether or not they are taken literally. For example, in Christianity the body of Christ, the new creation, the city of God, and other symbols may be and no doubt frequently are understood in the manner of Durkheim as indicating and re-creating important social and personal realities: The important thing (in terms of empirical effects) is that although they are transcendent they motivate people to action. Actually, we cannot be precisely sure what people mean when they say they believe or do not believe. It is not surprising that many people say they do not believe in God but nevertheless pray to him; Berger (1969, p. 30) cited a poll in Western Germany to this effect.

The statistics of church membership, attendance, and financial contributions fluctuate, of course, from year to year. According to an Associated Press report, the *Yearbook of American and Canadian Churches* (Jacquet, 1976) showed that membership in American churches and synagogues is climbing again after a few years of slight declines, which were due mainly to transitional turmoil in the Roman Catholic church. Sixty-two percent of the population are members of a house of worship. Nearly $12 billion were given to churches in 1975. In addition, no one knows how many of the billions of dollars given annually to hundreds of charities and good causes are given in part to implement religious commitments.

The anticlericalism of Europe, which is not the same as irreligiousness, is due to the historical coalition between established churches and conservative governments. Fighting for justice meant fighting against the established church. In reaction to the conservative coalition, secular religions developed, such as the religion of nature and reason in France and, later, Marxist socialism and communism. Ironically, these secular religions were profoundly shaped by the Judeo-Christian vision, about which the established churches had become complacent and neglectful (see Parsons, 1968, p. 444; Parsons, 1971, 1974, pp. 206-209). Like both Judaism and Christianity, Marxism stresses concern for the poor. Parsons, Fallding (1974), and many others found the element of the transcendent in the doctrine of the dialectical progress toward the end of history; the utopian theme in Marxism is remarkably similar to the eschatological theme in Judaism and Christianity of the final conquest of sin and death and the coming of the kingdom of God on earth.

Even so, the much discussed hostility or indifference of Europeans toward traditional religions is only relative. Most people continue to be believers (see the summary article by Swanson, 1968). France is a country with one of the strongest anticlerical traditions; yet LeBras (despite the railroad station in Paris) says that French Catholicism, relatively freed now from ignorance and coercion, is probably stronger and more "genuine" than it was before the French Revolution (cited in Shiner, 1967; see also Alston, 1973). In general, one of the great weaknesses in the "loss of relevance" thesis is the flimsy assumption that in ages past the great majority of any given population was more religious than the majority is now.

Sweden, with a highly educated population organized in a highly differentiated society, is often cited as the country most secularized. Yet, even there, about 90 percent continue to be baptized, confirmed, married, and buried by the established Lutheran church. A solid majority of the population still says that it believes in God. Only 23 percent actually disclaimed belief in life after death. Even as far as the organized church is concerned, a majority of the people says that it would join the church if it were disestablished; in 1957, 51 percent were actually against separation of church and state; and by the middle 1960s only 40,000 had left the church, although in 1951 a law had been passed permitting them to do so. Yet the article from which I take these facts is entitled, perhaps ironically, "Religion Is Irrelevant in Sweden" (Tomasson, 1971).

Conservative Influence of Religion

We are all familiar with the long list of problems for which we need careful analysis and concerted action, action by both private groups and governments supported by interested, informed, and idealistic citizens. In the United States several of these problems—poverty, unemployment, housing, and racism— are to a great extent urban problems. Are religious people among those who are interested, informed, idealistic, active, and supportive of constructive efforts?

We find a partial answer in studies whose *conclusions* might be regarded as pessimistic (Glock and Stark, 1965a; Hadden, 1969; for summaries of other studies, see Argyle and Beit-Hallahmi, 1975, chaps. 7 and 10). Glock and Stark and Hadden did not explore all the problems we mentioned; they primarily addressed the problems of racism and poverty. Briefly summarized, their conclusions are that (1) the clergy is more liberal politically than the laity, (2) theologically liberal clergymen are well ahead of theological conservatives, (3) the laity are complacent or obstructive with regard to social problems, and (4) whether the laity are theologically conservative or liberal, they tend to be politically conservative.

It is almost a commonplace in the sociology of religion that religion can be either a very conservative force or very dynamic or both at once at different levels. We are dealing here with some of the conservative aspects of American religion, presently leaving aside its more dynamic aspects. One reason for the conservative effects of religion is that one of the themes of Christianity from the beginning has been that salvation means, at least in part, going to heaven in an afterlife. For some Christians ever since, the Christian way of life has been interpreted somewhat negatively: Do nothing that will make you unworthy of the great reward of immortality. This attitude has frequently carried with it a ritualistic, devotional, mystical, or ecstatic tendency, as opposed to social activism in building the kingdom of God on earth. Of course, not all evangelicals, neoevangelicals, or fundamentalists (however one defines these terms) are politically indifferent or conservative. The fact remains that many are and that the religious orientation itself *can* contribute to this result.*

Another reason that many people do not concern themselves with great social issues is that they cannot; they do not have enough psychic energy or time after coping with their own demanding and changing work roles and the perplexities of their personal lives. Undoubtedly one reason for the increase in church membership since the middle 1940s is the increased need for spiritual guidance, comfort, and social support and reassurance. Providing for such needs is a genuine service of traditional churches.

One must ask about the role of the pervasive Protestant ethic as a potential conservative force. Parsons (1960) summarized it as follows: "Essentially by this system of values I mean the continued commitment to values of 'instrumental activism,' the subordination of the personal needs of the individual to an objective 'task' to which he is expected to devote

---

*My intention is not to make light of religious concerns for direct experience or for perfection in interpersonal relations; my point, rather, is that for some persons and even whole groups these concerns eclipse the potential religious motivation to create a more just society, which must go beyond any individual's personal relationships.

his full energies, and the subjection of the actions of all to universalistic standards of judgment" (p. 311). The Protestant ethic, which was strongest in the Calvinist tradition, stresses individualism and self-reliance. In the United States, this emphasis was reinforced by the long frontier experience. According to church historian Sydney E. Ahlstrom (1972, p. 169), "Puritanism provided the moral and religious background of fully 75 percent of the people who declared their independence in 1776." He added that "85 or 90 percent would not be an extravagant estimate" of those with a Calvinist background; this larger percentage would include many German, Swiss, French, Dutch, and Scottish people. There were, to be sure, significant numbers of Catholics in Maryland, Pennsylvania, and New York, and there were very small Jewish communities in many towns; but, according to Ahlstrom, there were no more than 2 or 3 thousand Jews in the United States as late as 1800.

In general, the individualism fostered by Calvinism and the frontier tradition helps to keep alive a conception of government that is no longer appropriate. The political ideals of John Adams, Thomas Jefferson, James Madison, and the other founding fathers were certainly derived in part from Christianity. But two facts tempered the activism that such ideals might have encouraged. One was that the founding fathers had a profound distrust of power (this too has deep Judeo-Christian origins), as expressed in the system of checks and balances and in the principle that "that government governs best that governs least." The second was that the new nation seemed to offer boundless opportunities to any individual (except slaves) willing to work. To early Americans, the great ideals of freedom and equality tended to mean freedom from governmental interference and the equality of self-reliant landholders, not rich but not poor.

After two world wars and the Depression of the 1930s, it is evident to most reasonably informed people that the old wisdom must be modified. Worldwide economic and political interdependence and the growing complexity of internal problems in industrialized and urbanized nations mean that the role of government at all levels must be greater than Thomas Jefferson contemplated. The ideals of liberty, equality, and democracy were correctly called liberal; but today the people who still insist on balanced budgets, a very limited role for government, and the almost exclusive role of private enterprise are likely to be called conservative, and the word *liberal* tends to be applied to those who add to the ideals of liberty, equality, and democracy the realization that public collective enterprise is vital for modern needs.

In rural areas and small towns, however, and where frontier standards are still cherished, rugged individualism and distrust of big government are still strong. Welfare policies are likely to be regarded as a form of coddling and encouraging idlers. The presence of communism is felt keenly. It is thought that we should maintain powerful military forces to protect ourselves, but we ought to be distrustful of the United Nations and chary of giving away our hard-earned money to idlers and socialists overseas. Protestants, regardless of class, region, or residence, tend to vote Republican far more often than would be expected on a chance basis, and proportionately more often than Catholics or Jews (Lenski, 1961, 1967).

The Protestant ethic is still alive. If it were not, the counterculture would make no sense. As Benton Johnson (1961) pointed out, the Pentecostal and Holiness sects, which are frequently but incorrectly accused of comforting people for their poverty and low status, "socialize in dominant values"—that is, encourage people to be steady and self-disciplined. There is probably no more common topic for sermons (both those given from pulpits and those preached by parents, teachers, novelists, filmmakers, and journalists) than the terrible temptations of the pursuit of hollow success as opposed to true achievement. Even the popular inspirational literature that urges one to pray because praying can help one to succeed in life is not necessarily a perversion of the Protestant emphasis on personal achievement; after all, success is not necessarily bad. Books of the type studied by Schneider and Dornbusch (1957) reveal the immense importance of personal ambition in American life.

There has been a great deal of debate about whether Catholics are as ambitious as Protestants (see, for example, Lenski, 1961, 1971; Bressler and Westoff, 1963; Greeley, 1964; Schuman, 1971). The results are perhaps not conclusive, but it is safe to say that in this respect Catholics are now very much like Protestants. As Nelson (1973, pp. 99-102) observed, recent comparisons between Catholics and Protestants bring out the enormous influence of the Protestant ethic in the United States; they do not refute Max Weber since, of course, many changes have occurred in both Catholicism and Protestantism since Weber's time.

Individualism, and thus conservatism, are also supported by a religiously based, naive conception of free will. In effect, if the poor are poor it is their own fault. Eighty-six percent of a national sample of Protestant, Catholic, and Jewish laity agreed with the statement "Negroes would be better off if they would take advantage of the opportunities that have been made available to them rather than spending so much time protesting"; thirty-five percent of the clergy also agreed (Hadden, 1969, p. 141). We can also note the national response to another statement, "Martin Luther King, Jr., is an outstanding example of making Christianity relevant and meaningful for our day." In 1967, only 29 percent of the laity agreed with that statement. This was before King spoke out against the Vietnam war; thus it was King's nonviolent Christian witness in behalf of civil rights for blacks that the majority of the laity was responding to. The Protestant laity was the least supportive (27 percent agreed); the Jews were the most (59 percent agreed); and the Catholics (30 percent) were in between (Hadden, 1969, pp. 136-137).

Glock and Stark (1965a) obviously thought that the public's naive belief in individual free will and responsibility, which underlies religious beliefs in rewards and punishments in life and after death, is an important obstacle to social progress, particularly as it conflicts with social science. The separation of church and state and the tax-free status of churches may also contribute to conservative views. Some people have taken the separation of church and state and the tax immunity of the churches to mean that the churches must scrupulously stay out of politics.

Types of Churches

In the eyes of many liberal clergy, the greatest scandal of the churches in the United States is the continued separation of blacks and whites. The end of slavery, the Civil War, and Reconstruction have been, of course, the most traumatic events in American history. A little later, the United States had to begin the difficult process of assimilating millions of immigrants from Europe. Virulent nativism (white Anglo-Saxon Protestant supremacy) was an ugly part of American life from about 1850 to World War II, rising with the tide of non-Anglo-Saxon immigration and subsiding after the passage of discriminatory new immigration laws in 1924 (see Ahlstrom, 1972, chap. 34; Higham, 1955; Woodward, 1966).

Most of the new European immigrants settled in the large cities; in the twentieth century, blacks began migrating in large

numbers from the rural South to southern and northern cities as
well. The churches to a great extent have moved out of the city
into the suburbs, avoiding the problem of trying to meet the
needs first of European immigrants and then of migrant blacks
from the South. Winter has told the story in his book *The Suburban Captivity of the Churches* (1961). Many liberal clergymen
concur in the negative judgment and feel a responsibility now to
rectify what they consider to be unjust and un-Christian insensi-
tivity by middle class whites (including many, now, who are not
Anglo-Saxon).

Despite the movement of white churches to the suburbs,
many kinds of churches remain in the cities. To address this
diversity we must classify churches. Fallding (1974) distinguished five elements that make up any religion: doctrine, an
ethic, fellowship, ritual, and religious experience (an unusual experience of exaltation associated with religious ideas, fellowship, ritual, or ethical action). We might add to this list organization in collectivities and roles. Churches vary in all these
respects and also in the emphasis they place on each element.
Thus, all churches are based on religious doctrine consisting of
myths and tenets of faith, but some (for example, the fundamentalist churches and certain special departures from orthodox Christianity, such as Christian Science and the Church of
Latter-Day Saints or Mormons) place a great deal of emphasis
on their members' having the right doctrines, while others, including mainstream Protestant denominations, are latitudinarian
in doctrine and do not require new members to accept precisely
defined beliefs. With regard to ethics, some churches are very
strict about specific details of conforming behavior, while
others stress general principles and largely leave interpreting the
principles in concrete situations up to the individual. All
churches enjoy and encourage fellowship, but some almost restrict the social life of their members to the church itself while
others are far less demanding. All churches have rituals, at least
in the sense of repetitive patterns of worship, but again some
attach particular importance to participating in rituals while
others put more emphasis on sermons. Some churches stress
emotional experience and in effect organize everything to attain
it, while others seem reserved and controlled by comparison.
Finally, there are several types of organization. Some churches
stress the difference between the clergy and the laity; others
minimize it. Some churches stress radical democracy in the
management of affairs at the level of the local congregation;

others have several levels of representative government, extending from the local congregation to the nation or even the world; others are organized bureaucratically; and still others are organized around the unpredictable revelations of a single living charismatic leader.

One of the things that make a big city cosmopolitan is its enormous religious variety. Shippey (1967) classified city churches according to parish geography and the population served. Churches of his "Type I" have a widely dispersed parish and a selected clientele; "Type II" churches have a compact parish and a dominant neighborhood penetration. In addition to these two main types, Shippey spoke of churches in transition (on their way to becoming Type II churches). There are four subtypes of Type I: the "downtown church" (often an old church, always located in the center of the city), the "prestige church" (located in an upper-middle class neighborhood and serving upper-middle class people), the "one-of-a-kind church" (the one church in the community for a numerically weak preference, such as a Methodist church in a New England city), and the "church-for-the-handicapped." All these subtypes are likely to have dispersed members. There are six subtypes of Type II churches: the "traditional church" (member of a large denomination with a clearly established tradition), the "institutional church" (which, in addition to Sunday worship, provides social services and often cooperates with social work agencies), the "store-front church" (a modest church rather informally run for the urban poor), the "sect church," the "foreign-language church," and the "suburban church" (which is highly variable in social class level and doctrine but is located in a suburb).

Shippey also gave seven subtypes of the transitional church, each of which reflects an inherently unstable state of affairs and an unstable constituency.

Shippey's classification is not ideal. For example, both main types really have selected clienteles; it is hard to see why the traditional church (in Type II) has a less selected clientele than the downtown church or the prestige church (in Type I). Further, the differences in degree of neighborhood penetration need not imply differences in the degree of member involvement; it is possible for a dispersed clientele (Type I) to be deeply "penetrated" by its participation in the church. An example is provided by the Pentecostal black church studied by Williams (1974). The members of this church were scattered over Pittsburgh and yet they composed a close community in the socio-religious sense. The same example shows that a sect may have dispersed members.

Stanley (1967) presented another classification of urban churches; he distinguished between the "involuted" and the "involved," with a transitional class in process of becoming involved. Generally speaking, involuted churches are solely concerned with the spiritual needs of their own congregations, while the involved churches are trying to do something for one or more wider communities beyond their membership—something beyond simply gaining new members. This distinction does not necessarily imply a value judgment. We have noted that modern life intensifies and complicates for many people religious and moral problems: problems of ultimate meaning, problems of interpreting religious and ethical doctrines in an ever differentiating culture and society. There are also certain sects that do not proselytize but are anxious to protect their comprehensive way of life against alien incursions. The best-known examples are rural groups such as the Amish and the Hutterites, but urban groups, such as the Hasidic Jews, also exist.

Stanley (1967) subdivided the involved churches into two subtypes, the "inclusive" and the "exclusive." The inclusive church seeks to attract most if not all strata and cultural groupings within its reach. An exclusive church tries to serve certain groups that it feels are neglected and whose interests it sees itself as representing. In turn, either the inclusive or the exclusive church may be geographically limited to a neighborhood, hence being local, or may reach out across a city or even a region, hence being "nonlocal."

The subtypes of inclusive local church are three: the "supplementary service church," the "neighborhood center church," and the "coordinating church." An example of a supplementary service church would be one that holds noon worship services in the business district—it supplements the members' regular residential churches. The neighborhood center church may be an interdenominational church in a heterogeneous community or a denominational church in an ethnically, economically, and religiously homogeneous community; in any case, it tries to be the center of local community life, starting with worship and going on to other kinds of service. The coordinating church is likely to be in a socially homogeneous neighborhood; for example, an all-black church in a lower class neighborhood may be the center not only of worship but of social and political action to improve the conditions of the people that it serves.

The exclusive involved church, whether local or nonlocal, is not trying to attract everyone; it may appeal to a language or racial minority, to a single class, or to people with narrowly defined theological beliefs. In addition, there are the "specialized ministries" to the blind, to artists, to college students, and to handicapped people.

A final classification of churches was suggested by Fallding's (1974) discussion, which has many precursors. In one class are churches that basically accept the existing society, with its social stratification and its basic institutional patterns; in the other class are the churches of social protest, whose members feel excluded or at least humiliated and do not accept their position as unchangeable. As Fallding made clear, these latter churches, called "sectarian movements," are fundamentally religious but of course have political implications; their members and leaders are to some degree alienated from society and demand a new social definition of their place. A good example is provided by the Black Muslims (Lincoln, 1961; Essien-Udom, 1962). In the most extreme phase of their development, the Black Muslims maintained that blacks were better than whites and specially chosen by God or that blacks *were* God. The movement originally appealed largely to highly alienated urban blacks, convicts and ex-convicts, illiterates, and other black people who felt there was no chance for ethnic pride and personal dignity as long as they accepted conventional white definitions.

The distinction between accepting and protesting religious groups requires at least one important qualification. No *religious* group wholly accepts society as it is; a religious group by definition is devoted to an ideal order that is only partly realized in the empirical world, and every religious group is therefore to some extent critical. The difference is between ideal types in Weber's sense: the society-accepting churches are composed of people whose religion and social position are already respected; the religious protest movements are composed of people who feel deeply that they are at least not respected enough and whose protest is not only against certain aspects of the social-political-economic order but also against existing religious groups.

Both the society-accepting and the society-rejecting groups in particular historical situations have been dogmatic and intolerant. The ideal type *ecclesia* was the established church in the society and was intolerant of other religious groups. Protest movements tend to be intolerant at first but tend to "mellow," as Fallding (1974) put it, after they begin to achieve respectability. Shortly after the death of Elijah Muhammad, long-time head of the Black Muslims, the new head began to lead the movement toward greater respectability and eventual incorporation into the wider society. Today the Black Muslims are trying to attract white as well as black members.

In the United States there may be no religious group, perhaps not even the communists, who wish to become an *ecclesia* of the pure type. The Roman Catholic Church in the United States has ultimately become one denomination among many. It is socially accepted and respected, it scarcely claims to have exclusive possession of religious truth, and it follows the rules of mutual respect and forbearance in its cooperative competition or competitive cooperation with the other denominations. Besides denominational churches and sectarian movements, we can distinguish the type of established sect, like the Amish, who certainly are satisfied with their position in the world but who feel religiously compelled to live somewhat separately from other churches.

The Future

Three trends are likely to continue into the future. These are the assimilation of minorities, the trend toward amalgamated religious organizations, and the ascendancy of liberal theology.

Continuing Process of Inclusion. The fundamental values and institutions of the United States were against the long-run success of the Pròtestants' attempt to establish themselves as a hereditary aristocracy (see Baltzell, 1966). The derisive term "Boston Brahmins," which was applied to the most vigorous pretenders, was a prediction of their failure. There have been three different conceptions of the assimilation process in the United States (Gordon, 1961). There is some truth in all three, but one has come to prevail. According to the largely outmoded "melting pot" conception, a new race and a new culture are being produced, fusing the best of all the heterogeneous peoples. Second, the somewhat anachronistic conception called "Americanization" tacitly assumed that Germans, Poles, Italians, and all the other latecomers would speak English and become as much like the Anglo-Saxon Protestants as possible. To a great extent this has happened, but it is obvious that ethnic groups, including various religious groups, have not simply disappeared. The conception that has come to prevail, both descriptively and normatively, is ethnic and religious pluralism. According to this conception in its ideal form, ethnic, racial, and religious groups should have equality of opportunity as full citizens in a democratic commonwealth. Equalitarian pluralism means, however, that religious, ethnic, and racial groups are free to maintain and develop a separate cultural and social life if they wish. It is up to the individual, in principle, to decide to what extent he or she wishes to retain and express his or her religious, ethnic, or racial identity and separateness.

The sociologist Talcott Parsons (1967) used the term *inclusion* to refer to the process by which religious, ethnic, and racial groups that were once looked down upon and discriminated against (excluded, as it were) gradually come to be accepted as full citizens in a pluralist society. Inclusion must obviously be distinguished from integration and assimilation. Parsons's analysis is too complex and subtle to summarize briefly, but two points must be made. First, the diversity that can coexist harmoniously is not infinite. As far as the United States is concerned, all groups must believe in religious tolerance (or at least practice it) and accept constitutional limitations on the procedures by which social change is sought. The second point is that in the process of including Catholics and Jews in the United States, all religious groups have had to change their practices or attitudes to some extent. Catholics and Jews have been by and large included, and they certainly have developed an American style. Obviously, most Protestant groups have also changed. In *Protestant-Catholic-Jew* (1955), the Jewish scholar Will Herberg maintained that ethnic differences had become less important in the United States and that we now had three great religious groups living peacefully side by side, but he lamented that in the process by which this harmony had come about, the Catholics, Protestants, and Jews, with some exceptions, had lost touch with their true religious traditions and now shared a vague, so-called culture religion (see also Herberg, 1967a, 1967b; Winter, 1967). In any case it is extremely unlikely, as Parsons (1967) noted, that Protestants, Catholics, and Jews could have achieved their present approximation to equalitarian pluralism if all three groups had not modified their traditional ways.

It was a turning point in American history when a Catholic was elected to the presidency. It is widely agreed that a Jew might well be elected in the future. We have Protestants, Catholics, and Jews on the Supreme Court. The rate of intermarriage

between Christians and Jews has become so high that some Jews
are actually worried that Jewish identity will be lost altogether
in the United States (Rosenthal, 1972; Sklare, 1964). The
process of inclusion of course continues. The religious basis for
the continued success of inclusion has been firmly established
(Parsons, 1960).

Herberg's characterization of the triple melting pot of
Protestants, Catholics, and Jews has been criticized. Glock and
Stark (1965a) have shown that many Protestants are closer in
their beliefs to Catholics than they are to some other Protestants. Mueller (1974), considering marriage, friendship, residence, occupations, and politics, concluded that there are three
groupings in the United States: white Christians, white non-
Christians, and blacks; but he saw increasing mutual acceptance
of Christians and Jews and impressive recent economic and
political gains by blacks. Political scientists and sociologists have
often noted the importance of the question of whether groups
are divided by many things and joined by none or few (Truman,
1951; Coleman, 1956). The divisions noted by Mueller (1974)
and others would be much more serious if the three groupings
were welded together by strong bonds and yet divided by various beliefs, values, or interests. Fortunately for the solidarity of
the United States, the three groupings Mueller distinguished are
not united within and separated without. All three, with statistically minor exceptions, speak English. The white Christians
are divided theologically and also ethnically (by nationality of
descent). Some are rich, some poor. Any sect that feels too
threatened by participation in the common life can largely cut
itself off. The white non-Christians are similarly divided; though
above average in wealth, they do not constitute a monolithic
bloc holding a great deal of wealth or political power; with the
white Christians, the non-Christians participate in the same
political parties. As for the blacks, they are overwhelmingly
Christian; they are not all poor and deprived of power; and they
are now free to participate in politics—if not equally, at least
more nearly so.

One of the most famous recent papers in the sociology of
religion is Bellah's "Civil Religion in America" (1970, pp.
168-189). The "civil religion" consists of those beliefs and practices about sacred things that provide an essentially common
religious meaning to the society. Although national heroes,
shrines, holidays, and rituals are in a sense the main focus of
American civil religion, Bellah emphasized that the founding

fathers and all the presidents (as amply shown in their inaugural addresses) have regarded this nation as being under God and subject to His judgment. The God referred to in public ceremonies is not specifically Christian or Jewish. The nation's highest ideals were given ideal words in the Gettysburg Address, the "New Testament" of the civil religion (the "Old Testament" being the Declaration of Independence). "Behind the civil religion at every point lie biblical archetypes: Exodus, Chosen People, Promised Land, New Jerusalem, and Sacrificial Death and Rebirth. But it is also genuinely American and genuinely new" (Bellah, 1970, p. 186).

The Protestant ethic is part of the American civil religion in the sense that a good society, for Americans, is one that provides opportunity and facilities for individuals and private groups to achieve worthwhile things, in the process of which individuals fulfill themselves and realize their capacities. The partial exclusion of blacks from this opportunity and facilitation is part of the betrayal of the civil religion.

Amalgamation of Religious Organization. Indicating a broad movement toward religious unity are the number and importance of mergers of Protestant denominations in recent years (Gaustad, 1968, p. 115). In 1939, three formerly independent Methodist organizations merged to form the Methodist Church; in 1957, the Congregational Christian Churches (themselves the result of a merger) joined with the Evangelical and Reformed Church to form the United Church of Christ; in 1958, two Presbyterian bodies joined to form the United Presbyterian Church in the U.S.A. (which publishes the magazine *A.D.* jointly with the United Church of Christ); in 1960, three Lutheran groups joined to form the American Lutheran Church; and in 1962, four other Lutheran groups joined to form the Lutheran Church in America. Consultations are presently going on to unite ten broad groups of Protestants (including three of the amalgamated groups named above).

There are several reasons for this movement toward unity among Protestants. First, the decline of dogmatism has made the separation of some denominations increasingly meaningless. Second, the gradual inclusion (or, in a sense, Americanization) of various ethnic groups (for example, the Germans and the Scandinavians) has of course eliminated language barriers and made it possible for religious similarities to become more salient. Finally, there is the movement toward involvement with the problems of this world (the here and now). Though for

Christianity this movement is gradual, uneven, and secular, it is unmistakable. The movement toward Protestant unity is partly based on the knowledge that the church could have greater influence in politics if it were united. The trend toward Protestant unity is not a movement of huddling together against a Catholic threat; on the contrary, Protestants in favor of Protestant unity also favor unity with Catholics, and Catholics in favor of ecumenicalism regard Protestant unity as a step in that direction (Kelly, 1972).

Gradual Ascendancy of Liberal Theology. There remain fundamentalists who not only continue to disfavor Darwin but, going further than many pre-Darwinian Christians did, continue to insist on the literal accuracy of the Bible in everything. There is a defensive quality to such fundamentalism, however. In an article on the Churches of Christ in America, which are definitely fundamentalist, Gaustad (1969) gave considerable evidence that this denomination, while growing, is also becoming more liberal. Students in the denominational colleges, he said, are beginning to treat with good-natured satire such controversies as whether musical instruments should be used in the churches.

Why the liberal clergy is so much further ahead in its liberalism than the liberal laity is not entirely clear. The clergy in most denominations are better educated than the laity. Since some of the concerns of the older theology have become less meaningful, the clergy have had to think harder about the functions of the church in a new situation. Clergy are probably less tied than the laity to various vested interests and worldly concerns. Finally, it has, of course, always been an important part of the clergy's role to activate people's religious and moral commitments. Even in the nineteenth century, when evangelical pietism was stronger than it is now, clergymen were among the courageous and determined leaders in the movement to abolish slavery.

The younger clergy tend to be more liberal theologically and politically than the older. Liberal clergy are also in positions of influence: in seminaries, in administrative positions at denomination headquarters, and on college campuses as chaplains and religious leaders. Hadden (1969) explained the greater activism of these clergymen—for example, participating in demonstrations, organizing rent strikes, getting arrested as a way of bearing witness—by reference to their "structural freedom" (see also Hadden and Rymph, 1971). Clergy without

local parishes are structurally free in that they are less concerned about the censure and reprisals of the conservative laity.
In contrast, clergy serving a local congregation run serious risks
if they become too active or speak too boldly from the pulpit.
(For an illuminating account of how local clergymen cope with
their consciences, see Campbell and Pettigrew, 1959.) Hadden
also suggested, however, that there was a selection process by
which the clergy in teaching, administration, and the campus
ministry are likely to be more liberal. He suggested that some
liberal clergymen may be escaping from the slow, frustrating,
less spectacular task of working with and for the suburban congregations to lead them out of their conservatism. He also said
that liberal firebrands are intentionally kept away from the
local churches, where they might stir up trouble and dry up
financial contributions, and at the same time are kept in the
service of the church.

Hadden found that liberal ministers in local churches can
and do have a liberalizing influence on their congregations (see
also Friedrichs, 1971). As we have seen, conservative congregations may sometimes influence clergy behavior, but the evidence suggests that clergy opinions remain unaffected.

Cox (1968) gave the characteristics of what he called the
"New Breed" of clergy. First, the New Breed includes Catholics
and Jews as well as Protestants, whereas the last revival, the
Social Gospel movement, which lasted from about 1865 to
about 1925, was a Protestant affair. Second, the New Breed includes blacks as well as whites. Most black clergymen, like their
flocks, are theologically conservative, and many are Pentecostal
and Holiness sect members. (For a good description of an old-
fashioned black Pentecostal church in Pittsburgh, which among
other things preserves some of the symbols of the rural South
for its dispersed congregation of little-educated, hard-working
southern migrants, see Williams, 1974.) Yet Johnstone (1974)
found that 20 percent of the black ministers of Detroit were
militants in race relations. These were theological liberals and
belonged to mainline denominations. Like the white liberals,
these black ministers were much more active and much more
influential. They belonged to many more organizations, taught
their congregations, engaged in protest, and voiced demands to
political officeholders.

Third, the activist movement has genuine and deep religious roots—in Jewish concern for justice, in Jesus' concern for
the poor and oppressed, and in the conception of the kingdom

of God. In addition, the New Breed centers in the cities; it cooperates with secular agencies working for the same ends; and though idealistic, it does not have the rather naive utopianism or excessive optimism that characterized the Social Gospel movement. The New Breed has been influenced in part by the neo-orthodox theology of writers, such as Reinhold Niebuhr.

Astute observers gave the northern clergy who demonstrated in the South (away from their own congregations) much credit for legitimating the civil rights movement and gaining passage of the Civil Rights Act of 1964. Hadden (1969) kept track of the clergy's participation in demonstrations and found that it was extensive. Many struggles remain, and neither the New Breed nor their admiring supporters expect the kingdom of God to be created in their lifetime.

It will likely be a long time before it will be reasonable to regard integrated churches as an indicator of progress in race relations. First, even if church congregations become more responsible and more responsive to social and political needs than they presently are, there will continue to be a certain tendency to regard the local congregation as an enlarged family, and hence a tendency for members to be comfortable with one another only if they are not too far apart socially as well as religiously. This means that church congregations tend to be homogeneous in social class, education, and ethnicity (as well as race). Second, and closely connected, the process of inclusion is not the same as amalgamation or acculturation. For some time to come, blacks in the United States will be developing their sense of self-esteem as blacks; the slogans "black culture" and "black nationalism" are highly ambiguous and imprecise, but their meanings include an emphasis on a consciously cultivated separateness. At the same time, those who are scandalized by the separation of black from white churches are of course fundamentally right. Inclusion ideally means that blacks, as individuals and families, may decide to belong to black churches but also that they will be entirely welcome if they wish to participate in white churches; and as the process of inclusion nears completion, it seems reasonable to expect that there will be more integrated congregations.

As Littell (1968) emphasized, the American institutional pattern of separation of church and state was not a matter of mere expediency; it was a matter of principle. By the time of the Revolution, many Americans felt (probably correctly) that churches flourish better if membership and support are entirely

voluntary and that government can perform its functions better
if it is not under the direct control of an ecclesiastical organization. Government would remain subject to the free consciences
of the citizens, from whom power in a democracy ultimately
flows, and these consciences might well be shaped in part by
religious belief and faith. Littell (1968) argued that "cooperative separatism " the term used by Paul G. Kauper of the University of Michigan Law School, "better describes the uniqueness of the American experiment than would either a modified
theory of Christendom or a dogmatic secularism" (p. 36). If a
church became an adjunct to a political party, its tax immunity
might well be called into question; on the other hand, the idea
that Christianity should have nothing to do with politics can be
regarded as extreme, and the idea that separation of church and
state somehow requires religious silence on controversial issues
might well be regarded as a rationalization of political conservatism. I suggest that the historically problematic right of freedom
of expression and the privilege of tax immunity (an endorsement of religion in general as opposed to any particular religion)
do put clergymen and churches in tension. They must not be
frivolous or partisan and they must ask themselves what causes
are in line with the most catholic interpretation of freedom,
equality, and justice. The causes officially espoused by churches
are likely to cut across denominations, sects, and political parties, and appeal to universalistic principles. At the same time,
clergymen and laypersons, as individuals, are free to express
themselves on even very specific issues, bearing the prestige of
their affiliations yet not legally or morally implicating the
churches to which they belong.

Part Three

Social Control
in Urban Society

Urbanization in the short run can be quite disruptive, but in the long run it can spur the development of new patterns of social control, both explicit and implicit. The four chapters of this section are concerned with these problems and patterns. Chapter Nine by Theodore N. Ferdinand analyzes changes in "Criminal Justice: From Colonial Intimacy to Bureaucratic Formality." It will surprise some readers that Ferdinand finds advancing urbanization and industrialization to be accompanied by a sharp drop in the amount and seriousness of crime. Chapter Ten by Steven T. Bossert looks at the socialization side of social control in "Education in Urban Society." A crucial question for Bossert is whether urban education is necessarily mass and standardized education. In Chapter Eleven, "Welfare in the Metropolitan Area," Diana Pearce and David Street examine changes in the system of help and control that constitutes wel-

259

fare, exploring the proposition that suburbanization produces a bifurcation of this system. The section concludes with Chapter Twelve, "Social Life and the Physical Environment" by Harvey M. Choldin. The chapter is concerned with the effects of the built urban environment and with exploring the evidence bearing on the hypothesis that density and crowding lead to social pathology.

9

Criminal Justice: From Colonial Intimacy to Bureaucratic Formality

Theodore N. Ferdinand

Between the reigns of Queen Elizabeth I and Queen Elizabeth II, Western civilization changed profoundly—from a loose collection of isolated villages and small towns casually linked through Christianity and weak national governments to a world system of interlocking, urban-rooted, economic and political megaliths. The whole fabric of Western life has altered, but few things have been affected more deeply than criminal justice and crime.

Note: The author thanks David H. Flaherty, David Street, and Michael Hindus for reviewing and criticizing an earlier version of this essay.

We generally understand the meaning of these changes for economic endeavor, government, and social structure, but as yet the impact of modern urban society on crime and its control is unclear. Accordingly, this essay will focus on two broad questions: How did crime change in both quality and amount as urban society developed in America in the eighteenth and particularly the nineteenth centuries; and what adjustments in law enforcement, judicial procedure, and penal policy took place during this period? By limiting ourselves in this fashion we can perhaps develop a better understanding of the links that exist between urbanization, crime, and its control and thereby build a foundation for more focused research into this basic problem.

Deviance and Control in Colonial America

The control of deviance in early America and particularly in New England depended basically on the firm grip that the family, the community, and the church maintained on each of their members. Parents were warned to supervise their children closely; husbands were expected to control their wives; and church members were admonished to oversee one another; as a result, very few, if any, in the community were not under constant, close supervision (Morgan, 1966; Flaherty, 1972, chaps. 2, 3, 5; Bushman, 1967, chap. 10; Lockridge, 1970, part 1). Those few newcomers who were not members of established families or the church were required to marry into such a family and join the church within a reasonable period—or leave the community altogether. There was no room, particularly in New England, for independent individuals, and those who would not submit their lives to close community control were not welcome. Moreover, members rooted in the community were regularly bombarded with orthodox views on a variety of basic matters ranging from personal conduct to current political issues. The church and the clergy effectively molded elite opinion using the pulpit and their pivotal role in community affairs, and the town meeting extended their influence to everyman in an almost irresistible fashion (Bushman, 1967, chap. 10).

In the absence of more ancient institutions, many New England communities instituted town meetings where pressing local matters could be considered, solutions proposed, and a policy established, often by voice vote. Although town meetings were not truly democratic, there can be little doubt that they effectively mobilized community opinion along locally approved lines. Few individuals felt strong enough to defy a con-

sensus established via the town meeting, and those who did
were often obliged to depart for more hospitable surroundings
by the pressure that ensued (Allen, 1972; Zuckerman, 1968;
Zuckerman, 1970, chaps. 4-6). The typical New England community, therefore, was well organized for establishing and maintaining community-wide agreement on most basic issues.
Through the church and town meeting local leaders were able to
define the proper stance on public issues and present their views
to key members of the community. And through the neighborhood and the family these views were imposed on young and
old alike. Thus, corporate control, that is, control by well defined, permanent groups, was the established method of insuring social conformity in the community, and for the most part
it worked very well.

There was very little crime, and what little there was reflected primarily the inability of individuals to discipline themselves within the narrow limits of colonial society (Erikson,
1966, chap. 4; Adams, 1927, pp. 160-161; Flaherty, 1973). For
example, Ferdinand (1973, table 3) reports that the rate of
criminal prosecutions in Boston between 1703 and 1732 was
less than one thirteenth the rate of arrests in the same city in
1884 and 1885. Formal legal institutions were available for
dealing with serious offenders, but the bulk of the deviants was
identified and sanctioned informally through the church (Zuckerman, 1970, pp. 61-65; Oberholzer, 1956, chap. 12; Flaherty,
1972, pp. 154-163).[1] Persistent transgressors were accused by
witnesses or the pastor before the congregation and, failing a
confession and the appropriate degree of contrition, were ex-
communicated from the church. If, however, they repented
their sins, reinstatement often followed.

Serious offenders were dealt with via more formal procedures, that is, by arrest and a court hearing. But even here the
law and criminal procedure were little more than an extension
of the community and its mores. Community sentiment was
more powerful in determining who was to be arrested than the
written law, and constables were keenly aware of this fact. They
regularly refused to interfere with illegal but popular activities.
Moreover, the law and its interpretation in the courts were left
largely to community leaders and not to trained lawyers or
judges (Goebel, 1969, pp. 109-120). The early criminal codes of
Massachusetts and Connecticut owed much to the Bible, and
the clergy were prominent in most important cases, such as the
Salem witch trials (Starkey, 1949).

Magistrates and justices of the peace often created law to

fit the cases that came before them, and summary judgments were frequently handed down after only a superficial examination of the evidence, a grand jury indictment being considered sufficient in many cases to establish guilt (Goebel, 1969, pp. 112-113; Goebel and Naughton, 1970, part 2). Jury trials were rare, and justices frequently cooperated with the prosecution by vigorously interrogating defendants and defense witnesses (Flaherty, 1972, pp. 227-232). But when cases did reach a jury, it often formulated law, weighed evidence, and rendered verdicts more in terms of local custom than legal precedent (Nelson, 1975, pp. 28-35). Lawyers were not even recognized as officers of the court until the first decade of the eighteenth century in the colonies of Massachusetts and Connecticut, and they were regarded with great suspicion until much later (Gawalt, 1970, p. 283). At the time of the Revolution, fewer than 100 were available to about 200,000 people in all of Massachusetts (Gawalt, 1973, pp. 27-50). Thus, the court and its officers were tied to the local community in many ways and followed closely the initiatives and guidelines established by community leaders. The principal bulwarks against deviancy and crime, therefore, were the community and the church, with the formal law and the courts simply reinforcing their authority in nearly all matters.

Breakup of Colonial Society

Several developments in the eighteenth century combined to shatter this orderly, sober existence in the American colonies (Bushman, 1967, chaps. 2, 9, 14, 16). The authority of the church was shaken at its foundations, first by the Enlightenment and later by the growing wealth of the middle classes, who were increasingly drawn to materialistic values. Moreover, the hegemony of the New England village was challenged by the expanding cities, which served as convenient havens for those who found the close, corporate control of the Puritan village too restrictive. In the late eighteenth century a variety of entrepreneurs, both legitimate and otherwise, congregated in America's growing cities to serve the needs of their citizens—pawnbrokers, tavern owners, gamblers, thieves, fences, and prostitutes (Bridenbaugh, 1965, p. 318; Inciardi, 1975, pp. 47-48; Lane, 1967, pp. 23-24). Finally, the eighteenth century was a riotous time in America, with its urban and rural populations frequently declaring their displeasure with public policy. The spirit of defiance and rebellion was strong, and in its wake many indulged in criminal behavior who might never have been tempted otherwise (Hindus, 1971; Maier, 1970).

The combined effect of these several developments was to weaken the authority of the church and the community, to heighten criminogenic pressures, and to confront the courts and law enforcement with the necessity of revising, reinforcing, and extending their structures for coping with the increasingly troublesome problems of crime and deviance. By the first decades of the nineteenth century, therefore, America was on the threshold of important changes in both its crime problem and its criminal justice system.

An Autonomous Criminal Justice System

During the first quarter of the nineteenth century, the crime rate turned upward, and by 1824 in Boston it was at an all-time peak (Ferdinand, 1973, table 3). There was little alarm among the citizens of Boston—perhaps because there were few, if any, comparative statistics that could detail the extent of the problem. (Handlin [1968, pp. 18-20] reported no concern among the citizens of Boston during this period; indeed, quite the reverse was true.) But it is clear that the constables in nineteenth-century Boston were a much more dedicated and thorough arm of the law than their eighteenth-century predecessors had been (Ferdinand, 1973; Flaherty, 1972, pp. 190-193; Greenburg, 1975, pp. 175-180; Zuckerman, 1970, pp. 85-88). It is also clear that the courts and even the penal system were beginning to adapt to the growing volume of crime in their own ways.

In 1823 a haphazard arrangement in which the constables essentially served the lower courts was replaced in Boston by the more efficient organization of the constables serving under a city marshall who could oversee their activity and redirect them when and where necessary (Lane, 1967, pp. 16-17). But even this step toward centralized law enforcement was inadequate, and in 1838 Boston's constables were augmented by a new force of full-time, paid police. The first major city in the United States to institute a full-time police force was Philadelphia in 1833, but by the Civil War most major cities had replaced their constables with police.

The law and the courts also experienced considerable ferment in the early decades of the last century. As American cities became larger and more impersonal, it quickly became evident that the informal, often arbitrary methods of the colonial period were inadequate. Communal solidarity was no longer sufficient in many cities to intimidate deviants; town meetings had become too large and unwieldy to mobilize public sentiment; and powerful factions had emerged on many important issues regarding criminal justice, such as the punishment of offenders. It was no longer possible, in other words, for community leaders to impose decisions on reluctant parties to many important disputes, and to fill this gap the American courts adopted a series of reforms that enhanced their authority in the community and enabled them to impose settlements where local dicta were insufficient. Specifically, the rights of defendants were significantly strengthened; courtroom procedures were rationalized; rules of evidence were tightened; the professional training of lawyers and judges became more rigorous and systematic; and punishments for felonies were substantially reduced.

Penal institutions also underwent a remarkable evolution following the Revolution. During the colonial period they had been used primarily as jails and workhouses for the temporary imprisonment of minor offenders in the local community (Powers, 1966, chap. 8). There were few if any statewide institutions for long-term imprisonment of serious offenders. But with the revision in the penal code that occurred in most states following the Revolution, the number of capital offenses was substantially reduced and alternative means of punishment became urgently needed. In response to these pressures, the states began building prisons, and an entirely new factor in the administration of criminal justice appeared: the prison system.

The several changes that I have sketched here will be documented in the sections that follow, but it should be noted that their ultimate effect was to transfer the administration of criminal justice from the control of local leaders to a professional or bureaucratic elite, who formulated criminal justice policy that was often far removed from the moral temper of the people they were serving. The new autonomy of the law and courts undoubtedly improved the quality of justice in nineteenth-century America by freeing courts from local prejudice and ill-founded rumor. The autonomy enjoyed by the police and the prisons in nineteenth-century America, however, had a less happy result. Let us examine these changes in greater detail.

Emergence of a Modern Criminal Court. In the libertarian mood that prevailed after the Revolution, the rights of defendants in the criminal court were substantially broadened

(Nelson, 1975, pp. 100-101; Warren, 1966, pp. 468-472). Defendants charged with capital offenses, for example, were no longer permitted to plead guilty at preliminary hearings and could do so at their arraignments only after sober reflection. Justices of the peace were no longer permitted to interrogate defendants regarding their offenses during preliminary hearings, and insanity was finally accepted as a defense in criminal cases.

The Revolution also had a profound effect on the organization of American courtrooms. Since witnesses were no longer assumed to be truthful simply because they had taken an oath, juries were required to weigh not only the evidence but also the credibility of witnesses in framing their decisions in criminal cases (Nelson, 1975, pp. 113-114). Also, the appellate courts were reduced from three presiding judges to one (Nelson, 1975, pp. 167-172). During the colonial period the appellate courts had had three or more judges, each of whom could give instructions to juries on questions of law. Since these instructions were often contradictory, juries were generally free to interpret the law according to their own standards—and often did so. The justice that emerged from this arrangement was often arbitrary, as we have already seen. In a series of cases decided between 1804 and 1810, however, this defect was remedied by taking the responsibility for interpreting the law from the jury and giving it entirely to the presiding judge (Nelson, 1975, pp. 168-169). This move, no doubt, had the desired effect of strengthening due process in American courtrooms, but it also enhanced the general authority of presiding justices at the expense of juries and thereby further diminished the influence of local sentiments and prejudices on criminal court cases. (Although this redistribution of responsibility was initially established in the civil courts, before too long juries in criminal courts were similarly restricted; Nelson, 1975, p. 257).

The advent of single-judge appellate courts meant, moreover, that it became much easier to fasten responsibility for the outcome of appeals and important rulings on individual judges. To render this accountability more precise, many judges began issuing written opinions to support their decisions and rulings in court. To give some significance to these reforms, appellate courts began to scrutinize the deliberations and verdicts of the lower courts more carefully and to reverse decisions that were manifestly in violation of due process or contrary to the evidence (Nelson, 1975, p. 168). As the record of these decisions (and in some cases their reversals) accumulated, a distinct legal perspective emerged, and the basis for a careful analysis of the legal principles underlying the rulings of American judges, that is, an American jurisprudence, took shape (Nelson, 1975, p. 168). The implications of these changes in American court-rooms were not immediately apparent, but there can be little doubt that on these foundations the American judiciary has emerged as perhaps the most authoritative in Western civiliza-tion. American courts today are asked to resolve disputes in almost every area of American life, but such authority would not have been possible without, first, the clear designation of the judge as the interpreter of the law at the expense of the jury, and second, the emergence of an American jurisprudence to lend the combined authority of tradition and consensus to the opinions of individual judges. These structural changes were nicely complemented by the timely appearance of several extra-ordinary judicial personalities, such as Chief Justice Marshall, but it is also clear that without these changes, a strong judiciary would have been, at the very least, much slower in developing.

Several improvements in the laws of evidence were also instituted during this period. If judges and juries were to be held to a stricter standard, it was important to clarify the standard itself and to close several notorious loopholes. To this end the hearsay rule restricting secondhand testimony before the jury was given much broader application in American courts in the early decades of the nineteenth century (Friedman, 1973, pp. 134-137). A court in which professional justices rendered the verdict, as in most European courts, need not protect itself so carefully from weak or improper evidence: An experienced, trained judge can recognize and disregard such evidence. But a court in which untrained laymen decide the question of guilt or innocence must institute laws of evidence to ease the task. The prohibition against hearsay, however, was not absolute, and several exceptions were recognized as experience in using the rule accumulated (Friedman, 1973, pp. 135-136). For example, the accusation of a dying murder victim and the routine records of a business firm were admissible as exceptions to the hearsay rule. But the basic intent of the rule was not undermined by these exceptions, and the discretion of the jury was further curbed by the clarification of the law of hearsay.

As the law became more intricate after the Revolution and as the commercial-industrial revolution gathered momen-tum, the demand for legally competent judges and lawyers grew rapidly. To meet this demand many colleges appointed professors of law to give regular lectures to their students, and private lawyers in several cities presented systematic courses of study for prospective lawyers (Warren, 1966, chap. 14). The most successful of these was the Litchfield Law School, established in 1784 by Judge Tapping Reeve in Connecticut; by 1833, when it closed, it had graduated more than 1,000 students, many of whom had gone on to prominent careers in American politics and law. The professional training of lawyers was firmly established, however, by the founding of Harvard Law School in 1817. It was the first university law school, and under its influence the traditional method of apprenticing young men to practicing lawyers was gradually replaced by systematic study in an established law school (Gawalt, 1973).

As lawyers became more competent and criminal cases were more carefully scrutinized, several defects in criminal proceedings became apparent (Warren, 1966, pp. 472-474). For example, under the old common law of England, individuals with a material or direct interest in a case (including the defendant) were prohibited from giving testimony before the court. Thus, in many important cases defendants were prevented from giving their interpretation of the evidence in person, and their defense was thereby seriously impaired. In the beginning American courts followed this ancient rule, but by the 1840s the disabilities it imposed on the court were no longer tolerable. Following the lead of the English Parliament, which passed Lord Benham's act in 1843, Connecticut passed legislation in 1848 that specifically enabled the parties to a case to give testimony. These innovations were gradually adopted by the other states, but it was not until 1878 that the federal courts were permitted by statute to hear testimony by defendants in criminal cases.

From the perspective of the criminal law and courts, the Revolution and the subsequent urban industrial society worked a profound transformation on the rights of defendants and clarified the responsibilities of both the judge and the jury in criminal proceedings. Due process received a more precise definition, and the adversarial system in American courts was strengthened. But as justice became more formal and objective, it also became more removed from the values of the local community. This fact probably improved the quality of justice in American courts in the first half of the nineteenth century by making guilt and innocence more certainly distinguished, but it also prepared the way for the American judiciary to play a much expanded role in American life and to hold other segments of society to a new and more rigorous standard of behavior. The full meaning of this development is far from clear even today, but its origins can be readily traced to the post-Revolutionary era, when the American judicial system was cut loose from both the immediate community and the authority of the English courts.

A Modern Police System. A parallel emergence of the police from within the community had a less salutary effect. At first American cities continued to enforce the law with constables and watchmen, but as the cities grew, these officers soon proved ineffective, not for law enforcement but for crowd control. Antebellum American cities were laced with serious riots almost annually: Proslavery and abolitionist groups, anti-Catholic mobs, antiimmigrant crowds, and poor people took their grievances to the streets regularly, with the result that by the 1830s civil disorders were becoming a chronic problem in many northern cities. The constables and watchmen were effective against disorganized criminality, but in the face of rioting mobs they were too thinly dispersed to have much effect (Ferdinand, 1973, p. 7; Lane, 1967, p. 27). In addition, the constabulary was unavailable at night, and the nightwatch was dispersed throughout the city and difficult to assemble quickly. In the 1830s Philadelphia and Boston organized police forces; New York did so in the 1840s, and Baltimore in the 1850s.

The new police force represented an advance over the ancient constabulary because it placed all law enforcement under one command and thereby enabled the deployment of an organized force relatively quickly in the face of civil disorder. It proved its worth in New York City in 1863 when police contained a city-wide riot of extraordinary dimensions (Headley, 1970, chaps. 10-19).

The first police departments had to overcome many problems (Costello, 1972, pp. 127-128; Richardson, 1970, pp. 64-65, 68). At first they wore no uniforms and carried no guns. An arrest usually meant transporting a reluctant suspect some distance through the streets to a lockup. The lonely patrolman had little more than his wits and commanding presence to cope with criminals and their supporters in the early years. The organizational problems of these early departments were substantial. When the New York police department was founded in 1845, it included a force of 800 men, and when the Baltimore department was established in 1857 it consisted of 405 men. Most of the early departments served growing metropolitan

areas with severe crime problems, and the new police departments were forced to organize themselves quickly to meet this
threat. Almost from the beginning, therefore, the major departments assumed bureaucratic structures with a centralized command and a rational organization in which distinctive functions
were performed by specialized bureaus (Costello, 1972, p. 81
and chap. 18; Lane, 1967, pp. 47-48, 60-62, 98-99). The detectives and patrolmen were differentiated early and vice and traffic bureaus followed soon after. Soon the chain of command
between the policeman on the street and the commanders at
headquarters consisted of at least three or four levels.

The bureaucratic structure enabled the various departments to mobilize rapidly in the face of threat, but it also
affected their relationship with the community (Bordua, 1968;
Tifft and Bordua, 1969). The commander became an important
public figure and relatively unapproachable by the average citizen; the bureaucratic structure itself isolated the men from
broad, informal contacts in the community; and most important, the lower ranks became virtually invisible to those in command. Thus, the larger departments in the nineteenth century
were already isolated from the public they served and vulnerable to more specific kinds of pressures.

Two influences quickly developed. Community leaders
realized that the police performed a strategic function and
needed to be controlled if their own political objectives were to
be accomplished. Accordingly, it became common practice to
appoint commanders who could be trusted to support the
mayor's policies and to remove those who could not (Haller,
1976). This practice posed no problem for the police if the
mayor was simply interested in effective law enforcement. But
there were many antagonistic factions in nineteenth-century
American cities (as now), and it was often difficult to develop
policies that all could endorse. As different factions gained control of city government, therefore, they routinely installed their
own appointments in key positions in, among others, the police
department. Police commanders, in other words, had to be politically adroit as well as effective law enforcement officers to
remain in office for any length of time. The resultant instability
at the top level inevitably weakened its authority and rendered
control of the department that much more difficult.

At the same time several different kinds of criminal factions were also affecting the police. In the early years of several
departments, men who specialized in solving property crimes

developed an easy familiarity with the thieves whom they were pursuing (Johnson, n.d.; Lane, 1967, chap. 8). A detective was only as effective as his underworld contacts, and many thefts were solved only through tips. To facilitate the solution of many crimes, handsome rewards were offered, and before long detectives and thieves were cooperating in order to split the reward. A thief and a detective would conspire to steal some goods and agree to return them for the reward when it was offered. The detective served as the liaison between the thief and the victim. To thwart this practice, most departments required that any reward earned by policemen be given to the police relief fund. Another but less easily suppressed activity was that in which vice operators sought to corrupt the police in return for permission to continue their activities. By the 1870s criminal elements controlled several New York precincts, and corruption became almost commonplace in the department.

This corruption of the police at both the top and the bottom resulted in the appearance of a novel kind of police department in several American cities in the 1870s (Richardson, 1970, pp. 153-155, 161-164, 180-189), which was especially responsive to the dominant political currents in the city and shaped their arresting and promotion policies accordingly. Enemies of the party in power could expect police harassment, and friends could expect easy promotion within the police hierarchy. These departments were readily corrupted by elements of the underworld, and their reputations in their communities suffered proportionately. Their budgets were minimal, morale was poor, and the momentum for change was nil. The periodic scandals simply completed the picture and confirmed what all suspected—the department was utterly corrupt. James Q. Wilson (1968b, chap. 5) has labeled this department the "watchman" department.

The fact that nothing effective was done for so long in the several cities plagued with such departments indicates clearly that the problem went much deeper than simply the quality of leadership. Watchman departments served an important function for an entrenched political machine: They helped protect the machine and its denizens from investigation, and as long as they had something to hide, it was essential that the police be controlled. The result in many American cities was a police department that lacked integrity, initiative, and respect. By the 1920s the problem had gained nationwide attention, and under the leadership of August Vollmer, chief of the Berkeley, California, police department, a movement to correct the deficiencies of many large-city departments gathered support, mainly from among chiefs of police (Carte and Carte, 1975, chaps. 3-5). The goal was to raise police work to a professional level by freeing police departments from political meddling and by raising the competence and quality of policemen generally so that corruption would be virtually impossible. The ideal was to create a department in which police matters were decided solely by police authorities and in which the rank and file were so deeply committed to excellence in police work that their subversion was difficult if not impossible. Over the years several departments have been relatively successful in reaching this ideal, for example, those in Los Angeles, Berkeley, Cincinnati, Kansas City (Missouri), and St. Louis; but several others have been unsuccessful: most notably the departments in Boston, New York, and Chicago.

The police department envisioned by Vollmer—and subsequently labeled the "legalistic" department by Wilson (1968b, chap. 6)—was to utilize science and skill in achieving police goals. Only the "highest type" of people would be recruited to police work; they would be given the best possible training; the expertise of specialists would be used whenever possible; and above all the law would be enforced without fear or favor. Unfortunately, the solution contained some problems of its own. When the police were released from the smothering control of the community in the early decades of the nineteenth century, the vacuum was filled by special interests that sought to use the police for their own purposes. But when these special interests were neutralized in the twentieth century, the only ethos available was professionalism, that is, an ideal that presumes a high degree of independence for the police.

Unlike the courts, however, the police are not guided by an ethos that is easily compatible with liberal, democratic government, and when granted autonomy to define their mission according to the highest standards of police professionalism, there is some risk that departments will violate the traditional freedoms that form the essence of liberal democracy (Skolnick, 1975, pp. 235-239). J. Edgar Hoover, for example, ordered his special agents to collect information for political purposes on a wide variety of public figures during the 1960s, and the Chicago police department has done the same at the local level. If the police can turn their expertise in crime detection on those who support unorthodox causes with impunity, democracy cannot thrive for long. The ideal of police professionalism, therefore, seems to collide with the ideal of a liberal democracy.

Perhaps the solution to this dilemma lies in the nature of

the controlling organization and the kind of leadership it culti-
vates among police agencies. As we have seen, when the controlling structure is politically determined at the local level, the
department can only be as effective as local leaders want it to
be. But if the controlling structure was located at the state level
and was constituted of responsible, appointed officials—for
example, supreme court justices—the quality of leadership in
local police departments would probably be considerably higher
over the long run, and the departments' freedom to pursue
criminality would probably be greater. Several states—for example, New York, Maryland, Massachusetts, Missouri, Michigan,
Ohio, and Louisiana—have experimented with variations of this
method of appointing commanders to major urban departments, and many European countries, for example, Belgium and
the Netherlands, follow a similar procedure today. No one has
carefully evaluated the results, but several observers have commented on the overall superiority of European police departments (Becker, 1973, chap. 5; Glueck, 1974, chap. 5). What
might happen over the long term in American departments if
such a procedure for appointing commanders was instituted can
only be guessed, but it is clear that professionalism in police
work is not the final answer to the problems that the police
pose for modern democratic societies.

   A Modern Penal System. The emergence of an urban civilization in nineteenth-century America had an equally complex
effect on American penal institutions. As we have seen, in the
colonial period minor offenders were punished informally
through public denunciations and warnings. More serious offenders were punished with public punishments of several kinds,
such as stocks and pillories, whippings, and ducking stools; the
most serious crimes were punished with death or banishment.
Houses of correction and prisons were also used for punishment
during this early period, but most of the sentences were short
and the number of offenders sentenced to prison was relatively
small (Powers, 1966, pp. 238-241). The bulk of the serious offenders received public humiliation, death, or banishment. Out
of eighty-one cases that came before the Court of Assistants in
Massachusetts Bay Colony between 1673 and 1683, only three
were sentenced to prison, twenty-one were sentenced to death,
and eight were banished (Powers, 1966, p. 408). During the
seventeenth century, fourteen crimes were punishable by death
in Massachusetts, including stealing, arson, robbery, sodomy,
polygamy, burglary, and counterfeiting; consequently, a sub-

stantial portion of those found guilty of any offense were punished in ways that did not require large prisons.

Shortly after the Revolution, however, the penal codes of several states were substantially changed. Pennsylvania, for example, restricted the death penalty to treason, murder, rape, and arson in its Penal Code of 1786, and although other states did not proceed as rapidly as Pennsylvania, many used its code as their guide. But if offenders were not to be executed as frequently as before the Revolution, some alternate punishment had to be found. Several methods were experimented with, but ultimately all the states settled on imprisonment as the primary solution and began to build prisons (Lewis, 1967, chap. 2).[2] At first these institutions were relatively small (for example, Walnut Street Prison in Philadelphia could house only seventy-two prisoners without overcrowding), but as the crime rate increased and as the number of capital offenses shrank, the number of prisoners inevitably soared. In 1819 in Auburn, New York, Auburn Prison was opened with a capacity of 458, and in 1825 work was begun at Sing Sing, where a prison with 800 cells was planned.

As penal institutions grew larger and more expensive, much thought was given to their design and purpose, and two competing philosophies evolved. The Auburn Prison pioneered the congregate system, in which the inmates worked together in silence during the day and returned to their individual cells at night. One aim of the congregate system was to teach inmates industrial skills and habits, but the most important result was that the prison more than covered its own expenses. Eastern Penitentiary, on the other hand, developed the separate system, which stressed the importance of personal grace and redemption, and imposed Bible reading and solitary confinement on each inmate for the term of imprisonment. Whatever the relative merits of these two philosophies, both were applied relentlessly, with the result that American prisons developed a worldwide reputation for the efficient way in which they managed large prison populations (Rothman, 1971, chap. 4).

These early attempts to design a penal system that was well managed and corrective failed for a variety of reasons—overcrowding, faltering leadership, inadequate budgets, but perhaps most of all because of an inexorable custodial drift. It is a truism that nearly all prisoners deeply resent their imprisonment, and this resentment often encourages resistance to prison programs and policies. But prisoner resistance kindles authoritarianism among prison staff members, which normally results in hostility between prisoners and prison supervisors and harsh custodial policies (Perrow, 1963). Thus, any policy for the treatment of inmates encounters steady pressure to become more custodial and in the absence of countervailing pressures will ultimately be so redefined. By the 1850s, therefore, both the congregate system and the separate system had lost any illusion of "correcting" the offender and had long since focused exclusively on using inmate labor to defray the costs of their imprisonment (McKelvey, 1968, chap. 2).

During this period America was an amalgam of religious and ethical perspectives, and many of them had applications to the prison and its goals (Mennel, 1973, chap. 3). The harsh conclusions of social Darwinism—though not yet formally defined by Spencer and Sumner—were implicit in the fierce struggle for survival in industrial America and justified an especially punitive regimen for those who lacked the good fortune, will, or talent to prosper during the antebellum period. At the same time, the belief in America's special mission to the world as ethical leader was also gathering support and seemed to stress society's obligation to lift offenders out of their criminal habitats and place them back into the mainstream of American social and industrial life. The latter view prevailed in 1868, when the New York Prison Association endorsed the idea of a reformatory devoted to training young men for industrial employment (McKelvey, 1968, p. 67).

Zebulon Brockway implemented the idea in 1877 when he opened the Elmira (New York) Reformatory. Its mission was not so much the religious salvation of inmates as their social rehabilitation. Prisoners were not seen as individual misfits who had slipped morally from grace but as unfortunates whose social or personal deficiencies prevented their full participation in the industrial economy. Instead of religious teaching and meditation, therefore, the emphasis was on training inmates in industrial skills. It accepted only men between the ages of 18 and 30, gave them educational courses and vocational training, provided graded rewards for progress in the program, and promised early release for those who successfully completed the program. Other states built similar reformatories, and soon many states had two types of prisons: a main prison for defiant, irredeemable prisoners and a reformatory for young, salvageable ones.

The concept behind the reformatory movement was worthy, and for a period reformatories actually seemed to achieve the reform of some of their inmates (Brockway, 1969, chap. 13; Barnes, 1974, chap. 9). But the abrasive forces of the penal system wore down the idea and eventually the movement withered. The goal of the reformatory was to reform youthful offenders, and to this end it required an indeterminate sentence and the fixing of release by prison officials based on their evaluation of each inmate's growth within the program.

But the reformatory was clearly a more relaxed, humane setting than the maximum security prisons in New York State, and before long it began to be used as a medium security institution. Those who failed at Elmira were transferred to one of the maximum security institutions (Brockway, 1969, chap. 12), and those at other institutions who needed only medium security were assigned to Elmira. The mission of Elmira, therefore, was slowly transformed from that of affording young inmates a chance to develop vocational skills to one of containing a relatively cooperative inmate population. The latter purpose gave much more attention to the attitude and demeanor of the inmate and rewarded only those who were cooperative with early release. As a result of this change of mission, the vocational programs became less crucial in determining release and finally became irrelevant in the eyes of both the inmates and the staff. Ultimately, a great variety of inmates—many of whom needed no vocational training—were assigned to Elmira on the basis of their ability to tolerate a medium security setting (Brockway, 1969, p. 370), and eventually the heterogeneity of its population overwhelmed the specialized vocational and educational programs. The same probably happened at other reformatories, and by World War I the reformatory movement in the United States was dead (McKelvey, 1968, chap. 4).

Steele and Jacobs (1975, pp. 149-158) offer an interesting interpretation of why such institutions as Elmira tend to lose their momentum. Such institutions are designed to function within a differentiated prison system, wherein each institution is assigned a specific treatment or rehabilitation mission with respect to its particular segment of the inmate population. Custodial concerns are secondary to the primary purpose of the institution—rehabilitation through specialized treatment or training—and only inmates who have a specific need for its programs are assigned to such an institution. But when a treatment institution is a member of a hierarchical prison system, that is, a system that is graded essentially in terms of security, its population is defined primarily in terms of custodial requirements, not rehabilitative needs; eventually both staff and inmates adapt accordingly.

Pattern of Crime in Industrial America

While the separate elements of the criminal justice system were developing in nineteenth-century America, the criminal world was also changing in response to shifts in social structure and organization. We have already noted the slight amount of serious crime in colonial New England. There is strong indication, however, that shortly after the turn of the eighteenth century, serious crime in New England reached record levels, changing its focus dramatically as urbanization gathered momentum. According to Ferdinand's (1973, table 3) study of the Boston police court, the rate of prosecutions in 1824 was more than eight times that between 1703 and 1732, and the largest increase was experienced in violent crimes. During the earlier period there were three property offenses for every violent crime, but during the later period there were five violent offenses for every three property offenses. Thus, as Boston became an urban, commercial center, crime became much more common and violent crime became the prevalent form.

An explanation of this broad shift in level and type of crime from the eighteenth to the early nineteenth century must be speculative. I incline to the view that the emerging urban society in nineteenth-century America provided city dwellers with attractive opportunities for deviant or criminal activity while confronting them with few restraints. The cities in the early nineteenth century were just emerging from their small-town status. Professional criminals of several types were finding comfortable niches within many cities, and the church and town meetings were no longer effective methods for insuring conformity. The cities were much more anonymous, and growth was so rapid during this early period that relatively few urban dwellers had roots in either stable neighborhoods or enduring careers (Knights, 1971). Those who wished to engage in deviant or criminal activity were relatively free to do so.

It is interesting that this is also a period of very high levels of premarital pregnancy in New England. Smith and Hindus (1975) found in a study of illegitimate births that the highest levels ever recorded were between 1761 and 1800. Any change in social organization that facilitated deviance could be expected to affect young people, and specifically their sexual activity, relatively quickly; the Smith and Hindus finding is entirely consistent with the thesis developed here. Finally, along these same lines Clinard and Abbott (1973, table 2, p. 18) reported that between 1955 and 1968, which was a period of rapid urbanization, Uganda reported an increase of 89 percent in total crime and an increase of 138 percent in violent crime—the same pattern observed in early Boston. Although the evidence is by no means conclusive, it appears that a rapidly urbanizing community releases its citizens from the pervasive controls of village life and presents them with the opportunity to engage in a variety of deviant and criminal activity.

After an initial transition period, however, the structure of urbanizing society becomes more settled and better defined, with the result that crime assumes proportions more typical of an urban community (Lane, 1968). As cities mature, their citizens become established in urban occupations and integrated into relatively stable urban neighborhoods. The police and other agents of control replace the informal methods of the village. After the transition from village to urban social patterns, therefore, we might anticipate a decline in serious crime and a shift to crimes more consistent with the conditions and ethos of urban life, that is, a shift from violent crimes to crimes against property and to vice.

There is considerable evidence that such a shift occurred in several American cities and European societies during the nineteenth century. Ferdinand (1973, table 3) found that the rate of prosecutions for serious crime in the Boston police court declined by 38 percent between 1824 and the 1860-1869 period and that prosecutions for violent crimes dropped most, by 52 percent. Prosecutions for property crimes dropped by only 15 percent during this same period. Moreover, the level of serious crime continued to decline through the remainder of the nineteenth century and on into the first half of the twentieth century (Ferdinand, 1967). There were several major fluctuations, reflecting wars or depressions, but the overall trend was downward, with property crime assuming an increasingly prominent position in the overall pattern.

Similar changes were observed in Salem, Massachusetts, and New Haven, Connecticut. In Salem, violent crimes outnumbered property crimes well into the twentieth century (see Table 1), and in New Haven the same was true until the 1880s. Ultimately, however, property crimes became dominant in both cities. Moreover, the rate of serious crime (violent crimes and

Table 1. Ratio of Property Crimes to Violent Crimes in Three
American Cities in the Nineteenth and Twentieth Centuries.

Salem, Massachusetts		New Haven, Connecticut		Rockford, Illinois	
Ratio	Period	Ratio	Period	Ratio	Period
0.52	1853-1861	–	–	–	–
0.71	1865-1870	0.54	1864-1873	–	–
0.60	1871-1879	0.83	1874-1882	–	–
0.59	1880-1888	12.63	1883-1891	3.13	1884-1892
0.76	1889-1897	15.85	1892-1900	1.53	1893-1901
0.93	1898-1906	21.98	1901-1909	1.11	1902-1910
0.74	1907-1915	14.74	1910-1918	1.71	1911-1919
1.26	1916-1924	6.97	1919-1927	2.04	1920-1928
1.85	1925-1933	4.68	1928-1932	2.14	1929-1937
1.64	1934-1942	–	–	2.94	1938-1946
2.00	1943-1951[a]	–	–	2.54	1947-1955
2.33	1952-1960	–	–	2.31	1956-1964
4.73	1961-1966	–	–	2.45	1965-1970

Note: Violent crimes include murder, manslaughter, aggravated assault, forcible rape, robbery, and assault. Property crimes include burglary, larceny, auto theft, and horse theft. These data were taken from earlier studies by the author (see Ferdinand, 1968, 1972, 1976).

[a]Data for 1946 through 1948 are missing. There are no data for years in which dashes are indicated.

property crimes together) declined steadily in both cities as they adapted to the developing commercial-industrial civilization. At the end of the series described in Table 1, the rate of serious crime in Salem was one seventh its level at the beginning, and in New Haven it was less than one eighth. Both cities were settled early in the seventeenth century and existed for roughly two hundred years as preindustrial villages before industrialism absorbed them in the early 1800s. Rockford, Illinois, which was established in the 1840s and developed virtually from the beginning as an industrial city, presents an altogether different picture (see Table 1). Property crimes outnumbered violent crimes consistently throughout its history, and the level of serious crime from 1965 to 1970 was more than eight times its level in 1884 through 1892. It never experienced the radical changes that Boston, Salem, and New Haven all underwent.

The only crimes in Boston to show a consistently upward trend during the nineteenth century were offenses against chastity, morality, or decency (Ferdinand, 1973, table 3). Between 1824 and the 1860-1869 period, the rate of prosecutions in this category for such offenses increased by 72 percent in the Boston police court, and by 1884 and 1885 such arrests constituted 66 percent of all arrests. The major problem, of course, was drunkenness.[3] Excluding drunkenness, the rate of prosecutions or arrests for vice declined steadily in the nineteenth century. Nevertheless, drunkenness was widely regarded in the nineteenth century as a vice, and it would be arbitrary to exclude it from that category because our view toward it has softened.

Several studies of European societies tend to confirm the general pattern described above. Gatrell and Hadden (1972, pp. 336-396) examined the historical pattern of crime in nineteenth-century England and Wales and found that indictable committals to trial for serious offenses declined by 79 percent between 1842 and 1891, and Lodhi and Tilly (1973) studied the criminal patterns of France between 1826 and 1954 and reported that serious crime dropped by nearly 90 percent. Finally, Ferracuti, Lazzari, and Wolfgang (1970, pp. 45, 47) found that as Sardinia became more urban, the percentage of homicides and serious assaults decreased from 40 percent of the total crimes in 1800 through 1829 to 8 percent in 1957 through 1960. It is difficult to compare such widely diverse communities and societies and assert confidently that advancing urbanization is the only factor causing these similar patterns, but the consistency of these patterns is suggestive.

This long-term decline in serious and especially violent crime seems to contradict the evidence of recent years, in which the rate of serious criminal complaints in the United States increased 179.9 percent between 1960 and 1975 and the rate of complaints for violent crime increased even more sharply, 199.3 percent, over the same period (*Uniform Crime Reports, 1975,* 1976, p. 49, table 2). These increases have been noted in virtually all sections of the country—even in New England, where the historical evidence clearly indicates a long-term decline. How can we reconcile the historical pattern with the current trend?

Apparently, the upsurge in criminality since the late 1950s reflects a real increase, and not simply more comprehensive and thorough reporting—it has been felt too broadly and recorded in too many different communities. Moreover, there can be little argument over the sources of the increase. The social liberation of blacks in American society, announced in 1954 with the Supreme Court decision of *Brown* v. *Board of Education, Topeka, Kansas* and culminated in the urban riots of the 1960s, left in its wake many young blacks who no longer feared or respected white society and its institutions. In Rockford, Illinois, for example, the percentage of blacks among all arrests never exceeded 12 percent during the 1950s but steadily increased to more than 25 percent by 1970 without a proportionate increase in the percentage of blacks in the population (compare Ferdinand, 1976, figure 5). Some of the upsurge in criminality in the 1960s may have reflected a release of pent-up anger that had festered for years—if not centuries—among blacks.

Another factor in this increase is undoubtedly a decided shift in values and behavior of young, middle-class Americans of every color. First, the student sit-ins at Berkeley and then the student riots everywhere as the Vietnam war reached fever pitch seemed to provoke an antiestablishment perspective among a substantial portion of American college students. The unity of the students as a social and political bloc was strengthened even as their opposition to established authority mounted. In the aftermath of student protests, a substantial portion of all young people rejected the authority of their parents, teachers, and everyone else who spoke for convention or conformity. These young people were not criminals in the traditional sense, but they were certainly more adventuresome than most of their parents, and many were drawn into sexual and psychedelic experimentation. Consequently, a substantial number were introduced to a segment of the underworld that their parents and most of their peers knew only remotely. Thus, criminality came to the suburbs in the 1960s, but it was a type that offended traditional limits of morality and responsibility more than common law definitions.

Thus, serious crime grew rapidly in the major cities to which blacks had migrated from the South, and sexual and drug-related deviance became commonplace in the middle-class areas of metropolitan centers, particularly in the Northeast and Far West. These changes, of course, are widely documented in a variety of studies, but whether they will be enduring or simply aberrations in the long-term downward trend is much less sure.

The most likely outcome at this point seems to be a permanent shift toward greater sexual permissiveness but a decline in both the use of debilitating narcotics and inner-city black crime. Young people today are not as suspicious of and rebellious toward authority as their counterparts were in the 1960s, and their urge to repudiate conventional values has moderated.

Thus, the symbolic importance of narcotics has weakened, and their dangers are too broadly recognized to permit widespread consumption. Young people, however, still yearn for sexual experience much as they always have, and in the absence of compelling reasons to avoid it (the advanced technology of birth control has eased the problem of unwanted pregnancy considerably), they seem likely to continue along the path forged during the 1960s.

Finally, the outburst of black crime that took place during the 1960s will probably subside somewhat as black suppression in America recedes. Racial unrest will probably never subside to its original level, because not all blacks will escape poverty and move into the middle or solid working class mainstream. But a sufficient number of blacks may enter this mainstream in the near future to repudiate the currently widespread belief that racism is largely responsible for the plight of the lower class black. Black leaders will increasingly adopt a moralistic, law-and-order perspective, not unlike that observed now among many ethnic leaders whose predecessors played a prominent role in the urban disorders of the nineteenth and early twentieth centuries. Thus, it appears that the sharp rise in the crime in the 1960s will probably be reversed in the 1980s, aided considerably by the advancing age structure of the American population, and will thereby resume the historical decline described earlier.

Summary and Conclusion

In essence I have argued here that the emergence of a thriving commercial civilization in America after the Revolution and into the nineteenth century fundamentally transformed crime and criminal justice. The growing complexity of commercial transactions forced the development of contract law (as it had in England earlier) and the growth of crime stimulated criminal law, with the overall result that lawyers were in considerable and growing demand following the Revolution. The old apprenticeship method of training lawyers was unequal to the task—just as it was inappropriate in an egalitarian society— and it was soon displaced by professional schools of law specifically organized to train lawyers in all aspects of the law. Both civil and criminal law were stimulated, but criminal law in particular was specially affected by the rigorous, systematic analysis it received at the hands of professors of law.

The penalties for a wide range of felonies were reduced from capital punishment to imprisonment; the procedural rights of defendants were extended; and the authority of trial judges was expanded at the expense of juries. Taken individually, these changes may not appear epochal, but together they transformed criminal justice in America. First, they created the basis for a responsible, active judiciary and a changing, socially responsive law in the early decades of the nineteenth century. As judges began defending their decisions in court with written opinions and as these opinions were tested via appellate review, a core of sound legal principles—a jurisprudence—emerged that was peculiarly fitted to the American experience. As society continued to develop, the case law that emerged in this fashion changed along with it.

Second, the reduction in severity of punishments forced the creation of a system of prisons essentially dedicated to containing the burgeoning number of felons sentenced in American courts. A variety of reforms have been introduced since imprisonment became the routine punishment for felony offenders, such as the Quakers' separate system, Auburn's congregate system or Brockway's reformatory, but all of them have succumbed ultimately to the inexorable drift of prisons toward a custodial and punitive policy, giving American prisons overall a distinctively brutal stamp.

Finally, as American courts clarified and extended the rights of defendants in criminal proceedings, the basis was laid for an evaluation in later decades of police practices, with the result that many American police departments came under severe criticism for their treatment of suspects prior to arraignment. The constables in most American cities had been responsible directly to the lower courts, with the result that any tendency to abuse suspects or to violate their procedural rights was quickly known to magistrates and if necessary easily corrected. When police departments were organized during the antebellum period, however, they were established as independent agencies beyond the direct influence of American courts, and after the Civil War a variety of abuses in New York City and elsewhere reached scandalous proportions (Richardson, 1970, pp. 157-160; Haller, 1976, pp. 314-320).

But the violation of the rights of suspects was not the only difficulty that plagued American police departments during the late nineteenth century. They were bedeviled by political manipulation at the top and by corruption at the bottom, and by the 1880s several American cities had invented that peculiarly American phenomenon, the watchman department. Finally, prohibition and the racketeers that it spawned in the 1920s enlarged the problem to a national crisis, and the International Association of Chiefs of Police led by Vollmer began to press for a professionalized local police. Policing inevitably occupies an ambiguous position in any society that is dedicated to freedom of expression and the presumption of innocence in criminal proceedings. The difficulties that American police have experienced in the last 125 years no doubt reflect the ambivalence that Americans feel toward policing and its power. But at the same time Americans are ambivalent toward certain types of crime, and this confusion has also contributed to the difficulties of the police.

There are several broad lessons to be drawn from this survey of the American criminal justice system. As the components of a criminal justice system emerge in a developing nation, the influence of the local community in directing their day-to-day activities necessarily diminishes and is replaced by three distinct kinds of pressures. First, the police, courts, and prisons begin to develop a structure and ethos specific to their particular functions: The police evolve a bureaucratic structure and a crime-control ethos, the courts tend to follow a due process model in their deliberations, and the prisons develop a custodial policy toward inmates.

At the same time, each component in the system begins to influence the others with the result that new, subtly indirect effects are felt by each. The sentencing policies of the courts indirectly affect the programs of the prisons by determining the length and type of sentence that inmates receive, and the police and their arresting policies contribute both to the pattern and the volume of cases processed by the courts. Finally, national associations and groups begin to make themselves felt on each component of the criminal justice system. The growth of university law schools serving the entire legal profession, for example, tended to unify the profession on a national level by exposing law students to similar kinds of training oriented not to local problems but to state and national legal problems. Similarly, the International Association of Chiefs of Police issued proposals to modernize police forces, and prison associations developed most of the reforms that shook penal institutions in the nineteenth century. The Pennsylvania Society for Alleviating the Miseries of Public Prisons was largely responsible for the development of Eastern Penitentiary in Philadelphia and its separate system, and the Auburn Prison with its congregate system was the child of the New York Society for the Prevention of Pauperism.

As the criminal justice system developed in the nineteenth century, therefore, it came under the influence of a variety of new and powerful forces that moved it a considerable distance from its origins in colonial America. These forces in combination have had a salutary effect upon the criminal courts, but their overall effect on the police and prisons has clearly been mixed.

The final question that we must consider here is the complex relationship between the crime problem and the criminal justice system. Does crime shape the criminal justice system? Does the criminal justice system inhibit or deter crime? It seems from the discussion here that crime very directly affected the organization of American police. Certainly the riots of the antebellum period were a prime factor in the consolidation of the constabulary and the watch and ward societies into a police force in several cities. The vice that took root in most American cities before and after the Civil War had a profound effect on American urban departments. Similarly, the confusions of prohibition in the 1920s and the civil disorders of the 1960s helped to galvanize public sentiment in favor of legalistic police departments throughout the nation.

But whether the criminal justice system has actually achieved a systematic reduction of crime is open to debate. The evidence seems to indicate that advancing urbanization and industrialization are accompanied by sharp drops in both the seriousness and the amount of crime. This, of course, does not take into account the increases in juvenile crime, organized crime, and white collar crime that also accompany industrial development. But even if we ignore these crimes, it is not at all clear that the criminal justice system can take credit for the long-term decline in crime that most Western nations have experienced since the nineteenth century. True, recent evidence suggests that certainty of punishment tends to suppress criminality (Silberman, 1976, pp. 442-461), but the relationship is not strong and there is plenty of room for other factors.

I incline to the view that social structure is the most powerful factor in defining the level and nature of the crime problem and that the steady decrease in crime since the early decades of the nineteenth century reflects a maturation of the communal structure such that both the severity and volume of crime have declined significantly. Certainly, national events affect the secular pattern. Economic depressions, wars, and shifts in ethnic and racial relations all have periodically affected the crime problem and altered the direction of change; of course, the United States is presently in the midst of one of these aberrations. The social liberation of blacks and the social revolution of middle class college students, both of which contributed to the turbulence of the 1960s, have had an extraordinary effect on the crime rate. But as we have suggested, these effects will affect the crime rate less and less as other issues increasingly occupy the minds of both blacks and young people.

In the long run, then, it seems to be the evolving social structure that shapes the human condition and thus the pattern of crime in society. The police and the criminal justice system— even when highly effective—can have only a minimal impact on the crime problem. The increases in crime since 1950 took place in spite of a substantial increase in police budget, equipment, and presumably effectiveness. It is not the police and the law that prevent crime; it is the community.

Notes

1. These informal methods of dealing with deviance in the colonies may have been a factor in their low crime rates. Many crimes that in a later era would have been dealt with via arrest and a court hearing were handled in the eighteenth century outside of formal procedures altogether (Zuckerman, 1970, pp. 86-87).

2. Before prisons were used in Philadelphia, gangs of convicts were used to repair the public roads. But they presented such a fearsome appearance—shaved heads, iron collars, and chains—and became so numerous that road gangs were soon abandoned in favor of prisons (Lewis, 1967, chap. 2).

3. It is difficult to say that an increase in drunkenness in Boston during this period simply reflected the disorganizing effects of urban, commercial life, because it was concentrated largely among the Irish. It is probably more accurate to say that it reflected the rigorous impact of urban life on an ethnic group that had already developed a strong pattern of male social drinking.

10

Education
in Urban Society

Steven T. Bossert

When we think of education in the urban society, many images abound: the large, decrepit, windowless inner-city schools which serve our minority population so poorly that many high school students cannot read; the dull, repetitive execution of lessons that stifles our children's individuality and love of learning; the centralization of administration and massive red tape that slow the functioning of the system sometimes bringing it to a halt, and impede attempts at innovation by teachers and parents alike; the alienation and aggression expressed by those students who are trapped within these schools because of the increasing minimum leaving age and who know that jobs will not be available even upon graduation. These are common con-

Note: The author wishes to express his gratitude to Ruth Horowitz and David Street for their helpful suggestions.

ceptions. They express a view that education in the urban society is mass education and as such involves an organizational structure that becomes more bureaucratized and standardized in its procedures and programs—an organization that attempts to serve everyone but serves none effectively and many badly.

Urban education conceived of as mass education fits well with the idea held by many sociologists concerning the character of institutional functioning in urban society. For example, Wirth (1938), in his classic essay on urbanism, has pointed out that "when large numbers have to make common use of facilities and institutions, an arrangement must be made to adjust the facilities and institutions to the needs of the average person rather than to those of particular individuals" (p. 18). In many ways, schools have operated as a leveling influence in urban society. They have been reasonably successful at providing minimal competency in English, math, and history. This has been accomplished, in part, through the establishment of compulsory attendance and a "common curriculum." The notion that public schooling should provide a set of basic skills necessary for full, adult participation in society has affected the development and organization of educational systems. Standardization has been a primary mechanism.

At the same time, however, schools have been asked to assume more and more functions. In addition to providing basic cognitive skills and citizenship training, education in the urban society is supposed to decrease the disparity among social groups, to provide collective experiences that will bring together diverse ethnic and racial groups, and to remain responsive to the desires of the local community and provide social and political integration. Some of these functions are inherently incompatible as urbanization increases the heterogeneity of city populations and as suburbanization increases the differential in both financial resources and student background characteristics between regions of the metropolitan area. In addition, the organizational arrangements that have been created to fulfill most of these functions are often inadequate. With each new function, a new set of programs has been attached to the school. The result has been a large but fragmented set of school systems, not a monolithic and standardized mass-education institution.

In this chapter, I will focus on three primary areas of school organization—governance and finance, school administration, and socialization and training—to analyze how schools are structured, how successful these structures are in meeting various changes in urban society, and why certain functions of the school, as well as the organizational forms established to fulfill these functions, are problematic. I shall try to avoid the descriptive and prescriptive orientation of other writers on urban education; much of my analysis will be speculative, raising more questions than providing answers. Education as an institutional system has not been closely analyzed and many of the processes to be noted here are in flux.

Rise of Public Schools: The Urban Context

Urbanization and industrialization have created many changes in American life. With the increasing migration of diverse racial and ethnic groups to the cities, the rise of technical labor, and labor union control of access to skill employment, the school has become the primary institution for providing basic citizenship training and technical skills. Other institutions —the family, the church, and the workshop—have seemingly lost their ability to provide common social, moral, and economic socialization in the cities precisely because of the increased heterogeneity in their forms among urban populations and the growing complexity of modern life. Historically, the idea of the common, modern school originated in the search for an institution to replace many of the functions previously fulfilled by other institutions. Yet in looking to the school to provide for these tasks, Americans also began expecting the school to solve more and more problems associated with urban life. (I cannot do justice to the complex and interesting historical trends in American education. For excellent accounts, see Cremin, 1964, and Veysey, 1965.)

Two basic values have shaped schooling in urban America. Early social reformers and educationists felt that the massive immigrant populations that filled the cities at the turn of the century needed to be educated in order for them to better their own condition and contribute to the betterment of society in general. This social reform ethic was particularly powerful, and early school curricula emphasized elements that would hasten assimilation and provide appropriate moral orientations. English, cleanliness, dress, manners, and the duties of citizenship were stressed in an attempt to Americanize the many foreign-born children who attended urban schools. Basic writing and arithmetic were also important, for these were seen as skills necessary for employment. Rather than organizing for specialized training to meet the specific needs and aspirations of this diverse body of students, public schooling was to provide a common core of knowledge, both social and technical, necessary for active and capable citizenship. This notion, in part, was reinforced by the strong value of contest mobility (Turner, 1960). Although the assimilation functions of education are less manifest today, our current concept of equality of educational opportunity derives from this idea, which underlies the organization of the common curriculum.

Another basic factor shaping the organization of education has been the commitment to local, nonpolitical governance and neighborhood schools. Unlike other countries that have established national or regional institutions, school systems in the United States have been organized, governed, and funded at the local community level, thus paralleling the local organization of governmental and social welfare functions in general. The result has been a proliferation of school districts as metropolitan areas have grown. Each new community establishes its own educational system, often before any other basic services are available, and many big-city school systems have decentralized portions of their administrative structure into smaller, local units. While actual parental involvement in school affairs remains quite low, most attempts to consolidate school districts, eliminate neighborhood schools, desegregate schools using a regional plan, or increase state and federal control of funding generate hostile reactions. Perhaps because childrearing and the home are strongly associated ideas, the neighborhood school is seen as most desirable. Whatever the basis, however, local school organization has created a massive duplication of facilities as urbanization processes enlarge the metropolitan population. It has made the school more sensitive to the effects of diversity in student composition and in resources as different social groups enter and disperse across the urban environment.

Increasing Functions. Within this context of educational values and with almost boundless faith in its ability to meet the new problems associated with industrialization and urbanization, the school has been asked to assume more and more functions. Basic cognitive and technical training have become almost exclusively the purview of the school. Other settings for skill training and apprenticeship work either are nonexistent or recruit only those persons who have already finished basic schooling. Despite the often disjoint relationship between occupational skill and educational requirements, level of schooling has been used increasingly to select job applicants (Berg, 1970; Collins, 1971). The rise in the minimum school leaving age reflects in part the notions that children need more technical knowledge in our modern society and that the school is the appropriate institution for such training. In many ways, education is seen as the institution through which the society advances, and new technical findings are incorporated into the curriculum at earlier and earlier grade levels. The rapid rise of junior college attendance since the 1950s indicates the growing demand that public education systems provide not only basic, general schooling but also advanced and specialized training. Schooling in the urban society has become more than common citizenship training.

The increasing emphasis on universal high school graduation and postsecondary education, however, has not been based solely on the need for more advanced technical training in modern society. In part, the raising of the minimum leaving age reflects the demand for the school to play a custody-control function. Historically, compulsory attendance laws, child-labor laws, and union control over employment opportunities are intimately related. The availability of child labor in urbanizing America threatened adult labor and the organization of industrial workers. While much of the social reformers' and labor unions' support for child-labor laws and public schools was aimed at eliminating unhealthy sweat shops in which children worked as much as sixteen hours a day and at providing training in basic skills and morals, efforts to establish compulsory school attendance laws also were supported because they reduced labor market competition. In several cases, where enforcement laws were unable to decrease child labor, compulsory school attendance laws with strict enforcement procedures were instituted (Cremin, 1964). Time in school has increased from about 45 days each year during the early 1900s to about 180 days currently, thus drastically limiting labor market participation by children and adolescents. Moreover, educational requirements for employment in many occupations have increased faster than the technical skills required for performing these occupations. Schools often serve to control labor pools and delay entry into many occupations without providing job-related skills. Collins (1971) and Berg (1970) have argued that this can result in increased status and power for occupations that control educational entry requirements as well as in decreased satisfaction and productivity among employees who are "overeducated." Yet postsecondary education is becoming an increasingly important and desirable commodity, and public education has responded by enlarging college facilities, especially at the junior college level, within local school districts.

In trying to provide for the basic citizenship training and custody-control functions, schools in urban areas have faced an immense task. In addition to the tremendous growth of the urban population and the associated problems of providing adequate facilities for this population, the increasing diversity in racial, ethnic, and socioeconomic composition has produced new problems. The goal of the common school, to provide collective experiences and basic skill training, has been modified to accommodate the needs or perceived needs of these various groups. Schools have incorporated countless new programs aimed at decreasing the educational disparities among children and, in doing so, have selectively ordered and batched students within the school system. Despite the relatively poor success of special programs, the school in urban society has actively accepted the mission of attempting to overcome social inequities.

Two programs that best reflect the inclusion of this function into education are school desegregation and compensatory education. In addition to issues related to providing equal access to educational resources, one goal of school desegregation has been to bring together diverse social groups and provide a core of collective experiences in which contact would foster intergroup understanding. Desegregation may be just another manifestation of the common school ethic, to assimilate certain groups into dominant middle class cultures. However, it also can be seen as simply promoting intergroup relations that will break down the prejudices that stem from segregation. (For a description of the contact hypothesis, see Pettigrew, 1964, 1967.) The idea of facilitating the understanding of different groups and cultures has been incorporated into many new curriculum materials and programs. Education, particularly the education of young children, is seen as the way in which the disparities between groups can be overcome, if not through actual changes in the abilities and customs of various social groups, at least through their common understanding and acceptance of their diversity.

Although compensatory education is partly based on the same social reform ethic that underlies the early foundation of public education, it has modified the common school ideal considerably. With the Great Society programs of the 1960s, the school actively became involved in the task of decreasing social inequalities. There has been a rapid increase in special programs aimed primarily at the disadvantaged child—the child raised in ethnic and racial urban ghettos without the intellectual and cultural "advantages" of middle class life. In fact, *urban education* is sometimes synonymous with the education of this type of child. It consists of remedial programs, special curriculum materials, Head Start, bilingual reading programs, free lunch and breakfast programs, and special tutoring. The result has been the addition of these numerous programs, special teachers, inservice training programs, consultants, and new administrative roles for handling federal input into education to already large and cumbersome urban educational systems. And while many "new" programs are nothing more than slight modifications of current practices (Street, 1967), schooling in urban society has meant increasing variations in the common curriculum and the identification and treatment of the special needs of different student populations—from preschool to university. Organizing to handle diversity has produced an extremely complex system that in itself fosters specialization (Janowitz, 1969).

With the rise of universal schooling for urban children and the associated complexity of programs, school administration has become increasingly centralized over the last forty years. The growth of city school districts and the consolidation of suburban and rural districts has increased administrative components. Even though there have been attempts to decentralize decision making within large city school systems, many parents feel that they have little control over their children's education. Moreover, many residents of the inner city feel that their views are not represented adequately by predominantly white, upper-middle class school board members and administrative staff. It is often argued that deteriorating buildings, poorly supplied staffs, and the lack of additional special education programs are the result of insensitive if not discriminatory administrative practices. Professional school administrators, just as the politicians who ran the big-city school systems before the Depression, are seen as serving their own interests. They are slow in responding to the growing diversity in ethnic and racial subgroupings within the urban setting. The result has been a call for local community control of schools.

The demand for neighborhood control over schools, however, has been more than an attempt to modify the administrative structure of school districts so as to insure better education for children. The community control movement is a political movement. It is an attempt to organize neighborhood groups in order to preserve the autonomy and uniqueness of communities and establish basic grass roots political organizations. As such, community control can be seen as a mechanism for the redistribution of power within the urban context. Schools have become the target of this political organizing because of the high value local residents place on education and the school's visibility in the local community. The result of the community control movement has been to add another function to education in the urban society, that of distributing political power.

The faith that education can solve the problems of our rapidly urbanizing society has made the school a target institution. It has been asked to take on more and more functions in response to the increasing diversity of the urban population it serves. As a result, the school is faced with a major dilemma: How do you provide for functions that are mutually incompatible? How do you provide common, collective experiences for children from different social groups *and* recognize and effectively treat the learning differences that exist among these groups? How do you distribute power of control among a diverse set of local communities *and* provide common schooling? How do you make the school a place that fosters learning *and* a mechanism for controlling access to the labor market? It seems that schools are asked to perform an impossible set of tasks. In analyzing education in the urban society—education that is to recognize and respond to the diversity of the urban population while providing common experiences—the organizational arrangements by which schools have attempted to meet these demands and the consequences of these arrangements for the lives of children become our central topic.

Organization of Governance and Finance

One of the major consequences of urbanization has been the proliferation of governmental units within metropolitan areas. The value of local community governance coupled with the expansion of urban populations and the movement out of the central cities into the suburbs has contributed to the multiplication of units and the duplication of services to the extent that most metropolitan areas have a jumbled, fragmented, and uncoordinated set of jurisdictions. In 1962, for example, there were more than 19,000 local governmental units within the 212 SMSAs (Minar, 1968; Zimmer and Hawley, 1968). The organi-

zation of school governance and finance has contributed to this
fragmentation and segmentation of metropolitan government.
Of the 6,604 school districts in metropolitan areas in 1962,
only 28 percent had boundaries that were coterminous with
some other governmental jurisdiction (Zimmer and Hawley,
1968).[1] A common pattern is the large central-city school district surrounded by small autonomous districts; Chicago is
exemplary, with over a half million students served by one large
city district and another half million students served by approximately 340 local districts within the SMSA. Because the local
school district is the basic unit for educational governance and
finance, the organization of education in the urban society has
been particularly sensitive to the basic ecological properties of
urbanization. The increasing heterogeneity of urban populations
and the concentration of racial and ethnic minorities and the
poor in the central cities place considerable pressures on city
school districts to provide an ever expanding set of special programs. Yet the movement of working class and middle class
families to suburban communities and the concomitant decrease
in the central-city tax base creates problems of financing these
special programs. Moreover, the demand for local control, representative of community composition, has created pressures to
further decentralize school governance, with the possibility of
more fragmentation and financial problems.

Finance. Local property taxes are the basis of educational
finance in the United States. Historically, this reliance on local
funding gave an advantage to urban areas. Prior to 1957, big-
city school districts were able to fund education at a level significantly higher than most suburban and rural districts (Sacks,
1972). Despite increasing enrollments within the central city
and the higher cost of special and advanced programs, city
schools could rely on a growing wealth and on the efficiency of
centralized administrative procedures to insure a high level of
expenditures (Callahan, 1962). Suburban schools, except for
those in the few older, very wealthy suburbs, had to allocate
much of their educational expenditures for building new
schools to accommodate growing populations, and hence spent
less on current operations than most city districts (Sacks, 1972;
Levin, Muller, and Sandoval, 1973). However, after 1957, central-city financial situations began to decline.

One reason for this decline in fiscal advantage has been
higher maintenance and basic operating costs. Construction of
schools in the cities peaked in the 1920s, so that the proportion

of city schools that are over fifty years old has been rising steadily. For example, in 1965 over 50 percent of the school plant in Boston, Cleveland, Pittsburgh, and St. Louis had been built prior to 1920 (Sacks, 1972). In most large cities, over one third of the schools are over fifty years old (Hummel and Nagle, 1973). The result has been that maintenance and replacement take up a larger share of the educational budget, decreasing the percentage of resources available for current expenditures (Sacks, 1968).

City school systems also seem to provide a more comprehensive and specialized set of programs for their students. Although there is little data on the range and cost of these offerings over time, city schools appear to have more students in more expensive programs. For example, vocational education programs in the cities, which usually cost 27 percent more than regular academic programs, typically have two to ten times the enrollment of noncity programs (Hummel and Nagle, 1973). Other compensatory and special education facilities cut deeply into a city school's budget. Moreover, desegregation, especially through busing, adds an enormous cost to school expenditures. The cost of buses, drivers, and maintenance decreases the resources available for instruction. (Recently, however, federal judges who have ordered busing for desegregation have also ordered state departments of education to defray much of the busing cost.)

The funding of education in the large cities has also been hampered due to their declining fiscal situation. There are fewer revenues to allocate to the increasing costs of city schools. While overall school expenditures in large cities have not decreased compared with all other areas, city school districts have had to tax themselves at a higher rate in order to maintain their spending levels (Hummel and Nagle, 1973; Sacks, 1972). This reflects the decline in city property tax base as middle and upper-middle class families have moved in increasing numbers to the suburbs. The processes of suburbanization and the concentration of minority and poor in the cities have undercut the fiscal solvency of school districts to the point that several large central-city districts have not been able to complete the academic year without special grants from their state governments. Several analysts attribute this to the fact that a high percentage of city property is devoted to public housing, transportation, and other public usage (Sacks, 1972; Hummel and Nagle, 1973). For example, 45 percent of all public housing is located in the thirty-five largest cities (Hummel and Nagle, 1973). Hence, schools compete with other social welfare programs for limited funds in large cities.

Suburban school districts are not immune to the problems of local tax funding. The image of the wealthy suburban school obscures the realities faced by newer working class communities in providing adequate funding for basic programs. Moreover, urban sprawl and localism in school operation have often created school districts that are too small to provide a full range of educational services. For example, many schools are unable to institute special education programs for the few educationally handicapped or gifted students in their districts. In order to offer these programs, new administrative units, such as special education and intermediate school districts, have been created to pool students and resources from several areas.

Most recently, the major concern in educational finance has centered on the inequalities among school districts in metropolitan areas, inequalities that arise from local tax funding of education. While there is about as much variation in educational spending among suburbs as between suburbs and their central cities, suburban communities in general have increased their tax allocation for education nearly twice as fast as the central cities since 1957, so that by 1965 central-city districts spent about $449 per child compared with $573 per child in the suburban ring (Hummel and Nagle, 1973; Sacks, 1972; Levin, Muller, and Sandoval, 1973). Moreover, suburban communities allocate a higher percentage of their total expenditures to current education: about 55 percent in the suburbs and 33 percent in the central cities (Sacks, 1968). These inequities are due to the same factors affecting city finance mentioned before: higher cost of maintenance and more expensive programs.

The result of local financing of education has meant that education in the urban society has been and remains inequitable —at least, inequitable in terms of expenditure.[2] Historically, the inequity has favored the large cities; now, however, the older, stable, middle and upper-middle class suburban districts hold the advantage. Several means have been proposed to reverse this disparity while recognizing the special program needs of central-city schools. First, there has been a massive influx of federal funds for education, particularly since the Elementary and Secondary Education Act of 1965. This has largely financed inner-city education programs aimed at helping racial minority children and the poor. Although federal support is difficult to document, in part because it reaches local school districts through a variety of circuitous routes (for example, through the Model Cities program), it appears that federal money has increased per-pupil expenditures in the central cities to the level of the wealthier suburban districts (Hummel and Nagle, 1973). However, federal funds do not provide a stable base on which to finance day-to-day school operations. Many grants are for start-up costs or demonstration programs that terminate, with the expectation (at least by the federal agencies) that local school resources will support successful programs. Besides, many federally funded projects do not involve financial assistance for basic programs. Breakfast and lunch programs, Head Start, and other special projects seem to account for the bulk of funds allocated to local school districts.[3]

State governments also have been asked to decrease the disparities between areas of the metropolitan community by providing "foundation programs." Most states do provide a base-level support system for local schools. (See Levin, Muller, and Sandoval, 1973, and Michelson, 1972, for analyses of state variations in educational funding.) Unfortunately, state aid has tended to favor suburbs over the cities. Beyond maintaining a minimal level of per-pupil expenditure, state aid usually is allocated to equalize the per capita tax expenditure. Therefore, central-city school districts receive less assistance than suburban districts because their school-age population, while large, represents a smaller proportion of the total city population than is the case in suburban areas (Sacks, 1972; Hummel and Nagle, 1973). Recent court cases have challenged the local property tax as a basis for funding education.[4] It has been argued that the inequities that result from different expenditures deny the child's constitutional right to equal opportunity in education: High-quality education is equated with high fiscal resources. While these cases have not been supported by the Supreme Court, many state governments have moved to assume more of the financial burden of funding education. (In the move to higher state support of education, the political position of suburban communities in metropolitan areas will be extremely interesting.)

In all, the organization of urban educational finance reflects several dilemmas. Local tax support of schooling may not be adequate for providing the special program needs of inner-city students or guaranteeing equal educational opportunity within the metropolitan area. The value of local control con-

flicts with the values of equality of educational opportunity and
of education as a means to overcome social inequalities. To
move school finance to the state or even federal level increases
the opportunity for providing these latter functions but decreases local control.

   Governance. Some writers have argued that changes in
educational finance will not equalize educational opportunity
unless accompanied by changes in school governance. Levin
(1976), for example, indicates that without political change
there is little assurance that additional funds will be transformed into school services that will improve education—particularly the education of racial minorities and the poor. This position reflects the growing distrust of school boards, especially of
central-city boards. They are depicted as slow in responding to
community pressures and as representing elite interests. There
has been increasing pressure to decentralize school governance
in the large central-city school districts. In effect, the school is
seen as a potential basis for local community social and political
integration. Can it serve this function in the inner city or even
in the suburban community, where the school is often the only
basic local institution in which citizens can participate?

   School governance has not changed significantly since the
end of the Depression, when school board membership was
taken out of the political arena and professional administration
was established. School boards primarily handle fiscal issues related to the total budget and tax rates and rarely become involved in the day-to-day operation of schools: They mostly
legitimize decisions made by the school superintendent (Kerr,
1964).[5] Moreover, while the processes of urbanization and suburbanization have significantly changed the population characteristics of inner-city school districts, school board composition
has not changed since Counts (1927) first studied their social
composition. School board members are mostly white, male
homeowners who have more than a twelfth-grade education and
are employed in professional or managerial occupations (Zeigler
and Jennings, 1974; Wirt and Kirst, 1972).[6] The social characteristics of school board members do not match those of families with school-age children (Hummel and Nagle, 1973; Levin,
1976).

   The nonrepresentativeness of central-city school boards
has stimulated the movement toward decentralization of school
governance through the establishment of local community
boards. The ideology of the community control movement cen-

ters on several beliefs: Inner-city school boards cannot respond to parental interests because they are not representative of the urban population and because large, centralized school districts are naturally slow to respond to any pressures for change; and local community residents should have a direct input into school decision making and will participate if given a community-based governance system (Gittell and Hevesi, 1969; Levin, 1970). Community control is not only an organization to insure local control but also a mechanism to redistribute political power within the central city. The local school becomes the focus for the establishment of grass roots politics (Firestone, 1972).

However, there is some question about the ability of the school to provide for this function and handle its other tasks. For example, Pfautz (1970) has pointed out that community control rests on the assumption that one can identify distinct communities within the central city. He notes that the high mobility in inner-city areas, particularly among black, lower-class families, may preclude a stable base of participation. Many inner-city schools have annual enrollment shifts involving 50 to 75 percent of their students. And despite the general faith that local community control will increase participation and the few cases in which participation has been relatively high in the first years (for example, Ocean Hill-Brownsville in New York City; Gittell and Hevesi, 1969), there is no evidence that local school governance units will increase resident participation: It has not done so in suburban districts (Carter, 1960).

Moreover, Pfautz (1970) questions the compatibility of the political and social integration function of community control with the school's basic function of socializing the young into adult roles. Drawing on Dreeben's (1968) theory on instructional activities and norm learning, Pfautz suggests that increasing local participation, particularly parental participation in a school's day-to-day functioning, decreases the ability of the school to serve as a transitional institution between the family and the wider society. Pfautz's hypothesis warrants examination, for it focuses attention on the possible consequences and contradictions of organizational structures that insure parental and local community involvement in schooling and structures that provide children with orientations and skills that allow them to attain full adult status.

The idea that schools can and should serve a social and political integration function is not confined to central-city governance issues. In the suburbs, schools comprise a central institution around which community ties form, often because the school is the first and most important institution in the new community: "The school becomes the surrogate for other kinds of community attachment lost in the suburbs" (Minar, 1962, p. 100).

There are several reasons why the school might serve as the most meaningful community polity for suburbanites. Education is highly valued, particularly among middle class suburban dwellers. Residential choice is often made with a concern for quality educational facilities. Middle class suburban families tend to be child oriented and hence involved in the institutions in which their children participate. Moreover, the school system is often one of the primary suburban institutions. It is the primary consumer of tax revenues and a major arena for local activity. Schools are seen as "nonpolitical" and "safe and respectable" for civic participation (Minar, 1962). Hence, the process of suburbanization may involve a situation in which suburbanites look to the school to satisfy basic needs for the community. (This view is supported by many observers of suburbanization; see Schwartz, 1976; Whyte, 1956; Riesman, Glazer, and Denney, 1950.)

However, examining actual participation in school governance, suburban residents do not seem to be very zealous. Many observers of community involvement in school affairs report extremely low levels of participation. For example, among residents in 1,054 school districts across the United States, Carter (1960) found uniformly low rates of participation in school board and tax rate elections, of parental interest in school governance and administration, and of participation in school-related organizations. Minar (1966), studying elementary school districts in Chicago suburbs, reports that the median proportion of registered voters casting ballots was 8.7 percent when board members were being chosen and 12.7 percent when taxing referenda were being held. Low participation typifies both central-city and suburban school districts (Martin, 1962; Zeigler and Jennings, 1974; Wirt and Kirst, 1972). Unfortunately, there has not been a detailed analysis of community participation differences that controls for the effects of social class, parental status, life-cycle status, the age of the community, or population changes. Although the school may not serve as a basis for the sociopolitical integration of suburban communities, schooling as part of the childrearing process may serve an integration function. Children seem to play an important role in the development of friendship networks and neighboring. However, there is little evidence to suggest that this function differs between urban and suburban areas when community age differences are considered (Keller, 1968).

While the claim of extensive suburban participation seems unsupported, interest-group involvement may be more effective in suburbs than central cities. While there are few data on the degree of interest-group participation, most writers indicate that suburban groups have a greater impact on decisions (Martin, 1962; Zeigler and Jennings, 1974; Levin, 1970; Iannaccone and Lutz, 1970). Recently, O'Shea (1975) has analyzed differences in suburban and inner-city parental interest-group effectiveness. Drawing on theories of organizational responsiveness, O'Shea notes that the power of suburban groups (like the PTA) rests largely in the high level of dependency of local school systems on local tax revenues. The PTAs serve as effective media for mobilizing community support (albeit small) for tax referenda and develop close, influential linkages between parents and school board members. By contrast, central-city districts are less dependent on small, localized interest groups for establishing support for school tax elections. In fact, neighborhood-based groups often find it hard to mobilize a local constituency for even major issues (Firestone, 1972). Therefore, local community groups in the inner city for the most part cannot develop the linkages necessary for effective influence.[7]

In general, while there are efforts to increase the meaningfulness of citizen participation in school governance, particularly through the decentralization of school boards in the inner cities, local control does not seem an adequate organization for insuring community involvement. Yet the value of local control rests at the base of educational systems despite the conflict generated between issues of providing both local control and equality of educational opportunity. Metropolitanism is often cited as the method by which the inequities of local tax fundings of education and government fragmentation can be overcome, as well as a means of organizing school desegregation in black-majority cities (Havighurst, 1968). However, metropolitanism is not supported by most residents in urban areas (Zimmer and Hawley, 1968; Zimmer, 1976). This reflects one basic conflict in the organization of urban education: The functions of maintaining local participation and control and of providing equality of educational opportunity may be incompatible within the context of urbanization and suburbanization, which have rapidly increased the size and heterogeneity of metropolitan populations, distributed them over a wide area, and segregated and localized racial and social class groupings.

Educational Administration

School administration, like school governance, has been under increasing pressures to decentralize. Educational administration in the urban society, especially the management of big-city school systems, is generally seen as overcentralized, overbureaucratized, and overprofessionalized. Many parents, teachers, and professors of educational administration complain that schools are unresponsive to change attempts, inefficient, and fouled with red tape: Big school systems are bad school systems.[8] Yet much of school decision making is not centralized. It resides with principals and teachers as they make moment-to-moment decisions about instruction. There are, however, two factors that may increase the professional administrative structure of schools—federal funding to local school districts and teacher unionization. The dilemma of educational administration in urban society, then, becomes how to remain responsive to local community interests and to handle effectively the numerous tasks placed on the institution in the context of an ever changing urban environment.

Professional school administration was established during the Depression era when in most places school decision making was taken out of the urban political arena. With the origin of the school superintendency and other specialized administrative roles, the "science of management" was introduced into the operation of school systems. During the urban school's rapid growth, professional administration was mainly responsible for maintaining adequate facilities and a relatively high level of educational expenditures (Callahan, 1962). Since the 1960s, however, the administrative staffs of big-city school districts have seemingly lost their ability to operate schools efficiently. Unfortunately, there are few studies comparing the relative growth of administrative staff functions with increases in the student population and the complexity of the instructional program and services. While the size of the student population may not correlate with bureaucratization and centralization (Bidwell, 1965), the increasing heterogeneity of pupils and of programs to serve them has led to larger, more differentiated administrative staffs.

School systems seem to respond to size and complexity by continually creating specialized roles (Street, 1967; Janowitz, 1969). Most urban school systems have highly differentiated staff roles throughout the administrative and teaching hierarchy, from special assistant superintendents to special teachers. The result has been the establishment of professional elite control (Iannaccone and Wiles, 1971).[9]

Despite elite, professional control and extensive centralization of administration in some areas, decision making in urban schools is far from monolithic. As Janowitz (1969, pp. 25-26) has observed,

> The term overcentralization . . . is too imprecise to characterize adequately the decision-making in the big city public school system. There is a profound limitation in the term overcentralization if a distinction is not made between decision-making about long-term goals or organization of the school system versus the procedures for administering the organization on a day-to-day basis. It is of course abundantly true that in short-term allocation of resources, in management of personnel, and in the modification of operating procedures, the approval of a few officials is required and in this respect, decision-making is highly centralized. Nonetheless, centralization of authority at the top levels of the big city school system is reduced and diffused by elements outside the institution. Such authority is greatly reduced by statutory and legal restraints which narrow the scope of authority of the Board of Education and its superintendent in the strategic management of the organization. Thus, state law has developed a web of rules and regulations which limit the scope of change by defining rigidly many procedures and setting professional standards. The superintendent is even limited in the appointment of his key assistants. The impact of schools of education has removed from the superintendent effective jurisdiction over the training of personnel. Professional associations and commercial groups have strong influence on curriculum and educational procedures.

In addition to the reasons mentioned by Janowitz, centralization and bureaucratization of long-term decision making are hampered by the organization of governance and finance discussed earlier. Local school systems are extremely sensitive to changes in community composition and tax base, changes associated with urbanization. Hence, planning for enrollment, teacher assignments, material acquisitions, and the like must remain short-term.

Moreover, in terms of day-to-day operational decisions, especially those concerning instruction, the organizational structure of large school districts limits administrative controls. As Rogers (1969) has illustrated, field administrators often subvert district policy to fulfill their own goals and perceived needs. This is possible because of weak links between central staff and school staff in obtaining adequate information about program results and procedures. Area superintendents and principals are given considerable autonomy. "Field superintendents and principals often reinterpret directives to mean that they should do what they can to implement them in the light of their own superior knowledge of local conditions. Such reinterpretations could be anything from 'passive sabotage' . . . to more active efforts" (Rogers, 1969, p. 300).

Control of classroom instruction is even less articulated than school administration. Having analyzed teacher-administrator relations, Lortie (1969, 1975) pointed out that schools have few resources for exercising extensive control over teachers. Because salary, advancement, vacations, and job security are usually independent of performance and performance ratings, principals have few sanctions or rewards to offer teachers. Merit pay and accountability procedures have been uniformly rejected by teachers. In addition, Lortie indicated that teachers primarily value the intrinsic rewards derived from classroom interaction. For the most part, administrators do not manage these intrinsic rewards and hence must rely on the exchange of advice in exercising control.

Administrative control of instruction may become even less effective as teacher unionization and specialization increase. Although no one has studied the relationship between union contracts or teacher specialization and teacher-administrator relations, one might hypothesize that both factors would further limit the basis of control. Recently, the scope of union contracts has expanded from bread-and-butter issues to class size, discipline procedures, textbook selection, transfer policies, promotion procedures, curriculum, evaluation procedures, and the establishment of new programs (Cheng, 1976). The specification of many administrative functions into union contracts decreases administrators' discretionary use of many control devices and bolsters teachers' claims of autonomous professional status. In addition, the increase of teacher specialization spurred by the growing number of special programs limits the principal's ability to use advice as control. The newly credentialed specialist is the expert.

The control over instructional organization in school systems has become extremely fragmented, not centralized. The lack of articulation between administration and instructional staff hinders change from either direction. For example, "death by incorporation" may refer more to the inability of administration staff to monitor and direct innovations adequately than to attempts to eliminate efficacious program elements during institutionalization. And "bureaucratic runaround" may stem from the lack of coordination and clear responsibility in administration rather than from an unresponsive and buffered central decision maker.

Nevertheless, two forces may be increasing bureaucratic control and centralization of some functions of school administration. The influx of federal funds to local school districts has created a special demand for administrators and teachers who are able to write grant proposals and prepare the numerous reports required by federal agencies. Many school districts have employed experienced "grantsmen" to manage the relationships between the district and federal departments. Unfortunately, little is known about the impact of federal involvement on local schools, either in terms of the number of special positions created at the district level or of the relative success of school districts that employ specially trained or experienced people in obtaining federal funds. However, it is clear that the need for such specialized staff increases the central bureaucracy of the school district.

Teacher unionization also seems to heighten district control of decision making to some degree. While union contracts may decrease administrative control at the school level (as argued above), it creates "an infrastructure of labor-relations experts" who ultimately control the basis of everyday administrator-teacher relations (Cheng, 1976). Special labor negotiators may become the exclusive arbiters of school contracts and thus acquire controls normally exercised by the local school board. As contracts begin to include greater specification of job duties and procedures, more control will be vested in those who negotiate the contracts. Functionally, this decreases control by the community, principal, and individual teacher.

Two consequences of these trends exemplify contradictions between the organization of educational administration and other functions of schooling. First, both the centralization of administrative functions and the fragmentation of control decrease the extent to which local community residents can participate effectively in school decision making. Special positions for teachers, administrators, and labor negotiators establish expert, professional control. This limits extensive parental and community participation in decision making because it is assumed that nonexperts do not have the appropriate knowledge to make decisions. Moreover, the low articulation between administrative staff and teachers over issues of instruction creates a system in which change or influence attempts have no real target. That is, there is no locus of control over classroom instructional organization outside of the individual teacher in his or her individual classroom. Attempts to change instruction often fail not because of overcentralization but because of the fragmentation of day-to-day administrative control: There is no one to organize, implement, and monitor changes in instructional policy. The organization of educational administration, therefore, limits the extent of local community control.

Second, to the extent that administrative staff increases faster than instructional staff, the organization of educational administration may function to decrease the degree of pupil achievement. Recently Bidwell and Kasarda (1975) have shown that school district structure, especially its administrative intensity, affects pupils' learning. There is a significant negative relationship between the ratio of administrators to classroom teachers and pupil achievement. Bidwell and Kasarda's work suggests that larger administrative components may restrict organizational resources utilized in instruction. By increasing administrative effectiveness through centralization, the organization of educational administration may decrease instructional effectiveness.

These trends in school administration are not characteristic of big-city schools only. However, urban school districts are faced with large influxes of federal assistance programs, extensive unionization, demands for local control, and problems in providing effective instructional programs for their diverse student populations. These problems are confounded by an urban environment that fosters significant shifts in population and tax revenues and increases the need for special programs and personnel. The result has been that educational administration in the urban society is extremely fragmented. It does provide a core of standardized and centralized decisions, particularly in the allocation of staff, the specification of basic curriculum units, and within-district budget distribution. However, it does not have control over day-to-day and long-term operational decisions. Educational administration has been neither responsive to local control issues nor effective in building instructional programs.

The Schooling Experience

The notion of the common school was founded on the idea that public education could provide common, collective experiences that would bring together diverse population groups. Bringing together meant more than creating a setting for intergroup contact, though this meaning was very important. It primarily meant decreasing differences in the cognitive, economic, and social development that existed among groups. The common school was to guarantee equality of opportunity by providing equal basic education. This goal was particularly salient in the context of urbanization, which brought large numbers of rural and immigrant people to the cities. Schools enrolled many foreign-born and illiterate children and were faced with the tasks of teaching manners, cleanliness, and dress in addition to reading, writing, and arithmetic. As Cremin (1964, p. 72) observes, "Not only baths, but a vast variety of other activities that could not be found in any syllabus began to appear [in public schools]." Special treatment and new programs were a necessary part of educating the heterogeneous urban population.

The inclusion of special programs into the school paralleled efforts to institutionalize the common curriculum. Much of the schooling experience in the urban society has been correctly typified as standardized, routinized, and rigidified. Historical as well as current accounts of urban schools demonstrate their dull, monotonous, repetitive nature. There has been substantial bureaucratic "success" in standardizing textbooks, curriculum units and their sequencing, and the age-graded structure. In looking at the experience of any given child, schools seem unitary and invariable. However, some common school elements have been institutionalized and others have been thwarted. The organization of training and socialization is considerably differentiated in urban school systems. Within schools, curriculum specialization and tracking create substantial variations in learning experiences. The urban area contains many different types of schools, each affected by its neighborhood social environment. This differentiation arises in part from the schools' necessary response to differences among children in the urban society: New procedures arise to handle new problems. Schools, therefore, face a significant dilemma. In the context of the urban society with its diverse population, the basic elements of a common school and the mechanisms necessary to insure learning and equality of educational opportunity seem incompatible.

While the establishment of special programs is not new—vocational education, for example, began in the 1920s—the Elementary and Secondary Education Act of 1965 probably did more to stimulate curriculum differentiation and specialization than any other event in educational history. The major focus of projects funded under this act has been to decrease the inequities in learning outcomes that occur between children of different racial and ethnic groups. Because of this, urban education is now often synonymous with education of inner-city, poor, and black children—the "culturally deprived" (Riessman, 1962; Miller, 1967). A variety of special curricula, training programs, and support programs (like free lunches and school social workers) have been initiated. Most urban school districts now contain special preschool programs, bilingual education, remedial curricula, vocational centers, and special in-service training for inner-city schoolteachers. While the success of these special programs has been contested, one definite result has been the increasing specialization and differentiation of educational practice and hence the increasing heterogeneity of children's schooling experiences in the metropolitan area.

The variety of children's educational experiences is quite apparent even within a single school. At the secondary level, tracking by ability and curriculum type (remedial, vocational, general, regular, and college preparatory) segregates children into subgroups, each receiving "appropriate" treatment. On face value, tracking seems a reasonable response to a heterogeneous student population: Different students have different learning needs and should receive special treatment. However, while tracking has not been shown to improve pupils' learning, it has reinforced distinctions between racial and social class groups. The upper tracks have an overrepresentation of white, middle- and upper-middle class children, while the remedial tracks contain predominantly lower class, racial-minority students (Hollingshead, 1949; Cicourel and Kitsuse, 1963; Goldberg, 1966). Rather than providing common collective experiences that will bring together diverse racial and ethnic groups, this organization of instruction perpetuates the separation of these groups in the everyday life of the school.

Moreover, even where formal tracking does not exist, differential teacher expectations cause variation in children's classroom experiences. Particularly in the early grades, teacher expectations can be crucial in a child's progression through school. For example, children often are separated into informal reading groups based on a teacher's initial impressions of ability or potential. This system becomes castelike when children are continually placed in the same group each year and constitutes significantly different classroom experiences for children (Rist, 1970).

Between-school differences in the metropolitan area become even more pronounced.[10] First, large cities seem to have a variety of school settings. Not only do alternatives to public education exist in a range of private and parent/cooperative schools, but alternatives within the public system are available as well. For example, most city school districts provide special training schools. In New York City there are specialized schools for art, drama, music, science, and various vocational skills, including aviation mechanics. In addition, city school districts often offer alternative school settings; Metro High in Chicago and Parkway in Philadelphia are noted examples, attracting students from various social class and ethnic groups and providing nontraditional, student-oriented and -initiated curricula. Moreover, many urban districts have both open and traditional options for students, especially in elementary schools. Recently, the ideas of providing special schools and an open format have been combined into the "magnet" school concept. This type of school is intended to provide an instructional setting that will attract and stimulate students who have lost interest in the regular curriculum. These magnet schools have been used with some degree of success to stimulate voluntary racial integration within city districts. Because of these options, large city school systems have a reasonably high level of differentiation between schools. Of course, this is not to say that every schooling option is available to each child, but rather that the overall organization of schooling in urban areas is heterogeneous. This heterogeneity provides some degree of dissimilarity in the schooling experiences children have.

Second, processes of residential segregation in urban areas
seem to affect schooling experiences. Residential mobility and
separation by race and social class have a strong impact on
schools since attendance districts are neighborhood based. It has
been clearly demonstrated that community context and the
social class composition of a school population affects the
achievement and aspirations of children (Rogoff, 1961; Turner,
1964; Boyle, 1966). "Variations in the modal socioeconomic
composition of a school and accompanying variation in cognitive development in the primary grades, generate norms of interpersonal behavior and role-expectations which acquire a force
of their own and have a resounding impact upon the students in
the situation" (Wilson, 1967, p. 181). Natural processes of
urbanization and suburbanization, then, heighten this effect
within the metropolitan area.

One attempt to ameliorate the differences in schooling
experiences associated with residential segregation has been
school desegregation. While sociological research indicates that
desegregation might be more effective if conducted along social
class rather than racial lines, racial desegregation of city schools
does lessen the contextual effects of socioeconomic segregation
because black students are disproportionately represented in
lower socioeconomic status neighborhoods and schools. School
desegregation rests on the goal of providing equality of educational opportunity through common schooling experiences; yet
residential segregation both within cities and between suburbs
of a city reinforces differences in children's schooling experiences.

The issue of school desegregation raises an interesting
though little studied question: What is the effect of educational
policy on the process of urbanization? Most often, the context
of urban society is seen as shaping the educational system. By
contrast, in examining school desegregation policy, Coleman has
recently argued that court-ordered busing for desegregation influences residential mobility and metropolitan segregation. In a
hotly contested series of papers, Coleman indicates that busing
for desegregation has caused "white flight" in many major cities
(see Coleman, Kelly, and Moore, 1975; Pettigrew and Green,
1976). Whatever the accuracy of Coleman's findings, he raises
an important question about the influence of an institution's
policy on processes of urbanization and suburbanization.

To summarize, while some elements of the common
school exist, there are a variety of differences among schooling

experiences within urban education. The heterogeneity of school settings and the proliferation of special programs aimed at treating differences in the urban student population have produced a highly specialized and differentiated schooling system. This does not imply that this system is effective in its treatment of student differences; rather, it suggests that the schooling experience in urban society is not uniform. It is not mass education in the sense of providing for the average.[11]

Another problem facing education in the urban society is the school's expanded custody control function. Increases in the minimum leaving age and in the fragmentation between school and work require the school to maintain student interest and motivation over longer periods. While all schools face this task, urban schools encounter particular problems. They face what Janowitz (1969) calls the "new crisis," the increase of minority and ethnic students in schools where before they were socialized into the labor market at earlier ages. One consequence of this has been to increase student alienation, particularly among students who do not sense a link between school activities and postgraduation employment opportunities (Stinchcombe, 1964). Not only does alienation seem to increase misbehavior, vandalism, and truancy, it also decreases the impact that any form of instruction has on the child (Spady, 1974). Custody control heightens the degree of compulsion and the reliance on institutional and coercive authority. These, in turn, decrease the teacher's ability to develop a relationship of trust and rapport with the child, elements necessary for stimulating learning. In this way, the organization of custody control conflicts with the organization of socialization and training. This conflict leads to one of the major problems for teachers in urban schools: How to motivate a captive and alienated set of youth. The schooling experience for many in the urban society is increasingly fragmented from other aspects of their lives.

Postsecondary schooling has not been immune to these problems and processes. Increasing educational certification requirements for employment have created demands for college education that, until recently, have exceeded facilities. Moreover, there has been an increase in educational consumerism involving older persons, especially older women, who are not seeking educational credentials for occupational advancement. The result has been a remarkable increase in public colleges, especially in the locally financed and governed junior college systems (Clark, 1960). Some of these colleges have declared that their mission is to serve inner-city youth who have not had the opportunity to attend college and benefit from higher education. This extension of equality of educational opportunity into postsecondary education has created several problems. Besides compounding the financial strain of already over-burdened central-city school districts, the openness of junior and community colleges brings students who are often completely unprepared for postsecondary work onto campus. Extensive remediation programs (the compensatory education of higher education) foster the same organizational outcomes as other special education programs in city schools—the increasing specialization and fragmentation of the college system (Karabel, 1972). Community colleges are becoming differentiated by program and prestige, hence adding to the already heavy differentiation among colleges and universities in general. Even though junior colleges have extended postsecondary education to working-class youths, it is unclear if attendance at inner-city junior colleges increases either college or occupational success. The "cooling out" function of the community college is still operating. The two-year college degree may do little more than extend the custody-control function into higher education.

The organization of training and socialization in urban schools is faced with a major dilemma, that of fulfilling the goals of the common school and of providing for the special needs of a heterogeneous and residentially segregated urban population. Coleman (1968, p. 6) has reflected part of this dilemma in analyzing the culture of the school:

> One of the explicit goals of the public school in the United States has always been to act as a common school bringing together diverse population groups and providing some joint and collective experiences for persons who might share very little in other arenas of life. A school is not the ideal institution for such socially integrative experiences, because school activities (apart from extracurricular ones, in particular, athletics) are highly individualistic, and offer little opportunity for close, shared experiences that can create strong interpersonal bonds.

Yet beyond these problems in the organization of instruction, the common school ideal conflicts with other goals. Providing special programs to serve the needs of diverse groups of pupils, guaranteeing equality of educational opportunity, and maintaining local schools demand structures that differentiate children by race, socioeconomic status, and ability. The result has been a system of schooling that fosters specialization and fragmentation and often perpetuates the differences it has been organized to alleviate. The schooling experience in the urban society reflects differences inherent among people and organizations in the urban context.

An Overview

That urban education is in the midst of a crisis remains a popular theme. It is a crisis of students who fail to learn, of administrators who fail to act, of curricula that fail to stimulate interest, of school boards that fail to represent their communities, of school districts that fail to integrate, and of finance structures that fail to guarantee equitable expenditures within the metropolitan area. Responses to this crisis entail curriculum reform, decentralization of administration, special programs, community control, desegregation, and federal assistance to local school districts. Unfortunately, these responses seem part of the problem itself, not part of a solution. The crisis of education in urban society is a crisis of fragmentation in organizational structure. This stems from attaching multiple functions to the school without developing an integrated institutional form. Schooling has been seen as the panacea for social ills, especially those associated with urbanization. In addition to handling basic cognitive skill training, schools have been expected to provide common, collective experiences and respond to the special needs of student groups within the heterogeneous metropolitan population; to provide expert, efficient, nonpolitical administration and serve a sociopolitical integration function within the community; to insure equality of opportunity and remain responsive to local variations in revenues and governance; to socialize children into adult status effectively and provide custody control. These conflicting goals and the organizational structures established to fulfill them have resulted in numerous small adjustments in educational practice rather than comprehensive institution building. New programs are continually added to schools without providing any comprehensive organizational change. The result has been a specialized and fragmented set of educational procedures, programs, and experiences.

As we have seen at the school district level, local community control and equality of educational opportunity goals are frequently incompatible. One of the mechanisms for providing community control, local district finance and governance, contributes to the unequal distribution of resources within the metropolitan area. In the context of urban growth and residential segregation by race and social class, local school districts have become increasingly varied because of differences in their ability to obtain adequate local tax revenues. Moreover, the current organization of local school districts insures the segregation of various student groups, thus eliminating one basis for the common school. Yet large centralized school districts are not the answer. They become unresponsive to the variety of interests reflected in the urban population and may have a negative effect on pupil learning to the extent that large administrative units utilize a higher proportion of school resources. However, decentralization of governance may limit the school's ability to socialize children into roles appropriate for full adult participation in the wider society. The heterogeneity and residential segregation of metropolitan populations resulting from processes of urbanization and suburbanization create dilemmas for school district organization and operation. Current practices involve the fragmentation of educational units and foster variations in schooling practice and outcomes.

At the school level, attempts to fulfill both the common school notion and the educational needs of a diverse urban population have also created dilemmas and conflicting organizational patterns. Instructional schemes that respond to the child's individual needs preclude many collective situations in which strong interpersonal bonds among different pupils are reinforced. Illustrative of this conflict is the pattern that occurs in many desegregated secondary schools: Tracking by ability segregates student groups within the school, replicating internally the pattern of residential segregation within the community. In addition to internal sorting mechanisms, special programs and schools further differentiate the schooling experience in urban society.

The expansion of custody control into secondary and postsecondary education has created further dilemmas for instruction and socialization. The rise in educational requirements for employment and the separation of school and work increase both the numbers and alienation of students within the educational system. The demand for more education and the introduction of remedial programs into higher education have stimulated considerable differentiation, especially at the junior college level, in order to accommodate students who have traditionally entered the work force after high school. However, for those students who do not find a linkage between their schooling experience and their probable occupational status, the custody-control function heightens their alienation, thus decreasing the socialization effectiveness of the school.

The complexity of multiple goals attached to schooling has created a massive but fragmented system of education in urban society. Wirth's (1938) predictions about institutions in mass society have not typified schools. While some standardization exists, variation at all levels, from classroom to school districts, creates considerable diversity in schooling experiences. In its attempt to incorporate a heterogeneous population, the school itself has been affected by processes of differentiation and segmentation operating in the urban context. Insofar as these processes continue to operate, education in the urban society will retain its diverse and specialized form.

Notes

1. The actual number of school districts has decreased recently. Zimmer and Hawley (1968) report a 20 percent decrease in independent school districts in the 212 SMSAs between 1957 and 1962, indicating some consolidation among educational units. However, the fragmentation of school governments in metropolitan areas is still considerable.
2. The relationship between expenditure and quality of education is a complex and hotly debated topic. See Coleman, Kelly, and Moore (1975), Mosteller and Moynihan (1972), and Summers and Wolfe (1975).
3. There are no data available on the stability and type of federal assistance to local districts, nor on the specific use of money within school districts. One observer, however, has indicated that a significant proportion of federal funding has done nothing more than increase the length of the school day and school year (Street, 1967).
4. *Serrano* v. *Priest,* 5 Cal.3d 584, 487 P.2d 1241 (1971).
5. This is not to say that school boards cannot be extremely important in setting policy. School board policy has been shown to have a crucial impact in integration processes (Crain, 1969) and teacher union formation (Rosenthal, 1969). While there is no comprehensive study of school board involvement, however, most observers indicate that the overwhelming proportion of school board activity is limited to approving superintendent's plans.
6. For descriptions of how school board members are selected, see Goldhammer (1964). Also, for discussions of the general politics of education at local, state, and federal levels, see Iannaccone and Lutz (1970), Zeigler and Jennings (1974), and Wirt and Kirst (1972).
7. Of course, the community control movement points to this as a

rationale for decentralization of school governance. However, community control plans have not given local boards full fiscal control or based funding solely on local tax revenues. To do so would drastically weaken most inner-city community districts (O'Shea, 1975; Levin, 1976).

8. Most treatments of bureaucratization and centralization of school administration consist of individual accounts of the problems of working in big-city schools. The best of these is Rogers's (1969) detailed description of the New York City system. However, there are very few studies of the degree and patterns of bureaucratic structures and processes or of their consequences for school-system operation (Bidwell, 1965).

9. By "elite control" is not meant control by upper-middle-class members of the community, but rather the control by a group (administrators) that generally certifies and selects its own members. School administrators form a fairly closed social group. Since advanced positions generally require state teaching and administrative certification plus experience, recruitment most often occurs within local or intrastate networks (see Carlson, 1972).

10. I do not intend to enter the debate on school effects here. Coleman and others (1966) and Mosteller and Moynihan (1972) have demonstrated that gross measures of school differences in resources and teacher characteristics do not predict differences in pupil learning. However, Summers and Wolfe (1975) found school-related differences in achievement when resource data was disaggregated at the school level within one school district.

11. While the organization of programs contains considerable variation, the process of instruction may be fairly uniform among all schools. Although there is no extensive empirical evidence concerning the types and relative usage of instructional modes in classrooms, many observers feel that recitation is the most common form of instruction. Therefore, despite content, program, and organizational differences among schools and districts, most children may experience the same type of instructional process. This is a consequence of educational technology, not of urbanization.

11

Welfare in the Metropolitan Area

Diana Pearce
David Street

Considered in its entirety, the topic of the relationship of social welfare to urbanization requires an extremely broad comparative inquiry into industrialization, social structure, ideology, and inequality. Our aim is much more modest: to explore the interaction of changing social welfare institutions in the United States with the changing social order of its larger and older metropolitan areas. That the topic is modest does not make it easy; information is scarce beyond what we could obtain in an exploratory study of welfare in the Chicago metropolitan area. In this chapter we intend less to summarize research findings than to raise theoretical and research issues.[1]

By *social welfare institutions* we refer to that heterogeneous, uneven, and poorly bounded collection of programs, per-

319

sonnel, and practices—both public and private—that attend to human needs in the name of the public good. Both the needs and the services set up to deal with these needs are collectively defined; many of the complexities and conflicts of urban social welfare revolve around defining not human needs but rather the collectivity that is responsible. What is the relevant community, and at what level? Social welfare institutions range from the Cub Scout pack meeting in a local church basement to the giant public hospital for the care of the poor with its attached clinics for alcohol and drug control, prenatal care, and out-patient psychiatry.

Ecology of Welfare

Characteristic of the American social welfare institution is the complexity, ambiguity, and localism of its organization. Ecologically, the institution shows striking but complicated patterns of differentiation in the location of clientele, personnel, facilities, and programs. Agencies and programs are unevenly distinguished, overlapping, and fragmented between private and public spheres and across states, metropolitan areas, and other units. Various welfare agencies and programs in close proximity to one another tend to have very complex interrelationships and to compete and coalesce in a local "ecology of games" (Long, 1958).

Welfare activities are justified in terms of serving the general good of a given community, which may range from being a local jurisdiction to the total society. A few important welfare programs, such as the Social Security insurance benefits, operate uniformly across the society, the placement of regional and local offices being largely an administrative convenience. In parallel to and in large part reflecting the decentralization of the nation's political structure, however, much welfare—both public and private—originated in and continues to be organized along the lines of, as well as a rationale for, the good of some local community. A continual problem is to settle on what is meant by that community. The fragmentation and ambiguities of the welfare system are highlighted when one contrasts it with public education. In the schools, although there is considerable dissension over the goals and appropriate methods of education, coherence is provided by the fact that a single local, accountable board of education usually exercises a substantial monopoly over the education that is provided across an unambiguous geographical area.

The relationship of welfare to the local community is further complicated by the problem of who is to benefit and how. Overall, welfare institutions may benignly serve the public good of social integration in an industrialized, urbanized, mobile society, but to do so they usually must target specific subpopulations for attention, and they often do so only at the behest of other, more privileged groups. Altruism in the United States very poorly masks self-interest (Titmuss, 1971). To do "good" *for* someone often means to do "good" *to* someone; the ultimate justification for counseling Mrs. Smith may be not so much to make her "better adjusted" in dealing with or leaving her errant husband as to reduce the chance that the Smiths' child will become a predatory delinquent. Thus to the ambiguities of political and administrative jurisdictions are added a politics of the self-defined "community of rectitude" targeting some other community for improvement. As Street and Davidson argue in Chapter Fifteen of this volume, suburbs tend to be highly defended communities; proposals involving the locations of welfare facilities and populations in suburbia often make defense of community a great concern.

Analysis of the ecology of welfare leads to a view that is substantially different from the human needs perspective of the conventional literature in social work, which tends to define needs and services in an individualized manner and to ignore the functions that welfare plays in the preservation of community order.

Metropolitan Change and Welfare

Social welfare has not always been identified as an urban institution. The earliest social welfare laws and institutions were set up to control wandering vagabonds and landless paupers. But with the growth of large urban-industrial complexes coupled with substantial movements of migrants to the cities both from home and abroad, the problems of unemployment, poor living conditions, and adjustment were quickly viewed as city problems.

In the extended city—or metropolitan area—of the 1970s, the shape of social welfare is influenced by many factors. In this chapter we will analytically separate three of these factors, discussing the trends in each and their effects on metropolitan social welfare. First, we will look at ways in which suburbanization directly influences welfare populations, programs, and resources, looking particularly to see if there is a growing dichotomy between the welfare institutions of the city and those of the suburbs. Second, we will look at the larger national structure of social welfare, noting important changes in sponsorship, resources, and professional ideology. Of special interest here is the apparent return to normalcy in social work since the end of the "War on Poverty," involving a shift back to great concern with individual adjustment and middle class problems compared with efforts at reform and provision of help to poor populations. Third, we will look at the role of the state, particularly the federal government, in social welfare as it has moved from laissez-faire in the pre-Depression years to pervasiveness by the mid 1960s. At present the state's role seems to be enlarged but more ambiguous and uneven, neither clearly dominant nor unimportant in making policy and developing programs.

Suburbanization and Welfare. As indicated at several points throughout this volume, suburbanization is the single most striking force in American urban life. In Chapter Two, Kasarda documents the great movement not only of affluent populations but also of industry from the central city to the suburbs. In Chapter Four, Janowitz and Street analyze the disarticulation of work and community of residence in terms of the problems that it creates for the political and social orders. The fragmentation of governance of suburbia means that the increase in the economic power of the suburbs has not been matched by an overall increase in political power. However, in spite of the incredible fragmentation into various districts, authorities, and local governments, which dilutes their political power, the suburbs have retained hegemony over some very important aspects of their development. In particular, they control zoning. Zoning is a political tool that is much more than annexing land and then subdividing it. It can be used to maintain economic as well as racial segregation, most often by establishing minimum lot-size requirements for houses. It can be used in quite subtle and complex ways, as in the Arlington Heights case.[2] Because of such zoning as well as other practices of the housing industry (Pearce, 1976), there has been little change in residential segregation patterns for decades (Taeuber and Taeuber, 1965). The movement of middle class blacks to the suburbs has been minimal and, in any case, has resulted in decentralization but not desegregation of the black population (Farley, 1970). Likewise, there are pockets of the poor who have migrated to the suburbs, often concentrated in pockets of poverty either in older industrial suburbs or in the interstices between suburbs, again reflecting the effects of zoning restrictions and discriminatory practices.

Obviously, the barriers of suburbia tend to exclude the poor who are recipients of public welfare or who would live in public housing were it available. Further, suburbia tends to be inhospitable to welfare programs and facilities no matter what the socioeconomic status of their users. Welfare programs often provoke great controversies over land use and location. They are frequently seen as series of treatments of the misbegotten, best done elsewhere. Like heavy industries, institutional facilities such as jails, mental hospitals, or public housing projects are generally a "noxious use" to the local community, which may want the benefits of the facility but certainly not its presence. The same kind of opposition arises with programs that have less visible facilities but might draw into the community undesirable people—drug addicts coming to a methadone maintenance clinic, delinquents living in a halfway house, recipients of public aid, or former mental patients and old people attracted by inexpensive rents.

The result of this resistance is often the restriction of welfare facilities to the central city, which are concentrated in the city's less well defended neighborhoods. Thus one finds what can be called "welfare minighettoes"—the nursing home row and areas like the Cass Corridor of Detroit. These are usually found in the dying districts near the central business district or in the areas around expressways. Even the rumored planning of a single facility can arouse a suburb to strengthen its barriers.[3] Not only are such facilities deemed objectionable in their own right, but for most communities the absence of welfare programs, as with the absence of minority groups, is deemed important as an indicator of affluence or at least respectability. It is true, of course, that not all communities reject welfare programs and facilities that serve the poor or deviant, even in the suburban ring. Poor communities naturally see public assistance as a necessary source of income, and some communities, perhaps primarily the "defeated neighborhoods" of the inner city that Suttles (1972) describes, will accept even a new jail for its jobs.

However, not all welfare services are rejected by even the most affluent suburbs. Some programs, which we will call *welfare amenities,* are desirable in all communities, rich as well as poor. These include an array of small clinics and private practices aimed at helping with individual adjustment to problems of marriage, divorce, strange children, phobias, or identity crises. Welfare amenities also include the provision—through YMCAs, churches, and (in working class communities) settlement houses—of benefits to normal youths and adults. Since life crises, such as "midlife" and "empty nest," are now normal, so are the services that deal with them. (The normality of these crises is indicated in the popularity of such books as *Passages* by Sheehy [1976].) Some welfare services, however, although widely used among the affluent and respectable and thus tolerated, have an ambiguous moral status and are concealed as much as possible. Thus, runaway centers are located above pizza parlors, abortion clinics are located among singles bars, and sex therapy clinics are found nestled within medical clinics.

Ultimately, suburbanization threatens to produce a *bifurcation of social welfare* between an inner-city "warehousing" and "containment" segment and a suburban "amenities" segment. The inner-city institutions, through increasingly public programs, emphasize support through public assistance and housing programs at subsistence levels along with direct social control discharged through juvenile courts, the mental health system, and related institutions. In contrast, the suburban segment is fundamentally concerned with providing adjustment counseling and consummatory services to the families of the middle class. In brief, the regulation of the poor (Piven and Cloward, 1971) seems to be becoming essentially a central-city phenomenon.

Of course, such a clean bifurcation cannot occur in practice, because nowhere does such a sharp differentiation of city-suburban populations occur and because there are substantial variations among metropolitan areas in the degree and effects of suburbanization. Bifurcation is also mitigated by the fact that many welfare programs that serve at least some of the middle class remain in the inner city because of heavy property investments, as with many medical-related facilities, or by the success of the suburbs in preventing their relocation. Not only property values but one's prestige and self-esteem are protected if the juvenile home where one's son is sent or the abortion clinic used by one's daughter are located in the next town or preferably downtown. The suburbanites' desire for a welfare-free environment is further complicated as the suburban ring spreads across the boondocks, thus encompassing the massive institutions built in an earlier era, when locating the asylum, prison, and sanatorium in the countryside was thought critical to cure.[4] The pace of suburbanization is uneven, as seen in Riska's (1974) study of the difficulties of bringing modern, specialized medical care facilities to a suburbanizing Long Island, where the small towns and doctors that predate suburbanization are parochial.

Despite the mitigations, the bifurcation of welfare may have progressed far beyond what the ecological and socioeconomic factors would seem to warrant. The suburbanite is not so clearly self-sufficient nor the city dweller so likely to be dependent or undependable as the character of the contrasting social welfare segments seems to suggest. Human need knows no boundaries (despite centuries of residence requirements to the contrary). Thus the artificial dichotomization by geographic area may dramatically neglect the needs of those who do not fit the stereotype for their area, for example, older people in the suburbs who need public housing.

Finally, this tendency for suburbanization to bifurcate social welfare is enhanced by the fact that the out-migration of resources includes an out-migration of both leadership and volunteers for private welfare efforts and of welfare professionals. Even when resources remain in the city, many professionals move to the suburbs and commute. The problems are of course compounded as the movements of welfare professionals coincide with the out-migrations of doctors and lawyers who also had served the inner city. With the large movement of whites comes a dispersion throughout the metropolitan region of old ethnic subcommunities that had been centers for traditional social welfare activities. The neighborhood houses and settlements that had served a broad clientele, including but not limited to the ethnic group sponsoring them, have declined (Switzer, 1973). Zald's (1970) study of the Chicago metropolitan YMCA is interesting as a deviant case—a neighborhood-based agency oriented to middle class services struggling to preserve its inner-city locations and divert some resources back into the city.

For most of the new suburbanites, however, their own community's needs become more apparent, the ways in which their new communities differ from the city are emphasized, and the needs of the city's people become more remote. Moreover, because contributions to the United Fund and many other individual charities are increasingly solicited at work—and away from the community of residence—both employees and their employers (most of whom are also suburbanites) are likely to become less enthusiastic supporters of private welfare activities in the city. In contrast, private welfare is encouraged in the suburbs because of a growth in third-party payments as part of corporate medical insurance packages made available in the workplace. These provide for access to such practitioners as child psychologists and marriage counselors and even for participation in esoteric "deep tissue" and "plays for living" therapies as well as now conventionally accepted transactional groups.

Suburbanization thus has profound effects on social welfare. The increasing segregation of our society into racial and economic ghettoes has its counterpart in the development of a bifurcated system that seems to warehouse the poor and provide amenities for the middle mass. Moreover, even in the suburbs, certain welfare services are provided surreptitiously or walled off in the interstices. The problems of the poor and less fortunate become literally as well as figuratively more distant from the average urban dweller.

Changes in the Welfare Institution. The shape and character of welfare in the metropolitan area cannot be seen simply as a reflection of processes of suburbanization. Also important are related short-term movements and long-term trends in the welfare profession, welfare institutions, and the political arena with which welfare interacts. Welfare today, with its multiplicity and ambiguity of programs, purposes, sponsorship, and functions, stands in stark contrast to its early years. Until the Depression there was a clear division of labor. Private efforts sought to ameliorate conditions of immigrants, industrial workers, and their families. They were considered the worthy poor, for their poverty was either temporary (for example, until they learned English) or the result of an uncontrollable misfortune (such as blindness or disease). Services and support were delivered under religious auspices or through the settlement house (Rose, 1963). A statement of the National Association of Settlement Houses, made in the 1890s, indicated a dual focus of the efforts on behalf of the worthy poor: direct services (including classes as well as food, clothing, and money) and lobbying on their behalf for social reforms. Settlement house workers like Jane Addams distinguished themselves around the turn of the century in their efforts for child welfare, labor unions, women workers, and related causes (Smith and Zeitz, 1975).

Public efforts, mainly through local governments, sought to control and support, at the most minimal level, the unworthy poor. Because their poverty was seen as the result of willful laziness or moral degeneracy, there was less concern with amelioration and more with suppressing the vices and perhaps inspiring the desire to work by stigmatizing those on the government dole and by the degradation of low living standards.

By the time of the Depression, voluntary and private social welfare had changed substantially. The wealthy and prestigious women and men who had actually formed the settlement were largely gone, having been replaced by paid, professional social workers. Social work crystallized as a profession in the early 1920s, and it did so around psychological and individualistic theories and techniques with a diminished interest in social reform (Pottick, 1977). As a result, social work's main concerns increasingly became the problems of those with the verbal skills and motivations appropriate for casework, and thus were increasingly addressed to the more educated and middle class. The movement of the function of distributing food, clothing, and money not only from private welfare to public but also from local to national auspices aided and abetted social work's disengagement from the poor (Cloward and Epstein, 1965).

The development of the social security system was of course done with the participation of and some leadership by prominent social workers, and one cannot overstate the consequences of the pension component and later Medicare for the welfare not only of the aged but also of the mass of the population who were freed from supporting aging kin. The public assistance categories of social security were spawned as well with a great deal of participation by professional social workers, but the unplanned growth of categorical programs occurred without professional control. A final effort to provide direct professional work for the poor came in the Social Security amendments of 1962, requiring that caseworkers certify that they had provided services to welfare recipients as a prerequisite to federal reimbursement of state welfare expenditures. However, in most jurisdictions the disproportionate number of recipients compared with the resources for hiring professional workers made this certification an empty ritual.

By the early 1960s, the settlement houses and neighborhood centers had developed an ideal staff model that posited professional social workers with appropriate specialties for all settlement house work: caseworkers (for individual and family counseling), group workers, and community organization workers. Although few city centers had more than one or two social workers with master of social work (M.S.W.) degrees, most directors of such agencies, when asked, said they would put any extra resources first into hiring more professional staff (Switzer, 1973). While the direct help provided by the settlement house and neighborhood center had changed in emphasis from goods and money to services, the social reform aspect of settlement house activity simply atrophied. The New Deal legislation and federal government policies had shifted the initiative to the federal government. The pre-Depression faith placed in the market to distribute resources equitably was now lodged in government. Private social welfare's role was seen to be that of innovation and flexibility in treatment modes, while the curing of social ills was best done by the state.

One of the best examples of the complexities of reform in metropolitan social welfare is seen in the history of urban public housing. The 1950s saw the advent of a massive public housing program based on the theory that the city's growing problems could be traced to its slums. In this view, the slums acted like a social swamp in which sloth, drunkenness, and disorder festered and grew, occasionally breaking forth in isolated incidents and sometimes epidemics of violence. If one eliminated the slum, then one could greatly improve the social health of both its residents and the city at large. Unfortunately, public housing and the land clearance and urban renewal that preceded it were administered more as a program in real estate than as a social institution (Rose, 1963). Communities were often uprooted and destroyed, frequently replaced with ecologically disastrous high-rise buildings that were artificially single-class and single-race in composition. (Of course, sometimes slum housing was replaced with middle-income and commercial developments, moving the housing problem elsewhere.) Even if the kind of settlement house services had been provided that earlier generations of the uprooted had received, there would have been no stable community and no leadership, for the successful families were forced to leave. Robert C. Weaver lamented, "It is no surprise that communities have swept their human tragedies into slums and forgotten them. But having embarked upon a program to tear up the slums, and having turned these tragedies up to the light, should the community *then* so blithely forget them?" (Rose, 1963, p. 383). Perhaps the community should not, but clearly the effectiveness of public housing is seen as much by its ability to house (or warehouse) the poor, out of sight and mind, as by its ability to solve the problems of poverty and crime.

In a later period, the War on Poverty seemed ready to transform social welfare; but although it had its roots in the social reform conception of government's role, it never embodied social reform in the old sense. Programmatically it was modeled after some of the relatively new programs that were private or semiprivate in nature, such as Mobilization for Youth on Manhattan's Lower East Side or the Ford Foundation's Gray Areas programs in various cities (Marris and Rein, 1967). Yet it was basically a political strategy and not a social welfare initiative. The Kennedy administration's razor-thin margin of victory resulted in a great debt to the urban black ghettoes. To settle this debt and consolidate the political base, the strategies chosen were a strange blend of very traditional programs, such as variations on educational and vocational training, together with programs that were seen as highly radical, such as giving power to the poor directly through community control, that is, "maximum feasible participation of the poor." The traditional programs resulted in the establishment of a heavily minority-staffed urban bureaucracy not unlike the patronage jobs of the old machine. The community participation efforts resulted in a heightened fragmentation of welfare and a mutually discrediting competition among various professional and citizens groups seeking their pieces of the antipoverty pie (see Grønbjerg, Street, and Suttles, in press). Behind the rhetoric, the radical efforts looked much like the machine as well. Thus in Mobilization for Youth, touted as speaking so genuinely in the name of the oppressed, Helfgot (1974) found a heavy staffing of middle-class minority group members apparently chosen to symbolically represent the poor. Indeed, new neighborhood service centers, which are the 1970s offspring of the War on Poverty programs, have been described as less the functional equivalent of the old-style settlement house than the ward-community center (O'Donnell and Sullivan, 1974). Even the VISTA volunteers, who are most like the original settlement house workers in that they live in and among the poor with whom they work, are deployed and supported by the federal government.

Even though politically motivated and ultimately politically undercut, the War on Poverty did influence the face of urban social welfare. The new multiservice neighborhood centers that were created in its aftermath reflected in their personnel more indigenous people, mostly as paraprofessionals, than would probably have been hired otherwise. The focus of activities also became more practical, for example, on how to deal with welfare bureaucracies, landlords, and stores. Activities did not, however, reflect the more radical strategies of participation of the poor or minority members in the decision-making structures. While one can debate the competence and inclination of those on the bottom to participate fully and effectively in organizational decision making (see Moynihan, 1969), it is apparent that the idea of such a radical shift in the power structure was threatening enough in itself, to mayors and congressmen alike, to produce the almost immediate dismantling of programs such as the Community Action Program (Donovan, 1967). At any rate, the inherent contradiction of the government sponsoring its own welfare reform, at some cost to itself, would seem to have led to its demise. Cahn and Cahn (1964) explored this problem for New Haven, Connecticut.

The civil rights movement that prompted the Kennedy-Johnson attack on poverty, along with the many liberation movements that followed—of women, senior citizens, gays, Latinos, consumers, and others—inherited much of the burden of social reform initiatives. For while there was some "greening" of the professionals in social welfare in the turbulent 1960s, the twin agenda of racism and poverty remained vague and nonprogrammatic. By the early 1970s dechlorinization was well along. Professional social workers increased the sophistication and multiplied the numbers of treatment strategies and specialties. Private practice, which almost by definition serves the affluent middle and upper classes, became a desirable goal for many. Miller (1977) found that about a third of social work students, when asked to write a hypothetical vita reflecting the next ten years of their lives, indicated that they expected to engage in some private practice. In parallel, enrollment in community practice curricula in schools of social work has tended to slide since the 1960s, while attention at many professional meetings has gone to new individual therapies to the exclusion of discussions of poverty.

While professional social work has been becoming even more private, middle class, and individualistic in orientation, there has developed outside of both public and private welfare programs what might be termed "movement" social welfare. Although lacking the neighborhood focus of the settlement house, the organizations spawned by liberation movements, like the settlements, are urban in character. They are even ethnic, if one defines *ethnic* broadly to mean a sense of peoplehood, shared fate, and commonality of world view (Geertz, 1963). Many a

women's center, for example, is clearly a more direct descen-
dant and functional equivalent of the settlement house than is
the neighborhood service center. Its combination of consciousness raising and classes, demonstrations in the street and lecture
series, and services (for example, abortion or legal counseling)
and agitation (for example, task forces on sexism in the schools)
resembles closely the 1890s description of the services-and-
social-reform settlement house cited above. The professionals
found in movement social welfare, like the Jane Addams figures
of the past, are generally not professional social workers, but
lawyers, city planners, doctors, and even academics. Thus while
many trends on the professionalized side of social welfare are
highly congruent with suburbanization and bifurcation of welfare, movement activities focus attention on problems of city
living—although frequently only on problems of the more affluent city dwellers.

In less than a hundred years, then, the pattern of urban
social services has moved from its dual focus on services and reform to a concentration on services. Moreover, as social work
became a profession, adopting an ideology of individualism and
a body of scientific knowledge, and as the Depression and the
massive relief and welfare programs it spawned moved the provision of material objects to the public sphere, the services provided through voluntary social welfare became more specialized.
The War on Poverty's newsmaking programs were noticeable for
their upsetting effects on political affairs, not on social welfare,
while the advent of movement social welfare reopened some
new social reform initiatives, but generally these were in the
area of middle class concerns.

Many of these changes are reflected at a micro level by
the transformations of the original settlement of Jane Addams,
the famous Hull House. Founded in 1889, it grew to an enormous complex of buildings, offices, classrooms, and recreation
facilities that continued to serve thousands of people until the
early 1960s. At that time, however, much of the immediate surrounding community and all of the complex but the original
house were leveled in the name of urban renewal and to make
way for the University of Illinois at Chicago Circle. Services
were still provided by what is now known as the Hull House
Association at several locations, not including the original Hull
House (it is now a museum). The new locations are scattered
about the city, in areas that serve as arrival points for new immigrants and in one "suburban" location. The centers almost all

include day care and counseling of one kind or another; some also include a theater, recreation, and job training and placement. Two of the centers are not actually community based, but are citywide senior citizen groups. Most are headed by professionals, and none—for reasons of time and not to jeopardize their nonprofit status—engages in social reform activities.

Trends in Government Involvement. The explicit efforts by the federal government to enhance the political position of inner-city poor populations during the War on Poverty clashed with the traditional ideologies of local and state control and the political powers vested at these levels. Dismantling the antipoverty program, the Nixon and Ford administrations substituted revenue sharing, which is characterized well by Wade (1976-1977, p. 3) as follows: "By spreading money among 39,000 communities throughout a complicated formula, it favored the suburbs and ignored the disproportionate needs of the larger and older cities. By moving money through the states, it enhanced the power of suburban representatives which now dominate most state legislatures."

On the contemporary scene, two subtle developments in social welfare are of interest and may have lasting if complicated effects. The first is a continuation of the recurrent trend for a concentration of welfare expenditures, with a parallel if less certain tendency to centralize power over welfare programs at the higher levels of government, particularly the federal level. This trend is obscured but not halted by a continuation of the rhetoric about citizen participation and gearing programs to the needs of local communities. The second trend is more clear-cut: An increasing tendency of government to buy social services from private agencies, thereby further blurring the line between public and private social welfare.

The localism of welfare in America is of course strong, and the fragmentation that results may have much to do with the failure of the nation, relative to Western European countries, to develop more than a "reluctant welfare state" (Wilensky, 1965). Yet some tendency to concentrate resources and some kinds of centralization seem apparent at each government level. The percentage of Aid to Families with Dependent Children (AFDC) funds that is federal has steadily risen, and in a study of the American AFDC rolls from 1960 to 1970, Grønbjerg (1977b) finds a powerful if uneven growth in the number of recipients and the level of welfare expenditures. She also finds that "the United States has been gradually and halt-ingly moving toward a mass society in which the definition of citizenship is being extended to include economic rights and duties as well as [more traditional rights like suffrage]" (p. 153). The federal government has also increasingly promulgated federal standards and imposed requirements that local governments coordinate their requests for monies. For example, government circulars such as A-80 and A-95 require review on a regional basis, usually that of a metropolitan area, to be conducted by a unit such as a council of governments. In practice, efforts at metropolitan coordination may involve less a centralization of power than a pattern of "accommodative cooperation" (see Chapter Fifteen of this volume by Street and Davidson), but in the long run these may ultimately yield increments of centralization.

Among social welfare agencies themselves, there is a continued tendency toward consolidation and coordination, especially in terms of funding. Major steps toward this came after World War I, with the development of the community chest type of organization, and were augmented in the 1950s and 1960s when foundations and then the federal government began to create special projects requiring agency cooperation as a prerequisite to funding (Grønbjerg, 1977a). Efforts at social service coordination or integration generally receive high tribute in public rhetoric but lag as agencies find them too disabling in the pursuit of their own goals (Zald, 1969). Further, coordination does not usually escape the competitive politics of "interest group liberalism" (Lowi, 1969). Centralization in the private sphere is thus even less clearly unidirectional than in the public arena, but nevertheless there is a trend toward treating neighborhoods as uniform and agencies in batches (Brilliant, 1973). Overall, one effect is that communities and neighborhoods are seen as having problems, not people; the symptoms treated are the rates (the juvenile delinquency rate or the crime rate); and when the rates decline or at least stabilize, the problem has been solved. Developments in both the public and private spheres of welfare, so long insulated from one another, have become interrelated. This interrelationship has occurred particularly as recipients of public assistance were sent to private agencies because of requirements that the recipients receive services and as the War on Poverty funds became available to such private agencies as well. The result is a blurring of the distinction between public and private that raises questions about the ultimate autonomy of the private sector (Grønbjerg, 1977a).

Presently the greatest blurring of public and private welfare societies is occurring because of the trend of "federalism by contract" (Brilliant, 1973). This has taken many forms, four of which will be mentioned here. The first is the straightforward contract for service; such contracts account for increasing proportions of governmental spending on social services. Beck (1971) estimates that 28 percent of institutional care of children and 100 percent of maternity home services are purchased by government from private agencies. The second form is the contract to business corporations for management consulting, fraud investigation, organizational overhauling, and the like. Third, there is the creation of hybrid organizations that resemble voluntary agencies in that they provide social services but are intended to make a profit. Nursing homes and day care centers, some supported almost entirely by government funds, are examples. Fourth, there are new private agencies created for the state or federal government and designed according to the specifications laid down in the administrative fiat or legislation. The latter agencies do not exist independently but are creatures of the state, private in name but public in all other respects. Even the community they represent may be an artifact of federal policy (Taub and others, 1977). Pifer (1967) suggests distinguishing between the voluntary association, which is controlled by its membership; the nongovernmental agency, which acts as if it were voluntary but is in fact dependent on government largesse; and the private agency, which is controlled by a self-perpetuating board of trustees (and whose money often comes from an endowment).

Considered together in the local community, these trends raise questions about the true character of a given social service organization. How local is an agency that is largely federally funded, and how much local control can be exerted over its activities? How neighborhood oriented is a neighborhood service center whose services are determined centrally? (Indeed, the services themselves are frequently offered in a central location as well.) Similarly, how private is a social service agency that is created along federal guidelines for the purpose of receiving federal monies and that is in no traditional sense accountable to a local board of supporters and fund raisers? Moreover, how public are services bought with public tax monies but delivered by private agencies that are sponsored by religious or other private groups or organizations?

This lack of distinction between private and public agencies and among neighborhood, local, regional, state, and federal levels has obscured and made more palatable the stronger role of government, especially federal government, in much of social welfare. And it has done so at a time when American cynicism about the ability of government to handle social welfare and other liberal programs both equitably and efficiently is quite high. The skepticism has particularly focused on questions of efficiency, the more so as questions of equity have diminished with the fading of civil rights and poverty as national concerns. In the interests of efficiency we have deinstitutionalized mental health and correctional populations and contracted for services from the profit as well as from the nonprofit private sectors. Whether the new face of social welfare thus obtained is an improvement is very much an open question.[5]

The provision of social welfare under public as opposed to private (especially religious) auspices ostensibly makes social services available to all those in need regardless of race, creed, color, or sex. But what is the effect of the "reprivatization" (Drucker, 1969) of social welfare services? The voluntary social agencies have always fought the loss of their functions to public agencies and sought to preserve themselves and their integrity by obtaining government money without strings attached. The Catholic Church has advocated, for example, that where the government must act it should do so through existing structures (Beck, 1971). The question of equity becomes crucial as federalization by contract becomes the norm, for the government is now engaging in direct grants to local agencies (Hill, 1971). When the federal government bypasses state and local governments to give monies to local social service agencies on a three-to-one matching basis, it is then giving over decision making about public funds to agency boards, small groups of people who are frequently not democratically selected and are self-perpetuating. These boards, of course, tend to represent neither the larger community nor the clientele served. Once again, the upright and well-to-do citizens become the Overseers of the Poor.

Consideration of the effects of federal involvement with welfare on equity and efficiency leads to new questions. In the end, the important issue may not be whether government has undermined and taken control of social welfare or whether governmental contracting for services disguises continuing control over social services by sectarian groups. Instead, the key question may be whether the results will not resemble a "social-industrial complex" (Harrington, 1968) that is not a genuine part of or controlled by either private or public agencies. The developments we have discussed complicate the understanding of social welfare in the metropolitan area, since they not only make the distinction between private and public ambiguous but also threaten further the already feeble legitimacy often accorded to definitions of *neighborhood, local community,* and *wider community.*

The Chicago Metropolitan Community: An Empirical Case

We have hypothesized an increasing bifurcation of the social welfare institutions in the older, established metropolitan areas as they have undergone intense suburbanization, and we have discussed ways in which these changes are reinforced and complicated by trends in the social work profession and in the extent and character of federal funding of welfare. We have also speculated that the bifurcation may go beyond segregation by socioeconomic status, race, and ethnicity and reflect a reification of the stereotypes of city and suburbia that produces a very sharp differentiation between the social welfare institutions serving the inner-city dweller and those serving the suburban resident. We have not asked whether there are countervailing forces of inertia and cultural lag which slow the suburbanizing processes that transform the system of social welfare, although such a question would be useful.

To this point our discussion has been short on systematic data. In partial response to this problem we present a preliminary analysis of data demonstrating change in the voluntary or private, nonprofit welfare programs in the Chicago metropolitan area. Although the growth of public as well as for-profit welfare in the Chicago SMSA clearly merits study, we have not focused on this aspect. As evidence of the suburbanization of affluence, under the federal poverty standards of 1969, 14.3 percent of Chicago residents were below the poverty level versus 4.2 percent among residents of the rest of the metropolitan area (U.S. Bureau of the Census, 1973b). With respect to the public assistance populations, one indicator of bifurcation is that in 1972 the AFDC recipient rate in Cook County (which includes Chicago) was 124 per thousand, compared with figures ranging from 10 to 36 per thousand in the other five SMSA counties (Illinois Department of Public Aid, 1974). Another indicator is that within Cook County, of the 722,281 public aid cases handled through regular district offices in July 1975, approximately 94 percent were on the books in twenty-two of the twenty-four offices located within the Chicago city limits (Illinois Department of Public Aid, 1975).

We will ask specifically what has happened to private welfare agencies over the past three decades. The source for our study is the "blue book," the social service directory, coded for five years: 1944, 1956, 1963, 1970, and 1976. The directory's primary usage is for referral; each agency listed has a brief description that includes its source of funds, client criteria, location, and services offered. The directory's coverage is metropolitan in scope, and it purports to include all agencies that are nonprofit organizations.[6] Four types of change in private social welfare will be discussed here: criteria for clientele, agency sponsorship, services offered, and locations of the agencies.

Criteria for Clients. In general, there has been a decline in the sectarian social service agency. While it is probably not surprising that agencies that served particular ethnic groups, such as the Bohemian Old Folks Home, have either closed or broadened their criteria for clientele, it is noteworthy that the number of agencies that exclusively serve new immigrants to the ethnic ghettoes of Chicago, such as blacks and Latinos, has also declined—from 2 percent of the agencies in 1944 to 1 percent in 1976. Agencies in the past reflected racial and ethnic segregation patterns of the city, so that each ethnic enclave had its own set of institutions—recreational, social, and religious. As these ethnic subcommunities have dispersed throughout the larger metropolitan community, the groups that have inherited their neighborhoods have not developed this pattern of institutions. At least, institutions have not been established with what today would be called "separatist" philosophies of serving particular groups exclusively. Of course, the difference in services delivered may be more apparent than real; since today's newcomers are much more segregated than white ethnics ever were, by location alone an agency may serve only one group without need of exclusionary criteria or a separatist philosophy. At any rate, it is clear that today's immigrants do not have title to sets of social services in the same way that their European predecessors did.

Services offered exclusively to groups having particular demographic characteristics, such as those of sex or age, have also declined. Most striking is that a decline in services to young women ("working girls"), which frequently consisted of housing or housing referral, accounts for most of this decrease. The newer agencies serving women exclusively, such as the women's liberation centers and feminist health groups, have engaged in new kinds of services to women, such as education, health care, and consciousness raising, services not unlike those offered earlier by the settlement houses to immigrants who were likewise new entrants to the urban labor market.[7]

Agency Sponsorship. Social service agencies have been overwhelmingly nonsectarian in their criteria for clientele; even in 1944, 84 percent of all agencies put no religious restrictions on whom they would serve. By 1976, 96 percent of the agencies had no such restrictions. In terms of agency sponsors, however, there has been a drastic shift. While in 1944 two thirds of the agencies listed in the directory were sponsored by or under the auspices of a church or religious organization, by 1976 the percentage had dropped to 43 percent. Some of this change was quite dramatic. Of Logan Square's seven agencies in 1944, three were sponsored by a Protestant ethnic denomination; by 1976, all but two of the twelve agencies serving this area were nonsectarian or private. It should be noted, however, that the decline in religious sponsors in Logan Square and elsewhere is less the result of the withdrawal of religious groups and organizations from the social welfare scene than the result of these establishments being overwhelmed by the many new agencies that are virtually all nonsectarian. Particularly in areas that did not have social service agencies in the early years, such as Uptown and the newer suburbs, there are now almost no religiously sponsored agencies.

It may be true, as Smith (1971) maintains, that some of the apparently nonsectarian agencies have disguised their religious underpinning or restructured themselves in order to be eligible for certain sources of funding (such as government or foundations). At the same time, there has been *de jure* secularization of organizations that are still titularly religious (for example, see Zald and Denton, 1963, on the transformation of emphasis of the Young Men's Christian Association from Christ to "gym and swim"). As many of the religious groups served primarily but not exclusively people of a particular ethnic as well as religious background, the secularization of sponsorship can be seen as one reflection of the decline of white ethnicity as a social force in general and of ethnic intragroup welfare efforts in particular. While it seems that the religious organizations of the newer groups are not involved in sponsoring social welfare to the extent that their predecessors were, the patterns are probably more complex than these data suggest. For example, some social services are contained wholly within religious institutions that are not formally organized or are restricted to members only (or both)—as with some of the Black Muslims' activities. Also, cultural differences between the old European immigrants and the newer groups may be such that similar needs for social services are satisfied within the community but not within the "voluntary social service agency" framework (see Stack, 1975).

Changes in sponsorship are also reflected in the sources of agency funding.[8] Contributions, fees, and dues have remained essentially constant as sources of funding, with contributions constituting approximately 37 percent of revenue sources throughout the period studied, and fees and dues about one third. Reflecting changing patterns of welfare described more generally above, Chicago's social service agencies cite endowment support half as often today as they did two decades ago, while governmental sources have increased fivefold. In 1944 only one agency in the entire directory mentioned the federal government as a source of money; it had not increased much by 1963 (to five), but in 1970 there were twenty-five, and by 1976 there were forty-four agencies receiving federal monies.

Services Offered. Each of the agencies listed in the directory in each of the five selected years was coded for the services it offered, up to three. In spite of the development of multiservice centers, apparently there are few actual establishments for which the coding of only three services was a limitation. As can be seen from Table 1, it is the services that have *not* increased as much as those that have increased that create the new patterns of social welfare. In education, for example, one would expect that food and nutrition programs and adult education increased greatly as social agency offerings. Instead, and despite health and medical breakthroughs, the special schools for the developmentally disabled have shown the largest increase among the educational services offered.

Particularly among services offered for two groups who are presumed to be dependent, children and the aged, it is surprising to note that there has been almost no response to newly recognized needs, such as child abuse, or increased problems, such as delinquency, in the voluntary sector. Homes for dependent and neglected children have actually declined, although it should be remembered that in this area, as with nursing

Table 1. Voluntary Social Services in the Chicago Metropolitan Area.

Service	1944	1956	1963	1970	1976
Education					
General	103	82	85	88	102
Special schools	12	8	10	24	46
Schools for immigrants	7	5	1	1	1
Adult education	3	3	4	5	11
Forums	5	7	7	9	10
Food and nutrition programs	2	1	2	3	9
Scholarships	3	2	3	3	3
Subtotal	135	108	112	133	182
Percentage	15.6	13.7	13.5	13.2	13.8
Child Welfare and Aged					
General	7	8	6	4	4
Child placement	10	16	15	15	21
Homes for dependent and neglected children	48	39	32	30	35
Homes for delinquent children	5	5	5	4	4
Day care centers and day nurseries	33	23	27	39	54
Child protection/child abuse	1	1	1	1	3
Noninstitutionalized services for the aged	0	0	3	3	14
Subtotal	104	92	89	96	135
Percentage	12.0	11.7	10.7	9.5	10.2
Health					
General	10	7	11	12	14
In-patient care	62	79	94	99	91
Separate clinics	30	28	29	36	50
Convalescent/nursing homes[a]	10	12	10	7	6
Rehabilitation	3	7	10	13	26
Dental clinics	5	4	5	6	11
Birth control	3	1	1	1	11
Subtotal	123	138	160	174	209
Percentage	14.2	17.6	19.3	17.3	15.8
Housing					
Emergency shelter	8	5	4	5	9
Room registries	9	4	1	1	1
Boarding clubs and hotels	36	19	21	13	8
Homes for aged	43	55	49	50	47
Subtotal	96	82	75	69	65
Percentage	11.1	10.6	9.0	6.9	4.9
Employment					
Employment services	12	10	13	23	38
Vocational rehabilitation	6	6	8	6	7

Table 1 *(Continued)*

Service	1944	1956	1963	1970	1976
Employment *(Continued)*					
Job training	0	1	5	10	21
Subtotal	18	17	26	39	66
Percentage	2.1	2.2	3.1	3.9	5.0
Legal and Criminal Institutions					
Legal aid and counseling	10	9	9	12	35
Law enforcement	6	3	3	5	5
Juvenile homes, prisons	3	3	2	1	1
Subtotal	19	15	14	18	41
Percentage	2.2	1.9	1.7	1.8	3.1
Mental Health					
Community mental health centers	5	4	9	19	19
Mental hospitals	11	9	12	9	5
Counseling services	12	8	39	58	118
Subtotal	28	21	60	86	142
Percentage	3.2	2.7	7.2	8.6	10.7
Recreation					
Camps	26	27	23	20	24
General recreation	74	65	84	91	110
Subtotal	100	92	107	111	134
Percentage	11.6	11.7	12.9	11.0	10.1
Advocacy and Community Groups					
Consumer protection	5	5	4	4	6
Civic and reform organizations	13	9	12	11	18
Women's groups (traditional)	6	4	5	6	7
Minority group organizations (including women's liberation)	5	10	8	8	14
Financial fund raising	28	24	22	21	21
Coordination of services	53	49	50	52	55
Regional and city planning	0	0	1	1	3
Research	6	11	14	12	13
Subtotal	116	112	116	115	137
Percentage	13.4	14.2	14.0	11.4	10.4
Miscellaneous					
Neighborhood, settlement, and multiservice centers	55	54	46	66	60
Disaster relief	23	18	15	14	17
Food services	3	3	3	3	12
Other	45	33	66	81	121

(continued on next page)

Table 1 *(Continued)*

Service	1944	1956	1963	1970	1976
Miscellaneous *(Continued)*					
Subtotal	126	108	130	164	210
Percentage	14.6	13.7	15.7	16.3	15.9
Total	865	786	829	1005	1321
Percentage	100.0	100.0	100.0	100.0	100.0

[a]Except homes for the aged, which are listed under Housing.

homes, there are private, for-profit institutions whose services are purchased by the state that do not appear here. Even where there has been an increase, it seems inadequate to the needs; given almost no public development of day care centers, are fifty-four centers throughout the metropolitan area enough? With a rapidly growing proportion of our population over sixty-five years of age, are fourteen programs for the senior citizens of Chicago reasonable?

In health services there has been an increase in almost every area. As mentioned above, the high investment in immovable buildings and equipment of a large hospital or medical complex mitigates against its withdrawal in spite of the flight from the city of much of its clientele. The pattern in health seems to be in contrast to other areas, with the continuing development of inner-city establishments concomitant with the development of newer services in newer areas.

Housing is clearly not a major area of social services today. Particularly striking is the decline of homes for the aged since the peak in 1956. Obviously, there has been an enormous increase in nursing or convalescent homes for the aged; what the figures here reflect is the decline in socially sponsored housing. It has been replaced in part by public institutions, but in the main by private, for-profit establishments. (For the effect of replacing social responsibility with the profit motive on the care provided nursing home residents, see Mendelson, 1975.)

The increase in employment services and training reflects both the greater problem of unemployment and the higher priority placed on the goal of helping people of all ages and both genders to become productive members of society. The larger number of services offered in the area of legal problems also reflects the increasing complexity of social structure; just as getting a job today requires skills and sometimes an advocate, so does getting justice—both in and out of the courtroom.

The services under mental health clearly reflect the process of deinstitutionalization. While the number of mental hospitals has been reduced by half in the last three decades, the number of community mental health centers has quadrupled. Services for those with less serious mental health problems have shown the most dramatic increase in any single category; clearly for old and especially new agencies, this is the single most important service offered.

Advocacy and community-wide groups have not shown the increase that one might expect. While minority group organizations doubled between 1944 and 1956, there has been a net increase since 1956 of only four organizations. Apparently, much of the unrest and upheaval of the 1960s did not leave a residue of new social service agencies or advocacy-oriented groups. Finally, among the miscellaneous services, it is apparent that the agency offering many services under one roof is not yet the predominant model. At the same time, a variety of new services are being offered; while they are a potpourri, in general the unclassified services are more specialized and technical, for example, donated architectural services or accountant advice to women on their credit ratings.

Location. The suburbanization of Chicago's population has been followed to some extent by a suburbanization of private social welfare services. While in 1944 less than 100 of the nearly 500 agencies were suburban, 36 percent of the agencies listed were suburban in 1976. While the city gained a net of less than 100 new agencies, the suburbs almost tripled their numbers. Particularly because the social service directory does not reflect individual private-practice or for-profit agencies, these indicators understate the city-suburban change.

Given that the suburbs have gained social service agencies and, at least relatively, the city has lost agencies, have these changes been evenly distributed? Examination of the data indicates that the answer is no for both instances. Thus, certain areas of the city experienced dramatic withdrawals of large numbers of social welfare agencies; for example, Kenwood had nine agencies in 1944, but only one by 1976. The Near West Side and its remaining people, subjected to urban renewal and bisected by two expressways, have been abandoned by twenty-one agencies at the same time that its status as an outstanding medical center for the metropolitan area as a whole has been reinforced. (The area also includes the old West Madison Street skid row; as is the case for the elderly, the people in this area have been left to the cheap hotels, hospitals, and the police.)

Other areas that lost agencies tended to be older areas near the center of the city that have experienced decline and sometimes depopulation.

In contrast, the areas that have gained agencies are, with two exceptions, suburbs—frequently new suburbs. The Loop gained almost two dozen agencies, an indication of some of the centralization and consolidation that has occurred over the period as well as the specialized nature of some of the newer services offered. The other nonsuburban area that has gained a large number of agencies over this time period was Uptown; this area has been the landing zone for several new groups to the city, including Appalachian whites and native Americans, as well as the site of many halfway houses, nursing homes, and other small institutions. It seems to be both a welfare ghetto, a place where establishments of doubtful respectability are found, and a colony in which new types of service delivery systems and treatment modalities are established on a trial basis.

Examining the suburbs, there is a distinct pattern to the growth of social welfare. The older suburbs, such as Evanston and Waukegan, seem to have gained the largest portion of the added organizations. This is in part due to the lower income of these suburbs relative to others. If the suburbs are divided into three groups according to mean income, the lowest third (using 1970 census figures) gained an average of 5.6 new agencies over the past three decades; the middle third gained an average of 2.1; and the high-income third an average of 3.9. The kind of agencies that are gained differs as well; in at least one instance a group of higher-income suburbs banded together to create a runaway center for their residents' teenagers, but built it in a nearby, older, less respectable suburb, and then debated as to whether children from the latter suburb should be included in the runaway center's clientele.

Finally, a comparison of the changes in distribution of services between city and suburbs reflects the tendency toward bifurcation of city services discussed above (see Table 2). Services that could be classed as amenities, such as counseling and recreation, have grown disproportionately in the suburbs compared with the city; over a period of two decades, for example, there was a net increase of only eight agencies offering recreation services in the city, while the suburbs moved from having none to having more than 25 percent of the recreation services offered in the Chicago metropolitan area. Services that emphasize warehousing or other kinds of social control, such as homes

Table 2. Selected Voluntary Social Services Offered, By City Versus Suburban Location of Agency, By Year.

Service	1944	Percent Suburban	1956	Percent Suburban	1963	Percent Suburban	1970	Percent Suburban	1976	Percent Suburban
Child welfare and adoption	12/5	29.0	18/6	25.0	16/5	23.8	15/4	21.0	15/10	40.0
Dependent and neglected children	29/19	39.5	18/19	51.3	19/15	44.1	22/11	50.0	26/18	40.9
Day care centers and day nurseries	31/2	6.1	21/1	4.5	21/6	22.2	26/13	50.0	34/19	35.8
General services and hospitals	62/6	8.8	70/11	13.6	71/32	31.1	71/38	34.9	66/37	35.9
Clinics	30/0	0.0	28/0	0.0	23/5	17.9	27/6	18.2	33/16	32.6
Nursing homes and homes for aged	34/19	35.8	40/26	39.4	30/25	45.4	28/29	50.9	24/29	54.7
Housing	48/2	4.0	24/3	11.1	21/5	19.2	15/4	21.0	14/4	22.2
Employment (all employment-related services)	22/1	4.3	14/1	6.7	24/0	0.0	32/7	17.9	38/15	28.3
Community mental health centers	3/0	0.0	2/0	0.0	2/2	50.0	7/6	46.2	8/11	57.9
Counseling services	8/3	27.0	7/0	0.0	28/9	24.3	39/17	30.4	63/55	46.7
General recreation	71/0	0.0	59/2	3.3	65/17	20.7	72/17	19.1	79/29	26.6

Note: The number to the left of the slash indicates the number of services of that type offered by agencies located in Chicago; the number to the right of the slash indicates the number of services of that type offered by suburban agencies. (Numbers of services offered differ slightly from Table 1 because of slightly different groupings and because some agencies could not be clearly located geographically.)

for delinquent children, maintained their proportionate share. Contrasting day care, which is an amenity needed by working parents with nonproblem children, with services for problem children who are dependent, neglected, and delinquent, makes this difference in distribution clear: While services of the latter group of children have maintained a 60/40 city/suburban split over the past two decades, the city/suburban ratio for day care has moved from 94/6 to 65/35. (This is in spite of the probably greater need for subsidized day care in the city.) Lastly, note that those services that are rooted by their irretrievable investments in facilities or require centralization, such as hospitals, have had some suburban growth while basically remaining in the city.

The overall picture of voluntary social welfare in Chicago is thus not simply one of flight from the city, although that is certainly a clear pattern. There has also been a sorting out of services. As services have become offered to a less narrowly defined client class, they have become more clearly middle class in their offerings, even under alternative sponsorship, and have followed the exit of the middle class from the city and the city's problems.

If we placed the results of this study of voluntary social agencies in the larger context of social welfare broadly defined to include the public and for-profit sectors, the contrasts drawn would be even greater. Not only do the suburbs house large numbers of private and for-profit amenities, such as tennis clubs, psychiatrists, and marriage (and divorce) clinics, but their affluence also creates additional public and private amenities as well that are not included here. On the public side are parks and playgrounds, swimming pools, arboretums, lapidary museums, and historical collections, some of which are donated by affluent citizens. On the private side are such things as wealthy churches that support ministers whose sole job is pastoral counseling or that fund expensive seminars and clinics for their members on such topics as parent-child relations. Our study has also understated the social control activities of social welfare in the city, which is largely in the hands of various public agencies such as the police and the schools.

The City as a Reservation

We have explored the interrelationships of changes in social welfare and community patterns in established major metropolitan areas. Theoretically we have emphasized the symbolic and political aspects of the ecology of welfare, particularly as the suburbanization of populations and resources seems to bifurcate welfare offerings. We have seen these patterns as related to and complicated by trends in social welfare institutions and government, the results blurring distinctions among levels of government, between public and private agencies, and between what might be called real and contrived community organizations. A preliminary examination of data on voluntary social welfare in the Chicago SMSA has somewhat substantiated our rather speculative analysis.

We must ask where our discussion leaves the residents of those cities that have been left behind by rampant suburbanization of people, wealth, and industry. Here we are principally discussing the older and larger cities in the Northeastern and North Central regions of the country. We seem to have come to the "end of the self-sufficient city" (Wade, 1976-1977), and projections of the dependency ratios of cities, relating wage earners to the numbers of young and old dependents, clearly support this conclusion. In Chapter Two of this volume, Kasarda suggests that governments will increasingly have to transfer funds to the less viable central cities. His formulation moves toward the familiar metaphor of the city as a federal reservation, a tragic end point at which the city is administered and financed from above, with resources provided at the level of subsistence or whatever other level, higher or lower, will keep the natives from storming the barricades. The notion of reservation implies two things: that the residents lose their capacity for self-governance and initiative and that their life space can be effectively confined to the city boundaries.

To evaluate the power and limits of the reservation metaphor, we must also ask (1) whether the generation of federal funding to support the reservation is automatic or at least feasible, (2) whether we have reached the point where in some cities the reservation is already in operation, and (3) whether the reservation truly must constitute an end point. With respect to the first of these questions, the generation of resources for the cities is clearly not automatic. This has been harshly demonstrated by the federal reaction to the New York City fiscal crisis. Obviously, distinctive features of the incredibly bloated New York municipal bureaucracy and of the politics of the time have played a role—but in addition there is sound reason to think that massive transfers of resources to the cities will simply be unfeasible. This is not only because the political power balance has tipped in favor of the suburbs but also because the federal cornucopia for progressively heightened expenditures on welfare and education is reaching a limit (Janowitz, 1976).

Determining whether some of our cities are not already reservations, if underfinanced ones, is made difficult by the blurring of private and public agencies, levels of government, purposes of programs, and social definitions of community, which our analysis has emphasized. We can tentatively conclude that some cities are already treated as reservations. But viewing a particular city in this way involves severe problems in deciding whether a given program of private services is in fact public, whether a given local program is in fact federal, whether a given metropolitan program truly is universal or largely diverts resources to one place or another, and whether a given community organization is more than a self-perpetuating and self-aggrandizing interest group. Our uncertainty on such questions is much less important than the concrete confusions of local residents. The welter of programs and accompanying rhetoric such as the "new federalism," or "revenue sharing," or "community development" make it uncertain whether the welfare state has not somehow arrived. It is also unclear whether the federal reservation is currently in operation, about to appear, or—with the end of the War on Poverty—already come and gone. The bifurcated system of social welfare seems to offer city residents subsistence and dependency along with some crude programs to provide social control for their most unruly offspring. These efforts are so penurious and mean spirited that none of the reaction of gratitude by the recipient that was idealized in an earlier day of private charity could possibly be expected. Also, the efforts are so clouded over with ambiguity and rhetoric that any demand for accountability also seems out of the question.

Finding an answer to the third question—about the reservation model as an end point—is the most important problem. The danger is that by undercutting local responsibilities and initiatives the reservation will be self-perpetuating. Let us assume that the reservation model is already, or soon will be, in operation in several American cities. If so, no doubt its operations are and will continue to be relatively invisible. For the city dwellers seeking an alternative to the vagaries of programs and claims, there might be some key to finding a solution in Camus's assertion that one is most free when one is in prison because at least one is freed of the illusion of freedom. Breaking through the ambiguities that obscure inequities and responsibilities to discover the "prison" of the reservation could be both terrifying and liberating, but a necessary first step. The aim of such a breakthrough would be to make possible an agonizing reappraisal, a wholesale deflation of rhetoric, and realistic but genuine efforts at institution building on the part of the poor and the remaining working and middle class city dwellers together. It is obvious that everywhere a sustained community life requires voluntary efforts. Community life cannot be administered from afar; it must be constructed locally in a way that is realistic about economic difficulties as well as freed from welfare-state ideologies that generate false optimism, confusion, and dependency. The aim must be to free human potentials for community building rather than to impose bureaucratic structure upon these potentials.

What might be done? We shall not deal with the broad range of policies that might reduce the general tendency to socioeconomic and racial segregation of the metropolitan area, although any efforts must be accommodated to these goals. Nor shall our suggestions be restricted to those policies that are immediately politically feasible; rather, they will highlight the implications of our analysis. We shall concentrate on a few hypothetical governmental policies addressed to the problem of enabling city residents to break out of the social welfare reservation. First, the federal and state governments should remove themselves from any further purchase-of-service arrangements—ones that are innocent in conception but that frequently corrupt local initiative. Such arrangements greatly obscure not only the distinction between public and private but even that between welfare and profit making. Further, the great interest of some corporations in moving into a social-industrial complex in welfare suggests the likelihood of great diversions of public funds from policy aims and a concomitant disenchantment with government and welfare. The evidence on nursing homes suggests that in many cases profit-making enterprises will reduce services below acceptable levels. To insure that profit-making firms perform adequately in the welfare field would require such an infrastructure of public controls that the purpose of utilizing such firms would be lost.

Second and more generally, governments should refrain from any further practices that blur the public/private distinction, perhaps forbidding grants to private welfare agencies altogether. Such a policy would be brutal to particular efforts and personnel, but in the end it would allow a rebuilding, at a lesser scale of affluence, of an institution of private welfare uncompromised by federal and state involvement and rooted genuinely in local interests and participation. Third, governments should refrain from creating the illusion of an integration of metropolitan welfare programs and planning when constituent bodies involve only weak efforts at coordination. Such activities only confound an understanding of governmental and welfare realities. Fourth, Congress should enact a proposal, which can be endorsed on many grounds, for full federalization of public assistance payments, which on balance would seem to be advantageous for local institution building. A possible objection, that removal of local taxation to support public aid could undercut conceptions of community responsibility, would seem to apply to cities that are reasonably solvent but has little meaning for cities heading for bankruptcy anyway. The countervailing advantage for these cities would be that the universalization of public assistance would reduce the tendency to perceive variations in benefits as gratuitous inequities.

The above changes made, a final and crucial policy change would become feasible: With inequities and responsibilities much less obscured, a relatively clear balance sheet of the debits and credits of the federal and state relationships to a city could be developed. A public audit of this type could greatly enhance accountability for governmental action at all levels. It would become more reasonable to talk of adjusting the levels of federal and state subsidies of the cities upward or downward in light of existing national or state resources and competing needs. The commitments of more affluent units to redistribution, if any, could be made explicit.

The cities on their side would be in a position to make their own hard choices about how to allocate their limited funds. For the residents of the city, a clarification of how much (or, more likely, how little) federal and state money would be forthcoming could stimulate conversion from the extreme tactics of either fawning or threatening to a more realistic approach. Such a conversion would seem to be a sociological necessity if the more troubled of our cities are to be more than reservations in the long run.

Notes

1. Our thinking about this chapter benefited from early conversations with Yeheskel Hasenfeld and Mayer N. Zald.

2. In this 1977 court case, the Supreme Court upheld a zoning ordinance passed by the Arlington Heights, Illinois, city council that had the effect of excluding black families from a housing development and thus from the community. The court ruled that intent had not been proved. The decision suggests that unless it is demonstrated that zoning actions are deliberately undertaken to exclude a particular racial or ethnic group, such actions will stand.

3. The possible location in a Chicago suburb of several households of self-supporting but mentally retarded adults resulted in the formation of several concerned citizens groups and rumors that long-ignored statutes forbidding unrelated groups of adults to share a residence would be invoked.

4. This problem has been exemplified on Long Island by the spread of suburbia around and past gigantic mental hospitals forty or more miles east of Manhattan, a problem compounded when deinstitutionalization has caused thousands of ex-mental patients to seek lodging in local resort and suburban communities.

5. Private nonprofit organizations are not necessarily more efficient than government institutions. McCullogh's study (cited in Beck, 1971) of Pennsylvania's century-long practice of buying child welfare services from private organizations found that quality or efficiency of service was of little importance in determining which agencies were funded. The primary criterion was historical precedent.

6. The directories are established for referral use. They do not include proprietary agencies, nor do they list services that are listed in other directories (for example, social services offered by public schools). It is also possible that some agencies that serve a very narrow ethnic-religious base are not included, but an attempt is made to be as comprehensive as possible.

7. Of course, these directories do not reflect the overall impact of the women's movement on the quality and quantity of services generally offered to women, such as in hospitals or courtrooms. They also do not include, as with racial groups, support groups and services for women that are informal, secret, or even illegal (for example, abortion collectives; see Bart, 1977).

8. The sources of funding were coded in order listed, up to three. The figures cited here do not reflect *how much* each of the funding sources contributes, but only whether or not the agencies indicate receiving income from that source.

12

Social Life and the Physical Environment

Harvey M. Choldin

Sociologists, in viewing the city, have focused on the actors and actions in the foreground, ignoring the setting, the buildings, streets, parks, and other features of the physical environment. They have examined the social organization, social psychology, and demography of the urban community without explicitly considering the ways in which these phenomena might be conditioned by their unique and remarkable environments. In reading much urban sociology, one might easily ignore the towers and the tenements, the freeways and housing projects, the shopping centers and airports. The urban environment has been "left behind in the dust" according to Michelson (1976). Analysis of urban life should benefit from explicit consideration of the physical environment. Since it is a *built* environment, it is the product of social processes—most elaborate ones. It is also the setting for social behavior and may affect it in various ways. In recent years, a few social scientists have studied the interplay between environment and social life, particularly within urban contexts, and have helped to explain social phenomena. (A few examples are works by Cooper, 1975; Michelson, 1977; Duncan, 1973; and Rainwater, 1970.)

The purpose of this chapter is to emphasize the interest and utility in incorporating the environment into sociological urban analysis by reviewing the place of the environment in social theory; discussing the special features of urban America, especially housing; and summarizing some proposals in applied sociology that would introduce social science into environmental design processes. Two environmental issues that have been studied sociologically—the density-pathology hypothesis and the effects of public housing—will be presented as examples of social analyses that have explicitly incorporated environmental variables. In conventional sociological usage, *environment* means the social surroundings more often than the physical (Rose and Rose, 1970), but in this chapter environment will refer only to physical features of the urban scene.

Environment in Social Theory

Rejection of the Environment. One reason the social sciences ignored the physical environment for so long was that they had a disastrous encounter with environmentalism early in the twentieth century. The theory of environmentalism in its extreme form held that physiographic and climatic factors controlled humanity in any given region. This deterministic argument, as propounded by Huntington, asserted that physiographic factors determine the fundamental character of civilization (Wallis, 1931). The reaction to environmentalism was drastic, particularly within the discipline of geography, and it was discredited and rejected (Platt, 1948; Spate, 1968).

Another major reason for the neglect of environmental factors in sociology was embedded in a fundamental assumption of the sociological point of view—that the reality of a situation is in the definition attached to it by the participating actors. The definition of the situation is seen as real. This implies that the physical properties of the situation may be ignored. This assumption is associated with the names G. H. Mead and H. Blumer, and it represents an element of sociological thought that is ordinarily unchallenged.

Recent Perspectives on the Environment. A reconsideration of environment occurred in anthropology in a theory of possibilism (Meggers, 1954), which held that while the environment does not determine the culture and social organization of a population, it sets limits as to what can take place within it. Elements such as climate and soil represent constraints on the type of social order that can exist in a given place. In the decades following this reconsideration of the environment, there have been other theoretical developments that help introduce the environment back into urban sociological analysis.

First, Gans (1968) differentiated between the potential and the effective environment. He stated that the physical features of the environment are simply potential in relation to social life. They do not necessarily affect the behavior of the persons who encounter them. Some features may impinge on behavior, but for the most part the physical is only potentially relevant. This is especially true with regard to built forms in the environment. The effective environment is "that version of the potential environment that is manifestly or latently adopted by users" (Gans, 1968, p. 6).

Gans's approach to environmental effects is analogous to the transition that occurred in mass media research in the 1940s and 1950s. Initially, media researchers were looking for the impact of various messages on audiences. Then, after discovering the limited impact, they began to look for the ways in which the audience *used* the media. Similarly, Gans was suggesting that the analyst must look at the effective environment, the uses of the environment by its occupants. In examining a situation, the observer must try to discover which aspects of the environment are activated by the actors.

Second, congruence between place and activity is emphasized in a recent theory of environment and urban life developed by Michelson (1976). Congruence refers to the fit between the physical environment and activities that may occur within it. A particular environment is congruent with an activity if it readily accommodates it. Conversely, an environment may prevent or limit an "inappropriate" activity. In approaching an environment-behavior situation, one must ask about opportunities: For which activities does a given environment provide opportunities (Michelson, 1976)?

A third approach emphasizes the latent functions of designed environments. This approach, developed by Zeisel (1975), originates out of a concern with the social effects of architectural design. Gutman (1976), Zeisel (1975), Broady

(1972), and others have noted that architects are typically environmental (architectural) determinists with respect to the behavioral aspect of their products. Such designers assume that occupants will behave in predictable ways in new structures and that the architects can influence the behavior patterns. Zeisel notes that often the intended behaviors do not occur and that many unplanned activity patterns arise. He calls these unplanned patterns "latent functions of the design."

Human ecology offers the potential for an integration of environment into sociological analysis, but the potential has so far gone unrealized. The ecosystem framework that organizes human ecology includes environment as one of the four main referential concepts (Duncan, 1959), but ecological analysis has typically been at the interface between population and social organization, with some attention paid to the impact of technology (Hawley, 1971). Environment has consistently been ignored. Nonetheless, the theory of human ecology is available, and it should be possible to apply it to environmental questions in much the same way that it has been used in relation to technology. Just as it was useful to study the effects of the change from trolley and train transportation to the automotive complex, it should be helpful to probe the effect of the change from high-density to low-density housing.

The Urban Environment

Special Qualities. Ecologists and environmentalists ordinarily conceive of the environment as natural, incorporating land, climate, and vegetation—preferably before the onset of human interference. The urban environment is quite unlike this. The special quality of the urban scene is apparent—it is a built environment. The surface is paved and covered with structures. Even those areas that are not paved or built up are covered with cultivated plants, such as grass. There is a regularity to the environment, especially in cities developed within a rectilinear grid pattern. Land use is highly intensive, especially in central areas. There is a verticality to the built forms, with high-rise structures prominent, especially in older and larger communities.

Parts of cities are designed environments, having been planned by professional designers such as architects, city planners, and landscape architects. Most parts of cities are not designed environments, since the city grows by the addition of elements at various times and the destruction of others.

Exceptions in the United States are planned communities (including utopian communities), company towns, planned suburbs, greenbelt towns, and new towns (Alonso, 1970; Lansing, Marans, and Zehner, 1970). There are also designed environments within large cities, the most common being neighborhood redevelopment projects (Rossi and Dentler, 1961; Gans, 1965), large downtown redevelopment projects, and large parks (Cranz, 1971).

Scale is a factor that is essential to a consideration of the urban environment. It refers to the size of the environmental unit in question. It ranges from the small, such as the single dwelling unit, to the large or macroscale, referring to the city or the metropolis. There are also intermediate large-scale features such as neighborhoods, residential areas, and districts.

Land-Use Decisions. Building the city is a social process, although it is rarely discussed as such, being seen more often in light of engineering, politics, or economics. Land-use decisions, determinations of what to locate at each place, are central to the process. The most influential sociological position regarding the social production of the city is that of Park (1925), one of the founders of urban sociology. Park emphasized a market mechanism for the allocation of land uses and the spatial location of population subgroups within the city. He saw competition as the basic ecological process determining the pattern of the city. More recent urban analysts, following Form (1954), insist that political decisions are also central to the processes that allocate people and uses to locations within the community. Form argued that Park's competitive-capitalistic conception of the city ignored important political processes. Meyerson and Banfield (1955) and Willhelm (1962) also emphasized the political aspects of land-use decisions. Meyerson and Banfield's examination of the process by which whites in Chicago prevented the construction of housing projects in their neighborhoods that were likely to house poor blacks demonstrates the fundamental importance of public opinion and political processes in environmental decisions. Willhelm studied zoning, a part of the environment-producing process that became important decades after Park stated his position. He found that a complex political process was involved in land-use decisions in one city.

Nonetheless, investors are still powerful actors in the building of the city, especially within the U.S. capitalist context, and they are more powerful than city planners. Thus, despite planners' attempts throughout the twentieth century to limit daytime densities in central Manhattan, investors continued to build additional office space there throughout the 1960s. Similarly, although the Chicago master plan did not call for such buildings, developers erected major apartment and office buildings northeast of the Loop.

Engineers, city planners, and other design professionals also influence the production of the urban environment. They often work on large-scale projects, but of course they can do no more than make modifications in existing cities already shaped by historical forces. The urban infrastructure, with its plan of streets and highways, is produced by these professionals interacting with politicians and investors. Recently, this city-building process has been influenced by other citizens who are neither professionals nor politicians, such as neighborhood groups who have become active in the process of locating (or resisting) highway development and other major projects at the local level.

Values and ideology underlie the social processes producing the built environment. The racism that permeated the dispute over Chicago public housing projects illustrates this (Meyerson and Banfield, 1955). Another set of more positive values was highlighted by Duncan (1965) in his interpretation of Chicago architecture. He argued that the democratic, free enterprise values of late nineteenth-century business leaders provided the basis upon which a new form and style of architecture could arise. In a study of the history of Chicago's parks, Cranz (1971) shows that the design of parks was influenced by ideology, as the dominant type changed from the grand city park to decentralized facilities—neighborhood parks and playgrounds.

Housing Standards and Preferences. There are two main social elements in the production of housing: public preferences, both formal and informal, and the social organization of the construction process itself. The formal expression of public preferences comes in official housing standards; the informal comes in taste, style, and purchasing decisions. Housing standards reflect prevailing social values (Hole, 1965; Ratcliff, 1952; Choldin, 1976). The official standards are established by municipal or national authorities attempting to improve the quality of housing. The history of such standards is that their bases evolve over time, starting with very elementary rationales for fire protection, prevention of epidemic diseases, and provision of air and light. Later, as these elementary shelter needs are satisfied, the bases of the standards shift toward social objectives such as the segregation of adolescent children by sex for privacy and healthy personality development.

The original basis of health and safety standards is exemplified in the history of English housing (Hole, 1965). In early industrial towns, workers were housed in slums surrounding the mills or factories (Hawley, 1971). The housing was extremely dense, occupancy was high, and there were no sanitation amenities. The housing was unsafe and unhealthy, providing little ventilation or fire protection. These conditions, combined with poverty and poor health habits, led to excessive mortality and severe epidemics of cholera and other diseases (Hole, 1965). England began to regulate and improve workers' housing in 1840 with a series of statutes that established minimum housing standards.

Since the introduction of the first standards, the prescriptions for space and amenities have continued to multiply so that now the standards are quite high. From 1840 to 1965 the minimum space standard rose from about 100 square feet per person to almost 200. This was accompanied by specifics pertaining to ventilation, sanitation, and other amenities. These standards were developed by a series of governmental commissions and by the efforts of reformers. During the same period, national wealth also rose, providing economic resources to support improved housing for workers.

The history of housing standards in the United States has paralleled that in Britain, although it started later. Reformers after 1850 noted the overcrowded and degrading environment of big-city immigrant workers residing in tenements. The reformers tried a series of solutions to this problem including "model tenement" plans (Friedman, 1968), which implied residential standards. The American Public Health Association began to develop housing standards in the late 1930s, which have been widely adopted by local communities (American Public Health Association, 1950). The Federal Housing Administration (FHA) has formalized building standards that are required in the many houses and apartments that have been built with federal financial assistance. The FHA and other generally accepted housing standards have risen over the years to the point where one room per person is considered minimum family housing. The codes represent a consensus of expert opinion, but there has not been definitive scientific research determining such standards. The constant rise in standards is consistent with the general wealth of the nation, but U.S. standards are not much higher than those of other nations, even those in Western Europe.

For most Americans, the ideal type of housing is a single-family detached dwelling; this is especially true for households with children. Americans generally prefer a good deal of interior space with an individual bedroom for each child and as much outdoor yard space as possible. Most couples with children who live in apartments regard their situation as a temporary deprivation.

In the literature on the social aspects of housing there is a confusion between needs and wants. Architectural research on housing has emphasized user needs as a basis for design, assuming that it is possible to discover such needs in social research and theory. This is not reasonable in a wealthy society such as the United States, because our existing housing, except for the very poor, already provides far more than minimal shelter. The human organism is highly adaptable and minimum shelter needs are easily satisfied (Dubos, 1965; Biderman and others, 1963). Beyond these, other specifications relate to cultural preferences and are arbitrary. There are a variety of wants rather than needs in housing.

Vernacular Architecture. Architectural scholars distinguish between vernacular architecture and high design. In agrarian societies dwellings are built by their eventual occupants, presumably without the aid of construction specialists (Rapoport, 1969). The design and the building techniques are traditional and knowledge of them is part of the common technology. Buildings produced in this way are known as vernacular architecture. In contrast, the modern profession of architecture produces designs according to prevailing styles known as high design.

Stylistic preferences combined with the housing production process have resulted in a new kind of vernacular architecture in the United States, which is housing produced according to standard plans by commercial builders. This process employs conventional plans to generate buildings. The tradition is carried out by home builders responding to their perception of public tastes. Vernacular housing is built for sale by builders and real estate developers (Venturi, Brown, and Izenour, 1973) and by manufacturers of prefabricated houses and mobile homes.

Private builders, small and large, produce the vernacular housing. Home building is one of the last vestiges of small-scale production in the U.S. economy, decentralized among numerous small contractors. The builders offer a small number of houses for sale. The builders are likely to be conservative in the introduction of stylistic or other innovations, having much of their capital and credit tied up in each house and not wanting to take risks on a potentially unpopular model. There are also some very large developers engaging in mass production, who were very evident during the housing boom of the 1950s, when they built large subdivisions and suburbs, such as the Levittowns (Gans, 1967). These large operators also produced standardized homes.

Thus, builders are tied into a conventional process of fashion, taste, and style, similar to those governing clothing and automobiles (Blumer, 1968). There is much less stylistic fluctuation and much slower change in house design than in these other items. Perhaps this is because a house lasts longer than an automobile or a dress or because houses are not usually either mass-produced or mass advertised.

Nevertheless, change and individuation do occur in vernacular housing, despite the forces for conservatism. Exterior decoration expresses some continuing themes such as plantation elegance or colonial community, displayed with white columns on green shutters, respectively. But there have been major changes in interior house plans over the course of the twentieth century. Large family rooms now predominate, and living rooms or parlors have become small, even vestigial; multiple indoor bathrooms are now common in middle class housing; and most houses have large garages. These and many other items distinguish the house of the 1970s from its Victorian counterpart. These innovations came in response to changes in family patterns, rising income, and technological changes in transportation and sanitation. One striking feature of contemporary residential development is the national adoption of regional styles. One is as likely to find a ranch house in suburban Detroit as in Phoenix and the so-called Cape Cod is equally well distributed, both with minor modifications by region and household income level. Apartment buildings, too, have prevailing styles, such as the complexes of two-story, wood-frame buildings with apartments over parking space. Banham (1971) generically refers to such buildings as "Los Angeles dingbats" and notes that they may be decorated with a variety of trimmings.

The Spread City. The distinctive feature of U.S. urban development is the prevalence of single-family detached housing. Worldwide, urban housing usually consists of dense, multifamily structures, a pattern exemplified in European cities. Indeed, high-density settlement is a defining feature of cities (Wirth, 1938). Yet the typical U.S. metropolis has about two thirds of its housing in single-family units. New York City and Chicago deviate from this pattern along with a few cities of the northeastern region, but most of the housing in dozens of large cities is comprised of single-family structures (see Table 1).

Table 1. Percentage of Single-Family Housing Units in Selected Cities.

City	1960	1970
Baltimore	75.9	67.6
Chicago	43.1	44.4
Cleveland	62.6	57.3
Houston	82.9	71.2
Indianapolis	78.0	67.0
Los Angeles	71.0	61.7
Milwaukee	54.7	51.8
New York	31.8	33.2
St. Louis	62.1	61.8
San Diego	76.1	66.2
San Jose	83.6	68.6

Note: Figures represent the percentage of year-round housing units that are one-unit structures.

Source: U.S. Bureau of the Census, 1962, 1973b.

Metropolitan areas in the United States have a distinctive pattern of housing tenure: widespread home ownership combined with a high rate of transience. While renting is the basic worldwide pattern of urban residential tenure, most American urban residents own their homes, and this proportion has increased in each decade of the twentieth century except during the Depression. By 1970, 65 percent of white and 42 percent of black families were home owners. Urban residents, especially renters, also change residences frequently. In the aggregate, approximately one out of five households moves annually, although this masks the fact that some households move repeatedly and others are stable for decades (Morrison, 1971).

By the end of the 1950s, the United States had developed the spread city. This was the culmination of the decentralizing suburban trend that had begun in the 1920s (Hawley, 1956). In addition to low-density residential areas, its environmental features are strict separation of residential from nonresidential land uses, the absence of multistory buildings, and a good deal of open space for lawns and parking. The spread city includes shopping centers rather than stores on residential or business streets, and it also includes freestanding single-purpose facilities such as churches, offices, and restaurants with accompanying parking areas. The spread city also includes some commercial strip development on major streets.

The development of the spread city has come from four sources: general housing preferences and traditions in the American public, government programs and financial structures, technological developments, and resources and environment. American housing preferences for the single-family detached dwelling are reflected in surveys (Hinshaw and Allott, 1972) and in the pattern under which so many actually own such residences. Throughout the nation's history, middle class families occupied individual homesteads, and this became a strong preference.

Traditional banking practices and recent governmental programs have facilitated and promoted this pattern of home ownership in the middle class. The mortgage system, with payments stretched over a period of decades, made home ownership possible for a wide range of employed persons. Following World War II, the federal government gave massive assistance to builders and would-be home owners through the mortgage loan guarantee programs of the Federal Housing Administration and the Veterans Administration (VA). The main type of housing constructed under such financing was the single-family detached home, located at the metropolitan periphery in the suburbs, where there was available land. These two housing programs gave powerful impetus to the decentralizing trend that was creating the spread city.

The other massive federal effort that fostered this trend was the interstate highways program, which built expressways connecting city centers with intercity arteries. Expressway construction was part of the overall conversion to transportation based on the internal combustion engine, which was integral to the emergence of the spread city. Other technological developments that facilitated this trend were the diffusion of the telephone and the conversion of manufacturing to electrically powered processes in single-story factories (see Chapter Two by Kasarda in this volume). Cars became the dominant form of intraurban transportation, and trucks supplanted railroads for many functions. Car ownership encouraged the continuing spread of housing, and cars and trucks facilitated the decentralization of manufacturing, wholesaling, and retailing.

The existence of great stretches of land and of the national wealth, including resources, in the United States was the precondition for the spread city. The national economy was so rich and personal income was so high that most middle class families could afford to own individual dwellings, especially with the help of the mortgage system. The environment and its resources were also adequate to support this pattern: There was ample lumber for massive construction of relatively large dwellings and sufficient fossil fuel to supply energy both to the dwellings and to the transportation system that made the dispersed pattern possible.

The Central City. Environmental trends in the central city offer a more mixed picture than the suburban areas. The U.S. cities have major segments with characteristically urban features in addition to the low-density elements. There is a great deal of high-intensity development, and there are distinctive urban land uses such as department stores, office buildings, parking garages, hospitals, railroad years, and trucking depots. There are also distinctive urban building forms, especially the high-rise building, used for many purposes. Environmental change within the city since 1945 has included the progression of residential areas through an aging cycle that leads to abandonment and destruction and then urban renewal, the development of specialized institutional districts, and construction of new types of housing projects.

The typical history of an urban residential area is a cycle of growth and decline (Guest, 1973). It starts with open land and adds a few and then many residences to it; later there is a lowering of density as the buildings and occupants age. This process was originally accompanied by successive invasions of ethnic and socioeconomic groups. As Guest found it, this process was widespread in the first half of the twentieth century. Since World War II, the cycle has developed three variations, the first one being the typical aging of housing along with an aging of the population or an ethnic succession. This still occurs in some older city districts. The second variation involves abandonment and destruction, a new process in U.S. urban history. This takes place in areas of older apartment buildings or older dilapidated houses (Sternlieb and Burchell, 1973; Moore, Livermore, and Galland, 1973). This process has a sequence of events —the landlord neglects services, some tenants move and leave empty apartments, the rest of the tenants move, vandals strip valuable building materials from the structure, arsonists burn the building, and a wrecker razes the shell. The environmental result is large areas of rubble-covered lots. The Woodlawn area in Chicago and the South Bronx are prominent examples. Residential areas in many cities were also destroyed for the large highways built in recent decades. Some older areas of warehousing and manufacturing in the zone of transition were also cleared for expressways.

In the third variation, some older residential areas go into a cycle of regeneration, including middle class in-migration, reconstruction of existing buildings, and construction of new housing. In some areas older houses are replaced by low- or high-rise apartment buildings. In others, the newcomers buy older residences and remodel them. In many of these areas, the new residents are middle or upper-middle class, replacing old lower class occupants. The result of this process is to establish or extend fashionable older middle class areas near city centers. Some of this is done in the context of the architectural historic preservation movement.

One type of residential development in the postwar period was slum clearance accompanied by large project construction. The underlying idea was that the only solution for slum areas was to raze them and start afresh with open land. There were numerous projects of this type financed under the provisions of the Housing Acts of 1947 and 1954 and carried out in the 1950s. This resulted either in large high-rise apartment projects for the poor or for the middle class. The former were provided by local housing authorities with federal funding and the latter were provided by large private-sector investors. These apartment projects followed two city planning principles: that there should be a maximum of open space surrounding buildings and that local traffic should be separated from through traffic (J. Jacobs, 1961). They were designed as "super-blocks," eliminating conventional city blocks and the small shops many of them accommodated. The objective of the "tower in the park" was pursued by providing as much grass as possible between the buildings where there were not parking lots. Despite their high population densities, the new apartment projects had lower ground coverage then conventional apartment buildings along city streets.

Gans (1965) has proclaimed the urban renewal program to have been a failure, and many others have echoed this evaluation. They criticize the program for destroying housing, albeit substandard, that was occupied by the poor and using the cleared land either for upper-middle-class residences or non-housing purposes. They note that while the stated objective of the program was neighborhood redevelopment, much of the money went for downtown rehabilitation. Many of the projects destroyed housing and turned over the cleared land for institutional development for hospitals and universities. One of the major trends since World War II was the creation of single-purpose zones and monumental facilities. Large medical centers containing several hospitals, clinics, and schools are found in many cities now. University campuses have tended to expand and to eliminate residential and commercial facilities in their areas. Urban renewal projects had similar effects in residential areas that were not destroyed, eliminating shops and other non-residential land uses to provide housing only. At the same time, monumental cultural and civic centers proliferated in the cities, projects like Lincoln Center in New York and the Kennedy Center for the Performing Arts in Washington. These, too, established single-purpose zones in the central areas.

In sum, the trends in the cities in the 1950s and 1960s were toward largeness in highways, housing projects, and civic facilities and toward uniformity of uses within subareas.

Uses and Effects

The Chicago School. Some sociologists of the Chicago School described and discussed the environment, but they did not develop the nexus between it and the social life it accommodated. Wirth (1947), in an essay entitled "Housing as a Field of Sociological Research," said that research was necessary to relate housing to social values and community life. He contended that housing should be studied as a social problem and a topic in public policy, but he did not make any theoretical connections to the physical environment. Hayner (1936) devoted an entire monograph to hotel life and came much closer to an environment/behavior connection. He delineated several types of urban hotels by size, location, and function—for transients and permanent residents, for the rich, for commercial travelers, and others. He described types of users of hotels, such as salesmen, theater people, and tourists. He discovered particular social effects of hotel life including liberation from conventional morality, which meant drinking, gambling, and sex. He described the interaction between hotel staff and tenants and presented the method by which workers estimated potential tips. He found a special kind of family life among residents and characteristic behaviors of children who lived in hotels. Anonymity was a theme of hotel life that he emphasized repeatedly. Park (1915, p. 20) referred to the hotel as the epitome of urban life:

> A very large part of the population of great cities, including those who make their homes in tenements and apartment houses, live much as people do in some great hotel, meeting but not knowing one another. The effect of this is to substitute fortuitous and casual relationships for the more intimate and permanent associations of the smaller community. It is probably the breaking down of local attachments and the weakening of the restraints and inhibitions of the primary group under the urban environment, which are greatly responsible for the increase of vice and crime in great cities.

Zorbaugh (1929), in *The Gold Coast and the Slum*, also showed a sharp awareness of the environmental features of the city and neighborhood. He presented the history of the construction of the area, the progression of building types, the importance of the construction of bridges over the Chicago River to permit residential development, and the mix of industry and residences. He described the mansions and large apartments of the Gold Coast, the rooming houses and boarding houses of "the world of furnished rooms," the garrets and coach houses of the bohemians, and the degraded tenements and houses of the slum. He noted, for example, that rooming houses and boarding houses were formerly large single-family residences. He also emphasized anonymity, especially in the rooming houses, and noted that coresidents were not acquainted in apartment buildings. This contrasted with an open-door life-style in the bohemian studios with much visiting and partying.

Both Hayner (1936) and Zorbaugh (1929) were basically concerned with these residential forms as organizations and not with the influence of the physical properties of the buildings. This is illustrated most clearly in Zorbaugh's distinction between rooming and boarding houses. Physically both originated as large houses; only their respective administrations differed. The rooming house landlady rented a room to each resident, offering no common room, meals, or kitchen privileges. The boarding house landlady maintained a dining room and served common meals as well as offering a sitting room. The rooming house arrangement offered the greatest anonymity and, presumably, loneliness. It was the different organization of the establishment, the uses of the buildings, that made the social difference.

Some General Effects. Studies and theoretical discussions of the urban environment in the past thirty years have dealt with general issues involving population heterogeneity and homogeneity in relation to housing and symbolic uses of housing and neighborhood. An important early study demonstrated a strong effect of proximity on the creation of friendships within a housing complex. Couples in married student housing at the Massachusetts Institute of Technology in the late 1940s tended to develop patterns of contact and friendship that corresponded with proximity and distance within the project (Festinger, Schacter, and Back, 1950). A series of studies on contact and friendship between blacks and whites that began at about the same time produced a different conclusion, however. Proximity yielded positive contacts, attitudes, and friendship only under special social circumstances. Only when the blacks and whites were of the same social class and did not pose much of a threat to each other did proximity foster positive contacts and friendship. In sum, the environmental effect depended on the particular social situation.

In effect, the underlying social situations for the MIT graduate student couples and the blacks and whites in the housing projects were the same. The graduate students were all in the same fundamental situation—young in age, students by occupation, and couples in family life cycle status. Similar underlying similarities, particularly in occupation and income, were required in the interracial housing projects. Given homogeneity, the locational factor could make a big difference.

The general trend of urban development and city planning has been toward greater homogeneity within urban districts, both of land uses and social categories. The extreme of this trend is in the newer suburbs, which tend to be internally very homogeneous with regard to social class (working class, upper-middle class, and so on). The overall homogeneity of the suburban ring, foretold by the critics who decried the "suburban myth," has not developed; the ring is a patchwork of different types of suburbs. But the patches are at least as homogeneous as city neighborhoods.

Homogeneity is high with regard to household types and

age composition within the populations. A very pronounced pattern of household location is for families with children to locate at the metropolitan periphery in the newer suburbs and subdivisions (Anderson and Egeland, 1961; Guest, 1972). This leaves an overrepresentation of the elderly in the central city along with households of young adults. The aged are not as segregated in the center as some of the alarmist imagery of "geriatric ghettoes" has implied (Pampel and Choldin, in press). But, certainly the young families at the periphery live at some distance from old people. This reinforces the contemporary family pattern of the modified extended family, with the nuclear family at least spatially separated from the grandparent generation.

These residential patterns often require a long journey to work, which can keep the father out of family life for most of the day. Because of the homogeneity of family suburbs, their low density and the exclusion of nonresidential activities require considerable driving in everyday routines. Working mothers must drive their children to day care and to many other kinds of activities. Indeed, suburban children are quite dependent on adult drivers.

Sennett (1970) and J. Jacobs (1961) have severely criticized city planners for fostering single-purpose, homogeneous urban areas. Sennett argues that members of different socioeconomic and ethnic groups have insufficient cross-group contact in the new city. He says that individuals tend to develop "purified identities" by living in purified or homogenized environments. In this he agrees with Jacobs, who advocates an environment with mixed land uses and mixed populations. In reality, it is difficult for members of different social categories to maintain an integrated neighborhood according to Gans (1961). People will choose residential areas of their own social category, or if they are upwardly mobile, areas housing people in a slightly higher category. There are powerful tendencies toward residential homogeneity.

Housing the Poor. Topics involving slums and housing for workers and the poor have dominated urban environmental social research over the decades. The earliest reports were by reformers who tended to be quite deterministic in their interpretations of the effects of slum conditions. In England, the reformers' focus on slums and workers' housing began in the first half of the nineteenth century (Hole, 1965). The rise of the factory town in seventeenth-century England brought with it a uniquely degraded residential environment, the slum near the factory (Hawley, 1971). Workers' housing may not have improved until the mid nineteenth century in that country. From 1840, in a series of statutes, some minimum standards for housing gradually evolved. The vast surveys of London by Booth (1882-1897) collected the facts of working class life. In the United States in the 1860s, social reformers noted the squalid conditions of immigrant workers in New York City and instigated a series of charitable and government programs directed toward improved housing. Some of the early programs were model dwellings and "model tenants," followed by the New York Tenement Acts of 1867, which set standards for such amenities as plumbing, fire escapes, windows for ventilation, and light (Friedman, 1968).

An environmental determinism ran through the arguments of the housing reformers. They recognized the slum as a subcommunity with a congeries of social problems, including crime and juvenile delinquency, vice, mental illness, and family strain and breakdown. They noted that these had severely deleterious effects on child development and that health was poor in the slum. They recognized that the housing was overcrowded and sanitation inadequate. The neighborhood offered few outdoor recreational facilities, and there were numerous other environmental deficiencies. The reformers reasoned that improved housing was necessary for these people and that it would improve their lives (Friedman, 1968). Large-scale systematic research was prepared for governmental commissions like the New York City Commission on Congestion of Population in 1911.

There has been a long debate as to whether the slum should be defined by its environment or by the behavior of the people living in it. Clinard (1966, p. 4) began an extensive definition of the slum by stating, "Of all the characteristics of a slum, the physical conditions have been emphasized most often. Slums have commonly been defined as those portions of cities in which housing is crowded, neglected, deteriorated, and often obsolete." He then adds social elements to the definition: slum culture, deviant behavior, social isolation from the larger community, and poverty. For the purposes of this chapter, we may sidestep the debates on the culture of poverty and on lower-class values and norms and note that the concept of the slum includes a degraded environment, with the important exception of the "federal slum," to be mentioned later.

The U.S. studies following World War II attempted to ascertain the differences between poor families housed in slums and those in better dwellings. One study in Boston was by Loring (1970), who compared the housing of "disorganized" families, that is, ones who came to the attention of social agencies. He found that the families in trouble had less space and fewer rooms, fewer heated rooms, and a generally poorer housing environment than the others. The most thorough and rigorous study was by Wilner and others (1962), who drew a sample of 600 black families residing in Baltimore slums in 1955. Half of these families then moved into a new housing project and the others stayed in the previous environment. Being interested both in health and social life, Wilner's group conducted interviews and physical examinations of the subjects while they all lived in the slums and then periodically after the move, using the nonmovers as a control group. The social impact of the new housing was minimal, but there were benefits to health. There was generally less illness and disability in the new housing, and children's health was noticeably better there, with fewer incidents of contagious diseases. There was no difference in family life between slum families and rehoused ones in terms of family activities, helping, fighting, or similar indicators. People in the project were more positive about their dwellings, but they had complaints about the community, such as distance to shopping and the presence of gangs. People in the project exchanged help with neighbors more than slum residents did. However, rehoused children did not perform better in school than children in the slum.

A decade later the liberal perspective on public housing for poor black families had changed dramatically—such housing was seen as a bad environment and a bad subcommunity. From 1945 through 1970, approximately 1.5 million units of federally assisted housing were provided in programs for low- and moderate-income households (Fried, 1971). Federal policy was that the housing projects should be inhabited by the poorest families, and many were filled with blacks receiving public welfare. Many projects became fearsome subcommunities with high rates of violent crime; the general failure of this system became apparent nationally.

About ten years after Wilner's survey, Rainwater and a group of students entered the Pruitt-Igoe housing project in St. Louis to study black family life, conducting intensive case studies of households as well as a survey of the modern high-rise environment. This time, though, there was no attempt to discover improvements in family or community life. Yancey (1971, p. 13) reports:

> In Pruitt-Igoe, the familiar aspects of slum living such as fires and burning, freezing and cold, poor plumbing, dangerous electrical wiring, thin walls, and overcrowding of children and parents into single rooms, were somewhat abated. Yet the amenities of lower-class neighborhoods had apparently been lost. Mothers fear the early introduction and socialization of their children into sex and other troubles. They also see the adults in the housing project as being irresponsible, deviant, and beyond control.

In concluding the study, Rainwater (1970) states that during the course of the research, the focus shifted from housing policy to the general situation of the poor in U.S. society. He discusses the "culture of poverty" theory in relation to the facts of social life in the project. Regarding housing he concludes, "In many cities public housing has simply become a more visible kind of slum " (p. 409). Rainwater offers the bitterly ironic concept of the federal slum in his book title.

Rainwater (1966) delineates the special housing needs of the poor, showing that they are different from those of the middle class. Housing provides certain elementary shelter functions, protecting people from the hazards of the natural environment, animals, and the like (Fitch, 1966). It performs these functions for all, including the poor. But the poor also require protection against other social hazards in the community, particularly abuse from their neighbors. Rainwater says that for the poor, the house is a haven from social dangers as well as the elements. Part of the failure of public housing is that although it provides improved elementary shelter functions, it exacerbates rather than protects against the dangers of the community. Yancey (1971) sets the scene for social life in Pruitt-Igoe by describing the open areas covered with broken glass, the plywood-boarded windows, and the stench of urine in the elevators. He criticizes the designers for dividing space into private and public, with no space intermediate. This division forces people into their apartments, atomizing them and preventing the formation of a neighborhood.

The incongruity between childrearing and high-rise build-

ings for the poor has been noted by several investigators
(Michelson, 1976). In the high-rise, poor mothers have no way
of supervising the outdoor activities of their little children and
cannot afford help to care for them. They must confine the
small children to the apartments or release them at early ages to
unsupervised play with older children.

Many public housing projects have high crime rates, and
Newman (1972) discovered some specific environmental features
that diminish their security levels. He analyzed crime rates in all
169 housing projects in New York City and found that there is
variation across projects that correlates with architectural features of the buildings. The projects with the highest rates have
high-rise buildings with "double-loaded" corridors—long halls
with apartment doors facing onto them from both sides. The
buildings are also sited over open areas designed to be parklike.
This plan deviates from traditional apartment areas, where the
buildings stand side-by-side along a street with entrances at the
sidewalk. The project plan yields dark areas at night where there
is no natural surveillance. It also makes places of entrance and
mailbox areas dangerous. Stairway arrangements are also related
to crime, according to Newman. Stairways in the high-rise buildings have numerous outlets, making it easy for a criminal to
escape within the building without being followed. A type of
project with lower crime rates has three-story buildings, with
only a few families using each stairwell. In these projects, neighbors recognize each other and are thus able to detect outsiders
in their building. There is natural surveillance of the area. Newman calls this "defensible space," which is much safer for the
residents than the high-rise open-site project.

The public housing projects have had a severe community
stigma attached to them from the outset. There is a reputational
dimension to these projects just as there is to housing and neighborhoods in the metropolis in general. One defining feature of
the slum is that its residents know that the outside community
considers them to be disreputable (Suttles, 1968; Clinard,
1966). This labeling is by no means ameliorated by the provision of new housing for the poor. If anything, the stigma seems
to be intensified by the visibility of urban housing projects.

Management practices and governmental policies controlling the use and occupancy of housing projects for the poor are
just as powerful in producing the eventual kind of community
life as is the architecture itself. One critical decision producing
the federal slum out of new housing was to populate it exclu-

sively with the poorest families. This meant that the members of the working poor who made slightly more than poverty-level incomes were driven out of the government projects, thus leaving the projects to the very poor, those receiving welfare, broken families, and the disabled. The projects simply created great concentrations of the people with the greatest number of problems and the least success in overcoming them.

A general policy, adopted by many local housing boards and administrators, was to treat the residents as temporary occupants who would eventually return to the regular housing marketplace. This policy led to the practice of giving the residents as few claims to the premises as possible. For example, in many projects the residents were not permitted to garden around their individual entrances; in most cases the premises were cared for by municipal employees, without any responsibility given to the residents.

Thus, it is not simply the buildings and their arrangement that produce the federal slum. Rather, it is the interplay of these factors with the composition of the residential population, the management policies, and the stigmatization of the outer community.

Density and Pathology

Much controversy surrounds the question of whether high density or overcrowding in cities produces pathological behavior. The issue has had some political importance as part of the general issues of city growth and population distribution as well as environmental policies. The density-pathology hypothesis has attracted some scientific attention, manifested in a series of sociological and psychological research projects.

Calhoun (1962a, 1962b, 1963) demonstrated that high density was harmful in a series of experiments on rats. In these experiments, rats were allowed to breed to abnormally high densities and given ample food. Once they became sufficiently crowded, many of their normal patterns of behavior broke down. Most became aggressive, snapping at each other. Mortality rates increased as mothers failed to nurture their offspring. Pansexuality was rampant among the adults. Calhoun called this total situation a "behavioral sink." Many other ethological studies of infrahuman species, conducted in the field as well as under laboratory conditions, showed that excessive density was harmful, causing severe physiological and behavioral damage

(Archer, 1971). Calhoun's findings, along with those of other ethologists, were disseminated widely (Zlutnick and Altman, 1972) and were cited by environmentalists who offered the analogy that U.S. cities were becoming behavioral sinks. During the 1960s, when urban crime rates and fear were increasing and there were many black ghetto riots, the analogy evidently was tempting.

The question of density effects offers a good theoretical example of an environment-behavior connection because it appears to be so very clear and simple. Density is the number of persons per unit of area. As such, it is a far simpler variable than most others in the built environment. Some more complex and subtle ones are environmental scale, complexity, or the presence of open space.

Crowding is another concept in many discussions of density and pathology. It refers to the occupancy level of dwellings compared with a given standard. The common U.S. standard is one person per room, and a residence with more occupants than rooms is considered overcrowded. Density and crowding represent the same ratio, persons to area, but density refers to ground area while crowding refers to internal occupancy. Thus it is possible to say that the density of a neighborhood is quite high but that a particular apartment within it is not overcrowded.

Pathology is a term that is variously used in the density-pathology discussions, ordinarily referring to some negatively valued condition or behavior. Some of the pathologies that have been studied have been health related, such as infant mortality, general mortality, and tuberculosis rates. Other pathologies are crime related: general and violent crime rates, arrest rates, and juvenile delinquency rates. Crime and delinquency rates are sometimes used as indicators of aggression in attempts to be consistent with the ethological theories based on studies of other species (see Schmitt, 1957, 1966; Winsborough, 1961, 1965; Galle, Gove, and McPherson, 1972; Choldin and Roncek, 1976; and Roncek, 1976, for examples of these various pathology rates in ecological analyses).

Theoretical Approaches. The experiments on rats suggested a simple model of density effects, one we will call the "rodent model." The central hypothesis of the model is that high density causes pathologies and social breakdown. Sociologists approaching the density-pathology question have questioned the applicability of this model to human populations

(Choldin, 1972; Baldassare and Fischer, 1976; Gans, 1968). They have pointed out that humans may mediate environmental effects through cultural and social organizational mechanisms not available to lower animals. Sociologists approach urban pathologies such as crime and delinquency from a perspective that emphasizes social structural factors. Sociological explanations of crime have shown that poverty or minority status account for variation in this phenomenon.

A second density-pathology model was proposed by Galle, Gove, and McPherson (1972). It combined social structural variables with density and crowding. Recognizing that the rodent model was simplistic, they said that while poverty and minority status may cause crime, crowded living conditions may accentuate the propensity to crime. Thus, crime rates should be higher in poor crowded areas than in poor uncrowded ones. In this model, density and crowding are incorporated as secondary intermediate variables.

Choldin and Roncek (1976) said that the second model is still too simple to explain the spatial distribution of some pathologies and proposed a somewhat more elaborate scheme. They contended that the family status of a neighborhood was an important determinant of pathologies—actually, a deterrent to pathology. They also suggested that the population composition of a neighborhood influences the risk factor regarding pathologies. Family status is important because areas with few families and households composed of unrelated individuals do not foster neighborhood organization and integration (Janowitz, 1967; Kasarda and Janowitz, 1974; Hunter, 1974). The age composition is important because young males tend to be involved in street crimes and older people may be victims of crime. The third model says that social structure and demography are central to understanding urban pathology and that density and crowding are minor variables.

Various Research Approaches. The social geography of the city itself makes it difficult to discover the independent effects of density on social life, that is, to discover the extent, if any, to which it causes pathologies. The spatial distributions of density, poverty, and minority status are quite similar in the typical large U.S. city: The densest parts are near the center, as are the residential areas of the poor and of newly arrived minority groups. Thus, there is a research problem of collinearity among the possible causal variables. The difficult research problem has been to extricate the effects of density from the effects of other variables. A variety of research methods have been used in this quest. These have included small-group laboratory experiments, psychological studies of children, and historical and comparative studies of crowded situations. Recent larger-scale urban studies have been done by ecological or spatial analyses.

An early urban psychological analysis of the effects of density and crowding was made by Plant (1930), who worked with children in a Newark slum. He contended that crowding adversely affected the children's psychosocial development. The slum children spent so much of their time in social situations that they became unable to function apart from the group, according to Plant's interpretation. They had no opportunities for solitude and were exposed to adult sexuality and other backstage activity at such an early age that they never developed ego ideals or role models among the adults. More recent social psychological research has not shown harmful effects of density and crowding (Freedman, 1975). For example, Loo (1972) conducted an experiment on nursery school children in which they were crowded for a limited amount of time. Some of the time they were in spacious surroundings and at other times they were crowded. She found less aggressive behavior in the crowded situation. In the crowded room there was less interpersonal behavior altogether as the children withdrew into solitary behavior.

Biderman and others (1963) conducted a historical study of incidents of extremely high crowding and found that crowding was never the primary factor when high death rates occurred. They studied documentary evidence of slave ships, prisoner of war camps, immigrant ships, and other episodes of extraordinary crowding. They discovered a complex of environmental factors including sanitation, heat, and lack of oxygen that contributed to high mortality rates in some of these incidents. There were also sociopsychological morale factors that affected death rates, but they concluded that crowding itself was never decisive.

Two surveys, one in Hong Kong and one in France, have discovered limited effects of overcrowding. In Hong Kong, Mitchell (1971) studied family life in housing projects with very high levels of density and crowding. He found that crowded families withstood the situation but when such households were located on the higher stories of the buildings the parents lost control of their children. In Paris, Chombart de Lauwe (1955) studied a sample of working class families, examining the mental health of the adults. The crowding levels of the households were measured precisely. The study revealed that there was a threshold point of eight to ten square meters per person. If the household was more crowded than this, the rate of social pathologies was likely to rise.

Density was mentioned in many of the ecological studies of the Chicago School, although it was a variable of central interest only to Wirth. Pathology was a major concern in many of the studies of the city. Several of the studies showed that the highest frequencies of pathologies occurred in the densest sections of the city, which were also the ones with the oldest, most deteriorated housing and which were populated by immigrants and other poor people. Some of the pathologies that were distributed in a radial pattern, with the highest rates near the city center, were boys' gangs, delinquency, crime, tuberculosis, and infant mortality. In these distributional studies it was impossible to ferret out a cause.

Recent Research. Ecological studies have carried on the tradition of the earlier Chicago studies, but with the addition of multivariate statistics that help to extricate the causal variables. The first uses of multivariate correlation and regression techniques on the density-pathology problem were by Winsborough (1961, 1965) and Schmitt (1966). Schmitt studied the city of Honolulu, assembling a large set of pathology statistics by location and combining these with social and economic data for census tracts. He attempted to control for two powerful social structural variables: income and education. His results showed that density was highly related to several pathologies and that crowding was not. His analysis was later criticized on methodological grounds, particularly for the way the income and education controls were dichotomized.

Galle, Gove, and McPherson (1972) studied Chicago statistics, also applying multivariate statistics (partial correlation) to the density-pathology question. Their central concern was with the collinearity between the social structural variables and density effects. The main finding was that the social structural variables were powerful predictors of the pathology rates, as was crowding, but that pathology rates were somewhat higher in poor minority areas with crowded housing than in similar areas with uncrowded housing. Thus crowded housing accentuated the tendency toward high pathology rates in poor minority areas. Neighborhood density was not important, whereas household crowding was. The study has been criticized for its statistical strategy (Ward, 1975) and for the use of community areas rather than more homogeneous areal units (Roncek, 1975), but it stands as a landmark.

Other researchers have made similar analyses of other cities, with differing results. Gillis (1974) essentially replicated the study by Galle, Gove, and McPherson (1972) in a smaller city, Edmonton, and had the same results. Schwirian and LaGreca (1971) reported that crowding is related to general mortality. They indicated this in a path analysis, in which crowding produces an effect in combination with income and education. Freedman (1975), however, studied the distribution of mental illness and juvenile delinquency in New York City and found that social class, race, and ethnicity were sufficient to account for these phenomena and that density was an unnecessary variable.

Choldin and Roncek (1976) questioned the importance of density and crowding reported in the Chicago project and studied two large cities in detail. They examined city block statistics in Cleveland and San Diego to minimize the statistical aggregation effects that they detected in earlier studies. They found that density and crowding had trivial relationships to crime, death, and birth rates. They discovered that the most important determinant of crime rates for city blocks was the household composition of the local population. Blocks with family households tended to have lower crime rates and blocks housing unrelated individuals tended to have higher rates, all other variables being equal. Other important social variables were race and income. The results clearly showed that neither density nor crowding was related to the distribution of crime rates.

Three major surveys have been conducted on density effects (Booth, 1976; Galle and Gove, 1974; Verbrugge and Taylor, 1976). The surveys yield more detail in the pathologies studied than do the ecological studies. Survey data collected for other purposes has been subjected to secondary analysis for density effects (Baldassare, 1975). The new surveys took place in Toronto, Chicago, and Baltimore. Although only some of the results have been published, it appears that the surveys yield contradictory findings.

The Toronto survey was complex in method and comprehensive in scope. It included both personal interviews and medical examinations of each subject. The medical portion was included to test the biopsychological theory stating that crowding

causes stress which is manifested physiologically as well as behaviorally. Among animals studied there is hyperactivity in the
adrenal-thyroid system with crowding, and the Toronto study
was designed to look for such effects in crowded humans. The
sample consisted of working class families in high- and low-
density tracts. Booth differentiated between objective and subjective crowding as well as between neighborhood density and
household crowding. He devised original measures for some of
these concepts.

The overall result of the Toronto study was that almost
no negative effects of density could be found, and the ones that
did emerge were quite weak (Booth, 1976). The major results
were: (1) Neither neighborhood density nor objective household crowding was associated with heightened aggression levels
among adults; (2) neighborhood density did not affect the quality of family life, and household crowding was associated with a
slight decrement in the quality of family life; (3) neighborhood
density was not related to the health of adults, whereas household crowding was associated with a greater prevalence of stress-
related diseases among males but not among females; (4) household crowding had a small negative effect on development,
health, and school performance of children.

Preliminary results from the two other surveys go in the
opposite direction, indicating negative effects of household
crowding. Neither of these two surveys shows that neighborhood density has harmful effects. The Baltimore survey shows
that crowded housing is associated with "conflicts over space,
irritation about noise and dissatisfaction with the amount of
privacy a person has" (Verbrugge and Taylor, 1976, p. 13). It
also shows that density is a far less important cause of stress and
other negative effects. The Chicago survey also shifts the focus
from density to crowding (Galle and Gove, 1974). Verbrugge
and Taylor also showed that length of residence in the neighborhood mediates the negative environmental effects. Long-term
residents are far less negative about crowding, density, and
other environmental features than are newcomers. Verbrugge
and Taylor argued that previous studies did not detect effects
because they did not look at the correct dependent variables.
Verbrugge and Taylor further stated that it is necessary to look
at phenomena that might be proximate effects of crowding,
such as perceived frequency of noise and feeling irritated about
outdoor noise, phenomena that might be directly influenced by
environmental features.

Survey data do not show more neighborhood interaction in dense residential areas than elsewhere. Baldassare (1975), in a secondary analysis of Detroit data, found that persons in dense areas were less likely to interact with neighbors than those in other areas. Otherwise, those in dense areas had sociability patterns with family and friends similar to those living elsewhere in the metropolitan area. Booth reported that in Toronto density is not related to neighboring. The Baltimore data show that neighborhood density is not strongly related to local social activities but that people on dense streets are slightly more likely than others to have some involvement with neighbors (Verbrugge and Taylor, 1976).

The density-pathology question seems to be essentially resolved at this point. Certainly, the rodent model is inappropriate for human populations in cities. All the spatial studies conclude that neighborhood density is at best a trivial variable in relation to the pathology rates and that social structure makes the difference. The relationship between neighborhood density and social integration is less clear. Verbrugge and Taylor (1976) found some positive social consequences of density, especially on the microneighborhood (street) level. Roncek (1976), following J. Jacobs (1961), suggested that high density may have positive effects on inhibiting crime. The relationship between household crowding and social phenomena shows few if any effects. Booth concluded that crowding is not harmful, while Verbrugge and Taylor argued that if one looks at proximate effects some negative consequences can be detected.

Sociology in the Design Process

Architecture and Social Research. Some sociologists and psychologists have suggested that the quality of the designed environment will improve if more social knowledge is injected into the design process (Gutman, 1972; Sommer, 1969, 1972; Michelson, 1976; Zeisel, 1975). They have proposed ways to accomplish this, and a few projects joining social research with design have been undertaken.

The design process has three phases: programming, design, and construction. Programming consists of determining which activities need to be accommodated in the new environment and how many people will use the facility, how often, and for what purposes. These questions are then converted into physical terms: How many rooms for each purpose are necessary and how large they must be? Design is the creation of the actual plan to accomplish these purposes, a plan that a builder may execute.

Zeisel (1975) showed how the changing relationship among architect, client, and user creates a need for social science involvement in the design process. In the past, the client who commissioned a design by an architect was the one who occupied the completed facility, as with a residence or a bank. Currently, the client is often not the ultimate user, especially in the case of large public buildings such as schools or housing projects, which are usually commissioned by a public board. Zeisel points out that there is a knowledge gap between the designer and the ultimate user, who may be of a different social class and cultural background. The social scientist can fill this gap by gathering information about the characteristics, needs, and wants of the users and conveying it to the designer.

Two examples of such work will illustrate the potential. Zeisel (1973) and an architect studied the living patterns and preferences of Puerto Rican families in New York City with the objective of remodeling the families' apartments. They discovered distinctive patterns that were not congruent with the existing environment and that would not be satisfied by a contemporary design conforming to middle class tastes. They found that the families used the living room as a formal, quasi-sacred area. This was inferred by the presence in these rooms of items such as statues of saints and pictures of John F. Kennedy. Furniture was kept covered, people with dirty shoes could not enter, and eating was prohibited. Based on this study, the architect offered a design in which this area was separated from other parts of the apartment and did not have an exterior entrance. Zeisel noted that a contemporary middle class design solution combining living and dining area in an open plan would have been totally inappropriate.

Henderson and Bauman (n.d.) studied another distinctive culture, the Arapaho and Cheyenne in Oklahoma. Their first discovery was that the Indians prefer to live in the country, not in a small town or city. This differs from the modal American preference for a town near a city. Second, they found intense kinship involvement—most preferred to live near their siblings or children rather than near their parents, cousins, or nieces and nephews. They also indicated a willingness to share outdoor space, workrooms, wells, septic tanks, laundry facilities, and storm cellars. Based on this, the authors, an architect and an

engineer, proposed a new type of housing development in the
country, which they called a "micro-community." It would
consist of adjacent, privately owned properties arranged around
a common node. This community area could accommodate
group activities such as cooking and eating. It would also include laundry facilities and areas for special games and other
joint activities. In addition, the common area would have shared
utilities such as a septic tank and well. This overall plan, which
conforms to the living patterns and preferences of the people, is
vastly different from conventional housing arrangements that
prevail in U.S. society, including those among the middle class
and the poor.

Social research has also been advocated after a new facility is in use. Sommer (1972) suggested that the design process
should become cyclical, with postconstruction evaluation feeding into the programming and design phases of the next similar
project. Ordinarily the designer's role in a project ends when the
construction is completed. Sommer (1972) and Zeisel (1973)
proposed that the users should be studied in the new environment to discover whether the architect's intentions were realized and what sorts of behavior actually take place. One study
in this mode was conducted by Cooper (1975) in a housing
project in San Francisco. She sought the architects' intentions
and their prior assumptions and expectations about the ways
people would behave in the environment that the architects designed. She anticipated a difference between the architects'
image of the people's needs and wants and the ones the eventual
occupants would express. After interviewing and observing the
residents, she discovered that most of their complaints had to
do with management policies of the housing authority rather
than the physical decisions made by the architects. For example, the authority provided no fences because they did not want
tenants to express any territorial rights to their places. The policy of renting only to the poorest families drove out many desirable neighbors. There were also some complaints about the
facility itself, particularly about the lack of recreational opportunities for teenagers.

Zeisel and Griffin (1974) analyzed architects' intentions
in conjunction with residents' responses in a housing development in an urban renewal project near Harvard University. The
researchers found that the architects' expectations about the
way people would behave were not always borne out by the
occupants. For example, the architects "arranged the units

opening onto a shared stair with the intent of increasing interaction between neighbors" (p. 66). The researchers discovered
that residents did not know the people in their own stairwell
better than others located elsewhere in the project.

The studies cited typify a new kind of collaboration between social scientist and designer. The recent studies and theoretical formulations may portend more input of social knowledge into the production of the designed environment.

Interaction Between Designers and Social Scientists.
Despite the prescriptions for social science in the design process,
there are major obstacles, some of them social-structural, to
such cooperation. The architect works on contract for a client.
This relationship imposes two major constraints; there is no
place in the regular fee structure for a charge for social research
and the ordinary project timetable requires rapid progress. Social research is usually a time-consuming process, and sociologists have not devised techniques to produce quick results.
Intellectual interaction between designers and researchers may
be very difficult due to their differing professional modes. The
architect is oriented toward solutions while the sociologist is
oriented toward explanations. The architect is synthetic, drawing together elements to produce a unique solution, while the
sociologist is analytical, dissecting a situation into a set of interacting variables. Architects are generalists, claiming competence
to design a vast range of types of facilities from factories to
schools. Sociologists are specialists, with different scholars
studying industrial sociology and the sociology of education.
Gutman (1972) says there have been failures in some attempts
at interaction because architects have consulted the wrong
sociologists, not knowing how specialized they are. He emphasizes the importance of recruiting a social scientist with appropriate substantive knowledge for a given design project.

Despite all these difficulties, there is increasing use of social science in design, as illustrated by the studies cited. In
recent years, two organizations have started to bring together
designers and social scientists—the Environmental Design Research Association and the Association for the Study of Man-
Environment Systems.

Conclusion

The overall argument is that comprehension of the urban
community is facilitated by recognizing that it is set within a

unique environment that is relevant to specific social phenomena. It is important not to lapse into environmental or architectural determinism but to use one or more of the moderated theoretical approaches to the interface of environment and social order. We first summarized a theoretical perspective emphasizing congruence between environment and activity. Second, we described the spread city of single-family residences occupied by homeowners, one unlike cities in history or in other societies. The trend has been toward single-purpose areas, dividing residential from commercial and other workaday activities. The social effects, while not well understood, seem to be congruent with a particular family and kinship structure and with U.S. patterns of social class, status, and racial and ethnic relations. Third, we addressed the density-pathology hypothesis and found it greatly overstated. One must look for the correct social effects before the environment becomes relevant. Urban density may not cause high mortality, but household crowding may exacerbate irritation with noise. Finally, we noted the emerging possibilities for the incorporation of social science into the environmental design process.

Part Four

Communication
and Politics

The urbanization of American society has involved a great enlargement in the scale not only of human settlement but also of
the webs of communication and polity. The parallel between
the growth of the "spread city" metropolitan area and the rise
of network television may have been largely historical accident.
Still, there is an especially fortuitous fit in that the normal
radius of both major metropolitan areas and VHF television
transmittal zones is approximately forty miles—the latter extended by cable systems as further metropolitan growth makes
such systems profitable. Given the coincident growth of the
metropolitan area and the area-wide media, it is no wonder that
the functioning of more localized governmental and political
structures becomes increasingly problematic and that proposals
for metropolitan-wide levels of government surface to general
consciousness.

The first two chapters of this part deal with mass communications in the urbanized society, presenting instructive contrasts. In Chapter Thirteen, "Television as a National Medium," Paul M. Hirsch assesses the workings and effects of that medium as it comes to dominate mass entertainment and news in a nationalizing fashion. Chapter Fourteen, "Print Media in Urban Society," by David Street and W. Paul Street, looks at the much more finely partitioned contents and audiences of the print media, particularly at the ways in which newspapers reflect the persistence and difficulties of addressing the changed local and metropolitan communities.

The remaining three chapters of the part directly address political process. "Community and Politics in City and Suburb," Chapter Fifteen by David Street and Jeffrey L. Davidson, examines questions of what happens to political organization, class cleavages, elite mobilization, and local participation in large cities and suburbs. Mark D. Gottdiener's "Social Planning and Metropolitan Growth," Chapter Sixteen, seeks to understand the sprawling patterns of the metropolis, despite and yet perhaps with the encouragement of energetic social planning activities. Finally, in Chapter Seventeen, "Changing Priorities for the Urban Heartland," Gerald D. Suttles analyzes the situation of the cities of the northeastern and north central regions of the nation and explores the potentialities for improvement through a realistic, scaled-down rehabilitation strategy.

13

Television as a National Medium

Paul M. Hirsch

Two key characteristics of an urban industrial society are a common culture and a shared national economy. By presenting popular national symbols sponsored by nationally advertised brand names, the mass media in the United States have encouraged and maintained the presence of both. Television in particular provides a steady flow of information and images to which all are exposed and that influence our perceptions of the world and affect us all.

Approximately 40 percent of all Americans' leisure time is spent attending to broadcast and print media. Television's content is almost entirely national in scope and orientation. The

Note: The author gratefully acknowledges grants from the Rockefeller Foundation and the University of Chicago Center for Urban Studies, which supported the research projects on which this chapter is based.

content of magazines and radio is less so, while newspapers are predominantly—though far from exclusively—local. The time investment with the media was substantially smaller before the advent of television, which now accounts for nearly three-quarters of all time spent with the mass media; television viewing is also correlated with spending less time visiting others, conversing, and sleeping (Robinson, 1969). On the average, Americans currently view television two hours daily. It is *the* primary source of both news and entertainment and is also the most trusted source of news (Roper Organization, 1971; Klein, 1976). In terms of audience size and reach, it is the largest and most prominent mass medium, and in many ways the most powerful: Nearly all of its programs are selected and disseminated nationally by three commercial networks, each seeking the same audience, and by the noncommercial Public Broadcasting System. During "prime time" evening hours when viewing is at a maximum, the images and information received on 92 percent of all sets in use across the nation are carried by the three commercial networks; fewer than 4 percent are tuned to "public" or educational broadcasting stations, and the remainder are divided among independent or nonnetwork-affiliated channels. Residents in virtually every American city can tune in, and often choose to watch, the same programs being watched by residents in every other American city at that time.[1]

While it is not clear whether viewers would abandon these programs if more channels and thus greater choice were available, it is now technically possible, with the advent of cable television and new video technologies, to produce more local programs on lower budgets for smaller communities than has been the case in the past. Precisely how the economics of greater diversity will be worked out and whether it will be facilitated by (at this writing, still restrictive) government policies remains to be seen. For the present and foreseeable future television network programs will continue as the predominant fare, defining much of our popular culture and providing many viewers with information that is useful at times but also distorting if not downright nonsensical at others. Gerbner and Gross (1976a, 1976b), for example, report that viewers of over four hours of television a day differ significantly from light viewers (of two hours or less) in believing that the likelihood of becoming involved in violence and the number of persons employed in law enforcement occupations are both unusually high and that strangers are untrustworthy. Officials of large corporations are reported to have moved company headquarters out of New York City partly because it "is always highly visible in the nation's news media: bombings and street violence in New York are likely to get more national attention than similar events in a midwestern city" (Clark, 1975, p. 9). This disproportionate concentration of news media coverage on a few cities, especially those in which television news crews are most conveniently dispatched (Epstein, 1973), often is included among reasons why managers resist transfers to some cities and corporations seek less publicized locations.

In return for providing programs that so many find attractive (or perhaps "settle for"), the television industry is able to efficiently deliver to advertisers of consumer goods enormous national audiences that are unprecedented in size (Rosenblatt, 1976). To reach the general public, preferably those between the ages of eighteen and forty-nine, national advertisers purchase time designated for broadcasting their commercial messages. For example, the audience for the Super Bowl spectacular in 1976 numbered over 75 million people, with advertising time sold at $230,000 per minute. Approximately 25 million households tune in one of the three networks' nightly national news programs. Millions of housewives loyally watch daily soap operas (this term derives from their principal sponsors, detergent manufacturers), and children stay home on Saturday mornings to watch action-adventure cartoon shows. No other American mass medium can rival television for audiences of these magnitudes.

What are some of the meanings of such a successful perceptual-image machine, encompassing all cities and communities, for a commercial, urban industrial society? How did this situation come about and how might it change? How much is known about television's effects on society as a whole and on categories of individual viewers? These are among the questions addressed in this chapter.

Urbanization and Mass Communication

Although the mass media are widely regarded as an essential prerequisite for modern, industrial societies, their appearance typically must follow the wiring of communities for electricity and telephone service, the building of roads, and the attainment of a standard of living meeting at least subsistence levels. Social scientists who study developing countries usually stress the appearance of mass media "hardware"—radio sets, movie projectors, and newspapers—as a significant contributor to a population's growing national consciousness and the "psychic mobility" stimulated by learning about new ways of life (Lerner, 1964). Statistically, "communication development" (the increasing presence of mass media hardware) is highly associated with other indices of modernization, such as the percentage of the population in cities over 50,000, rising literacy rates, and per capita income (Cutright, 1963; Olsen, 1968; Frey, 1973).

At the same time, the *content* of broadcast programs, that is, the actual images conveyed and people's reactions to them, are seldom examined, having been studied primarily in countries where a nationwide system of mass communication has already been built. It is only at this later point that the novelty effect of first having the media has worn off; it then becomes easier to find or assume high levels of a population's routine exposure to programs: By this time, the hardware has been widely distributed and is already in place. Thus, as a nation develops, we know that the appearance of movies, newspapers, radio, and television increases. A fascinating finding across nations (Robinson, 1969) is that the more widespread television ownership is, the more time owners themselves spend watching television. But while McLuhan (1965) and others suggest that the actual content of the images conveyed is of secondary importance, it is also the case that there is surprisingly little knowledge about variations in mass media content and its effects, not only in developing countries but in advanced industrial societies as well.

At the earlier growth stages, however, societal choices about which media will proliferate, at what rate, to whom, and with what content are key issues, strongly influenced by each nation's historical, economic, and political traditions. Thus, the character of the American mass media system has been determined largely by its long-standing commitments to private enterprise, local self-government, minimal government regulation, and a tradition of *caveat emptor* ("Let the buyer beware"). These commitments, also tied to the constitutional protection of press freedom, account for a tightly organized and highly profitable broadcasting industry: Local stations are licensed to provide service to communities but may meet this requirement by affiliating with national networks or syndication services that feature national programming. These commitments also suggest, as we shall see, that the "television of abundance" once promised by the cable television industry will be limited—an outcome which, from a sociological and policy perspective, may also prove to have some advantages.

Economics and Organization of American Broadcasting

The big wheel at the network started spinning,
The verdict was that "Hee Haw" had to go
'Cause city slickers don't believe in grinnin'
And who the heck needs jokes in Kokomo?[2]

The provision of mass-communicated information and images becomes "just another industry." Historically, the mass media have grown with and prospered from the large-scale urbanization of America over the past century. As a result of this process, about 80 percent of all retail goods are purchased in three hundred metropolitan areas, primarily by adults aged between eighteen and forty-nine. With few exceptions (such as the selection of Saturday mornings by each network to schedule programs directed at children or the appearance of advertisements directed at viewers over the age of fifty on the nightly news programs), this is the audience sought by the television industry and its advertisers. The total audience is evaluated in terms of each viewer's demographic characteristics (age, sex, and income) rather than place of residence. Signals from transmitters located in 235 metropolitan areas reach the entire U.S. population, with the coverage area of each television market basically coterminous with the large retail zone in which it operates. Programs and advertisements carried in the ten largest television markets reach one-third of the population; in the top fifty, 75 percent. By and large, the remaining majority of cities and towns and the minority of people who live in rural areas or are in the "wrong" age, education, and income categories are excluded from the target audience to which the advertisements, and therefore programs, are designed to appeal. Of course, such viewers are all welcomed as additional members of the national viewing audience, of which these groups are certainly a part; up to a point, in fact, the "standard English" used in program dialogues has been found to raise the English proficiency levels of the poorly educated and of children in largely rural areas. However, the programs and world view presented by American television are tailored almost exclusively to appeal to and reinforce the value structure of urban residents.[3]

This process clearly skews the images presented of people

and society and of what is funny or important. While the economic rationale behind these programming decisions is clear, the sociological functions served are seldom considered or investigated. There are instances when makers of economic and marketing decisions may distinguish only minimally between their "have" and "have not" consumers; for example, because of the retail zones in which they reside, programs whose appeal includes the urban poor may be more financially attractive to produce and sponsor than programs whose appeal includes the wealthy but rural (and hence scattered) farmer.

The economic basis for determining television programs is not a recent development. Rather, it follows arrangements pioneered during the heyday of radio, whose owners, in turn, had borrowed some of their own organizational strategies from mass-circulation newspapers and magazines. Two key organizational goals are to build and attract a national audience and to realize economies of scale by constructing networks or cooperatives that produce, select, or provide copy (as do the Associated Press and newspaper syndicates) and programming (as, for example, the National Broadcasting Company) to participating newspapers or broadcasting stations, which in turn can avoid producing material themselves individually and at a higher unit cost.

Creating a National Audience. "To say that media make markets means nothing more than that they create common interests and standards of taste. They tend to attract people who are alike socially or culturally or in certain dimensions of personality. The same psychological elements may help to dictate or influence a person's choice of medium as help to define his use of a product or choice of a brand" (Bogart, 1967, p. 92).

During the 1800s, the American newspaper was transformed from an elite to a mass medium. Rising literacy rates, the growth of cities, and an absence of political controls all contributed to the rise of privately produced and inexpensive newspapers written for a mass, heterogeneous audience. The new "penny press" prominently featured stories on crime, sex, and violence in addition to political news; within four years of the appearance of such a newspaper on New York City street corners it sold more copies per issue than all of its elite competitors combined, which featured more partisan political news written at higher levels of sophistication (DeFleur and Ball-Rokeach, 1975). This formula for success, immensely attractive to advertisers because of its ability to increase the number of readers exposed to their messages, set the pattern for each subsequent mass medium, all of which have adopted the techniques of the penny press for appealing to and creating a mass audience. Metropolitan dailies developed by providing information and entertainment to local residents, selling advertising space to area retailers, and stressing local news while also forming cooperative syndicates to lower the cost of reporting stories originating in faraway places. While national newspapers developed in many other industrial nations, this medium has retained a predominantly local orientation in the United States, partly because there are so many autonomous governmental units to report on as well as so many local merchants who can place advertising (Bagdikian, 1971).

As industry expanded and railroad links were completed, the first national magazines appeared. Initially produced for increasingly literate housewives, these featured in-depth biographies of public figures, short fiction, and information about fashions in clothes, cooking, and home furnishings. They also could be merchandised at low subscription rates by selling advertising space to emergent national manufacturers of brand-name household products and remedies, who found magazines with this editorial format an attractive vehicle for reaching their consumers. Some of these magazines, which helped to create new standards of taste among the growing middle class, soon broadened their appeal to include a wider cross-section of Americans and grew into such widely read paragons of popular culture as *Collier's, Life, Look,* and the *Saturday Evening Post.* While each of these had millions of subscribers when they ceased publication, their economic function—to gather together large numbers of "average" Americans for national (rather than local) advertisers—was made obsolete by the rise of television, a far more efficient medium with the same audience profile.

The emergence of radio initially posed numerous questions about its most likely audience, content, and sources of financial support. Unlike the print media, its progenitors were neither journalists nor particularly interested in competing for the now-established mass audience in providing the news of the day. Primarily, the corporations that developed this invention were concerned with promoting the sale of radio sets; the programs needed to attract buyers were conceived largely to supplement this marketing effort. By 1925, with all available air waves hopelessly flooded by amateur operators, the industry repeatedly requested the federal government to step in and impose order through licensing and regulation. At first, both Congress and the president, in accordance with American political tradition, refused, insisting instead on self-regulation by the new industry. The Federal Radio Act was finally passed in 1927, only after the industry proved incapable of agreeing on which operators could broadcast on specific frequencies at designated hours.

By this time, the Radio Corporation of America, formed by General Electric, Westinghouse, and American Telephone and Telegraph, had established two radio networks (which became NBC and ABC), whose immediate success prompted the formation of CBS in 1928 and a fourth network (Mutual) six years later. Each network contracted with individual stations (affiliates) across the country to simultaneously carry expensively produced programs employing well-known performers designed to appeal to a large and hitherto nonexistent national radio audience. Since it had also become clear by this time that listeners would not willingly pay to receive radio programs, the cost of programming was borne by national advertisers, who learned to the surprise of all that radio listeners did not protest commercial interruptions. In return for "clearing time" to broadcast network programs, local stations would receive a portion of the advertising revenues obtained; more importantly, they could also sell commercial time to local and regional advertisers who wished to take advantage of the opportunity to reach the large audiences attracted by the network programs broadcast in their retail territory.

These arrangements almost instantly resolved the initial set of questions concerning the content and financial base for the new medium. The government's reluctance to interfere in the new industry ruled out federal support for educational uses of either radio or television for many years. Instead, programs produced and sponsored by private industry sought out the largest possible audiences, providing entertainment formats with the widest appeal. Once cost sharing through network affiliation, or "the interconnection of a number of local stations to produce standardized programming with central control," became the dominant organizational pattern, the economic burden of producing programs was lifted from locally licensed stations. As described by William Henry, a former chairman of the Federal Communications Commission, local stations are thereby able "to throw the network switch, or open a syndicated film package as they would a can of beans" (Bagdikian, 1971, pp. 166, 171-172).

Local affiliates, however, have long tended to reject low-rated network programs, such as documentaries or symphonic broadcasts, when they are not contractually obliged to carry them. An interesting, unanticipated consequence of this arrangement is that when unsponsored congressional hearings—such as Senate and House committee hearings on the Watergate break-in and the impeachment of President Nixon—are broadcast live by the major television networks, local affiliates often find they must reluctantly "clear" these, if only because they have no alternative programs (or sponsors) to air in their place. Ironically, radio stations, which have locally produced programs, seldom if ever interrupt their scheduled programming to provide such coverage of public affairs. In short, while local stations are licensed to serve the communities in which they are located, network arrangements, first in radio and now in television, sharply reduce the number of hours devoted to programs geared to the metropolitan areas in which stations are licensed. Whether the national programs are preferred by viewers over the local alternatives and precisely what types of local television programs could fill the broadcast day are questions that have seldom arisen or only recently been investigated. We do know, however, that local news programs (that is, reports of major events within each station's large coverage area) are widely viewed and that some of the smaller independent and educational radio and television stations have long provided coverage of local athletic events and public affairs.

Impact of Television on Other Mass Media. The radio medium, followed by movies, newspapers, and magazines, has been transformed radically by the public's enthusiastic acceptance of television. Ownership of television sets, which were first tested in 1927, grew at an astonishing rate shortly after the end of World War II. Television networks, formed at this time and following the same audience-building strategies enunciated first by the mass newspaper and further developed by radio, "stole" many of radio's most popular programs and performers, and added the visual dimension. Television has forced on the radio industry new round-the-clock formats directed at individual listeners rather than families, with each format designed to appeal to a specific component of the formerly composite mass audience, hence the "all news," "country and western," "easy listening," "top 40," and "soul music" formats. Each of these is targeted at specific segments of the population and sold to advertisers seeking certain demographic profiles. All-news listeners, for example, tend to have high incomes and be well educated, while the profile of listeners to country-and-western formats is just the opposite. The impact of television on radio has thereby indirectly provided these listener aggregates, or subcultures, with far more access to cultural fare that each finds attractive than may have been the case when radio was a less diverse medium, with dominant networks seeking to appeal to everybody (Hirsch, 1969).

At the same time (excepting some talk shows), these radio formats, while locally produced, remain national in orientation, still bringing news of the outside world to their listeners —for example, the latest stories from Washington or a new record by the Rolling Stones—rather than suggesting (perhaps improbably) that events in the listener's life are of equal importance. One of the most important functions of the mass media in urban societies, in addition to helping citizens relate to the outside world, may be to effectively transport people "outside" of themselves and thereby continually reinforce the power of our national culture.

By providing new formats for listeners, the radio medium also had to build or create its new audience. As radio stations began programming more recorded music and losing their traditional audience to television, McPhee and Meyersohn (1955, p. 142) noted: "The greatest part of the adult audience for radio music during the day is surely a created phenomenon—something that has grown up in response to radio's own proliferation of material, talent (for example, disk jockeys) and time-availability in this field. Moreover, in this case one has a pretty good idea which one took the lead most of the way, radio's proliferation of offerings or the audience's growth in interests and habits. It is a good bet that the growth of local stations and local advertising, as well as the blows of television on radio—all these independent of audience demand for music—were probably pushing more stations and more disk jockeys into the recorded music field than, at the given time, there were existing interests in having music for the home."

Television's impact on radio also has had an indirect though substantial effect on which records are produced by the recording industry and made available to its consumers. When, as part of radio's adaptation to a new environment, some radio stations began featuring top 40 music, then rock and roll records, and later progressive rock, the diffusion of the new music and its associated life-styles contributed substantially to fostering new forms of "youth culture" by providing what was effectively a private communications medium for teenagers and college students. The lucrative prospect of radio air play for rock music has strongly influenced decisions taken by record companies concerning which styles and performers to record and promote. More generally, American radio now facilitates cultural solidarity within specific subgroups and subcultures (whose members remain tuned to one format, ignoring its competitors), while television functions as a major communications link *between* groups, collecting together the members of different cultural subgroups for common exposure to the larger, dominant popular culture (Hirsch, 1971).

Television's success also significantly altered the movie industry, which suffered a substantial drop in theater attendance as television viewers chose to be entertained at home. Over time, what used to be the second feature, or B, movie was dropped from production because it was no longer being shown in movie houses, only to be revived when television networks contracted them for exclusive showings during the prime-time evening hours. With what were once stock movie plots now the staple of popular television series, today's films (with notable exceptions) are produced for new audiences: those who are least likely to stay home and watch television. The age of the average movie goer has declined, and like radio formats, movies are now produced with narrower target-audience subgroups in mind. Consequently, movies are frequently far more violent than previously and feature more explicit sexual sequences than would appeal to the average television viewer (who may, however, see a severely edited-for-television version subsequently).

Newspapers, once able to deliver primarily just the news of the day and a few features, have adapted to the superior capacity of television to provide the same superficial service at the national level by presenting more in-depth features, local coverage, analysis, and commentary. And magazines, like radio, have sought more limited segments of the population. After the demise of *Life,* for example, Time, Inc., brought out two new publications, *Money* and *People,* geared to different audiences, with higher and lower income and education profiles, respectively, than characterized *Life* magazine, whose more heterogeneous readership was deemed too similar to television's audience by advertisers.

In sum, each of the mass media in America, privately operated and subject to minimal government regulation, has consistently sought to build and attract the largest possible audience and provide it with the types of entertainment and news that are most popular. Presently, television performs best at fulfilling this task, and its success has forced other mass media to adapt by attracting new audiences and offering greater diversity. An increasingly national audience for this created popular culture has been built, carefully nurtured and maintained for nearly a century by forces basic to the political and commercial tenets of American society. What are considered some of the outcomes and effects of these organizational arrangements and such widespread dissemination of cultural symbols?

Role of Television and Popular Culture in Contemporary Society

Television's impact on American society consists partly in its spectacularly successful continuation of a trend started by other media—developing content designed to create and attract massive audiences composed of people from all regions, classes, and backgrounds. Analytically, one of its most potent effects on American society—*the provision of a centrally produced, standardized, and homogeneous common culture*—is as much an artifact of how this medium's technological capacity has been organized as the inevitable result of the technology itself. This distinction is of great importance, for it suggests that some of the effects commonly attributed to the television medium should be conceived instead as following from its present organizational form, one in which nearly nine hundred separate channels are in effect mere conduits for four centralized television networks. It is for this reason and because of the consequent lack of diversity in program content that television now serves so well as a proxy for all of the mass media whenever questions arise over mass media effects. Many of the controversial effects often attributed to television and presumed to be unique to this medium were earlier attributed to the media that it displaced. These effects include concern over the impact of its reliance on action-adventure formats featuring stories about crime, sex, and violence to attract and maintain its present audience. For example, when AM radio stations were divided into affiliation patterns with a few dominant networks, similar fare or what is better thought of as the same "network effect" was mistakenly conceived by many observers as an effect of radio as a medium rather than as a product of organizational arrangements. (See, for example, *Billboard,* 1940.) Similarly, efforts by movie producers and magazine publishers to attract large, heterogeneous audiences were misinterpreted as inevitable characteristics of these media, which were also eliminated by television's appearance as a competing medium.

Over and above television's refinement of formats and organizational arrangements pioneered by others, however, its technical ability to present an unending montage of moving visual images—of fictional characters, aspiring political leaders, comedians, wars, and disasters, in living color and in the privacy of one's home—is a wholly new phenomenon. Its political and cultural power lie in this combination of a technical capacity superior to other media and organizational arrangements that encourage many millions of viewers worldwide to watch images produced and controlled by a handful of networks. The resultant "global village" unquestionably plays a significant role in the political and cultural life of contemporary America.

In television's short twenty-five-year history, the effects have been considered and examined from numerous viewpoints. That some interpretations may seem to conflict with others follows partly from the fact that observers tend to consider entirely different aspects of television's role in society and then offer broad generalizations about society based on whichever aspects of the topic they see as most important. Each view is then disputed by others as perhaps following logically and directly from an important perspective, but nevertheless being unrelated to aspects of the question that the disputants consider significant. For example, historian Daniel Boorstin (1973), noting statistics on Americans' pervasive exposure to TV and on changes in our use of time following television's introduction, concludes that its effects on society have been nothing short of "cataclysmic." Sociologist Joseph Klapper (1960), on the other hand, reviewing studies of whether individuals' attitudes are measurably affected by short-term exposure to single programs, concludes that the medium typically reinforces already existing viewpoints and predispositions, resulting in minimal change in the attitudes of the average viewer. Note that these evaluations are not actually contradictory, because each addresses different aspects of television's impact on society.

At least five such distinctive perspectives contribute to our understanding of television in America. These focus on: (1) the *political impact* of the medium on government and the electoral process—ranging from television's institutional effect on

political campaigns, candidates, and officeholders to efforts to
measure its influence on the perceptions and attitudes of individual citizens; (2) its *cultural impact* on the American people
(Does television's provision of nationally recognized and discussed symbols, heroes, and villains serve to integrate an increasingly fragmented society of isolated groups and individuals, or
does it deprive Americans of exposure to alternative viewpoints,
high culture, and the freedom to do and discover things for
themselves?); (3) the *demographic impact* of set ownership and
viewing on other cultural patterns and on time use; (4) the *latent and manifest functions* served by the program content and
the commanding presence of television throughout society (as,
for example, an agent of social control or a setter of agendas for
public discussion); and finally, (5) the *effects on individuals* of
exposure to television programs (Does violent content lead to
an increase in aggressive behavior? and Under what conditions,
if any, is television best able to convey information or motivate
individuals to purchase advertised products, vote for a political
candidate, develop new interests, or change their opinions?).
Three of these perspectives will be discussed separately.[4] It is
important to keep in mind that these perspectives are all analytically distinct and independent. We shall see that the decep-
tively simple question "What is the effect of television?" must
first be broken down by specifying the areas of concern and the
level of behavior and social organization that is of interest.

Television's Impact on the Political Process

As a commercial enterprise, supported by advertising
rather than government subsidies, American television is more
independent of direct state controls over its reporting of public
affairs than are the broadcasting media in practically all other
nations. Its national news coverage is produced entirely under
the supervision of the major networks, each of which (as with
entertainment programs) seeks to attract the largest possible
share of the national audience. Candidates for political office
seeking to reach the public directly must *purchase* television advertising time—which has become the single largest item in campaign budgets and greatly accounts for the rising cost of seeking
office and pressure to raise funds in ever increasing amounts.
Television news is both the first and most trusted source of
news for the majority of Americans (Roper Organization,
1971). In addition to a daily news summary consisting of short

segments and which has expanded from fifteen to thirty minutes (with forty-five-minute broadcasts projected for the near future), television networks produce a limited number of documentaries. They also preempt entertainment programs to present "live" a select number of special events, such as space shots, political party conventions, and election results.

Television coverage of public affairs departs from newspaper reporting in significant ways: the *visual dramatization* of stories, always delivered by *familiar and trusted personalities,* and viewed by *millions of people,* ranging from presidents and congressmen to the least educated and least interested members of the mass public. The combination of all these structural features has had a major impact on the political process. In a pluralistic society, in which elite interest groups are not always in agreement and must seek public support for their positions, the most significant aspect of the nightly ritual of television news is that national leaders and officeholders exercise so little control over the news judgments of broadcast journalists. And regional and local leaders, whose activities receive far less network coverage—and whose image of importance may thereby be diminished—exert far less influence.

Organizational Effects. In order to build and retain the interest of a nationwide news audience, a television network must feature those events that appear equally relevant to each member of its far-flung audience. This organizational constraint encourages a predisposition to focus on events in Washington, beginning with the president's schedule and extending to members of the Senate, rather than to report on events in a single state (excepting disasters and human interest stories) or on the activities of the governors or U.S. representatives (whose constituencies are too small). For similar reasons, events in large cities, which also are less expensive to transmit stories from and more accessible to camera crews (Epstein, 1973), are reported more frequently than those in outlying areas. Thus, unlike metropolitan newspapers (which emphasize local over national news), the overriding impression from network television news is that the most *important* events and activities occur at the national rather than local level, involve the federal rather than local government or private corporations, and arise in major population centers.

Local television news programs, while offsetting this somewhat by reporting on state capitals and the larger local cities, also contribute to this impression in at least three ways.

First, they are typically produced on lower budgets, with less professional news personnel who remain for shorter time periods as they jockey for positions in larger cities or with the national television networks. Second, because television stations' signals reach many cities, their "local" news coverage is largely regional, omitting much of what happens in individual mayors' offices and towns' council or school board meetings (Bagdikian, 1971). Much of the local television news received in some areas (northern Indiana, Delaware, and New Jersey) concerns the neighboring regions or states in which most of the transmitting television stations are located. In Grand Rapids, Michigan, for example, the signals from three television stations reach about 400,000 viewers in twenty-four counties spread over 17,000 square miles. Under such circumstances (which are quite typical, and more pronounced for larger metropolitan areas), television news departments come to broadcast regional news, now redefined as "local." Radio faces a similar set of conditions and constraints. Bagdikian (1971, p. 153) suggests that "If these 24 counties have their proportionate share of all Michigan governmental units, then the average broadcasting station heard in Grand Rapids-Kalamazoo has 26 minutes a day in which to report the news from 150 municipalities, 230 townships and 310 school districts." Finally, most of the time accorded to local news by television stations consists of reports on national sports results, local athletic teams, and the weather throughout the region. Much of the political news of the day continues to be delegated to the national networks and local press.[5] A content analysis of the issues and topics included in television's public affairs coverage will generally show that people are implicitly told that the nation rather than city or state in which they happen to live is important. Another implicit theme has been to emphasize problems rather than subsequently reporting on their outcomes (Robinson, 1975).

Local affiliates present live and unedited the television networks' daily news "feeds." Thus, for example, network affiliates in the South were unable to predict when stories on the civil rights movement would appear, nor could they have censored them easily had they known in advance. Similarly, whereas newspaper editors can rewrite wire service copy to their liking, local network affiliates during the Johnson and Nixon administrations transmitted images of American soldiers burning Vietnamese villages and mutilating enemy soldiers, and national news commentaries suggesting that official government

policies were poorly conceived and that the American public
was being deceived. While station managers who disagreed (as
they were asked to do by the Nixon administration; Porter,
1976) can protest the content of such broadcasts *after* they
have aired, station affiliates can seldom "pull the plug" on them
during broadcast without jeopardizing their highly profitable
network affiliations.

The unique ability of network television to present identical, privately produced, advertiser-sponsored, and visually
dramatized versions of news headlines to the American people
on a regular basis constitutes an extraordinary base of independent political power. President Johnson (who kept three
television monitors in the Oval Office, one for each network),
on seeing Walter Cronkite announce the war in Vietnam could
not be won, is reported to have interpreted this as meaning that
public support for its continuation could no longer be mar-
shalled (Halberstam, 1976). And Vice-President Agnew
([1969], 1972), representing an administration less willing to
countenance the credibility of television newsmen and the
medium's presumed power over public opinion, directly attacked (in a speech carried live by all three commercial networks) the "small band" of decision makers, "unrepresentative"
of the diverse regions and spectrum of political opinions in
America, who exercise such a powerful "monopoly" of judgments over what information is transmitted daily into living
rooms across the nation.[6]

Political leaders and officeholders are generally far more
alert and sensitive than social scientists and journalists to the
structural characteristics that distinguish television from other
news media and give it a different form of power. Elite journalists, for example, often stress the lack of depth and originality
in television news stories, while at the same time ignoring the
political significance of network television as a disseminator of
these headlines (Blumler and McQuail, 1969) and of the inability
or general disinclination of local affiliates to alter the amount
and tone of coverage accorded each story. The organizational
structure of television further underlies and makes possible a
wide variety of effects often proposed by social scientists as
being unique to this medium, but which also formerly characterized other mass media. For example, the prospect of favorable television news coverage has accelerated (though it did not
originate) the staging of conferences, political conventions,
press releases, campaign stops, and other "pseudo-events"

(Boorstin, 1961), often scheduled early in the day to "make the evening news" (Seymour-Ure, 1974). In addition, political candidates and leaders themselves turn to television news programs to learn which, if any, of their many activities in a given day were chosen for coverage in a brief segment and hence became publicly "real"; such coverage gives the nation perhaps its only glimpse of the actions or views of these political figures (Crouse, 1973; Novak, 1975). Participants and observers of the reported events often find, in addition, that the portrayal of what occurred does not accord with their own direct experience (Lang and Lang, 1953; Douglas, 1976). Topics emphasized by television news editors (generally the same topics receiving emphasis in other news media as well) are usually selected by respondents to public opinion polls as the most pressing issues of the day, a significant finding that attests to the role of the news media in defining political issues for public discussion (McCombs and Shaw, 1972; DeFleur and Ball-Rokeach, 1975).

Perhaps the most visible effect of network television news coverage on the political process has been to alter the conduct of elections and operating procedures of newsworthy organizations, political parties, and public agencies. In the area of political campaigns, the visual and dramatic bias of television is widely believed to be facilitating a significant change in the presentation (or "packaging") of candidates to the mass public as attractive, low-keyed ("cool") personalities. Also, there is less emphasis on issues, a greater search for "controlled" media situations, and an increased intrusion of concepts and techniques used in advertising campaigns for consumer goods (Mendelsohn and Crespi, 1970; McGinnis, 1969). The public relations profession has grown as efforts increase to "plant" stories and otherwise influence decisions taken by news editors (Rivers, 1970). National television coverage of a possible scandal almost invariably leads to congressional hearings or executive action, and officials and functionaries monitor television and newspaper stories about themselves and their colleagues very closely (Douglas, 1976). Brunner and Crecine (1971) report that the first question asked by U.S. House members when a vote is to be taken is whether the measure is controversial and therefore newsworthy. Live television coverage of Senate and House committee hearings on the Watergate break-in and its aftermath was widely considered to have altered the participants' views of the importance of their inquiry and the high stakes involved, more so than it measurably affected the attitudes of home viewers

(Robinson, 1974). That television publicity and news coverage provides a direct feedback function to political elites illustrates a major effect of the medium and highlights the institutional role played by the mass media in contemporary America (Janowitz, 1970).

Audience Surveys. At the less visible level of individual citizens, opinion surveys—the primary methodological tool employed to gauge levels of information diffusion and short-run attitude change—suggest that the public is far less concerned about or influenced directly by the content of television news than are political decision makers (Berelson, Lazarsfeld, and McPhee, 1954; Patterson and McClure, 1976; Kraus and Davis, 1976; Robinson, 1972). There is a wide variety of interpretations of the data in this area. In the absence of good baseline measures, for example, the finding that 50 percent of adults surveyed in 1964 knew some Americans were fighting in Vietnam (Robinson, 1972) can be viewed as either a testimony to the power of the mass media to alert so many people to what was then a relatively obscure bit of information or as evidence that a hard core of uninformed people simply will not be taught or reached through television news. Both propositions receive some support from the well-documented finding that where learning new information about society is concerned, the already well-informed are most likely to notice, comprehend, and actively seek out more information, while the poorly informed tend to ignore, misunderstand, and avoid it. Television, in reaching the largest audience of any media, may thus further contribute to the "knowledge gap" described by Tichenor, Donahue, and Olien (1970) and Donahue, Tichenor, and Olien (1975) for certain types of esoteric information, while also serving in other instances (such as times of national tragedies) to reduce it. It also has been suggested (Robinson, 1975) that the mass of television news viewers may indeed develop strong impressions about places, personalities, and the overall condition of the country while lacking the sophistication to follow or care about the specifics of each individual news story, although public opinion polls are phrased only in terms of the latter.

In sum, television's impact on the political process is seen as being strongest by political leaders and candidates, followed, in roughly descending order, by political scientists, historians, sociologists, survey researchers, and psychologists. This ordering reflects a difference between social science perspectives, in which "institutionalists"—scholars analyzing societies, communities, or organizations, or seeking to examine large-scale trends over time—find television to have a major impact on society, while "individualists," who use the sample survey respondent as the unit of analysis, aggregate individual responses, and often are concerned with the correlation between exposure to specific programs and short-run changes in attitude, typically find that the medium does not appear to exert any strong influence over its viewing audience. Both views may be correct in their own contexts. This difference in outlook and perspective will reappear as we consider the cultural implications of the typical American household having its television set(s) turned on for an average of six hours every day of the week.

Television's Impact on American Culture

"Whether it be papyrus scrolls or cable television, the immediate cause of widespread adoption of a communications medium is its content, not technical feasibility or price or promises of future utility. Amos 'n Andy and FDR's Fireside Chats impelled Americans to buy radio sets in the 1930s, Howdy Doody, Milton Berle, and national political conventions sold initial television sets in the 1940s. FCC regulations, national networks, and improved receivers helped, but they only made possible the programming that convinced consumers to participate" (Bagdikian, 1971, p. 163).

Television's coverage of national public affairs represents only about 3 percent of the programs it presents, usually at a financial loss and to fulfill part of its legal obligation to operate "in the public interest." It is far more widely and accurately perceived as a medium of mass entertainment.[7] As a business, television network profits derive from presenting entertainment shows that attract a nationwide audience for "delivery" to commercial advertisers. The term popular (or mass) culture has come to refer to such mass media content, packaged and designed to appeal to this huge audience. As an enterprise, television has been enormously successful at meeting its goal: The appeal of popular culture on television is pervasive and its presence insistent and continuous. To remain isolated from its content for an extended period is almost tantamount to being removed from the mainstream of American life (Wilensky, 1964); when a writer for TV Guide locates someone who has not seen "The Tonight Show," the discovery is grounds for a feature article patterned after Ripley's "Believe It or Not."

Inherent in the concept of such national programming is an implicit rejection of cultural differences among viewers in different regions of the country, from different income and education categories, or with different backgrounds and interests. The logic of reaching everybody encourages a disregard of differences, a minimum of sequences that might offend a significant amount of viewers, and a standardization of content and expectations. While there is little doubt concerning the validity of this observation, its cultural *meaning* and effects have long been a topic of widespread discussion and debate among humanists, social scientists, and professional critics—all of whom offer provocative interpretations and raise important issues, most of which remain unresolved (McQuail, 1969; Blumler and Katz, 1974).

Popular culture, to be a meaningful concept, depends on the set of structural conditions embodied in the organizational arrangements of television at present: a limited number of channels supplying entertainment to the widest possible audience of voluntary viewers. What makes top-rated programs like "All in the Family," "Kojak," and "NBC Nightly News" part of our popular culture is that their national audiences *cut across* demographic boundaries and present diverse groups of Americans a set of common symbols, vocabularies, information, and shared experiences. In these terms, the new audiences built by the radio, movie, and magazine media, once the original audiences were displaced by television, are less of a mass public, for there are now more outlets (radio formats, special interest publications, and movie genres), each geared to a smaller, more homogeneous segment of the population. In an important sense, these are no longer *mass* media, for their increased diversity and consequent fragmentation of a previously mass audience suggests they no longer are the primary carriers of popular culture. Rather, their new audiences consist of more clearly delineated subcultures: pop music radio stations service the youth culture, and soul music stations the black culture. Of all the mass media, then, television is unchallenged as the predominant source and distributor of popular culture. As noted earlier, it has thus inherited nearly all of the critical attention earlier directed toward the other media when they were primary carriers, starting with the urban newspapers that built circulations by developing formula stories about imaginary events, crime waves, violence, and sex (a tradition carried on until recently by the *National Enquirer*). In addition, television's unique ability to dramatize graphically each story visually and increase the number of hours people spend before home receivers has provided new foci for scholarly attention and critical concern. What are some of the predominant themes, messages, and story lines to which such an enormous audience has been so attracted?

Content of Television. TV program content has been analyzed in various ways. In the view of producers and literary critics, a key distinction lies in the type of program *genre* being discussed, for each type is written and paced differently according to implicit or explicit rules (Newcomb, 1974). Thus, situation comedies are often difficult to compare with variety shows, sports broadcasts, action-adventure westerns and detective series, talk shows, or soap operas; and program content shown in the late evening hours (such as "Mary Hartman, Mary Hartman") may bring forth protests if scheduled in prime time, either from too many viewers who would find it offensive or from network executives if its ratings were unsatisfactory. From this standpoint, it is interesting to examine the *form* of each genre and to learn how its plot lines and characterizations have changed over time. Lowenthal (1944) and W. Wright (1975) have performed this type of analysis for magazine biographies and movie westerns. It is a strategy too seldom applied to the television medium.

Television content is also very amenable to more ambitious efforts to analyze its formulas, patterned images, and thematic content. One such observation is that television's main characters, both fictional and nonfictional (excepting some villains), are nearly always intelligent, well educated, successful, affluent, and from the middle class (Novak, 1975). Note that this type of analysis can be performed *across* genres, as can a survey of the race and sex of the individuals on screen and a coding of whether these individuals are presented as competent, sympathetic, in positions of authority or subordination, and so on. Also, in television dramas, problems must usually be solved by certified experts and heroes through ingenuity rather than by mere luck. Upward mobility is desirable. In action-adventure programs and children's cartoons, on-screen violence is ubiquitous, though questions remain as to whether analysts should consider all violent acts categorically or consider whom they are committed by, under what circumstances, and to what end.

Perhaps the most consistent and significant theme, across all genres, is also the simplest: *The latest consumer goods are highly desirable and should be purchased.* This is the unambiguous message of the commercial advertisements that appear before, during, and after every program and, more subtly, on the stage sets and the television actors and personalities themselves. The cumulative effects of this exposure, viewed by so many millions each day, raises a host of questions about and interpretations of the impact of individual viewers. The interpretations divide roughly into three types: (1) those that view television as a public menace and essentially call for its abolition, (2) those that view its homogeneity of content, but not the medium itself, with dismay and advocate more diversity by decentralizing program production and distribution, and (3) those that either approve of the present state of television or seek to alter minor aspects of program content without significantly affecting the organizational arrangements by which television is now structured.

Abolitionist Position. The first and most radical school of thought about television conceives of popular culture as immensely harmful to the vitality of both high and folk culture, as the handmaiden of a totalitarian state, or as simply an inexcusable waste of the viewer's time—time that ought to be channeled into more rewarding, productive areas of social life. During the late 1950s the extent of the threat posed by mass culture to high culture and American society was debated extensively within the intellectual community (Rosenberg and White, 1957; Bauer and Bauer, 1960). Although Wilensky's (1964) finding that high culture is losing vitality only because so many of its own proponents embrace television entertainment fare enthusiastically defused part of this argument, an important part of the original indictment remains. This concerns the combined facts that the time people spend viewing television is time spent away from other activities and that the act of watching television is essentially passive, encouraging people to share the experiences of nonexistent others vicariously rather than joining more organizations and otherwise leading more active lives of their own. The policy implications of both observations, as phrased, do not encourage efforts towards better or more diverse program content. Rather, as McCarthy (1974, p. 17) has recommended, they lead to "ousting the stranger from the house"; after breaking a habit of watching over thirty hours a week of basically unredeemable programming, he proposed that television cease operation with the following announcement to all viewers: "Come forward and turn off your set. . . . Get up and take a walk to the library and get a book. Or turn to your husband or wife and surprise them with a conversation. Or call a neighbor you haven't spoken with in months. Write a letter to a friend who has lost track of you. . . . Meanwhile, you'll be missing almost nothing."

Related to the alleged consequences of the amount of time Americans spend passively viewing television are two further concerns. First, local and regional cultures may be affected adversely by more than the mechanical reproduction of live performances made possible by sound, movie, and videotape technologies. Combined with the nationwide dependence on a small number of technically proficient Los Angeles- and New York-based production companies contracted by the major television networks, these factors encourage members of the national audience to look far beyond their own geographical territory for standards of entertainment, talent, and aesthetic enjoyment. Locally gifted performers, if acknowledged, are thus more likely to move away to the few real centers of popular culture, while those remaining will be regarded by their public (and themselves) as second rate. Local taste cultures will also be seen by outsiders and possibly by their own defensive participants as quaint holdovers from times past. And finally, the automation of cultural production and its transference to the small screen accelerates the disbanding of many live-performance troupes, such as circuses, rodeos, and vaudeville, that find it increasingly difficult to compete for former patrons' time, money, and interest. The cultural consequences of centrally produced, standardized, slick, and nationally televised entertainment, therefore, include diminishing the number and quality of local productions and performers, lowering the amount of pride and interest taken in local and regional cultures, and narrowing the range of these cultures. This further increases the prestige and influence of the more homogeneous national popular culture.

A second implication, drawn by critics of mass culture and mass society, is that the *political* correlates of once distinctive local and regional cultural patterns will similarly decline in strength. That is, a nation whose population stays at home imbibing identical information and images will also become more homogeneous in cultural experiences and political knowledge and less amenable to mediating influences between the passive, possibly atomized individual and the state (Kornhauser, 1959; Wilensky, 1964). Here television, as the most national of the mass media, is seen to inhibit effectively political mobilization by interest groups independent of the state, thus serving as a primary agent of social control. As in the instances of time use

and the presumed threat to high culture, the simplest and perhaps sole solution to the problems posed by the abolitionist
position is to "oust the stranger from the house" and shut down
the medium.

Channel Diversity Position. A more realistic alternative is
suggested by a second group of concerned observers who accept
the continuing presence of television but wish to see its organization structure decentralized, the number of channels increased, and a greater degree of diversity in program content.
Cable television technology (discussed more fully in the concluding section) is admirably suited to this purpose, though
many of the same goals could be accomplished if existing stations relied less on the dominant networks and syndicators for
their programming and if more UHF channels were put into
operation. Under these conditions, several possible consequences can be anticipated. If, for example, the amount of time
invested by viewers in watching television remained constant,
they probably would see more entertainment programs featuring local or regional culture and performers; public affairs coverage of particular interest to members of each channel's viewing
audience would be very likely to rise also (exactly how much
would depend on policies adopted by the Federal Communications Commission, local performers' and craft unions, and the
costs of producing programs—which should decline with the advent of cheaper video production equipment). If, as industry
members maintain, viewer interest (and ratings) for such local
programs is low and people would choose to watch fewer hours,
then more direct patronage of local talent and culture might
well follow. Either way, local and regional cultures would be
vitalized by a decreased availability of the nationally dominant
popular programs that are now so well entrenched. An alternative version of more diversified, subcultural programming has
been proposed by Gans (1975). This would be directed, like
radio formats, to particular segments of the national audience.
Instead of focusing on issues and cultures of possible interest to
specific geographical localities, it would develop entertainment
and public affairs programs geared to particular demographic
segments, including the elderly, the poor, women, and minority
groups. Gans's proposition, unlike the others reviewed so far, is
that the impact of televised programs on culture and society is
minimal, and therefore it would be more equitable (at little
social cost) to provide each segment of the mass audience with
programs that it might prefer if only the choice was available.

Cultural Integration Position. The final interpretation of the cultural impact of television asserts that present network arrangements serve a variety of socially useful functions, agrees that the cultural influence of popular culture is substantial, and argues largely for a continuation of the present system. Following Durkheim (1964), it proposes that in contemporary America we already have a great diversity of economic, ethnic, cultural, and regional divisions that, further subdivided by a complex division of labor and patterns of occupational specialization, rely on a national, common popular culture to reintegrate and symbolically unify the many diverse elements. Television more than any other mass medium performs this important function by ensuring that virtually the entire population is exposed to the same jokes, sports events, presidential addresses, and dramatic fare. Consequently, if particular program genres are considered excessively violent or in poor taste, the solution is to insist on enriching or changing the content presented by existing networks rather than to encourage further cultural divisions by providing new channels and programs directed at each of the segments that now comprise the heterogeneous mass audience. In large part this has been the strategy followed by the Public Broadcasting System, with nationally distributed programs like "Sesame Street," and by groups seeking specific changes in the content offered by commercial networks, such as Action for Children's Television and organizations seeking a more positive portrayal of minority groups on popular television programs and commercials.

This position also sees network television as a cultural "melting pot" in which intergroup communication is facilitated when popular entertainment programs such as "M.A.S.H." and "All in the Family" present characters embodying different views on public issues, which provides the mass audience with information about how conflicting groups in society perceive the questions involved. Social psychologists often label such programs ineffective or harmful because they fail to convert viewers who agree with a negative character's position to the viewpoint of the positive characters (Vidmar and Rokeach, 1974). However, this criterion misses a larger point—that the key function most likely served is to expose the viewer and increase his or her awareness of differing tastes and views, all presented within a single broadcast. This type of intergroup communication, as characteristic of the old "Ed Sullivan Show" as of "All in the Family," is measured by whether viewers' information and awareness levels have risen rather than whether they were converted to a new value position. Finally, the cultural integration position argues that even broad educational purposes are best served by utilizing network facilities rather than by reaching selected target groups through separate programs on a less widely viewed channel. For example, a single episode of "All in the Family," in which Edith Bunker feared she had breast cancer, powerfully and effectively conveyed information to more people of all categories about a major health problem than did all of the episodes of "Feeling Good," an ill-fated series on public television devoted to health problems, which failed to reach the poorly educated viewers it most sought to inform.

It is important to note that each of the interpretations and policy positions just outlined is based on the same body of knowledge from social science. They differ in the conclusions reached because each seeks to relate what is known about television to different models of society. The abolitionist position conceives of American society as becoming too regimented, bureaucratic, and standardized. Television is seen as contributing to this problem, aggravating an already undesirable situation by providing a homogeneous mass culture for a mass society. The channel diversity position presents a less pessimistic model of recent social trends, suggesting the problems faced are more a matter of degree. Television's role is seen as a problem of organizational arrangement rather than as endemic to the medium itself. According to this position, a decentralization of network dominance would restore public attention to local culture and political affairs or to diverse national subcultures and thereby help deter nationwide trends toward cultural, and particularly televised, homogeneity. Finally, the cultural integration position conceives of society as already fragmented into stratified groups and in need of reintegration through shared symbols and a common culture. Here the precise content of that culture is less important than the fact that it be shared by all. Consequently, network television is seen as contributing to the social good by providing greater cultural cohesion. All of the three positions described agree on the facts about the organization of the industry and the content of its programs. To a lesser extent, all also share a common set of assumptions regarding the importance of television in America's popular culture and political processes and how audiences respond to the viewing experience.

Television and the Individual Viewer

While each of these institutional perspectives conceives of television as an important social force, the challenge of specifying the mechanisms by which individual audience members are influenced or affected is an exceedingly complex task. The topic of television's effects on individual viewers—as distinct from its impact on American culture and political institutions— has long been a topic of vigorous debate among social scientists.[8] Here, we provide a brief overview in the context of the three policy positions outlined.

A complete explanation about the influence of watching television on the individual viewer would have to take into account a great multitude of issues. At present, for example, we know how much time people spend viewing, but it remains unclear *why* individuals turn on the set, how television is watched and perceived, and to what degree viewers are involved while watching. In part, these remain mysteries because television diffused so rapidly throughout the country that there is hardly a population of nonviewers left to compare with the viewing audience. Instead, researchers have sought largely to infer effects through laboratory studies and sample surveys using structured questionnaires. Both techniques have generated few findings. A second limitation is in the narrow range of topics selected for study. Most research efforts have sought to ascertain either the effects of focused messages, such as advertisements for brand-name products, or of highly specific, discrete aspects of unfocused program content across genres, such as violent acts in dramatic or action-adventure entertainment. The coverage of political campaigns, first by radio networks and now television, has also been the topic of numerous studies, as have a wide variety of public health information campaigns. Historically the key questions investigated have been whether exposure to certain types of content presented by the mass media leads audience members (1) to alter their behavior measurably or (2) to alter their attitudes toward or opinions on specific topics. Out of these studies has emerged a fragile consensus of opinion among social scientists: There is negligible evidence that people's basic attitudes or behavior patterns are changed in direct response to exposure to individual programs, news stories, and short-term information campaigns (Klapper, 1960; C. Wright, 1975). Numerous studies have found that people tend to select the kinds of information and entertainment formats that are least threatening and to interpret or perceive news stories or dramatic plots in terms of existing preconceptions. Rather than affecting the viewer directly, television influences through a set of mediating factors—family and friends, organizations, past experience, and other social ties—that act as a perceptual filter through which the content is interpreted (Katz and Lazarsfeld, 1955; Janowitz and Shils, 1948).[9] Excepting times of widespread social unrest and confusion or when such mediating primary group affiliations are lacking, a widely drawn though exaggerated inference from these findings is that it does not make much difference what television program content is because it is unlikely to affect viewers' attitudes or behavior.

These empirical findings historically helped quiet popular fears about the vulnerability of audiences to political propaganda and the utilization of broadcasts to manipulate the attitudes and behavior of a susceptible mass audience. In debunking earlier stimulus-response-based theories of a direct, unmediated link between mass communication and individual action, social science research also challenged similar psychological assumptions underlying concern over mass media effects on individuals that were proposed by three of the schools supporting the abolitionist policy position: medical practitioners (Wertham, 1954; Rothenberg, 1975), humanistic critics (N. Jacobs, 1961), and some political theorists (Kornhauser, 1959). Where the contentions of these groups pertain directly to questions that have been examined by survey research methods, most of the evidence points *away* from any direct effects. The degree of overlap between topics of mutual concern here, however, is only partial; many of the issues addressed by the mass culture critique, for example, do not pertain to the impact on individuals or the short-term effects of popular culture, and others simply are not amenable to survey research (or possibly any other social science research).

Because individuals interpret the same information differently, it is all the more important to supporters of the cultural integration position that all viewers be exposed to similar television fare. This accords with a model of society that conceives of the mass media less as an agent of social control (to be feared) than as a force for holding together a divided society. Hence, some common information may be presumed to get through to audiences of the same programs despite the phenomenon of selective perception. In contrast, if everyone were to view different programs from multiple sources, then any likelihood of

television fostering or maintaining a common culture would disappear altogether (Brunner and Crecine, 1971; Klein, 1973).

Proponents of the channel diversity position are more
divided over the implications of the empirical findings. Gans
(1975) has suggested that precisely because individuals do *not*
appear to be affected directly by its program content, television
should become more diverse so that groups can have more
choices over the aesthetic contents and viewpoints in the programs that they watch. Alternatively, the findings of minimal
effects are implicitly rejected where others contend local culture and political affairs would be supported more actively if
they received more prominent attention from television. This
latter view is held most strongly by proponents of community-
oriented cable television. Within the channel diversity framework, then, the proposed decentralization of the medium would
work either to increase interest and participation in local culture and political affairs or to provide people with a more
democratic choice over program content, even if they still chose
to watch the same programs as at present. Much of the basis for
this difference in perspective rests in opposing assumptions
about how seriously the television audience is involved with the
programs it views.

While basic attitudes and behaviors are quite seldom affected by single programs or information campaigns, the mass
media may be far more effective in conveying generalized information to the mass audience than studies following traditional
research designs have so far suggested (Clarke and Kline, 1974).
This criterion for assessing television's effects, less frequently
employed in communication research, has yielded interesting
examples of how individuals may learn from and receive information through television. For example, heavy viewers, exposed
to frequent weather reports, exhibit greater knowledge than
light viewers of what terms like *low pressure zone* mean and
how such terms relate to the likelihood of rain (Robinson,
1972). Similarly, while viewers may not *choose* which candidate
to vote for as a result of election coverage, television news programs and campaign advertisements repeatedly announce and
convey information about coming elections: Viewers are inun-
dated with information about which issues and personalities are
most likely to be in contention. As a general rule, audience
members are more likely to recall portions of the messages conveyed when mass media content is focused and repeated than
when information is transmitted irregularly and with no distin-

guishing focus. Hence, consumers' awareness of television-advertised brands is extraordinarily high, whereas for occasional names in the news, such as the secretary of defense and guests on a talk show, awareness levels are characteristically, and not unexpectedly, lower. Often, the subjects of focused messages (advertised goods and services, for example) are also more salient to the viewer because people are familiar with and use them, whereas if a civil war breaks out in a faraway land, for instance, it is usually unclear (except to newsmen and educators) why the fact is worth remembering. In short, television's messages vary in the degree to which they are repetitive, narrowly focused, and salient to audience members; each of these variables must be distinguished when we seek to gauge the effect of television content on the mass public.

While these distinctions have proved to be very useful in enabling social scientists to explain why certain types of content may or may not affect the viewing audience, there remain a host of tantalizing, puzzling issues on the relation between contemporary television's images and their influence on the individual viewer. Social scientists and humanists are presently concerned with but find it quite difficult to answer such questions as: What are the likely long-range effects of individuals' daily exposure to network television's version of political affairs, comedy, drama, sports, and other elements of American culture? What roles does television viewing play in the socialization of children and in the images that various groups in American society hold of themselves and of others? What are the various styles of viewing employed by members of the mass audience? At what point should a correlate of viewing be conceived as an effect of viewing? And what additional latent and manifest functions are served by television? These types of questions are both underresearched and not amenable to study through either conventional laboratory experiments or survey research techniques. There is some evidence concerning each of these topics, however, and widespread interest in learning a great deal more.

For example, psychiatrists have observed a narrowing in the range of children's fantasies during the last twenty years as many youngsters increasingly see themselves in roles of television heroes—a relatively small group, with associated plot lines and characterizations that limit the range of imaginable possibilities (Kaplan, 1972). Among adult viewers, Gerbner and Gross (1976a, 1976b) found that when the education factor is controlled, heavy viewers believe the world to be more dangerous,

violent, and untrustworthy than do matched individuals who
are light viewers.

To determine the impact of television also brings up the
question of the criteria used in defining a significant effect. Is it
an effect if the amount of information people learn or perceive
about political and entertainment personalities, manners, popular styles, fads, and fashions is associated with watching television or with conversations in which others speak of what they
saw on television? Or should the definition more strictly require
that audience members take a specific action or undergo a conversion of attitude toward a subject as a result of the viewing
experience? Social scientists have traditionally selected the latter definition of effects, whereas humanists, advertising agencies, and political candidates include the broader informational
criteria.[10] If 5 percent of the viewing audience tries a new brand
of toothpaste or seriously considers voting for a different candidate because of a television commercial, the effect is enormous
from the standpoint of the election outcome or the product
sales curve, but it is likely to be seen as far less significant by
survey researchers concerned with effects on the entire viewing
audience. The importance of analyzing the content, formats,
and genres of television offerings is more strongly emphasized
by humanists than social scientists, because humanists believe
that there are limits on the number of ways common information can be selectively perceived or distorted. Also, humanists
maintain that changes in the presentation of cultural norms
(which will affect the individual indirectly) may be fruitfully
studied independently of how survey respondents interpret
what is shown at a single point in time (DeFleur and Ball-
Rokeach, 1975; Allen, in press).

A similar topic, subject to various interpretations by social scientists, concerns the relationship of television's effects on
individuals to its political and cultural functions in society.
Many of the programs are designed to emphasize situations and
behavior patterns with which viewers, at least urban ones, are
already familiar. Combined with knowledge that viewers tend to
interpret what they see according to preexisting attitudes,
a frequent interpretation of the viewing experience is that its
effect is minimal because both its content and the perceptions
of events portrayed serve only to reinforce the prior beliefs of
the audience. Depending on one's model of society, however,
such media-supported reinforcement of existing patterns may
constitute either an insignificant effect since it fails to act as a

change agent (Klapper, 1960) or a major consequence since it acts as an agent of social control by discouraging change (Schiller, 1973; Gerbner and Gross, 1976b). An additional effect or function, proposed initially by Lazarsfeld and Merton (1957) and still apt, is the conferral of status upon *anyone* who receives coverage by the mass media. Status conferral is an effect, whereby the television audience perceives those publicized as important simply by virtue of having been selected for such coverage.

Many students of mass communication are presently seeking to elaborate existing theories and models to include greater consideration of additional latent functions, multiple definitions of communication effects, content analysis, and the long-range impact of television on society. At the same time, both communications technology and the political and organizational arrangements that largely determine mass media content have been undergoing dramatic changes, which may in turn foster a host of new models relating television and its audience to society.

Prospects for Cable Television

"To the American public, there is apparently no such thing as too much television. . . . The size of the potential makes it plain that there is a bonanza waiting for cable if it can crack the big markets" (*Business Week,* 1969, pp. 101, 105).

Until recently, the term *television* has been closely associated with program content created for a national audience and offered by the major commercial networks. As stated throughout this chapter, however, such a description tells more about the organizational arrangement of television's commercial operation than about the medium itself. Theoretically, each locally licensed station could present many more hours of programming created specifically for viewers in its geographic coverage area. In addition, the initial choice by the Federal Communications Commission to limit the number of channels to about nine hundred was as much a political as a technologically required decision (Bagdikian, 1971; Kittross, 1960, 1975). As television has developed, however, the combination of network arrangements and a relative scarcity of channels makes the production of more local programs impractical because it would require a large financial investment per program, and (worse yet, from the industry's standpoint) also lead to a decrease in the size of the audience for each program. In this context the advent of cable, or community antenna television (CATV), presents a means of altering television's long-time focus on mass entertainment and news at the national level. Combined with the decreasing cost of cameras and film, cable technology's capacity to provide from forty to eighty separate channels, clearly transmitted to home receivers through coaxial cables, stimulates visions of ongoing coverage of city council and local school board meetings, more educational channels, more broadcasting of programs appealing to viewers with specialized interests and tastes, and greater access for individuals and groups who wish to convey ideas and information to interested viewers. In addition, CATV technology can provide better reception and direct, two-way communication between sender and receiver so that city agencies and advertisers, for example, could arrange for immediate feedback from viewers in response to televised messages. Separate channels could also be allocated for the private transmission of personal and business correspondence, newspaper columns, and microfilmed books from the public library.

Cable television began as a means of improving television set reception and has gradually expanded to the point where about 10 percent of U.S. households now subscribe to it. The key issues surrounding the questions of how rapidly CATV will continue to be adopted and what kinds of programs it will offer are financial and political. Cable firms, like commercial broadcasters, are privately operated, profit-seeking corporations and the sole investors in and major promoters of the new technology. Like other broadcasting corporations, they, too, will seek to offer the most profitable programs to the largest possible audience to the extent permitted by the regulatory agencies of government. Significantly, the regulation of cable firms has so far been divided between approximately 1500 municipalities that have awarded cable franchises to operate within their boundaries and the Federal Communications Commission. Unlike conventional radio and TV broadcasters, who are licensed solely by the federal government, CATV firms must also be licensed by municipalities in order to lay their cables on city property. The requirement that each cable firm be franchised by the cities in which it operates in turn provides municipal administrations and community groups greater leverage over how the larger channel spectrum of cable television will be divided up by the cable operator. For example, will there be a provision and funding for a public access channel? For educational channels? For a channel that city agencies can use to reach citizens?

Gradually, the Federal Communications Commission has extended its jurisdiction over these questions, and over time national rather than local standards of CATV programming and channel allocation are likely to evolve. National chains of cable companies, supplanting local ownership, have already emerged. Until a wide variety of legal, jurisdictional, and economic questions are resolved, a clear picture of how CATV will be integrated into the existing mass communication system will not emerge. At this point, however, several alternative scenarios can be suggested, with some estimates made of the probability of each.

The first possibility, and also the most attractive to proponents of the channel diversity position, is quite exciting while at the same time meeting the greatest resistance from the cable television industry. Although industry spokesmen themselves at first exhibited enthusiasm for this approach, its basic appeal— the promise of more special interest and local coverage as a *supplement* to what network TV now offers—is limited to a relatively small minority of citizens who are both dissatisfied with current television fare and willing to pay a monthly fee to receive special interest programs of limited appeal to the mass audience. Most cable operators ceased encouraging expectations of more local programs as soon as their legal challenges to barriers against importing "distant signals" (TV channels from other cities) and obtaining rights to what are currently network television offerings, such as movies and sports events, received some support from government agencies. In addition, current projections call for the establishment of CATV networks offering programs very similar to what presently appears on existing commercial networks and for increasing the number of distant signals "imported" as soon as the Federal Communications Commission lifts present restrictions on these activities.

A related, early scenario for the development of CATV was that it would offer entertainment (operas and roller derbys, for example) as well as public affairs programs prepared for select segments of the mass television audience, much as specialized radio formats today have divided up the mass audience into target subpopulations. This vision, also appealing to many proponents of the channel diversity position, might possibly compete successfully with television programs designed to appeal to everybody and thereby serve to effectively decentralize network television. Although this scenario, focusing on the demographic characteristics of the audience rather than its place of residence, is potentially more viable (for it is national in scope and program production costs would be lowered accordingly), it also is far less attractive to cable operators than the prospect of their own national networks to compete with the present television industry.

The arguments in favor of CATV becoming the new showcase for first-run movies and sports spectaculars are that this program content will stimulate consumers to adopt the new technology on a large scale; consequently, some of the resulting profits from mass programming could be channeled into community service. Without these profits, it is maintained, there would be no funds or audience available to fulfill the ideals of the earlier scenarios. With favorable rulings from the courts and the Federal Communications Commission, proponents suggest that this must be the direction in which CATV moves or else it simply will not develop as a new factor in the American mass communication system. The present television broadcasting industry opposes these plans with essentially the same argument —that is, its own ability to provide public affairs programming is contingent on profits from mass entertainment fare—and argues against permitting the newer cable interests to draw these programs away from their present position on advertiser-supported, free television. A possible alternative, though less likely, is that cable television will be declared a public utility, much like the telephone company, whose mission would be to lease channels to any producers of programs wishing to use its transmission facilities. Such an arrangement would bar cable operators from producing programs themselves or setting up their own cable networks; it is often suggested that this arrangement, if a large part of the public subscribed to cable television, would successfully open the air waves to all interested parties. As fewer people would view each program, this scenario also envisions an end to the domination of television by a few networks, each seeking to attract the mass audience (Dean, 1973; Smith, 1972). If cable television fails to deliver on its technological potential to provide improved programs for specialized audiences and for educational and civic purposes, it will join radio and television as private communications media that could have done so but whose organizational and financial arrangements combined with an absence of political regulation and public demand to prevent these types of programs from being featured (Scott, 1972). At the same time, many municipal agencies in charge of franchising cable firms have succeeded in reserving several channels for nonprofit, noncommercial uses.

More generally, there is a widespread belief among communications experts that the long-term trend for television and all of the mass media is towards greater diversity and audience fragmentation (Maisel, 1973; Bogart, 1967, 1973; Bagdikian, 1971). Even if cable television is not widely adopted, increased demand for diversity could be met by existing UHF stations if they received appropriate advertiser and public support. While political forces will continue to partially brake trends toward greater diversity in television programming, we can still expect that the trend will accelerate over the next twenty-five years. This projection of increased diversity again raises many of the same issues we have discussed in the framework of policy positions favoring the decentralization of network television news and entertainment versus the position that the social and cultural cohesion of American society is best maintained by the present arrangements.

Summary

Since 1950, television has increasingly become the dominant medium of mass entertainment and news in the United States. Its programs and orientation are urban and national in scope, tending to downplay cultural differences between regions, cities, races, classes, and all other sources of potential differentiation. The organizational structure of three commercial networks and the Public Broadcasting System insures that each part of the nation has access to virtually identical programs at all times, contributing further to a common popular culture.

Television's impact on America's political system and cultural life has been assessed by many observers and from numerous standpoints. Generally it is believed that television's influence has been greatest on American institutions and smallest on the behavior of individual viewers. The same body of information, however, often is interpreted differently by critics and advocates, ranging from those holding an abolitionist position to others stressing that television, as a cultural integrator, serves well as America's national mass medium. As a set of commercial organizations, television as we know it is intimately bound up with the desire of national advertisers to reach viewers between the ages of eighteen and forty-nine living in metropolitan areas. This mandate provides much of the basis on which programs are selected for production and distribution. Television has been so successful in attracting this audience that all other mass media—newspapers, magazines, radio, and motion pictures—have been forced to change their formats in order to continue attracting audiences and financial support. Despite experts' predictions that television will become more diverse in the long run, the outlook for the near future is for little or no major changes in the medium's operation. If more channels become available—through cable television, UHF stations, videocassettes, other technologies, or governmental encouragement of greater organizational or program diversity—then some transformation of the television medium away from national and perhaps towards more local programming may be expected. Barring such developments, television will continue as the most pervasive of the mass media.

Notes

1. The number of public television stations has grown from 56 in 1961 to 227 in 1972, at which time about 70 percent of the American audience could receive signals from a public television station. More generally, over 75 percent of the U.S. population report receiving three or more channels, and 15 percent say they receive eight or more (Bower, 1973). Only 3 percent of American households receive less than three channels. *Neither the number of channels received nor the quality of programs (for example, first-run or rerun programs) appears to make any difference in the amount of viewing time per household* (Bogart, 1972). The average amount of time spent watching television by individuals has increased in nearly every year in which national surveys have been conducted. Technically (with proper aerials), the typical American home is within viewing range of nearly seven television stations, including VHF and UHF. Where there are more than three channels, usually either network programs from nearby areas are duplicated or programs from an independent or public television station are available. People living on the West Coast watch slightly less television than people in the Midwest, but city size makes no difference in the amount of viewing time (LoSciuto, 1972): By 1972, viewers in major cities were watching television as much as viewers in rural areas, and 35 percent of U.S. homes (with 43 percent of the population) had more than one television set.

2. From "The Lawrence Welk-Hee Haw Counterrevolution Polka" by Vaughn Horton. © Happy Go Lucky Music, Nashville, Tenn.

3. This is a relatively recent development. Before 1970, the commercial value of network television programs was judged in terms of the sheer number of viewers attracted. Since then, however, the demographic composition (age and income) of each program's audience has become a crucial factor as well (L. Brown, 1971). The turning point was reached when the industry replaced popular entertainment programs appealing to rural and older viewers (Red Skelton, Lawrence Welk, "The Beverly Hillbillies," "Hee Haw," and "Gunsmoke") with others that attracted a wealthier urban and suburban audience ("Columbo," "All in the Family," and "Sanford and Son").

4. The demography of set ownership and time use was discussed briefly in the beginning of this chapter, and suggestions concerning television's latent and manifest functions appear throughout. None of these will be taken up separately in this section.

5. There often is substantial variation, however, among cities in the extent and quality of local reporting by both the broadcast and print media. Detailed discussion, critiques, and city-by-city comparisons are published bimonthly in the *Columbia Journalism Review* and annually in the Alfred DuPont-Columbia University *Surveys of Broadcast Journalism*, edited by Marvin Barrett.

6. The recurrent question of whether (and how much) network television news is biased to the left or right is symptomatic of its high visibility. To date, few scholars have analyzed the direction of bias or agreed on appropriate coding categories. By and large, where nonscholars have presented content analyses of network news, their findings are based on procedures that violate scientific norms of objectivity and thus have not been taken seriously by social scientists. Gans (1970) and others have noted that the format of dramatized presentations chopped into short time segments requires an oversimplification of issues, and that canons of journalistic news judgment dictate that bad news is more newsworthy than good news.

7. This statement, while especially the case in the context of its present organization structure in the United states, may also be true at a more generic level. I am unaware of any country that has employed television as a mass medium primarily for purposes other than entertainment or diversion.

8. For excellent recent summaries, see DeFleur and Ball-Rokeach (1975), Weiss (1969), Bogart (1973), and Robinson and Bachman (1972).

9. The sole exception to this generalization concerns young children, who do not have many prior experiences through which to interpret what they see. Here, there is some modest research support for the proposition that young viewers become more aggressive as a result of exposure to violent programs (Rubinstein, Comstock, and Murray, 1972).

10. This informational function of the mass media is stressed, however, in some social science models, mainly of innovation diffusion (Rogers and Shoemaker, 1971) and marketing (Ray, 1973). These emphasize the significance of mass media in increasing awareness levels about topics, rather than directly influencing behavior in the short run.

14

Print Media
in Urban Society

David Street
W. Paul Street

Reflecting his early background as a journalist, the preeminent urban sociologist Robert E. Park saw the intimate connection between communication and community and did an early study using the geographical outreach of newspaper circulation as an indicator of metropolitan dominance (Park, 1929). For Park, newspaper circulation not only reflected but helped define the community. More generally, essential to Park's theoretical view

Note: This chapter benefits from the pioneering work on the print media by Janowitz (1967), whose study of the urban neighborhood press in the "community of limited liability" dissuades us from overdrawing the distinction between gemeinschaft and gesellschaft in either the press or the community. The chapter also benefits from critical readings and suggestions by Morris Janowitz, Paul M. Hirsch, and John W. C. Johnstone.

was the assumption that communication transformed subsocial ecological processes into the social. A modern corollary is the notion that social constructions shape the ecological order.

This chapter makes connections among patterns of social change in communities, in society as it is linked to the community, and in the print media. It focuses on the period of 1920 to the present. Two initial questions guide the work:

1. To what extent has urbanization in its advanced form contributed to and reflected a "mass society" model of community, in which the focus of attention is directed away from local and regional events and toward the larger society? What effects has this had on the community? We have good reason to think that television fits a mass society model well, but what of the print media? Does the "diffuse phase" of urbanization end or diminish the influence of the community press? (See Hirsch's Chapter Thirteen on television and Hawley's Chapter One on the diffuse phase of urbanization.) Also, to what extent do changes in the print media alter community and society?

2. To what extent has urbanization and its correlates (such as the advance in education and literacy) produced changes in media content? Have gemeinschaft themes (or rural values) given way to gesellschaft themes (or urban values)? Have social changes transformed the prime emphases of mass culture? Have the print media become "massified," standardized, and bereft of community?

This chapter will provide indirect and partial answers to these questions and will raise new queries along the way. We will first present a relatively comprehensive analysis of change and problems in the structure of the newspaper media. We will look in particular at the suburbanization of the press, the rise of newspaper chaining, and problems in the contributions both local and metropolitan newspapers make to the political functioning of urban society. Second, we shall present a study of social change in the readership and themes of popular magazines and best-selling books from 1920 to the present. In assessing patterns of both magazines and books, we will be seeking to see whether the development of an urbanized society is accompanied by basic shifts in their content.

Newspapers and Continuing Urbanization

From 1920 to 1975 the population of the United States slightly more than doubled (from 105.7 million to 212.8), but

the number of daily and weekly newspapers published in the
country declined, the dailies by more than 22 percent and the
weeklies by more than 36 percent. Relevant data are in Table 1.

Table 1. Number of Newspapers, Daily Circulation, and
U.S. Population, 1920-1975.

Year	Number of Dailies	Total Daily Circulation (in millions)	U.S. Population (in millions)	Ratio, Daily Circulation to Population	Number of Weeklies
1920	2,343	31.9	105.7	0.30	13,964
1930	2,248	44.1	122.8	0.36	11,159
1940	2,015	39.4	131.7	0.30	10,860
1950	1,894	52.3	150.7	0.35	9,794
1960	1,841	57.6	179.3	0.32	8,959
1970	1,825	62.0	203.2	0.31	8,891
1975	1,819	59.3	212.8	0.28	8,824

Note: Data pertain to the forty-eight and then the fifty states. Daily circulation figures exclude data on Sunday editions. All figures on newspapers except daily circulation come from the *Ayer Directory of Publications* volumes for each of the years
indicated.

Total daily circulation almost kept pace with the population
growth, however, as a smaller number of larger papers emerged
overall. The ratio of daily circulation to population fluctuated
considerably over the period, reflecting economic trends, variations in the proportions of the population of reading age, and
other factors. Yet this ratio was almost identical in 1920 and
1970, at 0.30 and 0.31, respectively. Only in the more recent
years do the data show a value below this level—0.28 in 1975.
One result of the reduction in the number of dailies coupled
with rapid urbanization is a dramatic falling off in the number
of urban places that have their own dailies, from 90 percent in
1880 to 29 percent in 1961 (Bagdikian, 1971, p. 80).

    The readership of weekly newspapers as a whole and of
the various categories, such as "country," "small town," and
"city neighborhood" weeklies, is difficult to estimate. This is
true not only because no comprehensive compilation is made of
weekly circulations but also because many of the small-town
papers are becoming suburban papers and a multitude of publications exist at the fringes of the definition of *weekly* (for
example, "shoppers" that contain some news or newspapers
that community organizations publish regularly only during pre-
election periods). Yet it seems clear that weekly readership is at

least as great as ever. Janowitz (1967) and Sim (1969) provide evidence that although the number of different weekly publishers is declining, the number of readers is not. Seiden (1974, p. 36) concludes that the readership of weeklies is growing. He estimates that 8,800 weeklies published in 1973 had a combined circulation exceeding 28 million, a growth in circulation of over 45 percent in fifteen years. Further, the economies of centralized printing make it possible to start new weeklies with little capital (Bowers, 1969), and a trend can be seen in American cities toward a development of neighborhood newspapers and newsletters produced by citizen boards and volunteers (Ward and Gaziano, 1976). Sim points out that the weekly, particularly the rural or small-town paper, with its syndicated features and small news items about local people and events, is generally viewed with tolerant amusement by publishers of other papers. On the other hand, he suggests that those who "deprecate the vitality of the weekly might well note that even after a half-century of decline the community weeklies outnumber all other units of news-reporting media—dailies, radio and television stations, and news magazines—though no one of them has the visibility of the *New York Times, Los Angeles Times,* or *Time Magazine*" (Sim, 1969, pp. 3, 7). In his summary of changes in the local community press from 1950 to 1966, Janowitz (1967, pp. ix-xiv) concludes that not only has the suburban press grown rapidly, but also modest gains have been found in the inner-city press.

Although daily circulation over the long run has been relatively stable, shifts since 1950 have been greeted suspiciously in the industry. Titling his article "Prosperous Newspaper Industry May Be Heading for a Decline," Grotto (1974) sees 1950 as a watershed and contrasts the substantial growth in the general population from 1950 to 1970 (up 34.8 percent) with the slow growth in daily circulation over this period (up 18.5 percent). He also points to a marked decline in the ratio of advertising expenditures in daily newspapers to the GNP since 1950. The recent decline in the daily newspaper comes in part through small but steady diminution in daily newspaper circulation per family, from 1.28 in 1945 to 1.05 in 1967. This decline is thought to result from some dropping off of newspaper purchasing at the highest educational levels, less buying of two or more papers per family, a reduction in the number of two-paper cities, and a dying out of a number of the larger papers (Bagdikian, 1971, pp. 54-55).

The Suburbanized Press. Patterns of change in newspaper publication and circulation make the big-city newspapers less dominant over their metropolitan hinterlands. (For a study of papers in the Los Angeles metropolitan area, see Lyle, 1967.) Circulation patterns of successful big-city dailies once correlated highly with trends of population growth of both their cities and metropolitan areas. The pattern of collapse or merger of large-city papers so well publicized in the case of New York has been common to many American urban centers; the decrease in central-city dailies has come to be counterbalanced by a rise in the number of suburban dailies. Thus in the 10 largest SMSAs in the nation as defined in 1967, the net number of dailies was 205 in 1922, 181 in 1940, and 168 in 1950 and 1970 (Sterling, 1975, p. 247). Similarly, the number of dailies in the 25 largest SMSAs (in 1967) fell from 302 in 1922 to a relative plateau of 249 in 1940, 236 in 1950, and 246 in 1970. A similar pattern obtains in the 100 largest SMSAs. The overall net loss of papers has come elsewhere, in the smaller SMSAs or outside them.

Eberhard (1974) provides a striking portrait of the suburbanization of newspaper growth and of the loss of dominance of the major city papers in a study of a sample of daily newspapers that were published in both 1940 and 1970. Looking at newspaper "penetration," the ratio of circulation to occupied housing units, he finds no change overall during the thirty-year period. However, he finds that in 1970 penetration was inversely related to size of SMSA: In SMSAs with populations under 250,000, penetration was 52 percent in the metropolitan area and 51 percent in the home county; in SMSAs of a quarter million to a million, penetration was 43 percent in the larger area and 47 percent in the home county; in SMSAs of a million or more, 31 percent in the larger area and 39 percent in the home county. Over the thirty-year period, he found suburban papers making great gains—circulation rising 242 percent within home counties, and city papers in the larger SMSAs losing penetration by about 10 percent. It is noteworthy that this decline took place in the face of many mergers; the papers Eberhard studied were indeed the "successful" big-city papers and still they could not keep pace.

The suburbanization of newspaper growth is an uneven process. A goodly number of existing small-town dailies expand and modernize, seeking to capitalize on the opportunities provided by urban growth and on the potentials of advertising revenues of new shopping centers. Some weeklies upgrade them-

selves into dailies. Some papers die out in the face of new competition, and others remain parochial small-town papers that are
little affected by surrounding change. An occasional *Newsday*
(the Long Island paper) arises and attempts to appeal to an entire metropolitan subregion. Finally, big-city papers may attempt specialized regional suburban editions or the creation of
satellite publications in the suburbs.

A decline in penetration in the cities becomes understandable simply on the basis of the out-migration to suburbia
of people who are generally heavy readers of newsprint: the
better educated; persons in skilled, professional, or managerial
positions; the affluent; and persons aged thirty to fifty-four
(Bagdikian, 1971, p. 49). Further, a sound argument can be
made that the suburbanization of newspapers is functionally
necessary because the American newspaper is fundamentally
localistic. Grotto, Larkin, and DePlois (1975) found unsur-
prisingly that readers of a small daily newspaper perceived it as
a "source of local information." Various polls of local officials
and the public establish the general perception that newspapers
are far superior to other media on local affairs. A study of city
managers in cities of over 100,000 population found 51 percent
reporting newspapers as highly influential on their public affairs, with only 8 percent saying the same about television and 2
percent about radio (Bagdikian, 1971, pp. 81-82). The press is
fundamentally differentiating and localizing, while American
TV is fundamentally nationalizing and, when it focuses on
urban life, overrepresentative of the small number of cities in
which the networks own their own stations. Indeed, the fact
that U.S. newspapers are so localized when most other nations
have national-circulation newspapers can be explained as deriving in large part from the American political structure:

> The fundamental reason for this persistent localism
> in American news institutions is a peculiarity in American
> political organizations and the prevailing pattern of fam-
> ily money spending. More governmental functions are left
> to the local level. . . . Schools, property taxes, land use,
> public health, large areas of business regulation . . . are
> controlled by locally elected and . . . controlled bodies.
> . . . These locally controlled policies have maximum im-
> mediate impact on family life, such as schooling for chil-
> dren, design and location of homes, routes of local high-
> ways, and rates of personal property taxes. Such

decisions are made by a complicated but highly localized
set of political bodies . . . 18,000 municipalities and
17,000 townships . . . 500,000 local government units of
one kind or another directly elected by local residents.
. . . No national newspaper or national broadcast news
program can tell the local citizen what he needs or wants
to know about these local activities that affect his family
life. . . . What is relevant to one local jurisdiction is only
minimally significant for the next. . . . Another powerful
force for localism in the mass media is the large amount
of local money spending by the average family. . . . The
great majority . . . done locally. . . . Thus, there is both a
political and an economic base for the localized pattern
of American news media [Bagdikian, 1971, pp. 72-74].

With the large cities suffering a decline in resources, advertisers, and readership, many inner-city neighborhoods lose
their attractiveness to big-city dailies as places for promotion
and detailed coverage, despite the papers' economic and ideological commitments to the city. Seiden (1974, p. 25) sees the
situation of the big-city dailies as follows:

What lies behind the sudden, desperate pressure for
newspaper circulation in the nation's big cities? The explanation is found in the increasing decentralization of
America's urban centers. As the wealthy and middle class
whites move into the suburbs the retail shopping center
and department store branches follow them. And so does
the newspaper circulation and advertising revenue that
supported the old, established, big city dailies. . . . Newspapers are not becoming technologically obsolete. Rather, their markets are changing location and they are
now in a state of transition. The impact of these changes
is greatest in the major cities.

Specialized Papers. To speak of the suburbanization of
the press as a master trend does not deny the persistence and
development of alternative, specialized segments of the press.
Many are rooted in urban-based racial and ethnic groupings,
most prominently among blacks. Some of the earlier leaders of
the traditional black media have suffered death by integration
of their readership and personnel into the heretofore white
press—as with the *Pittsburgh Courier*'s drop in circulation from

247,000 in 1945 to 48,800 in 1974, or the *Chicago Defender*'s parallel drop from 202,000 to 33,300 (Seiden, 1974, p. 37). The incorporation of blacks into the media was seen as imperative once reflection on the 1960s riots brought a recognition that the media has almost totally disregarded minority groups (National Advisory Commission on Civil Disorders, 1968; Johnson, Sears, and McConahay, 1971). Nationally, however, very few blacks have penetrated the editorial ranks of the news media. A survey of daily and weekly newspeople in 1971 found only 3.9 to be black, and less than 3.0 percent if those in the black press are omitted (Johnstone, Slawski, and Bowman, 1976).

In 1974 there were (including magazines) 163 black-oriented publications with a total circulation of 5.1 million—or nearly one product for each black family in the land. This institution is highly centralized, however: almost 40 percent of the circulation comes from three publications: *Ebony*, 1.2 million monthly; *Jet*, 565,000 weekly; and *Muhammad Speaks*, 530,000 weekly (Seiden, 1974, p. 37). In counterbalance, Janowitz (1967, p. xii) attributes a decline of the black press in Chicago to the continuation or rise of local neighborhood papers in areas that had become black; territorial organization ultimately emerged as in the city at large.

Foreign-language periodicals are still significant. In 1974 there were 341 general interest periodicals published in twenty-six different languages with a combined circulation of over 2 million. The largest group was 29 Spanish-language newspapers, which had a combined circulation of about 450,000. Also noteworthy are underground papers. The first of these publications came in 1964. Seiden (1974) estimates that by 1970 there were 450 such papers, with an estimated combined circulation of about 5 million. Johnstone, Slawski, and Bowman (1976) estimate 800 alternative newspapers around 1970, with 4,800 editorial personnel. The underground papers with the largest circulations were the *Village Voice*, with 120,000 circulation; the *Los Angeles Free Press*, 95,000; *Berkeley Barb*, 85,000; and *East Village Other*, 65,000. In sharp contrast to the underground press is the huge religious press, which produces 1,300 religiously oriented newspapers and periodicals. This serves the largest specialized audience. Many of the publications have very small circulations, but nineteen major religious periodicals, each with circulations over 400,000, have a combined circulation of over 30 million (Seiden, 1974, pp. 34-38).

There is also a small partially nationalized press, reflected mostly in the readership of the *Wall Street Journal* (circulation of 1.46 million in several regional editions), the *Christian Science Monitor* (173,000), a substantial part of the readership of *The New York Times* (842,000 daily, 1.5 million Sunday), and some portion of the readership of the *Washington Post* (515,000 daily, 719,000 Sunday). The *Times'* circulation pales in comparison to the tabloid *New York Daily News* (1.9 million daily, 2.8 million Sunday), but of course the *News* gives no competition in its visibility and influence or in the education, affluence, and power of its readers. (All circulation figures derive from *Ayer Directory of Publications, 1976*). Nationalizing elements of the press have long come through the major wire and syndication services (AP and UPI), with the New York Times Service and the Los Angeles Times-Washington Post Service providing relatively elite syndications in recent years.

Competition and Chaining. The trends in rural, small-town, suburban, and urban newspaper publication and distribution certainly are not isolated from one another, though competition among and between newspapers is increasingly less discernible. Competition, as part of a conspiracy of social, economic, technological, and even political forces—all identifiable with urbanization—has eliminated many publishers though not many readers. Emery (1972, pp. 441-444) states:

> The Pulitzers, the Scrippses, the Gradys, and the Van Andas joined the Franklins, the Bennetts, and the Greeleys of the past who by achievement of new techniques and appeals enriched the total journalistic output. Their successes in creating newspapers with distinctly individualized appeals, combined with a doubling of the number of dailies between 1880 and 1900 . . . seemed to indicate that variety of competitive appeal was a permanent feature of American journalism. . . . But the forces which created the modern mass newspaper—industrialization, mechanization, and urbanization—made for less individuality and more standardization . . . as the twentieth century unfolded. . . . Competition for the mass market in the urban centers, and other socioeconomic pressures stemming from technological change, led to an inevitable contraction of newspaper publishing.

Emery cites the increases in one-newspaper towns and cities as evidence, pointing out that in 1900 more than half of all towns with a population of 15,000 or less had competing weeklies; by 1920 the proportion had dropped almost to 30 percent and by 1930 to less than one in four—so that by 1960 only about one town in twenty (5.2 percent) had competitive weekly papers (Emery, 1972, p. 630). Correspondingly, competing dailies existed in more than 60 percent of the 389 cities with dailies in 1900; of the 1,295 cities with dailies in 1920, almost half had more than one (Emery, 1972, p. 443); in 1971, of the 1,511 cities with dailies, only 37 had two or more competing dailies (Krieghbaum, 1972, p. 158). Additionally, only 5 cities had three or more competing dailies, and twenty-seven of the fifty states had no communities with competing dailies. Competition within the same city becomes difficult to support because advertisers want the largest audience for the least expenditure and prefer to support one expensive newspaper plant rather than two (Bagdikian, 1971, p. 127).

Citing these trends is not intended to suggest a grand cessation of competition. Between 1950 and 1967, when TV grew most rapidly, 330 dailies failed. But there were also 303 new dailies started, of which 166 survived, most successfully in cities of under a half million (Seiden, 1974, pp. 21-23). Certainly papers in single-daily towns do not gain noncompetitive access to revenues—particularly as many must compete with TV and radio for advertising dollars. The lengthened journey to work that accompanies suburbanization may reduce the newspaper habit, and the squeeze between commuting and endless early-evening TV news may be starting to hurt the big-city afternoon daily especially (*Wall Street Journal,* 1976). The issue here, however, is more political than economic, involving a drying up of alternative versions of local events. As Bagdikian (1971) has indicated, the scope of TV's local news tends to be regional, and local radio stations just "read the wire."

As daily competition has declined, the numbers of chains and syndicates has been increasing, interlocking not only dailies but also suburban weeklies and the older weeklies—and more recently linking them with other mass media (magazines, radio, and television). Hynds (1975, p. 169) reported that in 1970 more than half the nation's dailies, which as a group account for more than two thirds of the daily circulation, were owned by groups. "The combined holdings of groups, cross-media owners, conglomerates and firms related to the mass media encompassed almost three fifths of the daily newspapers, slightly more than three fourths of the television stations, and slightly more than one fourth of the AM and FM radio stations," he states. By the end of 1976, three out of five dailies belonged to chains (*New York Times,* 1977, p. 16). Chains owning weeklies are created on the one hand by careful corporate design, as when Time, Incorporated, came to own twenty-five weeklies in the Chicago area by 1969 (Seiden, 1974, pp. 36-37); on the other hand, they can emerge through a casual process in which printers acquire small papers that default on their bills. Thus competition and chaining occur in symbiotic fashion. Centralized printing of the weekly permits the starting of small papers with very little capital, allowing for competition in what had been one-newspaper areas, but again leading to concentration and perhaps again the end of competition (Bowers, 1969). Competition comes more and more between larger and larger combines (Clark, 1958, p. 76). A major change in organizational structure is the decline of competing papers within reading areas. The personal, the local, the national and international, and the cosmic in news are still in demand. The local press, as Janowitz (1967) points out, can still crusade for local causes, championing the community against outside evils and pressures, but its opponent is more likely to be those evils and forces than another newspaper.

Trends toward concentration and standardization are not new. The rural and small-town weeklies, beloved as indigenous "people" publications, felt the economic pinch during the Civil War and resorted to a device known as "patent insides" or "ready print," which was developed by a Baraboo, Wisconsin, publisher, A. N. Kellogg, first for use in his own paper but shortly vended to weeklies all about the nation (Mott, 1953, pp. 396-397). It started when, shorthanded by wartime personnel shortages, he ordered two pages (two and three) printed from type set for the *Wisconsin State Journal* at Madison with pages one and four left for him to fill with local news. Kellogg's example was soon followed by others, and space in the patent insides was sold shortly to advertisers who wished to reach readers on the "syndicate" subscription lists, thereby making the service cheaper for the weekly editors. Mott reports that by 1872 over one thousand papers were using such a service, Kellogg himself setting up a leading syndicate for the service in Chicago in 1865. Boiler plate, a casting of type or art materials, especially advertising stereotype, followed as part of the syndicated services serving both weeklies and dailies. This metal casting, which could be readily nailed to type-high wood blocks for assembly with other type, was later supplemented by mat materials (papier-mâché stereotypes), which could be nailed more cheaply than metal for those print shops with hot-metal facilities. Such services have been extended today—not to mention telephoto and computer linkages, so that standardized features and advertising, with pictorial and magazine-section inserts, are taken for granted. Whole magazine and cartoon sections are common "piggy backs," as discussed in the magazine section of this chapter.

The present growth of chains of dailies is unprecedented, however, and some distinctive features of the newspaper as an institution help to make it comprehensible. First, it is clear that the newspaper business *is* big and profitable. Daily papers take in close to $6 billion a year in advertising revenues (versus $3.7 billion for television, $1.3 billion for radio, and $1.2 billion for magazines) (Krieghbaum, 1972, p. 142), and newspaper profits run 12 to 15 percent on assets after taxes (Bagdikian, 1971, p. 131). Second, newspapers tend *not* to follow the paths of other large businesses. Although there is some tendency for them to become public corporations, they still tend to be held through family inheritance. Further, the limit is soon reached in the capacity of a newspaper to reinvest its profits in its own expansion. A successful paper gains a monopoly but has saturated its market if it is penetrating 80 percent of the homes, having no further local world to conquer. With high profits but seeking relief from taxes, it is pushed toward investment in chains or conglomerates. Third, while chains necessarily expand, they do not thereby become highly centralized or standardized. Because even chained papers must maintain separate production plants and staffs in each locality, expansion of the company does not involve the economies of scale found in many other expanding industries. As a result, many chains give their local outlets substantial autonomy (Bagdikian, 1971, pp. 75, 116-131).

The ultimate effect of widespread chaining on American communities is unclear, although Bagdikian (1971, pp. 117, 120) suggests some of the dangers. There is evidence that newspapers provide less local news when competition disappears, and certainly absentee owners are less likely to be sensitive to local problems. Further, there is little economic incentive to quality at least in the measurable short run; the monopolistic daily may be bought for its TV schedules, sports results, advertisements, or Ann Landers, no matter how undistinguished its news coverage. As a result, if a paper is to be excellent, some stimulus is required other than conventional corporate ambition, as in the

pride of the owning family: "The tradition of the personally involved owner is strong, and while it produces numerous cases of
entrenched moribundity, it also is the largest single factor in
papers of excellence" (Bagdikian, 1971, p. 117). Bagdikian suggests that chaining erodes this tradition, one that has traditionally played out through luck or "genetic roulette" as a community discovers whether the heir or son-in-law is an able leader
who produces a good daily or an ineffective leader who produces an indifferent one. Increasingly, there come to be too
many heirs and the paper is sold off to a chain, leaving the character and degree of local orientation of the newspaper un-
settled.

   Newspapers and the Politics of Urbanized Society. We
assume that newspapers are required to serve essential political
and social functions for their communities that no other institutions can provide. At the grass roots level, they provide the resident with the mundane reports on local persons, schedules,
ordinances, deaths, births, marriages, store openings, and sales
necessary for his or her local roles as citizen, consumer, and
neighborhood resident. We assume that this information facilitates the development of some minimum identifications with
the local community among residents. Neither radio nor television can provide these reports except on a sporadic, "slice of
life" basis. These functions are handled—well or poorly—by almost all weeklies and by many small-town dailies. The quality
of the journalism is less important than the question of covering
all the neighbors, insuring that no groups are ignored. Externally, the grass roots paper may play an important role by making a local community visible when otherwise it would not be, a
function especially important within the cities (on the political
importance of inner-city neighborhood papers, see Janowitz,
1967, pp. xiv-xvi).

   At the metropolitan level, newspapers are needed to provide reports on national, regional, and metropolitan developments and issues that are less superficial than those furnished by
radio or TV. Because in the urbanized society no community is
an island unto itself, newspapers must also mediate among the
factions, claims, and reputations of the various communities of
the metropolitan area, to make comprehensible the citizens' enlarged role and to produce a minimum necessary identification
that goes beyond the immediate local community. Many big-
city papers fulfill this function with varying effectiveness. Here
the quality of journalism is more important, but still significant
is the question of whether and how fully the paper incorporates

the diverse communities and groupings of the metropolitan area.

It follows that generally the urbanized society requires at least a two-tiered community press, at both the grass roots and metropolitan levels, although in some medium-sized cities that are relatively self-sufficient a single paper might be able to fill both roles. With these assumptions in mind, we can outline three crucial problems in the political functioning of newspapers in an urbanized society:

1. Excessive Parochialism. The grass roots press may be so "nice," so allergic to controversy, that it fails to provide the content necessary for resolving even very local issues. At the grass roots level, there is some corrective possible, as competing papers or newsletters can quickly be created out of the controversy heretofore suppressed (Ward and Gaziano, 1976).

When the metropolitan newspaper is monopolistic and parochial, there is no way to counterbalance. Apparently many newspapers in single-paper medium-sized cities resemble the "Little Old Daily of Dubuque" (Bagdikian, 1974) in combining excellent (and issue-oriented) coverage of local events with superficial national coverage. The latter is guaranteed by the fact that for reasons of cost the paper subscribes only to the press service wire furnishing condensed stories on international and national events (like TV coverage), although it takes the full wire reports on sports, financial, and regional news. Most American dailies assign their reporters exclusively to local news; an estimated 75 percent of state, national, and international news comes from the wire services (Roschco, 1975, p. 67). Apparently only 31 percent of American papers use more than one major wire or supplementary news service (not counting feature syndicates) (Schwarzlose, 1966), and most papers provide token or no coverage of events in their state capitals (Hoffman, 1967; Kane, 1967).

Parochialism is a critical problem with many suburban papers in light of the faltering penetration of the metropolitan press. Local news may be strongly overbalanced, and among newsmen in smaller cities and on smaller papers the style of reportage is more likely to be neutral and uncritical than investigative (Johnstone, Slawski, and Bowman, 1973, p. 533). Gans (1967, pp. 324-326) describes journalism as seen in his study of suburbanites as follows:

> Over time, the reporter becomes a part of the political institution, if only marginally, and his coverage be-

gins to be selective, sometimes deliberately but more often unconsciously. Getting to know his major news sources well, he forms likes and dislikes which cannot help but influence his reporting. . . . The reporter also begins to identify with the community, omitting uncomplimentary items, and helping people and causes he thinks deserve publicity. . . . It must be noted that most of the time the reporter's coverage is routine. . . . His everyday work is to cover the community and its myriad events, and he is not expected to delve deeply into government. In a small community, many decisions of the actual government have obvious or publishable explanations, and events that strain the system of mutual obligation are rare.

Another expression of excessive parochialism is to ignore the presence in suburbia of sizable numbers of poor and minority-group persons. Perhaps to incorporate them would itself be controversial, challenging the suburban myth that the populace is entirely white and middle class (Berger, 1961).

An important contribution to the understanding of the problem of parochialism in the suburban community press is provided by Greer (1967, p. 265), who studied the failure of metropolitan government in the St. Louis area:

In summary . . . the community press in St. Louis took a strong position against governmental integration of the metropolis. Identifying the existing political units with the totality of the local communities they served and earned a living from, they heatedly disputed the need or desirability of any larger framework for facing the problems of the complex metropolis. While they accurately reflected public opinion on the issue, it is doubtful that they have a major impact on the formation of that opinion. They did have an exciting issue to exploit, one on which they could take sides; they communicated their position to a large minority of the suburban residents. They probably helped activate some of the conservative social norms and belief systems which were evidenced by the voters in the postelection surveys. On the one hand, their authority to speak on the issue was seriously doubted by a sizeable proportion of their readership; on the other hand, few people accused them of self-interest

in the affair. They were seen, not as commercial enterprises searching for profits, but as organs of the local
communities and of suburbia as a whole.

Greer states the issue more generally: "Strengthening of the
sub-areas in a metropolis may, however, integrate the small area
at the cost of anarchy and anomie for the entire city" (1967, p.
265).

2. Lack of Orientation to the Larger Metropolitan Community. Beyond the fact that parochialism at the grass roots
level may be extreme is the fact that metropolitan newspapers
often have underdeveloped conceptions of and attachments to
the metropolitan area. This may come from bad luck with the
owner-heir or the absentee chain. Or it may come when the
metropolitan paper becomes so identified with specific segments or interests in the metropolitan area that it is discredited
with other segments. For example, it may come to be seen as a
patron of downtown interests celebrating an obsolete boosterism, of affluent suburbanites glorifying their expensive but lily-
white schools, of inner-city blacks hustling power, or of effete
intellectual snobs wallowing in cynicism.

The problem may also arise as the journalists, whatever
their identification with the metropolitan area, find it difficult
to overcome the power of the format of news, which at the
metropolitan and national levels thrives on controversy and
polarization. Interpretive reporting, no matter how sensitive,
may be unable to offset the messages of the headlines, which
generally pit blacks against whites, suburbanites against city
dwellers, and people against government. Mediation requires
more than conflict. Further, an increasingly centralized press
may generate alienation among the newsmen themselves (Johnstone, 1976) and thereby further undercut efforts toward creative solution.

3. Disarticulation of Media and Units of Community. We
are in the diffuse phase of urbanization, but establishing a tie
between newspapers and communities requires the intermediate
units of metropolitan area and local community. Bagdikian
(1971, p. 82) captures the economic side of the problem very
well: "The poor fit between community units and news media
comes largely because newspapers and radio and television stations, even though they carry a place name in their identification, do not arrange their output by civic boundaries but instead by merchandising territories. As the automobile

determines the range for shopping, merchandising territories increasingly ignore civil boundaries. And as these shopping territories enlarge, the growing production power of the mass media follows them through communities whose civic affairs they largely ignore." Further, as the merchandising function continues to favor ever larger geographic territories, "so the fit between advertising jurisdictions that tend to fix the limits of news media, and the local units by which most people live and work become ever more maladjusted" (Bagdikian, 1971, p. 86).

Thus both newspapers and metropolitan communities grow in somewhat disarticulate ways. The growth of suburban papers is uneven and may leave some local communities without newspapers adequate to the polity at either the grass roots or the metropolitan levels. The operations of the city dailies may little fit the polity either. Finally, some inner-city neighborhoods, bereft of the resources for their own papers or the attention of the metropolitan press, may find themselves and their problems sliding into oblivion. We have seen that the mass society model does not provide a good overall characterization of the press in America. The local press and the local community are part and parcel of one another and persist in old, modified, and new forms in the urbanized society. Still, trends such as the chaining of papers and growing disarticulations in patterns of urban and newspaper growth mean that in a large number of places mass society is left by default.

Magazines, Books, and Continuing Urbanization

We turn now to magazines and books, looking mainly at patterns of change and stability in the content of the most popular products. We will assess the media more humanistically than heretofore and gauge major shifts in the presumed values of an urbanized society. In this analysis we shall not attempt to describe or assess systematically such structural aspects of book and magazine publishing as the social characteristics of people who buy books, the character of the growth of bookstore chains, or the nature and influence of book clubs. Specialization —in content and in the tailoring of advertising—has been a major recent development in the magazine industry according to such observers as Wood (1971) and Tebbel (1969), and of considerable interest is the recent rise of city magazines (such as New York) that cater to the affluent and highly educated populations of metropolitan areas. Our focus on the most popular products will, however, give us a strategic way to understand the most visible content of these very heterogeneous media.

Trends in Popular Magazine Readership, 1920-1970

When the U.S. population almost doubled from 1920 to 1970, the numbers of magazines published did not keep pace. From some 3,100 monthly publications of all kinds reported for 1920, the figure rose to only 4,300 by 1970 (*Ayer*, 1920, 1970). On the other hand, total magazine readership has mounted much faster than the population. In 1920 there were only twelve magazines that had a circulation as great as 1 percent of the population, the two highest of these each having circulations a bit above 2.5 million, the other ten falling between 1.3 and 2 million. By 1970, however, there were twenty-five periodicals (excluding comics) with circulations above the 1 percent level, one claiming some 17.5 million readers, another more than 14.5 million, and several in the 4 to 10 million range. The most popular magazine in 1970, for example, had more than 8.5 percent of the population subscribing, whereas in 1920 the most popular claimed less than 2.5 percent. Obviously, the number of publications has increased (though proportionately less than the population), while the number of readers has increased in considerably greater proportion. More specifically, the number of popular periodicals (having a circulation of at least 1 percent of the population) had roughly doubled by 1970, and those most popular were much more than three times more popular (in terms of percentage of population subscribing or buying at the newsstand) than were the most popular in the 1920s.

The tendencies just outlined are not, of course, consistent. The vagaries of newsprint supply and price, changes in printing and photographic technology affecting both price and format, changes in postal regulations and rates, and fluctuations in income influence the figures. For instance, the number of those periodicals in the popular group cited above could be declining slightly, even though the more popular do appear to be becoming even more popular. A decade-by-decade survey, based on reports by *Ayer*, showed: for 1920 there were twelve magazines with circulations above the 1 percent level; in 1930, twenty-one; in 1940, twenty-two; in 1950, twenty-nine; in 1960, twenty-seven; in 1970, only twenty-five; and in 1976 (the last year for which figures were available for this study), only twen-

ty-two. (Again, these figures exclude comics, which had grown
rapidly by 1950 and have maintained their popularity ever
since.) As indicated, the number in the popular group made a
considerable jump from 1920 to 1930 and a somewhat impressive increase from 1940 to 1950, and then since have been fairly
stable, with a small but consistent drop between 1950 and
1976. It is noteworthy, however, that the twenty-two popular
publications in 1976 had an average circulation of more than
7.25 million each, compared with the average for the twenty-
five of 1970 of only 6.5 million each. There is a reasonable suspicion, nevertheless, that the market may be tightening for
magazine enterprises, for there were 170 fewer monthly publications reported for 1976 than for 1970. The figures therefore
suggest that a saturation point may have been reached as to the
number of publications that the market will support.

Character of Popular Publications. Of the twelve popular
magazines reported for 1920, two were weeklies: the American
Weekly, which was a syndicated Sunday newspaper insert, and
the old Saturday Evening Post. Both of these survived until the
1960s. The other ten were monthly, and most were home magazines, as the Post was somewhat. That is, their appeal was to the
family, particularly to the housewife; Cosmopolitan and American Magazine were perhaps less so than the others, but they
were still so inclined. These ten, in addition to Cosmopolitan
and American, were Comfort, Gentlewoman, Household Magazine, Ladies' Home Journal, McCall's Magazine, McCall's Monthly Fashion Sheet (a free publication that led the field with more
than 2.5 million distributed per issue), Pictorial Review (a
monthly for women), and the Woman's Home Companion. Of
these ten, only three, the Ladies' Home Journal, McCall's, and
Cosmopolitan, survive today. The Journal and McCall's are
perennials that are still on the popular list; Cosmopolitan has
dropped enough in circulation that it has not so qualified since
the 1950s.

Changes for 1930. Ten of the twelve magazines on the
popular list in 1920 remained in 1930 and eleven more were
added. The two that dropped from the list were Comfort and
Gentlewoman, both of which disappeared by the 1950s. Those
added were: Collier's (a weekly), Delineator, Farm Journal,
Good Housekeeping, Liberty (a weekly), Literary Digest, National Geographic, People's Popular Monthly (home and garden
magazine), True Story, Woman's World, and Blade and Ledger
(a fiction and special articles publication that disappeared before
1940). Obviously, appeal to home and housewife characterized

most of these, although *True Story* represented a different appeal, perhaps providing the reader a vicarious projection into roles more exotic than those of household realities. (The *True Story* success must have influenced other women's magazines to mix such an appeal with their traditional home content.)

The fact that five of the eleven new magazines were clearly household in character appears to support the notion, further validated in this study, that one perennially dependable formula for magazine popularity has been appeal to the housewife. The additions of *Collier's, Liberty, Literary Digest, National Geographic,* and *Blade and Ledger,* however, suggest a shift toward concerns beyond the home. The popularity of the *Farm Journal* bespoke the rural quality of life at the time.

Changes for 1940. The 1940 popular list kept fourteen from the 1930 list, lost seven, and gained eight new magazines. *National Geographic* fell below the 1 percent standard but recovered in the decade following and has been popular ever since. Phased out were *Blade and Ledger,* as mentioned, along with *Delineator, Literary Digest, McCall's Monthly Fashion Sheet, People's Popular Monthly,* and *Pictorial Review*—this last to be resurrected later for two decades as a Sunday newspaper supplement that again achieved popular rank, although it was a quite different publication. *Literary Digest,* which ended earlier than other literary periodicals, such as *Collier's,* the *Post,* and *Delineator,* is generally assumed to have died of embarrassment after it predicted the defeat of President Roosevelt in 1936 on the basis of its previously quite reliable straw polls (*Time,* 1938, p. 55).

The eight new magazines on the list were: *American Home, Better Homes and Gardens,* and the *Reader's Digest* (all three of which still thrive on the popular list today), and five others that are no longer published: *Country Gentlemen, Life, Look, Rural Progress,* and *This Week. This Week* was another newspaper supplement, but *Life* and *Look* represented an innovation by stressing pictures instead of printed matter, which became feasible because of advancements in photographic and printing technologies. Like *National Geographic* (which survives them), they reproduced exotic scenes and views of people around the world in realistic color; unlike the *Geographic* they added short news items and vivid graphics—something that kept them in business and popular well into the color television era of the 1970s. *Life* and *This Week* were weeklies, while *Look* was a biweekly.

Most noteworthy of all, however, was the arrival of the

Reader's Digest. The *Digest* accepted no advertising at that time and, in consequence, had no reported circulation; thus, it may have qualified for the popularity club in 1930. Its rise since its beginning in 1922 has been perhaps the most sensational in all magazine journalism. Its circulation was for several years somewhat a mystery, presumably because at first it got free permission to reprint from other magazines and later because the management wished to reprint at low cost (Bainbridge, Nov. 17, 1945, p. 40). In 1944 the estimates of its circulation ran between 8 million and 11 million (*Time,* 1944, p. 43; 1945, pp. 58-59; *Newsweek,* 1944, p. 92). In 1945 the *Digest* boasted, in promotional ads for its classroom edition (which removed materials inappropriate for youngsters), that its school edition alone had a circulation of 850,000 and was in use in 70,000 classrooms (*Journal of the National Education Association,* 1945, inside back cover). Also, by the 1940s it had developed a spectacular circulation abroad, reported in the millions in more than a dozen different languages (Rorty, 1944, pp. 78-84).

Even today, the only publications giving the *Digest* any real competition in terms of circulation claims are comics, newspaper supplements, and an entirely different kind of publication, *TV Guide. TV Guide* is necessarily produced with special adaptations to various areas of the country, so that in a sense it is not a single publication but a chain of differentiated ones. It is obviously no direct competition for the *Digest,* being actually symbiotic with television.

What is the magic of the *Digest* that brought it so quickly to its apparently perennially high position? A study of the *Digest* (Street, 1946) showed these reasons for its success:

1. It is compact, easily portable, convenient for the busy reader, and crammed with "quickie" articles and squibs that "he who runs may read."

2. It is written "down" for the reader (Bainbridge, Dec. 15, 1945, pp. 38-39). The Flesch (1974, inside front cover) formula for readability is observed. In rewriting and condensing articles, the editors informalize and personalize copy, shorten sentences, substitute shorter and more common words, incorporate colloquialisms, and convert third-person viewpoints to the first and second, effecting the "dear reader" device for "cuddling up" to its clientele (Street, 1946, p. 123). This character accompanies its promotional efforts too. Special bonus arrangements were made for it to follow the troops during World War II (Bainbridge, Dec. 15, 1945, p. 38), and subscrip-

tions were given as scholarships to high school valedictorians with certificates especially provided for personal presentation at graduation ceremonies.

3. Humor and human interest squibs are generously dispersed throughout the content—humor that often teases about sex to the edge of but not transgressing conventional morality.

4. It makes life exciting by being effusive and optimistic, exaggerating, sensationalizing, hero building, and emphasizing the drama of everyday life.

5. It stresses variety, despite the fact that ideologically the selection of articles for condensation as well as original articles are limited to those reflecting a somewhat circumscribed perspective (Street, 1946, p. 351; Bainbridge, Dec. 15, 1945, pp. 39-40), and it contains something for everybody. As originally conceived, the *Digest* was to be just that: an eclectic selection from a broad range of publications. Actually, it has only partly been a digest at all, as was exposed early in its rise to prominence (Bainbridge, Dec. 1, 1945, p. 42; Miller, 1942, p. 6; Street, 1946, p. 27) and as is easily verified by anyone who examines it for articles that are published simultaneously or in advance of publication elsewhere—articles "planted" by the *Digest* in other publications so that they can be reprinted in the *Digest*; some magazines, at least in the past, have been paid by the *Digest* for the arrangement. Nevertheless, by gathering materials widely, either from other publications or by its own initiative, and by presenting such material in condensed form for readers who have little time for leisurely reading, the *Digest* does serve a great diversity of interests.

6. The viewpoints taken in controversial articles in the *Digest* are congenial with those of the great proportion of the public who forms the clientele of the magazine. While the *Digest* takes stands on certain issues with clarity, vigor, and sometimes sensational forthrightness, those positions represent stereotypes of popular thinking—for example, government (in contrast to industry) is wasteful, taxes are too high, unions are generally corrupt, opportunity is available to the industrious and deserving, animals have a transcendent wisdom, the simple life is best, and life is sure to get better if men but persevere.

In addition, it is perhaps only reasonable to point out that the *Digest* has rather consistently employed a staff with a great deal of journalistic resourcefulness, at least for the *Digest* style and purpose. Some newspapers and captive-audience publications are somewhat insulated from competition; the *Digest* appears to have started with the advantage of new ideas and approaches that cannot, however, be patented. So far it has outhustled all competition. Nevertheless, it seems worth considering that the hypothesis that the *Reader's Digest* has a special formula that is peculiarly fitted to the needs and interests of people in an increasingly urbanized and technological age and that it perhaps supports both the existing value patterns of its readers and the changes that are taking place in those patterns. The *Digest* appears to have opened a new epoch—so far all its own—in U.S. (if not world) journalism; this epoch, initiated in the 1920s, is still in process and imitated by *Atlas* and the now defunct *Intellectual Digest* and *Coronet,* among others.

   Changes for 1950. Another kind of journalistic phenomenon appeared in the 1940s that emerged in the listing for 1950: the sudden prominence of comic publications, ten of which achieved the 1 percent minimum circulation level in 1950. These were *Archie Comic Group; Fawcett Comic Group; Harvey Comic Group; Lev Gleason Comics Group; Marvel Comic Group; National Comics Group; Preferred Comics Group; Puck, the Comic Weekly; Quality Comic Group;* and *Standard Comics.* All of these were monthly or bimonthly except *Puck,* which was a weekly syndicated to Sunday newspapers. Circulations, in terms of total circulation of all comic books for each group combined, were astronomical. *Puck,* however, though not a group, boasted the highest circulation, more than 8 million, and the lowest circulation of the group had more than 2 million. While these publications can only be classified as magazines in the broadest meaning of the term, they do reflect a significant interest and value orientation in the reading public, particularly for children and some adults. Each of the comic groups sells advertising as a package for all the units in its group; as a result, circulations are reported for the group as a whole. Though some units alone did not reach the 1 percent level, they did so in combination, and most groups far exceeded the 1 percent level.

   The twenty-nine magazines (excluding the comics) that made up the 1950 list included nineteen listed in 1940, only three being lost from the 1940 list (*Liberty, Rural Progress,* and *Woman's World*) and ten more being added. Of the ten new ones on the list, four were home magazines: *Redbook Magazine, True Confessions* (similar to *True Story* in its appeal), and *Family Circle* and *Woman's Day,* both circulated primarily through chain-store marketing. Since *Woman's World* dropped from the listing, the group representing housewife appeal was increased by three. Added to the list were two weekly newspaper inserts, *Parade* and *Pictorial Review,* the latter under the title once used for a popular monthly magazine for women. Four magazines of general and editorial character were new to the list for 1950: *American Legion Magazine, Coronet* (a digest competing with *Reader's Digest*), *National Geographic* (back on the list again), and *Time,* a weekly news review.

The 1940s showed, then, that the home magazine that appealed to housewives still had great popularity, with chain-store marketing bringing two new ones to the list. In addition, there was increased representation by weekly newspaper inserts, as well as one notable weekly news magazine, *Time.* The 1950 list contained thirteen magazines that appealed mostly to the housewife; ten of general appeal (news, editorial, and special comment); four newspaper supplements; and two survivals of the appeal to farm readers. The 1950 list is the longest among those compared here, showing that, compared to population, more magazines were popular for the decade represented by *Ayer's* 1950 report, though the number on the list has not dropped significantly since. In addition, certainly not to be completely overlooked, there were the comics.

Changes for 1960. Seven of the popular magazines of the 1950 list were missing from the list for 1960. Four of these were from the housewife category: *Household* and *Woman's Home Companion,* both no longer published, and *Cosmopolitan* and *True Confessions,* which are still published but have never since reached the 1 percent level. Two were of more general interest: the weekly *Collier's* and *American Magazine,* neither of which is presently published. One of the two rural-appeal publications, *Country Gentlemen,* also dropped off. (*Farm Journal* survived on the list into the 1970s.) The 1960 list, therefore, had twenty-two survivors from the 1950 list and five new additions: *Parent's Magazine and Better Family Living* and *Family Weekly* (another Sunday newspaper insert) came to the scene with the established housewife-appeal format. Appeal to the male appeared with *Boy's Life* for the young and *True* for the sports fan—both featuring outdoor action. Most spectacular, however, was the previously mentioned *TV Guide,* which started in 1953 and had by 1960 become a household basic in more than 7 million homes, destined to overtake *Reader's Digest* in circulation in the early 1970s.

While the loss of the two home magazines suggests that the market may have become a bit crowded for such publications, it should not be overlooked that eleven of the twenty-seven on the list were of this type and that some of the general group (*Reader's Digest* and *Coronet*, for example) were strong in housewife appeal. The "comic boom" appeared to have been cooled slightly, with only seven comic publications on the list, but those had astonishingly high circulations. Also, the Sunday newspaper supplement appeared to be clearly established. Only one farm-appeal periodical was left. Still surviving, it remained on the popular list for 1970 before dropping off. The popularity of *Boy's Life* and *True* represents success in new kinds of appeals, *Boy's Life* undoubtedly bespeaking the strength of the Boy Scout organization through which it is published.

Missing from the comics list, compared with 1950, were *Lev Gleason, Preferred, Fawcett,* and *Quality* comics groups and *Standard Comics*. Added for 1960 were *Charlton Comics* (bimonthly) and *Dell Comic Group* (monthly), *Charlton* with an estimated 5 million circulation and *Dell* reporting more than 9.5 million; *Puck,* however, still led this category, having grown to more than 11.5 million circulation.

Changes for 1970. Three of the newspaper supplements on the 1960 list, *American Weekly, Pictorial Review,* and *This Week,* were missing from the popular list in 1970. The first two were no longer published, and the last had fallen in popularity. The *Saturday Evening Post* ceased publication in February 1969.[1] *Coronet,* with a format comparable to the *Reader's Digest,* had dropped below the 1 percent standard and died in the early 1970s. In all, five on the list in 1960 were absent in 1970. This means, of course, that twenty-two of the 1960 list still remained, and three new ones were added to bring the total to twenty-five. (These figures exclude the comics.) The three new magazines were *Homemaker's Digest* (a free bimonthly that did not last long), *Newsweek,* and *Playboy. Playboy,* established in 1953, had risen to a position of considerable attention and debate because of its then shocking sexual appeal.

For 1970, *Reader's Digest* was still leading the pack (with *Coronet*'s competition dropping out), while *Newsweek* had joined *Time* in the weekly news group. *Life* (a weekly) and *Look* (a biweekly) had replaced the *Post* by 1970 as perhaps the most visible publications in doctor's and dentist's offices and barber shops; in the latter *Playboy* was also common, along with *Newsweek* and *Time* as well as *True* and other lesser outdoor magazines. *Life* and *Look,* however, soon ceased publication, and *True* had slipped off the popular list by 1976. Although the *Digest* outcirculates all general-appeal magazines today, it is less visible than several others because it appears only monthly instead of weekly. Also, especially until it began to accept advertising, its graphics were comparatively modest. It is, of course, still compact in format—small enough to disappear easily from the waiting room.

In 1970 the home magazine still occupied a plurality of nearly one half of the field—twelve of the twenty-five on the list. Comics still appeared to be gathering strength, while the newspaper supplements were reduced to only two. *Playboy* was strong, as it still was in 1976, but it now is in competition with *Penthouse*, which, established in 1969, reached a circulation of 4 million in 1976 by imitating *Playboy* if not outdoing it (*Newsweek*, 1975, p. 76).

By 1976, in addition to *Penthouse*, the popular list included the new entries of *Modern Maturity* (published by the National Association of Retired Persons), the *National Enquirer* (a sensationalist weekly of tabloid format, usually displayed strategically at chain stores), *Sports Illustrated* (a weekly that has now become highly visible in barber shops), and *Travel and Leisure* (a publication subsidized by the credit card and travel industries). It seems possible that *Sports Illustrated* has partially displaced *True* (which still survives but below the popular level) and that *Modern Maturity* and *Travel and Leisure* represent deference to the interests of older persons, a growing proportion of the population.

Boy's Life, although still strong with a circulation of more than 2 million reported in the 1976 directory, fell below the 1 percent mark by that year, as did *Farm Journal, Homemaker's Digest, Parent's Magazine,* and *True Story Magazine. Homemaker's Digest,* a bimonthly giveaway, is no longer listed. *True Story* continues with a circulation only a bit below 1 percent, its exciting factual stories perhaps less attractive in the less inhibited context of today's journalism.

Particularly of note are the demise of *Life* and *Look,* both of which had been consistently popular as well as visible since their births in the late 1930s. Both had circulations near or above 8 million each before they died. It appears that their production costs were such that the more copies they sold the greater their losses.

Added to the list of popular comic publications was *Gold Key Comics,* a monthly sold at the newsstands, with *Dell Comic Group* dropping off. The list for 1970, therefore, had the same number of comic entries as for 1960. The 1976 popular comic publications, however, were more popular than the popular group in 1970, circulating more than 11 million more copies.

1920-1970 Trends. Magazine reading is much more popular now than fifty years ago, but this phenomenon is not recent. The number of magazines read by more than 1 percent of the population more than doubled from 1920 to 1950. Since then, though, there has been some decline in the number in the popular group, although the change does not seem great enough to be significant. Television has created the best seller of all, *TV Guide,* and television appears to have affected news-picture magazine demand adversely. It does not, however, appear to have reduced the demand for weekly news magazines—*Newsweek* and *Time* are both on the popular list and are increasing their circulations as of 1976.

The home magazine remains the mainstay in appeal for the popular magazine. As the urban community newspaper appeals as a communicator of the local scene to the homemaker (Janowitz, 1967), these magazines appear to serve as communicators to the resident in more remote areas. They focus on the personal, the relevant to family, and they deal with those things that both embellish home life and provide some escape from its monotony. These qualities in appeal have prevailed over five decades and show little sign of decline.

A virtual monolith appears to have emerged in the *Reader's Digest,* which represents the compressed, succinct, sensational, informal, and personal approach in presenting a broad range of materials, albeit from a limited perspective when interpreting controversial issues. Born in the 1920s and taking a commanding lead in circulation before the 1940s, it still maintains that lead quite substantially, its only competitor in circulation figures besides *TV Guide* being Sunday newspaper supplements *Parade* (with almost 19 million) and *Puck* (with more than 17 million) in 1976. The *Digest* reported a bit less than 18.5 million in circulation in 1976, with foreign editions making it a leader in some other countries also. For that year it reported twenty-six international editions. In 1970 its circulation was running above 1 million each in British, Canadian, French, and German editions, with a total foreign distribution of more than 13 million. It is to be noted that none of the publications with *Reader's Digest*-size circulations are really competitive in the field in which the *Digest* operates—and its major imitator, *Coronet,* is gone.

Magazines appealing to the male, in sports, adventure, and sex, have come to claim a place in the popular rank. The crisis of values of the 1960s appears to have resulted in a breaking down of the taboos, especially about sex and obscenity, that had prompted a staid decorum in magazine content. It is perhaps too early to tell whether the change is permanent, but at least for the 1970s the content of popular magazines is clearly more open to four-letter words, outspoken considerations of sex, and graphic exposure of the human anatomy. It is symptomatic of this trend that in the 1972 directory *Ayer* provided a new classification for publications, "Underground," which was later changed to "Underground and Alternative." By 1976 there were fifty-six publications on this list from nineteen states. The list included gay, lesbian, leftist, and avant-garde publications.

The explosion of the comics appears to parallel somewhat the rise in popularity of the paperback novel. The comics, particularly the comic groups, represent a dramatic and rather innovative development. In the *Ayer* reports before 1950 that are used here, there was no "Comics" classification and any such publications (none satisfying the 1 percent criterion) were listed under "Humor." With the 1950 explosion came ten comic publications reporting extraordinary circulations above 1 percent of the population.

What Marks the Casualties? Perhaps the demise of some of the most popular publications points to trends in magazine reading as clearly as does survival and popularity of others. The *Saturday Evening Post*—which had been in the top group for every decade reported until its death at age 238 in 1969, with its nameplate designating Benjamin Franklin as its ancestor editor and Philadelphia as its home—appears, like the dinosaur, to have reached an age to which it could not adapt. Its traditional pattern of installment novels and its Norman Rockwell covers and art reminiscent of elm-shaded small towns and idyllic rural byways may not alone have marked it as an anachronism. Economics certainly had a part—printing costs and advertising patterns—but it seems reasonable to conclude that it would have had to become a different magazine to survive. Mooney, writing in the *Atlantic Monthly* (1969, pp. 70-71) wrote:

> In April 1955, the *Post* started a series called "The Face of America." The first layout showed the Brandywine in spring. "The Brandywine, a jewel among rivers, is

so small mapmakers call it a creek. But it looms large in American history, poetry and art."

Yes, well it turned out later that the Brandywine was polluted, and America knew, the *Post* did not. . . .

The failure of the *Post* is not just the story of another magazine going under, but the failure of a style, a system, a regime. In the beginning the *Post* and its style stood for all the hopes of free enterprise. In the end, the *Post*—old King *Post*—could no longer understand the sense of things.

Newsweek (1969, p. 52) in "Death of an Institution," observed: "Rockwell's paintings were supposed to mirror the America that read the *Post*. But more and more the reality wasn't there any more—if it ever was. . . . America was going urban and was mesmerized by TV."

Both Mooney and *Newsweek* provide a view that can be checked with former readers of the *Post*. Both, however, attribute the death of the magazine to the ebb of competition for advertising, with the mergers of small production units, and with television bidding for the national advertising market. The *Post* was obviously competing with television's comedies, detective stories, and soap opera novels—all of which imitated the *Post* by installment presentations. The Neilsen ratings were hard evidence against the *Post*'s bid for $40,000 for a page of advertising. It is also true that in the early 1960s the *Post* lost a libel suit to football coaches Wally Butts and Paul "Bear" Bryant (Mooney, 1969, pp. 70-71) over a muckraking story charging them with game fixing. In a last-minute effort to rescue itself the *Post* went to biweekly production; it purged all but the presumed elite from its subscription list to reduce production and postage costs and to limit its distribution to a select clientele so that it could justify high advertising rates, but presumably it lost more by antagonizing its faithful readers.

In all, it seems reasonable to conclude that the leisurely *Post,* with its novel installments expected to hold a reader for a week, could not keep up with "quickie," compact journalism— epitomized in the *Digest, Time, Newsweek,* and television. Also, the paperback press, with novels in tantalizing, garish displays, obtained at comparatively low cost with no need to read in plodding installments, was flooding the market. It appears likely that there is an inverse relationship between popularity of the paperback and the popularity of such publications as the *Post*.

The *National Review* in "The Post RIP" (1969, p. 64) perhaps summarizes the passing well, although with a bit of sympathetic nostalgia, "Well shucks, runs the consensus, the Saturday Evening Post represented the vanished America of farmers, small merchants, church socials, and spooning on the porch swing; it couldn't survive in the age of jets, bombs, space, and riots."

The disappearance of *Life* and *Look,* which occurred in the early 1970s, requires a somewhat different explanation. Postage rates, printing costs, and competition from news weeklies as well as television appear to have conspired to end the publication of both; certainly lack of popularity is not an explanation. Perhaps the doom of *Life* and *Look* were portended in the earlier passing of *Collier's* and *Woman's Home Companion* back in the 1950s. *Commonweal* ("Death of Two Magazines," 1957, p. 398) observed that "prosperity, it seems, is going to kill more magazines than the depression did" and that "serious magazines of opinion and criticism . . . face mass-circulation methods"—ignoring the fact that both *Collier's* and *Companion* were mass circulated. The conclusion was that they were closed to protect stockholder investments, a reason *Commonweal* seemed to regard as hardly valid morally.

A mechanical detail that might be noteworthy is that all five of these magazines (*Life, Look, Collier's, Companion,* and the *Post*) were of a large, unwieldy format—the opposite of the *Reader's Digest.* They were all very popular, but they became expensive to print, deliver, and mail. Both *McCall's* and *Ladies' Home Journal* reduced format in the early 1970s, apparently to reduce costs—and both are still alive and strong on the popular list. *Life,* on the eve of its surrender, anticipated a 170 percent increase in postal rates over the coming five years (*Newsweek,* 1972, p. 109). Cousins (1971), discussing the departure of *Look,* pointed out that television can reach more people more cheaply for advertising purposes, seeing this fact and the postage increases as environmental pressures that such publications must face. The same *Newsweek* quoted a "vintage reader" of *Life* as lamenting its departure: "It was my television." Then *Newsweek* declared: "The real TV, of course, helped do *Life* in."

Of course, accidents happen—of fiscal reorganization, breaches with readers, and libel hazards. The *Post*'s misfortune with the football coaches has been cited, and *Collier's* had its trial with readers not long before it gave up, when one of its fiction editors was cited by the House Un-American Activities

Committee and an article defending teaching about UNESCO in California public schools brought a strong negative reaction from its readers (*Time*, 1953, p. 50). A Saturday Evening Post Company remained after the closing of the *Post* and some of the funds salvaged were reinvested in radio and television, representing simply a reshuffling of the investment pattern of the owners (*Business Week*, 1969, p. 26). Such accidents were probably not, however, the basic causes of collapse.

In all, it appears that the magazine is far from gone—indeed, it is prospering—and that, to the extent that it can adapt itself to rising printing and distribution costs and focus on particular interests of special groups of readers, it has a reasonable chance of maintaining its popularity. It must, of course, have a substantial financial base and must expect to face the competition of television, other magazines, and the paperback and adapt its format, printing process, and content accordingly. Finally, it does well to reflect viewpoints with which its readers generally agree and be identified with the cultural patterns and respectful of the mores of that part of society that constitutes its clientele, although testing its readers' moral boundaries (in its humor, for instance) can be quite profitable. Furthermore, informality, personal directness, and attention to things relevant to the lives of its readers seem perennially identified with success.

It should be clear that our methodology has had a limitation: By looking at the popular magazines, we have focused on mass publications and have not studied the rise of specialized magazines that have found a stable market with a particular reader segment. Thus we have not inquired into such processes as the way in which Time, Incorporated, may have partially revived *Life* in the more specialized forms of *Money* and *People*. However, it is apparent that aside from some obvious changes, such as the relative decline of farm journals, popular magazines do not show a great transformation from rural to urban values in the diffuse phase of urbanization. It is not stretching the point to say that the top magazines have become suburbanized, appealing broadly to the specialized tastes diffused throughout the metropolis and nation.

Trends in Best-Seller Books, 1920-1970

The parallel between the amount of book reading and population growth seems self-evident, even though radio and television must certainly have displaced reading time in the lives of many. An analysis of media consumption trends by Frase (1967, pp. 30-31) reported that from 1947 to 1963, when the population rose by under 30 percent, newspaper circulation had increased 134 percent; magazine circulation, 111 percent; book publications, 231 percent; miscellaneous publications, 277 percent; radio consumption, 84 percent; television consumption, 17,357 percent; and movie consumption, 97 percent.

Television, of course, grew the most. It is noteworthy that book and miscellaneous publications led the printed media. Lacy reported that book sales rose from some $500 million in 1952 to $2,500 million in 1967 and that the size of publishing houses in the same period had gone from a point at which selling $5 million a year in 1952 was "large," to 1967 when several houses had a total of at least $100 million in sales each and quite a few more were doing at least $25 million. Membership in the American Booksellers Association increased from 1,125 in 1955 to 2,400 in 1966 (Lacy, 1967, pp. 3-7). Lacy attributed much growth to the marketing of high-priced paperbacks and the booming college market.

Schick (1958, pp. 79-83), suggesting that 1939 was the beginning of the enduring trend of paperback popularity, states that in 1945 there were only 112 paperback titles published; by 1952, 1,572 such titles; and that from 1944 to 1952 paperback publishing had grown from less than six to more than six dozen firms. *Publishers' Weekly* (1970, p. 78) updates these records of growth well into the television age, reporting a 7 percent annual increase in paperback books sold from 1963 to 1968—a 34 percent increase for the five-year period. While hardcover sales may have been slowed by such competition, they have nevertheless increased also. From 1959 to 1967, the number of new titles of books published increased by 380 percent, and the sales of serious books have climbed steadily upward (Bagdikian, 1971, p. 187).

Tastes in Book Reading. The different kinds of media constitute an ecological system of a sort, with a symbiotic relationship existing between hardcover books, cheap paperbacks, quality paperbacks, magazines, various kinds of newspapers, radio, television, and the movies. The big daily is read for one purpose, the hometown weekly for another, the shopper for another, and the book for still another. There is competition, but radio, television, and the newspaper verify, rather than duplicate, the news for their common audiences. The book and the magazine provide substance for readers' reflection and vicarious experience beyond readers' immediate settings. Each medium

helps shape the other but does not displace it in any practical
sense. While books, magazines, or newspapers may have
changed their respective characters, the change may simply
represent an adjustment to each other and other media. The
Western novel, so popular in the 1920s, for example, is not so
popular today, but the Western still has been very much alive
in television on "Gunsmoke"; and its modern counterpart, a
law man in a siren-heralded police car instead of a cowboy
sheriff in chaps and on horseback, is far from extinct. Edgar
Rice Burrough's Tarzan, even though in black and white, still
runs on television, and the superman stereotype that Tarzan
represents is very much with us in "Six Million Dollar Man" and
"Bionic Woman."

To characterize the trend in book-reading tastes since
1920, we chose to analyze the more popular authors at three
points in the past half century, taking those in the five-year
periods 1918 to 1922, 1943 to 1947, and 1968 to 1972. The
following are the authors who appeared more than two times on
best-seller lists during these periods, as reported by Hackett
(1956, pp. 124-133, 176-187) and by *Publishers' Weekly*, from
which her reports were drawn (*Publishers' Weekly* reports are
based on monthly bookstore reports of sales, those in the top
ten being listed as best sellers for the year):

1918-1922

Fiction
> Zane Grey: *The UP Trail, The Desert of Wheat, The Man of the Forest, The Mysterious Rider, To the Last Man,* all published by Harper.
> Mary Roberts Rinehart: *The Amazing Interlude, Dangerous Days, The Poor Wise Man, The Breaking Point,* all published by Doran.
> Eleanor H. Porter: *Oh, Money! Money!, Dawn, Mary-Marie,* all published by Houghton Mifflin.
> Harold Bell Wright: *The Re-Creation of Brian Kent* (twice), published by Book Supply Company; *Helen of the Old House,* published by Appleton.

Nonfiction
> Frederick O'Brien: *White Shadows in the South Seas* (twice), *Mystic Isles of the South Seas,* both published by Century.

1943-1947

Fiction
 Lloyd C. Douglas: *The Robe* (three times), published by
 Houghton Mifflin.
 Thomas B. Costain: *The Black Rose* (twice), *The Money-
 man*, both published by Doubleday.

Nonfiction
 Ernie Pyle: *Here is Your War* (twice), *Brave Men* (twice),
 Last Chapter, all published by Holt.
 Betty McDonald: *The Egg and I* (three times), published by
 Lippincott.

1968-1972

Fiction
 Taylor Caldwell: *Testimony of Two Men, Great Lion of
 God, Captains and the Kings*, all published by Doubleday.
 Frederick Forsyth: *The Day of the Jackal* (twice), *The
 Odessa File*, both published by Viking Press.

Nonfiction
 Rod McKuen: *Listen to the Warm, Lonesome Cities, Stan-
 yan Street, In Someone's Shadow, Twelve Years of
 Christmas, Fields of Wonder*, all published by Random
 House.

These works are presumed to epitomize the interests of
book readers for the respective five-year intervals. The characterizations offered below are made accordingly.
 1918-1922. The writings of Zane Grey were of Western
outdoor adventure and action. Mott (1947, p. 238) cites *Book-
man* for June 1, 1906, as describing Grey's typical hero as "a
superman whose will was iron, whose nerves were steel, and
whose manners were brass." Mott places Grey with the "rough-
and-tough school of letters of the Roosevelt-Kipling era," saying
that "if Grey mixed blood with his ink, that too was part of the
technique of his school." His appeal must not have been in
"boy meets girl," for Mott says, "His love passages are far too
downright funny, not in intention, but in their naive attempts
to depict passion." Mary Roberts Rinehart wrote the detective
story puzzle, using a middle-aged spinster narrator (Mott, 1947,
p. 265). Her works were in the tradition of Arthur Conan Doyle

and Ellery Queen. Eleanor H. Porter and Harold Bell Wright had something in common in their writing: They moralized. She was perhaps best known for an earlier work, *Pollyanna,* which preached cheerfulness to the extreme in the face of adversity. Wright was a Church of the Disciples minister for some time (Mott, 1947, pp. 222-229). The works of both writers were obviously sentimental as well as didactic, both reinforcing the traditionally respected virtues. Mott characterizes Eleanor H. Porter and Gene Stratton Porter (a contemporary who authored two best sellers of the period, *A Daughter of the Land* and *Her Father's Daughter,* published by Doubleday, Page) together, saying that their writings, though directed toward girls, were also read by millions of adults, adding that "we must not forget that the average educational attainment of American readers was not then . . . very high." Wright, he points out, was extremely critical of the established church for its failures to live up to its own standards. Both Wright and the Porters appealed to the nostalgic in people who yearned for both the rustic past and uncomplicated morality.

Outdoor adventure and action, detective mystery, and didacticism in story form appear to represent the most popular reading interests of people of the 1920s. Interests were nostalgic. The most popular writers did not deal with the controversy of society's movements; rather they looked on the immediate past of simple folk on the eve of more urban sophistication. In nonfiction for the 1918-1922 period, the range of interest was perhaps wider. Considerable attention for the first three years of the period went to World War I, with such works as Arthur Guy Empy's *Over the Top;* Pat O'Brien's *Outwitting the Hun;* two books by James W. Gerard, *Face to Face with Kaiserism* and *My Four Years in Germany;* G. H. Clark's *Treasury of War Poetry;* John McCrae's *In Flanders Field;* Phillip Gibbs's *Now It Can Be Told;* and *Poems of Alan Seeger.* Nevertheless, the only writer who had as many as three best sellers in nonfiction was Frederick O'Brien, with his vivid travel anecdotes and descriptions of idyllic life in the South Seas and criticism of the white man's influence there (Hackett, 1956, pp. 36-43). The war writings, as may be noted by their titles, were not critical of war or society and its part in war. Immediate events and issues were touched little in the nonfiction of the time.

1943-1947. Another preacher, Lloyd C. Douglas, headed the popularity list for this period. While his plots were not particularly simple, his religious messages were: *The Robe,* for instance, was another life of Jesus, this time from the perspective of a Roman soldier and his Greek slave. Quite different are the writings of Thomas B. Costain, a storyteller who wrote historical romances that dramatized a hero's overcoming of perils and his victories over those who plotted against him (Mott, 1947, p. 284). Like the 1918-1922 fiction readers, the 1943-1947 readers consumed morality; unlike them they also turned to the remote and exotic in adventure—and neither Douglas nor Costain dealt with people readers might have known in any direct sense, as they might have known Wright's rustics of the Ozarks or the Porters' cheery characters.

World War II, raging at the time, affected the popular fiction comparatively little; Hackett observed that in the 1943 list, "Novels reflected the war only slightly" and that there were no war novels in the 1945 list (Hackett, 1956, pp. 177, 183). The remote tended to appeal to the fiction reader. In contrast, the influence of World War II cannot be overlooked in the popular nonfiction of the period. It obviously prompted the tremendous popularity of Ernie Pyle's writings, with his graphic, detailed accounts of war incidents. Said Mott (1947, p. 277): "The reporter who lived with the boys (and died with them at Ie Shima, 25 April, 1945), sharing all their hardships and dangers —their chow, their own reactions under fire, their rough joking, their homesickness, cold, insects, disease—and who got next to the real heart of the GI as no other writer ever did: That was Ernie Pyle. And he put down names and addresses like a country correspondent for the home paper."

However, Betty McDonald, with *The Egg and I,* which has the basis of autobiographical reality but with the perspective of the colorful and humorous reflections that match fiction, was perhaps comic relief. Mott (1947, p. 284) comments: "Was ever autobiography more amusing? From the unconventional account of an unconventional birth to the story of the fire, it is all written with gusto and verve—and often hilarity— hard to match." One element in the popular writings of this period is perhaps notable—though it is extremely intangible: Character stereotypes are less discernible in comparison to the writings of the previous period.

1968-1972. Taylor Caldwell and Frederick Forsyth had fiction best sellers three times in this period; Rod McKuen, with poetry, was the only author of that period to do so in nonfiction. Caldwell's writings are difficult to characterize because of their wide range in setting and theme. Some of her writings, such as *Great Lion of God,* have a religious theme, although didacticism is hardly obvious; all are historical but not religious; all are vividly drawn in scene and character with an immediacy in detail that makes the reader feel the author must have "been there." Indeed, one interviewer of Mrs. Caldwell suggests that perhaps she has a mystical power for reliving the experiences she describes (Stearn, 1972, p. 86). Her books do not tend, however, to deal with here-and-now problems of common people, and they are sizable volumes compared with the popular books of earlier days. She writes with much detail; the three books that headed the lists in the 1968-1972 period averaged about 600 pages. Frederick Forsyth continues the mystery-detective motif, placing it in a setting of modern technology and political intrigue. His *The Odessa File* entangles the reader with the concentration camp records of Germany in World War II; *The Day of the Jackal* is about an assassination attempt on a French official—dramatic in the conflict between the would-be assassin and the shrewd though plodding detective. The detective story is obviously still popular.

McKuen, whose poetry obviously claims a large audience, appears to appeal tremendously to some but not at all to others. Marcia Seligson (1972, p. 12) reports an interview with McKuen under the revealing title, "The Million-Dollar Loneliness of Rod McKuen," saying that a unique quality of McKuen is the "bizarre character of his audience" and that he is "revered by his fans and held in such mocking contempt by his nonfans." Certainly to his "nonfans" he exhibits a whimsical, mystical bent in the public interest, but to his followers, as Seligson suggests in quoting one of them, "He speaks to me, says exactly what I feel most deeply and can't say myself." One glance at his poetry reveals it as simple reading indeed. His books are short, with few words on a page.

In fiction it is a sharp contrast between the stereotypes of the 1918-1922 best sellers of Grey, Rinehart, Porter, and Wright to the more varied, colorful, and realistic characterizations and detailed descriptions of Caldwell and Forsyth. It must not be overlooked, however, that those who want the simple can get it on television—and certainly the older writings, and many like them, are still available. Indeed, there appears no clear trend away from adventure and mystery, and even mystical appeals.

Overall. There are connecting threads through the years. The Bible is still, year after year, the best seller of all, with new translations and editing from time to time (Mott, 1947, p. 297).

In the fifty-year span from the 1920s to the 1970s, there were three writers of fiction and one of nonfiction who had best sellers in either both the 1918-1922 and the 1943-1947 periods, or the 1943-1947 and the 1968-1972 periods. Sinclair Lewis, whose *Main Street* headed the fiction list in 1921 (Hackett, 1956, p. 131), had *Cass Timberlane* in fifth place in the 1945 list (p. 182) and *Kingsblood Royal* in eighth in 1947 (p. 187). His incisive critique of society appears to have some perennial appeal—enough to reach across more than two decades. Similarly, Taylor Caldwell, second with *This Side of Innocence* in 1946 (p. 184), had the successes already reported in the 1968-1972 period. Also, Irving Stone, tenth in the list in 1945 with *Immoral Wife* (p. 182), was third in the 1971 list with *The Passions of the Mind* (*Publishers' Weekly*, 1972, p. 51).

It can be argued, of course, that writers do vary the content and style of what they write from book to book. Also, it must be considered that while these writers were the most consistent producers of best sellers, there were others—that the reading tastes of people cannot be characterized so simply. These arguments must be admitted. Indeed, a review of the listings of best sellers as well as other substantial successes is impressive in the variety and range of the material. With the population explosion has come space in the market for tremendous sales to groups who have, from the perspective of the majority of readers, fantastic, "far-out," and even perverted reading tastes. A best seller may appeal to only 1 percent of all readers but still make the list. Fad interest must not be overlooked—nor the whimsies of book club selections, sales promotional drives, and fortuities of advertising and media attention.

Even assuming the validity of the approach taken in this study of books, however, it seems unsafe to generalize that any great change has taken place in book-reading tastes since 1920. Our findings seem consistent with Tebbel's conclusion (1974, pp. 382-383) that the amazing thing about the book industry is how little it changes. Action, adventure, and settings remote from the reader all still attract. Characters are portrayed more incisively—less stereotyped—and detailed scenes more concretely in Caldwell's and Forsyth's writings than in Grey's and Wright's generally. Yet, O'Brien's descriptions of South Sea life in the 1920s had vivid detail, in contrast to the contemporary simplicity of McKuen's poetry. Mott (1947, p. 285) was presumably correct in his statement: "There is no formula which may be depended upon to produce a best seller." Perhaps the firmest conclusion that we can draw on the basis of this study is that urbanization and other social changes seem to have generated more, but not necessarily different, reading in the best-seller category.

Conclusion

One might have expected to find substantial changes in the print media over a period of a half century in which the society moved into the diffuse phase of urbanization. This was the era of television, a period of continued improvement in literacy, and a time at which educational levels rose dramatically— all developments that hypothetically could have revolutionized reading tastes and altered the structure of the print media in fundamental ways.

Our study shows more continuity than change. No doubt the improvements in education together with the economics of production for enlarging markets have contributed to the economic health of the print media in the urbanized society. Our research on the character of popular magazines and best-selling books indicates that despite social change at large and structural changes in the organization of publishing there have been few changes in dominant media themes toward gesellschaft or other values.

Yet certain important changes are seen in the newspaper industry, which relate to the movement into the diffuse phase of urbanization. The print media have become diffuse as well. To speak of a mass society press is to overstate the issues. A critical trend has been the uneven suburbanization of the press and the decline in dominance of the metropolitan newspaper. We have posited that the political health of the urbanized society requires a two-tiered press, serving both very localized or grass roots functions and metropolitan-wide functions. The political functions are threatened by tendencies to excessive parochialism, a lack of an orientation to the larger metropolitan area, even in the metropolitan dailies, and a disarticulation between units of media and units of community. If we are correct in assuming that citizenship requires a consideration of public issues less superficial than what television can provide, then our concerns for the functions of newspapers become more pressing, given the recurrent finding of polls that Americans place more trust in televised news than in printed news (Roper Organization, 1975).

We do not have the data to answer many important questions about the future. Foremost among these is the question of the long-run effects of very high levels of chaining of papers with attendant absentee ownership. Will this produce a further standardization of content and inability to contribute to the resolution of grass roots and metropolitan issues? As newspapers—metropolitan or very localized—decline, so may their communities and polity.

Note

1. In title and format the *Post* still survives, although it is a completely new publication. It appears nine times annually, is produced in Indianapolis rather than Philadelphia, and has a circulation of perhaps a half million. It is really a souvenir to satisfy the nostalgia of old *Post* readers.

15

Community and Politics in City and Suburb

David Street
Jeffrey L. Davidson

It is widely known that most of the major older metropolitan areas in America have experienced great changes since World War II that have deeply altered the balance of population and resources between the city and suburbia. Critical changes have included the massive migration to suburbia of millions of persons who were disproportionately middle class and white (Farley, 1976); the great buildup of roadways, housing, shopping centers, and urban infrastructure in suburbia; a sharp decline in industrial employment in the city and some growth of employ-

Note: This chapter benefits from a discussion at the Inter-University Metropolitan Seminar (Loyola University, Chicago) and, early on, from a discussion with Gerald D. Suttles.

ment in this sector in the suburban rings (Kasarda, 1976); a dangerous weakening of the tax base in many cities; and an increase in suburban representation to state legislatures following reapportionment (Reichley, 1970). Some of the effects of these changes are obvious, such as the fiscal crisis in New York City and the rising dependency ratios in cities throughout the nation; other effects are less apparent. One might expect that the great growth in population and resources in suburbia would transform the politics and ultimately the polity and power of suburbia. Yet no clear-cut transformation can presently be discerned.

This chapter aims to analyze the relationships between the community and politics in the older cities and their suburbs as they have experienced the kinds of changes just indicated. We are fundamentally interested in comparative analysis—in describing and explaining social change and similarities and differences between cities and suburbs and among different types of cities and suburbs. We will be able to provide less in the way of empirical generalization than informed speculation and a general consideration of how to think about the problem. Further, although we recognize the existence of sizable heterogeneity among suburbs and the need for a typology of suburbs, we have not settled on such a typology nor do we consistently respect the danger of making simple city-suburban contrasts.

Starting Points

We proceed from the intersection of three theoretical starting points. First, we are interested in the political sociology of communities. This implies that we are interested in both the social stratification and the organizational approaches to political sociology (Janowitz, 1968). Applied to communities, the former approach gives rise to an analysis of social class as it shapes community politics, stressing the social bases of political cleavage and cooperation; the latter approach leads to an analysis of community decision making and the problems of developing consensus and effective elite groupings across metropolitan areas.

Second, we start with a macrosociological conception of the metropolitan community as an ultimate object of analysis. Communities are appropriately seen as being in continuing social change. Currently, to quote Hawley (personal communication), "The urban unit may be viewed as a communication system. And changes in communication are threatening to tear it apart." Related to politics, our approach is illuminated by the imagery of Greer (1962a) when he speaks of the disarticulation of the economic city and the political city. Historically, these two aspects of the city could be kept in rough correlation as long as cities were so dominant that they could annex their growing fringes. With the massive suburbanization since World War II, in most locations the economic city has sprawled beyond the control of the political city. From this perspective, the end of our analysis is to make an assessment of change in terms of the capacities for manageability and governance of the "spread city" of the metropolitan area.

Third, Janowitz and Suttles (1977) provide a conception useful for our task by suggesting a model wherein naturally occurring social blocs progressively aggregate into a larger polity that weakly integrates and represents the total metropolitan area. In ideal form the model assumes some coherence across sectors and along levels and a reasonable isomorphism of levels —although the authors suggest many of the complexities involved and clearly intend not to reify a structure but to highlight the problems of aggregation. We present the model schematically in Figure 1, together with an indication of some of the major complexities that make the social construction of larger political communities so difficult. In understanding the typical complexities of aggregation in the suburbs compared

Figure 1. Model of Natural Aggregation and Further Complexities.

Simplified Janowitz-Suttles (1977) Model of Tiering	*Some Further Complexities*
	Fragmented and even capricious federal policies complicate further aggregation
	↑
	Arbitrary and fragmenting state boundaries and policies
	↑
"Aggregated metropolitan area"	Fragmented and polarized metropolitan area
↑	↑
"Organizational community"	Organizational community fragmented (by municipal and subdivision boundaries, other governmental units, neighborhoods)
↑	↑
"Social bloc"	Social bloc

with those normally found in the city, it is helpful to recognize
that the boundaries of various governmental units or salient
physical and social groupings (such as school districts, fire districts, sewer districts, municipalities, townships, and subdivisions) may simply not be coterminous and may not nestle
smaller units within larger ones in any reasonably coherent fashion. Units may be quite disarticulate. Beyond this and what is
indicated in the figure, one can mention other important complications of aggregation: the fact that tiering of levels of government is frequently unrelated to any tiering of levels of mass
media, the incessant change in the system due to continuing
suburbanization, the complications of racial differentiation and
polarization, and the effects that the "politics of accommodation" (of which we will say more later) have in generating ambiguity.

One assumption of the foregoing is that politics throughout the metropolitan area consists of much more than the official actions of such formal levels as the city government or village board. Not only is the settling of issues problematic, but so
also is settling on the units within which issues are to be addressed. In the suburban fringes the sociologies of politics and
community become almost indistinguishable.

Governance and Public Services

The focus of this chapter is the older, settled cities of the
nation and their metropolitan areas, and not the "Sun Belt"
metropolises of the South and Southwest. Our overall approximation of the key trends in problems of governance in these
older metropolitan areas is summarized in Figure 2, which indicates problems of social cleavage, aggregation, and elite activities separately for the city, the suburbs, and the metropolitan
area. We shall consider each in turn.

The Cities. Within the cities, we see a continued strong
racial cleavage as blacks increasingly move toward the majority
population. We also see some reduction in class cleavage or at
least in the abrasiveness of cross-class relations as the bulk of
the population, regardless of race, becomes more homogene-
ously low in socioeconomic status. The out-migration of white
middle and working class groups tends to reduce the political
strength of nationality groups in the city, and this in turn weak-
ens the political machine already softened by decades of reform.[1] The changes may produce a strong conflict between

Figure 2. Approximate Characterization of Changes in Problems of
Governance in Metropolitan Areas, Post-World War II.

	Cities	Suburbs	Metropolitan Areas
Social Cleavage	Continued race cleavage, diminished class cleavage	Increasing heterogeneity masked by "myth of suburbia"	City/suburb cleavage increases
Aggregation	Breakdown of old machine to manage cleavages and forge consensus	"Toy governments"	Accommodative co-operation
Elite	Breakdown of old coalitions; professionalization; unionization	Amateur politicians	No overall elite; some media figures

black working class groupings and predominantly white police, fire, and other public service departments. The reforms that undercut the machine frequently weaken the formal political structure, as in San Francisco, where as Wirt (1970) indicates, successive charter reforms have produced the "politics of hyper-pluralism," thus disorganizing politics and putting city agencies in strong competition with one another.

The breakdown of the old political machine tends to reduce the ties of locality groups to the political system and vice versa, and is related to a partial bureaucratization, professionalization, and unionization of city government and municipal employee groups. In Lowi's (1969) terms, there is substituted a "new machine" for the "old machine." This analogy has its difficulties, however. It is true that both old pols and new professionals operate in self-serving ways. However, the old pols served themselves by relating to the array of interest and locality groups of the city so as to generate both large voter turnouts and considerable consensus on political decisions. With the new professionalized machines, the constituencies, although powerful, seem narrow and extremely self-interested, and it is difficult for them to aggregate public opinion toward effective action.[2] The result then is that new machines are weak. Greer's (1962b) conclusion that the mayor becomes increasingly professional but unable to halt the fundamental trend of city deterioration still seems justified.

The crises of erosion of the tax base, loss of affluent populations, deterioration of housing, and increases in depen-

dent populations further debilitate the political structure. Fiscal
woes reduce or eliminate the exercise of discretion in funding,
programming, and goals, and require minimal funding of those
public programs able to get their share in the life-and-death
struggle of agencies for subsistent resources for operation. The
public nature of the struggle may create the appearance of a
great centralization of power among the competing components
of the new machine, but centralization on a zero-sum basis constitutes a weak center. In cities where blacks are coming into
the majority, by the time they inherit the power there may not
be much left.

The Suburbs. Suburbanization involves processes of
homogenization, with images of megalopolis, "spread city,"
mass society, and, in Boorstin's (1973, p. 273) phrase, the tendency of "everyplace to become anyplace." Suburbanization
also involves differentiation. New suburban housing developments and shopping centers perpetually seek at least marginal
differentiation and the symbols of distinctiveness, and older
suburbs continue to reassert their traditions. Much as Suttles
(1972) finds defended neighborhoods in the city, the student of
the metropolitan area frequently finds defended suburbs and
defended suburban neighborhoods. We may be witnessing the
end of the ultimate defended area, the "exurbia" of lush estates
in Fairfield and Nassau counties, but we find prime specimens
of the defended suburb in such communities as Oak Park and
Shaker Heights (defended against nearby racial change), the
northern shore towns of Long Island (defended against the construction of a bridge across the sound), and Ann Arbor (defended against the fact that it really is part of the Detroit
metropolitan area).

Objectively, suburbia becomes more heterogeneous, in
terms of population, occupational structures, incomes, and to a
very small degree race. These changes tend to be masked by the
"myth of suburbia," that is, by the tendency for suburbanites
to visualize themselves and their neighbors as being affluent and
respectable no matter what the reality (Berger, 1971). Politics,
then, is cast in a rhetoric of progress and amenities, even when
the new residents of an American dream community of $80,000
homes find that their youngsters' sparkling new high school is
on a double shift. Suburban populations that do not fit the
model of affluence may find themselves and their problems disregarded, as the poor of suburbia are undefended and much
more the "invisible poor" than the poor of the city.[3]

When one asks how the political structure of suburbia

changes with massive suburbanization, the answer must be "the more things change, the more they stay the same." The new populations are essentially accommodated by and become part of the existing political structures of villages, townships, and other units (Zimmer, 1976), and these governmental units reflect more the character of community development of the 1950s than present realities. Suburban development grafts onto and largely adds to the "polycentric metropolis"—in the New York area, to Wood's *1400 Governments* (1961). The small units are what Greer (1962a) termed the "toy governments," characterized by amateur politicians.

The pattern, of course, is not quite this simple. Suburbia tends to have higher levels of resources than the cities, particularly for supporting schools, and it is no accident that the greatest aggregate activity in suburbia is to create large and highly bureaucratized and professionalized school systems. Some suburban areas also have highly developed county governments. The resources available even to the more affluent suburbs are limited, however, particularly in light of the great expense of creating new school systems and an infrastructure of roadways, water systems, and sewage systems in the open countryside. Given these expenses and the lack of economies of scale in the operation of small governmental units, there is often no way to generate the full round of amenities that the suburban myth implies and particularly to build social and cultural institutions besides the schools. The provincialism of the communities that make up suburbia hinders this growth as well. Riska (1974) has documented how localism impedes the development of modern medical facilities on affluent Long Island.

Some suburban municipalities are likely to be highly homogeneous and may feature a substantial fit between the grass roots emphasis of government, the ideologies of the residents, and residents' social characteristics (Gans, 1967). Relative to the well-publicized difficulties of the city, suburban problems are not ominous, and the answer to the question "How does your local government work?" is likely to be "I don't really know, but it must be OK." As Wood (1958) argued long ago, the rooting of suburban politics in local real estate taxes produces a politics of differentiation and competition. When these atomized units face sizable increases in the incidence of urban problems (such as crime and drugs) or of problems requiring federated or cooperative relations (such as the need for water, sewage, or mass transportation), the politics of the suburban myth and the politics of differentiation and competition stand in the way. The suburbs are so atomized that they even limit the rational planning that could facilitate the arrival of more industry (Wood, 1959)—ironically a great blessing for cities.

The Metropolitan Area. It follows that governance at the metropolitan level is weak and that the provision of public services is atomized and therefore uneven. The creation of true metropolitan governments is the exception (major instances being Miami, Nashville, Jacksonville, Baton Rouge, and Indianapolis), and evidence exists that when metropolitan governments are created, they tend to disappoint their proponents by retaining existing politicians and programs (Greer, 1963). In most of the nation the metropolitan government solution remains only a continuing aspiration of reformers who have become realistic enough to refrain from even launching a campaign (Zimmer, 1976). In addition to the guaranteed opposition of suburban residents (Adrian, 1961) and the reluctance of politicians and others in the city to see their jobs jeopardized (Ylvisaker, 1961), there is now the added fact that metropolitan government may seem a special threat to blacks coming into power in the cities.

Fundamentally, then, the governance of the metropolis is left to the market system and to efforts at cooperation in limited spheres, seeking in small ways to overcome the fact that the suburbs are defended against each other. Ostrom, Tiebout, and Warren (1961, p. 838) analyze the metropolitan area as a "polycentric political system" providing "quasi-market choice for the local residents in permitting them to select the particular community in the metropolitan area that most closely approximates the public service levels they desire." In this view the system works by permitting cooperation through contractual arrangements among communities (as with the Lakewood Plan, wherein municipalities arrange with Los Angeles County for specific service packages), by fostering other cooperative arrangements on matters where benefits are likely to be uniform across communities, and through litigation. Perhaps even more than in the city, the suburban ring provides fertile territory for bargaining and an "ecology of games" (Long, 1958, 1962). Limited-purpose government units can provide sensible programs, but they may be so limited and therefore so small as to be uneconomic. Or, if given substantial resources (as with the New York Port Authority), they may become self-serving, skimming off resources and undercutting other units of government (Doig, 1966). As Dye and others (1963) have shown in a study of the Philadelphia area, intergovernmental agreements are infrequent among communities that are not very similar socially and economically. Gottdiener (Chapter Sixteen of this volume; also Gottdiener, 1977) has documented the superficiality of land-use planning on Long Island, a process that blends professionalism in planning with grass roots democracy and frequently results in land developers getting their way. Private interests are much better organized than are localities, and although the forces for community betterment win most of the battles, eventually the developers, whether corruptly or legally, win many wars.

The planning rituals that Gottdiener observed illustrate well the pattern of "accommodative cooperation" of metropolitan politics. Danielson (1971, pp. 193-194) describes this pattern and indicates some dynamics for change implicit within it, as follows:

> The fragmented, small scale suburban political system uses [such devices as the Lakewood plan], as well as growing state and federal involvement, to accommodate itself successfully to the steadily rising pressures for more public goods and services. The system of accommodation has shortcomings. . . . It encourages proliferation and differentiation, diffuses responsibility, weakens the representative processes, handles some kinds of problems far more effectively than others, and lacks any commitment to the general welfare. Nonetheless, the system of accommodation works sufficiently well to foreclose more extensive approaches to the provision of public services in suburbia. Since it preserves the autonomy of the individual suburban jurisdiction, most suburbanites see it as a successful system.
>
> But local autonomy is preserved at a price. The principal feature of the politics of accommodation is the growth of functional autonomy. Increased use of special districts, assistance programs, and other devices shifts control over broad areas of public policy from local officials and the electorate to relatively autonomous agencies responsible for particular functions of government. More and more key decisions . . . are made by independently financed agencies responsible for one function and insulated from the local political process.

Diminished land control is an ironic development since the desire to maintain the political and fiscal integrity of the community underlies the system of accommodation. Functional autonomy only partially diminishes local control, however, since it rarely threatens directly the most critical of all local political concerns, the regulation of land use. In addition, the system of accommodation is highly flexible because most relationships are voluntary.

What we see, then, are incomplete efforts at aggregation, made possible only if directed at specific purposes like the provision of water, sewage systems, and transportation (Janowitz and Suttles, 1977) or created as carefully honed efforts to improve metropolitan coordination directed by the legislature (as presently in the Twin Cities). The need for aggregation does not create a political leadership that could bring aggregation into being (see Greer and Greer, 1976, on the invisibility of public figures in the unsuccessful fight for metropolitan government in St. Louis). Robert Moses, the power entrepreneur of the New York Port Authority, is the great exception, and a disquieting one at that. Further, the racial changes of the city reinforce the city-suburban cleavage and make the development of area-wide leadership even more unlikely.

Character of Local Citizen Political Participation

While the need to aggregate suburban and city politics into a metropolitan system has not produced the political leadership necessary to bring this aggregation about, local politics continues to be practiced in both cities and suburbs. Residents of the metropolitan area frequently resort to overt political action to get streets repaired, taxes lowered, trash collected, parks built, public housing banned, schools improved, and crime stopped. While these "domestic affairs" may seem trivial compared with other glaring social problems faced by the metropolis, these purely local, sometimes personal issues possess a motivational power that contributes to the vitality of the local political arena in the face of the nagging realization that local government may in large part have outlived its usefulness.

Here we will make a statement about local political participation that is in part substantiated empirically and in part based on a hypothetical extension of the findings of a study of

Ann Arbor, Michigan (Davidson, 1977). Theoretically, citizen participation in local politics may be viewed as having four interrelated functions. First, participation by locality and interest groups may draw attention to wants and needs to which local government officials may have been insensitive. Most attempts by citizens groups to influence local officials involve a desire to gain some favorable outcome on a substantive issue or set of issues. In any community, delivery of services is likely to be uneven, creating the likelihood that some groups of citizens will mobilize to seek redress. Regardless of whether these efforts succeed, groups that participate will at least increase the recognition of their needs by local officials.

A second function is that community residents who mobilize on a local issue may place that issue on the general political agenda. For example, a neighborhood group concerned about sewage polluting a nearby pond may, through repeated attempts, bring the issue before local decision-making bodies by directing the attention of local officials not only to the pollution of the nearby pond but also to similar problems occurring elsewhere in the community. By pursuing their parochial position on an issue, the group may cause other groups, their elected officials, and the administrative machinery of local government to become concerned about an issue at large. Citizen participation in local politics, then, can contribute to the flexibility of local government by providing it with a continuing stream of new issues to consider.

Third, citizen participation can produce new leaders for the political system. People active in the affairs of their neighborhood may be drawn into the political arena when an issue affecting their neighborhood arises. As their awareness of the intricacies of local politics increases, these neighborhood politicians may find that they have talents that should not be confined to a single neighborhood and consequently may become more actively involved in larger issues that concern their own neighborhood only indirectly. Frequently local political organizations will identify promising neighborhood politicians and recruit them first for precinct work and later for candidacy for local office. In most cases, the ranks of local political leadership may not be as permeable as we have implied, but in communities characterized by high mobility—including both cities and suburbs—a housewife lobbying a council member for more efficient trash collection one week may find herself working for that council member's reelection the next.

The final function of local political participation is its importance in creating and maintaining community boundaries and community political identities. In the process of lobbying local officials for parks or against shopping centers or low-income housing, locality groups may refer to their neighborhood as an entity with certain wants and needs that transcend the people who happen to live there. If these groups persist in their attempts, these definitions of community identity are communicated to local public officials, who may use these definitions in determining neighborhood boundaries and neighborhood identities (Davidson, 1977). These definitions can also be useful to public officials as guidelines as to how seriously they should weigh subsequent lobbying attempts by residents from a particular area and how sensitive officials should be to concerns expressed by various locality groups. Requests from residents of an area perceived as populated by transients will thus be treated differently from requests by residents of areas perceived as stable and involved in local affairs. The definitions communicated by local citizen activity can therefore be more important than the outcomes of specific issues. For example, the implications of the political identities that local officials construct for a neighborhood may be more far-reaching than whether the local city council votes to rezone a nearby piece of land for apartments. Once the apartments are built, local residents can adapt to them regardless of their earlier views; however, political identities resulting from lobbying efforts can affect a whole range of decisions involving a neighborhood over a period of years. In analyzing the effectiveness of local citizen participation, therefore, one is advised to examine both the short-run outcomes and the long-run effects.

Diversity of Local Political Systems. The functions served by citizen participation in local politics can, of course, vary considerably, depending on the nature of the local political system in which it occurs. Activity by a locality group in a city of over a million people with a strong mayor and board of aldermen and with partisan, ward-based local elections does not have the same effect as similar activity in a town of 5,000 with a professional town manager and a largely impotent town council. Taking into account the great diversity in communities in both cities and suburbs, it is difficult to generalize about the nature and effects of local citizen participation. We confront local political systems that differ in their affluence, organization, geographical scope, autonomy, authority, competitiveness, and responsiveness to local residents. The cities and suburbs comprising these local systems may be very large or very small, rich or poor, new or old, largely industrial or residential, and relatively tranquil or extremely tense. The functions played by citizen participation in local political systems is affected by all of these variables.

Participation in the Suburbs. Nowhere do the seemingly trivial domestic affairs of local government constitute so important a source of political participation as in the suburbs. Both popular literature (Keats, 1956) and more scholarly work (Wirt and others, 1972; Greer and Greer, 1976) have found higher rates of local political participation among suburban residents than among urban dwellers. Explanations for this difference in participation have been sought in the characteristics of the suburban population, the nature of suburbs as communities, and the character of suburban governments. Because suburban residents are more likely to be white and middle class than are residents of the central city, they exhibit higher scores on measures of participation, which have traditionally been related to socioeconomic status (SES) and to race. Many researchers note these social differences and argue that suburban residence has no independent effect on participation (Verba and Nie, 1972). Some research indicates, however, that while the traditional relationships between SES and political participation do hold among suburban residents, suburbanites of a given social class tend to participate more than their urban counterparts (Greer and Greer, 1976). This conclusion assumes that the explanation of at least part of the suburbanites' higher rates of political activity lies beyond class and racial characteristics.

A number of social scientists have looked to the characteristics of suburbs as communities to explain differential participation. Fischer and Jackson (1976) suggest that the peripheral location of suburban communities increases the costs of maintaining social networks across the metropolitan area, leading to the creation of social worlds centered primarily within the suburban neighborhood. This constriction of the suburbanites' social world leads to an increased concern among suburban residents with the well-being of the local area. Increased citizen participation in the domestic affairs of suburban municipalities may then be viewed as an expression of their increased localism.

The City: Machine and Reform. While recent work has analyzed the importance of localism in generating much suburban activity, this emphasis runs counter to a persistent theme in the literature on suburbanization, which maintains that as urban areas grow, a set of economic, occupational, and other nonterritorial interests replace locality as the organizing basis of politics (see discussion in Greer, 1962a). The replacement of the old-time machine with an alternative form of political organization clearly indicates this trend (Lowi, 1969). Where this change has occurred, groups whose primary interest in the political system rests with its ability to serve their neighborhoods are left without adequate institutional channels for their political activity. Replacement of ward-based, partisan electoral systems with at-large reform government structures has reduced political corruption but weakened an important organizing force by which the interests and concerns of locality groups were expressed within the political system. Where once locality found its expression through participation in machine politics, the general trend is toward the elimination of poorly organized locality groups from the urban political arena.

One can sensibly ask why reform in the cities decreases the participation of locality groups when participation is so high in the suburbs, which have had a reform structure almost from the outset. To understand this, we must consider how the old-time machines facilitated the political participation of locality groups. One of the machine's primary functions was to reduce the distance between the locality group and decision-making authorities. The machine's representatives served as intermediaries who helped residents organize and articulate their interests and who communicated those interests to the responsible decision makers. The machine was thus an external agent active in creating both the locality groups and their requests for assistance. The machine's payoff, of course, was continued electoral support by the locality groups and, in many instances, the financial benefits made possible by control of city government.

The absence of the machine as an intermediary between the locality group and local government thus has different effects on large cities and suburbs. Locality groups in large reform cities have few institutional bridges between themselves and the authorities. The officials' interests lie with the well-being of either the city as a whole or of particular interest groups (business, labor, or various ethnic groups) rather than with the well-being of particular neighborhoods. Of course, locality-group members may present themselves as representatives with general "informed opinion" in the city at large, but frequently they are discredited once their ties to locality are discerned. Thus "liberal opinion" in New York may be discounted as representing "those nuts from the upper West Side." Because of the size of large reformed cities and the number of votes required to elect candidates in at-large elections, no single neighborhood (or even collection of adjoining neighborhoods) has sufficient electoral strength to draw candidates' attention to the neighborhood's needs. Even if the locality group can gain access to high-level city officials, there is no assurance that the officials will pay attention to it. (Witness the ineffective attempts of neighborhood groups to affect park construction in New York City under Robert Moses.)

Suburban Government Participation. Contrast the city's pattern of participation to that of most suburbs. Due to the size and homogeneity of many suburban communities, the social distance between locality groups and public officials tends to be small (Wood, 1958; Danielson, 1976). Where the principal unit of government in the suburb is larger than the municipality—for example, the township or county—social distance is presumably increased and responsiveness decreased. Because elected officials in the suburbs are likely to live in a neighborhood similar to that of the locality group, persons interested in securing something for their neighborhood are generally more comfortable attempting to influence their local officials. This may be one of the factors behind the increased political efficacy and political participation of both lower class and working class suburban residents (Wirt and others, 1972; Greer and Greer, 1976).

Where local political systems are relatively small (as in many suburban systems), the absence of a political machine intermediary is mitigated because the electoral activity of each neighborhood can be more crucial in local elections, therefore making elected public officials more sensitive to their wants and needs. In his study of Ann Arbor, Davidson (1977) discovered that candidates for city council spent more time campaigning in neighborhoods that by virtue of their size and homogeneity had a great potential for affecting the outcome of local elections. This differential investment of campaign activity made council members more sensitive to the wants and needs of these neighborhood residents and more responsive when they sought to influence city council. Although Ann Arbor has a partisan, ward-based electoral system, it seems likely that even in smaller systems with reform structures, concerted electoral activity by the residents of one or a few adjoining neighborhoods can play a similar role in attracting the attention of candidates for public office. Suburban political systems with reform structures would, of course, vary in the extent to which a neighborhood's voting behavior would offset the effects of the lack of a machine-organized electoral system. The size of the system, the diversity of local interests, the amount of political conflict in the community, and the role of elected officials in local government would presumably play important roles in determining the importance of neighborhood electoral activity to a locality group's political efficacy.

Political Differentiation of Neighborhoods. Our discussion suggests a substantial degree of political differentiation of neighborhoods. Analyses of suburban local politics have generally concentrated on the suburban community as a whole, sometimes focusing on how suburbanites defend their community from encroachments by inner-city forces (Danielson, 1976). Exclusionary zoning practices, opposition to busing, refusal to maintain inefficient local hospitals, sewage treatment plants, and police forces all evidence this protectionist posture. Parallel to this pattern, however, one finds that residents of suburban communities, like their urban counterparts, organize to defend their individual neighborhoods rather than the communities as a whole from changes that they believe will lead to a deterioration in the quality of life or the value of their investment in their own neighborhoods. These organizing efforts are at the heart of what we call the domestic affairs of suburbia.

This emphasis on the internal differentiation of suburban communities may seem curious given the image of the suburb as a reborn New England town governed by a town meeting in which all citizens participate (Wood, 1958). While some suburban communities may conform to this model, an alternative picture of suburbia consisting of endless tracts of subdivisions, each with its own developer-provided name and identity, seems to fit the reality of most metropolitan areas today. Rather than being made up of quasi-rural, semiisolated estates as the town meeting image implies, suburban areas are frequently collections of "artificial communities" (Suttles, 1972), which provide residents with social categories that enable them to locate themselves in an otherwise undifferentiated landscape. While "Nottingham Green" may not seem particularly different from "Covered Bridge Farms" to the outside observer, residents of these subdivisions know where one begins and the other ends, and know what it means to be a resident of one rather than the other. When an issue arises that residents see as a threat to their neighborhood, they frequently define that neighborhood in terms of their subdivision. Thus, subdivision names are useful not only as locational referents, but also as symbols in the local political culture.

While subdivision names and identities are important sources of differentiation for suburban residents, these identities are perhaps more interesting for their usefulness for local public officials. Not only do subdivisions have identities in terms of their population characteristics (rich, white, working class, and so on), they also have political identities that local officials use to locate residents in the political landscape. Davidson (1977) found that elected council members defined some neighborhoods as particularly well organized, active, and politically sophisticated entities (political neighborhoods), while others were seen as disorganized collections of apathetic individuals. Political neighborhoods were seen by council members as potentially powerful political entities by virtue of the pivotal role they could play in local elections. Council members were therefore highly sensitive to requests from residents of these neighborhoods. By maintaining informal working relationships with council members, residents of political neighborhoods were able to get inside information on issues, which in turn reinforced their ability to calmly and rationally influence other council members in the name of their neighborhoods (subdivisions). The matter-of-fact tone of their influence attempts further contributed to the neighborhoods' reputation as organized, sophisticated entities, and further increased the likelihood that those influence attempts would gain listeners.

Furthermore, residents of subdivision neighborhoods with low or fluctuating voter turnout are unlikely to attract the sustained attention from local officials necessary for political neighborhood definition to be created, even if they make repeated attempts to influence those officials. In short, to obtain the advantaged position in local politics accompanying definition as a political neighborhood, an area must have a core group of persistent neighborhood activists willing to speak for the good of the neighborhood; it must have recurrent issues around which that group of activists can rally; it must have voters capable of turning out in sufficient numbers to affect the outcome of local elections; and it must be located in a political system where locality is salient. Clearly, this combination of characteristics is not shared by most neighborhoods.

Ironically, the creation of political neighborhoods in the

suburbs gives locality there an importance parallel to what it had in the nonreformed city, where the machine always was attentive to the wants and needs of residents of neighborhoods where their supporting voters resided. The core of political activists of suburban political neighborhoods serve much the same function as the machine's local ward and precinct workers. It is in the reformed city where the concept of political neighborhood is least useful, and if the needs and identities of neighborhoods are still important to their residents, their influence on public officials has decreased markedly.[4] This loss of influence in the reformed city should not be overstated, however. While local groups lose their negotiating power with elected officials, they may retain it with officials of the new machines. This occurs because government and government-supported programs have been addressed to specific neighborhoods identified as target areas for services or experiments in health, welfare, or other fields. Such programs frequently require consultation with local residents and so advisory boards of citizens, who presumably are representative, are sometimes created. This consultation provides a new route for influence for locality groups and may add to the concept of political neighborhood the related concept of "bureaucratic neighborhood."

Local Participation and Metropolitan Aggregation. Another source of difference between city and suburban political participation lies in the issues that the two communities habitually confront. Large-city governments continually face both issues centering on the delivery of residentially based services (such as police protection, trash collection, education, and street repair) and issues emerging from large-scale social problems (such as unemployment, welfare, and drug addiction). While shrinking resources make both types of issues increasingly difficult for big-city governments to handle, the former type of issue is clearly more amenable to successful resolution than the latter: City officials can sometimes get the trash collected, but unemployment and welfare services are usually beyond their control.

On the other hand, suburban governments have until recently dealt almost exclusively with issues of the first type. While these issues may seem trivial when compared with the problems of the city, they do have the appealing feature of being easier to resolve. Because local governments are thus more likely to be effective in resolving these issues, groups of residents are more willing to enter the political arena. Thus, not only do suburban residents have high levels of personal political efficacy, but also the political systems in which they live seem more effective than big-city governments.

With the urbanization of suburbia (Masotti and Hadden, 1973), however, the capacity of many suburban governments to resolve even the trivial issues that confront them is being seriously undermined. Not only are many suburbs beginning to suffer the same constriction of resources that have long plagued big-city governments (indeed, many older, less affluent suburbs have suffered from insufficient funds for a long time), but an increasing concentration of population and industry in suburbs that were once exclusive islands of single-family dwellings creates problems of management and social control that are often beyond the capability of suburban toy governments (Greer, 1962a). As the problems facing suburban local governments become increasingly complex and as local resources become increasingly complex and as local resources become more scarce, the capricious boundaries of these governmental units begin to inhibit the successful management of such growing problems as crime control, sewage treatment, medical care, education, and control of spreading blight. In addition, the intervention of the federal, county, and state governments; the courts; and regional special-purpose districts on matters that were formerly within the purview of local governments further constrains the ability of suburban governments to act effectively, even on such sources of suburban pride as education or land use. Like city governments, even those suburban governments that were effective in the past are becoming increasingly feeble (Newton, 1976).

This diminishing capacity to act effectively can have serious consequences for government and politics both within suburbs and within the metropolitan area as a whole. It can discourage suburbanites from trying to influence their local officials on important issues. Participation in local politics can be increasingly considered a waste of time. Even in suburban political neighborhoods, the recognition that local government cannot find solutions to local problems itself can inhibit political activism. While residents of a political neighborhood might have inordinate influence within a particular suburb, they are likely to have no more influence than any other neighborhood when the issue is decided at a higher level of government or when no level of government exists that can make the necessary decision. Indeed, where the decision is to be made by the courts, such residents may have no legal standing.

Recognition by politically active suburbanites that their local governments can no longer serve their neighborhoods can, however, have a different result. Instead of diminishing participation by residents, it can lead to a redirection of that participation. No matter what changes occur in the government's ability to handle local problems, the predominantly local orientation of suburban residents will probably not change, and they are likely to continue to want government to maintain high levels of service delivery. Yet when their local governments can no longer provide adequate services, the focus of politically active suburban locality groups could shift from attempts to secure better services to an effort to join other communities in aggregating sufficient support until a new political entity is formed with the necessary scope to deal with problem issues.

Two strategies are available to such locality groups. They can coalesce with locality groups in other communities into regional interest groups that attempt to influence a higher level of government (Hunter and Suttles, 1972). Or they can combine their locality with other local units to form a regional interest group with its own resources and the legal standing to take part in judicial proceedings. The impetus for both of these forms of aggregation would emerge from the purely localist orientation of suburban residents, an orientation that has until now been a major obstruction to meaningful aggregation. Given the progressive decline in the ability of individual suburbs to manage their own domestic affairs, if suburban residents wish to maintain the levels of service to which they have become accustomed, one or the other of these forms of aggregation should be considered. Of course, moving to another suburb that can provide adequate services (as in the "community of limited liability" model of Janowitz, 1967) is an option many suburbanites would choose over aggregation.

The consequences for metropolitan aggregation of local citizen participation thus depend largely on the focus of that participation. Up to now, citizen participation in local politics in most cities and suburbs has been parochial, reinforcing community definitions emphasizing autonomy and exclusivity. A major consequence has been to inhibit the development of metropolitan aggregation. If as local governments become less able to meet the needs of their neighborhoods, locality groups redirect their influence attempts toward larger units of government, quite different definitions of community identity and boundaries could result. Rather than defining themselves as local groups pursuing their own parochial interests, groups en-

gaging in participation on issues of broader geographical scope
are likely to refer to larger entities, leading the public officials
they try to influence to construct broader definitions of community identity. While these new community definitions would
probably not involve very large segments of the metropolitan
area, they could constitute first steps in the emergence of a
more fully articulated metropolitan political community. Thus,
while the political leadership among city and suburban government officials necessary for aggregation and cooperation in the
metropolitan area has been lacking, the prospects for the creation of at least partial, temporary forms of meaningful metropolitan aggregation may not be entirely bleak. As in the past,
the leadership for this coordination will probably come not
from the enlightened leadership of public officials in either the
cities or the suburbs: It will have to be a by-product of the desires of locality groups, primarily in the suburbs, to keep their
neighborhoods from suffering the fate that many suburbanites
moved to the suburbs to avoid—the progressive deterioration of
their residential environments.

The Future

We have looked at patterns of stability and change in
politics and government in America's older cities and metropolitan areas as the society has moved into the diffuse phase of
urbanization. In the cities we have seen continued racial change
and cleavage, a general breakdown in the old machine and coalitions as means to forge consensus, and the rise of professional
and union interest groups managing local government. In the
suburbs we have seen an increasing heterogeneity in the population masked by the myth of suburbia and a continued proliferation of toy governments managed by amateur politicians mainly
in the interest of suburban defense. Across metropolitan areas
we have seen the cleavage between the city and suburbs increasing (although lessened in terms of the traditional distinction
between the Democratic city and the Republican suburb), and
we have seen attempts at aggregation to be limited and weak,
suffused with accommodative cooperation and lacking area-
wide leadership. We have also analyzed the continued viability
of local participation, particularly in the suburbs, and have identified mechanisms through which, given the continued frustrations of metropolitan change, local participation might produce
efforts to enhance aggregation. Overall, we see a disarticulated

and fragmented system; the transformation in the scale of the economic city does not give rise to a transformation in scale of the political city. Still, we also see some motivation for change from the local level.

The social costs of the predominant patterns of metropolitan change are heavy and in many respects grow heavier. Suburbanization continually generates inequities, particularly as the movement of population, tax base, industrial jobs, and other resources from the city leaves in its wake a weakened and segregated school system, deteriorating and abandoned housing, a large number of unemployed and underemployed youths, and conditions that invite crime and additional out-migration. The patterns of metropolitan sprawl begin to create high social costs for suburbanites as well, as they must support the perpetual reconstruction of the urban infrastructure (schools, roads, and sewers) and as they fail to create political structures and agencies with the capacity to handle the urban problems that inevitably begin to seep into suburbia. In particular, many of the suburbs are beginning to suffer the costs of having woefully overcapitalized their school systems as both communities and resident populations age. The benefits of the flow of resources from city to suburb accrue principally to the individual householder in terms of the rising value of housing and the amenities of personal life-style; few of these resources go to any collective and long-term effort to preserve and enhance the common good.

These patterns are not merely the result of impersonal economic and ecological trends; they are also stimulated by political activities and government policies at many levels. The localism and parochialism of suburban politics of course contribute mightily to the failure to develop political structures that would address planning and the reduction of inequities over the entire metropolitan area. The interest-group competitiveness of municipal, "new machine" groups has a similar effect. As is well known, federal and state policies have made a critical contribution to the patterns of unguided sprawl. This is particularly true of the federal stimulation of suburban housing development through the VA and FHA loan programs and of federal and state programs of highway construction. The higher units of government spend great amounts of money in both the cities and suburbs, but spending in the cities tends to take the form of welfare transfer payments. Governmental spending in the suburbs tends to have the effect of investment through the construction of expressways that attract the wealth of shopping center and subdivision development, the latter further aided by federally insured loans. In recent years federal policies have been especially fateful for older metropolitan areas, as they have disproportionately directed investment and other funds away from the cities of the "urban heartland." (On the special problems and prospects of these cities, see Suttles's Chapter Seventeen of this volume.)

Looking ahead, several scenarios seem possible. One is a simple continuation of unending sprawl, fragmentation, the decline of the central city, and accompanying social costs. This scenario seems unlikely to occur because the costs are becoming so widely recognized and they sometimes sharply affect even the heretofore best-defended suburbs. Another and more probable scenario involves the painful and uneven steps that ultimately result in some increase in the level of cooperation among the governmental units of the metropolitan area. This would occur when the lag between suburbanization and the polity becomes too stressful. The suburban myth becomes more difficult to sustain as the economics of construction require that an increasing proportion of new suburban homes be apartments and condominiums and as the class and ethnic base of suburbia broadens, more industrial and commercial development occurs, and new economic leaders with new perspectives emerge (Danielson, 1971, p. 370). The assumptions of suburbia are also battered when middle-aged suburbanites find that their emancipated offspring are unable to afford to live nearby and when residents of the inner suburban rings confront decay of commercial strips, subdivisions, and schools and growth of welfare and crime problems. Under this scenario, cooperation would be enhanced by the increasing activities of dissatisfied local groups. Their crystallization, however, would require the emergence of new economic or other elites.

Unanswered in this scenario is the question of whether the central city would genuinely be included in metropolitan aggregation. The periphery might strengthen at the further expense of the center. In benign form, the suburbs could develop cooperation with cities on such matters as water distribution systems and regional transportation, in the latter case cementing the independence of suburbia by investing more in intrasuburban transportation than in facilitating the journey to and from the center. At its worst, this scenario would find the suburbs more insulated from the central cities' populations and problems, presumably under the assumption (but perhaps not the reality) that the cities had become a federal responsibility. Further civil disorders could finally make the city-suburban dichotomy nearly complete and leave the city as a federally administered reservation. The preferred scenario is, of course, one of a strengthened metropolitan polity, sharing both the benefits and costs of the urban social order in both the center and the periphery.

There are no master solutions to the concrete social problems of the metropolitan area or to the problems of developing a more adequate structure of metropolitan governance. Among policy proposals that seem likely to be effective but are unfeasible politically, the following seem especially attractive: stopping all further highway construction and issuance of sewer permits, thus halting suburban sprawl; and putting a prohibitive user's fee on airline tickets while creating high-speed intercity train service, making the neighborhoods of the old downtown railway stations attractive to businessmen again. Such actions could quickly impose a "Spaceship Earth" mentality on the metropolitan area, but they remain unfeasible unless and until an energy crisis transforms the nation's ecology drastically. Appropriate policies must be realistic and therefore incremental. In Chapter Seventeen in this volume, Suttles argues the benefits of civic leadership giving up the "renaissance" mentality of city reconstruction for more modest but feasible goals. Similarly, those who would reform the metropolis are generally sensible to avoid proclaiming the overall cure of a metropolitan government.

We have not made a policy analysis. But we can suggest a few possibilities for exploration: (1) raising federal subsidies to regional transportation authorities that attend to the journey *out* to work and not just the journey in; (2) resisting where possible further freeway construction and exacting financial benefits for mass transportation where it cannot be halted; (3) fighting through litigation and legislation to require the suburbs to allow low-cost housing and to mandate cross-district school desegregation; (4) withholding revenue sharing funds from suburban units that levy low property taxes; (5) equalizing federal spending among regions of the nation; (6) encouraging the linking of private to public investment in the cities, as by arranging for industries to build next to junior colleges, which would facilitate the development of cooperative training and work programs; and (7) requiring thorough environmental impact

Communication and Politics

studies, applying to the entire metropolitan environment, for all
sizable investments, public and private.[5] These are not startling
proposals; they are part of ongoing metropolitan and federal
politics. The resolution of the issues they address will be fateful
for America's metropolitan areas. The most important general
strategy is that federal funds should be used as incentives to
metropolitan cooperation. A significant corollary is that these
funds should not reward "cooperation for cooperation's sake"
but should in each instance be designed to ameliorate inequities,
particularly those between suburbs and cities.

Finally, to analyze the glaring social and political problems of the metropolis is not to subscribe to the entire "urban
crisis" ideology and "end of the city" angst of the 1960s. Most
of America's cities have been strongly resilient in the face of
massive suburbanization and the widely presumed antiurban
bias of the culture—perhaps in part because there are many cultural themes celebrating the city center. Whatever the politics of
the metropolitan area, certain life cycle and life-style characteristics and certain cultural tastes make city life especially attractive to certain groups—particularly to many minority groups,
rich and poor, to "mainstream," educated groups before they
have children and, for some, after their children have grown.
The cultural, educational, and communal institutions that attract these groups resist diffusion (see Kornblum and Williams,
Chapter Three of this volume), and this fact seems to imply a
continued viability of city life for the foreseeable future.

Notes

1. As Banfield and Wilson (1963) indicated years ago, two aspects
of the environment of the city inescapably offer inducements to reform:
the lure of federal monies available in return for producing large Democratic pluralities, requiring heavy Democratic voting not only in the city
but without; and the suburbanization of voters. Together these aspects require the Democratic mayor to submit to further reform in order that the
party not be discredited in the eyes of suburbanites.

2. The new machines do not seem to have grown uniformly across
the cities. They are well developed in the Northeast, the West Coast, and in
a few other cities (for example, New Orleans and Kansas City) in which
the unions and minority groups seem to have forged alliances. These alliances may be falling apart and probably were never very stable (Suttles,
1976, personal communication).

3. A drapery salesman in an affluent Levitt development on Long
Island told us that he is often called on to install draperies in great haste to
conceal the fact that the incoming residents have not yet purchased respectable furniture.

4. That the needs of the neighborhood are still important to residents is indicated by the frequency with which locality groups petition the municipal government over some abuse or lack of service by going on the local television news, which also indicates the lack of mechanisms for direct communication to political structure. Problems of communication in the reform city are also illustrated by the fact that one of our students, a community organizer working in Detroit in 1976, was given the task of figuring out how a message from the Latino community in which he served could be routed to the black mayor, Coleman Young. He was unable to trace a likely route, in marked contrast to the ease in which a route could be sketched in a political structure comprised of aldermen and ward committeemen, as in Chicago.

5. Many of these suggestions and the more extreme ones mentioned earlier came up at the *Chicago Daily News* Seminar on "Chicago and Its Suburbs," April 6, 1977.

16

Social Planning and Metropolitan Growth

Mark D. Gottdiener

Urban growth in the United States can be characterized by great migratory patterns that have often mirrored historical stages in the nation's development. In the nineteenth century the social fabric was strained by rapid industrialization and the massive influx of relatively poor immigrants into the cities. On the one hand, such growth signified the remarkable strength of a new nation embarking on a path of large-scale capital development and supported by a steadily growing pool of low-wage laborers eager for work. On the other hand, the enormous successes of private industrialists in every region stood in glaring contrast to the inequities of urban social life. Rapid, unbalanced growth left a small part of the nation's population extremely well-off with considerable leisure time. At the same time, the majority of city residents was saddled with abysmal housing and sanitation conditions, limited educational opportunities, neighbor-

494

hood crime, frequent public health crises, and predatory political regimes controlled by bosses. Early social legislation and religious reform programs in the nineteenth century sought to overcome these evils of capitalist development by combining to
articulate a political and voluntaristic response to rapid, uncoordinated growth.

Amelioration was pursued, for the most part, by identifying the city itself as a social landscape in need of repair
(Scott, 1971). Turn-of-the-century efforts progressed on at least
three distinct levels—political reform, social legislation, and
urban planning. Political reforms were designed to promote
"good government" and anticorruption municipal forces. Legislation, such as child-labor laws and statutes on compulsory
education, was intended to guarantee minimal living standards
for the large immigrant working class. Perhaps the most innovative aspect of these efforts, however, was the formulation of
an early version of urban planning. The social and religious
reformers believed that adequate living and working arrangements for the city could be realized by the appropriate and
"rational" application of municipal land-use measures that
would control the private decisions of businessmen for the public good. The challenge faced by these early urban planners in
America, however, was to conceive of planning tools that were
compatible with the public philosophy of laissez-faire and a
commonly held belief in the virtues of limited government
intervention. This was not then, nor is it now, an easy task for
planners, and their early efforts were only partially successful
(Delafons, 1969).

Contemporary problems of the urban environment have
somewhat different causes overall, but large-scale population
changes remain a factor. In the present case, however, it is regional migration to the suburbs and not city population growth
that is of primary concern. The social responses to uncoordinated development, however, do seem to be repeating history.
Social reformers in the United States have retained their three-
pronged approach of legislation, political reform, and land-use
planning, and they continue to lack a comprehensive connection between the efforts made within each of these realms. Consequently, the society continues to experience limited success in
integrating and controlling growth. Before discussing present-
day aspects of social planning, however, let us examine the
unique patterns of modern metropolitan growth and their associated causes.

Patterns of Metropolitan Growth

The post-World War II era ushered in a new phase of urban development involving a massive dispersal of city residents and activities into the hinterland of metropolitan regions. This pattern, the opposite of the nineteenth-century implosion, is a centrifugal flow of people, housing, jobs, cultural institutions, and commercial establishments from the central city to the surrounding regions (Zimmer, 1975). Its features include the large, rapid increase in the physical size of metropolitan areas, the general decline of urban population densities, the shift in population centers from the central cities to the suburban areas, and the progressive separation of work, commerce, and social activities from residences, thereby requiring extensive individual commuting. As the outlying regions have become the locale for rapid centrifugal expansion, the central cities have experienced large-scale deterioration in housing and the quality of neighborhood life, the loss of jobs and people (especially the middle class), and a mushrooming taxonomy of urban pathologies, which have been so sensationalized by the media and so exhaustively scrutinized by academic reports that they barely need mentioning.

Until the 1960s, thought on urban styles of social organization postulated the city-suburb contrast as a very fruitful analytical device for understanding newfound differences between two stereotypical places of residence and their associated patterns of everyday life (Fischer, 1972). This analytical dichotomy fueled the development of theories by an urban science that was struggling to accommodate the needs generated by regional patterns and problems of growth. Since 1960, however, it has become progressively clearer that the city-suburb contrast and an urban theory based on it is of limited value in the face of large-scale centrifugal development (Schnore and Jones, 1969). Clearly we must now conceive of the areas comprised of central cities and their adjacent zones of urban growth as metropolitan regions. These are not separate central cities and suburbs tied together principally by the residential locations of affluent city professionals. Instead, they are extensive areas of residential, municipal, commercial, industrial, and recreational activities that are experiencing an increasingly complex pattern of interregional and hierarchical relationships and of differential growth. This large-scale development is a consequence of powerful forces including governmental, corporate, banking, and real estate activities in addition to the role of consumer housing preferences. New approaches to urban science incorporate the magnitude and complexity of the regional residential array (Gottman and Harper, 1967). The boundaries of the New York City urban area, for example, stretch roughly from Trenton, New Jersey, to New Haven, Connecticut, and include Nassau and Suffolk counties on Long Island as well as Rockland, Westchester, Putnam, and Dutchess counties in upstate New York. The region is at least 150 miles long and 200 miles across, contains a population of almost 20 million and more than 1,400 separate municipal districts, including 16 SMSAs. Regions associated with other cities, such as Detroit, Los Angeles, Houston, and Boston, have experienced similar scales of growth and interdependence. One geographer has recently estimated that the average radius of present-day regional metropolitan development in most U.S. areas is about 70 to 80 miles (Berry, 1973a).

The key feature of contemporary society that sustains such immense urbanized regions is the post-World War II development of national corporate and bureaucratic forms of business and government decision making, along with their associated technologies (Greer, 1962a). Coordination and activities are mediated by advances in communications and transportation innovations that have enabled organizations to become regional and even national in scale. Social activities formerly located in compact central cities, such as banking and manufacturing, are presently spread out along with population, commerce, and housing in relatively low-density regions. Outlying suburban areas have accumulated a complement of public- and private-sector institutions that presently provide a great degree of independence from the city. At the same time, however, both the central city and its suburbs have become increasingly dependent on government and business decision making as well as media information systems that operate at the state and national levels. Some of these agents, such as the television networks, are still located in the city, but they represent organizations that are really national or even international in scope.

The emerging patterns of regional development and centrifugal urban growth are rather old concepts to most urban analysts, who tend to agree that the present-day reorganization into massive metropolitan areas heralds a qualitatively new form of human settlement and that the concept of the city is outmoded (Blumenfeld, 1967). Everyday life organized in low-density, large-scale metropolitan areas matches the more mature phase of twentieth-century industrial society. Such a settlement pattern, for example, cannot merely be considered a larger version of the traditional inner-city-suburban-exurban-agricultural landscape array first conceptualized by Von Thünen. Instead, there are several cities, suburbs, and differentiated patterns of residential development within the region.

The same analysts, however, differ greatly on what to label the emerging new urban form. Names vary from Geddes's and Mumford's "conurbation," Gottman's "megalopolis," Berry's "daily urban system," Blumenfeld's "metropolis," and Pickard's "urban region." Descriptive terms. such as "growth cities," "radial cities," and "multimodal and polycentric cities" have also been suggested. Perhaps, however, the Regional Plan Association of New York has characterized best the tenor of modern-day centrifugal urban development by calling it "spread city," for it is clearly the case that in every metropolitan region of the United States, land use appears as a mindless and almost unending sprawl.

Low-density residential and commercial growth exploded out of the central cities after World War II and followed the lines of residential commuting. Initially, these were railroad links, but by the 1950s ambitious highway construction programs, funded by all levels of government, criss-crossed agricultural, recreational, and undeveloped land and opened it to mass-produced suburban developments. The land-use patterns of this sprawl include commercial strip zoning of highways, which has led to massive traffic congestion despite low population density; inflation of land values, forcing farmers and low-income wage earners outward toward the ever-receding fringe areas; the conversion of public open space into the backyards of low-density single-family houses; environmental damage of land, including water and sewage problems; and finally, the essential and total dependence on automobile transportation with its consequent social compartmentalization and high energy costs. As early as 1958, observers like William H. Whyte, Jr., were calling public attention to these patterns. Whyte wrote: "Flying from Los Angeles to San Bernardino—an unnerving lesson in man's infinite capacity to mess up his environment—the traveler can see a legion of bulldozers gnawing into the last remaining tracts of green between the two cities, and from San Bernardino another legion of bulldozers gnawing westward. High over New Jersey, midway between New York and Philadelphia, the air traveler has a fleeting illusion of green space, but most of it has already been bought up and outlying supermarkets and drive-in theaters are augurs of what is to come" (1958, pp. 115-116).

The sprawl patterns of centrifugal development have also had institutional and social consequences. Of primary concern is the fragmentation of government units across the region as local municipalities attempted to keep pace with the social service demands of rapid population migrations. The progressive generation of governments and special service districts has led to a confusing mosaic of overlapping jurisdictional lines. In 1967 the total number of local governments in selected SMSAs was 1,113 for Chicago, 876 for Philadelphia, 551 for New York City, and 474 for St. Louis (Campbell and Dollenmayer, 1975). Wood (1961) estimated in 1961 that the entire New York metropolitan region was comprised of 1,467 separate municipal service districts. This decentralization often results in neighboring townships competing with each other for scarce employment and tax-producing resources. Administrative fragmentation also makes regional coordination an extremely complex task performed by nonelective superagencies such as the Port of New York Authority, which then must often fight with local interests over home rule in order to plan.

Second, the decentralization of urban activities has led to soaring tax rates as individual regions expropriate scarce revenue-producing resources to support social services. Property tax financing of schools in particular has led to grave budget problems for local school systems. The fiscal crises of central cities are only the more extreme phase of a regional municipal cash flow problem, which is manifested by soaring suburban property tax rates for home owners. For example, average property tax rates for suburban Long Island home owners are over $3,000 a year in many areas.

A third social effect of regional growth is racial and income segregation, which develops on an area-wide scale. There is a lack of community balance across the urban continuum from central city to suburban fringe area. Minority groups are confined for the most part to ghettos even in suburbia, where they constitute a very small proportion of the population. There are wide differences in community wealth, with poverty pockets and deteriorating housing in both the city and outlying areas.

Our taxonomy of regional ills merely suggests the dimensions of postwar sprawl problems and is not meant to be comprehensive. The important aspect here is that the present metro-

politan landscape appears chaotic and unplanned. An individual
resident confronts a bureaucratic and physical environment that
is difficult to comprehend and lacks a coherent community.
Only the immediate personal activities of everyday life fit into
an integrated scheme that works with some degree of coordination.

Planning and Growth

One view blames these problems of centrifugal growth on
the lack of social planning in our society and the inequitable
effects of unbridled free enterprise. This is a misconception.
There is considerably more planning in the United States than
either the proponents of the private marketplace or their critics
care to admit. Metropolitan expansion, despite its rapid nature
and massive scale, has involved extensive planning and resource
management by private builders, real estate speculators, and
banks as well as a legion of federal, state, county, and municipal
professional planners and programs. In addition, at least since
the Depression years, Congress has legislated and substantially
financed a wide variety of planning schemes at all social levels.
In fact, the efforts of government agencies and programs combined with private-sector land development, banking, and building activities have produced the rapidity and extensiveness associated with central-city decay and suburban expansion. As
Downie (1974, p. 87) recently wrote: "Suburban development
has not been happenstance. In fact, it has been exactly as real
estate speculators, builders, bankers, and even suburban home
buyers have wanted, because it has been so profitable for them.
They have forced government at all levels to plan suburban
growth their way through the administration of zoning laws,
construction of highways, laying of sewers, writing of tax laws,
and supervision and subsidy of mortgage banking."

The random growth patterns, for example, are due to at
least three distinct elements—rapid population migration, especially by whites, from the central city; the mass production of
single-family homes with the correlated deterioration of central-
city housing; and the extensive highway construction program.
The growth resulting from these factors can be illustrated by
the New York City region. Between 1950 and 1970 two million
people, most of them white, left New York City for suburban
communities. Many of them settled first in Nassau and later in
Suffolk counties on Long Island. This bicounty area went from

almost 1 million inhabitants at the beginning of the period to over 2.5 million by 1970. As early as 1951, the first large-scale suburban tract housing development, called Levittown, numbered 17,544 homes.

The feasibility of change in home construction from small-scale custom building to the mass market of tract housing called "suburban community development" was aided greatly by the ease of home financing across the country. Postwar legislation, such as the GI bills, Federal Housing Administration (FHA) mortgages, and the Housing Act of 1968, which included HUD 236 subsidies, made it possible and profitable for individuals to invest in single-family homes. This planned government support supplemented earlier precedents, such as the 1934 legislation that established FHA along with the Federal National Mortgage Association (FNMA), all of which guaranteed support and, therefore, subsidized the mortgage banking and housing industries (Clawson and Hall, 1973).

Central-city flight to Long Island was also aided by other factors, including the relative affluence enjoyed by the "middle mass"—the blue and white collar workers—due to the increased defense spending of the Vietnam war years; racism and real estate speculation, including blockbusting techniques that exploited racial tension and broke up central-city communities; and a dislike for high-density city living by families and their pursuit of a more private way of life. The immense exodus of residents who became suburban home owners, however, was also greatly facilitated by the highway construction planning program. The Federal Aid Highway Act of 1956 established support for the national system of interstate highways. These roads subsidized state and county highway projects that eventually tore open the countryside and provided a crisscrossing commuting web for residents. Nassau and Suffolk counties, for example, have 9,746 miles of roads in a region roughly 80 miles across and 30 miles wide. Most of the roads were constructed or improved since 1950. Interstate 495 runs across the center of the island from New York City to the eastern end. Although it has limited access, adjacent areas all along its length coupled with state and county highways allow development and have become strip zoned with a seemingly endless ribbon of commercial establishments sprawling into suburban tract housing for at least 60 miles.

The deterioration of central-city communities, however, was not planned by government programs. In fact, much of the housing legislation aimed specifically to prevent it. Since the U.S. Housing Act of 1937, subsidies have been provided to set up local housing planning authorities for the construction of low-income apartments. Subsequent acts, such as the one in 1949, the 1961 Section 221.d.3, and Section 235 of the 1968 act, also provided subsidies to support the planning and construction of such housing. Second, the "gray areas" problem of deterioration and blight was attacked by legislation such as Title I of the Housing Act of 1949 and the Redevelopment Act of 1954, which expanded the extensive planning machinery called "urban renewal." Attempts to discourage "white flight" were also tried, as with the 1955 Mitchell-Lama program, which enabled the middle class to purchase cooperative apartments in renewed areas of the city. Finally, innovative measures in renewal and new community construction forms were supported and encouraged by the 1968 and 1970 New Towns planning legislation under Title IV and Title VII.

The stimulation of metropolitan expansion by housing and highway legislation also supported the creation of a rather broad and somewhat fragmented administrative apparatus designed to plan and implement social change. Housing authorities and professional planning agencies were set up independently or incorporated as adjuncts to municipal departments at every stratum of government. These planning bureaucracies form hierarchies of responsibility and power within metropolitan regions. They also engage in considerable public relations efforts for each new project so that the public is given the impression that they live in a society in which the metropolitan landscape is scientifically designed. A typical resident in a city or suburban community, for example, would fall initially under the jurisdiction of a local town planning board or city planning district. This in turn might be part of a municipal planning agency or county board. Such agencies are often then consolidated into multicounty or regional planning "superagencies." Above this regional level of the bureaucratic hierarchy, planning agencies begin to spin off in a complex horizontal array, so that states often have numerous departments involving various facets of planning coordination and regional development, frequently involving overlapping jurisdictions. Finally, we reach the labyrinth of federal government departments that are set up to provide for planning, financing, development, and coordination across the country. Combining these separate levels, the extensive apparatus blankets the nation in a hierarchical administrative web that employs thousands of planners, economists, and administrators and that represents a multi-billion-dollar investment in social planning. Furthermore, the individual is provided with countless opportunities to participate in this social planning apparatus through the mechanism of public forums, town meetings on proposed projects and development schemes, and conferences with government and planning officials.

One indicator of this growth of planning activity in the United States is the extent to which academic programs in planning have developed since World War II. Between 1958 and 1974, for example, the total enrollment in planning programs went from 586 to 5,667, according to an American Institute of Planners survey. In 1971 there were eighty-three separate programs in planning at various universities across the nation and an additional seventy-one in related fields. A second indicator of the importance of planning as a profession is revealed by the number of individuals employed in the field. The American Institute of Planners estimated in 1974 that there were 13,000 individuals working as planners. This figure is conservative, for many other positions are held in planning bureaucracies that do not have the professional title of planner.

Federal planning programs and related efforts at state and local levels have had some success over the years, particularly as measured by the amount of construction. In 1949 and in every year of the 1950s, for example, more than 1 million units of housing were built. Across the nation between 1950 and 1970, 30.5 million units were constructed—over 10 million units greater than the net increase in households for that period (Berry, 1973a). Even on a per capita basis, this quantity is barely approached by European countries, which still suffer severe housing shortages originally resulting from World War II.

Several urban counties have also achieved success in social planning. For the most part, these have been relatively wealthy areas adjacent to large cities, which have taken advantage of municipal autonomy by utilizing land-use legislation and exclusionary zoning practices to restrict growth. Westchester County in New York, for example, has been dedicated to preventing less affluent city residents from moving into the area and discouraging high-density development. They have called this a public policy against "Bronxification" (Wood, 1961). In 1975, court cases against Mt. Laurel township in New Jersey and Petaluma County in California called attention to the ongoing and widespread use of similar policies, which many city residents perceive as being restrictive and unconstitutional. In the former case, the New Jersey state court ordered the township to cease restrictive zoning, while in the latter a federal court upheld Petaluma's plans. Nevertheless, the issue of exclusionary zoning as an aftermath of centrifugal growth will persist in the future in all areas of the nation (Babcock and Besselman, 1973; Davidoff and Gold, 1970; James and Windsor, 1976).

Many cities have also achieved moderate success in planning as a consequence of postwar programs. Boston, for example, was able to take advantage of the boom in service and white collar employment by embarking on an ambitious office construction plan, which thoroughly revitalized the long-depressed inner core of the city. In Minneapolis redevelopment has resurrected the downtown shopping district from consumer abandonment in favor of suburban malls. Municipal planners there worked closely with business leaders, such as Dayton's and Donaldson's department stores, to redesign the area into a public environment featuring a pedestrian mall, which became a focal point for commercial, civic, and social activities.

The sheer quantity and scope of government programs along with the substantial social investment in planning agencies at all levels has not, however, been able to alter the general shape of metropolitan development. First, the programs did not deter central-city decay or solve the low-income housing needs of its residents. Second, planning programs have done little to offset the basic patterns of segregation of racial and income groups in residential housing, which are now regional in scale. Problems associated with this dual segregation are still with us both in the central city and the suburb.

Third, local political control of highway and housing programs has supplied party regimes with significant command of social resources. This has increased the supply of patronage at the local level and has provided politicians with substantial bargaining powers in dealing with private business. Although political control has resulted in benefits to the polity, as in the New Haven urban renewal project (Dahl, 1961), it has also provided politicians with opportunities for party and personal gain, sometimes at federal expense. The limited success of several urban renewal projects, such as in Philadelphia and Newark (Bellush and Hausknecht, 1959), and the common complaint that the "federal bulldozer" provides a bonanza of private gain for politicians, speculators, and developers, are only a few examples of the weakness of social planning as it is structured by the unregulated marriage between government and business.

Fourth, the programs have only partially reflected the social needs of urban dwellers and have not provided for adequate community participation. While some federal subsidies, such as FHA programs that supported home mortgages for the middle class, have directly benefited local groups, many programs have ignored the desires of residents or have limited their involvement. This was the case, for example, in the West End of Boston and in the West Bank community of Minneapolis, inner-city neighborhoods destroyed by federally sponsored and privately implemented programs.

Finally and by far the most important limitation of postwar social planning is the lack of initiative in formulating programs to help coordinate growth. Decision making was left to local municipalities, an expanding and complex bureaucratic apparatus, and the private marketplace without benefit of any compelling regional framework or integrated programs designed to guide the judgments of businessmen, politicians, or administrators in the broad social interest. Due to the dominance of local home rule, integration on a metropolitan scale does not exist and the result has been the dual processes of centrifugal expansion and central-city decay. As we have already seen, the new, sprawling urban land use has many undesirable features. There seems to be no capacity to shape social growth at the local level to avoid the accompanying problems of metropolitan expansion, and both central cities and suburbs are becoming increasingly more dependent on federal supports, thereby losing their much-prized autonomy. The presence of government legislation and planning bureaucracies at all levels does not appear to impede the regional reproduction of urban-style social problems or provide the coordination so needed in the growing areas. In fact, the inert presence of planning agencies may make their limited impact all the more perplexing.

Ironically, the uncoordinated sprawl pattern of suburban development and its correlate of central-city devastation occurred with the full benefits of foresight. As early as 1948 the congressional hearings on the housing bill were informed by professional planners of the need for a national land-use regulatory policy to accompany social planning legislation. In 1950 the American Institute of Planners warned against uncoordinated metropolitan expansion and proposed alternatives modeled after the New Town legislation in England. In response Congress appeased the planning profession by requiring local areas requesting federal aid for housing and urban renewal to produce a comprehensive master plan for development. This requirement fell short of initiating the necessary national land-use legislation, but it did supply an incentive to establish planning agencies at every level, create jobs for the profession, and encourage the production of advisory master plans.

In trying to understand the limited success of planning and coordination in the United States, many problems can profitably be considered. The morphology of urban-suburban pathologies has already been comprehensively defined by a plethora of research projects, public commissions, studies, and monographs exploring the megalopolitan condition in general and the deficiencies in particular. We shall dispense with a review of these activities and concentrate instead on analyzing two phenomena. The first is the overall weaknesses of social planning in the United States, and the second is the political problems of land-use control and metropolitan regional coordination. These analyses will concentrate on the social perceptions of these activities rather than on specific case studies. In part, our emphasis is inspired by the judgment that the drafted programs themselves cannot bear the entire blame for their limited success and that the social context of legislated planning program implementation, including several public ideologies that constrain their local application, must be examined.

Weakness of the American Conception of Planning

Planning in the United States since its early stages has always been hedged by a strong commitment to market mechanisms. Federal and municipal efforts at obtaining the power to plan comprise a history of repeated clashes with the private orientation of citizens (Scott, 1971). First, it was believed that unfettered market forces would be beneficial to society. Second, the system of free enterprise was held to be secure only if private property rights were sanctified. This double-edged resistance to government coordination fostered the sacred charter of local political control, or home rule, and the reliance of government programs on private-sector implementation and execution. Home rule meant that political control, while a necessary evil in a free society, should be decentralized in order to be most responsive to the needs of local residents. At the same time, government programs to improve living conditions in the cities were designed to allow extensive participation by local businesses. Social planning evolved within this limited framework.

During the turn-of-the-century municipal planning crusade, two distinct trends emerged as a consequence of such ideological constraints, backed by court-supported judgments supporting private property rights and against planners. These also characterize social planning today. First, planning was reduced to coordination of physical design, and second, the social reform measures were separated from the purview of professional planners and retained as a political activity of government legislative bodies at all levels. Due to limits on their constitutional powers, municipal governments, for example, could not engage in the comprehensive social planning envisioned by early reformers that would regulate social and economic activities. Instead they confined their efforts to the manipulation of land use and controls of construction technology. They worked primarily with municipally owned land and attempted to landscape and develop it in a way that would modify the inequities of early urban industrialization. Cities annexed land for future use in the hope that they could control their growth. They developed parks to alleviate slum congestion and proposed and developed civic centers that expressed the aspirations of government in the form of monumental architecture and served as a municipal wedge against land speculation. In 1893 these elements of planning became fused in the physicalist "City Beautiful" movement following the famous Chicago Exposition of that year (Scott, 1971). Social reforms for the city were viewed by this approach as being implemented primarily through the mechanism of physical landscape design.

By the early 1900s the tool of zoning became the focal point of such municipal control. This involved a comprehensive land-use approach that would provide a rational ordering of societal activities by coordinating *where* the activities could take place rather than the regulation of *what* private businesses themselves did. Social planning progressed by concentrating on such control of location and land-use design that did not conflict significantly with individual private property rights. In 1926, after almost a century of urban industrial growth, the U.S. Supreme Court upheld the constitutional validity of zoning by municipalities, in the case of *Euclid* v. *Amber Realty* (Haar, 1959; Babcock and Besselman, 1973).

These early responses to metropolitan growth were inspired by European attempts to address the evils of industrial urbanization. The City Beautiful movement, for example, took its cues from the garden city planning approach of Ebenezer

Howard in England. The use of zoning and building codes as social reform measures was modeled after the rational ordering of societal activities fostered by the city ordinances of the German towns at the time. The essential difference between the European and the American experience, however, centers on the contrasting political climates. The U.S. commitment to free enterprise was certainly not matched in England, which was caught up in the turn-of-the-century Fabian socialist movement, nor matched by the evolving state capitalism of Germany. In this country, unlike Europe, the attempts to achieve the necessary integration of physical planning with the political process and social reform legislation have been unsuccessful.

This situation continues today. Policies concerning the redistribution of wealth, control of the environment, and the regulation of social activities are disconnected, as are the legislative, administrative, and design approaches to planning. Despite the efforts of the early reform movements in the 1900s, for example, the federal government did not take the initiative in developing a comprehensive social planning function utilizing the zoning mechanism and physicalist design principles. It respected, instead, the traditional sanctity of private property. Decisions on land-use policy were left by the federal government to the judiciary, which made them reluctantly. To this day, national land-use policy is one of the least developed areas of litigation. Consequently, no clear initiative was taken then for comprehensive planning by any branch of government, and the rights of citizens in obtaining relief from piecemeal municipal programs have never been explicitly stated. Despite warnings by professionals of the social need for such controls, Congress failed to respond again when it passed subsequent planning legislation in the years after the Depression. Coordination of social legislation and municipal planning programs today simply does not seem to exist, and the society relies very heavily on the courts to arbitrate matters of conflict and relief that arise from the efforts of planners, politicians, and local businessmen to coordinate the process of growth.

The combination of private enterprise supported by federal planning legislation and subsidies and implemented politically through local home rule, which is social planning American style, leaves professional planners in a curious role. For the most part they are government employees who are involved primarily in the task of composing, upgrading, and revising municipal and regional master plans. These are comprehensive guides for social growth that are submitted to political leaders on an advisory basis. They evaluate the demographic, business, and housing trends in a region and then describe in detail the preferred land-use patterns for future growth on the basis of that information. Master planning, therefore, aims to outline the rational steps that can be taken by local government to control development for municipal purposes (Altshuler, 1965). The comprehensive suggestions made to the political leadership are meant to replace any piecemeal attempts to use municipal control of land use and public works, such as highway construction, on an ad hoc basis in response to social growth needs.

The primary characteristic of master planning is that planners have little power beyond the persuasiveness of their own recommendations. There is a separation between the planning function and political control. The former advises while the latter makes decisions. While it might be argued that such a state of affairs is preferred in a democracy, professional planners have been greatly handicapped by their advisory status. On the one hand, the profession conceives of schemes and master plans that involve the commission of the physical fallacy, which assumes that changes in physical design will in themselves reshape behavior (Gans, 1968). These plans rely heavily on a technical, limited notion of rational decision making. On the other hand, professional planners are required to face what we will call the elitist/populist dilemma, which greatly restricts their ability to gather wide public support.

The physical approach to planning assumes that social and cultural patterns of interaction can be successfully manipulated by the proper design of environment (Gans, 1968). It concerns itself with satisfying adequate living and working patterns for society through the use of construction and landscaping technology, while taking the relations and mediations of those activities for granted. The problems and processes of urban growth, therefore, are viewed primarily in terms of design. Planners today are taught, for the most part, to follow in this architectural and landscaping tradition, which dates back to the City Beautiful movement. As Gans has shown, reliance on physical control of the environment for planners uses reductionist logic and is fallacious.

Planning that emphasizes physical design is a special case of the exclusive use of technical rationality. This is the adoption of efficient means for the attainment of a given goal, but leaves the choice of the goal open-ended. Confined to this limited perspective, the recommendations of planners can be considered to be neutral. In effect, professional planners could be equally proficient in designing cities or concentration camps. The social, economic, and political processes of development are usually given a more efficient and suitable form so that the results of growth are determined by the operation of those activities. The planners, therefore, take the social environment for granted and deal little with its reconstruction. At the very least, they have a rather naive view of the values and judgments on resource allocations that operate in our society on an everyday basis. They ignore, for example, the actions of speculators, the effects of racism and socioeconomic segregation, and the incentives created by government programs that support many undesirable trends, such as the abandonment of decent central-city housing.

Diesing (1962) has pointed out that there is in fact a taxonomy of rationalities that must be dealt with in viable social planning. Social, political, and economic considerations are as important as the technical aspects of landscaping or design. The planning profession must develop an approach that follows advocacy practitioners and explicitly deals with the nature and selection of goals for growth in order to help envision what society ought to be.

The professional planning approach also involves a mixture of the elitist assumption that the planner is best at community design and the populist belief that there is an easily aggregated public interest that planning can fulfill. This perspective does not address the broader questions of the public's participation in the selection of goals for growth, the search for alternative choices and technologies, or the adequate monitoring of outcomes in the plan (Davidoff, 1965; Bolan, 1971). This elitist approach leads to a dilemma. On the one hand, planners feel that, as professionals, they are best entrusted with the responsibility for making such decisions. On the other hand, they are limited in their ability to implement their schemes because of their advisory status. They need the public's support and must include residents' participation in the planning process. Most often this citizen involvement is spurious. It involves the use of pseudo-forums, public information meetings, and public relations efforts. This process tends to ignore the real interest of the public. Most often the residents are allowed to participate in the planning process only by their acquiescence to the plan or by the exercise of political veto power as planners, political leaders, and businessmen face the public with their proposal.

The fait accompli nature of such decision making was evident in the Minneapolis "new town" of Cedar-Riverside and in the controversy involving scattered-site low-income housing in the Forest Hills section of New York City. The problem of substantive citizen involvement on the one hand and the planners' need to advance the public interest on the other has yet to be resolved by the profession (Aleshire, 1970). To date the dilemma has been overcome by moving toward elitist expertise at local residents' expense. In this sense the profession has discouraged rather than broadened public support for more planning. There are real fears present here. Residents have been provided with ample evidence of the callous way that local citizen interests have been ignored, as in the long record of urban renewal. If given the choice, the public would probably prefer the continued operation of market forces to more ambitious government schemes for social planning.

Local Political Control and Regional Coordination

In the United States, centralized government planning does not exist. The many federal programs that support social growth rely on local implementation. Decentralized control is tailored to the home rule levels of the federated government structure. Planning has served to sustain political regimes in both the central city and the suburbs through community command of federal funds and local control of land use. Recent programs such as revenue sharing have reinforced this sacred charter of localism in the United States. This approach, however, has several limitations.

First, local political control does not always operate in the public interest. Local party organizations need to support themselves because community political resources are often very limited. Local government powers associated with control of land-use and federal funds have in many areas become convenient sources of revenue for party organizations and personal gain for political leaders. This feature, commonly referred to as corruption, seems to be a consistent one in American political life. Gardner and Olson (1974) have documented its effects in the central city. Gottdiener (1977) has shown that on suburban Long Island, conflict of interest in political control of land use has subverted the power to plan. Expedient zoning decisions made there for party and personal gain seem to have aggregated over the years to produce a pattern of uncoordinated suburban sprawl as if government land-use control did not even exist.

Studies on corruption most often highlight the abuse of

national or city public office either to consolidate political
power or to realize personal gain. Central-city political regimes,
for example, have long histories of boss rule and graft. In contrast, the suburbs have acquired an image of professional and
communal management reflecting enlightened leadership. To a
great extent such a reputation rests on the popularization of the
nonpartisan town manager form of government studies in suburbs, such as Westchester County in New York in the 1950s.
Presently suburban regions contain a variety of governing forms
and most utilize partisan party control (Greer, 1962b; Gilbert,
1967). What is now clear is that such regimes have difficulty
supporting themselves, lack broad backing among the voters,
and possess little patronage. Suburban parties have been described as "toy governments," and they often attract leaders
with narrow interests who do not distinguish themselves once
elected. In areas such as Suffolk County, the weaknesses of
political control have made the political parties heavily dependent on the decision-making powers of government to generate
revenue for support. In particular, political control over land
use has often been utilized for party and personal gain and has
been dependent on the real estate and construction industries.
Since the 1950s, Suffolk County has had a tradition of periodic
political scandals involving the abuse of zoning codes and building controls (Gottdiener, 1977). While such activities cannot
match the scale of party and personal gain associated with city
or federal corruption, they nevertheless demonstrate clearly the
correlated presence in suburban regions of the everyday abuse
of political power.

    The ability of political organizations at all government
levels to maintain the public trust and at the same time to use
the political control of the government decision-making apparatus for party and personal gain needs to be examined better.
Although the public perceives these abuses as periodic outbreaks of scandal, their presence and character suggest an important property of the state in our society. It is that the decision-making powers of government constitute a significant
productive resource that can create value for personal and party
gain in much the same way that capital is a resource that can
create profit for businessmen. Political control of public office
by parties can be considered as a somewhat autonomous unit of
social organization that cannot be reduced to either elitist or
pluralist conceptions of power (Gottdiener, 1977). Djilas
(1957), for example, considers the government decision makers

of the communist party as the new ruling class of Eastern European communist countries because of this autonomous state power. In a democratic society such as the United States, political control of the decision-making apparatus possesses dual properties. On the one hand, the state is part of society by being responsive to the public trust and to articulated versions of the polity's needs. On the other hand, it can stand apart from society to create value of its own through public decisions that generate personal or party gain. Sometimes, in fact, both objectives can be achieved with the same decision.

In view of the importance of such properties of the state, providing the government with additional powers to plan without required reforms may simply supply added opportunities for conflict of interest and the abuse of political control. The reforms necessary for viable social planning, however, would not be easy to accomplish. This is so because the polity seems reluctant to assume a more active monitoring role and because political parties and individuals running for office still need ways to support themselves as campaigns become progressively more expensive.

Local political control of land use has a second limitation. The power to zone has frequently been used at the local level to exclude lower-class and racial groups from developing regions. Local control of planning, especially in suburban areas, has been characterized as exclusionary zoning. Land-use patterns in such metropolitan subregions have mandated house construction that is relatively expensive by increasing the subdivision acreage requirements and insisting on restrictive building codes. In suburban regions the single-family detached house on at least one third of an acre seems to be enforced as the only desirable mode of home construction. This has resulted in extreme socioeconomic and racial segregation, preventing many segments of the population from owning their own homes. As we have seen, such practices have been challenged in the courts, but no national legislative land-use policy has resulted (Babcock and Besselman, 1973; Davidoff and Gold, 1970).

Local political control of zoning represents an extremely limited approach to the problems of rapid metropolitan growth. Low-density land-use policies that restrict low-income and minority groups from access to suburban housing help to create urban sprawl and foster the opportunistic political use of zoning. This is a very high price to pay. Suburbanites have protected their property values through local home rule, but they

have also destroyed available open space, encouraged strip development of highways, and made the automobile the only
viable mode of transportation. Evils of the spread city patterns
have been proclaimed by a myriad of metropolitan analysts,
including those of the Regional Planning Association. Home
rule control of land use, exclusionary zoning, and low-density
development, however, remain as the preferred approaches of
most metropolitan residents. Thus, there appears to be no voluntary way to maintain a balanced community of racial and
socioeconomic mixture or to implement rational land use in
most of the United States. Residential integration and enlightened planning, as attempted in the new town of Columbia,
Maryland, have not been generally practiced, despite the incentives of the 1968 and 1971 New Town legislation.

Consequently, the prospects for land use and social
change in the absence of judicial mandates presently seem remote. Both the judiciary and the executive branches appear to
be growing more reluctant to carry the burden—as in the case of
school busing. It is apparent that the legislative branch of the
federal government must take the initiative by drafting a national land-use policy. This long-awaited move would coordinate metropolitan expansion so as to eliminate local exclusionary practices and at the same time preserve environmental
quality along with whatever is left of the wilderness. The much-
needed legislation, however, would also have to tackle the major
task of drafting safeguards against the abuse of land-use powers
and planned residential development by local politicians, real
estate speculators, construction firms, and banks. This is so because of the rather long history of co-optation and conflict of
interest associated with the implementation of federal planning
legislation. Despite the critical need, it seems unlikely that such
reforms can be accomplished by Congress, for it would have to
defy its basic support of a minimally regulated free enterprise
system.

Local political control of land use has led to exclusionary
zoning and a pattern of metropolitan sprawl that would exist
had there been no planning at all. In addition, a third consequence of present-day patterns is that the patchwork mosaic of
municipal districts created by such centrifugal growth presents
grave problems of regional coordination. Federal programs have
so far failed to recognize the need to consider the central city
and the suburban hinterland as integrated areas of the metropolis. For example, Nassau and Suffolk counties were recently

given independent census status by the bureau as a separate SMSA adjacent to New York City. This fragmentation into special districts and the wide regional disparities in social services and fiscal resources make coordination of metropolitan growth a difficult task. At present, governance itself has become problematic for local municipalities, which must operate without the aggregated resources of the regional socioeconomic base. This is seen most clearly in the central city, which suffers from a lack of municipal control over suburban resources. It is also apparent at the state level within metropolitan regions. The area-wide disparities of contrasting poverty and wealth, of adequate and deteriorating housing, and of declining social services and abundant resources illustrate the uneven character of regional development. Programs such as revenue sharing have reinforced these patterns so that states as well as local municipalities continue to quibble with each other over scarce regional resources in "beggar thy neighbor" policies, such as grabs for business relocations within the same metropolitan region.

A reorganization of the fragmented political apparatus would be very unlikely due to great public reluctance to abandon home rule. However, areas like Dade County in Florida, which includes Greater Miami, and Nashville-Davidson in Tennessee have successfully accomplished this task. Other cities such as Houston have been fortunate enough to enjoy the legislative ability to annex suburban land, thereby providing the mechanism for regional urban governance (Siegan, 1972).

Most American cities, however, have been unable to accomplish either metropolitan reorganization or suburban annexation. Political fragmentation with its consequent lack of planning coordination persists. Recently several "patchwork" measures have been tried (Zimmerman, 1975). These include councils of government, which are voluntary associations of intraregional local governments without powers of planning implementation; intergovernmental service agreements that provide for the purchase of social services by one municipality from another; and metropolitan councils, which are comprised of county governments representing a metropolitan area and which can formulate policy but not implement it. Control over resources by such regional agencies has been strengthened by federal legislation, such as the 1971 Office of Management and Budget Circular A-95, which gave powers of review to state and regional planning agencies regarding federally financed projects. These measures and the creation of such voluntary regional councils and agencies, however, have had limited success in co-ordinating centrifugal growth. They have not, for example, effectively challenged home rule and localism, nor have they im-plemented land-use policies that have measurably constrained private property rights of real estate speculators and sprawl pat-terns of zoning.

Alternative approaches to regional coordination at the state level or by superagencies have also been tried. The Port of New York Authority, for example, has been successful in sup-plying the transportation infrastructure needs for the New York-New Jersey-Connecticut tristate region. State departments of education, for example, often coordinate school activities by supplying guidelines for local district performance and financ-ing. These activities are designed to deal with specific needs, however, and cannot meet the overriding requirement for com-prehensive and integrated coordination of urban regional growth.

Consequently, the lack of provision for metropolitan coordination in federal planning programs is matched at the local level within the politically fragmented urban region. In such a state of affairs and given the ideological adherence to pri-vate property rights and local political home rule, the entire notion of social planning seems to have little relevance or im-pact for the average resident.

Conclusion

The metropolitan region has acquired a complex social organization of large-scale, intraregional community interdepen-dence and a hierarchical system of overlapping government planning and administrative bureaucracies. The critical need for social coordination and integration during the period of rapid centrifugal growth, however, has not been adequately met by either political initiatives or local community efforts. Conse-quently, the intricate structure of regional metropolitan life is fragmented and social planning has enjoyed limited success, despite a large social investment in programs and coordinating agencies. Problems with regional social control and interagency cooperation have several sources, which have been linked with the weaknesses of planning in the United States. First, the fed-eral government failed to take the initiative to develop coordi-nating plans during its postwar passage of housing, highway, and regional development legislation. Second, the social ideology that supports private property rights and a government of limited size and scope is manifested in citizen demands for home rule. This has kept regional planning agencies from acquiring political control over land use. Mechanisms that would allow regional agencies to coordinate growth while preserving home rule control of the local community have yet to be fully worked out. Lacking stronger state and federal legislation for planning implementation, local political control of zoning leaves planners and coordinating agencies with a primarily advisory status. Without metropolitan powers of coordination, fragmentation continues and regional cooperation becomes a matter of trying to convince separate municipalities and even states to cease pursuing policies that are in their best local interests, such as attracting job- and tax-producing industries from neighboring areas. Such appeals by planners interested in rational land use and local citizens groups concerned about the quality of regional environments have had limited success.

The history of state-supported efforts to overcome local resistance to regional planning by establishing nonelective superagencies with land-use powers, such as the Urban Development Corporation in New York, also does not inspire optimism for future guidance. The Urban Development Corporation first lost its necessary power to override local zoning in a legislative dispute with a suburban township and then defaulted when the banking community ceased its financial support for overextended central-city construction projects. Alternatively, at the judicial level, legal efforts to override local land-use practices, such as exclusionary zoning, and to acquire legal powers to plan have met with limited success and have not gathered national support. Consequently, restrictive local segregating patterns with their attendant problems continue to persist, and judicial efforts do not appear promising as an additional area for developing stronger planning powers.

For these reasons social planning at all levels seems, for the most part, to be a facade. Behind the rhetoric of proliferating government legislation and development programs, planning bureaucracies have expanded their own hierarchical structure and regional jurisdictional powers without coordinating growth or avoiding the problems of urban sprawl. Behind the very same rhetoric and officially composed master plans, local political organizations have, for the most part, used home rule control of zoning to support themselves and the real estate industry, and in some cases to realize personal gain. Although satisfying the voters in most cases with narrowly defined use of planning powers, such as exclusionary zoning policies, local governments have not demonstrated the desire to overcome metropolitan fragmentation and to articulate the needs of coordinated regional development. From the federal government to the local village, therefore, there has been a failure of initiative in regional coordination and a lack of political cooperation, despite much planning activity. Consequently, spread city sprawl along with urban-style social inequities, such as housing blight, racial and socioeconomic residential segregation, predatory real estate speculation, and corruption in government-supported projects have now become regional in scale (Gottdiener, 1977).

With such a state of affairs prevailing, further calls for the expanded support of housing, urban renewal, and highway programs by government at all levels without social reconstruction and adequate governance mechanisms must be regarded with caution. The metropolitan regional political apparatus has grown bigger and more complex since World War II, but it has not necessarily become better equipped to plan. It seems reasonable, instead, to say that necessary political, social, and land-use reforms must be enacted before further social investment is made in planning programs or their associated administrative agencies. In particular, the entire metropolitan region requires new mechanisms of integration and coordination so that local community and municipal needs can be articulated and implemented in the best interests of the entire area while protecting individual rights. Such reconstruction would fit better the new mode of social settlement that has developed in the advanced stage of industrial growth and that presently appears as a metropolitan region of unplanned urban sprawl.

17

Changing Priorities for the Urban Heartland

Gerald D. Suttles

The American urban crisis has taken on so many forms that it is difficult to see its basic continuities. At various times our attention has been riveted on growing racial segregation (Taeuber and Taeuber, 1965) and conflict (Spilerman, 1970), the centrifugal drift to the suburbs (Zimmer, 1975), the job-residence mismatch (Kain, 1975), and most recently the urban fiscal crunch (Clark, 1976). Such a welter of issues makes it difficult to obtain an overall grasp of the urban crisis and to evaluate a concerted social policy aimed at remediation.

Note: An earlier version of this chapter was prepared for the Workshop in Community and Society, Department of Sociology, University of Chicago. In the course of preparation, the chapter benefited from the comments of a number of people; I would especially like to thank Morris Janowitz, Kirsten Grønbjerg, and David Street.

519

At the risk of gross oversimplification, I wish to argue that a general effort to understand our urban crisis can be most effectively pursued by looking at the intersection of long-term market forces in the competition among urban regions and the conscious urban policies of the last twenty-five years. The market forces have worked by and large to extend urbanization to almost all regions of the United States and to reduce the dominance of any one urban center or spatially concentrated set of urban institutions within a single urban center. The urban policies, however, have been based largely on the assumption of a very stable urban hierarchy and the continued dominance of a commercial-industrial central business core. A more successful urban policy, I suggest, would recognize the limits to central-city commercial-industrial growth and dominance and adopt a more flexible and favorable attitude toward mixed land use, upgrading the residential infrastructure of the older cities and investing in the human resources of the populations that are likely to predominate in the future of these central cities.

The market forces that have played such an important role in the urban crisis have occurred primarily at two competitive interfaces—between the old urban heartland and its hinterland and between the central city and its suburbs. The general trend in the United States has been toward the regional dispersion of urban centers so that the more vacant areas of the country have progressively acquired their own regional centers capable of self-sustained growth. This has led to a relative decline in the dominance of the northeastern and midwestern urban regions and to an intensification of competition between all regions for the same jobs, governmental installations, and work force. Such an intensification of regional competition finds many of the older, larger central cities of the heartland at a relative disadvantage compared with an earlier period.

These disadvantages are exacerbated by their competitive position relative to their own suburbs. The inflexibility of their boundaries and the comparatively low quality of life they can offer their residents reduce their capacity to hold residents and to shoulder the burdens associated with aging physical plant and an increasingly dependent population. The suburbs have the advantage of recent construction as well as continued access to many of the public facilities of the central cities.

Both of these observations have been made before, and the general pattern is well described by Hawley's phrase "diffuse urbanization" (Chapter One of this volume). However, urban policies over the last twenty-five years have either failed to recognize the momentum of these market forces or have paradoxically supported the deconcentration of urban places while still investing in intensive land use in the casualty areas left by this deconcentration. Thus, public investments and tax incentives for downtown commercial development have been accompanied by massive highway construction, public investments, and tax incentives for regional commercial development. Huge cultural and sports plazas have been developed in the central cities at the same time that their patrons were moving to the suburbs. Most central cities have their new "miracle miles," which compete with both their own central business districts (CBDs) and the regional shopping centers of the suburbs. Attempts to improve mass transit are often paired with efforts to improve parking facilities for automobiles. In fact, the central cities seem to have grasped at every opportunity for additional investment heedless of their long-term consequences, especially their contribution to further urban deconcentration.

At times this opportunistic mix of investment policies has even acquired its spokesmen, and city leaders have been urged to think that any investment in central-city amenities will have positive multiplier effects (Gottman and Harper, 1967). We are speaking here not only of public investments but also the way that public investments and public policy help shape private investment. The result has not only been a relatively high level of central-city investment, but a pattern of investment that tends to favor the development of the CBD, the growth of "high culture" amenities, and the promotion of high-wage industries. All of these investments were attractive in part because they seemed directly to reverse the outward flow of central-city income, prestige, and authority. However, they were also a rather piecemeal set of investment strategies that could be defended because they tended to meet separately each urban problem that had an identifiable constituency and they did not require a reassessment and, to some degree, a humbling of central-city ambitions.

The general pattern is what we may call a "growth policy": more and better jobs, more office space, more cultural institutions, more public buildings, and more recreational centers. The assumption seems to have been that growth was limitless, that it always brought net benefits to the central city, and that a failure to grow would bring not stability but stagnation. I would argue instead that in the older, larger cities of the urban heartland, or for that matter in any city where growth requires massive conversion of existing facilities, growth policy imposes such high social overhead costs that it furthers urban decay and public costs. Growth policies do so in a variety of ways: because of the stresses and strains accompanying massive land conversion, because of their disproportionate stimulus to suburban expansion, and because of the declining quality of central-city life that accompanies metropolitan growth.

Taken together the social and financial costs accompanying growth policies in our older and larger cities are so great that further national investments seem unwarranted, and there are many reasons to think that the diversion of most new urban growth to the "Sun Belt" or hinterland is advantageous to national growth. In short, the net gain for further public and private investment in the growth of some heartland metropolitan areas is so small compared with the benefits of public investment elsewhere that they contribute little to the increase of national wealth. Undoubtedly, the general situation is far more complex, and I present it in this bald manner to dramatize the fact that what may be seen as an advantage in these older cities need not amount to much in the way of national economic growth. As I shall try to point out later, certain kinds of investments in our declining central cities seem to be well justified. However, many of the structural problems of our declining central cities are not easily rectified by short-term growth policies, and in many instances these problems must be regarded as a permanent or incorrigible burden. For example, the massive suburbanization around some cities is not likely to be reversed (Campbell and Dollenmayer, 1975) and will continue to exercise a considerable burden on these cities in the foreseeable future (Kasarda, 1972). Cities having high-wage industries tend to push up wages in other private industries, making them less responsive to the effective demand for labor and raising the wages of public employees.

One could point to numerous other examples which suggest that the high overhead costs associated with some central cities are an indication of stubborn structural conditions rather than just an inequitable and inadequate distribution of federal funds between the older urban regions and the new emerging ones. However, this does not mean that those cities already in trouble should simply be written off and allowed to flounder in their weak competitive position. It is one thing to say that they represent poor candidates for *further growth* and another to consider the cost resulting from a *decline* in their populations and current activities. In at least one way the urban policies of the last twenty-five years have been a success: They have extended the advantages of urbanization to a vast portion of the nation's periphery of depressed regions. However, there is some danger that we shall replace one set of depressed regions with another unless we understand the limits of these policies.

The Urban Heartland

Although it is difficult to identify exactly which cities are most threatened by the urban crisis, two things seem to stand out at the present time. First, many of the cities affected seem to lie in the old urban heartland, that region most heavily urbanized in the United States stretching from about Minneapolis on the west, south to the upper Ohio Valley, east to Washington, D.C., north to Boston, and back along the shore of the Great Lakes (Berry, 1973a, pp. 1-9). Second, the urban crisis seems to be most severe among the older cities that reached their population peaks by World War II.

These conditions, age and location, are obviously closely related, but there are strong reasons to think that they converge to highlight the two most important causes of the urban crisis: the declining dominance of the urban heartland and the obsolescence of the infrastructure of our older cities. In order to appreciate the significance of these changing conditions, it is necessary to step back a bit and examine each within a historical perspective.

Competitive Position. The eastern part of the urban heartland took shape almost at the beginning of the country, and its dominance has persisted for almost two hundred years. While most of the regions in the country tried to exploit their limited natural resources, it was in the Northeast and later the upper Midwest that urban settlements sought to find a role for themselves by processing, consuming, and marketing the products produced locally and elsewhere (Boorstin, 1965). In the end the urban gamble of the Northeast and upper Midwest paid off. As the most intense areas of urbanization, these areas provided the emporium within which U.S. products were refashioned for final consumption and gained an outlet to international markets.

The great strength of the urban heartland was its market power: its sheer volume of consumers relative to the rest of the nation and its access to wider markets in Europe and elsewhere. Primary production may have been more active elsewhere, but it was the Northeast and Midwest that reigned as consumer, processor, and conveyor to wider markets. This relatively compact region contained over half of the U.S. population from 1870 to 1960, and in time it became a tightly integrated area, dense in population, transportation arteries, sales outlets, and the talent for finishing and marketing goods. As an opportune place for investment, it attracted capital from the remainder of the country and its financial institutions reached a scale where they were most able to support and shape the development of primary industries elsewhere (Berry, 1973a).

With its initial market and financial strength, the urban heartland was able to initiate the development of other regions so that these areas were tributary to the industries and consumers located in the heartland. Specialized agriculture in the South, coal mining in the Appalachians, wheat farming in the Great Plains, and specialized mineral extraction in numerous locations all added to the inventory of primary products for processing and distribution in the heartland. Such a process was "circular and cumulative" (Pred, 1966) in increasing the dominance of the urban heartland. Up to a point, its growth in population, market power, income, special skills, and financial resources was self-perpetuating and even self-increasing.

Much the same can be said for the urban core of these heartland cities. For most of these early cities, the CBD was literally the center, the downtown, where political, economic, and cultural authority resided. It held a near monopoly on high-income jobs, cultural entertainment, political advancement, high-quality merchandise, and intellectual pursuits. Communication and transportation arteries met only within its boundaries, and indeed they were the basic underpinning for its dominance over the remaining metropolis. It was in the central city that entertainers and merchants could hope to find the most numerous and most affluent audiences and clients. It was also that part of the city which sought to convey through art, architecture, and public expositions the collective enterprise that attracted people to the city—its ball games, its cultural centers, its press, its parades, and its persistent shows of boosterism. It was where employers, entrepreneurs, and fortune seekers gathered. Above all, it was the receptacle that brought together the metropolis's elite so that they could thrash out their differences and establish a set of relatively coherent policies.

By the time of the Depression, this process had reached the point where the dominance of the heartland and its urban cores seemed almost uncontested; each city was surrounded by a series of economically dependent, specialized regions. At an even earlier period, however, certain self-limiting processes seem to have started. First, as wages increased in the heartland, some low-skill and highly competitive industries were unable to meet the high-wage levels established in the heartland and moved elsewhere: textiles to the Piedmont, meat packing to the Great Plains, and food processing to the Pacific coast and Florida.

Second, by 1950 there appears to have developed a number of what Berry calls "footloose" industries, that is, industries that were not heavily dependent on close proximity to mass markets (such as aerospace) or industries that could use a vastly improved communications system to conduct business over great distances (such as research and development). The result was a considerable migration of these industries to areas in the hinterland that provided sufficient social services and amenities. It was not simply a matter of movement to low-wage areas, for only a few areas of the hinterland were able to provide the necessary infrastructure of social and economic services. But those that could grew rapidly: the West Coast, parts of the Gulf coast, and the Piedmont in the Southeast. Of course, much of the nation's hinterland remained a sort of rural slum, underserviced for urban residents and unable to provide either the skilled manpower or economic services needed by industry (such as waste disposal, energy, and transportation). However, even these areas were upgraded considerably as the money available for public expenditures increased enormously during the last two decades. The interstate expressway system, the expansion of electrical power grids, the nationalization of medical and welfare programs, and the spectacular growth of institutions of higher learning combined to provide much of the infrastructure that had been absent in the more remote regions of the country.

As this pattern of more uniform growth progressed, it pushed many urban areas in the hinterland over the threshold to the point where their market was sufficient to support local industries. This was a self-generating process that was also circular and cumulative. One of its most important consequences was the general growth of the population and market power of the entire hinterland. In terms of purchasing power alone, the old urban heartland was still dominant, but far less so than previously. Producers and distributors could look elsewhere for a healthy and apparently increasing demand for their goods and a new location for commercial and industrial growth. Indeed, from the point of view of private employers and distributors, the difference in advantages of various urban markets and labor pools is now small, and one can choose from a multitude of large American cities, all having a qualified labor force and a sufficient market, when seeking a good location. Where in 1940 there were about 200 places with 50,000 or more population, there are now over 396, and they are far more widely distributed among national regions.

Very nearly the same thing has happened to the business districts of our larger and older cities. Where once they had one clearly identifiable center, now they have many. It is no longer true that the best plays and most promising ball teams come only to the central city. The California Angels make it clear that their market is not just Los Angeles, as do an increasing number of sports associations and commercial enterprises in other cities. In some of our metropolitan areas the suburbs have literally engulfed the central city, and their market strength is far stronger in both dollars and numbers (Zimmer, 1975). There are two causes for the growing importance of the suburbs and the diminishing importance of the urban core. First, there is the relative inflexibility of the boundaries of the central cities, which is especially evident in the older metropolitan regions of the urban heartland. Second, and most important, is the capacity of the suburbs to create their own nodes of communication and transportation. Anyone who thinks that the suburbs are mere bedroom commuter sheds has not visited them lately. The vast urban sectors that Hoyt (1941) first identified have grown to the point where they are practically cities in their own right (Gottdiener, 1977; Logan, 1976). They are the locations of huge new shopping centers, industrial developments, and many new public facilities.

The communications and transportation revolution is part of the reason for this polynucleated metropolis, but in large measure it is the result of policy decisions that have expanded communication and transportation to the suburbs and the hinterland. Through such developments as the highway trust fund, a variety of measures that have tended to attract or subsidize new construction in the suburbs, and the general emphasis on the automobile as the sole means of transportation, many of our suburbs now sport commercial and industrial centers rivaling those of their central cities. The consequences of this have been profound because it fragments the management of the metropolis (Janowitz, 1961) by producing many elites with no common urban *oikonomus*. Most especially, it has perpetuated contradictory urban policies that subsidize the growth of the commercial urban core and the polynucleated metropolitan areas.

Aging Infrastructure. Both of these patterns of dispersion have been complemented by two other conditions that moved people away from the urban heartland and its central-city core. First, there was the early and continuous movement of people westward and southward as the more vacant regions of the country were brought into productive economic use, usually by investments from the heartland. This movement, of course, was highly selective, and in general the tendency was to produce urban rather than rural growth, especially in recent decades. In fact, many of the rural areas of the hinterland are less populous today than they were earlier. This pattern of urban growth increased purchasing power disproportionately and added to both the market strength and the stock of urban amenities and services in the hinterland.

What may have been of greater importance was a relative decline or obsolescence of the infrastructure of the older cities in the urban heartland and a weakened competitive position in holding their residents despite relatively high wages. By now many of the physical installations of the urban heartland are shabby, aging, and enormously expensive to maintain. In fact, there may be an oversupply of housing for the poor and dependent and an undersupply for middle-income or self-supporting groups. The streets of these cities are narrow, pockmarked, and in some places so frequently resurfaced that the curbs have practically disappeared. Moving across the urban centers of some of our older cities is a nightmare for truckers, pedestrians, and commuters alike. Old and outdated transportation terminals, bridges, rail lines, and multistory plants and warehouses represent less a capital asset than a physical obstruction to modernization and the employment of new technology.

Above all, the central cities of the heartland are checkered with residential areas that have a deteriorating physical base for public and private services and have undergone a serious decline in the quality of housing relative to that emerging in the suburbs. Their shopping areas are often shabby, without parking, and unable to attract the latest in fashionable distributors. Cleared lots full of rubble, steel-grated windows, and perennial construction and repair mar what little claim some neighborhoods have left to aesthetic appeal or to being a retreat from the frictions and troubles of congested living. The amount of clearance and abandonment is awesome, and Harrison (1974) estimates that there is 1,349,000 vacant acres in a sample of 86 cities above 100,000 population. The situation is growing in Chicago and must be worse in St. Louis and Detroit. Clearance projects, fires, and the scars of past riots present the impression of the aftermath of street warfare in some areas. Huge high-rise public housing projects dot some of this open land but, despite their monolithic proportions, manage to house fewer persons than the less intensive housing they replaced (Greer, 1965).

Admittedly this image is overdrawn. There is practically no city in the old urban heartland which does not have a sizable sector that is still the chosen residence of many of the affluent and is so attractive to residents that they pay a ransom to live there. The Northwest section of Washington, D.C., the North Side of Chicago, the Upper East Side on Manhattan—all are still appealing places to live, although exceptionally expensive and often heavily subsidized by public expenditures (Blair, Gappert, and Warner, 1975). But aside from these typically pie-shaped islands (Hoyt, 1941), there has been a general deterioration in the quality of life in the central cities of the urban heartland, and it often seems to have deteriorated most in those central cities that are embedded in a rapidly growing metropolitan area (Carroll, 1975). Over the last three decades, for example, the Chicago metropolitan area has grown faster than almost any of the larger metropolitan areas of the urban heartland (Berry and others, 1976a), yet the central city of Chicago was among the first of the heartland cities to experience a loss in population. Banfield (1974) may be right in saying that most of our older cities are no more disagreeable than they were in the past, but now people have other, better places in the suburbs to which they can move. Those who can afford to live in the suburbs but choose to live in the central city often do so at increased costs, especially if they share the American dream of home ownership, a single-family dwelling, or some yard space.

To these exceptional costs incurred by those who continue to live in the central city, we must add a number of public costs that increase the burden of these older central cities. It is sometimes pointed out that central-city residents usually demand a high level of expensive public services compared with suburbanites and especially people living in small towns or rural areas (Hawley and Zimmer, 1961). One reason for this is a relatively small but vital population of affluent elites who have very high standards of public service and, like high-wage earners in the central city, tend to push up standards for everyone else. Already there is strong evidence that there is a net transfer of public funds for public services from poorer to richer areas in our central cities (Blair, Gappert, and Warner, 1975). This, however, is not an entirely avoidable public expenditure, since the alternative is to turn our central cities into "sandboxes" for the poor.

A second reason for these high levels of public service and expenditures is that they may be a necessary compensation for foregoing the benefits of living elsewhere. Thus, high expenditures on police protection, road repair, education, health care, and fire control may be necessary enticements to retain those who have the alternative of going where there is less danger of victimization, a less conflict-ridden school system, greater availability of doctors, and less chance of arson or the spread of fire. Some of these hazards seem to be built into urban living (Fischer, 1976), and they are frequently aggravated in our older, larger central cities by the shoddy housing available and the constant land conversion that accompanies metropolitan expansion.

All of this has contributed either to a reduced quality of life in many older central cities or to a very expensive effort to maintain a high quality of life for selected portions of the central-city population. Many of the old central cities of the urban heartland continue to be important centers for the performing arts, expensive shops, higher education, and exposition halls for sports, art, and natural history. However, most of these amenities have a rather narrow appeal, and while they make life more liveable for the cultured and young singles, they do little to hold the masses of people who depend heavily on the local tavern, ball park, school district, parish, or church for their entertainment and social life. A recent study by Campbell, Converse, and Rogers (1976) shows that the quality of community life is fundamental to resident satisfaction and attachment to place. But as their findings also show, high culture is not prominently mentioned among those items that most people see as important to the quality of community life. Those who participate in high culture appear to be a very small segment of the urban or suburban population (Gruenberg, 1975). This is no argument for the reduction of high culture establishments, but it does suggest that there has been an imbalance between public investments that enrich local neighborhood life for the masses and downtown expositions that achieve front page news. In fact, the older central cities may not have lost much of their elite, those with very high incomes and sophisticated tastes who make the downtown their playland. What the central cities have lost are those whose lives focused on their families, neighbors, church, and age peers.

Some of these urban residents have moved no further than to the suburbs surrounding these older central cities. But others have taken more drastic steps and moved out of the urban heartland. Often they have done so at some cost in terms of income and amenities, but usually the cost is not too great in comparison, since it is so expensive to maintain a tranquil quality of life in the older central cities. The impulse to leave the older central cities seems especially great among those who depended heavily on local shopping, entertainment, and amenities but had limited incomes: the diligently working and the lower- to middle-income groups. For them the glories of the bright-lights areas, the swinging singles' district, and the high culture of the CBD have had little lasting appeal. Often they went to the suburbs, but frequently they opted for the hinterland.

Impact of Public Policy. Certainly this massive reassemblage of residents, taxpayers, workers, and voters was not simply a subsocial process in which market forces relocated diverse populations without any form of public intervention. Important public policy decisions were made along the way that heavily affected the operation of free market forces. One of the most important of these was to favor housing construction and reconstruction outside the older central cities by mortgage loan guarantees and a general policy that kept property values in the central cities high so that land could be converted or maintained for residential use only at great cost to private investors. The abortive experience at public housing, sporadic and uncertain building programs, and coercive efforts to push angry low-income black and low-income whites together into the same school district often did little more than convince some people that the central city was not a fit place for habitation. Most of the antipoverty programs begun in the mid 1960s seem to have increased the uncertainty and apprehensions already epidemic in the central cities of the old urban heartland.

But if these social programs did much to alarm people about the fate of these cities, they seem to have done little to reverse the trends already under way. Human management in

the urban heartland probably accelerated existing trends and increased public costs by increasing the number of public employees (Edel, Harris, and Rothenberg, 1975) and the panic of
urban residents.

While the declining competitive position of the urban
heartland has been widely recognized by urban geographers,
local urban investment policies have remained relatively unchanged. In general they seem to have encouraged a high investment in the CBD, conversion to more intense land use, and the
growth of high-wage industries. These policies may have some
immediate benefits for the older central cities of the urban
heartland, but they may also be producing serious diseconomies
while doing little in the long run to retain their self-supporting
residents. Both public and private investment in the CBDs of
these older cities have been little less than spectacular. The new
skyline of Chicago, the Golden Triangle in Pittsburgh, the
Renaissance Center in Detroit, and Lincoln Center and the
World Trade Center in New York—to mention a few—represent
grandiose attempts to give a facelift to downtown districts. Undoubtedly this construction provides some new tax sources and
urban amenities. However, such development also tends to keep
up land values adjacent to the CBD in the expectation that
intense use is likely. Thus these new and awesome downtown
areas are often surrounded by an enlarged zone in transition,
where both residents and land owners are reluctant to invest in
maintenance or home construction. What the cities have gained
in new taxable resources in the CBD may have been lost in the
declining worth of housing and other buildings in this enlarged
zone. One must add to this loss a vast amount of housing and
other taxable property that has been displaced by the construction of highways.

The expectation of ever increasing intensity of land use
has distorted patterns of both personal and commercial investment in the cities. Private builders have come to assume that
housing construction in the central cities is not profitable unless
they are allowed to build multistory apartments. New, available
housing is extremely scarce, and home owners and renters are
dissuaded from needed repairs because of the assumption that
conversion or destruction lies in the near future. Massive highway construction and the building of large public structures do
much to keep these expectations alive, despite a large and growing amount of vacant land in many central cities (Harrison,
1974).

The effort to attract high-wage industries to the central

cities seems at first glance unobjectionable, and certainly the cities need to find ways of employing their large, dependent populations. High-wage industries, however, also demand high skills, and a large portion of the population of the central cities is currently unable to compete for these jobs. Indeed, a dramatic increase in the number of such jobs may only increase suburbanization, since high-wage industries will sponsor the movement of some or most of these people to the suburbs. Some central cities may already be in the position where *new industries simply sponsor outward movement to the suburbs and a corresponding increase in the fiscal burden that suburban growth places on the central cities.* Throughout the period of 1963 to 1967 many of the older central cities gained jobs in the private sector at a higher rate than did their suburbs (Fremon, 1970), although this was also a period in which suburban residential growth accelerated. As Harrison (1974) points out, the growth of public jobs in most central cities usually compensated for the loss of jobs in the private sector throughout much of the recent past, especially during the last decade when so much suburban growth took place.

While the diseconomies of these employment and commercial policies may not always produce obvious losses to the central cities, the cities' ability to gain much from them seems quite limited. Modest efforts to improve the CBD and selected, confined areas for more intense land use might create some gains in taxable wealth, but when these growth policies become dominant, they seem to do little more than frighten away or price out large numbers of central-city dwellers who can afford to live elsewhere. The key weakness of the older central cities in the urban heartland is their inability to retain or attract people of middling social status. The high culture of the CBD, the promise of more intensive land use, and the development of high-wage industries may only push residents toward the suburbs or out of the region entirely.

These concerns with population loss might not be so pressing if they were less selective in terms of socioeconomic status and residential area. But it is mainly the middling status people, those who contribute to the tax base, who are leaving, and it is mainly the areas adjacent to the CBD and large nonresidential areas that are being abandoned. The consequences of the loss of these taxpayers are fairly obvious, but of equal importance is a thinning of the ranks of those—of high and low income—who provided much of the informal social surveillance and social control that made nearby nonresidential areas fairly safe (Janowitz and Suttles, 1977). With the disappearance of residents interested in maintaining some level of order around them, many industrial and commercial areas have been given over to roving bands of teenagers, drug addicts, and footloose predators. The cost of adequate police protection for these areas is simply outside the reach of municipalities and is not that effective without citizen cooperation.

Further, the general loss of population near the city center reduces the influx of nighttime visitors and the capacity of the cities to assure shoppers, concert goers, tourists, and conventioneers that the downtown is safe for recreation and late-hour activities. Some areas of Manhattan that are quite lively and apparently safe during the daytime look like ghost towns at night. The Chicago Loop area has lost many whites who have moved to the Near North Side, and the city seems determined to build a second CBD. The costs that attend this loss of a nighttime population mix are not modest, for it is very doubtful that most of these heartland CBDs can survive at their present scale without nighttime business—convention trade, evening shoppers, and cultural patrons.

Undoubtedly much of the decline in the quality of urban life is the consequence of major shifts in residential and industrial locations, and central-city growth policies have only added fuel to the general conflagration. But as Popenoe (1977) documents for Sweden, it is possible for governmental policies to counter effectively the forceful trends of the marketplace, even to the point of producing their own separate sources of popular dissatisfaction. The American experience with urban planning is very limited and embedded in a history of voluntarism and boosterism that tends either to favor downtown growth or to leave initiative to diverse groups (Suttles, 1975). The countries of Western Europe have the advantage of a national culture, which legitimates centralized efforts to reproduce or maintain a common way of urban life. Also their major cities are cultural artifacts as well, which usually contain not only the seats of national and regional governments but also the accumulated relics of the feudal, Renaissance, and industrial periods. U.S. cities are relatively impoverished; few of them are the seat of regional government and most are lucky to have one national landmark. Very direct federal efforts at urban design and development, then, may have little popular support, and we may already be straining public tolerance of governmental intervention. It is largely through indirect efforts to shape the operation of the private market that U.S. efforts at planning might achieve greater legitimacy while also counterbalancing the further deterioration of our older central cities in the urban heartland. Such policies, however, face a major obstruction in the new public economy that has been constructed in these cities.

Structural Inflexibility. One of the obvious advantages of the newer cities outside the heartland is that their physical plant is technically superior and developed for the postautomobile period. A less visible advantage is the degree of organizational inflexibility that seems to have accumulated over time in the older cities of the heartland. It has become accepted wisdom that the old city political machines are moribund, but as Lowi (1968) has pointed out, these machines were really replaced by new ones consisting largely of public employees and diverse clients of the city—in short, those directly dependent on municipal expenditures. These new machines seem especially characteristic of the central cities in the urban heartland, where established traditions of direct union participation in politics and long-term relations to favored city contractors and suppliers have matured to the point that they make up the most significant constituency that city government must satisfy. Indeed, these groups and city government tend to constitute a sort of self-contained subeconomy in which debtors, contractors, and city employees compose so much of the city's "industry" that the failure or depression of the city government means a failure or depression for the city itself. Although New York is an extreme example, it is instructive to consider that if the city defaulted, it also would mean bankruptcy for many of the city's banks, employee retirement funds, and countless other businesses that service or sell to city government. City government and its associated industries are so big and so dominant that if they cease to grow, the whole urban economy ceases to grow or begins to shrink.

Not only does this lock some urban governments into a spiraling pattern of public expenditures, but it also reduces their flexibility almost entirely. Businesses and employees dependent on city government must somehow be kept going lest their decline spread to all other businesses and employees. Since neither city employees nor those businesses serving the city are very able or willing to "retool" themselves for alternate functions, a city government must generally spend its money the same way one year as it did the year before (Crecine, 1970). Sometimes new programs or capital movements can be started with federal funds, but once initiated by "creative federalism," these programs and investments tend to be incorporated as a part of the local responsibility and the political economy of central cities.

In fact, creative federalism may have partially reinforced a local economy in the urban heartland in which many people forget their roles as taxpayers and consumers and focus their attention on the federal government as the arbiter of their wages and prices. For example, the construction industry has set its wage and price demands almost entirely according to what government employers will pay. This pay schedule, along with built-in price rises guaranteed to contractors, has pushed the price of home repair and construction so high in many central cities that it has frightened many prospective home owners and tenants into the suburbs, where they can obtain nonunion labor and deal with unprotected construction firms. One of the great advantages for the suburban builder George Levitt was that he could hire nonunion laborers and give his prospective clients a firm price without built-in escalator clauses upheld by government decree. Construction or repair in the city, especially the older ones and those most firmly linked to past political coalitions, is far more problematic. In New York City this difference between the public and private economy has become so great that the labor unions have relented recently and argued that they need a two-price system, one for private home owners and another for federal, state, and local governments.

The difference between the public and the private economies in some cities is so great that entrepreneurial pirates have been lured into home maintenance; one can find construction firms, nonunion employees, part-time public employees, and diverse efforts to cut prices below the levels that have been regulated into existence by government. These firms and employees often do shoddy work and the buyer must beware, but their presence indicates how far the regulated marketplace has outdistanced the private one. More importantly, these entrepreneurs disclose the corruption of a society that claims to be a free enterprise system while attempting to yoke urban consumers to a contractual agreement with federal, state, and local backing that protects only the seller. This suspicion of corruption is confirmed when these agreements are enforced by city inspectors who seem constitutionally unable to recommend a builder, repairman, or licensed plumber who is not a member of the local public economy—unionized and incorporated into the servicing of public facilities.

The political economy of these cities expands but does

not change. Above all, programs and investment schemes seldom are eliminated. It is city and state expenditures that have grown most rapidly, and as long as the beneficiaries of these expenditures have the power to topple city and state governments, this situation will be difficult to change except by default.

  Costs of Rapid Growth. Faced with such uncompromising problems, it is expected that city leaders in the urban heartland would search for new policies to rescue themselves from self-defeat. One of the most important is the proposal for metropolitan government, or at least combining the tax bases of the cities and the suburbs (Committee for Economic Development, 1967). This argument is made on the assumption that suburbanites use central-city services but pay little in return. There is a good deal of analysis that tends to show that the growth of suburbs is associated with the growth of costs in the public management of central cities (Kasarda, 1972). There are problems in interpreting these analyses, and it is unclear whether the exceptional costs of central cities with large suburban populations are due to the use of city services by suburbanites or a result of the general stresses and strains that accompany massive outward movement and the reshaping of older central cities to accommodate this new form of urbanization. In a recent analysis Carroll (1975) has argued that suburban usage of central-city services is less important than the sheer difficulties of urban adaptation to the massive spread of housing and the required expansion of public and private establishments to serve both the central-city and suburban populations. Such a reassemblage requires high capital expenditures on new schools, sewers, roads, service agencies, hospitals, and sports plazas. It also means the premature abandonment of older schools and similar facilities. Simply the rate and magnitude of change required by massive suburbanization imposes great cost.

  To choose New York again, a prime example of this can be found in the inner suburbs, which are closing numerous elementary schools and high schools because of a shortage of students, while the outer suburbs are building new schools to accommodate families that are fleeing from the inner suburbs. Earlier the city invested heavily in parking structures to lure suburbanites back to Manhattan, at a time when public transportation was undergoing a serious decline in riders. New shopping malls opening in the suburbs stimulated publicly subsidized efforts to make those in New York competitive. The spread of the city in every direction increases travel distances and raises the cost of road repair, traffic management, and new road construction. When the city attempts to keep its high-income doctors, it must build large research-oriented hospitals. The city's effort to keep its sports facilities (such as Yankee Stadium), entertainment centers, and powerful institutions (such as the stock exchange) exacts a high public cost when these establishments threaten to leave for the nearby suburbs.

Some of these costs of suburbanization have been imposed on the central city of New York. Many others are beginning to be realized in the adjacent suburbs themselves. The suburbs have little infrastructure of their own and the costs of developing such an infrastructure are beginning to rise rapidly: the need for sewage disposal; the purchase and maintenance of parkland; the maintenance of aging housing and roads; the treatment of blight caused by industry; the special services and tax exemptions accorded the elderly; and the provision of recreational, higher education, and cultural amenities. By now it should be clear to both New York City residents and those in its suburbs that metropolitanization would provide little or no fiscal advantage to the city. In fact, property taxes in the inner suburbs are generally as high as those in the city itself. The tax bonus that might have existed at an earlier period has largely evaporated as the New York suburbs have run into the problems of financing their own growth and accumulated deficits.

Admittedly, New York and its suburbs are not the world or for that matter representative of other metropolitan areas in the urban heartland. We have probably overestimated the costs of suburbanization in terms of uncompensated usage of central-city facilities and underestimated the public costs of "spread city," or rapid growth itself. Since suburbanites—or suburban builders—tend to run exactly in those directions in which the social overhead is lowest, it always pushes development into areas with little or no urban infrastructure and its associated costs. As older, built-up suburban areas encounter the obstacles of providing their own public services, the less expensive homes at the margin draw development away from the center. Heavy suburbanization means the expansion of urban areas and the readaptation of functional locations to new uses. Whether these processes occur within the city or adjacent areas, they have similar consequences: the increasing pace of obsolescence, the greater likelihood of conversion, and the heavy burden of public expenditures to keep alive the central, dominant functions of the older cities.

Moral Claims of the Urban Heartland

One of the consequences of the past growth of the metropolitan areas of the urban heartland is that their central cities have been progressively reduced to a CBD, a zone in transition, and a well-guarded "Gold Coast." The resultant concentration of the poor and the growth of the welfare state has prompted some to argue that the federal government should assume the total costs of welfare. Although simple enough, this proposal rests on some tenuous assumptions and might have several consequences that have not yet been closely examined.

One assumption seems to be that the poor, particularly the minority poor, are primarily responsible for frightening away many of the self-supporting residents of the central city and that there is a national moral obligation to support these "asylums of the poor." The most direct expression of this outlook is the argument that poor blacks, Puerto Ricans, and Mexicans have led to "white flight" and a reduction in the number and affluence of taxpayers. Since this poor and apparently fearsome population originated outside the central cities, it seems only fair that the rest of the nation help support it.

However, despite strong efforts to identify white flight, the results are puzzling (Molotch, 1973; Piccagli, 1975). It would seem clear that once a low-income minority group enters a neighborhood, the previous residents do not replace themselves, and there is a gradual building up of blacks, Puerto Ricans, or Mexicans (Duncan and Duncan, 1957). But there is little or no evidence of sudden white flight, or a tipping point. Rather the general observation seems to be that working and middle class whites are able to view the entire metropolitan area as an accessible housing market, and when they move they tend to move to areas that have few or no minority racial groups; often these are in the suburbs. But there seems to be no precipitous exodus instigated by the proximity of minority racial groups. Rather, the general finding seems to be that once a residential area starts to "change," it undergoes a general deterioration and moves only in the direction of decline, poor servicing, and minority dominance.

There seems to be a good deal of truth to the apprehension about white flight, and city leaders and administrators appear to have been quite ineffective in countering this belief. Indeed, in subscribing to the infectious doctrines of rapid growth and conversion, there has been a tendency to simply "write off" changing neighborhoods and regard them as likely candidates for clearance, conversion, or new construction. The new residents were not seen as a resource or the potential citizens and employees of the city, but as a passing misfortune that had to be put up with until new construction brought in new taxpayers or residents. Every city seems to have its Robert Moses, and the prospect of bright, shiny new buildings seems to have regularly won out over the prospect of trying to develop the existing physical plant of the city or upgrade its new population (Caro, 1974).

Under present circumstances, that orientation may be undergoing some changes, because the prospects of new construction are dim and it appears that the current residents are likely to be the long-term residents of the city. However, if the cities are entirely relieved from supporting their poor, then they may lose what incentive they have for upgrading both the abilities of their poorer citizens and the neighborhoods in which they live. Indeed, full federal assumption of welfare costs might allow city leaders—the unions, construction firms, and those who sell to the city—to revert to their former practice of regarding the city's slums and ghettos as red-lined way stations where the federal government will bear the major expenses until the land can be improved. This prospect and the past performance of the old cities of the heartland hardly gives cities a moral claim on the national assumption of their welfare costs.

Moral Realism. The key weakness of the older central cities of the urban heartland seems to be their inability to provide a high enough quality of life to retain their self-supporting residents. They are in the grip of a growth strategy, but by any reasonable judgment of their market strength, unable to compete with either their own suburbs or the hinterland. Any questioning of this growth strategy is apt to encounter strong objections and seriously wound the pride of city leaders, who are accustomed to setting the national pace for urban bigness and change.

The alternative approach must seem especially modest or downright shameful for cities that have advertised themselves as the "big apple" or "city of broad shoulders." The basic ingredients in this alternative strategy are some efforts to improve housing and services to residents of moderate social standing and to invest in the social training of the majority of their current residents on the assumption that they will be the central city's future residents and major human resource. Slow and

modest improvements in housing and education seem to be
what is left to the urban leaders in the old urban heartland. Undoubtedly, these prospects are totally uninspiring to most civic
leaders or boosters, but they have a certain realism.

The most desired outcome of this realism would be for
such leaders to publicize the inherent weakness of the older
urban centers and alter the overly ambitious expectations of
landholders, speculators, and the real estate industry. Land
prices in the cities tend to remain exceptionally high, and they
are accompanied by inflated prices for clearance, repair, rentals,
and new construction. Everyone seems to be waiting for the
federal government or some other big spender from the East to
step in and pay top dollar for any usage or conversion of central-city properties. Often very little gets done or built outside
of the CBD. Occasionally HUD buys urban land and more rarely
develops high-rise housing for the poor or erects some public
buildings that lead to an enormous profit for a few landholders,
construction firms, unions, and those engaged in urban clearance. Sometimes vast high rises or public buildings can be lured
into or near the CBD by ad hoc arrangements that also strain
the public purse. Yankee Stadium and the World Trade Center
are notable examples.

But genuinely private developers in the older central
cities have been noticeably shy at sinking their own money into
the development of central-city residences and commercial
buildings. The older central cities of the urban heartland remain
a comparatively bad investment for private capital, and investors must be cajoled or bribed to invest venture capital into the
central cities. The costs of labor, bureaucratic obstacles, lengthy
estimates for construction time, and the costs of clearance make
life so unpredictable for the urban builder that he is apt to look
at his cost-opportunity schedule and decide that the suburbs or
the hinterland is a better investment.

But there are strong reasons for trying to lure the private
developer back into the central cities of the urban heartland.
Public housing and city-financed efforts to renew neighborhoods have had such limited success that one cannot endorse
them as a general approach to urban renewal. They involve, on
the one hand, grandiose plans that feature the central city as a
sort of future moonscape of high-rise buildings and elevated
transportation arteries, while on the other hand timidly recoil-
ing from any investment not supported by the banks and construction industry. With some minor exceptions, the federal

government has supported loan policies, depreciation allowances, and planning commissions that are only a little more adventuresome than the banks, who have already red-lined vast
areas in the central cities. Federal programs are as bureaucratic
as those of local city government and present one legal or administrative barrier after another. Both city government and
federal government programs tend to be highly centralized,
making them inflexible in the face of varying tastes and capacities in different communities. This same centralization lends
itself to heavy influence by the well-paid construction unions
and firms, who have generally demanded a large, exclusive, and
expensive role for themselves in any effort to reconstruct or improve housing in the central cities.

Luring private capital back into the older central cities
and increasing home owner confidence in the worth of investment is obviously a long-term and complicated problem. An
indication that land conversion is going to slow down or halt
completely may restore home owners' confidence in further investments. If some of our central cities are forced to drop these
pretensions, then they may once again attract private capital.
Most important, they may be able to recapture the interest and
investments of their own residents, who have a considerable
capacity to reshape, maintain, or simply avoid harming the
housing stock that remains. By and large, the maintenance of
housing is a responsibility of the occupant. Where the occupant
is led to believe that there is little hope in retaining his home for
long-term usage, he is unlikely to make much investment in
maintenance.

New federal loan guarantees and tax allowances may also
help to make available a portion of the needed capital. But it is
probably even more important to reduce the bureaucratic tangle, the centralized drive for standardization, and the strangle-
hold of construction unions and firms. Obviously, it is unlikely
that city and federal governments will be able to alter their own
programs directly in order to reduce the role of their most active political supporters and thus make their controls over housing and construction more flexible. For this reason there may
be merit in the argument that government should retreat from
direct construction and housing management in favor of local
community corporations or resident organizations. Such groups
do have flexibility, and while they may not always observe the
highest standards of construction, they may be able to retard
the pattern of deterioration and abandonment that has followed

previous housing policies. Even then, the hopes for restoring the housing stock of our older cities would involve a long-term plan with the expectation that only some subcommunities would be able to mobilize effectively to improve the quality of their housing and neighborhood life. Some areas of the central cities have such concentrations of the poor and unskilled that the prospects of self-help are quite limited unless accompanied by efforts to improve their capacity for employment and community participation.

Human Resources and Education

Although many of the minority poor have made significant advances in education and employment (Lieberson, 1973), community leaders have failed to see them as the main human resource on which the older cities must depend in the future. Dispersing the large-city ghettos and attracting high-income residents back to the central cities are long-term and limited strategies, albeit still favored ones. The most immediate objective, then, must be to upgrade large populations in the central cities so that they can effectively revive urban life themselves. Dispersal to the suburbs may help obscure or redistribute the problem of their support and have other benefits, but it does not immediately or clearly insure a substantial reshaping of the talents and abilities of minority group members.

One of the most significant failures of the central cities—those in the hinterland or the heartland—is their inability to adapt the school system to the new urban migrants in the post-World War II period. There are many ways to interpret the Coleman Report and its subsequent challengers and followers (Coleman and others, 1966). But one thing seems clear: As currently organized, variations in the primary and secondary school systems seem to make only modest contributions to the academic performance of children beyond what might be expected on the bases of their family backgrounds. What seems to be called for is not a discounting of the schools—their elimination in favor of the "hidden [and cheaper] curriculum" at home—but radical experimentation to find out if any variations in primary and secondary education can be effective.

Expectably, urban educational leaders have been especially reluctant to try much experimentation, especially of the kind that starts with some general idea of improvement and subsequently adopts variations to perfect the method in order to meet the special requirements of local students (Janowitz, 1969). Instead, most efforts at educational innovation have been fought out on a grand scale: tracking or no tracking, local control or central control, the use of volunteers or the use of professionals, the open classroom or the regimented classroom, productivity measures for teachers or none whatsoever, and investments in hardware or investments in teaching personnel. Faced with these technocratic approaches to education, it is not surprising that teachers and school administrators have generally retreated to a highly standardized curriculum and centralized forms of control that protect them from both accusations of favoritism and individual responsibility. Like other city administrators, the construction unions, and city planners, educators have interpreted *fairness* to mean standardization, uniformity, and centralized supervision (Street, 1969). This lockstep version of equality tends to eliminate innovation as being a sign of favoritism. A better conception of equal opportunity would provide equalizing resources but would give different groups great leeway in how the resources were to be used.

This insistence on uniformity as equality is far from the U.S. tradition of education, despite the declaration of defenders that it is a time-worn precedent of democracy. Public education in the United States has always been complemented by a wide range of alternatives that have supplemented or substituted for the routine classroom experience in a city-owned building. Parochial schools, high school equivalency examinations, vocational schools, night classes, commercial schools, and correspondence schools have been regular alternatives to the model of a twelve-year attendance at a red brick school building.

With a narrowing conception of what public education should be, it is understandable that some public support should develop for a thorough "market system" of education, giving free choice in how children are educated, provided they pass standardized exams. The most widely discussed plan is that of Milton Friedman (1973), who has suggested that the entire public education system be cashiered and replaced by a system of voucher payments that would allow parents to enroll their children as they please and encourage private education entrepreneurs to enter the market for training youngsters. There are numerous problems with this scheme, the central one being that high-income families would probably try to reduce public funding of education, since they could finance the education of their own children themselves. Public education at the lowest levels probably does represent a transfer payment from the well-to-do to the less well-off. A totally private system of education would allow the rich to pay for their own children's education and would designate pitifully small sums for the vouchers to be received by the remaining parents and the educational establishments they could afford. The popularity of this thinking at least indicates the extremes to which some Americans are willing to go to recapture some flexibility in their school system.

It is not necessary to abandon public education in America in order to make it more flexible. However, unless the central cities can find some way to use their massive primary and secondary systems of education to improve the capacities of the urban poor, they can only hope that these large residential concentrations can be broken up and scattered—and perhaps hidden —elsewhere. Scatter-site public housing is a special version of this argument. Aside from the rather dim likelihood that such housing will be adopted on a wide scale, it would do little to alter the basic problems of poverty and would give the cities little moral claim on the public support of the rest of the nation. Despite their weakening position, the older cities of the heartland retain comparatively great sources of wealth and public income. In the last two decades they may have used this wealth ineffectively, but it would appear that they could justify further public investments only if they could show that those investments will bear fruit in developing their human resources.

Prospects for the Urban Heartland:
From Production to Consumption

What the older cities of the heartland have lost is not their tax base or wealth but their ability to engage in perpetual deficit spending. Deficit spending—primarily through municipal bonds—is encouraged primarily by a growth strategy that always assumes that an ever increasing tax base will diminish the relative size of the costs of borrowing. This strategy is also fueled by the idea that urban growth is guaranteed by attractive amenities that lure high-income residents and industries (Gottman and Harper, 1967). There appear to be sharp limits to these policies, especially when urban amenities are read to mean those generally situated in the CBD. The social and economic overhead of such policies are themselves self-limiting and destroy the quality of life for the masses of urban dwellers who do not share in the grand style of life anticipated.

This, of course, has not kept urban leaders from retreating only a few steps to get their financial house in order, preparing for the time that they can reenter the money market. This short-run policy may do little more than dig deeper the hole in which older central cities already find themselves. Reconstructing their own infrastructure of housing and neighborhood life and developing their own human resources are very long-term goals. Vague hopes of reentering the money market or shipping the poor to the suburbs only delay a genuine evaluation of their long-term predicament. It would be quite shortsighted, however, to see in the present urban fiscal crisis and its specific correlates (Clark, 1976) the central cause of the U.S. urban crisis. The fiscal crisis is only another tip of the same iceberg that has been endangering our older central cities since the close of World War II. Racial segregation, the centrifugal drift to the suburbs and hinterland, the job-residence mismatch, and widespread public discord help to chart its course, but no single one of these problems indicates the total magnitude of this urban reassemblage or helps us to plot a safe course. Taken together they do suggest that governmental policies must remain indirect, that the prospects of urban growth strategies must be selective, and that the general quality of life in our urban centers should be the parameter of evaluation rather than the particular manifestation of each urban crisis.

In the long run, the prospects for the older cities of the heartland are not that dim provided that their leaders can accept the modest view that growth is unlikely and improvement apt to be slow. Already the migration of the poor to the cities seems to have slackened, especially in the older central cities. For the cities there may be a breathing spell in which they can gain from the rehabilitation of their resident talent rather than simply exporting it to the suburbs.

Also, despite the weakness of urban school systems and welfare programs, there does seem to be a self-healing process at work in the older cities' ghettos and slums. Especially among the blacks there are signs that the general pattern of generational mobility (Lieberson, 1973) is taking hold, and with some stability black neighborhoods may be able to exercise their own measures of social control (Warren, 1975). Under the pressure of a growth strategy, our city ghettos and slums have been mere revolving doors, entrepôts housing the most disabled and ill informed until they can move elsewhere. In the future, the ghettos and slums of the older central cities may come to more

closely resemble stable communities—poor but able to exert
their own brand of social control.

In addition, as urbanization occurs in the more remote
areas of the country, it helps eliminate the lingering pools of
concentrated poverty in the nation. Anyone who takes a long-
term view of urban poverty and its consequences for the quality
of urban life must recognize that the major burdens on our central cities during the last twenty-five years have been produced
by out-migration from the less urbanized parts of the nation's
hinterland. Growth centers in the nation's hinterland have done
much to reduce this population influx into urban areas. In this
respect urban growth in the hinterland has reduced the burden
of the older central cities. The only limitation to this process is
that it has not gone far enough and that there are still large
areas of Appalachia, the Mountain states, the upper Midwest,
and the Northwest where the long distance to an urban center
provides people with such limited opportunities that they must
join long-distance migrants if they wish to seek a better life in
the older cities of the heartland. There are, of course, those who
want to maintain such areas of rural poverty as a sort of natural
zoo, in which the resident humans and animals grub for a living
according to a set of primeval rules so that the well-paid residents of urban centers can look at the remnants of clean air,
desert, and self-inflicted poverty that prevail in areas like
southern Utah, Montana, or the Missisippi delta. Such an outlook can do little more than promote a breeding ground for
poverty and its eventual importation to the older central cities.

Most importantly, the newer urban centers in the hinterland seem to be quickly endangering themselves by adopting a
strategy not too different from that previously followed by the
older cities of the heartland. Their encouragement of unbridled
growth, their extensive investment in their CBDs, their neglect
of housing and education for those with moderate incomes,
combined with a heavy entry into the credit money market—all
this is reminiscent of the pattern that has so weakened the older
cities in the urban heartland. It seems altogether likely that
these adventures at urban growth are equally self-limiting, and
in due time they will bring about a new balance in the competition between urban places so that the older central cities will be
seen as comparatively good places to settle, if not the best
imaginable. Already, it appears that Los Angeles, the largest
growth center for the last two decades, has reached such a point
in pursuing its low-density pattern of growth. Regarding every

change as advantageous, these hinterland cities seem to be quickly rectifying the imbalance in their competitive advantage over the older central cities of the urban heartland.

There are other marginal changes that may aid the older central cities of the urban heartland. As the birth rate falls and as one- and two-child families increase, a number of families may find the central city more manageable and attractive, either because of its cultural advantages or because of affordable private education and day care. The lengthening delay in marriage and the growing population of relatively well-off divorcees may help replenish the stock of urbanites wanting to find a tolerant place for them to reconstruct their lives. Even such subcultural populations as homosexuals and the remainder of several social movements (hippies, yippies, and urban pioneers) may add a trickle to urban migration. In its own way, the energy crisis may favor those amenable to high residential densities, which lower transportation, heating, and maintenance costs.

Yet again, for some cities in the urban heartland, probably those at its periphery such as Cincinnati or Minneapolis, the prospects of growth may continue if they are able to lend their own services to the growth in the adjacent hinterland. In this respect, growth and rehabilitation strategies can be a mixed blessing for some cities. For the majority of the cities in the old urban heartland, however, the prevailing strategy—the one that would pay off in more taxable property and an improved quality of life—must be a rehabilitative strategy. Such a strategy finds few political supporters, but its moral realism may gain popular support as the trials and errors of municipal investment reach a clearer outcome. In America the past profits of urban growth have been so general that it has been hard for the electorate to make a discerning judgment about the wisdom of municipal expenditures. With the arrival of hard times, voters may become more discerning and more judgmental. In the high-growth economy that has prevailed since 1950, any municipal investment seemed warranted. One hopes that in the future new urban ventures will be more closely circumscribed by the potential delivery of income back to the municipal investor.

Part Five

Variations
in Urbanization

The two chapters in this section view urbanization from a broader perspective. Chapter Eighteen, "Urbanization of Rural Areas" by Robert O. Richards, looks at the ambiguities of urban-rural differences in the contemporary period and, among other concerns, probes the question of whether America's small towns have ever existed outside the context of a mass society. In Chapter Nineteen, Bryan R. Roberts develops "Comparative Perspectives on Urbanization" in the United States, Britain, Western Europe, and Latin America. In so doing, he questions whether the U.S. pattern of urbanization represents a modal pattern and argues that patterns of urbanization vary according to the location of the society in the core and peripheral sectors of an international economic order.

18

Urbanization
of Rural Areas

Robert O. Richards

New social change processes in rural areas are implicit in the
shift from the metropolitan to the diffuse phase of urbanization, which Hawley has described in Chapter One of this volume. The dominant sociological generalizations about urbanization were formulated in the context of the metropolitan phase.
If a transition such as Hawley delineates to a more diffuse pattern of urbanization is now under way, those generalizations
must be scrutinized.

Urbanization can be viewed as having three major dimensions: ecological, social organizational, and sociocultural. Each
of these dimensions provides a theoretical context for examination of prevailing sociological generalizations about the urbanization of rural areas. The validity of those generalizations as
they apply to the metropolitan phase of urbanization must be
considered. If they prove inadequate in describing the era from

which change is believed to be occurring, it will be impossible to make serious use of them either to describe base points from which new trends can be analyzed or to predict principles transcending specific phases of change dynamics.

Inspired by Kuhn's (1970) criticism of persisting outdated paradigms, Bernard (1973) cogently questioned the appropriateness of prevailing generalizations of four community paradigms, including the ecological and sociocultural. With incisive rhetoric, she encouraged reevaluation of popular generalizations from "normal" social science in the face of contradicting data and the emergence of new trends. In that spirit, two classic principles of ecology will be reviewed in the context of urbanization in both its metropolitan and diffuse phases. The social organizational proposition to be questioned is the popular generalization that during the metropolitan phase of urbanization, rural communities have lost autonomy in their decision-making structures and are now being absorbed into mass society. The sociocultural generalization to be considered is that urbanization results in a break with the attitudes and behavior surrounding the tradition, familism, and primary interpersonal contacts believed to characterize rural society.

Empirical studies and commentary from the literature on rural urbanization will be presented in evaluating sociological generalizations associated with the ecological, social organizational, and sociocultural dimensions. Thus, the purpose of this chapter is twofold—to explore findings related to each dimension and to interrelate these dimensions in assessing the state of sociological knowledge regarding the urbanization of rural life.

The Ecological Dimension

The ecological principles inherited from studies of the metropolitan phase of urbanization stressed the spatial dominance of cities in the impact of urbanization on rural areas. The dynamics of growth implied in the concept of diffuse urbanization require new ecological formulations that encompass the entire nation as an ecological community rather than conceiving of rural ecological change as essentially an extension of urban nodal expansion. The extent to which popular ecological generalizations accurately describe urbanization in rural areas during the metropolitan phase will be considered before describing new trends that may require reexamination of those generalizations.

Historically, the dominant themes in the ecological impact of urbanization on rural areas have dealt with population trends and socioeconomic specialization. During the metropolitan phase of urbanization, the urban population has been characterized as creating a sprawl outward from cities into the surrounding countryside in an ever expanding arc; rural communities in the path of this advancing urban frontier have been depicted as being simply swallowed whole and transformed into residential or industrial enclaves within the larger metropolitan ecology. Meanwhile, new urban centers were born from rustic villages in the immediate hinterland of metropolises; more distant rural regions surrendered their children to this metropolitan expansion and quietly withered away.

These population trends were formally summarized in the ecological "gradient principle," according to which "the extent of urban-influenced changes in rural areas varies inversely with the distance to the nearest city and directly with the size of that city" (Martin, 1957, p. 176).

Simultaneously with these population trends, the socioeconomic dynamics of the metropolitan phase of urbanization also display centrifugal expansion from cities. These dynamics involve increasing specialization in function and differentiation of subareas. As the rural hinterland becomes the urban fringe, it no longer has a simple, undifferentiated agrarian structure. Instead, it develops new specializations not only in agriculture but also in industry and commerce, thereby finding a functional niche within the larger urban ecological order. Small communities, incapable of meeting the competition in this specialization process, may lose many local enterprises and become increasingly dependent on other towns to meet employment and consumer needs. These socioeconomic trends were formally summarized in the ecological "principle of differentiation," according to which "the extent of specialization of functions and differentiation of subareas varies inversely with distance to the nearest city and directly with the size of the city" (Martin, 1957, pp. 176-177).

As America enters the "diffuse" phase of urbanization, these principles provide a heuristic device for describing the course of ecological change during the metropolitan phase of urbanization. They also provide reference points for describing changes in the diffuse phase that suggest the need to formulate new ecological principles.

Gradient Principle and Population Change. During the

metropolitan phase of urbanization, population growth rippled out from centers of population concentration in a pattern consistent with Burgess's (1923) description of different urban land uses succeeding one another along a gradient of concentric circles, with the impetus for expansion emanating from ever increasing growth at the center. Gradually the focus of growth expanded into metropolitan fringes (Beale, 1975). Hawley has noted that suburban growth was evident from the beginning of industrial city growth, but it was not until later that the rate of growth was highest in the suburban rings surrounding the central cities.

Metropolitan sprawl has characterized population growth for the last three decades. Fuguitt (1972, p. 112) noted that since 1940, "for each region, for each decade, the proportion of places growing is greater in metropolitan than nonmetropolitan places." Duncan and Reiss's (1956) analysis of the 1950 census pointed to an "urban gradient" that distributed demographic and occupational characteristics of the urban place along a gradient of consistently diminishing density from central cities. The effect of that sprawl on the surrounding countryside displayed the rippling consequences of urbanization. Utilizing variables employed earlier by Duncan (1961a) to represent a shift away from reliance on agriculture by rural populations, K. M. Brown (1971, p. 54) wrote that "the whole country is becoming more urbanized. Rural landowners near the cities are more likely in 1960 than in 1950 to sell their land at a profit for more intensive use than farming or to turn to commercial production."

This outward expansion of metropolitan population growth was believed to be fed in some measure by migrants moving from distant rural hinterlands in quest of metropolitan opportunities. The result was seen as the death by attrition of remote, small rural towns, while larger towns within the metropolitan region grew. Thus, in describing the population trends of small towns during the metropolitan phase of urbanization, Fuguitt (1972, p. 125) portrayed "a total picture of growth. ... The declining number and proportion of villages under 2,500 in size is not due to their decline and disappearance but basically due to growth." Studies utilizing either census data for all small communities (Taeuber and Taeuber, 1958, p. 115) or case studies of selected towns (Smith, 1974; Richardson and Larson, 1976) tend to display a general pattern of growth among small towns.

The popular notion that small towns have been dying was perpetuated by not distinguishing crossroads hamlets, which never enjoyed a firm lease on life, from larger small towns, which have occupied secure niches within the larger ecological order. In general, the crossroads hamlets were the last to be developed and are the weakest, and it is their demise that gives apparent statistical support to the generalization that all small towns are threatened. In the Midwest, the last stage of town development occurred just before the mass appearance of the automobile (Hart, 1972). The resulting pattern was a fine mesh of towns, including new crossroads hamlets, doomed to extinction. The impact of the automobile and technological advances in agriculture diminished the need for such closely spaced market towns. These towns were therefore among the first to succumb in the face of these changes. This may explain the pattern of town growth in Wisconsin, which Fuguitt (1965, pp. 19-21) described as conforming to the gradient principle: "Thus, despite aggregate increases [in the number of small towns] many individual small towns are declining, especially smaller ones in remote rural areas. No matter where studies were done, [they] show that larger places are more likely to grow, and to grow at a faster rate, than smaller places." Thus both open country and rural towns appeared to reflect the dynamics of population distribution expressed by the gradient principle during the metropolitan phase of urbanization.

In suggesting the emergence of a new, diffuse phase of urbanization, Hawley has noted, in an analysis of post-1970 trends, that growth is now shifting to nonmetropolitan regions. In analyzing county census data, Beale (1975) found a nonmetropolitan growth rate of 4.2 percent during the three years following the 1970 census. In contrast, he found a 2.9 percent growth rate in the metropolitan areas. These trends are evidence that population growth is occurring in what have previously been rural areas and not necessarily in a gradient pattern from metropolitan centers.

The recent growth of nonmetropolitan areas is not simply due to the spillover of urban population into adjacent nonmetropolitan regions (Beale, 1976). Even counties that in the past provided the archetype of rural decline—those not adjacent to a metropolitan area and having no town with at least 2,500 inhabitants—grew by 3 percent between 1970 and 1973. This occurred despite a decline in those rural counties of 4.5 percent during the previous decade. As Beale (1975, p. 3) noted: "There were still nearly 600 nonmetropolitan counties declining in population during 1970-73, but this was less than half as many as the nearly 1,300 declining in the 1960's."

Beale's studies of the repopulation of rural areas strongly suggest that urbanization is now not described by the distance gradient concept and that remote towns and open areas, once emptied by the pull of metropolitan opportunities, may now be exerting their own pull in retaining and attracting population. Although Beale (1976) noted town data were not as reliable or as complete as the county data with which he first detected a rural repopulation trend, these data nonetheless suggested that "in a very real sense the current trend of population distribution is one of renewed rural residential growth—open country and village. A majority of it is occurring in counties that have no places of 10,000 population, and it is especially pronounced in counties that lack any town of even 2,500 people" (pp. 10-11).

These findings indicate a new ecological trend for the repopulation of relatively remote regions. The trends which Duncan and Reiss (1956) found in the 1950s may well have followed the gradient principle, but the dynamics of rural population growth now suggest the presence of some impetus other than central-city growth. Although the repopulation of rural areas that Beale detected displays a rippling out from the center, just as the gradient principle would predict, now the center does not hold. Rather than being spurred by the expansion of healthy, growth-oriented centers, as the gradient principle implies, diffuse urbanization carries its own generating impulse, even in the face of declining central cities. Beale (1976, p. 7) argued that his findings have made a "complete shambles of the former strong positive association between density of population and growth." Thus, the conceptual underpinnings on which the gradient principle rests may require revision to be applicable today.

Social Differentiation Principle and Socioeconomic Change. As urbanization moves from the metropolitan to the diffuse phase, differentiation of ecological functions both between and within rural communities can be expected to undergo change. This section first reviews studies useful for evaluating the social differentiation principle as it applied during the metropolitan phase of urbanization to specialization among rural communities as socioeconomic units of the larger ecological order. New functions being performed in rural areas currently experiencing growth will also be considered as an aspect of the diffuse phase of urbanization. In addition, studies concerning the internal socioeconomic differentiation within small communities will be reviewed to aid future researchers in delineating rural socioeconomic structures as the dynamics of the diffuse phase of urbanization become more evident.

Proximity to urban centers has been viewed as essential to explaining the ecological interdependence of rural towns and cities during the metropolitan phase of urbanization. According to Martin's (1957) statement of the social differentiation principle, each community survives and finds its ecological niche within society by meeting the needs of the larger urban socioeconomic order through specialization; the closer the community is to an urban center, the more easily that function is met. During the metropolitan phase of urbanization, that principle was reflected in a community economic development policy that pegged the survival of small rural towns to the promotion of local industry—usually the manufacture of products for urban markets.

The urbanization of rural towns during the metropolitan phase of urbanization indeed has sometimes been synonymous with industrialization. Rural population growth appeared to follow a shift from an agricultural to an industrial economy (Tarver and Beale, 1969; Tarver, 1972). Haren (1970) found that from 1962 to 1969 more than a third of the growth in manufacturing employment occurred in the nonmetropolitan sector. McKinney and Bourque (1971) noted that the marked urbanization of the South (from 11 percent of the national urban population in 1900 to 21.5 percent in 1960) was accompanied by industrialization.

The socioeconomic characteristics of rural areas where Beale has detected a repopulation trend suggest that a more complex relationship between industrialization and population growth is emerging in the diffuse phase of urbanization. These new trends also indicate that these advanced and sophisticated urban socioeconomic functions appear in formerly remote rural regions, contrary to the pattern predicted by the gradient principle. Beale suggested a limited measure of industrialization may be necessary to provide a base for rural repopulation but that urbanization may now be occurring without an equivalent increase in industry. In the two rural southern regions where Beale detected the beginnings of population growth in the 1960s, the rapid population decline of the 1950s resulted in only one sixth of the labor force remaining in farming. These regions "were major beneficiaries of the decentralization trend of manufacturing that gathered speed in the mid 1960s" (Beale, 1975, p. 5).

Nonetheless, the association of industrialization with recently emerging rural urbanization is not a direct causal relationship. Beale (1975, p. 4) noted that despite the relationship between industrialization and growth, "population growth has not been high in 1970 in areas with heavy concentration of manufacturing activity. . . . From 1969 to 1973, manufacturing jobs comprised just 18 percent of all nonmetropolitan job growth, compared with 50 percent from 1962 to 1969." The effect of industrial development is believed to create an element of heterogeneity in the division of labor, and consequently a more complex, more urban stratified structure, such as Smith (1974) found in his midwestern studies. This heterogeneity results in socioeconomic development beyond manufacturing; recreational and educational activities representing advanced levels of specialization in urban functions play significant roles in regions that recently were characterized by marginal agrarian economies.

The specific kind of functions performed in growing rural communities also indicates that differentiation in societal level functions is spurring rural population growth. Beale (1975) pointed to the increase of retirement and recreation activities in these recently growing areas. The lower cost of living, the smaller scale of institutional structures, and the creation of recreational facilities attract urbanites seeking leisure or retirement opportunities to rural areas. Beale (1975) argued the net immigration to rural areas since 1970 has also been fueled by the growth of state university towns; rural counties housing these universities have grown by 5.8 percent since 1970. The role of college towns in rural urbanization was empirically confirmed by Irwin's (1971) multiple-regression analysis of all nonmetropolitan counties between 1960 and 1970. Such communities tended to spawn so-called fourth-order industries (for example, data analysis and processing, and testing and other educational services).

Recreational, retirement, and educational functions all represent the most advanced level of urban society; their roles in the new growth of rural areas indicate not a rebirth of traditional rural socioeconomic functions but the incursion of urban functions further into the hinterlands. The dissemination of these higher-order urban functions suggests contemporary urbanization of rural regions is not following a linear evolution from subsistence to cash crop agriculture, followed by urbanization through increasing levels of industrialization. The new southern growth areas that Beale (1975) described were left behind by the revolution of modern agriculture and are now leaping directly from subsistence agriculture into an era of advanced urban specialization, which has followed only modest industrialization. Conversely, the region most benefited by the industrialization of cash crop agriculture—the Great Plains—is the only major region of the nation where a large number of counties with declining population are still evident (Beale, 1975, p. 3). The Great Plains has specialized to serve the diverse urban-national and international economy with more agricultural products provided by decreasing labor inputs (Hart, 1972). Meanwhile, other rural regions with less intensely industrialized farming activity have become repopulated by meeting other needs of the urban-national socioeconomic order.

Analysis of the effects of the metropolitan phase of urbanization on internal differentiation has yielded contradictory generalizations. These contradictions have complicated the prediction of socioeconomic differentiation trends in rural communities as America experiences the diffuse phase of urbanization. For example, there are logical arguments and empirical data that suggest urbanization at the community level has brought both an increase and a decrease in social differentiation within small towns. Smith (1974) concluded, on the basis of changes he observed in twelve upper midwestern towns between 1900 and 1970, that urbanization resulted in a uniformly high level of socioeconomic differentiation and specialization in those relatively isolated towns. Despite a decline in the number of farm residents, farm/town economic relationships in all the communities that Smith studied involved increasingly sophisticated technology which required a proliferation of community services related to improved ways of farming. Coupled with an expansion of services facilitated by changes in communication and transportation, these agricultural changes resulted in a more heterogeneous local socioeconomic order. Smith maintained that technological changes represented a common experience for all such communities. In short, all communities became more uniformly urban.

A similar pattern of increasing internal social differentiation has been observed by Richardson and Larson (1976) in their longitudinal analysis of thirteen rural New York communities. Although the level of services displayed considerable stability in these small communities between 1960 and 1974, services associated with quality of life were a conspicuous addition. An increase in voluntary associations related to social services and community improvement was also noted. Finally, the industrialization pattern reflected greater social differentiation. There was an increase between 1964 and 1974 in the total number of industries but a decrease in agricultural industries. Most new industries involved the manufacture of small machinery; however, a few food and kindred product industries were added. The evidence from these studies by Smith and by Richardson and Larson suggests that rural communities are moving toward the internal differentiation in retail services, associational activities, and industrial development characteristic of urban places.

There is the suggestion of a countertrend to the generalization that communities respond to urbanization with increasing internal differentiation; the long-range trend for the structure of communities may be toward a diminution in the differentiation of retail services. As Hawley (1971), Tilley (1974), and others have observed, the automobile has freed rural residents from their home towns and permitted them to travel elsewhere for jobs, entertainment, shopping, and health services. In that process, the automobile has also robbed those towns of a consumer market for their services. Fuguitt (1965, p. 20) succinctly described this process of centralization:

> At the same time [that transportation widens shopping opportunities] the demand for goods and services becomes so varied and specialized that their satisfaction is far beyond the scope of an individual small town. So-called "economies of scale" operate to put the small store, creamery, or cheese factory at a competitive disadvantage. The growing complexity of farm machinery means that a store offering complete sales and services must be a relatively large one, drawing on a wide clientele. Hence, one cannot be located in every small town. Technological changes make for fewer but larger establishments to furnish inputs and to serve as markets for farm products. The operation of the same kinds of constraints, moreover, has led to the centralization of professional services (such as private medical practice) and public institutions (such as high schools and hospitals).

The impact of the centralization of retail activities upon small towns is reflected in studies recording the diminished availability of services in rural communities. Johansen and Fuguitt (1973) plotted a decline from 1939 to 1970 in the variety of services offered by rural Wisconsin villages regardless of whether a community was gaining or losing population. Neither the services lost nor others gained by villages over the three decades were necessarily related to agriculture. This indicates a decrease in the general capacity of local communities to meet an array of community retail needs.

Several studies document the proliferation of urban socioeconomic functions within small towns; others record the deterioration of such functions in that setting. In resolving this confusion regarding the relationship between urbanization and internal differentiation of communities, the introduction of various intervening variables may enhance the research design of future studies. Distance to urban centers would be an appropriate variable to use in testing the gradient principle. However, if the diffuse phase of urbanization has diminished the effect of distance from urban centers as a factor in differential internal socioeconomic structures, use of that variable may prove insignificant. Regional, population, and socioeconomic function variations might also be profitably investigated in better delineating the impact of urbanization on the internal ecological structure of rural communities.

The dawn of a new phase of diffused urbanization suggests that communities will find new ecological niches at the societal level, as Beale (1975) indicated, and also that the internal social differentiation of rural communities may follow a new course. Until the forces affecting differentiation within rural towns are better understood, it will be difficult to predict whether newly growing small towns will find themselves in the future with more or less industry and business. Hawley notes that potential energy shortages also interject an unpredictable element in these differentiation patterns. Such shortages could cause a resurrection of some retail services in small towns if fuel shortages restrain intercommunity travel. The possibility of dramatic changes in transportation occasioned by a reduction in gasoline supplies further complicates predicting future differentiation trends.

Ecological Trends and Analytical Limitations. Recent ecological literature suggests several generalizations concerning population and differentiation trends in rural America. First, urbanization is occurring in even remote rural regions in the form of growing population. Second, rural communities are finding new niches in the national ecological order as the differentiation of urban functions is dispersed throughout the nation. Together these generalizations illustrate the development of a diffuse phase of urbanization.

Findings of increasing urbanization in rural areas must be interpreted cautiously in the face of evidence indicating some significant ecological and demographic differences that continue to exist between rural and urban populations; differences in fertility, age composition, family status, education, employment, and income indicate that the diffusion of urban attributes has not proceeded to the extent that ruralists are now indistinguishable from urbanites. Historically, higher birth rates have been associated with rural society, and lower rates with urban society. Over the past two decades, comparative rates have not demonstrated conclusively that rural and urban fertility trends are converging. Writing in the 1950s, Westoff (1954) examined the hypothesis that differential fertility ratios between urban and rural areas in the United States have been contracting. Westoff (1954, p. 561) found the available evidence to be inconclusive: "Although the urban rural fertility ratios in 1950 are the closest they have ever been in this time series (1900-1950) . . . this is due to the greater increases in urban fertility during the baby boom and is not prefaced by an observable trend toward contraction before 1940 except among nonwhites." Similar patterns were apparent in the 1960s. Irene Taeuber (1972, p. 47) noted "metropolitan-nonmetropolitan differences in birth rates were reduced even further in the sixties, while the excess in the death rates in nonmetropolitan populations were accentuated. . . . The rate of natural increase was *higher* in the metropolitan than in the nonmetropolitan population" (emphasis added).

In analyzing post-1970 trends, Beale (1972, p. 675) detected a continuing divergence between urban and rural birth rates: "Since the fertility rate tipped downward in January, 1971, the well-publicized drop in births had been limited to the Northeast, North Central region, the Pacific states, and that part of the South north of the Potomac River. In the rest of the country, births continued to increase. In the declining regions, the population was 22 percent rural; in the regions of continued birth increases, 36 percent rural. Thus, the differential contribution of the more rural areas to national fertility does not seem to be ended."

Using national samples of U.S. census data, Johansen and Fuguitt (1973) found marked differences between metropolitan and nonmetropolitan populations in age composition, family status, education, employment, and income. Within the nonmetropolitan samples, urban populations differed from village and rural farm populations, particularly in income. Table 1 displays the variation between samples in a variety of census characteristics.

Table 1. Dissimilarity Between Nonmetropolitan Urban, Village, and Nonvillage Nonfarm Characteristics in the United States, 1970.

Characteristic	Index of Dissimilarity		
	Urban/Village	Village/ Nonvillage Nonfarm	Urban/ Nonvillage Nonfarm
Age	6.2	9.2	6.3
Family status	2.7	4.9	3.9
Migration	6.0	2.8	3.6
School completed	7.5	7.4	11.8
Labor force: male	5.1	2.8	3.1
Labor force: female	4.1	2.4	6.1
Occupation	7.7	9.7	16.7
Industry	5.2	10.5	14.3
Income	8.6	1.6	8.9

Source: Johansen and Fuguitt (1973, table 8).

In addition to limitations that complicate any ecological generalizations about the urbanization of rural areas that are based on the gradient and differentiation principles, Beale's recent studies pose specific problems of their own. Beale (1976) answered questions about the reliability of his data and about the extent to which rural repopulation is widespread. Nevertheless, several issues remain. Given the long history of rural population decline, social scientists may wish to have a trend of longer duration rather than proclaiming the dawn of a new era based on data gathered only since 1970. It might be argued the trend has been observable for at least a decade, since Beale (1975) discerned its appearance in southern areas in the 1960s. In the long term, Beale's evidence may represent an isolated regional phenomenon. This possibility must be entertained, given Beale and Fuguitt's (1975, p. 14) conclusion that "there is not a single generalization from the demographic data here examined [from subregional analyses of 1960 and 1970] that can be made validly about all regions."

The three-year period during which Beale gathered his

data included a marked trough in the national economic cycle. The economic recession in urban America in the early 1970s could have generated a "back to the land" movement, which has been the historical response of rural-to-urban migrants who encounter economic misfortune. For example, Mapstone's (1975) study of rural immigration in a declining northern New York county indicated that in his sample of thirty heads of migrant families, immigrants were predominantly returnees from urban regions. They tended to be blue collar and had a low median income, characteristics of relative marginality in the contemporary urban labor force. Kirschenbaum's (1971) finding that rural immigrants offer specific attributes well suited to the urbanized employment opportunities developing in rural society might well apply to returnees who indeed have acquired urban industrial skills but were unable to successfully maintain satisfactory employment in cities.

Given the absence of increased industrial employment noted by Beale (1975) in the growing rural areas of the South between 1970 and 1973, the notion that rural growth was absorbed through existing tertiary employment opportunities remains to be demonstrated. The persistence of poverty, hidden and overt unemployment, and underemployment in the very kind of regions Beale points to as harbingers of change should inhibit the prediction of a repopulation of hitherto declining rural areas.

Finally, the sources of rural repopulation that Beale identified may ultimately prove to be tenuous. Despite the large proportion of the national population currently available as customers for retirement, leisure, and education oases that dot the rural landscape, the degree to which the great transformation of rural regions can be sustained from such sources over time is problematic.

The Social Organizational Dimension

Students of social organization have focused on the generalization that urbanization during its metropolitan phase has appeared in rural America in the form of the "mass society," uncoupling the bonds of local integration by orienting the rural community toward the larger society. This view has been incorporated into contemporary conventional wisdom about small towns. Acceptance of that wisdom has occurred with little critical examination of the several issues that it raises. For example, do organizational attributes of urban society that are apparent in rural places represent the recent coming of a "Great Change" (Warren, 1963) due to the simultaneous burgeoning of urbanization, industrialization, and bureaucratization (Stein, 1960)? To what extent can the development of vertical ties between rural communities and mass society be demonstrated to create a corresponding decrease in horizontal ties within communities?

The attractiveness of the "Great Change" perspective on the loss of local social organizational autonomy can be explained in terms of elementary American values concerning communities. The influential case study of Springdale, New York, *Small Town in Mass Society* (Vidich and Bensman, 1958), accompanied by several similar community case studies, will be briefly reviewed to establish the empirical referent for the conventional wisdom concerning rural social organizational structure. The work of Warren (1963), which provides a theoretical statement paralleling those studies, will be described. Finally, serious criticisms of this conventional wisdom will be raised, focusing on its historical and logical accuracy.

The American ethos is saturated with the gemeinschaft imagery of the rural small town, not simply as an idyllic community but as the natural social unit for the polis. "Grass roots democracy" is nearly a sacred value, and it permeates not only the ideology of the American polity, but is valued as the organizing principle in all community group activity (de Tocqueville, 1956). Thus, the rural community has not only provided the prevailing image of the prototypical American community; it is also a popular, albeit usually implicit, metaphor for harmonious collective life. From that viewpoint, it is understandable that urbanization of rural communities is perceived as a threat to the organizational integrity of small towns, which are believed to be the wellspring of democratic social life.

In the classic 1939 documentary film "The City," Lewis Mumford clearly expressed these ideological themes in the American perception of the impact of urbanization on the social organization of rural communities. The opening scene depicts a village basking in the sun, nestled among gently rolling hills and framed by ancient trees. The steeple of a serene church dominated the nest of neat, unpretentious homes clustering about it. This compact rural community offers the picture of innocently complacent self-sufficiency, wherein even the physical appearance of the town bespeaks a well-integrated social order. In the blacksmith shop, the men of the village and its surrounding area nod and joke, passing the time of the day, and in so doing weave the fabric of a gemeinschaft community. The scene then shifts to the landscape of a train yard and a row house in a slum. Filthy children play between resting trains belching soot. Their elders stand apart from one another, staring in despair. Urbanization, the film tells us, precipitated our fall from the village Eden, where a healthy social structure was inherent in the form itself. In Springdale's fall we all sinned.

The study of social organization in Springdale, located in upstate New York, provided much of the contemporary conventional wisdom about the effects of urbanization on rural communities (Vidich and Bensman, 1958). The title of that book, *Small Town in Mass Society,* well captured the thrust of the evaluation of the plight of rural communities. The authors depicted town residents as willing yet unwitting captives of mass society and argued that this condition resulted in an incapacity of villagers to control decision-making authority, resulting in the demise of local community autonomy.

Vidich and Bensman portrayed a community with a myriad of linkages to the larger culture that culminate in a "political surrender to mass society." Formal agents of cultural diffusion, such as extension personnel and heads of the local branches of business and translocal government, were designated by Vidich and Bensman as disseminators of the values of mass society. "The intrusion of the mass media is so overwhelming that little scope is left for the expression of local cultural and artistic forms" (Vidich and Bensman, 1958, p. 86). Newcomers bring with them the values of the larger—and urban—culture. Various occupational groups find the parameters of their activities defined by external conditions. Thus, contemporary conventional wisdom describes increasing urbanization as inevitably responsible for decreases in the social organizational autonomy of local communities.

This conventional wisdom is also well represented in Martindale and Hanson's (1969) study of Benson, Minnesota, *Small Town and the Nation.* The similarity of their book's title to that of the study by Vidich and Bensman reflects a similarity in outlook. Martindale and Hanson (1969, p. 57) described the traditional social organization as pitted against urbanization in a losing battle:

Historically, Benson demonstrated to a high degree the small-town virtues once thought to be so distinctive

of America: spirited individual free enterprise, civic consciousness, and pride in local self-sufficiency. . . . However, the inventory of Benson's institutional order in the
mid 1960s reveals a structural confrontation of institutions locally founded, owned, and operated on the one
hand and branch offices, representatives, or affiliates of
translocal structures on the other.

Evidence of the "small-town virtues" that Martindale and Hanson claimed Benson has historically displayed is not documented in their study. Indeed, the most obvious disadvantage of
studies such as the Springdale and Benson monographs is that
they purport to delineate social organizational change on the
basis of observations made at a single point in time.

One of the few longitudinal analyses of community
change (Gallagher, 1961) has documented the appearance of
translocal institutions as a major event in the course of change
within the social organization of small towns. In comparing the
social structure of a Missouri village, Plainville, in 1939 with
that in 1955, Gallagher (1961, p. 227) emphasized the impact
of urbanization on the social organization introduced by the
New Deal programs of the 1930s and expanded in the post-
World War II years. He found that those programs "substitute
external for internal authority in areas of Plainville life where
decision-making responsibility has heretofore been considered
autonomous" (Gallagher, 1961, p. 255).

The interplay of ecological and social organizational dimensions of the urbanization process was well explicated by
Pratt (1957) in his longitudinal analysis of changes in a metropolitan fringe community in Michigan. He utilized a variety of
data-gathering techniques to contrast the community as it
existed in 1900 with its development in 1950. Pratt (1957, p.
438) maintained that in the earlier period "the village center
was the mechanism of adjustment." The village gradually became more specialized, with the community becoming "an
adaptive agency, with different areas of the enlarged community performing different functions. A fundamental change
in community structure has been the tendency of farm and village business systems to shift from a position of balanced interdependence to one of parallel economic structures, each directly related to the enlarged community" (Pratt, 1957, p. 438).

The theoretical significance of the ecological differentiation that Pratt well documented and that other community
researchers had commented on was expressed by Warren (1963)

in the phrase the "Great Change." As the community specialized in its exchanges with the society, Warren viewed it as developing a localized infrastructure with a more highly articulated
division of labor very similar to what Smith (1974) and Richardson and Larson (1976) described in their studies. Main Street
once served only as a conduit for exchanging food products for
consumer goods needed on farms. Now a new retinue of sophisticated services may be added to meet the needs not only of
local residents but also nonagricultural markets outside the local
community. Local economic, educational, and government services become the bureaucratized outreach of the larger urbanized
society. Under the "Great Change," Warren saw a complex division of labor and system of social stratification and organizational networks characteristic of urbanized mass society to be
inundating local communities. The differentiation at the local
level is not seen as being generated by the intrinsic needs of the
community but by translocal institutions. Therefore, the local
community is increasingly conceptualized as being integrated
more through vertical ties to the larger community and less
through horizontal ties among local groups. For the most part,
this process is believed to result in identification of a social
change in all local communities, whether urban or rural. Therefore, the commentary on phases of community change in this
general case articulated by Warren is applicable to rural communities, and has been cited in that context (Wilkinson, in
press).

In describing the increase in the scale of social organizational structures, Greer (1962a, p. 195) also noted the process
of "vertical integration": "In brief, the organizational necessities that once produced spacial density and a high degree of
local autonomy are no longer coercive. The independent factory
becomes the branch plant, while the nation-wide governmental
agency pre-empts tasks once locally performed. Organizational
space is a function of the shrinking space-time ratio."

Warner (1974, p. 309) argued that the bond of vertical
integration exists not between small towns and undifferentiated
mass society but between small towns and specific metropolitan
centers that are the headquarters for "corporate actors—both
private corporations and public bureaus" who control "the decisions and actions of consequence in society." He adds, "Although there are urban metropolitan dominance effects on a
rural area from the nearest metropolitan area, many of the lines
of interdependency and social bonds go to quite remote centers
rather than the nearby ones."

Whether power is now perceived to flow on a one-way street from either specific metropolises or from an undifferentiated mass society, has the dissemination of urban functions into rural communities produced an eclipse of small towns? Are they surviving only as population aggregates, sacrificing to mass society their community autonomy as social, political, and economic entities? The affirmative answers given to these questions by contemporary conventional wisdom are based on these few but influential community studies performed during the two decades following World War II, when the concept of mass society almost obsessed social scientists and social commentators. That preoccupation provided the impetus for associating the diffusion of urban functions with the conclusion that an "eclipse of the community" (Stein, 1960) had occurred in the social organization of small towns. The extent to which that association is sociologically defensible raises questions about the adequacy of these studies for establishing the empirical relationship between urbanization and the loss of autonomy in rural communities.

Social Organization Trends and Analytical Limitations. In its most simplified form, the "Great Change" generalization postulates that American rural towns are being absorbed into the larger culture through the development of vertical ties between the individual institutions of the local community and mass society along with simultaneous deterioration of horizontal ties among local institutions. Several limitations within the available literature can be specified which result in only qualified support for this generalization. First, evidence for this generalization is derived primarily from ahistorical case studies, which have their own methodological limitations. The consequence of these limitations appears in the assertion that vertical integration of rural communities represents a revolutionary change for small towns, an interpretation of American community history somewhat at odds with the mainstream of literature concerning rural settlement. Second, the universality of lost autonomy as an inevitable response to urbanization cannot be demonstrated either logically or empirically. Some studies that strongly indicate that indigenous factors such as leadership condition the way communities respond to urbanization will be reviewed below.

Reliance on case studies not only raises questions about the representativeness of the subject studies; it also permits use of research methods that invite highly subjective and impressionistic techniques of variable designation, data gathering, and data analysis. Under these circumstances it is difficult to determine the extent to which the investigators were victims of selective perception, given the prevalence of the mass society theme in post-World War II social thought. While Vidich and Bensman (1964, p. 313) asserted their study had "no a priori theory," their rhetoric uses a language that was part of the intellectual spirit of the times; what others, such as Riesman and Fromm, had assumed was the meaning of mass society for the individual, Vidich and Bensman stood ready to discover in the community.

The most obvious limitation of the case studies that support the "Great Change" interpretation of rural social organization is that their methodology was severely restricted in its capacity to analyze any element of community change. These ahistorical studies implicitly or explicitly reconstructed a past for the communities based on the assumption that there must have been a time when these towns were relatively unfettered by ties with the larger society. Without that assumption, there is little reason for concern about the fate of the small town in mass society.

Whether longitudinal observations within the communities studied would have validated that assumption remains a matter of conjecture. But intriguingly enough, there are brief passages within both of these monographs that invalidate the assumption that these communities have undergone any significant change in the degree of their autonomy. At one point, Vidich and Bensman (1958) said: "Basically, an historically indigenous local culture does not seem to exist. The cultural imports of each decade and generation and the successive waves of migration associated with each combine to produce a local culture consisting of layers or segments of the mass culture of successive historical eras. . . . The conflict between 'spurious' and 'genuine' culture appears to be a conflict between two different ages of 'spurious' culture" (pp. 87-88). Similarly, Martindale and Hanson (1969, p. 17) also recognized the historical presence of external societal forces that according to their thesis were insignificant until recently:

> However, while there were significant forces inclining Benson to form a close-knit autonomous local unit, there were others that ran counter to such self-sufficiency. From the beginning Bensonites envisioned the need to export their farm products to the outside and to import a wide variety of manufactured products. . . .

They were, moreover, faced with the financing of their farms and businesses and concerned with access to the money and credit facilities of the wider society. Moreover, it early became evident that they were rearing more children than their community could absorb; they had to train their children for survival not only in Benson, but to some extent, in the wider world outside. . . . Nevertheless, throughout the nineteenth century it is not unfair to estimate that the drive toward local self-sufficiency outweighed the counter-forces there.

Literature describing the history of community social organization portrays vertical integration as a significant factor from the beginning of American settlement, despite the celebration of an earlier small-town autonomy that appears in studies proclaiming the eclipse of those towns by mass society. Historical studies suggest that the prototypical American rural community has always been integrated primarily through vertical ties to the larger community and that those ties are not the hallmark of a recent "Great Change" in the social organization of rural towns. Rubin (1970, p. 89) pointed out that early in the nineteenth century "American interior regions . . . went through a process of urban-industrial development despite their relative isolation." He also maintained that a symbiotic relationship had always existed between the growth of urban and rural America and that urban growth was dependent, among other factors, on the extent to which rural America was "commercialized, industrialized, and linked to [urban] ports." He noted pioneer villages in the remote hinterland often displayed a remarkably complex division of labor attributable to "the highly commercialized background of the interior population, . . . limited but significant relations with the (urbanized) coast, and the constant stream of migrants which in some respects took the place of a movement of goods" (Rubin, 1970, p. 90). As Rubin's description suggests, far from being superimposed upon autonomous communities, vertical integration provided the genesis of the American rural community.

This historical role of vertical integration in sustaining rural communities leads to questioning the thesis that continuation of or even increases in those ties necessarily bodes ill for the future autonomy of small towns. A diversity of agricultural, industrial, and governmental ties to urban society may now assure these communities of greater latitude in decision making than when villages were totally at the mercy of urban farm-commodity markets. A populist cartoon of the late nineteenth century displayed a kind of exploitative vertical integration more threatening to the autonomy of rural communities than the extralocal ties of today: A scrawny, elongated cow was depicted being fed by the harassed farmers of the Plains and milked by capitalists in New York City.

In addition to limitations stemming from research methods and a questionable historical perspective, the "Great Change" studies involved a leap of logic from findings to an interpretation that is difficult to accept. In the intellectual milieu of the mass society construct, perhaps it was believed sufficient for one to infer from the presence of translocal organizations within communities that autonomy was thereby diminished. The conclusion that diffusion of urban functions causes a loss in local decision-making autonomy was sustained as much by the acceptance of the mass society proposition itself as by objective evidence. Having noted the presence of exogenous economic and governmental organizations in local communities, few researchers other than Vidich and Bensman (1958) have gone on to describe explicitly the actual displacement of local power by these external agents in specific decision-making episodes. Pointing to increased absentee ownership and increased presence of extralocal governmental agencies provides at best only inferential evidence of declining horizontal integration. Indeed, Schulze (1969) did find that national firms had become economically dominant in the small city he studied, but the firms did not participate in community decision making.

There is no logical imperative that requires the abandonment of local autonomy to be the inevitable consequence of vertical integration. For example, a dual structure of local decision making may emerge in which local groups or individuals are most influential on some issues and external actors on other issues (French, 1969). In other cases, the presence of extralocal organizations may have little impact on local power structures. For example, despite the introduction of an extremely powerful form of vertical integration into a heavily rural area—the construction of a large mill for U.S. Steel—Seiler (1973, p. 7) found little evidence of any changes in the local decision-making structure. He found that forty-three of fifty-nine community leaders named no "persons outside the community of substantial importance in influencing (local) decisions." The steel mill manager was the only person associated with that firm who received as many as two designations as being influential in local decisions. Nonetheless, the contention of lost community autonomy is a seductive thesis: Despite evidence to the contrary, Seiler devoted the bulk of his analysis to speculating over strategies of covert company involvement in the local power structure.

It is more logical to view the impact of vertical integration on local autonomy as varying according to such factors as community leadership and attitudes than as the precursor of the inevitable collapse of local autonomy. Adams (1969) concluded from his study of six rural towns in Wisconsin and Missouri that the attitudes of local leadership were the most significant among a host of variables investigated that might influence community growth or decline. "Risk taking" and "external orientation"—that is, a willingness to compete with neighboring communities—were attributes of leaders in growing communities. Simon and Gagnon (1969) performed a similar study in three southern Illinois towns and explicitly challenged the notion that vertical integration inexorably leads to loss of local autonomy. They concluded that whether a small town succeeds may be independent of the urbanization trend. Instead, the community decision-making organizational structure and values may explain the difference between successful and unsuccessful towns.

Further evidence of the importance of attitudinal factors appeared in a study of a declining small town, Bellefonte, in rural Pennsylvania. Lewis (1972) found that its deterioration was catalyzed by the "fear, resignation, and cynicism" that he believed had characterized the town. In recounting the story of Bellefonte, Lewis stressed that it shared with "hundreds of villages and towns across the county" the inability "to achieve the economies of scale of a Pittsburgh, a Chicago, a Minneapolis, or any of a host of lesser places." But not all rural towns have shared this fate: While Bellefonte declined, the nearby state college town it once dominated prospered. In the college town, the rewards of specialization in education noted by Beale (1975) were augmented by an exuberant speculative spirit that the city fathers of Bellefonte lacked.

In summary, the most influential studies of rural town social organization have popularized the generalization that increasing ties with the larger society have decreased ties within the community, with a resulting decline in the ability of the local community to determine its own affairs. While there is little question that mass society has made its presence known in small towns across the country, there is considerable reason to doubt that such a presence constitutes a juggernaut for communities. To advance the understanding of how vertical integration affects the social organization of communities, more comparative studies should be performed that transcend the methodological limitations of ahistorical case studies. Lacking longitudinal studies, methods must be developed to tap historical materials for a better delineation of the degree of decision-making autonomy present in the development of American rural towns. Finally, to overcome the illogic of the mass society-as-demiurge thesis, comparative studies must be promoted that will consider vertical integration as a variable capable of causing a variety of possible social organizational consequences.

The Sociocultural Dimension

A grand tradition in sociology declares that urbanization creates a way of life unlike that of rural society. That tradition finds urbanism to be expressed in liberal normative attitudes, depleted familism and other social interaction patterns, and alienation in mental life. These conclusions by social scientists, based on their observations during the metropolitan phase of urbanization in Europe and America, lead to widespread acceptance of an evolutionary model of community change from folk to urban society and culture. However, sociologists and anthropologists have now amassed a body of empirical findings that challenge this model.

A classic statement incorporating ideal-type characteristics of preindustrial, preurbanized rural communities in contrast to modern society appears in Tönnies's (1957) distinction between gemeinschaft and gesellschaft. That formulation was a precursor to Redfield's (1947) anthropological observations, which are strongly identified with the folk-to-urban evolutionary model of sociocultural change. The application of Redfield's description of folk society to the rural community in preurban America requires some extrapolation from the ideal type. Few American rural communities of the nineteenth century were illiterate to the degree that Redfield believed characterized the folk society. However, the idea of a continuum between the polar ideal types has permitted social scientists to consider the typical small, isolated American rural community as more folk than urban.

Rural America has historically been characterized by

small, isolated farm homesteads and small, isolated communities. Redfield (1947, p. 293) typified the small, isolated communities of folk society "as contrasted with modern urbanized society in exhibiting a strong sense of group solidarity. . . . Behavior is traditional, spontaneous, uncritical, and personal. . . . Kinship, its relationships and institutions, are the type of categories of experience and the familial group is the unit of action. The sacred prevails over the secular; the economy is one of status rather than of the market." Uzzell and Provencher (1976) suggested that Redfield perceived the small, isolated aspect of folk culture as a causal factor, resulting in the emphasis on kinship and traditional values in rural life. Thus, ruralists are expected to be more conservative than urbanites in political and moral values, and their behavior more oriented to family and other primary contacts.

Controversy over the adequacy of the folk-to-urban thesis has dominated sociological investigation of the impact of urbanization on the sociocultural dimension of American rural life. Therefore, three aspects of this thesis will be reviewed. First, studies comparing rural and urban attitudes will be reviewed for evidence of the purported change from rural conservatism to urban liberalism. Second, studies of rural family life and other social patterns will be reviewed for evidence of the purported change from rural primary-group integration to urban secondary-group integration. Third, studies of rural psychological adjustment will be reviewed for evidence of a change from rural levels of mental health to alienation and maladjustment purportedly characteristic of urban society and culture.

Urbanization and Rural Values. The traditional values that characterize rural society may have been somewhat liberalized by the ecological and social organizational processes of urbanization, but most studies do not show a merging of rural values with more liberal urban values on either political or moral issues. Polling data has continued to display a greater political and moral conservatism among ruralists. Stouffer's (1955) data of twenty years ago indicated less tolerance of deviant religious and political values among rural populations, even when controls for level of education and for region were introduced. More recently, acceptance of amnesty for draft evaders, of marijuana, of abortion, and of other liberal causes is shown to be lower than in urban areas (Fischer, 1976, pp. 193-196). Nelson and Yokley (1970) found in a study of 7,500 Presbyterian ministers and elders that rural respondents were substantially more conservative in attitudes concerning race relations than urban respondents. Yet Nelson, Yokley, and Madron (1971) pointed out in a related study that differences between rural and urban populations concerning one value are not generalizable to other values. While Gallup Poll data that they analyzed indicated greater religious orthodoxy among ruralists, there were no significant differences from urbanites in religious ritualism, experiential or intellectual involvement, or church attendance.

In reviewing the responses to ninety-two general attitude questions from twenty national polls conducted by the Gallup Organization and the National Opinion Research Center from 1953 to 1965, Glenn and Alston (1967, pp. 384-391) concluded that significant value differences continued to exist between farmers and three white and blue collar occupation groups:

> Farmers are unambiguously less informed, more prejudiced, less favorable to civil liberties, less tolerant of deviance, more ethnocentric and isolationist, more work-oriented and ascetic, more puritanical, less favorable to birth control, less trusting of people, and more favorable to early marriage and high fertility than most or all categories of urban workers. Some of the differences are quite large. . . . The leveling of traditional rural-urban differences, if there has been such a trend, has not progressed as far as some observers seem to think.

However, Glenn and Alston (1967, p. 394) note that "evidence on the (political) conservatism of farmers is ambiguous" and contradictory. Farmers were more likely than others to favor a liberal party but to have voted for Goldwater, and to evince lower levels of interest in politics but to have voted in the 1964 election. Glenn and Alston also suggested that "there are large rural-urban differences that are not plausibly explained by differences in socioeconomic status, age, region of residence, religious composition, or economic interests. Some of these differences may reflect the more pervasive Protestant influence in rural areas, but others probably result more or less directly from differences in the size, density, and heterogeneity of the population" (1967, p. 400).

In performing a multivariate analysis of 1974 data similar to that reported in the 1967 study, Glenn and Hill (1977) echoed the conclusion of Dewey (1960) that rural-urban differences can be demonstrated to be "real, but relatively unimportant." While arguing that distinctly rural values will continue to appear, particularly among rural-to-urban migrants, Glenn and Hill (1977, p. 50) noted "the predictive utility of the rural-urban variable is modest at best."

A generation ago Beers (1953) plotted other pitfalls in comparing urban and rural survey samples that complicate the search for urbanized trends reflected in attitudes. Beers noted that the data from polls conducted between 1935 and 1950 in general displayed greater conservatism among farmers than among other occupational groups—a pattern to be expected given the traditional values attributed to country folk. Despite this apparent conservatism of farmers, Beers emphasized the overlapping distributions of their attitudes compared with others on almost every issue. The conservatism detected by these polls is not the exclusive province of ruralists. The distribution of farmers' responses showed some similarity in their conservatism with the patterns displayed among executives, proprietors, businessmen, and white collar samples—occupational groups characteristic of urban society. Beers suspected that the representation of farmers in national polls may be inadequate at all strata of rural society. This again suggests class differences, as well as differences in region, function, tenure, and a variety of other variables masked by the occupational designation "farmer" that may be significant in attitude determination above and beyond the variable of holding a rural occupation.

Turning from national to regional studies, research investigating the same or similar variables has yielded contradictory results, raising the issue of whether local cultures intervene in the urbanization experience. Willets, Bealer, and Crider (1973) investigated the proposition that attitudes are leveling in American mass society, wiping out urban-rural distinctions. Using data from studies of sophomores in 1947, 1960, and 1970 in seventy-four Pennsylvania high schools, they found that in both urban and rural samples, traditionalism scores have reflected a decline in conservative morality. However, the country school populations reflected a slower rate of change than the town students, resulting in a "significant gap" between town and country students in 1970 findings. Likert-type items involving such factors as church attendance, divorce, alcohol and tobacco consumption, card playing, and appropriate Sunday behavior were included. However, it is difficult to conclude much about

urban-rural differences from this study, inasmuch as only
schools serving communities of 2,500 or less were included in
the sample.

Christenson and Dillman (1973) replicated many aspects
of the study by Willets, Bealer, and Crider (1973) with a sample in the state of Washington and found no significant differences in values by community size. However, this may be a regional phenomenon that does not necessarily reflect the effects
of any contemporary, nationwide convergence of rural and
urban attitudes. In 1952 Haer attributed the lack of support for
the contention that rural Washingtonians were more conservative than urban Washingtonians to regional cultural effects.

Both national and statewide studies point out the urban-
rural value differences are not as salient as differences usually
associated with socioeconomic status. There is at least as much
—if not more—variation within rural populations as between
rural and urban groups in attitude structures. Flinn and Johnson
(1974, p. 187) found a higher incidence of "agrarianism"—traditional rural values—among Minnesota farm operators who are
relatively "1) low income earners; 2) less educated; 3) older; 4)
small farm operators; 5) owners; 6) long-time farmers; 7) debt
free; 8) seldom in personal contact with extension agents or
agricultural college specialists; and 9) negative toward collective
bargaining, although the magnitudes of the correlations were
low."

Several studies (for example, Vidich and Bensman, 1958;
West, 1945) have noted farm operators can often be categorized
and tend to be locally stratified in terms of their orientation
toward either traditional agrarianism or modern entrepreneurship and management. Using the same rural Wisconsin sample
analyzed by Flinn and Johnson (1974) and comparing it with
residents in towns of more than 2,500 population, Buttel and
Flinn (1975) found attitudinal differences between the two
groups minimal, but variations within both groups were related
to educational differences. Mean scores and standard distributions in agrarianism, criminal justice, and anticommunist value
scores varied little between the urban and rural samples.

Photiadis and Ball (1975, pp. 62-63) detected variations
in adjustments to urbanization between rural Appalachian
groups that parallel the processes of vertical integration of community social organization:

> Integration into the larger society has been facili-
> tated through a process of differentiation of local norma-

tive structures. For instance, through the past two decades we have observed that certain subgroups within the
mountain villages tend to develop distinct normative patterns of their own. There is a tendency for such subgroups to differentiate themselves from the previously
homogeneous village life and to identify with subgroups
located outside the village systems. . . . These are in large
part the urban groups corresponding to their own. The
data also indicate that the process of normative reorganization is not uniform; some normative subsystems change
more slowly than others and some, by resisting change,
are even strengthened.

In summary, the evidence indicates that at the least urbanization has had little effect in altering traditionally conservative moral and political values among ruralists; at the most
urbanization has differentially affected certain areas of belief
and certain segments of rural society. Some have generalized
that urbanization as such has not brought rural values to presently existing levels of urban liberalism but that the aggregate
effect of sociocultural modernization has been to liberalize the
values of both rural and urban society. This results in a continuing gap between rural and urban values. The hold on the sociological imagination exerted by the proposition that rural traditional values become transformed into urban liberal values,
despite the paucity of evidence supporting that thesis, is amus-
ingly illustrated by a summary of the relevant literature by Larson and Rogers (1964). They conclude that rural-urban differences in values are declining as the nation moves in the direction
of a mass society. After explaining as fact how this change has
occurred, Larson and Rogers retreat to the position that any
conclusion must be cautious due to the lack of adequate research. This retreat is completed by their statement that "There
is currently a paucity of data, on a national or representative
basis, to portray in any scientifically adequate way the values
currently held by the farm people of the nation" (p. 55). In
point of fact, findings both prior to and following the Rogers
and Larson commentary would lead to the diametrically opposite position that rural-urban value differences remain substantial.

   Urbanization, the Rural Family, and Social Interaction.
While evidence suggests that urbanization has not resulted in the
wholesale changes in traditional values posited by descriptions
of folk society, the literature concerning familism and primary

interactions leads one to doubt that the initial differences between folk and urban society have ever really been significant in
American culture. The folk-to-urban evolution motif posits a
diminution in the functional salience of the family and a corresponding weakening of extended family ties as urbanization
shifts emphasis from primary- to secondary-group integration.
In this process, the individual is believed to become oriented to
the nuclear rather than the extended family, since the latter is
assumed to lack the flexibility and mobility required to meet
the challenges of urbanized society. This flexibility and mobility are thought to be achievable through interpersonal relations
that are facilitated by the "open system" of the nuclear family.
These are the characteristics that the marriage and family literature of sociology have conventionally attributed to changes
resulting from urbanization (Bossard, 1948; Burgess and Locke,
1945; Loomis and Beegle, 1951; Mirande, 1970).

There has been surprisingly little research performed in
rural settings that addresses this proposition. Greater interaction
within extended families has been noted among Wisconsin ruralists than among urbanites (Winch and Greer, 1968). Contrary to
the folk-to-urban evolution thesis, the pattern that emerges
from most other studies suggests that urban and rural families
are both capable of maintaining close extended family ties and
simply incorporate into their lives whatever additional secondary-group experiences necessity or desire imposes in the course
of urbanization. Rather than substituting secondary for primary
relationships, families superimpose the one upon the other. For
example, Miner (1969, p. 291) found that "Social organization
of the rural French in Canada is losing its folk character. Nonetheless, . . . many of the old culture traits are so closely allied to
the thrifty, close-family economy that they have resisted change
to a remarkable degree." Similarly, Schaffer (1958) reported
that while the North Carolina urban fringe community he
studied exhibited "greater administrative complexity of
churches and schools, an expanded middle class, and an increase
in part-time farming," the extended family retained much
strength and was one factor in a decrease of out-migration from
the community.

Complicating these analyses is the lack of empirical evidence to support the contention that there are distinctively different properties of urban and rural family structures and values
in America. Studies of urban family life (for example, Young
and Willmott, 1957) have displayed the importance of extended

family ties in the everyday life of urbanites conventionally ascribed to rural societies. Bultena's (1969) study demonstrated
rural families may actually display less contact among family
members than urban families.

In summary, research investigating changes in American
rural family life has failed to exhibit clear-cut effects of urbanization. The primary reason for this is that the dominant family
form in rural America has never been the close-knit extended
family attributed to rural society. In speaking of the settlers of
rural America, Halpern (1967, p. 110) noted they migrated to
the farmland as nuclear units: "Such nuclear families were often
part of larger kin groups, but the economic and social ties linking the constituent nuclear units appear to have been looser
than in many parts of the old world."

Data on other forms of interpersonal contacts outside the
family tend to yield the conclusion that the folk-to-urban transformations posited by the Redfield (1947) model cannot be
documented in the American experience. While both urban and
rural residents exhibit similar kinds and levels of interpersonal
contact (but not necessarily as predicted by the folk-to-urban
model), it is not necessarily the case that secondary contacts
drive out primary ties.

In the tradition of the gemeinschaft-to-gesellschaft
change model, urbanization is believed to have drawn rural individuals out of their homes and away from the family bond into
the networks of voluntary associations said to typify urban society. According to this model, a decreasing difference in the
levels of associational activity of urban and rural folk might be
expected. Indeed, in a study of Nebraskans, Babchuk and Booth
(1969) found a high rate of participation in rural, rural nonfarm, and metropolitan populations, with no significant differences between them. As noted above, Schaffer (1958) suggested
in his study of an urban fringe community that secondary-group
participation was increasing; churches and schools had increasingly developed such structures.

Empirical findings fail to demonstrate the hypothesized
course of urbanization on interpersonal interaction posited by
the folk-to-urban change model. For example, the impersonality
of urban places is supposedly reflected in fewer primary-group
attachments; therefore one seeking evidence of increasing
urbanization in rural areas would expect participation levels to
decrease. On the contrary, in his study of associational behavior
in rural, rural nonfarm, and urban settings, Reiss (1959)

pointed out that the greater opportunity for interpersonal contact in nonfarm jobs resulted in more primary contacts among
urban males. Fischer (1976, pp. 106-107) concluded that
"membership in formal organizations does not vary by size of
community," and, as the above studies suggest, "the formal organizations of cities come not to replace or overshadow, but
perhaps only to supplement [and provide the context for] persisting informal subcultures."

   Urbanization and Rural Mental Life. If urbanization were
to have the effects on familism and other primary contacts postulated by the folk-to-urban/gemeinschaft-to-gesellschaft change
models, it would be logical to expect the resulting impersonality
to produce a greater incidence of psychological maladjustment
and alienation. The writings of both Simmel (1950) and Wirth
(1938) are classic statements of a hypothesized link between urbanization and "mental life." Of course, as the previous section
noted, empirical support for their conceptualization of the impact of urbanization on interaction is scant. Thus it is not surprising that data do not entirely support their views about the
sociopsychological consequences of urbanization.

   Writing at the turn of the century, Simmel perceived the
market economy as a model for urban interpersonal interaction,
resulting in an alienating impersonality that the structure of
rural society was incapable of producing. If such differences had
indeed been typical of the mental life of urban and rural society, evidence of alienation and other pathologies found in rural
populations could be interpreted as another mark of increasing
urbanization.

   Summaries of studies of alienation, anomie, and related
issues tend to minimize differences between urban and rural
populations or differences among communities of various size
categories. Killian and Grigg (1962) reported that levels of education, rather than residence, accounted for apparent urban-
rural differences in anomie among whites in two southeastern
communities; among blacks, no urban-rural differences in levels
of anomie appeared whatsoever. (Racism has its own dynamics;
it is doubtful that high levels of anomie among rural blacks attest to their urbanization.) The significance of controlling for
education in explaining apparently greater anomie in the rural
population is questionable, since lower educational opportunity
has been historically intrinsic to rural society. Mizruchi (1976,
p. 647) also found factors other than a simple urban-rural differentiation to be significant in producing the incidence of

anomie: "Malaise is more likely to characterize selected segments in the rural community. High participation and age
(under fifty-five) proved to be significant factors related to
anomie."

Photiadis (1967, p. 229) went so far as to suggest that
"the positive relationship between anomie and size of community which Durkheim and others have discussed is now reversed." Having conducted interviews with more than 600 Minnesota businessmen from communities ranging from 300 to
312,000 population, Photiadis found very small (less than 0.2)
but negative correlations between community size and "anomie,
bewilderment and confusion, powerlessness, and need invio-
lacy." Photiadis suggested that people in small towns, including
businessmen, are more remote from mass society and therefore
more alienated than urbanites. Thus the Simmelian hypothesis
is turned upside down.

A finding of *greater* anomie in small towns, such as Photiadis reported, raises additional questions about the association
of anomie with urbanization. Is such rural pathology the result
of a "cultural shock" from urbanization, or is rural anomie
often produced by structural characteristics endemic to rural
society itself? There is evidence that strongly suggests the latter.
For example, Youmans (1976) reported that a metropolitan
sample yielded significantly more positive responses than a rural
sample on fifteen out of twenty-four attitude scales. Were these
differences the result, as Youmans (1976, p. 7) speculated, of
the inadequacy of the "traditional and folk quality of life in
helping rural and small town people cope with the complex
problems of an industrialized society into which they have been
thrust?" Or did these findings simply reflect the possibility, as
Oscar Lewis and others have argued, that folk society does not
intrinsically provide qualitatively healthier mental life than urban places?

Some suggestion that rural mental health is not superior
to urban mental health appears in research comparing the socialization of youth in rural and urban settings. The Wirth-Simmel
view of urban society as intrinsically productive of a higher incidence of social pathology is not borne out in comparative
studies of adolescent personality adjustment. The majority of
studies indicate that urban high school students attain scores
indicating better adjustment on pencil-and-paper personality
tests. For example, Munson (1959) administered the California
Test of Personality to 500 children from New York City, New

York suburbs, and rural upstate New York. The urban sample displayed higher (that is, "better") scores in areas such as self-reliance, sense of personal worth, "freedom-belongingness," antisocial attitudes, and family and community relations. Munson noted that three out of four previous studies of high school students obtained similar results.

Studies of satisfaction with community services also fail to indicate the more sanguine attitude of ruralists toward their social surroundings that would follow from the Simmel proposition. A positive relationship between population size and community satisfaction appeared in several studies. A study of 495 North Dakotans (Johnson and Knop, 1970, p. 547) in communities ranging from rural townships to towns with populations between 25,000 and 50,000 displayed similar trends showing "urban residents more satisfied with shopping and medical facilities, teacher ability, employment opportunities and entertainment-recreation potentials" and rural residents to be "more satisfied with local democratic process and the general geographic milieu." But many items related to the Simmel proposition, such as progressiveness, leadership, cooperation, local pride, general satisfaction, optimism, and recognition yielded no significant differences between urban and rural samples. This study yielded no data regarding the possibility that such differences would be apparent in more metropolitan settings.

In summary, ruralists are somewhat more conservative in political and moral beliefs than urbanites. Nonetheless, intervening factors such as differential educational levels rather than residence itself may produce some of the attitudinal differences between urban and rural samples. These attitudes are apparently unrelated to family and friendship behavior patterns or to satisfaction and psychological adjustment. The literature of social psychology has continually produced studies indicating frequent incongruity between attitude sets, as well as incongruity between what we say and what we do (Deutscher, 1973; Wicker, 1969). Thus, it is not unreasonable that ruralists may be more conservative than urbanites on many issues (although the groups overlap one another); yet these beliefs may be compartmentalized and may not be indicative of a traditional behavior system in the Redfieldian sense. The farmer who espouses conservative political beliefs may be as capable of embracing progressive business practices as his equally politically conservative urban executive counterpart.

Sociocultural Trends and Analytical Limitations. It is difficult to overstate the degree to which American rural society prior to twentieth-century urbanization did not resemble the folk society of Redfield's ideal type in attitudes and behavior. This being the case, it is no wonder that the impact of urbanization does not represent a linear, unidimensional historical transformation from all that was folk to all that is urban. The American countryside was not settled by yeoman farmers with peasant values; "the cultural gap between peasant and townsman so prominent in the history of continental Europe was from the beginning a minor affair in North America" (Rubin, 1970, p. 86). Rural settlers had a "highly commercialized background" and subsistence farming "was only a frontier condition to be overcome as rapidly as means of transport could be built up" (p. 91). Rubin cited "the historian of that region" in noting that the erroneous stereotype of the American ruralist as a peasant farmer emerged from a caricature of bumpkinish northern New Englanders who lived in one of the few northern pockets of near-subsistence farming. "The characteristics of the farmer there have determined to a remarkable degree the popular image of the American farmer, yet they had little in common with those of agriculturalists farther west" (p. 91). In short, Rubin noted that most of rural America outside the South was settled by a population living in "an urbanized tradition," which accounted for the "central point" concerning rural settlement: "the cultural similarity of townsman and farmer."

As Taylor and Jones (1964, p. 24) observed, "The notions of both systematic agriculture and industrialism were a part of the new nation's culture from its very inception." As a result, "conditions of systematic and scientific inquiry into food and fiber production were available to the earliest settlers." It is this heritage that results in the fact that "there are no precise distinctions between the way of life in the cities and on the farms." Schlesinger (1971, p. 72) noted that beginning as early as the last years of the nineteenth century technological advances "lent a new attraction to country existence" and "brought urbanizing influences to nearly every rural home." Thus, the majority of ruralists came from an "urbanized tradition"; technological and marketing changes further welded their ties to an urban culture. It is difficult to discern whether their contemporary relative maladjustment as reflected in written tests is caused by frustrations in dealing with an urban world or by the fact that rural life offers little psychic nourishment.

In summary, the sociocultural dimension of urbanization

has traditionally focused on transformations in attitudes and behavior postulated to occur in the process of moving from folk to urban society. The applicability of that postulate to the American case cannot be readily demonstrated. Attitude surveys continually indicate that ruralists are more conservative than urbanites, but the absence of longitudinal evidence makes it impossible to trace the possible impact of urbanization on rural attitudes. Also, these attitudes are not necessarily associated with other purported characteristics of rurality. Patterns of familism and other gemeinschaft behavior appear in similar measure in both urban and rural settings. The incidence of various forms of social pathology is as likely to represent indigenous strains as the impact of urbanization. In short, the American rural place is the scene of both folk and urban patterns, and the sociocultural impact of urbanization as either ecological or social organizational phenomena is not as easily charted as some of the classic social change postulates would lead one to believe.

With hindsight it now appears that social scientists falsely blamed urbanization for the loss of "Rousseauean Romantic Rural Society (RRRS)" (Uzzell and Provencher, 1976). The folk-to-urban change model now has been enthusiastically attacked from all sides. Depiction of RRRS as a historically pervasive experience is now regarded as fictitious—particularly in America. In those aspects in which the depiction of RRRS seems empirically accurate—for example, in the traditionalism of some rural values—the impact of urbanization in changing those values is not consistently demonstrable. A coherent analysis of the values and other sociopsychological concomitants of urbanization in rural areas requires that the confusing complex of findings about the attitudes and behavior of ruralists be unsnarled.

Summary and Conclusion

The course of urbanization has produced a composite of themes and counter-themes in its impact upon American rural life. The resulting patterns have been delineated in their ecological, social organizational, and sociocultural dimensions for insight into their significance in describing a shift from metropolitan to diffuse urbanization.

Within the ecological dimension, two major propositions —the gradient and the social differentiation principles—may require substantial modification if recent indications that previously declining rural areas are repopulating prove to reflect diffuse urbanization trends over time. The gradient principle has been utilized to describe the distribution of population throughout a hinterland as its central city grows and expands during the metropolitan phase of urbanization. The gradient principle is believed to express limitations imposed by the frictions of time and space (Clark, 1951). It now appears that the repopulation of remote regions may indicate the obliteration of those restraints on an even distribution of urban characteristics across the countryside. If the propulsion of current expansion no longer comes from central-city growth, new growth dynamics must be operating in the diffuse phase of urbanization.

The principle of differentiation has been employed to describe the extent to which socioeconomic functions of rural communities within the hinterland of given central cities specialize in relation to urban ecological functions. In the internal structures of these communities, there is evidence of both increasing and decreasing differentiation. Some rural communities can be shown to gain retail services associated with urban lifestyles; others can also be shown to lose such services to larger communities. The differentiation principle offers a possible explanation for this apparent contradiction by introducing community size and distance as causal variables; however, studies have not usually taken into account both size and distance factors in explaining the distribution of ecological functions within communities.

Industrialization alone does not appear to be the only route by which rural communities survive a loss in agricultural roles. In describing the course of repopulation in rural areas, Beale noted that communities with retirement, recreation, and educational functions have experienced recent growth. Communities previously supported by the most marginal agriculture may now enjoy the benefits of the proliferating demands of an affluent urban society. While the post-1970 census data recording a reversal in rural population trends may have revolutionary impact on both the gradient and differentiation principles, further data will be required to establish the long-term existence and consequences of the trends as indicators of diffuse urbanization.

During the metropolitan phase of urbanization, students of the social organization dimension have argued that these local communities have lost autonomy in their decision-making abilities. There are two limitations to that proposition. First, it is difficult to display empirically the conjunction of increasing vertical integration of community social organization and decreasing local power structure autonomy. Second, there is reason to question exactly how much of a "Great Change" this vertical integration has meant for American rural communities. For many communities, recent trends have simply represented a substitution of more diversified ties to urban society for entirely agricultural ties. These two limitations lead to questioning the accuracy of the "Great Change" paradigm in interpreting the meaning of urbanization of rural communities during the metropolitan phase. Students of the diffuse phase of urbanization may well wish to consider new paradigms that more accurately conceptualize the relationship between vertical integration and autonomy and portray the social structure of these communities prior to change.

The sociocultural transformations in rural life brought by urbanization fail to demonstrate a consistent pattern. To oversimplify, findings suggest that rural-urban attitude patterns reflect some differences predictable from classic sociological literature, but behavior patterns do not reflect such differences. Ruralists are more conservative than urbanites, but the two populations display gemeinschaft and gesellschaft behavioral characteristics to a similar degree. Apparent rural incorporation of some urban attributes can only be delineated through conjecture, which must rely on the assumption that at some earlier time rural Americans were substantially closer to the folk society pole of the community continuum and were more primary-group-oriented than they now appear to be; however, historical studies of the cultural backgrounds of early rural settlers cast doubt that this was the case. Incongruence between traditional gemeinschaft values and "market mentality" over several generations may not only have been tolerated by ruralists; it may have been a source of psychological adjustment. Rather than representing repulsion from impinging urbanity, findings of greater psychological maladjustment among ruralists than among urbanites may well represent frustrations experienced by market-oriented ruralists whose mobility opportunities are restricted by traditional rural values. This conflict between expansive personal goals and inhibiting rural values may be a greater source of frustration among ruralists than any confrontation of simple folk mentality with the complex, impersonal demands of urban society.

The prevailing paradigms of both the social organizational

and the sociocultural dimensions of urbanization bear the mark of the conservative tradition in sociological thought (Nisbet, 1966). It is this image of social life that Nisbet noted has been challenged by the emergence with industrialization of the concept "society," (and, for that matter, "mass society"). Those sociologists who have mourned the demise of local autonomy and of gemeinschaft values have celebrated a community that they believe existed before industrialization, which was "characterized by a high degree of personal intimacy, emotional depth, moral depth, commitment, social cohesion, and continuity in time" (Nisbet, 1966, p. 47). These are the values of sociological conservatism anchored in a traditionalism that romanticizes our rural past. Sociologists who see urbanization as depriving rural communities of attributes believed to be a part of the communities' preindustrial, preurban past are indeed "prophets of the past."

Throughout this chapter the ecological, social organizational, and sociocultural dimensions of urbanization have been dealt with relatively independently of each other. By way of concluding, a few observations may be made that cut across these dimensions. First, the specificity and precision with which research findings address sociological generalizations about urbanization are related to the extent to which variables are readily measurable. Findings result in increasingly confusing conclusions when moving from the ecological to the social organizational to the sociocultural dimensions. Such a progression involves an increase in measurement problems as one moves from the demographic and economic data of ecological research to the division of labor and decision-making structures of social organizational research, and finally to the attitudinal and behavioral data of the sociocultural dimension.

Ecological propositions can be readily stated using the continuous, quantified, interval data of population counts, economic unit censuses, and monetary values. Measurement of social organizational properties poses a variety of issues in making concepts operational; derivation of appropriate measures of "community power structure" stirred debate within political science and sociology for years. Nonetheless, within given conceptual frameworks, power networks can be delineated, vertical integration can be observed, and the organizational life of communities can be readily portrayed. Within the sociocultural dimension, measurement of variables may seem comparatively straightforward. Ordinal measurement in the form of attitude scales permits a level of quantification less common in the other two dimensions of urbanization, but propositions of the socio-cultural dimension, as represented in the work of Redfield (1947), Simmel (1950), and Wirth (1938), involve revealing transformations in the *quality* of mental life in the course of urbanization. The validity of available attitude and behavior measures as indicators of that quality is very difficult to assess.

Second, there is no readily demonstrable sequence of causation in the relationship between the ecological, social organizational, and sociocultural dimensions of urbanization. Common sense would suggest that increasing size and social differentiation would lead to greater complexity in local social organization; the resulting sophisticated social structure and immersion into national social networks might be expected to produce urban attitudes and behavior—and urban social pathology. However, the relationship between the three dimensions is not that simple. Wirth (1938) asserted that increases in the ecological variables of size, density, and heterogeneity resulted in "urbanism" as a sociocultural attribute, but this assertion has not received consistent confirmation in even the largest, most crowded, and most diverse of cities (Hunter, 1975). Furthermore, it is empirically difficult to bond directly ecological changes with either social organizational or sociocultural changes. For example, neither increased vertical integration nor decreased autonomy of communities necessarily follows from these ecological changes. Some postulated changes in rural behavior and attitudes are occurring; others are not. The extent to which those behavior changes are related to either ecological or social organizational changes is not clearly demonstrable. Few studies have systematically investigated the interrelationships between the three dimensions of urbanization reviewed in this chapter. In fact, most studies of the impact of urbanization on rural America have been descriptive, describing population and differentiation changes or social structure and sociocultural features at a specific time. Rarely if ever have longitudinal studies been performed that display the effects of one dimension on another.

In concluding this review, it is useful to note that half a century ago Sorokin and Zimmerman (1929) perceived the diffuse phase of urbanization as representing the culmination of a social change pattern spanning human history. They described the "historical curve of differentiation" between urban and rural society as:

something similar to a parabolic curve: at the initial stages of mankind or of a single society the rural-urban differentiation did not exist; later on, it appeared, but at the beginning was very slight and insignificant; it continued to grow in subsequent periods of history of a society or of all mankind; finally, having reached its climax, it has begun to become less and less sharp, less and less intensive, and, at the present moment, in several Western countries it tends to decrease [Sorokin and Zimmerman, 1929, p. 610].

Sorokin and Zimmerman (1929, p. 624) recognized that "urbanization of the rural world means only an approach of its characteristics to the characteristics of the urban world but does not mean a complete obliteration of all differences between them." Nonetheless, they saw "many reasons to think that the climax of the differentiation between city and the county, in the United States of America and in European societies, is already over."

In describing the process by which this climax of differentiation between urban and rural society occurs, it is clear that Sorokin and Zimmerman (1929) were delineating aspects of what Hawley describes as the diffuse phase of urbanization. They (pp. 611-612) noted "the weakening of the rural-urban geographic isolation, growth of the cities, an increase of rural-urban interaction, and rural-urban migration of the population. Invention of the railway and steam transportation, domestication of steam and electricity, development of the telephone, telegraph, press, airplanes, automobiles, and recently, radios—these and similar factors are particularly responsible for weakening of the rural-urban isolation and a more intensive diffusion of the urban traits in the rural, and some of the rural traits in the urban world."

As evidence has accumulated to indicate that the diffuse phase of urbanization that Sorokin and Zimmerman foresaw has brought new social change processes to bear upon rural society, there is all the more reason to reassess the ecological, social organizational, and sociocultural paradigms that have dominated in the past.

19

Comparative Perspectives on Urbanization

Bryan R. Roberts

The increasing urbanization of the world's population has become a familiar topic of discussion and enquiry. The major trends are impressive enough. From the early nineteenth century and beginning with Great Britain, the other European countries, and North America, the increasing concentration of population in urban places has become a relatively uniform pattern of change throughout the world. By 1975, almost 30 percent of the world's population of 4 billion lived in towns and cities of more than 20,000 people (Frisbie, 1977). The extent of this urbanization and its consistent increase in the modern period contrast with the low level of urbanization and the sharp fluctuations in urban populations in previous historical periods

(Lampard, 1965). Even in some countries that are now highly urbanized, the experience of urban living is a relatively recent phenomenon for most of the population: In 1920, almost half the population of the United States lived in settlements of less than 2,500 people (Lampard, 1968).

Contemporary urbanization and the increasing international trade, technological, and cultural exchange associated with it have meant a certain standardization of the terms of communication between nations. This process has been interpreted as a powerful force making for convergence in the patterns of economic and social development throughout the world. Hawley, for example, concluded his detailed account of urban society by stressing that urbanization is a single process that, over time, tends to produce similar patterns of behavior and organization wherever it occurs (Hawley, 1971, pp. 313-315). Hawley was careful to point out that convergence does not denote identity in all respects of social and economic organization and that underdeveloped countries are far from a state of development comparable with that of the developed nations. From his perspective, the study of urbanization is one means of evaluating the relative progress of nations towards modern forms of social and economic organization. My approach is different, since I shall emphasize that urbanization produces divergent processes as well as convergent ones, both within nations and between them. This diversity of urbanization experiences is not the result of the cultural uniqueness of different countries and regions, but, I shall argue, of the increasing economic interdependence of the world.

Both the perspective that I adopt and that of Hawley are based on seeing urbanization in the modern period as entailing a profound process of social and economic transformation. Agriculture employs a small fraction of the population in developed countries, and even in the underdeveloped world the majority of the economically active population is often employed in nonagricultural activities. Modern urbanization has also been based on an increasing territorial division of labor. Agricultural areas become specialized in the production of certain crops to provide foodstuffs for urban populations at home and abroad; towns and cities specialize in branches of industrial activity. Urban and rural areas become increasingly interdependent economically, and this interdependence is reproduced at the world level by the specialization of nations in different branches of production for export. In a survey of forty countries, including both developed and underdeveloped countries, Gibbs and Martin (1962) showed fairly close correlations between an index of urbanization (percentage of population in metropolitan areas) and dimensions of the division of labor such as industrial diversification, technological development, and the territorial dispersion of the sources of imported consumer goods.

Specialization and interdependence are the products of industrialization, and it is the consequences of industrialization for urbanization that distinguish the modern period from previous historical periods. As Lampard (1965) indicated, there is a long history of urban civilization in which cities were inhabited by elites, craftsmen, and traders and served as centers for the organization and appropriation of the agricultural surplus; it is only industrialization that has given rise to an incessant, worldwide urbanization based on increasing specialization and interdependence.

One of the most common approaches to this theme is similar to Hawley's (1971) emphasis on convergence and stresses the positive and necessary contribution that urban industrialization makes to economic development. Economic development is measured in terms of growth in national productivity and rise in per capita incomes. From this perspective, the concentration of people in urban-industrial places contributes to economic development over time by reducing the proportion of agricultural subsistence employment in a nation's economy (Rosenstein-Rodan, 1943).

Rosenstein-Rodan's program for promoting urban industrialization in the depressed areas of eastern and southeastern Europe found echoes, after the war, in the declarations of leaders of underdeveloped countries seeking to escape dependence on the industrialized countries. Nkrumah in Africa and the Economic Commission for Latin America were some among many who wished to embark on a pattern of urban industrialization similar to that of the developed world (Brookfield, 1975, p. 71). It was recognized that increases in the urban populations might not initially be absorbed into industrial employment, but it was claimed that an available urban labor force stimulated industrial investment and represented potential consumers of agricultural and industrial commodities. Other commentators stressed the advantages of urbanization from a sociological and psychological perspective. Levels of education were thought to improve with urbanization because of urban educational facilities and the stimulation that the urban milieu provides for the development of literacy (Lerner, 1964). Likewise, patterns of traditional behavior were thought to be less likely to persist in an urban environment (Sjoberg, 1965). Some traditional patterns such as kinship structures and ritual observances may persist, but unless they are compatible with modern urban economic organization and residential arrangements, their functions become increasingly ceremonial (Hawley, 1971, p. 314). These perspectives can be categorized as theories of modernization.

It is not my purpose to provide an extensive review of the literature on modernization, nor is it my intention to present the modernization perspective as a homogeneous or simplistic one. The analysis of the ways in which traditional forms can acquire a new and vigorous content during economic development has been an important part of modernization analysis (Feldman and Moore, 1962). Likewise, modernizers such as Wilbert Moore have emphasized the important differences between the development experiences of underdeveloped and developed countries (Moore, 1963), stressing, for example, the importance of state intervention in underdeveloped countries. What modernization perspectives have in common is a view of development as, in the long term, a convergent and evolutionary process in which simpler forms of organization are increasingly centralized into more complex ones.

Reissman (1964, pp. 155-179), for example, analyzed urbanization in underdeveloped countries as a replication, albeit in a more concentrated and uneven form, of the urbanization experience of the European nations at the time of their urban industrialization. The similarities that he emphasized are the rural-urban migration process, the rapid growth of cities, and the social problems found within the cities of nineteenth-century Europe. On the basis of this analysis, Reissman created a typology of change that represents the stages through which a society must pass to achieve a balanced urban-industrial development. The factors that he identifies as complementing each other in this development process are urban growth, industrialization, the presence of middle classes, and nationalism. Imbalances between these factors, such as urban growth without industrialization, create social problems and hinder progress to the next stage. Societies in these phases of development are described as transitional to more complex forms of organization; this viewpoint is similar to Sjoberg's (1965, p. 220) categorization of cities in underdeveloped countries as transitional to the urban-industrial structure of the developed world.

I question the usefulness of the concepts of "transition" and "convergence" and argue that their use has obscured important differences in the urbanization experiences of even the advanced capitalist countries. My own approach is to use comparisons between urbanization processes to isolate differences between these processes. This can be done by comparing countries that are urbanizing in the same historical period. My illustrations will be taken from Britain, some countries in continental Europe, and the United States at the end of the nineteenth century. I will use the comparative perspective to provide a further and quite distinct focus. I shall argue that urbanization processes in different parts of the world are indeed related: They are interdependent processes. Urbanization is the product of capitalist development and expansion. This expansion has not occurred evenly or at the same historical periods throughout the world, but it has affected, to different degrees, most areas. The industrial expansion of the first developed countries, such as England, led to rapid urbanization at home, but it also created different patterns of urbanization elsewhere. Ports and trading towns developed in the colonies and in Latin America as a consequence of the trade that developed between industrializing Europe and the regions that supplied the primary products needed for industry and to feed the urban population of Europe.

The development of an interconnected world system has the effect of alleviating scarcity for some at the cost of increasing the relative impact of scarcity on others (Brookfield, 1975, pp. 205-209). This world system is based on the specialization of different regions in different stages and aspects of the production process. Regarding the early modern period, Wallerstein (1974b) distinguished between the core industrial regions, such as England; semiperipheral regions specializing in commerce and in organizing the production of primary products, such as Spain; and peripheral regions, such as Latin America and eastern Europe, which were organized to provide primary products for the core countries.

This interdependent world structure produces the diverse patterns of urbanization found historically and contemporaneously. Concepts such as "transitional" or "mature" forms of urbanization are inappropriate because the various forms, ranging from the large urban-industrial complex of the developed world to the squatter settlements and nonindustrial cities of the underdeveloped world, are in part the product of each other's existence. Friedmann (1972a, 1972b) recently extended this line of argument to provide a detailed critique of growth point theories of regional development. These theories take the United States as their model and stress the elimination of regional inequalities through interfirm linkages and the spread of the advantages of technological innovation (Lasuen, 1969; Hermansen, 1972). In contrast, Friedmann emphasized the political dimensions that are important for regional development and stressed the concentration of power that develops in the most economically dynamic regions. He calls these regions "core regions" and examines the processes whereby they organize the production of peripheral regions; this organization concentrates resources at the core and creates an increasing economic and political dependence of the periphery on the core.

Friedmann's (1972a, 1972b) major point is that the dominance of core regions is a self-reinforcing process, since innovations in technology or culture tend to be developed first in core regions. Proximity to centers of decision making, the presence of a highly developed consumer market, and the presence of organizational resources for innovations are among the many factors that Friedmann cited to explain this concentration of innovation. Economic advantages accruing to the early adopters of innovation reinforce and extend the control of the core over the periphery. More traditional competitors in the periphery will be forced out of business, and less productive enterprises will be displaced from the core to the periphery. Dominance of the core creates what appears to be inefficiency or traditionalism at the periphery. Indeed, the dynamism of the core depends in great part on creating conditions of scarcity at the periphery. Thus, Friedmann argued that in the case of Chile, the predominance of Santiago has deprived provincial city governments of any financial resources; in this situation, local government appears inefficient since it does not provide adequate urban services or foster local economic development. Taxes and local banking deposits channel capital to Santiago, where it promotes the economic growth of the core region. In face of the dominance of the core, provincial elites in many countries may espouse regionalism, stressing the traditional virtues or ethnic characteristics of their region as a means of challenging the dominance of the core.

The persistence of cultural variations in the face of metropolitan dominance occurs even in the advanced capitalist countries. Thus Mellor (1975, p. 285) argued that societies

might better be analyzed in terms of metropolitan dominance and provincial dependency, in which pre-existing
variations deriving from the relational position of one
community vis-à-vis the others are continually being reac-
tivated. Even in a country as compact and highly centralized as Britain, the continual recreation of locally based
cultures cannot be overlooked—the "Mersey Beat" from
Liverpool, the gangs of the Glasgow housing estates,
Welsh and Scottish nationalism, Geordie pride and trucu-
lence—the peripheral regions and provincial communities
outside the golden circle of metropolitan England are
generating cultures as pervasive as those from the heart of
the metropolis.

The potential conflicts between the periphery and the core may
in the long term limit the expansion of the core, giving rise to
counterelites at the periphery and perhaps to the eventual withdrawal of the periphery from the influence of the core. To
understand how the dominance of a core region or city is weakened or how that region loses its dynamism requires an analysis
of changes in political power resulting from class, regionalist, or
nationalist struggles. My perspective, then, emphasizes that the
study of urbanization and urban structure must be integrated
with the study of the political economy of development.

In the sections that follow, I shall provide only the broadest outlines of the urbanization processes in the advanced capitalist countries and in Latin America. These urbanization
processes affect each other through the movement of people
and of capital. Large-scale migrations from Europe to the Americas involved the movement of some 50 million people in the
nineteenth and early twentieth centuries (Thomas, 1973, p.
244). These migrants went predominantly to the United States,
but millions also went to Canada, Argentina, and Brazil. Migrants to the two latter countries were more likely to return to
Europe, and, indeed, in Argentina some of this international
migration was seasonal migration of Italian workers who returned home after three months' work in the Argentine harvest
(Scobie, 1964). British capital and technology helped develop
railroads and industry on the continent of Europe, and outflows
of European, especially British, capital helped develop the
Americas, financing the railroads, agriculture, commerce, and,
in North America, industry.

The direct interrelationships of Europe and the Americas

are not the only sources of variation in urbanization. I will also examine agrarian transformation and will claim that this differed significantly between Europe, the United States, and Latin America. Another important variable is the nature of the market for industrial production; the pattern of urban industrialization varies on this dimension from the export orientation of British industry to the internal, mass consumption market of the United States and to the internal but highly income-concentrated markets of underdeveloped countries. Finally, the historical timing of the urbanization process has enduring effects on urbanization in the countries we consider.

My discussion will be organized in terms of brief case studies of the urbanization process in Britain, some continental European countries, the United States, and Latin America. I am not able to cover all the factors outlined above in equal depth in each case. Also, many of the suggestions should be regarded as speculative, hopefully intended to encourage further research. My aim is to·show that the content of urbanization is significantly different in the various countries in ways that are likely to prevent any substantial convergence in these countries' patterns of economic and social development.

Urbanization and the Advanced Capitalist World

We can begin by considering the urbanization of selected European countries and the United States during the nineteenth century (Table 1). England and Wales were the first to urbanize significantly, and it was not until the end of the century that the United States, Germany, and France had significant proportions of their populations in places of 20,000 and more people. Even by the end of the century, Italy is still massively a country of farms, villages, and small towns. These differences in urbanization correspond to differences in the timing and impact of the Industrial Revolution.

British Urbanization in the Nineteenth Century. In Britain, more perhaps than in any continental European country, the urban industrialization of the nineteenth century was preceded by a substantial transformation of the agrarian structure in a capitalist direction. Before the emergence of the large industrial towns, England had developed a substantial network of small but thriving market centers; some of these were already centers of important manufacturing activity. In Oldham, which later became one of the most important cotton towns, there

Table 1. Urbanization in the United States and Selected European Countries, 1800-1890.

Approximate Date of Census	England and Wales			Germany			France			Italy			United States		
	20,000-99,999	100,000 and over	Total	20,000-99,999	100,000 and over	Total	20,000-99,999	100,000 and over	Total	20,000-99,999	100,000 and over	Total	20,000-99,999	100,000 and over	Total
1800	7.2	9.7	16.9	–	–	–	3.9	2.8	6.7	–	4.4	–	3.8	–	3.8
1850	12.4	22.6	35.0	6.0	–	–	6.0	4.6	10.6	–	6.0	–	3.8	6.0	9.8
1890	21.8	31.8	53.6	9.8	12.1	21.9	9.1	12.0	21.1	6.4	6.9	13.3	8.3	15.5	23.8

Note: Figures represent the percentage of the total population living in cities with the indicated population sizes. Blanks for Germany and Italy indicate that data are not available for those categories; the blank for the United States is because no city had a population of 100,000 or over in 1800.

Source: Weber, 1963, p. 144.

were, before the end of the eighteenth century, some 15 thousand people living in the sixteen square miles of the borough; Foster (1974) estimated that most of the area's working population were unpropertied wage laborers, such as miners, hatters, and especially weavers.

At the beginning of the Industrial Revolution, then, there was a substantial supply of labor available to man the factories. There was also a supply of local, relatively small-scale capital to construct the factories (Hobsbawn, 1968). In Oldham, those who constructed the new mills came from families that had a long history of local entrepreneurship and landholding often as outwork manufacturers and traders (Foster, 1974, p. 11). Local entrepreneurship and a local labor supply meant substantial continuity in the early period of urban industrialization. Thompson (1970, pp. 401-429) stressed the cultural manifestations of this continuity in the regional customs and dialects that persisted in the factory towns. The predominant pattern of short-distance migration that populated the factory towns was another factor contributing to this continuity (Redford, 1926; Weber, 1963, p. 255). This short-distance migration was carefully documented in a study of the growth and industrialization of the Lancashire cotton town of Preston (Anderson, 1971). Kinship and places of origin continued to be an important means whereby migrants established relationships in the town and coped with the problems of work and finding accommodations (Anderson, 1971).

By the end of the nineteenth century, it is likely that Britain's urban population had become stabilized relative to that of Europe and especially the United States. Weber (1963, p. 263) pointed out that England was unique in that a manufacturing county like Lancashire had fewer residents born outside the county than did some rural counties. This stabilization took place toward the end of the nineteenth century, since during the nineteenth century there was considerable internal migration and, of course, emigration to North America, Australia, and New Zealand. The 1901 census showed that in Lancashire 77.5 percent of resident males had been born in their county of residence. There was some long-distance migration, and 3.3 percent of the population was Irish born. The major sources of migration from outside the county were, however, the contiguous counties. Of all those born in Lancashire and still resident in Britain, 89.3 percent were still resident in Lancashire itself (1901 Census of England and Wales, 1902-1903, tables 38 and

39). In the manufacturing towns of Salford and Oldham, with populations in 1901 of 221,000 and 137,000, respectively, 74 percent and 81 percent of the male population had been born in the local county of Lancashire and, most probably, in or near the towns themselves.

Residential stabilization continued, and in the early twentieth century there is evidence that residential turnover within towns was declining relative to the nineteenth century (Robson, 1973, p. 96). The available labor supply appears to have been adequate for the needs of industry in this period. Indeed, the inability of many northern manufacturing towns to hold their populations at the end of the century, let alone attract new migrants from Ireland or the rural areas, suggests that labor was not a minor factor in production.

A further characteristic of Britain's urbanization in the nineteenth century was that the traditional urban centers were bypassed. Many of the large cities at the end of the nineteenth century were essentially new towns that previously had not ranked significantly in Britain's urban hierarchy. Robson (1973, pp. 45-89) points to the large number of towns that grew rapidly from origins of less than 2,500 people. In contrast, in Germany, it was predominantly the established urban centers that grew fastest during the period of rapid urbanization; Weber (1963, pp. 84-86) showed that the great cities of Germany in 1819 were the urban centers that grew fastest by 1890.

The new urban-industrial centers in England and Wales were often no more than extended villages, rows of cottages in a river valley clustered around a mine or a mill. Close to these villages, there developed industrial towns, frequently based on a single industry, such as the northern mill towns. Metropolitan centers such as Manchester grew as a result of the industry of their region, but such centers differed substantially from the industrial towns and villages in their social composition. Manchester, for example, was and remained a more cosmopolitan place with a greater concentration of long-distance immigrants from the southern counties, Ireland, and overseas.

The most important contrast was with London. London grew rapidly in the nineteenth century, but not as rapidly as the provincial cities and not on the basis of manufacturing industry (Jones, 1971; Weber, 1963, p. 56). London's growth was based on its position as the administrative and commercial center of the country and as the organizing point of overseas commerce. Employment in transport and storage activities was the largest single employment category for males in the 1861 census with 13.44 percent and in 1891 was only surpassed by employment in retail and distribution activities (Weber, 1963, pp. 358-359). Manufacturing in London was seriously affected by competition from the factory production of the northern towns, resulting in the impoverishment of many craft workers (Jones, 1971). A high proportion of London employment was casual labor in the docks and in construction or sweatshop labor in the garment and shoe industries.

The growing towns and cities clustered in distinct regions of the country. This growth pattern reflected stages in industrialization: first, the rise of the textile industry then the growth of the port cities, the development of the iron and steel industry, coal, engineering, and shipbuilding (Weber, 1963, pp. 51-57). In regional terms, the sequence of urban growth was, first, the cotton towns of the North-West, soon followed by the woolen region of the West Riding of Yorkshire and by some manufacturing towns of the Midlands; then urbanization occurred in the coal and engineering areas of the North-East and South Wales. The metropolitan growth of London was considerable by the end of the century (Robson, 1973, figures 4.1-4.11).

British urban-industrial development was less economically and administratively centralized than that of continental Europe; in the United States, economic centralization in the form of large corporations also appeared early during urban industrialization. In Britain, a pattern of relatively small-scale industrial and commercial entrepreneurship persisted until well into the twentieth century. These small-scale enterprises were unable to introduce the costly technological innovations brought by the later stages of the Industrial Revolution (Hobsbawn, 1968, pp. 180-184). Robson (1973, pp. 221-228) showed how this weak economic and administrative centralization inhibited the introduction of both electricity and improved forms of public transport. In Britain, lack of cooperation and suspicion between contiguous townships and between private and municipal interests delayed many innovations, so that both continental and American cities were soon ahead of their British counterparts in providing the urban infrastructure for economic growth.

The final factor to consider underlay, in many respects, the others that we have considered. This is the export orientation of British industry. From its beginning, the revolutionary form of industrialization, factory production, was oriented to export. Cotton, the mainstay of British industrial production for much of the nineteenth century, exported over half the total value of its output at the beginning of the nineteenth century and almost four fifths at the end (Hobsbawn, 1968, p. 112). The expansion of the coal, iron, and steel industries in the second half of the nineteenth century did little to modify this export orientation. Iron and steel relied on overseas markets for about 40 percent of their gross production from the mid nineteenth century (Hobsbawn, 1968, p. 112). Engineering and shipbuilding industries produced mainly for the overseas market.

The export orientation of its industry meant that Britain depended on an international territorial division of labor. From the mid nineteenth century Britain relied increasingly on agricultural imports for feeding its population; some of its major industries, such as cotton, depended on the import of primary materials. It is this territorial division of labor that made possible the early and rapid urbanization of Britain; it meant that a very high proportion of the British work force could be absorbed into the transformative sector of industry (manufacturing and construction). By 1901, almost 40 percent of the British labor force was employed in industry and construction, and until the 1960s this concentration of employment was to remain at the same or slightly higher levels. Agriculture in 1901 provided employment for some 15 percent of employed males (1901 Census of England and Wales, 1902-1903, p. 82).

Britain's position as the "workshop of the world" meant a population concentration in the industrial regions. Since industry was not oriented to an internal consumer market and since it did not in its early development depend on finance from London, location was determined by regional advantage. Moreover, the first sixty years or so of industrialization took place without railways. In this context, regional advantages were easy access to good ports, the availability of coal and a labor supply, and the presence of local entrepreneurial capital. Britain's lead in the Industrial Revolution meant that it captured overseas markets for industrial products with a relatively simple and inexpensive production technology. This technology was accessible to those without great reserves of capital; and singly or in combination, many provincial businessmen invested in factory production. In this way, much of British industry was committed to the production of basic and relatively unsophisticated commodities for an overseas market that would constrict over time as new industrial nations emerged and as even underdeveloped countries developed their own industrial production.

Britain became tied to maintaining and creating an overseas market for basic industrial products, and these overseas interests were significant factors in producing the patterns of urbanization in the Americas in the nineteenth century. They meant that British capital was attracted overseas to create the infrastructure that would promote trade exchanges (Thomas, 1973, pp. 244-289). British investment in Argentine, Brazilian, or North American railroads increased, directly and indirectly, demand for British industrial products. These railroads also opened up the interior of the Americas for the production of primary products for export. In the long term, however, the slow rate of technological change in British industry meant that the cycles of investment overseas and renewed investment in Britain did not lead to sustained economic growth at home.

The above factors interacted to produce a pattern of urbanization in Britain that had little potential for supporting economic growth. There is little evidence in Britain for a self-sustaining pattern of regional development based on diffusion from growth centers, such as occurred in the United States. Robson (1973, p. 119) concluded from his survey of urban growth in the nineteenth century in Britain that it is not possible to talk of regional sets of cities with uniformly high growth rates, a fact reflecting the expansion of successive growth industries.

By the early twentieth century, London had reasserted its predominance in the national economy, with population and economic activity increasingly concentrated in the south of England. The development in recent years of regional political identities and, in the cases of Wales and Scotland, of nationalisms can be interpreted as the political response to the institutionalized patterns of regional inequality produced by British urbanization.

Urbanization in Britain created a permanent core-periphery pattern within the country. The peripheries were the industrialized regions in which a predominantly working class population received relatively low wages, which were spent on basic necessities. This population was to an extent trapped in its situation. To secure adequate incomes, several members of a family sought employment and in times of depression and emergency relied on the help of neighbors or kin. Even when wages improved at the end of the century, access to the better-paid jobs often depended on apprenticeship and following a family member or kinsman in his line of work. Housing tenure often reinforced these local commitments. Housing in the industrial towns and villages was constructed by the factory or mine owner or by local tradesmen. For local tradesmen, housing the working class was a source of income that often complemented their existing businesses. The owner of the corner shop was often the owner of the houses in the row; likewise, the landlord might also employ female members of a household as seamstresses for a garment business. The working class did not constitute a significant internal market for British industry, and there were few incentives for the capital accumulated from factory production to be invested locally. Instead capital drained south to London and overseas. Local commitments also inhibited labor mobility, thus perpetuating patterns of local exploitation.

The class consciousness and class organization that developed in Britain reflected the pattern of urbanization. Class consciousness and organization developed rapidly and powerfully during the early stages of industrialization (Foster, 1974). Over time, however, urbanization did not result in the development of a uniform working class culture. Rather, differences between regions in their industrial base, in the origins and stability of their populations, and in their dependence on exports contributed to the development of distinctive working class cultures. Also, the struggle for survival in the community environment of the industrial towns and villages generated a set of institutions —cooperatives, temperance and friendly societies, benefit clubs, and Non-Conformist Chapels—that reduced the sharpness of the class struggle. The structure of production contributed to the fragmentation of working class organization; in the industrial towns, numbers of small craft unions arose that catered to different specialties and different segments of labor: male and female, skilled and unskilled. Working class organizations and politics acquired a provincial flavor. Thus, Jones (1971, pp. 337-349) suggested that the "nonindustrial" nature of London in the nineteenth century prevented the development of a radical socialist, metropolitan labor movement and left the leadership of the working class movement to the syncretic socialism of the provinces. Such an analysis suggests the importance of understanding the class structures produced by different patterns of urbanization. Class relationships and class organization are crucial factors in determining the capacity of peripheral regions and populations to secure concessions from the center.

Continental Europe. Urbanization on the continent was affected in various ways by the prior industrialization of Britain. Coming later to industrialization, continental countries could take advantage of existing technology and, often, of British capital; also, the increase in industrial production was accompanied and stimulated by an efficient system of transport (railways). These countries followed a protectionist industrial strategy in face of Britain's existing preeminence, which made state protection and assistance for domestic industry an important element in their politics.

Though continental countries industrialized to different degrees and differed in the timing of their urbanization, we can note certain similarities in their urban-industrial organization. We have already noted that, on the continent, the fastest growing urban centers were likely to be existing centers of commerce and administration. Efficient transport systems and the importance of the internal market for industrial production meant that industrial activity, with exceptions such as the mining industry, tended to locate near to or in the established centers. Centralization of production was encouraged by the size of investment needed for the technology of the late stages of the Industrial Revolution. Investments were often so considerable that they were not easily met by the type of small-scale entrepreneurship found in Britain. By the end of the nineteenth century, and especially in Germany, large industrial trusts were forming and acquiring monopoly positions in various branches of industry. The financial power and size of these trusts enabled German industry to take the lead in the new growth industries, such as chemicals and electromechanics. In the less advanced industrial countries of the continent, large-scale industrial enterprise was also the predominant form of industrialization. For example, Italy industrialized through the participation of large banks and trusts in ways similar, in certain respects, to Germany (Gerschenkron, 1962, pp. 72-90).

This economic centralization encouraged and in part was made possible by administrative centralization, though there are important exceptions, such as Italy, to this generalization. The direct collaboration of the state and industrial enterprise characterizes much of the industrialization process on the continent and contrasts with the fragmentation of interests and jurisdictions that we noted in England and Wales. This centralization promoted the growth of the existing political and commercial centers on the continent and especially the growth of the capital cities.

One outcome of this process of centralization was the concentration of the industrial working class in large metropolitan centers and often in large conglomerate enterprises in which the gulf between owners and workers was, necessarily, a great one. The organization of large industrial combines produced a centralization of working class organization, adding a dimension to class organization and conflict that was absent, in this period, in Britain. Jones (1971), for example, cited Lenin's and Trotsky's accounts of the success of the Russian Revolution. Their accounts stress the concentration of the industrial proletariat in factories that were among the largest and most advanced in the capitalist world. Trotsky gave figures to show that in Russia the giant enterprises of more than a thousand workers employed 41.4 percent of the workers, while similar-sized enterprises in the United States employed 17.8 percent. Though the levels of employment in manufacturing industry on the continent did not begin to reach those of Britain until well into the twentieth century, this employment was concentrated in fewer urban centers.

By 1925, 38.9 percent of the labor force in Germany was employed in manufacturing and construction and 51.3 percent in 1961; in these two years, 30.9 percent and 6.8 percent, respectively, of the population was employed in agriculture (Singelmann, 1974, pp. 114-167). In France, employment in manufacturing and construction rose from 29.7 percent in 1921 to 37.7 percent in 1962; agriculture employed 42.4 percent of the population of France in 1921 and 20.6 percent in 1962. In Italy, 24.2 percent of the population was employed in manufacturing and construction in 1921 and 40.0 percent in 1961; agriculture employed 56.7 percent in 1921 and 29.1 percent in 1961.

Since industrialization occurred in or close to established centers, accommodation for the growing mass of workers had to be fitted into a preexisting and well-defined pattern of spatial organization. Some workers might find accommodation in tenements close to the center of the city, but large concentrations of workers were located on the outskirts close to the factories. Musil (1968, pp. 250-255) described this pattern of residence for Prague in the first part of the twentieth century. Manual workers were increasingly moving into the central zones of

Prague as the upper classes abandoned their former residences; but the concentration of workers was highest in the outlying zones and lowest in the intermediate zones. Though the different social classes were segregated in distinct subsections of the city, their spatial distribution was heterogeneous, with middle and working classes occupying the outskirts of the city as well as being juxtaposed in more central zones.

This residential organization is a possible further factor that differentiates class consciousness and organization in continental European cities from those of British cities. The industrial working class in Europe lived closer to the centers of power and wealth than was the case in nineteenth-century Britain. Under continental conditions, the working class living in metropolitan centers may have been less permeated by paternalistic institutions than were the British working classes living in industrial villages and towns. This suggestion, however, requires systematic comparative research. What is clear is the different political outcome: On the continent, communist and radical socialist working class movements have had a much greater importance than has been the case in Britain.

Urbanization on the continent reflects the semiperipheral position of many of these countries within the capitalist world system. Most continental countries lacked sufficient internal resources to be able to develop rapidly on the basis of their internal market, yet the opportunities for economic expansion through exchanging industrial products for primary materials were limited by the dominance of the core industrial countries: Britain and subsequently Germany and the United States. Thus, on the continent, the agrarian structure was to varying degrees less thoroughly transformed in a capitalist direction prior to and even during urban industrialization than had been the case in Britain. This pattern of uneven capitalist development meant that in many countries the relative backwardness of the agricultural sector contrasted with the advanced industrial-capitalist organization of the cities.

For the less advanced industrial countries of Europe, this contrast has been a source of social and economic tension. These countries could not rely on industrial productivity and market mechanisms to gradually transform the agrarian structure. Because of the interdependence of their economies and those of the core countries, more efficiently manufactured imported goods harmed domestic industrial production, while excessive protection of domestic production was likely, in a free market situation, to discourage peasants from exchanging their crops for manufactured goods. Consequently, in many European countries, the state has intervened to force the pace of agrarian transformation through taxation, land reform, and development projects. In Russia in the 1920s, the debate over how to incorporate the peasant sector into the industrial economy led to the forced collectivization of the peasantry to concentrate investment in rapid industrialization (Preobrazhensky, 1965).

In varying degrees, the pattern of urban industrialization on the continent has made the agrarian structure into a significant and persisting political issue. At times, this issue has taken the form of severe imbalances in development between agrarian regions, such as the south of Italy or the south of Spain, and urban industrial regions in the same country, such as the north of Italy or Catalonia. Also, the persistence of peasant forms of agriculture in, for example, the Mediterranean European countries has meant the availability of a migratory labor force that to this day adds a vital component to the urban-industrial expansion of the core European countries (Castles and Kosack, 1973).

Such processes have led to significant divergences in urban organization from that of Britain or the United States. In many European countries, a proportion of the industrial labor force commuted to work from nearby villages. Weber (1963, pp. 105-106) referred to this pattern in Russia, and Berry (1973b, pp. 143-144) cited cases of such commuting in Hesse and northeast Bavaria in Germany, Switzerland, southwest Germany, the Czech lands, parts of eastern France, and the Low Countries. This pattern of commuting has persisted in many countries to the present day, and factory work is frequently combined with agricultural small-holdings. In some European countries, such commuting has been encouraged as a means of saving investments in urban infrastructures. Eastern European countries are, for example, relatively "underurbanized" in terms of the housing available for the urban work force. A substantial proportion of industrial labor in Hungary lives in villages and journeys to the cities to work. This situation has been created by a deliberate policy of rationing urban housing to concentrate investment in industry. The contrast between the ecology of continental industrial cities and that of Chicago and other American cities, as described by Burgess (1923), is not the result of the cultural peculiarities. It is the consequence of the pattern of economic development on the continent of

Europe. Urban spatial organization has been an integral part of the uneven pattern of industrial capitalist development in many parts of Europe. The urbanization experiences of European countries, such as Russia and other central European nations, are, in fact, useful points of contrast with urbanization in many contemporary underdeveloped countries in which a numerically preponderant peasantry persists during industrialization.

Urbanization in the United States. One of the most striking differences between the United States and Europe is the lesser tie of urbanization to employment in manufacturing and construction. In 1870, 23.5 percent of the American labor force was employed in construction and manufacturing; at that date 50.8 percent was employed in agriculture and 11.5 percent in distributive services (transport, utilities, and trade). By 1920 the transformative sector generated 32.9 percent of total employment and by 1960, 35.9 percent was so employed, by which time agriculture employed 7 percent of the population. The ratio of employment in distributive services to that in the transformative sector remained fairly constant throughout the period 1870 to 1960; by 1900 the ratio of employment in distributive services to that in the transformative sector was 0.60, and in 1960 the ratio was 0.61 (Browning and Singelmann, 1975).

These figures suggest that a different pattern of economic development underlies urbanization in the United States. It was through the development of urban centers that the agricultural regions of the West and Midwest were opened up (Berry, 1967). In contrast to the situation whereby the needs of a scattered farming population gave rise to centrally located market centers, urban settlements preceded agricultural development in many parts of the United States. Urbanization in the United States was an active agent in developing agriculture as well as industry and the services.

In contrast, urbanization in Europe concentrated populations that could no longer find adequate work in agriculture. Industrialization displaced population from the rural areas of Europe by producing cheap manufactured goods that removed the source of livelihood of rural artisans and that encouraged the rationalization and mechanization of farming. This process eventually occurred in the United States also; but in the early period of urbanization from 1870 to 1920, employment opportunities in agriculture *increased* in the United States from 6,430,000 jobs to 11,120,000 (U.S. Bureau of the Census, 1975c, p. 138).

International migrations linked the U.S. pattern of urbanization with that of Europe. The rapid development of American industry as well as the development of agriculture and the distributive services was made possible by the immigration of European labor power at the turn of the century. This immigration was itself produced by the broader patterns of economic interdependency. While high rates of population increase and population pressures on scarce land resources were the main factors behind the availability of Europe's agricultural population, European industrialization also contributed to this out-migration. High rates of population increase were themselves the indirect consequence of the economic transformation of Europe. The contribution was less the result of any direct dislocations produced by industrialization than of the indirect consequences of industrialization in flooding the European market with cheap foodstuffs from the Americas and other parts of the world. As first England and then other European powers brought countries into their orbit as markets for manufactured products, so too did European capital stimulate the specialization of countries as producers of primary products. American and Canadian wheat, Argentine wheat and beef, New Zealand and Australian mutton, sugar, and other tropical foodstuffs entered the European market, driving down food prices and making the situation of the small European farmer more precarious.

The result was a redistribution of population in keeping with a newly emerging territorial division of labor. In Europe, the out-migrations relieved, to a certain extent, the pressures on employment in the cities. Indeed, as some commentators have suggested, it is possible that without emigration, European cities would have shown more evidence of a "surplus" population (Graham, 1972). The occupational distributions of these cities might, consequently, have been more akin to cities in the underdeveloped world today with a heavy concentration in service employment. European immigrants not only helped develop the American economy, but they also helped turn Argentina into a major wheat producer and Brazil into a major coffee producer.

Urbanization in the United States was also facilitated by the investment of substantial amounts of European capital and the import of capital goods from Europe. The development of the United States could be accomplished rapidly and without a prior concentration in heavy manufacturing. In the United States, industrialization was accompanied by the early predominance of cartels, monopolies, and large-scale finance; also, large industrial conglomerates were rapidly formed. Yet this industrial concentration could make use of sufficient supplies of immigrant labor and still leave enough labor to build the railroads and open up the farming lands of the West.

Labor was scarce for most periods of American economic development; European investments of human and money capital helped prevent this scarcity from becoming a bottleneck to development. Conversely, emigration and capital investment in the United States influenced urban development in England and Wales. While there is some disagreement on this point, it seems probable that house building in England and Wales was inversely related to emigration and capital investment abroad (Thomas, 1973, pp. 202-222; Habakkuk, 1962). Britain's position at the end of the nineteenth century as a *rentier* nation meant, in effect, that local urban-industrial development often took second place to more attractive investments abroad. This was an important limitation, not only on technological development in Britain but also on the evolution and spatial differentiation of its towns and cities.

Industrial production in the United States in the late nineteenth and early twentieth centuries was predominantly for the internal market; agricultural commodities and other primary products, especially cotton from the South, composed the major exports of the nineteenth century. The urbanization statistics show that under these conditions even a massive industrialization did not entail a high degree of population concentration. At the period (1896 to 1900) when United States manufacturing production was nearly double that of Great Britain, some 60 percent of the American population lived in places of less than 2,500 people (U.S. Bureau of the Census, 1975c). This degree of population dispersion was accompanied by the growth of large cities in certain regions of the United States. Indeed, the pattern of urbanization in late nineteenth-century United States diverged widely by region; in 1900, 61 percent of the population of the Northeast lived in places of 2,500 people or more, 18 percent of the population did in the South, 38.6 percent in the North Central region, and 39.9 percent in the West (Lampard, 1968, table 2).

The type of large city that emerged in the United States as a result of the interdependency of the Atlantic economy was quite distinct from that of Europe and became the basis for a different pattern of economic development. My concern is not with the issue of whether the large American cities of the first part of this century encouraged a distinctive urban style of life

that over time would influence the behavior of all urban inhabitants (Wirth, 1938). The discussion over urbanism as a way of
life has made clear the importance and persistence of urban subcultures in American cities; in some of these cities, ethnicity
and kinship are important means of economic and social solidarity, while for other social and economic groups urban location
may have little significance for behavior (Gans, 1965; Hawley,
1971, pp. 134-135).

For the international comparisons of this paper, I will
limit myself to general features of the organization of the large
American city. First, American cities had more and cheaper
space available for expansion, partly because land monopoly
was not as strongly entrenched in the new country; the use of
this space was facilitated by the early introduction of streetcars
and electricity. Weber (1963) reported the average densities of
cities in the United States, England, and Germany at the end of
the nineteenth century as being, respectively, 15.2, 38.3, and
25.9 persons per acre. By the end of the nineteenth century,
Weber was able to document an extensive movement of both
industry and residence to suburban locations, showing the
greater dispersal of the American compared with the European
urban population (Weber, 1963, p. 469).

International migration, which was mainly directed to the
cities, contributed to a low degree of working class organization
and consciousness in American cities. This migration became
part of the pattern of economic expansion at the end of the
nineteenth century. Thomas (1973, pp. 163-174) showed how
the American economy became geared to using, profitably, the
large numbers of unskilled and often illiterate workers that
came from Europe. Factory production and especially assembly-line methods of production were encouraged by the abundance of unskilled labor; industrial expansion created technical
and supervisory job opportunities for workers displaced by the
new processes. Jobs in commerce and the services also expanded
with mass production and the need to distribute and service the
commodities produced. The successive waves of migration from
Europe meant that American industry had an almost perpetual
pool of unskilled labor for expanding production cheaply. The
sons of the first generations of unskilled migrants acquired the
educational and technical skills to consolidate their hold on the
better-class jobs in society (Thomas, 1973, p. 153).

This economic structure generated the patterns of urban
residential succession that became characteristic of American

cities. Newly arrived immigrants settled in central-city tenements that were cheap and gave access to various job possibilities; unskilled and unstable work fixed these immigrants in ethnic ghettoes (Ward, 1968). As individuals and ethnic groups acquired skills and education, they obtained better-paying and more stable jobs and moved to outlying residential districts of the city. Residential instability, due to economic expansion, affected even supposedly unchanging New England towns, as Thernstrom's (1964) restudy of Warner's Yankee city showed (Warner and Lunt, 1941). Thernstrom (1964, pp. 215-216) reported a high degree of population and social mobility for nineteenth-century Newburyport and linked these mobilities to the lack of working class consciousness in American cities.

The social and spatial structure of American cities was an integral part of the pattern of industrial expansion. The segregation of skilled, stable, and often unionized jobs from unskilled, unstable work was accomplished through successive waves of immigrants, ethnic ghettoes, and residential succession. The effectiveness of this segregation of the labor force—the existence of what recently has been called a "dual labor market"—promoted American industrial expansion and technological innovation (Gordon, 1972, pp. 67-70). The contrast with British patterns of urban industrialization is helpful: In Britain, industrial production tended, as we have seen, to stabilize labor power in working class communities. The distinction between skilled and unskilled work was often internal to the community and embodied in the difference between skilled male and unskilled female operatives or between apprentice sons and skilled fathers. Along with the export orientation of industry, the relative solidarity of British working class communities reinforced the tendency of capital in Britain not to innovate technologically. The exceptions to this were those areas such as the London area where relatively mobile and unskilled labor power was available by the end of the century.

Urbanization and Economic Development. Our discussion can be deepened and linked to the case of Latin America by considering the overall pattern of urbanization in the United States by the end of the nineteenth century. I will approach this theme by using Morse's (1975) distinction between the plantation and homestead models of economic development. Morse developed his argument on the basis of the work of Baldwin (1956), Dowd (1956), Rothstein (1966), and others who traced the relationship between patterns of agricultural production and

patterns of urbanization. Morse used the distinction to understand why agricultural exports stimulated urban industrialization under some conditions but not under others. The plantation produced high export earnings, but these earnings did not
stimulate widespread local development. Instead, earnings were
channeled through one or two major urban centers where they
were consumed in sumptuous living, thus stimulating the import
of luxury manufactures and the development of commerce
dominated by the major centers. In contrast, small-scale homestead farming required a local infrastructure of small towns to
service the farms, and a considerable share of the earnings of the
farm product remained to stimulate local commerce and industry (Morse, 1975). In Morse's argument, the overall differences
in the urbanization patterns of Latin America and the United
States in the nineteenth century were due to the predominance
of the homestead in the development in the United States.

The low levels of urbanization in the South of the United
States were, conversely, due to the predominance of the plantation economy (Rothstein, 1966). As Rothstein (1967) indicated
elsewhere, the issue was not one of the noncapitalist or non-
entrepreneurial character of the planter elite. The southern
plantation operated as an economic enclave in its surrounding
territory. The slave labor had low levels of consumption, and
these consumption needs were met mainly by production on
the plantation. The cotton crop was tended, harvested, and
ginned by the resident labor; it was directly shipped in bulk to
the ports. Dowd (1956) pointed out that even after the abolition of slavery, institutional patterns kept the South underdeveloped and relatively unurbanized. Planters used sharecrop-
ping arrangements with poor whites to obtain cotton cheaply;
the hostility toward and fears of the blacks by poor whites were
used to keep factory and farm labor unorganized and cheap.
The profits made were channeled to northern banks, and investors' levels of consumption remained low in the South and insufficient to extend local commercial and industrial development.

The Northwest and West of the United States were as dependent on eastern capital and markets as was the South, but
this dependence did not inhibit local development. Unlike the
situation in the South, the profits of eastern financiers in the
West were not linked as closely to the direct institutionalized
exploitation of labor, such as using racial stereotypes and patterns of land tenure to keep consumption levels at a subsistence

level. Instead, the small-scale nature and technical requirements of wheat production generated a variety of middleman activities and demands for agricultural inputs (Rothstein, 1966). Grain was stored in bulk in small towns, stimulating the development of means to classify and standardize the various small harvests that made up the bulk. Complicated chains of brokerage developed around warehouse receipts, leading to innovations in the financial management and organization of the grain trade, which became increasingly centered in cities such as Chicago and St. Louis. Using these and many other examples, Rothstein argued that homestead wheat production helped develop a pattern of urbanization in which commercial and other service activities could flourish in small towns, generating profits that were often invested locally. Furthermore, the increasing voting power of the western populations combined with the interests of eastern finance to secure the development of transport and urban infrastructure.

The analyses of Dowd (1956) and Rothstein (1966, 1967) provide insight into the processes by which urbanization becomes an active agent of economic development. Particularly important is the account of the type of feedback mechanism that stimulates innovation in technology and in economic organization. In wheat production, innovation arises from the need to coordinate the activities of a large number of small-scale producers. The innovations are often technological, as in the case of grain elevators, harvesting equipment, and drying and fanning machinery. The network of intermediaries, ranging from the local storekeeper to specialized local dealers and large-scale urban merchants trade centers, was in a position to assess demand for products and to recognize opportunities for introducing new products. Merchant capital could thus be invested in the industrial production of farm machinery or domestic consumer goods. This network of commercial and financial organization helps account for the sectoral distribution of the labor force in the United States at this period and later. Manufacturing employment did not become as dominant in the United States as it did in Europe because commercial and distributive activities were an integral part of the efficiency of industrial production and stimulated technological innovation. The pattern of urbanization in which large manufacturing and commercial cities were complemented by a network of very small commercial and service centers is the spatial expression of this pattern of economic development.

The contrast with Britain is that there the distributive services did not attain the same structural importance for the economy; the chains of small-scale marketing and distribution activities were largely located outside the national boundaries. For most of the modern period, there was a division in Britain between large-scale commerce and finance, oriented to the external market and concentrated in London, and local commerce and distribution, catering mainly to a low-income market. Berry (1967, p. 90) contrasted the ratio of stores, including service establishments, to the population in Britain, the United States, and Canada; though the ratio is the same for all three (1:74 people), stores in Britain concentrate in providing necessities and their average size is smaller. The internal market in Britain was, under these conditions, a weak source of innovation in production, and the early concentration of population in large urban-industrial centers expresses this pattern of economic development.

Our historical discussion can be linked to more formal theorizing about spatial organization by considering central-place theory and its relationship to the rank-size rule of urban size distribution (Berry, 1967, pp. 35-77). When the sizes of urban places in a given region can be ranked so that the sizes of smaller places bear a standard exponential relationship to the size of the largest place, then this urban distribution is said to be log-normal. A log-normal distribution contrasts with the primate city pattern, in which a large city predominates and other centers are small and economically insignificant (Jefferson, 1939). A log-normal distribution is evidence that urban places in a region or country are integrated economically, forming a system of economic specialization and exchange. Central-place processes suggest that intense economic exchanges generate a systematic size hierarchy so that, for example, additions of population at lower-order centers generate demands for goods and services from higher-order centers and lead to population expansion in higher-order centers. This is the process described by Rothstein as taking place in the West and Midwest of the United States. Conversely, a primate city pattern implies that there is little economic interdependence among urban places and that the growth of one center does not necessarily generate growth in the system. The primate city pattern applies to urbanization in the South of the United States until World War II and to urbanization in many Latin American countries.

The metropolitan region is the ultimate expression of the

central-place form of integration, and metropolitan areas in the United States tend to fit the log-normal distribution. The metropolitan center provides the most specialized goods and services for a large territory and organizes, commercially and financially, the various forms of production found within that region. Centers such as Chicago and Detroit organize industrial and agricultural production in their regions, providing mass media and other specialized services. It is beyond the scope of this discussion to detail metropolitan organization in the modern period; the analysis of this organization has become a highly sophisticated branch of modern ecology (Duncan and others, 1961a). The point I wish to make is that the contemporary metropolitan region acquires some of its characteristics as a generative center of economic development from a particular historical pattern of urbanization in the United States and that this pattern has been infrequently replicated elsewhere in the world.

Urbanization and Underdevelopment

In examining the pattern of urbanization that accompanies underdevelopment, the contrast to keep in mind is that between the type of core-periphery relationship present in the homestead model of urbanization and that present in the plantation model. Under the homestead form of core-periphery organization, peripheral regions and peripheral people, for example, farmers in the Midwest in the nineteenth century, may still be economically exploited as income concentrates at the core, but opportunities exist at the periphery for standards of life to be raised through local economic and political organization. In the plantation model of urbanization, core-periphery relationships are such as to reduce the possibilities of independent economic and political organization at the periphery. Also, the core-periphery relationship is likely to change when the core is an economically dynamic metropolitan society, like the United States, and not a relatively stagnant industrial power, such as Britain.

Many regions of the world had urban civilizations before coming into economic and political contact with Europe and the United States. Yet contemporary patterns of urbanization in many underdeveloped countries are direct consequences of their involvement in the modern period with the advanced capitalist nations. Nations became peripheries in the sense that their economies were organized to serve the needs of capitalist expansion. Up until the nineteenth century, the degree of articulation was relatively weak; in Latin America, for example, there were few products other than precious metals that were demanded on the European market (Cardoso, 1975). Even this relatively weak articulation meant, however, a drastic reorganization of social and economic structures. In Latin America villages were relocated and reorganized to provide labor for mines and for large landed estates, and indigenous economies were disrupted by the forced sale of European products. With the Industrial Revolution, the articulation of developed and undeveloped countries became much stronger. In Latin America, exchanges were diversified and increased as local products acquired value in the European market as a consequence of the Industrial Revolution and urbanization. Examples of these products are cotton, sugar, rubber, cacao, agricultural foodstuffs, and non-precious metals such as copper. Other regions of the world, such as Africa and parts of Asia, were incorporated through imperialism into the European economy (Wallerstein, 1974b).

The pattern of urbanization in underdeveloped regions became part of this territorial division of labor. The bulk of the population were peasant farmers dispersed in small farms, villages, or plantations, while a few large cities arose as places of residence for local elites and as places to organize and control production for export. In Southeast Asia, the typical city became the port city in which urban ecology reflected the dimensions of colonial domination (McGee, 1967). Thus, the European commercial and administrative elites lived in distinct areas, usually those that afforded some protection from the climate and its health hazards. Other ethnically distinct areas developed to cater to foreign commercial groups such as the Chinese; remnants of the precolonial structure might persist around the temples and palaces of local rulers. The bulk of the native population lived on the outskirts of the city or in occupational communities, such as those of fishermen near river and dock areas.

The predominant pattern of urbanization was that of the plantation model. Despite the increasing volume of the export trade, a flourishing network of small- and intermediate-size urban places did not develop. Wealth was concentrated in a few urban centers, creating a luxury market for European manufactured imports, while the bulk of the population remained at subsistence levels of living. In this period the primate city phenomenon developed and became marked in Latin America and other areas (Browning, 1958). The ecology of these primate cities resembled that of the preindustrial city in some respects; the elites concentrated near the central area and centers of power, and the city was often organized into neighborhoods with distinctive identities and distinctive occupational bases (Sjoberg, 1960; Schnore, 1965a). This urban organization was the product of the economic relationship with Europe; in consumption patterns and cultural influences, these cities were oriented to Europe.

This pattern of urbanization corresponded to the British phase of economic dominance. Until the 1880s Britain was the dominant industrial power in the world, and it was the major source of capital investment for other countries until the early twentieth century (Thomas, 1973). The predominant orientation of British capital to underdeveloped areas was selling basic manufactures and stimulating the local production of primary products. British capital investments were designed to facilitate such primary production through the building of railroads and the financing of large-scale farming and mining operations. At times, the maintenance and expansion of these forms of exchange required the suppression of local manufactures, as occurred in India in the early nineteenth century (Hobsbawn, 1968, p. 33).

This core-periphery relationship engendered increasing tensions. Britain became unable to exchange industrial products for primary products with the industrializing nations, such as the United States and Germany (Thomas, 1973, pp. 121-122). Even the less industrial nations found that this pattern of exchange made their economies too dependent on the core countries. Thus, Argentina, Britain's "natural" trading partner, began to have increasing doubts in the 1920s about the equity of an exchange relationship that at times left Argentine wheat and beef without a market. The feeling by primary producing countries that the exchange of primary products for industrial ones was unequal was a major factor in nationalist and anticolonialist policies to protect the domestic market from foreign imports and to stimulate local industrialization.

This rebellion of the periphery against the core has been a major factor in Britain's economic decline; it has meant that in some underdeveloped countries a relatively independent process of urban industrialization has taken place for a limited period. In the early twentieth century there were several examples in Latin America of a process of urban industrialization based on local capital accumulation, notably Monterrey in Mexico, Medellin in Colombia, and São Paulo in Brazil. The growth of Medellin is, in part, an example of the homestead model of urbanization with capital accumulation based on flourishing intermediary activities and small-scale coffee farming (McGreevey, 1971). In Monterrey, distance from the capital city, mineral resources, and a strategic location near the North American market created the basis for an early industrialization (Balan, Browning, and Jelin, 1973). In São Paulo, the profits from coffee exports were enticed into industrial investment by the presence of cheap immigrant labor from Europe (Dean, 1969). In most underdeveloped countries, however, capital was unwilling to invest in industry in the absence of a developed internal market, with governmental instability, and in face of relative labor scarcity. This scarcity was relative partly because labor remained tied to traditional forms of agricultural exploitation in peasant villages and in large, semifeudal landholdings.

The possibilities of an independent urban industrialization in underdeveloped countries were soon foreclosed by the development of a new type of core-periphery relationship at the international level. This relationship was based on the technological superiority of the core countries. The sale of basic industrial products by core to periphery was replaced by investments in industry in underdeveloped countries, some through the collection of royalties on patents for advanced technological processes and others through exports of machinery and sophisticated consumer durables. The major core country is the United States. The expansion of the American economy overseas became evident after 1919, when private, long-term United States investment abroad exceeded for the first time foreign investment in the United States. This expansion stimulated a new pattern of urbanization in underdeveloped countries, which was based on industrialization. The association between U.S. domination of the world economy and the rapid urbanization of underdeveloped countries is suggested by data on decennial urbanization rates since 1920 (Table 2). This rapid urbanization was not simply the product of American economic intervention; internal demographic, economic, and political processes were equally important. The economic and political relationships of the United States and underdeveloped countries did, however, give this urbanization a special character. The area that is most integrated into the U.S. economic system—Latin America—is also the underdeveloped region to urbanize most extensively.

Table 2. Urbanization in the World.

	1920	1930	1940	1950	1960	1970	1975
World total	14.3	16.3	18.8	21.2	25.4	28.2	29.7
More-developed major areas	29.8	32.8	36.7	39.9	45.6	49.9	52.1
Europe	34.7	37.2	39.5	40.7	44.2	47.1	48.2
Northern America	41.4	46.5	46.2	50.8	58.0	62.6	65.4
Soviet Union	10.3	13.4	24.1	27.8	36.4	42.7	46.4
Oceania	36.5	38.0	40.9	45.7	52.9	57.9	57.1
Less-developed major areas	6.9	8.4	10.4	13.2	17.3	20.4	22.2
East Asia	7.2	9.1	11.6	13.8	18.5	21.7	23.7
South Asia	5.7	6.5	8.3	11.1	13.7	16.0	17.4
Latin America	14.4	16.8	19.6	25.1	32.8	37.8	40.5
Africa	4.8	5.9	7.2	9.7	13.4	16.5	18.1
More-developed regions[a]	29.4	32.6	37.0	40.0	46.0	50.5	52.8
Less-developed regions[b]	5.8	7.0	8.6	11.4	15.4	18.5	20.3

Note: Figures represent the percentage of the total population living in cities with populations of at least 20,000.

[a]Europe, northern America, Soviet Union, Japan, temperate South America, Australia, and New Zealand.

[b]East Asia without Japan, South Asia, Latin America without temperate South America, Africa, and Oceania without Australia and New Zealand.

Source: Frisbie, 1977, table 4 (based on United Nations, 1969, table 31).

From approximately the 1940s, the United States became the dominant trading partner in Latin America, replacing the previously predominant European powers (United Nations, 1964, table 159). The U.S. economic influence varied between countries and was greater in Mexico and Brazil than in countries such as Argentina, Uruguay, and Chile, which had most come under European influence. The U.S. investment in Latin America was considerable in this period; in the 1940s Latin America was the major location for U.S. direct private investment abroad (U.S. Bureau of the Census, 1975c, p. 870). Indeed, during the 1950s, this direct private investment in Latin America was greater than U.S. direct private investments in Europe and in all other countries of the world (except Canada) combined. It was not until 1962 that investments in western Europe exceeded investment in Latin America. The U.S. investment in Latin American manufacturing surpassed investment in agriculture by 1950 and by 1960 was approximately three times as great as investment in agriculture.

The salient feature of contemporary patterns of urbanization in Latin America is the concentration of production in
capital-intensive industries whose major markets are the high-
income populations present in a few large cities. This type of
industrial production employs relatively few workers and contributes to urban income concentration. High rates of natural
increase, which are in part due to modern techniques of health
care, relative land shortages, and the switch of the economic
dynamic from agriculture to industry, have led to massive rural-
urban migrations in the contemporary period. Rapid urban
growth has been concentrated in a few large cities, which on the
average have grown more rapidly than the smaller urban centers
(Frisbie, 1977). It is also important to note that rural-urban
migration is often not the major component in rapid urban
growth (Davis, 1972b). High urban rates of natural increase in
Latin American countries are themselves sufficient to double
the size of urban populations in a period of between twenty-five
and thirty years; when the city's population has reached that of
Mexico City—12,500,000 in 1976—even natural increase poses
severe problems to urban planners.

The combination of rapid urban growth and capital-intensive industrialization has resulted in what have been described as
dualistic urban structures. Urban economies have employment
profiles in which a large section of labor is employed outside
the modern sector of the economy in a wide variety of jobs in
workshop production, petty trading, and personal services. Residential patterns show marked contrast between luxury housing
for upper-income groups located near the city center or in
newly developing suburbs and a variety of low-cost housing for
low-income groups dispersed throughout the city. Shanty towns
and high-cost housing are often juxtaposed. Likewise, ultra-
modern infrastructure such as superhighways or elaborate street
lighting are found in cities whose densely populated peripheries
have no paved roads, public lighting, or sanitation services.

The mistake is to think of this dualistic pattern of urban
development as transitional to a more balanced form; contemporary urban dualism in underdeveloped countries is the product of the present phase of development of the world capitalist
economy. Capital-intensive industrialization in underdeveloped
countries creates the market needed by the advanced technologies of the developed world; at the same time, capital-intensive
industrialization is made feasible by a high degree of income
concentration and by the exclusion of the mass of the rural and

urban population in underdeveloped countries from direct participation in the benefits of modern economic development. The marginal populations of cities in the underdeveloped world provide the cheap labor in services, in construction, and in some manufacturing processes that increases the profitability of capital-intensive enterprises. At times, even the cost of labor in the capital-intensive sector is indirectly subsidized by practices such as that of workers building their own homes in squatter settlements (Oliveira, 1972).

Capital-intensive industrialization has been a major factor in producing state intervention in the economies of underdeveloped countries. Compared with the role of the state in the advanced capitalist countries at their time of urban industrialization, the state in underdeveloped countries is a more important agent of economic development. Soares (1976) reviewed a set of data from different historical periods for both developed and underdeveloped countries to show that in underdeveloped countries the state invests more in the economy and less in social services than did, historically, the state in developed countries. Faced with a situation of scarce capital, the state in many underdeveloped countries seeks to increase its capital by investment in the high-productivity, capital-intensive forms of industrialization. Often it is only the state that has sufficient resources to make the necessary investments in both urban infrastructure and in technological processes.

The type of core-periphery relationship embodied in current patterns of urbanization in underdeveloped countries contains significant tensions. Some of these appear in forms of nationalism, as governments in underdeveloped countries seek to restrict ownership and control of national industries. These forms of nationalism are often accompanied, as in the case of the current Peruvian military regime, by collaboration with foreign enterprises in the development of new resources. The technology required to exploit productively oil resources or mineral deposits, or to set up heavy industry is obtained through such collaboration. Dependence on foreign technology and the desire to keep up with its advances reduce the capacity of both government and individual entrepreneurs to innovate technologically and weaken the chance for self-sustaining economic development.

The slow rate of economic progress accompanying urbanization in underdeveloped countries is apparent in the continuing increase in the inequality of income distribution between social classes in both urban and rural areas (Adelman and Morris, 1973). In some underdeveloped countries that are relatively highly urbanized and industrialized, such as Brazil, it is probable that the income of the poorest sector of the urban population has declined in real terms. The consequent social and political tensions are further factors in current core-periphery relationships.

Concluding Remarks

The argument concerning the nature of core-periphery relationships at the international level can also be applied to the relationship between regions within the same country. Regional political discontent has become the counterpart, in certain areas of Europe, to the nationalistic, antiimperialistic position of many underdeveloped countries. Such developments indicate the essentially political nature of successful regional or national development.

Even in the United States, the equalizing of regional incomes in the recent period must be examined in political terms. Though the American patterns of urbanization were uniquely generative of economic development, there were marked regional imbalances in income, in urbanization, and in employment in manufacturing in 1920 and substantial differences in 1960 (Lampard, 1968, table 11). There is no reason to suppose that these regional inequalities would have been corrected to the extent that they have been without state intervention in dispersing the advantages of technological innovation. This intervention was the product of political action by deprived regions. The issue, however, remains why state intervention was so successful in the United States in correcting regional imbalances; in Britain, for example, despite determined efforts by government to correct them, regional imbalances persist.

In this survey of urbanization in the capitalist world, I have used the concept of interdependent development to show that developments in one part of an interconnected system necessarily condition the possibilities of change in other parts. In this sense, there is no normal pattern of urbanization by which urbanization in underdeveloped countries can be assessed. The pattern of urbanization most closely associated with rapid economic development—that of the United States—is the product of exceptional historical circumstances.

Moreover, the interdependency of core and periphery im-

plies that the organization of the core is affected by and becomes dependent on the relationship with the periphery. We
have already noted the negative consequences of this for Britain's economic development. A similar analysis needs to be
applied to current patterns of development in the United States.
Quijano (1973), for example, has commented on the tendency
of American industry to locate its more labor-intensive production in underdeveloped countries; he points out that this is likely, in the long term, to reduce employment opportunities in the
United States. The development of the American economy on
dualistic lines means an increasing contrast between high-
income employment in technologically advanced production
and associated services and an increasing pool of unemployed
urban labor. The urban spatial expression of this contrasts the
difference between the inner-city ghettoes and the middle class
suburbs.

Conclusion: Life in Urbanized America

David Street

The United States enters the final decades of the twentieth century fully urbanized in the sense that all but the most remote pockets of countryside and intentionally isolated populations are daily incorporated into ecological exchanges with one or more metropolitan areas. Contemporary patterns of living reflect the workings of complex and often contradictory processes of social change as the society has entered a diffuse stage of urbanization involving massive deconcentration—recently expressed in spurts of population growth in nonmetropolitan areas. This chapter will attempt to address these processes and their important results, both concrete and problematic. I will selectively utilize a variety of conclusions and concepts presented within this volume but will not attempt the nearly impossible task of providing a systematic summary of the rich array of materials that has been presented.

The chapter restricts itself to the United States, first, because the overwhelming proportion of the materials in the book have been American, and second, because, as Roberts argues (Chapter Nineteen), urbanization in other nations may take a different form or at any given point in time may express a different phase. More than is desirable, this chapter and the volume concentrate on the older, established cities of the northeastern part of the country, for there is where the bulk of research has been done. This chapter, like most of the volume, also focuses not on all aspects of life in America but only on those that have an urban element. In a highly urbanized society, the distinction between urban and rural (or urban and folk) loses much of its meaning, and urban becomes a general analytic construct pertaining to social organization as it has a territorial base and to processes of differentiation and integration as they affect this organization.

The Urbanized Society

Significant trends analyzed throughout this volume include the massive deconcentration of populations throughout metropolitan areas across the land; the dramatic suburbanization of population and industry in the older metropolitan areas of what Suttles (Chapter Seventeen) calls the "urban heartland"; a related reduction in the advantage of the heartland region over the rest of the nation; and a great rise in the proportion of city dwellers who are members of minority groups. The results of such trends are extremely complex, reflecting twin patterns of integration and differentiation. The changes wrought by urbanization are complicated as well by changes in the size and scale of government, business, and other organizations and by patterns of bureaucratization and professionalization.

Mass Society and the Local Community. The urbanization of America shows a spread of a mass suburban culture, as seen in the nationwide similarities of subdivision developments, the uniformity of freeway construction and patterns of community growth around freeway exits, the blurring distinction between small town and suburb within the metropolitan area, and the ubiquitous blighting of the older suburban highway strips by franchises serving the same menus from California to Maine. The feeling that "anyplace becomes everyplace" (Boorstin, 1973, p. 273) is reinforced by the omnipresence of network television, which in Hirsch's view (Chapter Thirteen) serves a strong nationalizing function, and by the content of this medium, especially its advertising. Yet to say that there are elements of a mass culture of suburbanism is by no means to assert that there develops a mass society, as conceived by Kornhauser (1959), in which the population is atomized, attention is focused on remote events, and the mass is ready for mobilization by inaccessible elites. Traditional social bonds and associations continue to have great power, as, for example, when institutionalized family and sex roles resist change in the face of a major increase in the number of women in the labor force (Harkess, Chapter Six). Parallel patterns are seen in the continued strength of ethnicity despite an apparently long-term decline (Kronus, Chapter Seven) and the continued vitality of religious organizations (Johnson, Chapter Eight).

In addition, local communities continue to have great significance. While there is an apparent decline in the use of local services, there does not seem to be a reduction in local social bonds or community satisfaction, sentiment, or participation. Indeed the activities of local voluntary associations in the political system may be increasing in importance (Janowitz and Street, Chapter Four). Wirth's (1938) classic essay "Urbanism as a Way of Life" has been so provocative of study precisely because it was so overstated; subsequently, no modal tendency toward a city life-style high on cosmopolitanism and impersonality and low on attachments to community and kin has been found. Further, the strength of the local community is seen recurrently as it shapes the patterns of large-scale bureaucratic and professional organizations. In urban school systems, local variations intrude into standardization (Bossert, Chapter Ten). In welfare systems, localism contributes to confusion and to the fragmentation of efforts (Pearce and Street, Chapter Eleven). The metropolitan press, however imperfectly, still serves a localizing influence (Street and Street, Chapter Fourteen). In metropolitan politics, grass roots efforts still seem to have great potential (Street and Davidson, Chapter Fifteen), and in metropolitan planning, traditional local political structures continue to intrude, following traditions of corruption (Gottdiener, Chapter Sixteen). Indeed, historical study seems to indicate that even the rural village may never have really had a golden age of local autonomy (Richards, Chapter Eighteen), further undercutting the hypothesis of the dramatic decline of the importance of the local community.

Altogether, the findings suggest that for understanding an urbanized America, the mass society model of Kornhauser might better be replaced with that of Shils (1962), which stresses the progressive incorporation of diverse elements into the center of the society. Hunter (Chapter Five) properly argues that if this substitution is made, the mass society can be seen as *facilitating* the expression of local community sentiments.

Differentiation. Community life in the nation reflects great differentiating trends as well as movements to cultural and political integration. The urbanization of virtually the whole society does not involve a concomitant reduction in the importance of physical location; indeed, it reflects the continued and even heightened salience of location and results in highly segregated if complicated patterns of land use throughout metropolitan areas. By permitting a great spreading out and freedom of movement, the diffuse phase of urbanization also creates the conditions for increments in differentiation in life-styles, since life-style groupings can reside in separate communities.

Differentiation is far more complicated than either the older distinction of urban-rural or the contemporary distinction of city-suburb suggests. One display of some of the variations in community life, largely confined to the city, was presented by Suttles (1975, pp. 265-276). He pointed to contrasts found when comparing the research literature on seven types of local community: the ethnic center, the black ghetto, the working-class neighborhood, the gold coast, the exclusive suburb, the cosmopolitan center, and the suburban development. Variations are seen in patterns of participation in voluntary, occupational, ethnic or racial, political, and religious organizations; in informal associations; in family relations; in relations with the wider community; and in other aspects of life. Such variations are related to but not explained by variations among residents in ethnicity, race, socioeconomic status, and life cycle. As indicated by Kornblum and Williams (Chapter Three), the pursuit of leisure becomes a further and important base of community differentiation in life-styles. The result becomes an often changing mosaic of patterns of living that defies any straightforward description in terms of such dichotomies as folk-urban, gemeinschaft-gesellschaft, or traditionalism-modernism, and the objects of our empirical study must often be the outcomes of the tensions between such polarities.

Problems of Community Life-Styles

To say that in the urbanized society location is a crucial factor and that local community organization is pervasive and important is not to propose that local organization is strong or clearly defined. In order to understand modern urban life, it has been necessary to break out of the classical conception of community as all-encompassing, an effort facilitated greatly by Janowitz's (1967) notion of the "community of limited liability." Under this concept, the degree of local attachment is problematic, as is the ease with which residents can move if their attachments become too low. Yet in a society in which suburbanization and differentiation now permit a search by many residents for communities expressing particular life-styles, the Janowitz concept becomes insufficient in that it does not explicitly address the problems of the social definition of community. At the present time, local communities gain strength insofar as they can be constructed as enhancing a given valued life-style, and commitments to life-styles are reinforced as viable community organizations can seem able to defend or enhance them. Thus in considering the problems of community life-styles, we shall add to the Janowitz concept the notion of the "social construction of communities" (Suttles, 1972), in which the character of community is also problematic and in which the construction of community images is critical.

Suburbanism as a Way of Life. The most prominent life-style in the highly urbanized society is suburbanism, pursued successfully by millions as cities have offered the push and suburbia the pull. The suburban life-style can be described adequately only by invoking both the positive and the negative images that accompany it: on the one hand, the ranch house, the yard, the good schools, the respectable neighbors; on the other, the "little boxes on the hillside," the preponderance of middle class whites, the flight from collective problems. Suburbanism as a way of life is partially a myth, since suburbia is more heterogeneous economically than is popularly believed (Berger, 1971) and since distinctions between familistic and urban styles of household life exist across the boundaries between city and suburbs (Greer, 1962a). Yet the realization of the suburban myth has been extremely profitable in the most literal sense as the massive spread of suburban housing construction has produced a continued dramatic rise in housing values.

The suburban life-style is haunted by its own success. The

economic pressures of suburbanization have made the protection of the true exurbia, where one can still live in the country, extremely costly. The exurban ideal now often requires a second home, and increasingly the "wilderness" is enjoyed from the balcony of a luxury condominium. Unconventional lifestyles intrude in suburbia and beyond as many towns become college towns. The costs of building a new urban infrastructure of utilities, roads, and schools, together with inflated housing prices, press even upper-middle class family incomes greatly. Increasingly, such families find it necessary to give up some aspects of the suburban ideal by sending wives back to work while the children are still young; job opportunities are limited because the families are landlocked in suburbia. The suburbanization of jobs, detailed in Kasarda's Chapter Two, provides a partial solution. However, it also requires the development of industrial and commercial facilities and transportation corridors and provokes persons to move in who were heretofore distant—working class people, blacks, and homosexuals—further threatening the suburban ideal. Inevitably, Schwartz (1976, p. 338) suggested, suburbia will generate an ambivalent negativism that will fade only if there is a "sustained deconcentration of the productive and destructive forces of the city," an unlikely prospect at present. Alternatively stated, in the event of a continued great deconcentration of resources, the city might ultimately become the periphery and suburbia in some sense the center. In this scenario, however, the bucolic myth of suburbia, particularly the defensive component viewing the residence as a retreat, could hardly be sustained.

The continued spread and change of the suburban landscape, then, involve a continued threat to and defense of the suburban myth and an uneven process of sustaining and changing community life-style definitions. The most well-defended suburban enclaves (for example, the Grosse Pointes of Detroit) successfully preserve an elegant style of life. For others, community defense involves a continuing necessity to reconcile the imagery of suburbanism as a way of life with unpleasant realities, such as the intrusion of new highways and industrial plants or fiscal crises in the schools caused by residents voting down bond issues. Quite "unsuburban" patterns of suburban life can occur in the interstices between settled communities and new subdivisions, and the development of multiunit condominiums and rental projects facilitates the entry of singles, even "swinging" ones, into the suburban scene. A continuing strain in much of suburbia derives from the aging of both residents and communities, which causes a reduction in the school-age population, a concomitant loss of state aid, and the embarrassment of modern but empty schools. Yet it is precisely in such aging communities that—given the findings of Kasarda and Janowitz (1974) that length of residence is correlated with community attachment and participation—the residents may best be able to defend their communities in the long run.

Inner-City Life-Styles. Suburban life features a strong component of voluntarism, a choice to go to a "better" community. Sizable proportions of central-city dwellers express such a choice, too, as they select residence from the variety of neighborhoods and developments that appeal to affluent young professionals, intellectuals, students, the recently divorced, upper class consumers of high culture and gourmet food, and swingers, gays, bisexuals, and the like. Such groupings often celebrate their decision to remain in the city, some seeing their residence as an affirmation of universal and fraternal values, and in almost all cities, and especially in New York, Boston, Chicago, and San Francisco, they are collectively able to sustain a quite cosmopolitan life.

But for most city dwellers, the freedom of choice of community life-style may be severely constrained, particularly for minority group members and for poor whites (especially the elderly) reacting to the barriers of racial and income segregation and to their own beliefs about such barriers. The least choice exists for those residents in black or Spanish-speaking ghettoes, although as Janowitz and Street (Chapter Four) have suggested, within such ghettoes there may develop substantial community institutions and sizable differentiation by residential location. Voluntarism is also low for those, regardless of race or ethnicity, whose poverty or personal deficiencies rule out escape from the neighborhoods into which welfare hotels, detoxification centers, and buildings full of ex-mental patients are concentrated or in which a vice industry serving the entire metropolitan area is blatantly visible. Intermediate between the ghetto model and the freedom of choice of the affluent are neighborhoods whose populations are on the one hand contained to some extent by income limitations but on the other are attracted by local ties, primarily the ethnic center and working-class neighborhoods. Efforts at community organization might reasonably see the latter neighborhoods, bereft of their present white racism, as models for institution building. Indeed, with minority groups becoming the majority population in cities, this institution building would sensibly incorporate elements of racial and ethnic pride.

I shall not catalogue the great variety of urban life-styles beyond what I have already listed. Suffice it to say that the cities offer an incredible array of life-styles, including esoteric and deviant ones, and that even in the most impoverished neighborhoods of the cities, rich associational and life-style patterns emerge around kin and relations, friendships, churches, and bars and clubs of all kinds, and that these have survived despite urban decay and turmoil. Yet, except for the affluent urban types who can find their own protected locales, the processes of suburbanization further threaten the maintenance (and where appropriate, rebuilding) of community life and the credibility of urban life-styles in the inner cities. First, both white and minority residents, business people, professionals, and others who live or work in integrated neighborhoods suffer from the withdrawal of mortgage money, other capital, and supporting facilities and services as residential areas continue to experience racial turnover because blacks continue to be contained within the central city. Second, the issue becomes one of maintaining a minimal economic base that is required to sustain community participation and organization, felt the more deeply as blue collar jobs move to suburbia while transportation problems for inner-city residents loom ever larger (Kasarda, Chapter Two). Third, the important symbolic side of the problem comes from the fact that inner-city residents are also exposed and socialized to the myth of suburbia as the good life, particularly as it is purveyed in the mass media. This exposure continuously undermines inner-city efforts to develop self-respect and participation, given the absence of signs that there is some urban progress rather than unremitting urban decay. Further withdrawal of capital and the suburbanization of jobs compound the damage.

Thus, community life-style patterns are widely differentiated and their futures are unstable in large parts of both the central cities and the suburban rings. Self-respect as an outcome and component of residence is problematic in both center and periphery. Further deconcentration across metropolitan areas threatens the credibility of suburbanism as a way of life and simultaneously undercuts the nourishment of community organization necessary to sustain and enhance life-styles in the city.

Cosmopolitanism. We can ask about the effects of the

spread of urbanization across the entire society upon the cosmopolitan life-style, long identified as a crucial by-product of the growth of cities and a prerequisite to scientific and other progress (Weber, 1961; Mumford, 1968). Does urbanization bring the residents of remote areas more genuinely into a cosmopolitan network? Does the dispersion of intellectuals and specialists from the central city prevent the assembling of the critical mass of cosmopolitans necessary for creativity? Our answers must be partial and speculative.

First, we have already spoken of the role of selected central-city persons in maintaining cosmopolitan life. As a by-product of their affluence and connections, museums, symphonies, and other repositories of high culture can be kept alive even where the base for mass or middle class participation has eroded. Second, the incorporation of rural areas into the metropolitan core, together with the spread of the mass media, especially television, have no doubt drastically reduced the amount of "hard core" parochialism everywhere. Relevant here is the notion that by the time children enter first grade, television has already substituted for the public school in introducing the world outside the immediate environment. Hard core parochialism probably persists much more in the city than in outlying areas, lodged principally in inner-city ethnic centers and other neighborhoods where English is not spoken in the home, and especially in closely tied communities of the "urban village" type (Gans, 1962b).

Third, the movement to suburbia of professionals, the slow but continued pressure to develop cultural institutions there, the suburban emphasis on good educational systems, and the growth of decentralized systems of higher education seem likely to make cosmopolitan culture and contacts available in most of the broad stretches of the metropolitan landscape. Still, there are great lags in cultural development, wide interstices between cultural centers, and great isolation of suburban youths of predriving age, and so it seems probable that many suburbanites come of age educated but parochial. On suburban Long Island, for example, we observed that many middle class college students had been to the Caribbean and California, and some to Europe, but few had had more than token contact with either the objects of high culture or the persons of low status and often foreign origins residing in New York City—unless the latter were relatives. Finally, the failure of city school systems to retain and motivate youths to advance their education indicates a failure at socialization to cosmopolitanism as well, one shown most dramatically as youths fail to appreciate the realities of a metropolitan opportunity structure in which jobs increasingly require travel to the downtown business district or the distant suburbs. Efforts at political and other reforms that have stressed the self-contained nature of inner-city life can reinforce parochialism by preventing an understanding of the realities of metropolitan life within which key public decisions will be reached.

Finally, we simply cannot answer the question of whether suburbanization undercuts a critical mass of face-to-face contacts that are crucial to cosmopolitan life. It seems likely that the high mobility and communication that are part and parcel of the modern world permit adequate cosmopolitan contact within professional groups and among members of specific bureaucratic organizations. Thus the physicists of Stanford, Ann Arbor, and Cambridge are in healthy contact across the nation, as are the General Electric officials of Schenectady, New York, and California. More problematic is the question of whether suburbanization sufficiently diminishes contacts among differentiated elite groups to diminish the quality of common cultural life. Certainly suburbanization seems to play such a role for differentiated elites in connection with the common political life.

The Metropolitan Polity

The urbanization of American society has involved the reduction of inequities across the entire nation while it has featured an increase in inequities within most metropolitan areas, especially those of the urban heartland. Deconcentration enlarges the advantages of the suburban rings over the center: The cities lose population relatively and sometimes absolutely; city populations become poorer and more dependent; the city tax bases erode as industry, commerce, and jobs move to suburbia; these movements create transportation problems for inner-city residents; and the cities continue to bear the costs of providing both daytime cultural and commercial amenities and nighttime facilities for entertainment and vice for their suburban visitors. Ironically, the central business districts often thrive as their new office installations provide employment for white collar workers who are increasingly suburbanites, while for blue collar workers the mismatch of residence to employment is reversed. (For a treatment of many of the points of this paragraph, see

Kasarda, Chapter Two.) Employment problems for inner-city residents are exacerbated as U.S. corporations use inexpensive labor in foreign lands (Roberts, Chapter Nineteen). Federal policies, including insurance of mortgages and investment in the freeways of suburbia, have facilitated these developments.

These patterns, of course, vary across metropolitan areas that differ in size, region, and age; but wherever they appear, they place great strains on a metropolitan polity that is fragmented by localism and by the complexity of levels and jurisdictions of public and private programs. Fragmentation is greatly exacerbated by the disarticulation of the communities of work and residence that accompanies suburbanization. Localism and the ambiguities of community membership and jurisdiction woefully disable the attempt to develop coherent welfare programs and may as a result facilitate a bifurcation of welfare programs, with the inner-city component oriented to warehousing and containment and the suburban segment devoted to counseling of individuals and providing the amenities of community life (Pearce and Street, Chapter Eleven). Simultaneously, the ambiguities of the welfare system may prevent any realistic appreciation of the situation of the central city and invite a drift to a poorly supported "reservation model" for administering the central city. Localism also complicates the administration of the educational system (Bossert, Chapter Ten), where it prevents the implementation of metropolitan-wide desegregation necessary if any real desegregation is to occur in many metropolitan areas. Efforts to create metropolitan governments largely fail, and existing metropolitan governments and other efforts at metropolitan aggregation are usually compromised by the politics of "accommodative cooperation" (Street and Davidson, Chapter Fifteen). Conceptions of professional reform seem accommodated as well to localism and existing political realities, exemplified in the ways in which theories of social planning have not halted but instead may have facilitated the pattern of suburban sprawl (Gottdiener, Chapter Sixteen).

All of these patterns, and especially the disarticulation of the communities of work and residence, undercut not only the possibilities for political aggregation but even the calculation of self-interest on the part of the individual resident of the metropolitan area. The citizen is even uncertain how to vote to serve economic self-interest as citizens groups and administrative agencies battle over such issues as the location of new freeways, school district consolidation, or the construction facilities for welfare programs. Such ambiguities both reflect and enlarge a general deterioration in the meaning of electoral choice in American society (Janowitz, in press). The weakness of the metropolitan polity undercuts the capacities not only of the cities but also of the suburbs. The result is not a city or metropolitan time bomb as existed in the cities in the 1960s. With all the fragmentation and inequities, the daily operations of the metropolitan polity show fairly reasonable intentions, cooperation, and patterns of decision making. A more appropriate metaphor is one of a vague but pervasive metabolic disorder, one that will probably never kill but may disable.

Institution Building. Despite the problems of the metropolitan political system, one can see the potentials of a variety of efforts at institution building in urbanized America. At the most local level, continual efforts at voluntary action and community building occur almost by definition if they are not undercut by ambiguity or demoralization. Cities show efforts to reattract industry and to capitalize on the success of central business district redevelopment by creating new areas attractive to middle class residents. Several of the chapters of this handbook are reassuring about the general possibilities for improvement. For example, Choldin (Chapter Twelve), analyzing social life and the physical environment, reassures us that city residents are not simply prisoners of their architecture or their densities, and Ferdinand (Chapter Nine) suggests that crime and delinquency may substantially recede after community patterns and demographic patterns stabilize. There is certainly the possibility that the rise to dominance of minority groups in certain cities will facilitate a rebuilding under new auspices.

Important to institution building in the urbanized society is the development of a new realism, involving a scaling down of aspirations so that they do not obstruct accomplishment. Suttles (Chapter Seventeen) argues that the leadership of the cities of the urban heartland has been the victim of a cultural lag, a boosterism seeking immediate "save our city" solutions. This attitude has prevented a recognition that the heartland cities are now at a competitive disadvantage with other regions, having an aging infrastructure that requires disproportionate expenditures to retain their middle classes and high-wage industry and having investment patterns that inflate property values, thereby leaving many areas fallow. Such boosterism will have to be deflated, allowing an anticipation of reasonable further dispersal of population and resources and a renewed concentration of investment in the human capital, particularly through the education system, of those persons that remain. This strategy would seek goals and programs of institution building that are between the "renaissance" that is officially proclaimed for Detroit and the "reservation" that is actually feared for that city.

At the metropolitan level, community building is found in continued efforts to aggregate political activities in and beyond those substantive areas in which some genuine cooperation can presently be seen, that is, metropolitan transportation and sewage and water systems. Ultimately, higher levels of cooperation and even coordination might occur as selected suburbs age and experience their own "urban problems." At all levels only an incremental model of reform is possible, for it is in the nature of urbanized society that, except during crises in communities that are most defended against urban change, people will rarely seek radical alterations or man the barricades to preserve community life. The long-term development of the metropolitan polity might be aided by an official designation of the boundaries of subcommunities, permitting pinpointed data gathering and accountability for public services that these areas receive; recognition of leaders or groups from these subareas as negotiators; adjustment of boundaries of public agencies to the new subareas; and other means to rationalize and clarify a decision-making structure so as to allow for clear-cut representation and accountability in the metropolitan polity (Suttles, 1975, pp. 276-290).

Research Potentials

The issues of community life-styles, of the metropolitan polity, and of institution building at both the local and the metropolitan levels of course impress this author as viable research topics. I do not, however, wish to suggest that these issues preempt promising priorities in research. Almost every chapter in this volume implies a variety of important research and relatively distinctive issues for study. As the materials of this handbook attest, the specialty of urban sociology has survived a period in which "urban" almost became the equivalent of the cataloguing of "inner-city problems." Such problems reflect outcomes of urban processes but are not their equivalent. Similarly, urban sociology has survived the tendency to see urban processes largely as those that involve the esoteric and the deviant, although the maintenance of such life-styles as the terms imply can stimulate fascinating research questions for the student of contemporary urban life.

In urbanized America, "urban" becomes primarily a theoretical construct referring to the problems of those forms of social organization and attachment that operate along territorial lines. It is possible to give a short, very partial list of guidelines to the further study of urban life looking forward to 2000:

1. The further study of urban life should be pursued at least as much without Chicago as within it. Research on urban life should occur not only in cities but in such locales as Harlan, Kentucky; Riverhead, New York; Livonia, Michigan; and Lemon, South Dakota.

2. The relationship of the conceptions of urban sociology to both the most general theoretical approaches to society and to the social psychology of modern life should be understood. In connection with both of these perspectives, urban sociology suggests the continued significance of a problematic but permanently rooted territorial component of social life.

3. Urban sociology is that area of study in which there has been the greatest payoff from utilizing a catholicity of research methodologies, integrating field research, surveys, and census data. Such methodological pragmatism is fruitful and should be continued, particularly if the field data can be collected in a fashion that facilitates comparative study. The change to collect census data on a five-year cycle should be helpful to this effort.

4. If and when there is finally an energy crisis that forces great reductions in the use of the automobile, it will stand suburbanization on its head. Students of society should be forewarned.

5. For the foreseeable future, the weakness of the capacity of the metropolitan polity for handling the continued strains of suburbanization seems likely to provide continuous fodder for the gloomy diagnoses of social scientists and journalists alike. Still, changes on the national political scene could ultimately provide some political realignments that would provide incentives for new and more effective aggregations at the metropolitan level. In the highly urbanized society, the community and the nation-state become highly interdependent.

References

Abrahamson, M. "The Social Dimensions of Urbanism." *Social Forces*, 1974, *52*, 376-383.

Abu-Lughod, J. "Testing the Theory of Social Area Analysis: The Ecology of Cairo, Egypt." *American Sociological Review*, 1969, *34*, 198-212.

Abu-Lughod, and Foley, M. "The Consumer Votes by Moving." In R. Gutman and D. Popenoe (Eds.), *Neighborhood, City, and Metropolis*. New York: Random House, 1970.

Adams, B. "The Small Trade Center: Processes and Perceptions of Growth and Decline." In R. French (Ed.), *The Community*. Itasca, Ill.: Peacock, 1969.

Adams, J. T. *Provincial Society, 1690-1763*. New York: Macmillan, 1927.

Adelman, I. G., and Morris, C. T. *Economic Growth and Social Equity in Developing Countries*. Stanford, Calif.: Stanford University Press, 1973.

Adrian, C. R. "Metropology: Folklore and Field Research." *Public Administration Review*, 1961, *21*, 148-153.

643

Agnew, S. "Speech on Television News Bias" (November 14, 1969). In W. Hammel (Ed.), *The Popular Arts in America.* New York: Harcourt Brace Jovanovich, 1972.

Ahlstrom, S. E. *A Religious History of the American People.* New Haven, Conn.: Yale University Press, 1972.

Aldrich, H., and Reiss, Jr., A. J. "Continuities in the Study of Ecological Succession: Changes in the Race Composition of Neighborhoods and Their Businesses." *American Journal of Sociology,* 1976, *81,* 846-866.

Aleshire, R. "Planning and Citizen Participation: Costs, Benefits, and Approaches." *Urban Affairs Quarterly,* 1970, *5,* 369-393.

Alihan, M. *Social Ecology: A Critical Analysis.* New York: Columbia University Press, 1938.

Alinsky, S. *Reville for Radicals.* Chicago: University of Chicago Press, 1946.

Allen, D. G. "The Zuckerman Thesis and the Process of Legal Rationalization in Provincial Massachusetts." *William and Mary Quarterly,* 3rd Series, 1972, *29,* 443-468.

Allen, I. L. "Mass Communication and Social Integration." In G. Gerbner (Ed.), *Current Trends in Mass Communication.* The Hague, Netherlands: Mouton, in press.

Almond, G., and Verba, S. *The Civic Culture.* Boston: Little, Brown, 1965.

Alonso, W. "What Are New Towns For?" *Urban Studies,* 1970, *7,* 37-55.

Alston, J. P. "Selected Religious Attitudes and Beliefs of the French Population." *Journal for the Scientific Study of Religion,* 1973, *12,* 349-351.

Altshuler, A. *The City Planning Process.* Ithaca, N.Y.: Cornell University Press, 1965.

Altshuler, A. *Community Control.* New York: Pegasus, 1970.

American Public Health Association. *Planning the Home for Occupancy.* Chicago: American Public Health Association, 1950.

Anderson, M. *Family Structure in Nineteenth-Century Lancashire.* Cambridge, England: Cambridge University Press, 1971.

Anderson, N. *The Hobo.* Chicago: University of Chicago Press, 1923.

Anderson, N. *Work and Leisure.* New York: Free Press, 1961.

Anderson, N. *Man's Work and Leisure.* Leiden, Netherlands: Brill, 1974.

Anderson, T. R., and Egeland, J. A. "Spatial Aspects of Social Area Analysis." *American Sociological Review,* 1961, *26,* 392-399.

Angell, R. C. "The Moral Integration of American Cities." *American Journal of Sociology,* 1951, *57,* 1-140.

Angell, R. C. "The Moral Integration of American Cities, 2." *American Journal of Sociology,* 1974, *80,* 607-629.

Archer, J. "Effects of Population Density on Behavior in Rodents." In J. Crook (Ed.), *Social Behavior in Birds and Mammals.* New York: Academic Press, 1971.

Argyle, M., and Beit-Hallahmi, B. *The Social Psychology of Religion.* London: Routledge and Kegan Paul, 1975.

Aronson, S. "The Sociology of the Telephone." *International Journal of Comparative Sociology,* 1971, *12,* 153-167.

Automobile Manufacturers Association. *Automobile Facts and Figures.* Detroit, Mich.: Automobile Manufacturers Association, 1971.

Ayer Directory of Publications. Philadelphia, Pa.: Ayer Press, 1920.

Ayer Directory of Publications. Philadelphia, Pa.: Ayer Press, 1930.

Ayer Directory of Publications. Philadelphia, Pa.: Ayer Press, 1940.

Ayer Directory of Publications. Philadelphia, Pa.: Ayer Press, 1950.

Ayer Directory of Publications. Philadelphia, Pa.: Ayer Press, 1960.

Ayer Directory of Publications. Philadelphia, Pa.: Ayer Press, 1970.

Ayer Directory of Publications. Philadelphia, Pa.: Ayer Press, 1972.

Ayer Directory of Publications. Philadelphia, Pa.: Ayer Press, 1976.

Babchuk, N., and Booth, A. "Voluntary Association Membership: A Longitudinal Analysis." *American Sociological Review,* 1969, *34,* 31-45.

Babcock, R., and Besselman, F. *Exclusionary Zoning.* New York: Praeger, 1973.

Bachman, J. S., and others. *Youth in Transition.* Vol. 3: *Dropping Out—Problem or Symptom?* Ann Arbor: Institute for Social Research, University of Michigan, 1971.

Bagdikian, B. H. *The Information Machines.* New York: Harper & Row, 1971.

Bagdikian, B. H. "The Little Old Daily of Dubuque." *New York Times Magazine,* February 4, 1974, pp. 14-15, 30-35.

Bainbridge, J. "Little Magazine." *New Yorker,* November 17, 1945, pp. 33-42; November 24, 1945, pp. 36-47; December 1, 1945, pp. 40-51; December 8, 1945, pp. 38-59; December 15, 1945, pp. 38-40.

Baker, F., Broskowski, A., and Brandwein, R. "System Dilemmas of a Community Health and Welfare Council." *Social Science Review,* 1973, *47,* 63-80.

Balan, J., Browning, H., and Jelin, E. *Men in a Developing Society.* Austin: University of Texas Press, 1973.

Baldassare, M. "The Effects of Density on Social Behavior and Attitudes." *American Behavioral Scientist,* 1975, *18,* 815-825.

Baldassare, M., and Fischer, C. S. "The Relevance of Crowding Experiments to Urban Studies." In D. Stokols (Ed.), *Explorations in Environment and Behavior: Conceptual and Empirical Trends.* New York: Plenum, 1976.

Baldwin, J. *Nobody Knows My Name.* New York: Dell, 1961.

Baldwin, R. E. "Patterns of Development in Newly Settled Regions." *Manchester School of Social and Economic Studies,* 1956, *24,* 161-179.

Ball-Rokeach, S., and DeFleur, M. "A Dependency Model of Mass-Media Effects." *Communication Research,* 1976, *3,* 3-21.

Baltzell, E. D. *The Protestant Establishment: Aristocracy and Caste in America.* New York: Vintage Books, 1966.

Banfield, E. C. *Political Influence.* New York: Free Press, 1961.

Banfield, E. C. *The Unheavenly City Re-Visited.* Boston: Little, Brown, 1974.

Banfield, E. C., and Wilson, J. Q. *City Politics.* Cambridge, Mass.: Harvard University Press and M.I.T. Press, 1963.

Banham, R. *Los Angeles: The Architecture of Four Ecologies.* New York: Harper & Row, 1971.

Barbera, L. "The Very Young Child: Status and Social Systems." Unpublished doctoral dissertation, Northwestern University, 1977.

Barnes, H. E. *A History of the Penal, Reformatory, and Correctional Institutions of the State of New Jersey.* New York: Arno Press, 1974.

Barnett, J. *Urban Design as Public Policy.* New York: Architectural Record Books, 1974.

Bart, P. B. "Seizing the Means of Reproduction: An Illegal

Feminist Abortion Collective." Paper presented at the annual meeting of the American Sociological Association, Chicago, Ill., September 1977.

Bauer, R., and Bauer, A. "American Mass Society and Mass Media." *Journal of Social Issues,* 1960, *16,* 3-66.

Baumol, W. J., and Bowen, W. G. *Performing Arts: The Economic Dilemma.* New York: Twentieth Century Fund, 1966.

Beale, C. L. "Rural Nonmetropolitan Population Trends of Significance to National Population Policy." In S. M. Mazie (Ed.), *Population Distribution and Policy.* Vol. 5. Washington, D.C.: U.S. Commission on Population Growth and the American Future, 1972.

Beale, C. L. *The Revival of Population Growth in Nonmetropolitan America.* ERS-605. Washington, D.C.: U.S. Department of Agriculture, Economic Development Division, Economic Research Service, 1975.

Beale, C. L. "A Further Look at Nonmetropolitan Population Growth Since 1970." Paper presented at the annual meeting of the Rural Sociological Society, New York City, August 1976.

Beale, C. L., and Fuguitt, G. V. "Population Trends of Nonmetropolitan Cities and Villages in Subregions of the United States." Working Paper 75-30. Madison: Center for Demography and Ecology, University of Wisconsin, 1975a.

Beale, C. L., and Fuguitt, G. V. "Recent Nonmetropolitan Trends in the United States." Unpublished manuscript, University of Wisconsin, Madison, 1975b.

Beck, B. "Governmental Contacts with the Nonprofit Social Welfare Corporations." In B. L. R. Smith and D. C. Hague (Eds.), *The Dilemma of Accountability in Modern Government: Independence Versus Control.* New York: St. Martin's Press, 1971.

Becker, H. K. *Police Systems of Europe.* Springfield, Ill.: Thomas, 1973.

Beers, H. W. "Rural-Urban Differences: Some Evidence from Public Opinion Polls." *Rural Sociology,* 1953, *18,* 1-11.

Bell, W., and Boat, M. D. "Urban Neighborhoods and Informal Social Relations." *American Journal of Sociology,* 1957, *62,* 391-398.

Bellah, R. N. *Beyond Belief: Essays on Religion in a Post-Traditional World.* New York: Harper & Row, 1970.

Bellush, J., and Hausknecht, M. (Ed.). *Urban Renewal: People, Politics and Planning.* New York: Doubleday, 1959.

Berelson, B., Lazarsfeld, P., and McPhee, W. *Voting.* Chicago: University of Chicago Press, 1954.

Berg, I. *Education and Jobs.* New York: Praeger, 1970.

Berger, B. *Working Class Suburb.* Berkeley: University of California Press, 1960.

Berger, B. "The Myth of Suburbia." *Journal of Social Issues,* 1961, *17,* 38-49.

Berger, B. *Looking for America.* Englewood Cliffs, N.J.: Prentice-Hall, 1971.

Berger, P. L. *A Rumor of Angels: Modern Society and the Rediscovery of the Supernatural.* New York: Doubleday, 1969.

Bernard, J. *The Sociology of Community.* Glenview, Ill.: Scott, Foresman, 1973.

Bernard, J. "Note on Changing Life Styles, 1970-1974." *Journal of Marriage and the Family,* 1975, *37,* 582-593.

Berry, B. J. L. *Geography of Market Centers and Retail Distribution.* Englewood Cliffs, N.J.: Prentice-Hall, 1967.

Berry, B. J. L. *Growth Centers in the American Urban System.* Vol. 1. Cambridge, Mass.: Ballinger, 1973a.

Berry, B. J. L. *The Human Consequences of Urbanization.* London: Macmillan, 1973b.

Berry, B. J. L., and Dahmann, D. C. *Population Redistribution in the United States in the 1970s.* Washington, D.C.: Assembly of Behavioral and Social Sciences, National Research Council, National Academy of Sciences, 1977.

Berry, B. J. L., and Kasarda, J. D. *Contemporary Urban Ecology.* New York: Macmillan, 1977.

Berry, B. J. L., and Rees, P. "The Factorial Ecology of Calcutta." *American Journal of Sociology,* 1969, *74,* 445-491.

Berry, B. J. L., and others. "Attitudes Toward Integration: The Role of Status in Community Response to Racial Change." In B. Schwartz (Ed.), *The Changing Face of the Suburbs.* Chicago: University of Chicago Press, 1976a.

Berry, B. J. L., and others. *Chicago: Transformation of an Urban System.* Cambridge, Mass.: Ballinger, 1976b.

Beshers, J. *Urban Social Structure.* New York: Free Press, 1962.

Biderman, A., and others. *Historical Incidents of Extreme Overcrowding.* Washington, D.C.: Bureau of Social Science Research, 1963.

Bidwell, C. E. "The School as a Formal Organization." In J. G. March (Ed.), *Handbook of Organizations.* Chicago: Rand McNally, 1965.

Bidwell, C. E., and Kasarda, J. D. "School District Organization and Student Achievement." *American Sociological Review,* 1975, *40,* 55-70.

Billboard. "Broadcasters Defend Soap Operas Against Critics." March 23, 1940, p. 8.

Billingsley, A. *Black Families in White America.* Englewood Cliffs, N.J.: Prentice-Hall, 1968.

Bingham, R. D., and Kirkpatrick, S. A. "Providing Social Services for the Urban Poor: An Analysis of Public Housing Authorities in Large American Cities." *Social Service Review,* 1975, *49,* 64-77.

Blackwell, J. E. *The Black Community: Diversity and Unity.* New York: Dodd, Mead, 1975.

Blair, J. P., Gappert, G., and Warner, D. C. "Rethinking Urban Problems: Inequality and the Grants Economy." In G. Gappert and H. M. Rose (Eds.), *The Social Economy of Cities.* Beverly Hills, Calif.: Sage, 1975.

Blake, J. "The Changing Status of Women in Developed Countries." *Scientific American,* 1974, *231,* 91-104.

Blau, P. *The Dynamics of Bureaucracy.* Chicago: University of Chicago Press, 1955.

Blau, P. *Exchange and Power in Social Life.* New York: Wiley, 1967.

Blumenfeld, H. *The Modern Metropolis.* Cambridge, Mass.: M.I.T. Press, 1967.

Blumer, H. "Fashion." *International Encyclopedia of the Social Sciences.* New York: Macmillan, 1968.

Blumler, J., and Katz, E. (Eds.). *The Uses of Mass Communication.* Beverly Hills, Calif.: Sage, 1974.

Blumler, J., and McQuail, D. *Television and Politics.* Chicago: University of Chicago Press, 1969.

Bogart, L. *Strategy in Advertising.* New York: Harcourt Brace Jovanovich, 1967.

Bogart, L. *The Age of Television.* (3rd ed.) New York: Ungar, 1972.

Bogart, L. "As Media Change, How Will Advertising?" *Journal of Advertising Research,* 1973, *13,* 25-32.

Bogue, D. J. *The Structure of the Metropolitan Community: A Study of Dominance and Subdominance.* Ann Arbor: University of Michigan Press, 1949.

Bogue, D. J. *Population Growth in Standard Metropolitan Areas, 1900-1950.* Washington, D.C.: U.S. Government Printing Office, 1953.

Bohm, R. A., and Patterson, D. A. "Interstate Highways and the

Growth and Distribution of Population." Paper presented at the American Statistical Association, Fort Collins, Colo., 1971.

Bolan, R. "The Social Relations of the Planner." *AIP Journal*, 1971, *38*, 389-396.

Bollens, J. C., and Schmandt, H. J. *The Metropolis: Its People, Politics, and Economic Life.* (2nd ed.) New York: Harper & Row, 1970.

Boorstin, D. J. *The Image: A Guide to Pseudo-Events in America.* New York: Harper & Row, 1961.

Boorstin, D. J. *The Americans: The National Experience.* New York: Random House, 1965.

Boorstin, D. J. *The Americans: The Democratic Experience.* New York: Random House, 1973.

Booth, A. *Urban Crowding and Its Consequences.* New York: Praeger, 1976.

Booth, A., and Edwards, J. N. "Crowding and Family Relations." *American Sociological Review,* 1976, *41*, 308-321.

Booth, C. *Life and Labour of the People in London.* (2nd ed.; 9 vols.) London: Macmillan, 1882-1897.

Bordua, D. "Comments on Police-Community Relations." *Connecticut Law Review,* 1968, *1*, 306-331.

Bossard, J. *The Sociology of Child Development.* New York: Harper & Row, 1948.

Bott, E. *Family and Social Network.* New York: Barnes & Noble, 1971.

Bowen, W. G., and Finegan, T. A. *The Economics of Labor Force Participation.* Princeton, N.J.: Princeton University Press, 1969.

Bower, R. *Television and the Public.* New York: Holt, Rinehart and Winston, 1973.

Bowers, D. R. "The Impact of Centralized Printing on the Community Press." *Journalism Quarterly,* 1969, *46*, 43-46, 52.

Boyle, R. P. "The Effect of the High School on Students' Aspirations." *American Journal of Sociology,* 1966, *71*, 628-639.

Bracey, H. F. *Neighbours: Subdivision Life in England and the United States.* Baton Rouge: Louisiana State University Press, 1964.

Bradburn, N., and others. *Side by Side: Integrated Neighborhoods in America.* New York: Quadrangle, 1971.

Brazer, M. C. "Economic and Social Disparities Between Central Cities and Their Suburbs." *Land Economics,* 1967, *43*, 294-302.

Breckenfeld, G. "Downtown Has Fled to the Suburbs." *Fortune*, October 1972, pp. 80-87, 156, 158, 162.

Bressler, M., and Westoff, C. F. "Catholic Education, Economic Values, and Achievement." *American Journal of Sociology*, 1963, *69*, 225-233.

Bridenbaugh, C. *Cities in Revolt*. New York: Knopf, 1965.

Brilliant, E. L. "Private or Public: A Model of Ambiguities." *Social Service Review*, 1973, *47*, 384-396.

Broady, M. "Social Theory in Architectural Design." In R. Gutman (Ed.), *People and Buildings*. New York: Basic Books, 1972.

Brockway, Z. *Fifty Years of Prison Service*. Montclair, N.J.: Patterson Smith, 1969.

Brookfield, H. *Interdependent Development*. London: Methuen, 1975.

Brown, K. M. "Farm Tenancy and Urbanization." *Rural Sociology*, 1971, *36*, 52-55.

Brown, L. *Television: The Business Behind the Box*. New York: Harcourt Brace Jovanovich, 1971.

Browning, H. L. "Recent Trends in Latin American Urbanization." *Annals of the American Academy of Political and Social Science*, 1958, *316*, 111-120.

Browning, H. L., and Singelmann, J. "The Development of the Service Sector in Latin America: An International Historical Perspective." Mimeograph. Austin: Population Research Center, University of Texas, 1975.

Brunner, R., and Crecine, P. "The Impact of Communication Technology on Government: A Developmental Construct." Discussion Paper No. 30. Ann Arbor: Institute of Public Policy Studies, University of Michigan, 1971.

Bugelski, B. R. "Assimilation Through Intermarriage." *Social Forces*, 1961, *40*, 148-153.

Bultena, G. L. "Rural-Urban Differences in Familial Interaction." *Rural Sociology*, 1969, *34*, 5-15.

Bumpass, L. "Comment on J. Blake's 'Can We Believe Recent Data on Birth Expectations in the United States?' " *Demography*, 1975, *12*, 155-156.

Burgess, E. W. "The Growth of the City: An Introduction to a Research Project." *Proceedings of the American Sociological Society*, 1923, *18*, 85-97.

Burgess, E. W. "The Growth of the City: An Introduction to a Research Project." In R. E. Park, E. W. Burgess, and R. D. McKenzie (Eds.), *The City*. Chicago: University of Chicago Press, 1925.

Burgess, E. W. *On Community, Family, and Delinquency.* (L. S. Cottrell, A. Hunter, and J. F. Short, Eds.) Chicago: University of Chicago Press, 1972.

Burgess, E. W., and Bogue, D. J. (Eds.). *Contributions to Urban Sociology.* Chicago: University of Chicago Press, 1964.

Burgess, E. W., and Locke, H. J. *The Family: From Traditional to Companionship.* New York: American Book Company, 1945.

Bushman, R. L. *From Puritan to Yankee.* Cambridge, Mass.: Harvard University Press, 1967.

Business Week. "Ackerman Looks Beyond the Post." January 18, 1969, p. 26.

Business Week. "Cable TV Leaps into the Big Time." November 22, 1969, pp. 100-108.

Buttel, F. H., and Flinn, W. L. "Sources and Consequences of Agrarian Values in American Society." *Rural Sociology,* 1975, *40,* 134-151.

Cahn, E. S., and Cahn, J. C. "The War on Poverty: A Civilian Perspective." *Yale Law Journal,* 1964, *73,* 317-352.

Calhoun, J. B. "A Behavioral Sink." In E. L. Bliss (Ed.), *Roots of Behavior.* New York: Harper & Row, 1962a.

Calhoun, J. B. "Population Density and Social Pathology." *Scientific American,* 1962b, *216,* 139-148.

Calhoun, J. B. *The Ecology and Sociology of the Norway Rat.* Washington, D.C.: U.S. Government Printing Office, 1963.

Callahan, R. *Education and the Cult of Efficiency.* Chicago: University of Chicago Press, 1962.

Campbell, A., Converse, P. E., and Rogers, W. L. *The Quality of American Life.* New York: Russell Sage Foundation, 1976.

Campbell, A. K., and Dollenmayer, J. A. "Governance in a Metropolitan Society." In A. H. Hawley and V. P. Rock (Eds.), *Metropolitan America in Contemporary Perspective.* New York: Halsted Press, 1975.

Campbell, E. Q., and Pettigrew, T. F. "Racial and Moral Crisis: The Role of Little Rock Ministers." *American Journal of Sociology,* 1959, *64,* 509-516.

Campbell, R. "Beyond the Suburbs: The Changing Rural Scene." In A. H. Hawley and V. P. Rock (Eds.), *Metropolitan America in Contemporary Perspective.* New York: Halsted Press, 1975.

Caplovitz, D. *The Poor Pay More.* New York: Free Press, 1963.

Cardoso, F. E. "The City and Politics." In J. E. Hardoy (Ed.), *Urbanization in Latin America.* New York: Doubleday, 1975.

Carlson, R. O. *School Superintendents: Careers and Performance.* Columbus, Ohio: Merrill, 1972.

Carnahan, D., Gove, W., and Galle, O. R. "Urbanization, Population Density, and Overcrowding: Trends in the Quality of Life in Urban America." *Social Forces,* 1975, *53,* 62-72.

Caro, R. *The Power Broker.* New York: Random House, 1974.

Carroll, R. "Metropolitan Taxation and the Suburban Exploitation Hypothesis." Unpublished paper, University of Cincinnati, 1975.

Carte, G. E., and Carte, E. H. *Police Reform in the United States.* Berkeley: University of California Press, 1975.

Carter, L. J. *The Florida Experience.* Baltimore: Johns Hopkins University Press, 1975.

Carter, R. F. *Voters and Their Schools.* Cooperative Research Project No. 308. Washington, D.C.: U.S. Office of Education, Department of Health, Education, and Welfare, 1960.

Castells, M. *The Urban Question.* Cambridge, Mass.: M.I.T. Press, 1977.

Castles, S., and Kosack, G. *Immigrant Workers and Class Structures in Western Europe.* London: Oxford University Press, 1973.

Center for Community Change and the National Urban League. *National Survey of Housing Abandonment.* Washington, D.C., 1971.

Chapin, Jr., F. S. *Human Activity Patterns in the City: Things People Do in Time and in Space.* New York: Wiley, 1974.

Cheek, Jr., N. H., and Burch, Jr., W. R. *The Social Organization of Leisure in Human Society.* New York: Harper & Row, 1976.

Cheek, Jr., N. H., Field, D., and Burch, Jr., W. R. *Leisure and Recreation Places.* Ann Arbor, Mich.: Ann Arbor Science Publishers, 1976.

Cheng, C. W. "Community Participation in Teacher Collective Bargaining: Problems and Prospects." *Harvard Educational Review,* 1976, *46,* 153-174.

Chinitz, B. (Ed.). *City and Suburb: The Economics of Urban Growth.* Englewood Cliffs, N.J.: Prentice-Hall, 1964.

Choldin, H. M. "The Metro Subcommunity in Ecological Perspective." Paper presented at the Conference on The Future of Sociological Human Ecology, Seattle, Wash., 1977.

Choldin, H. M. "Population Density and Social Relations." Paper presented at the annual meeting of the Population Association of America, Toronto, 1972.

Choldin, H. M. "Housing Standards Versus Ecological Forces:

Regulating Population Density in Bombay." In A. Rapoport (Ed.), *The Mutual Interaction of People and Their Built Environment.* The Hague, Netherlands: Mouton, 1976.

Choldin, H. M., and Roncek, D. W. "Density, Population Potential and Pathology: A Block-Level Analysis." *Review of Public Data Use,* 1976, *4,* 19-30.

Chombart de Lauwe, P. "Le Logement, Le Menage, et L'espace Familial." *Informations Sociales,* October 1955, pp. 956-991.

Christenson, J. A., and Dillman, D. A. "Rural-Urban Value Patterns." Paper presented at the annual meeting of the Rural Sociological Society, College Park, Md., August 1973.

Christian, C. M. "Emerging Patterns of Industrial Activity Within Large Metropolitan Areas and Their Impact on the Central City Work Force." In G. Gappert and H. M. Rose (Eds.), *The Social Economy of Cities.* Beverly Hills, Calif.: Sage, 1975.

Cicourel, A. V., and Kitsuse, J. I. *The Educational Decision Makers.* Indianapolis: Bobbs-Merrill, 1963.

Clark, B. R. *The Open Door College.* New York: McGraw-Hill, 1960.

Clark, C. "Urban Population Densities." *Journal of the Royal Statistical Society,* Series A, 1951, *114,* 490-496.

Clark, L. "New York, Which Sees Office Jobs as Key to Future, Loses Them." *Wall Street Journal,* June 5, 1975, p. 1.

Clark, T. N. "Fiscal Strain in New York and Elsewhere—Is New York Still First?" *New York Affairs,* 1976, *3,* 18-27.

Clark, W. C. *Journalism Tomorrow.* Syracuse, N.Y.: Syracuse University Press, 1958.

Clarke, P., and Kline, F. G. "Media Effects Reconsidered: Some New Strategies for Communication Research." *Communication Research,* 1974, *1,* 224-240.

Clawson, M., and Hall, P. *Planning and Urban Growth.* Baltimore: Johns Hopkins University Press, 1973.

Clawson, M., and Knetsch, J. *Economics of Outdoor Recreation.* Baltimore: Johns Hopkins University Press, 1967.

Clena, B. *Changing Neighborhood.* Los Angeles: University of Southern California Studies, 1929.

Clinard, M. B. *Slums and Community Development: Experiments in Self-Help.* New York: Free Press, 1966.

Clinard, M. B., and Abbott, D. G. *Crime in Developing Countries: A Comparative Perspective.* New York: Wiley, 1973.

Cloward, R., and Epstein, I. "Private Social Welfare's Disengagement from the Poor: The Case of Family Adjustment Agencies." In M. Zald (Ed.), *Social Welfare Institutions.* New York: Wiley, 1965.

Coleman, J. S. "Social Cleavage and Religious Conflict." *Journal of Social Issues,* 1956, *12,* 44-56.

Coleman, J. S. *The Adolescent Society.* New York: Free Press, 1966.

Coleman, J. S. "Education and Urbanism." *Education and Urban Society,* 1968, *1,* 5-9.

Coleman, J. S., Kelly, S. D., and Moore, J. A. *Trends in School Desegregation, 1968-73.* Washington, D.C.: Urban Institute, 1975.

Coleman, J. S., and others. *Equality of Educational Opportunity.* Washington, D.C.: U.S. Government Printing Office, 1966.

Coleman, J. S., and others. *Youth: Transition to Adulthood.* Chicago: University of Chicago Press, 1974.

Collins, H. "The Sedentary Society." *Scientific Monthly,* 1954, *79,* 285-292.

Collins, R. "Functional and Conflict Theories of Educational Stratification." *American Sociological Review,* 1971, *36,* 1002-1018.

Commission on the Review of the National Policy Toward Gambling. *Gambling in America.* Washington, D.C.: U.S. Government Printing Office, 1976.

Committee for Economic Development. *Modernizing Local Government.* New York: Committee for Economic Development, 1967.

Commonweal. "Death of Two Magazines." January 18, 1957, pp. 397-398.

Congressional Budget Office. *New York City's Fiscal Problem.* Background Paper No. 1. Washington, D.C.: U.S. Government Printing Office, 1975.

Cooper, C. C. *Easter Hill Village: Some Social Implications of Design.* New York: Free Press, 1975.

Coser, R. L. "Stay Home, Little Sheba: On Placement, Displacement, and Social Change." *Social Problems,* 1975, *22,* 470-480.

Costello, A. *Our Police Protectors.* Montclair, N.J.: Patterson Smith, 1972.

Counts, G. S. *The Social Composition of Boards of Education.* Chicago: University of Chicago Press, 1927.

Cousins, N. "The Death of Look." *Saturday Review,* October 2, 1971, pp. 26-27.

Cox, H. G. "The 'New Breed' in American Churches: Sources of Social Activism in American Religion." In W. G. McLoughlin and R. N. Bellah (Eds.), *Religion in America.* Boston: Beacon Press, 1968.

Crain, R. L. *The Politics of School Desegregation.* New York: Doubleday, 1969.

Cranz, G. "Models for Park Usage: Ideology and the Development of Chicago's Public Parks." Unpublished doctoral dissertation, University of Chicago, 1971.

Crecine, J. P. *Financing the Metropolis.* Beverly Hills, Calif.: Sage, 1970.

Cremin, L. *The Transformation of the School.* New York: Vintage Books, 1964.

Cressey, D. *The Taxi Dance Hall.* Chicago: University of Chicago Press, 1932.

Cressey, P. "Population Succession in Chicago: 1898-1930." *The American Journal of Sociology,* 1938, *44,* 59-69.

Crouse, T. *The Boys on the Bus.* New York: Random House, 1973.

Curry, J. P., and Scriven, G. D. "Dwelling Type and Fertility: A Cross-Cultural Replication and Extension to Minority Groups." Paper presented at the annual meeting of the Midwest Sociological Society, St. Louis, Mo., 1976.

Curtis, J. "Voluntary Association Joining: A Cross-National Comparative Note." *American Sociological Review,* 1971, *36,* 872-880.

Cutright, P. "National Political Development." *American Sociological Review,* 1963, *28,* 250-260.

Dahl, R. *Who Governs?* New Haven, Conn.: Yale University Press, 1961.

Dalton, M. *Men Who Manage.* New York: Wiley, 1959.

Danielson, M. N. (Ed.). *Metropolitan Politics: A Reader.* (2nd ed.) Boston: Little, Brown, 1971.

Danielson, M. N. *The Politics of Exclusion.* New York: Columbia University Press, 1976.

Darian, J. C. "Convenience of Work and the Job Constraint of Children." *Demography,* 1975, *12,* 245-258.

Darian, J. C. "Factors Influencing the Rising Labor Force Participation Rates of Married Women with Preschool Children." *Social Science Quarterly,* 1976, *56,* 514-630.

Darwin, C. R. *On the Origin of Species by Means of Natural Selection, or the Preservation of Favoured Races in the Struggle for Life.* London: Murray, 1860.

Davidoff, P. "Advocacy and Pluralism in Planning." *AIP Journal,* 1965, *31,* 331-337.

Davidoff, P., and Gold, N. "Exclusionary Zoning." *Yale Review of Law and Social Action,* 1970, *1,* 58-60.

Davidson, J. L. "The Social Construction of Political Neighbor-hoods." Unpublished doctoral dissertation, University of Michigan, 1977.

Davis, K. "The Origins and Growth of Urbanization in the World." *American Journal of Sociology,* 1955, *60,* 429-437.

Davis, K. "The American Family in Relation to Demographic Change." In C. F. Westoff and R. Parke, Jr. (Eds.), *Demographic and Social Aspects of Population Growth.* Vol. 1. Washington, D.C.: U.S. Commission on Population Growth and the American Future, 1972a.

Davis, K. *World Urbanization 1950-1970.* Vol. 2. Population Monograph Series No. 9. Berkeley: University of California Press, 1972b.

Dean, S. "Guidelines for Planning a Cable Television Franchise." *Urban Telecommunications Forum Supplement,* 1973, pp. 1-8.

Dean, W. *The Industrialization of São Paulo, 1880-1945.* Latin American Monographs No. 17. Austin: Institute of Latin American Studies, University of Texas, 1969.

DeFleur, M., and Ball-Rokeach, S. *Theories of Mass Communication.* (3rd ed.) New York: McKay, 1975.

DeGrazia, S. *Of Time, Work, and Leisure.* New York: Twentieth Century Fund, 1962.

Delafons, J. *Land Use Controls in the U.S.A.* Cambridge, Mass.: M.I.T. Press, 1969.

De Tocqueville, A. *Democracy in America.* New York: Mentor Books, 1956.

Deutscher, I. *What We Say/What We Do: Sentiments and Acts.* Glenview, Ill.: Scott, Foresman, 1973.

Dewey, R. "The Rural-Urban Continuum: Real but Relatively Unimportant." *American Journal of Sociology,* 1960, *66,* 60-66.

Diesing, P. *Reason in Society.* Urbana: University of Illinois Press, 1962.

Dinnerstein, L., and Reimers, D. M. *Ethnic Americans: A History of Immigration and Assimilation.* New York: Dodd, Mead, 1975.

Djilas, M. *The New Class: An Analysis of the Communist System.* New York: Praeger, 1957.

Dobriner, W. M. *Class in Suburbia.* Englewood Cliffs, N.J.: Prentice-Hall, 1963.

Doig, J. W. *Metropolitan Transportation Politics and the New York Region.* New York: Columbia University Press, 1966.

Donahue, G., Tichenor, P., and Olien, C. "Mass Media and the Knowledge Gap: A Hypothesis Reconsidered." *Communication Research,* 1975, *2,* 3-23.

Donovan, J. C. *The Politics of Poverty.* New York: Pegasus, 1967.

Douglas, J. "Framing Reality: The Growing Power of the News." Unpublished manuscript, Department of Sociology, University of California, San Diego, 1976.

Dowd, D. F. "A Comparative Analysis of Economic Development in the American West and South." *Journal of Economic History,* 1956, *16,* 558-574.

Downie, Jr., L. *Mortgage on America.* New York: Praeger, 1974.

Downs, A. *Opening Up the Suburbs: An Urban Strategy for America.* New Haven, Conn.: Yale University Press, 1973.

Downs, R. M., and Stea, D. *Image and Environment: Cognitive Mapping and Spatial Behavior.* Chicago: Aldine, 1973.

Drake, S. C., and Cayton, H. R. *Black Metropolis: A Study of Negro Life in a Northern City.* New York: Harcourt Brace Jovanovich, 1945.

Dreeben, R. *On What Is Learned in School.* Reading, Mass.: Addison-Wesley, 1968.

Drucker, P. F. *The Age of Discontinuity: Guidelines to Our Changing Society.* New York: Harper & Row, 1969.

Dubos, R. *Man Adapting.* New Haven, Conn.: Yale University Press, 1965.

Dulles, F. R. *A History of Recreation: America Learns to Play.* (2nd ed.) New York: Irvington, 1965.

Duncan, B., and Lieberson, S. *Metropolis and Region in Transition.* Beverly Hills, Calif.: Sage, 1970.

Duncan, H. D. *Culture and Democracy: The Struggle for Form in Society and Architecture in Chicago and the Middle West During the Life and Times of Louis H. Sullivan.* Totowa, N.J.: Bedminster, 1965.

Duncan, Jr., J. S. "Landscape Tastes as a Symbol of Group Identity: A Westchester County Village." *The Geographical Review,* 1973, *63,* 334-355.

Duncan, O. D. "Human Ecology and Population Studies." In P. M. Hauser and O. D. Duncan (Eds.), *The Study of Population.* Chicago: University of Chicago Press, 1959.

Duncan, O. D. "Community Size and the Rural-Urban Continuum." In Jack Gibbs (Ed.), *Urban Research Methods.* New York: D. Van Nostrand, 1961a.

Duncan, O. D. "Note on Farm Tenancy and Urbanization." *Journal of Farm Economics*, 1961b, *38*, 1043-1047.

Duncan, O. D., and Duncan, B. "Residential Distribution and Occupational Stratification." *American Journal of Sociology*, 1955, *60*, 493-503.

Duncan, O. D., and Duncan, B. *The Negro Population of Chicago*. Chicago: University of Chicago Press, 1957.

Duncan, O. D., and Reiss, A. J. *Social Characteristics of Urban and Rural Communities, 1950*. New York: Wiley, 1956.

Duncan, O. D., Schuman, H., and Duncan, B. *Social Change in a Metropolitan Community*. New York: Russell Sage Foundation, 1973.

Duncan, O. D., and others. *Metropolis and Region*. Baltimore: Johns Hopkins University Press, 1961a.

Duncan, O. D., and others. *Statistical Geography: Problems in Analyzing Area Data*. New York: Free Press, 1961b.

Duncan, R. P., and Perrucci, C. C. "Dual Occupation Families and Migration." *American Sociological Review*, 1976, *41*, 252-261.

Durkheim, E. *On the Division of Labor in Society*. (G. Simpson, Trans.) New York: Macmillan, 1933.

Durkheim, E. *The Division of Labor in Society*. (G. Simpson, Trans.) New York: Free Press, 1947.

Durkheim, E. *The Division of Labor in Society*. New York: Free Press, 1964.

Dye, T. R., and others. "Differentiation and Cooperation in a Metropolitan Area." *Midwest Journal of Political Science*, 1963, *7*, 145-155.

Eberhard, W. B. "Circulation and Population: Comparison of 1940 and 1970." *Journalism Quarterly*, 1974, *51*, 503-507.

Economic Research Service, U.S. Department of Agriculture. *Rural People in the American Economy*. Agricultural Economic Report No. 101. Washington, D.C.: U.S. Government Printing Office, 1966.

Edel, M., Harris, J. R., and Rothenberg, J. "Urban Concentration and Deconcentration." In A. H. Hawley and V. P. Rock (Eds.), *Metropolitan America in Contemporary Perspective*. New York: Halsted Press, 1975.

Eichler, M. "Women as Personal Dependents." In M. Stephenson (Ed.), *Women in Canada*. Toronto: New Press, 1973.

Emery, E. *The Press and America*. Englewood Cliffs, N.J.: Prentice-Hall, 1972.

Epstein, E. *News from Nowhere*. New York: Random House, 1973.

Erikson, K. T. *Wayward Puritans*. New York: Wiley, 1966.

Essien-Udom, E. U. *Black Nationalism: A Search for Identity in America*. Chicago: University of Chicago Press, 1962.

Fallding, H. *The Sociology of Religion: An Explanation of the Unity and Diversity in Religion*. Toronto: McGraw-Hill Ryerson, 1974.

Farber, B. "Bilateral Kinship: Centripetal and Centrifugal Types of Organization." *Journal of Marriage and the Family*, 1975, *37*, 871-888.

Farber, B. "Kinship—Now You See It, Now You Don't." *Sociological Quarterly*, 1976, *17*, 279-288.

Faris, R., and Dunham, H. W. *Mental Disorders in Urban Areas*. Chicago: University of Chicago Press, 1939.

Farley, R. "The Changing Distribution of Negroes in Metropolitan Areas: The Emergence of Black Suburbs." *American Journal of Sociology*, 1970, *73*, 15-31.

Farley, R. "Components of Suburban Population Growth." In B. Schwartz (Ed.), *The Changing Face of the Suburbs*. Chicago: University of Chicago Press, 1976.

Feldman, A., and Moore, W. *Industrialization and Industrialism: Convergence and Differentiation*. Transactions of the 5th World Congress of Sociology, Vol. 2. Montreal: International Sociological Association, 1962.

Felson, M., and Solaún, M. "The Fertility-Inhibiting Effect of Crowded Apartment Living in a Tight Housing Market." *American Journal of Sociology*, 1975, *80*, 1410-1427.

Ferdinand, T. N. "The Criminal Patterns of Boston Since 1849." *American Journal of Sociology*, 1967, *73*, 84-99.

Ferdinand, T. N. "The Criminal Patterns of New Haven since 1861." Paper presented at the annual meeting of the American Society of Criminology, 1968.

Ferdinand, T. N. "Politics, the Police, and Arresting Policies in Salem, Massachusetts, Since the Civil War." *Social Problems*, 1972, *19*, 572-588.

Ferdinand, T. N. "Criminality, the Courts, and the Constabulary in Boston: 1703-1967." Paper presented at the annual meeting of the American Society of Criminology, New York City, 1973.

Ferdinand, T. N. "From a Service to a Legalistic Police Department: A Case Study." *Journal of Police Science and Administration*, 1976, *4*, 302-319.

Ferracuti, F., Lazzari, R., and Wolfgang, M. E. (Eds.). *Violence in Sardinia.* Rome: Mario Bulzoni, 1970.

Festinger, L. Schacter, S., and Back, K. *Social Pressures in Informal Groups.* Stanford, Calif.: Stanford University Press, 1950.

Field, D., Barron, J., and Long, B. *Water and Community Development.* Ann Arbor, Mich.: Ann Arbor Science Publishers, 1974.

Firestone, W. A. "Community Organizations and School Reform: A Case Study." *School Review,* 1972, *81,* 108-120.

Firey, W. "Sentiment and Symbolism as Ecological Variables." *American Sociological Review,* 1945, *10,* 140-148.

Firth, R., Hubert, J., and Forge, A. *Families and Their Relatives: Kinship in a Middle Class Sector of London.* New York: Humanities Press, 1970.

Fischer, C. S. "Urbanism as a Way of Life: A Review and an Agenda." *Sociological Methods and Research,* 1972, *1,* 187-242.

Fischer, C. S. "The Effect of Urban Life on Traditional Values." *Social Forces,* 1975, *53,* 420-423.

Fischer, C. S. "The Study of Urban Community and Personality." In A. Inkeles, J. Coleman, and N. Smelser (Eds.), *Annual Review of Sociology.* Vol. 1. Palo Alto, Calif.: Annual Reviews, 1975a.

Fischer, C. S. "Toward a Subcultural Theory of Urbanism." *American Journal of Sociology,* 1975b, *80,* 1319-1342.

Fischer, C. S. *The Urban Experience.* New York: Harcourt Brace Jovanovich, 1976.

Fischer, C. S., and Jackson, R. M. "Suburbs, Networks, and Attitudes." In B. Schwartz (Ed.), *The Changing Face of the Suburbs.* Chicago: University of Chicago Press, 1976.

Fishman, J. A. *Language Loyalty in the United States.* The Hague, Netherlands: Mouton, 1966.

Fitch, J. M. *American Building.* Vol. 2: *The Environmental Forces that Shape It.* Boston: Houghton Mifflin, 1966.

Fitzpatrick, J. P. "The Intermarriage of Puerto Ricans in New York City." *American Journal of Sociology,* 1966, *71,* 395-406.

Flaherty, D. *Privacy in Colonial New England.* Charlottesville: University Press of Virginia, 1972.

Flaherty, D. "Criminal Justice in Provincial Massachusetts." Paper presented at the Conference of "Atlantic Society 1600-1800," 1973.

Flesch, R. *The Art of Readable Writing.* New York: Harper & Row, 1974.

Flinn, W. L., and Johnson, D. E. "Agrarianism Among Wisconsin Farmers." *Rural Sociology,* 1974, *39,* 187-204.

Foley, D. L. "Neighbors or Urbanites?" Mimeograph. Rochester, N.Y.: Department of Sociology, University of Rochester, 1952.

Foley, D. L. "Accessibility for Residents in the Metropolitan Environment." In A. H. Hawley and V. P. Rock (Eds.), *Metropolitan America in Contemporary Perspective.* New York: Halsted Press, 1975.

Form, W. F., and others. "The Compatibility of Alternative Approaches to the Delineation of Urban Sub-Areas." *American Sociological Review,* 1974, *19,* 434-440.

Form, W. H. "The Place of Social Structure in the Determination of Land Use." *Social Forces,* 1954, *32,* 317-322.

Foster, J. *Class Struggle and the Industrial Revolution.* London: Wiedenfeld and Nicolson, 1974.

Frase, R. W. "The Economics of Publishing." In K. Henderson (Ed.), *Trends in American Publishing.* Urbana: Graduate School of Library Science, University of Illinois, 1967.

Frazier, E. F. *The Negro Family in the United States.* Chicago: University of Chicago Press, 1939.

Freedman, J. *Crowding and Behavior.* New York: Viking Press, 1975.

Freedman, R. "Distribution of Migrant Population in Chicago." *American Sociological Review,* 1948, *13,* 304-309.

Fremon, C. *Central City and Suburban Employment Growth: 1965-67.* Washington, D.C.: Urban Institute, 1970.

French, R. M. "Change Comes to Cornucopia-Industry and the Community." In R. French (Ed.), *The Community—A Comparative Perspective.* Itasca, Ill.: Peacock, 1969.

Frey, F. "Communication and Development." In I. Pool, F. Frey, W. Schramm, N. Maccoby, and E. Parker (Eds.), *Handbook of Communication.* Chicago: Rand McNally, 1973.

Frey, W. H. "The Implications of Selective Migration and Residential Mobility for City-Suburban Differences in Age Structure." Paper presented at the annual meeting of the Population Association of America, Seattle, Wash., 1975.

Fried, J. P. *Housing Crisis U.S.A.* New York: Praeger, 1971.

Fried, M. "Grieving for a Lost Home." In Leonard Duhl (Ed.), *The Urban Condition.* New York: Simon & Schuster, 1969.

Friedlander, S. *Unemployment in the Urban Core.* New York: Praeger, 1972.

Friedman, L. M. *Government and Slum Housing: A Century of Frustration.* Chicago: Rand McNally, 1968.

Friedman, L. M. *A History of American Law.* New York: Simon & Schuster, 1973.

Friedman, M. "The Voucher Idea." *New York Times Magazine,* September 23, 1973, pp. 23ff.

Friedmann, J. "Cities in Social Transformation." *Comparative Studies in Society and History,* 1961-62, *4,* 86-103.

Friedmann, J. "A General Theory of Polarized Development." In N. M. Hansen (Ed.), *Growth Centers in Regional Economic Development.* New York: Free Press, 1972a.

Friedmann, J. "The Spatial Organization of Power in the Development of Urban Systems." *Comparative Urban Research,* 1972b, *1,* 5-42.

Friedrichs, R. W. "Decline in Prejudice Among Church-Goers Following Clergy-Led Open Housing Campaign." *Journal for the Scientific Study of Religion,* 1971, *10,* 152-156.

Frisbie, W. P. "The Scale and Growth of World Urbanization." In J. Walton and D. E. Carns (Eds.), *Cities in Change: Studies on the Urban Condition.* (2nd ed.) Boston: Allyn & Bacon, 1977.

Fuguitt, G. V. "The City and the Countryside." *Rural Sociology,* 1963, *28,* 246-261.

Fuguitt, G. V. "Small Town in Rural America." *Journal of Cooperative Extension,* 1965, *3,* 19-26.

Fuguitt, G. V. "The Places Left Behind: Population Trends and Policy for Rural America." *Rural Sociology,* 1971, *36,* 449-470.

Fuguitt, G. V. "Population Trends of Nonmetropolitan Cities and Villages in the U.S." In S. M. Mazie (Ed.), *Population Distribution and Policy.* Vol. 5. Washington, D.C.: U.S. Commission on Population Growth and the American Future, 1972.

Fuguitt, G. V., and Zuiches, J. J. "Residential Preferences and Population Distribution." *Demography,* 1975, *12,* 491-504.

Gale Research Company. *Encyclopedia of Associations.* Detroit, 1975.

Gallagher, A. *Plainville Fifteen Years Later.* New York: Columbia University Press, 1961.

Galle, O. R., and Gove, W. R. "Some Effects of Crowding on

Behavior in Urban Areas of the United States." Paper presented at the 1st World Congress of Environmental Medicine and Biology, Paris, 1974.

Galle, O. R., Gove, W. R., and McPherson, J. M. "Population Density and Pathology: What Are the Relationships for Man?" *Science,* 1972, *176,* 23-30.

Gans, H. J. "The Balanced Community: Homogeneity or Heterogeneity in Residential Areas?" *Journal of the American Institute of Planners,* 1961, *27,* 176-184.

Gans, H. J. "Urbanism and Suburbanism as Ways of Life: A Reevaluation of Definitions." In A. M. Rose (Ed.), *Human Behavior and Social Processes.* Boston: Houghton Mifflin, 1962a.

Gans, H. J. *The Urban Villagers: Group and Class in the Life of Italian-Americans.* New York: Free Press, 1962b.

Gans, H. J. "The Failure of Urban Renewal: A Critique and Some Proposals." *Commentary,* 1965, *39,* 29-37.

Gans, H. J. *The Levittowners.* New York: Random House, 1967.

Gans, H. J. *People and Plans: Essays on Urban Problems and Solutions.* New York: Basic Books, 1968.

Gans, H. J. "How Well Does Television Cover the News?" *New York Times Magazine,* January 11, 1970, *119,* 30-45.

Gans, H. J. *Popular Culture and High Culture.* New York: Basic Books, 1975.

Gardner, J. A., and Olson, D. J. *Theft of the City.* Bloomington: Indiana University Press, 1974.

Gatrell, V. A. C., and Hadden, T. "Criminal Statistics and Their Interpretation." In E. A. Wrigley (Ed.), *Nineteenth-Century Society.* Cambridge, England: Cambridge University Press, 1972.

Gaustad, E. S. "America's Institutions of Faith: A Statistical Postscript." In W. G. McLoughlin and R. N. Bellah (Eds.), *Religion in America.* Boston: Beacon Press, 1968.

Gaustad, E. S. "Churches of Christ in America." In D. R. Cutler (Ed.), *The Religious Situation: 1969.* Boston: Beacon Press, 1969.

Gawalt, C. W. "Sources of Anti-Lawyer Sentiment in Massachusetts, 1740-1840." *American Journal of Legal History,* 1970, *14,* 281-289.

Gawalt, C. W. "Massachusetts Legal Education in Transition, 1776-1840." *American Journal of Legal History,* 1973, *17,* 27-50.

Geertz, C. *Old Societies and New States.* New York: Free Press, 1963.

Gerbner, G., and Gross, L. "Living with Television: The Violence Profile." *Journal of Communication,* 1976a, *26,* 172-199.

Gerbner, G., and Gross, L. "The Scary World of TV's Heavy Viewer." *Psychology Today,* 1976b, *9,* 41-45.

Gerschenkron, A. *Economic Backwardness in Historical Perspective.* Cambridge, Mass.: Belknap Press, 1962.

Gibbs, J. P., and Davis, K. "Conventional Versus Metropolitan Data in the International Study of Washington." In J. P. Gibbs (Ed.), *Urban Research Methods.* New York: D. Van Nostrand, 1961.

Gibbs, J. P., and Martin, W. T. "Urbanization, Technology, and the Division of Labor: International Patterns." *American Sociological Review,* 1962, *27,* 667-677.

Gilbert, C. *Governing the Suburbs.* Bloomington: Indiana University Press, 1967.

Gilkey, L. "Social and Intellectual Sources of Contemporary Protestant Theology." In W. G. McLoughlin and R. N. Bellah (Eds.), *Religion in America.* Boston: Beacon Press, 1968.

Gillis, A. R. "Population Density and Social Pathology: The Case of Building Type, Social Allowance, and Juvenile Delinquency." *Social Forces,* 1974, *53,* 306-315.

Gittell, M., and Hevesi, A. G. (Eds.). *The Politics of Urban Education.* New York: Praeger, 1969.

Glazer, N., and Moynihan, D. P. *Beyond the Melting Pot.* Cambridge, Mass.: M.I.T. Press, 1963.

Glazer, N., and Moynihan, D. P. *Beyond the Melting Pot.* (rev. ed.) Cambridge, Mass.: M.I.T. Press, 1970.

Glenn, N. D., and Alston, J. P. "Rural-Urban Differences in Reported Attitudes and Behavior." *Southwestern Social Science Quarterly,* 1967, *3,* 381-400.

Glenn, N. D., and Hill, L. "Rural-Urban Differences in Attitudes and Behavior in the United States." *The Annals of the American Academy of Political and Social Science,* 1977, *429,* 36-50.

Glick, P. C. *American Families.* New York: Wiley, 1957.

Glick, P. C. "Family Trends in the United States, 1890-1940." *American Sociological Review,* 1942, *7,* 512.

Glick, P. C. "Some Recent Changes in American Families." *Current Population Reports.* Series P-23, No. 52. Washington, D.C.: U.S. Government Printing Office, 1975.

Glock, C. Y., and Stark, R. *Religion and Society in Tension.* Chicago: Rand McNally, 1965a.

Glock, C. Y., and Stark, R. "Is There an American Protestantism?" *Trans-action,* 1965b, *3,* 8-13, 48-49.

Glueck, S. *Continental Police Practice.* Springfield, Ill.: Thomas, 1974.

Goebel, Jr., J. "King's Law and Local Custom in Seventeenth-Century New England." In D. H. Flaherty (Ed.), *Essays in The History of Early American Law.* Chapel Hill: University of North Carolina Press, 1969. (Originally published in *Columbia Law Review,* 1931, *31,* 416-448.)

Goebel, Jr., J., and Naughton, T. R. *Law Enforcement in Colonial New York.* Montclair, N.J.: Patterson Smith, 1970.

Gold, N. N. "The Mismatch of Jobs and Low-Income People in Metropolitan Areas and Its Implications for the Central-City Poor." In S. M. Mazie (Ed.), *Population Distribution and Policy.* Vol. 5. Washington, D.C.: U.S. Commission on Population Growth and the American Future, 1972.

Goldberg, M. L. *The Effects of Ability Grouping.* New York: Teachers College Press, Columbia University, 1966.

Goldhammer, K. *The School Board.* New York: Center for Applied Research in Education, 1964.

Goldstein, S., and Goldscheider, C. *Jewish Americans: Three Generations in a Jewish Community.* Englewood Cliffs, N.J.: Prentice-Hall, 1968.

Goode, W. J. *World Revolution and Family Patterns.* New York: Free Press, 1963.

Gordon, C. W. *The Social System of the High School.* New York: Free Press, 1957.

Gordon, D. *Theories of Poverty and Unemployment.* Lexington, Mass.: Heath, 1972.

Gordon, M. M. "Assimilation in America: Theory and Reality." *Daedalus,* 1961, *90,* 263-285.

Gordon, M. M. *Assimilation in American Life.* New York: Oxford University Press, 1964.

Gosnell, H. F. *Machine Politics.* Chicago: University of Chicago Press, 1939.

Gottdiener, M. *Planned Sprawl: Private and Public Interests in Suburbia.* Beverly Hills, Calif.: Sage, 1977.

Gottlieb, D., and Reeves, T. *Adolescent Behavior in Urban Areas.* New York: Free Press, 1963.

Gottman, J., and Harper, R. A. (Eds.). *Metropolis on the Move.* New York: Wiley, 1967.

Graham, D. H. "Foreign Migration and the Question of Labor Supply in the Early Economic Growth of Brazil." Mimeograph. São Paulo, Brazil: Economic History Workshop, University of São Paulo, 1972.

Gras, N. S. B. *Introduction to Economic History.* New York: Harper & Row, 1922.

Greeley, A. "The Protestant Ethic: Time for a Moratorium." *Sociological Analysis,* 1964, *25,* 20-33.

Greenburg, D. "The Effectiveness of Law Enforcement in Eighteenth-Century New York." *American Journal of Legal History,* 1975, *19,* 171-207.

Greenstone, J. D., and Peterson, P. E. *Race and Authority in Urban Politics, Community Participation, and the War on Poverty.* New York: Russell Sage Foundation, 1973.

Greer, A., and Greer, S. "Suburban Political Behavior: A Matter of Trust." In B. Schwartz (Ed.), *The Changing Face of the Suburbs.* Chicago: University of Chicago Press, 1976.

Greer, S. "Urbanism Reconsidered: A Comparative Study of Local Areas in a Metropolis." *American Sociological Review,* 1956, *21,* 19-25.

Greer, S. *The Emerging City.* New York: Free Press, 1962a.

Greer, S. *Governing the Metropolis.* New York: Wiley, 1962b.

Greer, S. "The Mass Society and the Parapolitical Structure." *American Sociological Review,* 1962c, *27,* 634-646.

Greer, S. "Social Structure and Political Process in Suburbia: An Empirical Test." *Rural Sociology,* 1962d, *27,* 438-459.

Greer, S. *Metropolitics.* New York: Wiley, 1963.

Greer, S. *Urban Renewal and American Cities.* Indianapolis: Bobbs-Merrill, 1965.

Greer, S. "Postscript: Communication and Community." In M. Janowitz (Ed.), *The Community Press in an Urban Setting.* (2nd ed.) Chicago: University of Chicago Press, 1967.

Greer, S. "The Family in Suburbia." In L. H. Masotti and J. K. Hadden (Eds.), *Urban Affairs Annual Reviews.* Vol. 7: *The Urbanization of the Suburbs.* Beverly Hills, Calif.: Sage, 1973.

Greer, S., and Kube, E. "Urbanism and Social Structure: A Los Angeles Study." In M. B. Sussman (Ed.), *Community Structure and Analysis.* New York: Crowell, 1959.

Greer, S., and Orleans, P. "The Mass Society and the Parapolitical Structure." In S. Greer and others, (Eds.), *The New Urbanization.* New York: St. Martin's Press, 1968.

Grønbjerg, K. "The Interface Between Private and Public Welfare." Working paper, Department of Sociology, Loyola University of Chicago, 1977a.

Grønbjerg, K. *Mass Society and the Extension of Welfare, 1960-70.* Chicago: University of Chicago Press, 1977b.

Grønbjerg, K., Street, D., and Suttles, G. D. *Poverty and Social Change.* Chicago: University of Chicago Press, in press.

Grotto, G. L. "Prosperous Newspaper Industry May Be Heading for a Decline." *Journalism Quarterly,* 1974, *51,* 498-502.

Grotto, G. L., Larkin, E. F., and DePlois, B. "How Readers Perceive and Use a Small Daily Newspaper." *Journalism Quarterly,* 1975, *52,* 711-715.

Gruenberg, B. "How Free is Free Time?" Unpublished doctoral dissertation, University of Michigan, 1975.

Guest, A. M. "Retesting 'The Burgess Zonal Hypothesis': The Location of White Collar Workers." *American Journal of Sociology,* 1971, *76,* 1094-1108.

Guest, A. M. "Patterns of Family Location." *Demography,* 1972, *9,* 159-172.

Guest, A. M. "Urban Growth and Population Densities." *Demography,* 1973, *10,* 53-69.

Guest, A. M., and Weed, J. A. "Ethnic Residential Segregation: Pattern of Change." *American Journal of Sociology,* 1976, *81,* 1088-1112.

Gustavus, S. O., and Henley, Jr., J. R. "Correlates of Voluntary Childlessness in a Select Population." *Social Biology,* 1971, *18,* 277-284.

Gutman, R. "The Questions Architects Ask." In R. Gutman (Ed.), *People and Buildings.* New York: Basic Books, 1972.

Gutman, R. "The Social Function of the Built Environment." In A. Rapoport (Ed.), *The Mutual Interaction of People and Their Built Environment.* The Hague, Netherlands: Mouton, 1976.

Haar, C. *Land Use Planning.* Boston: Little, Brown, 1959.

Habakkuk, H. J. "Fluctuations in House-Building in Britain and the United States in the Nineteenth Century." *Journal of Economic History,* 1962, *22,* 198-230.

Hacker, A. (Ed.). *The Corporation Take-Over.* New York: Doubleday, 1965.

Hackett, A. P. *60 Years of Best Sellers, 1895-1955.* New York: Bowker, 1956.

Hackett, A. P. "Hardcover Best Sellers of 1968 in the U.S. Book Trade." *Publishers' Weekly,* March 10, 1969, p. 30.

Hackett, A. P. "Hardcover Best Sellers of 1969 in the U.S. Book Trade." *Publishers' Weekly,* February 9, 1970, p. 40.

Hackett, A. P. "Hardcover Best Sellers of 1970: The Year of the Love Story." *Publishers' Weekly,* February 8, 1971, pp. 34-37.

Hadden, J. K. *The Gathering Storm in the Churches.* New York: Doubleday, 1969.

Hadden, J. K. "Introduction." In J. K. Hadden (Ed.), *Religion in Radical Transition.* Chicago: Aldine, 1971.

Hadden, J. K., and Rymph, R. C. "The Marching Ministers." In J. K. Hadden (Ed.), *Religion in Radical Transition.* Chicago: Aldine, 1971.

Haer, J. "Conservatism-Radicalism and the Rural-Urban Continuum." *Rural Sociology,* 1952, *17,* 343-347.

Haggerty, L. J. "Another Look at the Burgess Hypothesis: Time as an Important Variable." *American Journal of Sociology,* 1971, *76,* 1084-1093.

Haig, R. M. "Toward an Understanding of the Metropolis. II. The Assignment of Activities to Areas in Urban Regions." *Quarterly Journal of Economics,* 1926, pp. 421ff.

Halberstam, D. "CBS: The Power and the Profits." *Atlantic,* January 1976, pp. 33-71, and February 1976, pp. 52-91.

Hall, P. *The World Cities.* New York: McGraw-Hill, 1966.

Haller, M. "Historical Roots of Police Behavior, 1890-1925." *Law & Society Review,* 1976, *10,* 302-323.

Halpern, J. M. *The Changing Village Community.* Englewood Cliffs, N.J.: Prentice-Hall, 1967.

Handlin, O. *Boston's Immigrants.* New York: Atheneum, 1968.

Hansen, M. L. *The Problem of the Third Generation Immigrant.* Rock Island, Ill.: Augustana Historical Society, 1937.

Hanson, N. *Growth Centers and Regional Economic Development.* New York: Free Press, 1971.

Haren, C. C. "Rural Industrial Growth in the 1960s." *American Journal of Agricultural Economics,* 1970, *52,* 3.

Harrington, M. *Toward a Democratic Left: A Radical Program for a New Majority.* New York: Macmillan, 1968.

Harris, C. D., and Ullman, E. L. "The Nature of Cities." *Annals,* 1945, *242,* 7-17.

Harrison, B. *Education, Training, and the Urban Ghetto.* Baltimore: Johns Hopkins University Press, 1972.

Harrison, B. *Urban Economic Development.* Washington, D.C.: Urban Institute, 1974.

Hart, J. F. "The Middle West." *Regions of the United States.* New York: Harper & Row, 1972.

Harvey, D. *Social Justice and the City.* London: Edward Arnold, 1973.

Hauser, P. M. *Population Perspectives.* New Brunswick, N.J.: Rutgers University Press, 1961.

Havens, E. "Women, Work and Wedlock: A Note on Female Marital Patterns in the United States." In J. Huber (Ed.), *Changing Women in a Changing Society.* Chicago: University of Chicago Press, 1973.

Havighurst, R. J. *Metropolitanism: Its Challenge to Education.* Chicago: National Society for the Study of Education, 1968.

Hawley, A. H. *Human Ecology: A Theory of Community Structure.* New York: Ronald Press, 1950.

Hawley, A. H. *The Changing Shape of Metropolitan America.* New York: Free Press, 1956.

Hawley, A. H. *Urban Society: An Ecological Approach.* New York: Ronald Press, 1971.

Hawley, A. H., and Rock, V. P. (Eds.) *Metropolitan America in Contemporary Perspective.* New York: Halsted Press, 1975.

Hawley, A. H., and Zimmer, B. "Resistance to Unification in a Metropolitan Community." In M. Janowitz (Ed.), *Community Political Systems.* New York: Free Press, 1961.

Hawley, A. H., and Zimmer, B. *The Metropolitan Community: Its People and Government.* Beverly Hills, Calif.: Sage, 1970.

Hayner, N. S. *Hotel Life.* Chapel Hill: University of North Carolina Press, 1936.

Headley, J. T. *The Great Riots of New York: 1712-1873.* Indianapolis: Bobbs-Merrill, 1970.

Heckscher, A. *Open Spaces: The Life of American Cities.* New York: Harper & Row, 1977.

Helfgot, J. "Professional Reform Organizations and the Symbolic Representation of the Poor." *American Sociological Review,* 1974, *29,* 475-491.

Henderson, A., and Bauman, R. D. *Indian Environmental Studies: The Cheyenne and Arapaho Tribes of Oklahoma.* Norman: University of Oklahoma, n.d.

Hendrix, L. "Kinship and Economic-Rational Migration: A Comparison of Micro- and Macro-Level Analyses." *Sociological Quarterly,* 1975, *16,* 534-543.

Henle, P. "Recent Growth of Paid Leisure for U.S. Workers." *Monthly Labor Review,* March 1962, pp. 249-257.

Henle, P. "Leisure and the Long Workweek." *Monthly Labor Review,* July 1966, pp. 721-727.

Herberg, W. *Protestant-Catholic-Jew: An Essay in American Religious Sociology.* New York: Doubleday, 1955.

Herberg, W. "Religion in a Secularized Society: Some Aspects of America's Three-Religion Pluralism." In R. D. Knudten (Ed.), *The Sociology of Religion: An Anthology*. New York: Appleton-Century-Crofts, 1967a.

Herberg, W. "Religion in a Secularized Society: The New Shape of Religion in America." In R. D. Knudten (Ed.), *The Sociology of Religion: An Anthology*. New York: Appleton-Century-Crofts, 1967b.

Herendeen, Jr., J. H. "Quantitative Evaluation of the Relationship Between the Highway System and Socio-Economic Changes in Nonurban Areas." Unpublished doctoral dissertation, Pennsylvania State University, n.d.

Hermansen, T. "Development Roles and Related Theories: A Synoptic Review." In Niles M. Hansen (Ed.), *Growth Centers in Regional Economic Development*. New York: Free Press, 1972.

Higham, J. *Strangers in the Land: Patterns of American Nativism, 1860-1925*. Brunswick, N.J.: Rutgers University Press, 1955.

Hill, R. *The Strengths of the Black Family*. New York: Emerson Hall, 1972.

Hill, W. G. "Voluntary and Governmental Financial Transactions." *Social Casework*, 1971, *52*, 356-361.

Hillery, Jr., G. A. *Communal Organizations: A Study of Local Societies*. Chicago: University of Chicago Press, 1968.

Hindus, M. S. "A City of Mobocrats and Tyrants: Mob Violence in Boston, 1774-1863." *Issues in Criminology*, 1971, *6*, 55-83.

Hines, F. K., Brown, D. L., and Zimmer, J. M. *Social and Economic Characteristics of the Population in Metro and Nonmetro Counties, 1970*. Agricultural Economic Report No. 272. Washington, D.C.: Economic Research Service, U.S. Department of Agriculture, 1975.

Hinshaw, M. L., and Allott, K. J. "Environmental Preferences of Future Housing Consumers." *Journal of the American Institute of Planners*, 1972, *38*, 102-107.

Hirsch, P. M. *The Structure of the Popular Music Industry*. Ann Arbor: Institute for Social Research, University of Michigan, 1969.

Hirsch, P. M. "Sociological Approaches to the Pop Music Phenomenon." *American Behavioral Scientist*, 1971, *14*, 371-388.

Hobsbawn, E. *Industry and Empire*. London: Weidenfeld and Nicolson, 1968.

Hodge, R. W., and others. "Occupational Prestige in the United States: 1925-1963." In R. Bendix and S. M. Lipset (Eds.), *Class, Status, and Power.* New York: Free Press, 1966.

Hoffman, L. W. "Effects on Child." In L. W. Hoffman and F. I. Nye (Eds.), *Working Mothers: An Evaluative Review of the Consequences for Wife, Husband, and Child.* San Francisco: Jossey-Bass, 1974.

Hoffman, P. "The Neglected Statehouse." *Columbia Journalism Review,* 1967, *6,* 21-24.

Hole, W. V. "Housing Standards and Social Trends." *Urban Studies,* 1965, *2,* 137-146.

Hollingshead, A. B. *Elmtown's Youth.* New York: Wiley, 1949.

Homans, G. C. *The Human Group.* New York: Harcourt Brace Jovanovich, 1950.

Hoover, E. M. *Anatomy of a Metropolis.* Cambridge, Mass.: Harvard University Press, 1959.

Hoover, E. M. "Reduced Population Growth and the Problems of Urban Areas." In S. M. Mazie (Ed.), *Population Distribution and Policy.* Vol. 5. Washington, D.C.: U.S. Commission on Population Growth and the American Future, 1972.

Hoskin, F. P. *The Functions of Cities.* Cambridge, Mass.: Schenkman, 1973.

Howell, J. T. *Hard Living on Clay Street: Portraits of Blue Collar Families.* New York: Doubleday, 1973.

Hoyt, H. *The Structure of Growth of Residential Neighborhoods in American Cities.* Washington, D.C.: U.S. Federal Housing Administration, 1939.

Hoyt, H. "Forces of Urban Centralization and Decentralization." *American Journal of Sociology,* 1941, *46,* 843-852.

Hummel, R., and Nagle, J. M. *Urban Education in America.* New York: Oxford University Press, 1973.

Humphrey, C. R., and Sell, R. "The Impact of Controlled Access Highways on Population Growth in Pennsylvania Nonmetropolitan Communities, 1940-1970." *Rural Sociology,* 1975, *40,* 332-343.

Hunter, A. *Symbolic Communities: The Persistence and Change of Chicago's Local Communities.* Chicago: University of Chicago Press, 1974.

Hunter, A. "The Loss of Community: An Empirical Test Through Replication." *American Sociological Review,* 1975, *40,* 537-552.

Hunter, A., and Suttles, G. D. "The Expanding Community of Limited Liability." In G. D. Suttles, *The Social Construction of Communities.* Chicago: University of Chicago Press, 1972.

Hurd, R. *Principles of City Land Values.* New York: Record and Guide, 1903.

Hutchinson, E. P. *Immigrants and Their Children, 1850-1950.* New York: Wiley, 1956.

Hyman, H. H., and Wright, C. R. "Trends in Voluntary Association Membership of American Adults." *American Sociological Review,* 1971, *36,* 191-206.

Hynds, E. C. *American Newspapers in the 1970s.* New York: Hastings House, 1975.

Iannaccone, L., and Lutz, F. W. *Politics, Power and Policy: The Governing of Local School Districts.* Columbus, Ohio: Merrill, 1970.

Iannaccone, L., and Wiles, D. K. "The Changing Politics of Urban Education." *Education and Urban Society,* 1971, *3,* 255-264.

Illinois Department of Public Aid. *Current Caseload Data—Cook County.* Chicago: Bureau of Research and Statistics, Illinois Department of Public Aid, 1974.

Illinois Department of Public Aid. *Current Caseload Data—Cook County.* Chicago: Bureau of Research and Statistics, Illinois Department of Public Aid, 1975.

Inciardi, J. A. *Careers in Crime.* Chicago: Rand McNally, 1975.

Institute for Social Research. "Measuring the Quality of Life in America: A New Frontier for Social Science." *Newsletter,* 1974, *2,* 3-8.

Intercom. "Women and Men: Changing Roles in a Changing World." *Intercom,* 1976 (no. 81), 2-32.

Irwin, R. "Nonmetropolitan Population Change: 1960-1970." Paper presented at the annual meeting of the Population Association of America, Washington, D.C., 1971.

Jacobs, J. *The Death and Life of Great American Cities.* New York: Random House, 1961.

Jacobs, N. *Culture for the Millions.* New York: D. Van Nostrand, 1961.

Jacquet, Jr., C. H. (Ed.). *Yearbook of American and Canadian Churches, 1976.* Nashville, Tenn.: The Abingdon Press, 1976.

James, Jr., F. J., and Windsor, D. W. "Fiscal Zoning, Fiscal Reform and Exclusionary Land-Use Controls." *American Institute of Planners Journal,* 1976, *42,* 130-141.

Janowitz, M. "Introduction." In M. Janowitz (Ed.), *Community Political Systems.* New York: Free Press, 1961.

Janowitz, M. *The Community Press in an Urban Setting.* (2nd ed.) Chicago: University of Chicago Press, 1967.

Janowitz, M. "Political Sociology." In D. L. Sills (Ed.), *International Encyclopedia of the Social Sciences.* New York: Macmillan, 1968.

Janowitz, M. *Institutional Building in Urban Education.* New York: Russell Sage Foundation, 1969.

Janowitz, M. "Mass Communications and the Political Process." In M. Janowitz, *Political Conflict: Essays in Political Sociology.* New York: Quadrangle, 1970.

Janowitz, M. *Social Control of the Welfare State.* New York: Elsevier, 1976.

Janowitz, M. *Macrosociology and Social Control: Socio-Political Changes in the United States, 1920-1976.* Chicago: University of Chicago Press, in press.

Janowitz, M., and Shils, E. A. "The Cohesion and Disintegration of the Wehrmacht in World War II." *Public Opinion Quarterly,* 1948, *12,* 280-315.

Janowitz, M., and Suttles, G. D. "The Social Ecology of Citizenship." Paper presented at the Wingspread Conference on Management of Human Service Organizations, Racine, Wisc., June 1977.

Jarrett, H. *Environmental Quality in a Growing Economy.* Baltimore: Johns Hopkins University Press, 1966.

Jefferson, M. "The Law of the Primate City." *The Geographical Review,* 1939, *29,* 226-232.

Johansen, H. E., and Fuguitt, G. V. "Changing Retail Activity in Wisconsin Villages: 1939-1954-1970." *Rural Sociology,* 1973, *38,* 207-218.

Johnson, B. "Do Holiness Sects Socialize in Dominant Values?" *Social Forces,* 1961, *39,* 309-316.

Johnson, D. A. "Museum Attendance in the New York Metropolitan Region." *The Curator,* 1969, *12,* 201-230.

Johnson, D. R. "The Detective in America, 1800-1860." Unpublished manuscript, n.d.

Johnson, P. B., Sears, D. O., and McConahay, J. B. "Black Invisibility, the Press, and the Los Angeles Riot." *American Journal of Sociology,* 1971, *76,* 698-721.

Johnson, R. L., and Knop, E. "Rural-Urban Differentials in Community Satisfaction." *Rural Sociology,* 1970, *35,* 544-548.

Johnstone, J. W. C. "Organizational Constraints on Newswork." *Journalism Quarterly,* 1976, *53,* 5-13.

Johnstone, J. W. C., Slawski, E. J., and Bowman, W. W. "The Professional Values of American Newsmen." *Public Opinion Quarterly,* 1973, *53,* 522-540.

Johnstone, J. W. C., Slawski, E. J., and Bowman, W. W. *The Newspeople.* Urbana: University of Illinois Press, 1976.

Johnstone, R. L. "Negro Preachers Take Sides." In P. H. McNamara (Ed.), *Religion American Style.* New York: Harper & Row, 1974.

Jonassen, C. T. "Functional Unities in Eighty-Eight Community Systems." *American Sociological Review,* 1961, *26,* 399-406.

Jones, G. S. *Outcast London.* Oxford, England: Clarendon Press, 1971.

Journal of the National Education Association. January 1945, *34,* inside back cover. (Advertisement for classroom edition of *Reader's Digest.*)

Kahn, A. "Service Delivery at the Neighborhood Level: Experience, Theory, and Fads." *Social Service Review,* 1976, *50,* 23-56.

Kain, J. F. "Post-War Metropolitan Development: Housing Preferences and Auto Ownership." *American Economic Association Papers and Proceedings,* 1967, *57,* 223-234.

Kain, J. F. "The Distribution and Movements of Jobs and Industry." In J. Q. Wilson (Ed.), *The Metropolitan Enigma.* Cambridge, Mass.: Harvard University Press, 1970.

Kain, J. F. "The Distribution and Movement of Jobs and Industry." In J. F. Kain (Ed.), *Essays on Urban Spatial Structure.* Cambridge, Mass.: Ballinger, 1975.

Kando, T. M. *Leisure and Popular Culture in Transition.* St. Louis, Mo.: Mosby, 1975.

Kane, D. N. "Illinois: Good Guys and Bad." *Columbia Journalism Review,* 1967, *6,* 57-59.

Kanter, R. M. *Commitment and Community.* Cambridge, Mass.: Harvard University Press, 1972.

Kantrowitz, N. "Ethnic and Racial Segregation in the New York Metropolis, 1960." *American Journal of Sociology,* 1969, *74,* 685-695.

Kantrowitz, N. *Ethnic and Racial Segregation in the New York Metropolis.* New York: Praeger, 1972.

Kantrowitz, N. *Residential Patterns Among White Ethnic Groups, Blacks, and Puerto Ricans.* New York: Praeger, 1973.

Kaplan, D. "Psychopathology of Television Watching." *Intellectual Digest,* November 1972, pp. 26-28. (Also in *Performance,* July 1972, pp. 17-19.)

Karabel, J. "Community Colleges and Social Stratification." *Harvard Educational Review,* 1972, *42,* 521-562.

Kasarda, J. D. "The Impact of Suburban Population Growth on Central City Service Functions." *American Journal of Sociology,* 1972, *77,* 1111-1124.

Kasarda, J. D. "The Structural Implications of Social System Size: A Three-Level Analysis." *American Sociological Review,* 1974, *34,* 19-28.

Kasarda, J. D. "The Changing Occupational Structure of the American Metropolis: Apropos the Urban Problem." In B. Schwartz (Ed.), *The Changing Face of the Suburbs.* Chicago: University of Chicago Press, 1976.

Kasarda, J. D., and Janowitz, M. "Community Attachment in Mass Society." *American Sociological Review,* 1974, *39,* 328-339.

Kasarda, J. D., and Redfearn, G. "Differential Patterns of Urban and Suburban Growth in the United States." *Journal of Urban History,* 1975, *2,* 43-66.

Katz, E., and Lazarsfeld, P. F. *Personal Influence.* New York: Free Press, 1955.

Keats, J. *The Crack in the Picture Window.* Boston: Houghton Mifflin, 1956.

Keller, S. *The Urban Neighborhood: A Sociological Perspective.* New York: Random House, 1968.

Kelly, J. R. "Attitudes Toward Ecumenism: An Empirical Investigation." *Journal of Ecumenical Studies,* 1972, *9,* 341-351.

Kennedy, R. J. R. "Single or Triple Melting Pot? Intermarriage in New Haven, 1870-1950." *American Journal of Sociology,* 1952, *58,* 56-66.

Kerner, O., and others. *Report of the National Advisory Commission on Civil Disorders.* Washington: U.S. Government Printing Office, 1968.

Kerr, N. D. "The School Board as an Agency of Legitimation." *Sociology of Education,* 1964, *38,* 34-59.

Killian, L. M., and Grigg, C. M. "Urbanism, Race, and Anomie." *American Journal of Sociology,* 1962, *67,* 661-665.

Kirschenbaum, A. "Patterns of Migration from Metropolitan to Nonmetropolitan Areas: Changing Ecological Factors Affecting Family Mobility." *Rural Sociology,* 1971, *36,* 286-314.

Kiser, C. V., Grabill, W. H., and Campbell, A. A. *Trends and Variations in Fertility in the United States.* Cambridge, Mass.: Harvard University Press, 1968.

Kittross, J. *Television Frequency Allocation Policy in the United States.* Unpublished doctoral dissertation, University of Illinois, Urbana, 1960.

Kittross, J. "A Fair and Equitable Service, or a Modest Proposal to Restructure American Television to Have All the Advantages Claimed for Cable and UHF Without Using Either." Paper presented at the annual meeting of the Association for Education in Journalism, Department of Communications, Temple University, Philadelphia, 1975.

Klapper, J. *The Effects of Mass Communication.* New York: Free Press, 1960.

Klein, C. "Cable Television: The New Urban Battleground." In G. Gerbner, L. Gross, and W. Melody (Eds.), *Communication Technology and Social Policy.* New York: Wiley, 1973.

Klein, F. "Big Afternoon Papers Still Losing Readers; Many Factors Blamed." *Wall Street Journal,* May 26, 1976, p. 1.

Knights, P. R. *The Plain People of Boston, 1830-1860.* New York: Oxford University Press, 1971.

Kobrin, F. "The Fall of Household Size and the Rise of the Primary Individual in the United States." *Demography,* 1976, *13,* 127-139.

Konig, R. *The Community.* New York: Schocken Books, 1968.

Kornblum, W. *Blue Collar Community.* Chicago: University of Chicago Press, 1974.

Kornblum, W. *Survey of Fire Island Residents.* Cooperative Research Unit Paper No. 5. New York: Graduate School, City University of New York, 1975.

Kornhauser, W. *The Politics of Mass Society.* New York: Free Press, 1959.

Kornhauser, W. "Mass Society." In D. L. Sills (Ed.), *International Encyclopedia of the Social Sciences.* New York: Macmillan, 1968.

Kraus, S., and Davis, D. (Eds.). *The Effects of Mass Communication.* University Park: Pennsylvania State University Press, 1976.

Kreps, J. M. *Lifetime Allocation of Work and Leisure.* Research Report No. 22. Washington, D.C.: U.S. Department of Health, Education, and Welfare, 1968.

Kreps, J. M., and Clark, R. *Sex, Age, and Work: The Changing Composition of the Labor Force.* Baltimore: Johns Hopkins University Press, 1975.

Kreps, J. M., and Spengler, J. J. "The Leisure Component of Economic Growth." In *The Employment Impact of Techno-*

logical Change, Appendix, Vol. 2, Commission on Technology, Automation, and Economic Progress. Washington, D.C.: U.S. Government Printing Office, 1966.

Krieghbaum, H. *Pressures on the Press.* New York: Crowell, 1972.

Kronus, S. *The Black Middle Class.* Columbus, Ohio: Merrill, 1971.

Kuhn, T. S. *The Structure of Scientific Revolutions.* (2nd ed.) Chicago: University of Chicago Press, 1970.

Lacy, D. "Major Trends in American Book Publishing." *Trends in American Publishing.* Urbana: Graduate School of Library Science, University of Illinois, 1967.

Ladner, J. A. *Tomorrow's Tomorrow: The Black Woman.* New York: Doubleday, 1971.

Lampard, E. E. "The History of Cities in the Economically Advanced Areas." *Economic Development and Cultural Change,* 1955, *3,* 81-136.

Lampard, E. E. "Historical Aspects of Urbanization." In P. M. Hauser and L. F. Schnore (Eds.), *The Study of Urbanization.* New York: Wiley, 1965.

Lampard, E. E. "The Evolving System of Cities in the U.S.: Urbanization and Economic Development." In H. S. Perloff and L. Wingo, Jr. (Eds.), *Issues in Urban Economics.* Baltimore: Johns Hopkins University Press, 1968.

Lane, R. *Policing the City: Boston 1822-1885.* Cambridge, Mass.: Harvard University Press, 1967.

Lane, R. "Crime and Criminal Statistics in Nineteenth-Century Massachusetts." *Journal of Social History,* 1968, *2,* 156-163.

Lang, K., and Lang, G. "The Unique Perspective of Television." *American Sociological Review,* 1953, *18,* 3-12.

Lansing, J. *Residential Location and Urban Mobility.* A Report to the U.S. Department of Commerce, Bureau of Public Roads. Ann Arbor: Survey Research Center, Institute for Social Research, University of Michigan, 1966.

Lansing, J. B., Marans, R. W., and Zehner, R. B. *Planned Residential Environments.* Ann Arbor: Survey Research Center, Institute for Social Research, University of Michigan, 1970.

Larrabee, E., and Meyersohn, R. *Mass Leisure.* New York: Free Press, 1958.

Larrabee, E., and Meyersohn, R. "The Suburban Dislocation." In A. N. Cousins (Ed.), *Urban Man and Society.* New York: Knopf, 1970.

Larsen, O. N., and Edelstein, A. S. "Communication, Consensus, and the Community Involvement of Urban Husbands and Wives." *Acta Sociologica,* 1960, pp. 15-30.

Larson, O. F., and Rogers, E. M. "Rural Society in Transition: The American Setting." In J. H. Copp, *Our Changing Rural Society: Perspectives and Trends.* Ames: Iowa State University, 1964.

Laslett, B. "The Family as a Public and Private Institution: An Historical Perspective." *Journal of Marriage and the Family,* 1973, *35,* 480-492.

Lasuen, J. R. "On Growth Poles." *Urban Studies,* 1969, *6,* 137-161.

Lazarsfeld, P., and Merton, R. "Mass Communication, Popular Taste, and Organized Social Action." In B. Rosenberg and D. White (Eds.), *Mass Culture.* New York: Free Press, 1957.

Lenski, G. *The Religious Factor: A Sociological Study of Religion's Impact on Politics, Economics, and Family Life.* (rev. ed.) New York: Doubleday, 1961.

Lenski, G. "Religion's Impact on Secular Institutions." In R. D. Knudten (Ed.), *The Sociology of Religion: An Anthology.* New York: Appleton-Century-Crofts, 1967.

Lenski, G. "The Religious Factor in Detroit: Revisited." *American Sociological Review,* 1971, *36,* 48-50.

Lerner, D. *The Passing of Traditional Society.* New York: Free Press, 1964.

Levin, B., Muller, T., and Sandoval, C. *The High Cost of Education in Cities.* Washington, D.C.: Urban Institute, 1973.

Levin, H. M. (Ed.). *Community Control of Schools.* New York: Simon & Schuster, 1970.

Levin, H. M. "The Effects of Expenditure Increases on Educational Resource Allocation and Effectiveness." In M. Carnoy and H. M. Levin (Eds.), *The Limits of Educational Reform.* New York: McKay, 1976.

Levine, M. P. "Gay Ghetto." Paper presented at the annual meeting of the American Sociological Association, Chicago, September 1977.

Levy, Jr., M. "Aspects of the Analysis of Family Structure." In A. J. Coale and others (Eds.), *Aspects of the Analysis of Family Structure.* Princeton, N.J.: Princeton University Press, 1965.

Lewis, O. F. *The Development of American Prisons and Prison Customs, 1776-1845.* Montclair, N.J.: Patterson Smith, 1967.

Lewis, P. F. "Small Town in Pennsylvania." In J. F. Hart (Ed.), *Regions of the United States.* New York: Harper & Row, 1972.

Lieberson, S. "Generational Differences Among Blacks in the North." *American Journal of Sociology,* 1973, *79,* 550-565.

Liebow, E. *Talley's Corner.* Boston: Little, Brown, 1967.

Lincoln, C. E. *The Black Muslims in America.* Boston: Beacon Press, 1961.

Linder, S. P. *The Harried Leisure Class.* New York: Columbia University Press, 1970.

Lineberry, R. (Ed.). "The Politics and Economics of Urban Services." *Urban Affairs Quarterly,* 1977, *12,* entire issue.

Lipman-Blumen, J. "The Vicarious Achievement Ethic and Non-Traditional Roles for Women." Paper presented at the annual meeting of the Eastern Sociological Society, 1973.

Lipman-Blumen, J., and Tickmayer, A. R. "Sex Roles in Transition: A Ten-Year Perspective." In A. Inkeles, J. Coleman, and N. Smelser (Eds.), *Annual Review of Sociology.* Vol. 1. Palo Alto, Calif.: Annual Reviews, 1975.

Littell, F. H. "The Churches and the Body Politic." In W. G. McLoughlin and R. N. Bellah (Eds.), *Religion in America.* Boston: Beacon Press, 1968.

Lockridge, K. A. *A New England Town: The First Hundred Years.* New York: Norton, 1970.

Lodhi, A. Z., and Tilly, C. "Urbanization, Crime, and Collective Violence in Nineteenth-Century France." *American Journal of Sociology,* 1973, *79,* 296-318.

Lofland, L. H. "The 'Thereness' of Women: A Selective Review of Urban Sociology." In M. Millman and R. M. Kanter (Eds.), *Another Voice: Feminist Perspectives on Social Life and Social Science.* New York: Doubleday, 1975.

Logan, J. "Industrialization and the Stratification of Cities in Suburban Regions." *American Journal of Sociology,* 1976, *82,* 333-348.

Long, L. H. "The Fertility of Migrants to and Within North America." *Milbank Memorial Fund Quarterly,* 1970, *48,* 297-316.

Long, L. H. "The Influence of Number and Ages of Children on Residential Mobility." *Demography,* 1972, *9,* 371-382.

Long, L. H. "Women's Labor Force Participation and the Residential Mobility of Families." *Social Forces,* 1974, *52,* 342-348.

Long, L. H., and Glick, P. C. "Family Patterns in Suburban Areas: Recent Trends." In B. Schwartz (Ed.), *The Changing Face of the Suburbs.* Chicago: University of Chicago Press, 1976.

Long, N. E. "The Local Community as an Ecology of Games." *American Journal of Sociology*, 1958, *64*, 251-261.

Long, N. E. *The Polity.* Chicago: Rand McNally, 1962.

Loo, C. "The Effects of Spatial Density on the Social Behavior of Children." *Journal of Applied Social Psychology*, 1972, *2*, 372-381.

Loomis, C., and Beegle, J. A. *Rural Social Systems.* Englewood Cliffs, N.J.: Prentice-Hall, 1951.

Loring, Jr., W. C. "Housing Characteristics and Social Disorganization." *Journal of Social Problems*, 1970, *3*, 160-168.

Lortie, D. C. "The Balance of Control and Autonomy in Elementary School Teaching." In A. Etzioni (Ed.), *The Semi-Professions.* New York: Free Press, 1969.

Lortie, D. C. *Schoolteacher.* Chicago: University of Chicago Press, 1975.

LoSciuto, L. "A National Inventory of Television Viewing Behavior." In E. Rubinstein, G. Comstock, and J. Murray (Eds.), *Television and Social Behavior.* Vol. 4. Rockville, Md.: National Institute of Mental Health, 1972.

Lowenthal, L. "Biographies in Popular Magazines." In P. Lazarsfeld and F. Stanton (Eds.), *Radio Research 1942-43.* New York: Bureau of Applied Social Research, 1944. (Reprinted in W. Peterson (Ed.), *American Social Patterns.* Doubleday, 1956.)

Lowi, T. J. "Gosnell's Chicago Revisited Via Lindsay's New York." In H. F. Gosnell, *Machine Politics.* Chicago: University of Chicago Press, 1968.

Lowi, T. J. *The End of Liberalism.* New York: Norton, 1969.

Lyle, J. *The News in Megalopolis.* Scranton, Pa.: Chandler, 1967.

Lynch, K. *The Image of the City.* Cambridge, Mass.: M.I.T. Press, 1960.

Lynch, K. *What Time Is This Place?* Cambridge, Mass.: M.I.T. Press, 1972.

Lynd, R. S., and Lynd, H. M. *Middletown.* New York: Harcourt Brace Jovanovich, 1929.

Lynd, R. S., and Lynd, H. M. *Middletown in Transition.* New York: Harcourt Brace Jovanovich, 1937.

MacCannell, D. *The Tourist: A New Theory of the Leisure Class.* New York: Schocken Books, 1976.

MacIver, R. *Community: A Sociological Study.* (3rd ed.) London: Macmillan, 1936.

Maier, P. "Popular Uprisings and Civil Authority in Eighteenth-

Century America." *William and Mary Quarterly,* 1970, *27,* 3-35.

Maisel, R. "The Decline of Mass Media." *Public Opinion Quarterly,* 1973, *37,* 159-170.

Manners, G. "The Office in the Metropolis: An Opportunity for Shaping Metropolitan America." *Economic Geography,* 1974, *50,* 93-110.

Mapstone, J. R. "Moving to the Country: Return Migration to a Rural Urban." Paper presented at the annual meeting of the Rural Sociological Society, San Francisco, August 1975.

Marris, P., and Rein, M. *Dilemmas of Social Reform: Poverty and Community Action in the United States.* New York: Atherton, 1967.

Marshall, T. H. *Citizenship and Social Class.* Cambridge, Mass.: Cambridge University Press, 1950.

Martin, R. C. *Government and the Suburban School.* Syracuse, N.Y.: Syracuse University Press, 1962.

Martin, W. T. "Ecological Change in Satellite Rural Areas." *American Sociological Review,* 1957, *22,* 173-183.

Martindale, D. "Prefatory Remarks: The Theory of the City." In M. Weber, *The City.* (D. Martindale and G. Neuwirth, Trans. and Eds.) New York: Free Press, 1958.

Martindale, D., and Hanson, R. G. *Small Town and the Nation.* Westport, Conn.: Greenwood, 1969.

Marx, K. *Karl Marx: Selected Writings in Sociology and Social Philosophy.* (T. B. Bottomore, Trans.) New York: McGraw-Hill, 1956.

Masotti, L. H., and Hadden, J. K. (Eds.). *Urban Affairs Annual Review.* Vol. 7: *The Urbanization of the Suburbs.* Beverly Hills, Calif.: Sage, 1973.

Mayo, E. *The Social Problems of an Industrial Civilization.* Boston: Harvard Graduate School of Business Administration, 1945.

Mazie, S. M. (Ed.). *Population Distribution and Policy.* Vol. 5. Washington, D.C.: U.S. Commission on Population Growth and the American Future, 1972.

Mazie, S. M., and Rawlins, S. "Public Attitude Towards Population Distribution Issues." In S. M. Mazie (Ed.), *Population Distribution and Policy.* Vol. 5. Washington, D.C.: U.S. Commission on Population Growth and the American Future, 1972.

McCarthy, C. "Ousting the Stranger from the House." *Newsweek,* March 25, 1974, p. 17.

McCombs, M., and Shaw, D. "The Agenda-Setting Function of Mass Media." *Public Opinion Quarterly*, 1972, *36*, 176-187.

McGahan, P. "The Neighbor Role and Neighboring in a Highly Urban Area." *Sociological Quarterly*, 1972, *13*, 397-408.

McGee, T. G. *The South East Asian City*. London: Bell, 1967.

McGinnis, J. *The Selling of the President, 1968*. New York: Trident Press, 1969.

McGreevey, W. P. *An Economic History of Colombia, 1845-1930*. New York: Cambridge University Press, 1971.

McHarg, I. L. *Design With Nature*. New York: Doubleday, 1969.

McKelvey, B. *American Prisons*. Montclair, N.J.: Patterson Smith, 1968.

McKenzie, R. D. *The Neighborhood: A Study of Local Life in the City of Columbus, Ohio, 1923*. Chicago: University of Chicago Press, 1923.

McKenzie, R. D. "Ecological Succession in the Puget Sound Region." *Publications of the American Sociological Society*, 1929, *23*, 60-80.

McKenzie, R. D. *The Metropolitan Community*. New York: McGraw-Hill, 1933.

McKinney, J. C., and Bourque, L. B. "The Changing South." *American Sociological Review*, 1971, *36*, 399-411.

McLuhan, M. *Understanding Media*. New York: McGraw-Hill, 1965.

McPhee, W., and Meyersohn, R. *Futures for Radio*. New York: Bureau of Applied Social Research, 1955.

McQuail, D. *Towards a Sociology of Mass Communications*. London: Collier-Macmillan, 1969.

Meggers, B. J. "Environmental Limitations on the Development of Culture." *American Anthropologist*, 1954, *56*, 801-824.

Mellor, R. "Urban Sociology in an Urbanized Society." *British Journal of Sociology*, 1975, *26*, 276-293.

Mendelsohn, H., and Crespi, I. *Polls, Television, and the New Politics*. Scranton, Pa.: Chandler, 1970.

Mendelson, M. A. *Tender Loving Greed: How the Incredibly Lucrative Nursing Home "Industry" is Exploiting America's Old People and Defrauding Us All*. New York: Random House, 1975.

Mennel, R. M. *Thorns and Thistles*. Hanover, N.H.: University Press of New England, 1973.

Merton, R. K. *Social Theory and Social Structure*. New York: Free Press, 1968.

Meyer, J. R., Kain, J. F., and Wohl, M. *The Urban Transportation Problem.* Cambridge, Mass.: Harvard University Press, 1965.

Meyer, M. W. "Size and the Structure of Organizations: A Causal Analysis." *American Sociological Review,* 1972, *37,* 434-440.

Meyersohn, R. "The Second Home." In *Leisure Time and Recreation.* New York: The Rockefeller Foundation Hudson Basin Project, 1976.

Meyerson, M., and Banfield, E. C. *Politics, Planning, and the Public Interest.* New York: Free Press, 1955.

Michelson, S. "The Political Economy of Public School Finance." In M. Carnoy (Ed.), *Schooling in a Corporate Society.* New York: McKay, 1972.

Michelson, W. "Environmental Change." Paper No. 60. Toronto: Department of Sociology and Centre for Urban and Community Studies, University of Toronto, 1973.

Michelson, W. "The Reconciliation of 'Subjective' and 'Objective' Data on Physical Environment in the Community: The Case of Social Contact in High-Rise Apartments." In M. P. Effrat (Ed.), *The Community: Approaches and Application.* New York: Free Press, 1974.

Michelson, W. H. *Man and His Urban Environment: A Sociological Approach.* (2nd ed.) Reading, Mass.: Addison-Wesley, 1976.

Michelson, W. H. *Environmental Choice, Human Behavior, and Residential Satisfaction.* New York: Oxford University Press, 1977.

Miller, B. "Career Expectations of Social Work Students." Unpublished paper, Department of Sociology, College of Social Work, University of Illinois at Chicago Circle, 1977.

Miller, H. L. *Education for the Disadvantaged.* New York: Free Press, 1967.

Miller, H. R. "The Reader's Digest and the Schools." Unpublished report of the Committee on Magazines of the National Council of Teachers of English, Evanston, Ill., 1942.

Mills, E. S. "Urban Density Functions." *Urban Studies,* 1970, *7,* 5-20.

Minar, D. W. "School, Community, and Politics in Suburban Areas." In B. J. Chandler, L. J. Stiles, and J. I. Kitsuse (Eds.), *Education in Urban Society.* New York: Dodd, Mead, 1962.

Minar, D. W. *Educational Decision-Making in Suburban Communities.* Cooperative Research Project No. 2440. Washington, D.C.: U.S. Office of Education, Department of Health, Education, and Welfare, 1966.

Minar, D. W. "Interactions of School and Local Nonschool Governments in Metropolitan Areas." In R. J. Havighurst (Ed.), *Metropolitanism: Its Challenge to Education.* Chicago: National Society for the Study of Education, 1968.

Miner, H. "Old and New." In Robert French (Ed.), *The Community.* Itasca, Ill.: Peacock, 1969.

Mirande, A. M. "Extended Kinship Ties, Friendship Relations, and Community Size: An Exploratory Inquiry." *Rural Sociology,* 1970, *35,* 261-266.

Mitchell, R. E. "Some Social Implications of High Density Living." *American Sociological Review,* 1971, *36,* 18-29.

Mittlebach, F. G., and Moore, J. W. "Ethnic Endogamy—the Case of Mexican Americans." *American Journal of Sociology,* 1968, *74,* 50-62.

Mizruchi, E. H. "Social Structure and Anomie in a Small City." *American Sociological Review,* 1976, *25,* 645-654.

Molotch, H. *Managed Integration: Dilemmas of Doing Good in the City.* Berkeley: University of California Press, 1973.

Molotch, H. "The City as a Growth Machine." *American Journal of Sociology,* 1976, *80,* 309-332.

Mooney, M. M. "Death of the Post." *Atlantic Monthly,* November 1969, pp. 70-71.

Moore, T. "The Demand for Broadway Theater Tickets, 1966." In M. Blaug (Ed.), *Economics of the Arts.* London: Martin Robinson, 1976.

Moore, W. *Social Change.* Englewood Cliffs, N.J.: Prentice-Hall, 1963.

Moore, Jr., W. *The Vertical Ghetto.* New York: Random House, 1969.

Moore, Jr., W., Livermore, C. P., and Galland, Jr., G. F. "Woodlawn: The Zone of Destruction." *The Public Interest,* 1973, *30,* 49-51.

Morgan, E. S. *The Puritan Family.* New York: Harper & Row, 1966.

Morgan, J. M. "A Note on the Time Spent on the Journey to Work." *Demography,* 1967, *4,* 360-362.

Morrison, P. A. "Chronic Movers and the Future Redistribution of Population: A Longitudinal Analysis." *Demography,* 1971, *8,* 171-184.

Morrison, P. A. *Demographic Trends that Will Shape Future Housing Demand.* Rand Paper Series P-5596. Santa Monica, Calif.: Rand Corporation, 1976.

Morrison, P. A., and Wheeler, J. R. *Working Women and "Woman's Work": A Demographic Perspective on the Breakdown of Sex Roles.* Rand Paper Series P-5669. Santa Monica, Calif.: Rand Corporation, 1976.

Morse, R. M. "The Development of Urban Systems in the Americas in the Nineteenth Century." *Journal of Inter-American Studies and World Affairs,* 1975, *17,* 4-26.

Moskos, C. "Why Men Fight: American Combat Soldiers in Vietnam." *Trans-Action,* 1969, *1,* 13-23.

Mosteller, F., and Moynihan, D. P. *On Equality of Educational Opportunity.* New York: Vintage Books, 1972.

Mott, F. L. *Golden Multitudes.* New York: Macmillan, 1947.

Mott, F. L. *American Journalism.* New York: Macmillan, 1953.

Mowrer, E. *Family Disorganization.* Chicago: University of Chicago Press, 1927.

Moynihan, D. P. *The Negro Family: The Case for National Action.* Washington, D.C.: U.S. Department of Labor, 1965.

Moynihan, D. P. *Maximum Feasible Misunderstanding: Community Action in the War on Poverty.* New York: Free Press, 1969.

Moynihan, D. P., and Glazer, N. "Why Ethnicity?" *Commentary,* 1974, *58,* 33-39.

Mueller, C. W. "City Effects on Socioeconomic Achievements: The Case of Large Cities." *American Sociological Review,* 1974, *39,* 652-667.

Mueller, P. O. *The Outer City: Geographical Consequences of the Urbanization of the Suburbs.* Resource Paper No. 75-2. Washington, D.C.: Association of American Geographers, 1976.

Mueller, S. A. "The New Triple Melting Pot: Herberg Revisited." In P. H. McNamara (Ed.), *Religion American Style.* New York: Harper & Row, 1974.

Mulvihill, D. J., Tumin, M. M., and Curtis, L. A. *Crimes of Violence.* Staff Report to the National Commission on the Causes and Prevention of Violence. Washington, D.C.: U.S. Government Printing Office, 1969.

Mumford, L. *The Culture of Cities.* New York: Harcourt Brace Jovanovich, 1938.

Mumford, L. "City: Forms and Functions." In D. L. Sills (Ed.), *International Encyclopedia of the Social Sciences.* Vol. 2. New York: Macmillan, 1968.

Munson, B. E. "Personality Differences Among Urban, Suburban, Town, and Rural Children." *Rural Sociology,* 1959, *18,* 256-264.

Musil, J. "The Development of Prague's Ecological Structure." In R. E. Pahl (Ed.), *Readings in Urban Sociology*. Oxford, England: Pergamon Press, 1968.

National Advisory Commission on Civil Disorders. *Report*. New York: Bantam, 1968.

National Commission on Technology, Automation, and Economic Progress. *Employment Impact of Technological Change*. Appendix. Vol. 2: *Technology and the American Economy*. Washington, D.C.: U.S. Government Printing Office, 1966.

National Review. "The Post RIP." January 28, 1969, p. 64.

National Tourism Resources Review Commission. *Destination U.S.A.* Washington, D.C.: U.S. Government Printing Office, 1973.

Neenan, W. "The Suburban-Central City Exploitation Thesis: One City's Tale." *National Tax Journal*, 1970, *23*, 117-139.

Neenan, W. *Political Economy of Urban Areas*. Chicago: Markham, 1972.

Nelson, B. "Weber's Protestant Ethic: Its Origins, Wanderings, and Foreseeable Futures." In C. Y. Glock and P. E. Hammond (Eds.), *Beyond the Classics? Essays in the Scientific Study of Religion*. New York: Harper & Row, 1973.

Nelson, H. M., and Yokley, R. L. "Civil Rights Attitudes of Rural and Urban Presbyterians." *Rural Sociology*, 1970, *35*, 161-174.

Nelson, H. M., Yokley, R. L., and Madron, T. W. "Rural-Urban Differences in Religiosity." *Rural Sociology*, 1971, *36*, 389-395.

Nelson, W. E. *Americanization of the Common Law*. Cambridge, Mass.: Harvard University Press, 1975.

Newcomb, H. *TV: The Most Popular Art*. New York: Doubleday, 1974.

Newman, O. *Defensible Space*. New York: Macmillan, 1972.

Newman, W. M. *American Pluralism*. New York: Harper & Row, 1973.

Newsweek. "Digest in the Doghouse." February 21, 1944, p. 82ff.

Newsweek. "Death of an Institution." January 20, 1969, pp. 52-53.

Newsweek. "The Lingering Death of Life." December 18, 1972, pp. 109-111.

Newsweek. "From Here to Obscenity." November 17, 1975, p. 76.

Newton, K. "Feeble Government and Private Power: Urban Politics and Policies in the United States." In L. Masotti and

R. Lindberry (Eds.), *The New Urban Politics*. Cambridge, Mass.: Ballinger, 1976.

The New York Times. "More Newspapers Change Hands." January 15, 1977, p. 16.

1901 Census of England and Wales. London: Her Majesty's Stationery Office, 1902-1903.

Nisbet, R. *The Quest for Community*. New York: Oxford University Press, 1953.

Nisbet, R. *The Sociological Tradition*. New York: Basic Books, 1966.

Novak, M. "Television Shapes the Soul." In D. Cater and R. Adler (Eds.), *Television as a Social Force: New Approaches to TV Criticism*. New York: Praeger, 1975.

Oberholzer, Jr., E. *Delinquent Saints*. New York: Columbia University Press, 1956.

O'Donnell, E. J., and Sullivan, M. N. "Service Delivery and Social Action Through the Neighborhood Center: A Review of Research." In H. W. Demone and D. Harshberger (Eds.), *A Handbook of Human Service Organizations*. New York: Behavioral Publications, 1974.

Ogburn, W. F., and Duncan, O. D. "City Size as a Sociological Variable." In E. W. Burgess and D. J. Bogue (Eds.), *Contributions to Urban Sociology*. Chicago: University of Chicago Press, 1964.

Oliveira, F. de. "A Economia Brasileira: Critica a Razao Estudos." *Cebrap*, 1972, *2*, 5-82.

Olsen, M. E. "Multivariate Analysis of National Political Development." *American Sociological Review*, 1968, *33*, 699-711.

Olsen, M. E. "Social Participation and Voter Turnout: A Multivariate Analysis." *American Sociological Review*, 1972, *37*, 317-333.

Oppenheimer, V. K. "Demographic Influence on Female Employment and the Status of Women." In J. Huber (Ed.), *Changing Women in a Changing Society*. Chicago: University of Chicago Press, 1973.

Ornstein, A. C. *Race and Politics in School/Community Organizations*. Pacific Palisades, Calif.: Goodyear, 1974.

O'Shea, D. W. "Urban Community Control: What Can We Learn from the Suburban Experience?" Paper presented at the annual meeting of the American Educational Research Association, 1975.

Ostrom, V., Tiebout, C. M., and Warren, R. "In Defense of the Polycentric Metropolis." *American Political Science Review*, 1961, *55*, 831-842.

Palm, R., and Pred, A. *A Time-Geographic Perspective on Problems of Inequality for Women.* Working Paper No. 236. Berkeley: Institute of Urban and Regional Development, University of California, 1974.

Pampel, F. C., and Choldin, H. M. "Urban Location and Segregation of the Aged: A Block-Level Analysis." *Social Forces,* in press.

Pappenfort, D. M. "The Ecological Field and the Metropolitan Community: Manufacturing and Management." *American Journal of Sociology,* 1959, *64,* 380-385.

Parenti, M. "Ethnic Politics and the Persistence of Ethnic Identification." *American Political Science Review,* 1967, *61,* 717-726.

Park, R. E. "The City." *American Journal of Sociology,* 1915, *20,* 607-608.

Park, R. E. "The City: Suggestions for the Investigation of Human Behavior in the Urban Environment." In R. E. Park, E. W. Burgess, and R. D. McKenzie (Eds.), *The City.* Chicago: University of Chicago Press, 1925.

Park, R. E. "Urbanization as Measured by Newspaper Circulation." *American Journal of Sociology,* 1929, *35,* 60-79.

Park, R. E. *Human Communities.* New York: Free Press, 1952.

Park, R. W., and Burgess, E. W. *Introduction to the Science of Sociology.* Chicago: University of Chicago Press, 1921.

Park, R. E., Burgess, E. W., and McKenzie, R. D. (Eds.). *The City.* Chicago: University of Chicago Press, 1925.

Parsons, T. "Age and Sex in the Social Structure of the United States." *American Sociological Review,* 1942, *7,* 604-616.

Parsons, T. *Structure and Process in Modern Societies.* New York: Free Press, 1960.

Parsons, T. *Societies: Evolutionary and Comparative Perspectives.* Englewood Cliffs, N.J.: Prentice-Hall, 1966.

Parsons, T. "Full Citizenship for the Negro American? A Sociological Problem." In T. Parsons and K. B. Clark (Eds.), *The Negro American.* Boston: Beacon Press, 1967.

Parsons, T. "Social Science and Theology." In W. A. Beardslee (Ed.), *America and the Future of Theology.* Philadelphia: Westminster Press, 1967.

Parsons, T. "Christianity." In D. L. Sills (Ed.), *International Encyclopedia of the Social Sciences.* Vol. 2. New York: Macmillan, 1968.

Parsons, T. "Belief, Unbelief, and Disbelief." In R. Caporale and A. Grumelli (Eds.), *The Culture of Unbelief.* Studies and proceedings from the First International Symposium on Belief,

Rome, March 22-27, 1969. Berkeley: University of California Press, 1971.

Parsons, T. "Religion in Postindustrial America: The Problem of Secularization." *Social Research,* 1974, *41,* 193-225.

Parsons, T., and Shils, E. A. (Eds.) *Toward a General Theory of Action.* New York: Harper & Row, 1951.

Patterson, T., and McClure, R. *The Unseeing Eye.* New York: Putnam, 1976.

Pearce, D. "Black, White, and Many Shades of Gray: Real Estate Brokers and Their Racial Practices." Unpublished doctoral dissertation, University of Michigan, Ann Arbor, 1976.

Peck, E., and Senderowitz, J. (Eds.). *Pronatalism: The Myth of Mom and Apple Pie.* New York: Crowell, 1974.

Perrow, C. "Realty Shock: A New Organization Confronts the Custody-Treatment Dilemma." *Social Problems,* 1963, *10,* 374-382.

Pettigrew, T. F. *Racially Separate or Together.* New York: McGraw-Hill, 1971.

Pettigrew, T. F. "Extending Educational Opportunities: School Desegregation." In M. Gittell (Ed.), *Educating an Urban Population.* Beverly Hills, Calif.: Sage, 1967.

Pettigrew, T. F. *A Profile of the American Negro.* New York: D. Van Nostrand, 1964.

Pettigrew, T. F., and Green, R. L. "School Desegregation in Large Cities: A Critique of the Coleman 'White Flight' Thesis." *Harvard Educational Review,* 1976, *46,* 1-53.

Pfautz, H. W. "The Black Community, the Community School, and the Socialization Process: Some Caveats." In H. M. Levin (Ed.), *Community Control of Schools.* New York: Simon & Schuster, 1970.

Photiadis, J. D. "Social Integration of Businessmen in Varied Size Communities." *Social Forces,* 1967, *46,* 229-236.

Photiadis, J. D., and Ball, R. A. "Patterns of Change in Rural Normative Structure." *Rural Sociology,* 1975, *41,* 61-73.

Piccagli, G. "Racial Transition in the Chicago Public Schools." Unpublished doctoral dissertation, University of Chicago, 1975.

Pifer, A. "The Quasi Nongovernmental Organization." In *Annual Reports.* New York: Carnegie Corporation, 1967.

Piven, F. F., and Cloward, R. *Regulating the Poor: The Functions of Public Welfare.* New York: Random House, 1971.

Plant, J. S. "Some Psychiatric Aspects of Crowded Living Conditions." *American Journal of Psychiatry,* 1930, *9,* 849-860.

Platt, R. S. "Environmentalism Versus Geography." *American Journal of Sociology*, 1948, *53*, 351-358.

"Plummeting PMs." *Wall Street Journal*, May 25, 1976, pp. 1, 18.

Pohlman, E. "Changes in Views Toward Childlessness: 1965-1970." In E. Peck and J. Senderowitz (Eds.), *Pronatalism: The Myth of Mom and Apple Pie*. New York: Crowell, 1974.

Popenoe, D. "Urban Residential Differentiation: An Overview of Patterns, Trends, and Problems." In M. P. Effrat (Ed.), *The Community: Approaches and Applications*. New York: Free Press, 1974.

Popenoe, D. *The Suburban Environment: Sweden and the United States*. Chicago: University of Chicago Press, 1977.

Porter, W. *Assault on the Media: The Nixon Years*. Ann Arbor: University of Michigan Press, 1976.

Pottick, K. J. "Social Workers' Perception of Their Professional Environment." Unpublished preliminary examination, Ph.D. Program in Social Work and Social Science, University of Michigan, Ann Arbor, 1977.

Powdermaker, H. *Hollywood, Dream Factory*. Boston: Little, Brown, 1972.

Powers, E. *Crime and Punishment in Early Massachusetts*. Boston: Beacon Press, 1966.

Powers, M. G., and Thacker, C. "Mobility and the Fertility of Wives in an Urban Neighborhood." *International Migration Review*, 1975, *9*, 211-219.

Pratt, S. "Metropolitan Community Development and Change in Sub-Center Economic Functions." *American Sociological Review*, 1957, *22*, 434-440.

Pred, A. *The Spatial Dynamics of U.S. Urban Industrial Growth, 1800-1914*. Cambridge, Mass.: M.I.T. Press, 1966.

Preobrazhensky, E. *The New Economics*. Oxford, England: Clarendon Press, 1965.

Preston, S. H. "Female Employment Policy and Fertility." In C. F. Westoff and R. Parke, Jr. (Eds.), *Aspects of Population Growth Policy*. Vol. 6. Washington, D.C.: U.S. Commission on Population Growth and the American Future, 1973.

Preston, S. H., and Richards, A. T. "The Influence of Women's Work Opportunities on Marriage Rates." *Demography*, 1975, *12*, 209-222.

Publishers' Weekly. "New Survey Shows Paperback Growth Rate." June 29, 1970, p. 78.

Publishers' Weekly. "Best Sellers 70-71." February 7, 1972, p. 51.

Publishers' Weekly. "Best Sellers: The Year of the Bird and the Bible." February 5, 1973, p. 41.

Quijano, A. "Redefinicion de la Dependencia y Proceso de Marginalizacion en America Latina." In F. C. Weffort and A. Quijano (Eds.), *Populismo, Marginalizacion y Dependencia.* San Jose, Costa Rica: Editorial Universitaria Centroamericana, 1973.

Rainwater, L. "Fear and the House-as-Haven in the Lower Class." *Journal of the American Institute of Planners,* 1966, *32,* 23-31.

Rainwater, L. *Behind Ghetto Walls: Black Family Life in a Federal Slum.* Chicago: Aldine, 1970.

Rapoport, A. *House Form and Culture.* Englewood Cliffs, N.J.: Prentice-Hall, 1969.

Ratcliff, R. U. "Housing Standards and Housing Research." *Land Economics,* 1952, *28,* 328-332.

Ray, M. "Marketing Communication and the Hierarchy of Effects." In P. Clarke (Ed.), *New Models for Mass Communication Research.* Beverly Hills, Calif.: Sage, 1973.

Redfield, R. "The Folk Society." *American Journal of Sociology,* 1947, *52,* 293-308.

Redford, A. *Labour Migration in England, 1800-1850.* Manchester, England: Manchester University Press, 1926.

Reichley, A. "The Political Containment of the Cities." In A. K. Campbell (Ed.), *The States and the Urban Crisis.* New York: Columbia University Press, 1970.

Reiss, A. J. "Rural-Urban Status Differences." *American Journal of Sociology,* 1959, *65,* 182-195.

Reissman, L. *The Urban Process: Cities in Industrial Societies.* London: Collier-Macmillan, 1964.

Richardson, J. F. *The New York Police: Colonial Times to 1901.* New York: Oxford University Press, 1970.

Richardson, J. L., and Larson, O. F. "Small Community Trends: A 50-Year Perspective on Socio-Economic Change in 13 New York Communities." *Rural Sociology,* 1976, *41,* 45-59.

Riesman, D. "Work and Leisure in Post Industrial Society." In E. Larrabee and R. Meyersohn (Eds.), *Mass Leisure.* New York: Free Press, 1958.

Riesman, D., Glazer, N., and Denney, R. *The Lonely Crowd.* New Haven, Conn.: Yale University Press, 1950.

Riessman, F. *The Culturally Deprived Child.* New York: Harper & Row, 1962.

Riska, E. "Urban Growth and Local Health Care Policy." Unpublished doctoral dissertation, State University of New York at Stony Brook, 1974.

Rist, R. C. "Student Social Class and Teacher Expectations." *Harvard Educational Review,* 1970, *40,* 411-451.

Ritter, K. V., and Hargens, L. L. "Occupational Positions and Class Identifications of Married Working Women: A Test of the Asymmetry Hypothesis." *American Journal of Sociology,* 1975, *80,* 934-948.

Rivers, W. *The Adversaries.* Boston: Beacon Press, 1970.

Robinson, J. "Television and Leisure Time: Yesterday, Today, and (Maybe) Tomorrow." *Public Opinion Quarterly,* 1969, *33,* 210-222.

Robinson, J. "Mass Communication and Information Diffusion." In F. G. Kline (Ed.), *Current Perspectives in Mass Communication Research.* Beverly Hills, Calif.: Sage, 1972.

Robinson, J. "Public Opinion During the Watergate Crisis." *Communication Research,* 1974, *1,* 391-405.

Robinson, J. P. *How Americans Use Time.* New York: Praeger, 1976.

Robinson, J., and Bachman, J. "Television Viewing Habits and Aggression." In G. Comstock and E. Rubinstein (Eds.), *Television and Social Behavior.* Vol. 3. Rockville, Md.: National Institute of Mental Health, 1972.

Robinson, M. "American Political Legitimacy in an Era of Electronic Journalism: Reflections on the Evening News." In D. Cater and R. Adler (Eds.), *Television as a Social Force: New Approaches to TV Criticism.* New York: Praeger, 1975.

Robson, B. T. *Urban Growth: An Approach.* London: Methuen, 1973.

Rogers, D. *110 Livingston Street.* New York: Vintage Books, 1969.

Rogers, E., and Shoemaker, F. *Communication of Innovations: A Cross-Cultural Approach.* New York: Free Press, 1971.

Rogoff, N. "Local Social Structure and Educational Selection." In A. H. Halsey, J. Floud, and C. A. Anderson (Eds.), *Education, Economy and Society.* New York: Free Press, 1961.

Roncek, D. W. "Density and Crime: A Methodological Critique." *American Behavioral Scientist,* 1975, *18,* 843-860.

Roncek, D. W. "Space and Crime in Two Large Cities: A Block-

Level Analysis." Paper presented at the annual meeting of the American Sociological Association, New York, 1976.

Roper Organization. *An Extended View of Public Attitudes Toward Television and Other Mass Media.* New York: Television Information Office, 1971.

Roper Organization. *Trends in Public Attitudes Toward Television.* New York: Television Information Office, 1975.

Rorty, J. "The Reader's Digest." *Commonweal,* May 12, 1944, pp. 78-84.

Roschco, B. *Newsmaking.* Chicago: University of Chicago Press, 1975.

Rose, A. "The Social Services in the Modern Metropolis." *Social Service Review,* 1963, *37,* 375-389.

Rose, A. M., and Rose, C. B. *Sociology: The Study of Human Relations.* (3rd ed.) New York: Knopf, 1970.

Rosenberg, B., and White, D. (Eds.). *Mass Culture.* New York: Free Press, 1957.

Rosenberg, T. J. "Ghetto Residence, Employment Opportunities, and Mobility of Puerto Ricans in New York City." Paper presented at the annual meeting of the Population Association of America, New Orleans, 1973.

Rosenblatt, R. "Report from the Dream Game." *The New Republic,* February 14, 1976, pp. 31-33.

Rosenstein-Rodan, P. "Problems of Industrialization in Eastern and South-Eastern Europe." *Economic Journal,* 1943, *53,* 202-211.

Rosenthal, A. *Pedagogues and Power.* Syracuse, N.Y.: Syracuse University Press, 1969.

Rosenthal, E. "Acculturation Without Assimilation? The Jewish Community of Chicago, Illinois." *American Journal of Sociology,* 1960, *66,* 275-288.

Rosenthal, E. "Jewish Intermarriage in the United States." In A. M. Rose and C. B. Rose (Eds.), *Minority Problems.* (2nd ed.) New York: Harper & Row, 1972.

Rosenthal, E. R. "Working in Mid-Life." In A. Stromberg and S. Harkess (Eds.), *Women Working: Theories and Facts in Perspective.* Palo Alto, Calif.: Mayfield, 1978.

Rosenwaike, I. "Interethnic Comparisons of Educational Attainment: An Analysis Based on Census Data for New York City." *American Journal of Sociology,* 1973, *79,* 68-77.

Rossi, P. H. *Why Families Move.* New York: Free Press, 1955.

Rossi, P. H., and Dentler, R. A. *The Politics of Urban Renewal.* New York: Free Press, 1961.

Rossides, D. W. *The American Class System: An Introduction to Social Stratification.* Boston: Houghton Mifflin, 1976.

Rothschild, E. *Paradise Lost: The Decline of the Auto Industrial Age.* New York: Random House, 1973.

Rothenberg, M. "Effect of Television Violence on Children and Youth." *Journal of the American Medical Association,* 1975, *234,* 1043-1046.

Rothman, D. J. *The Discovery of the Asylum.* Boston: Little, Brown, 1971.

Rothstein, M. "Antebellum Wheat and Cotton Exports: A Contrast in Marketing Organization and Economic Development." *Agricultural History,* 1966, *41,* 91-100.

Rothstein, M. "The Antebellum South as a Dual Economy: A Tentative Hypothesis." *Agricultural History,* 1967, *42,* 373-382.

Rozak, T. *The Making of a Counterculture.* New York: Doubleday, 1969.

Rubin, J. "Growth and Expansion of Urban Centers." In A. M. Wakstein (Ed.), *The Urbanization of America: A Historical Anthology.* Boston: Houghton Mifflin, 1970.

Rubinstein, E., Comstock, G., and Murray, J. *Television and Social Behavior.* Vols. 1-5. Rockville, Md.: National Institute of Mental Health, 1972.

Rybeck, W. *Property Taxation: Housing and Urban Growth.* Washington, D.C.: Urban Institute, 1970.

Sabagh, G., Van Arsdol, Jr., M. D., and Butler, E. "Some Determinants of Intrametropolitan Residential Mobility: Conceptual Considerations." *Social Forces,* 1969, *48,* 88-98.

Sacks, S. "Central City and Suburban Public Education." In R. J. Havighurst (Ed.), *Metropolitanism: Its Challenge to Education.* Chicago: National Society for the Study of Education, 1968.

Sacks, S. *City Schools/Suburban Schools.* Syracuse, N.Y.: Syracuse University Press, 1972.

Safilios-Rothschild, C. "Family and Stratification: Some Macrosociological Observations and Hypotheses." *Journal of Marriage and the Family,* 1975, *37,* 855-860.

Salem, M. "The Seattle Opera." Unpublished doctoral dissertation, School of Business, University of Washington, 1974.

Sawhill, I. "Discrimination and Poverty Among Women Who Head Families." *Signs: Journal of Women in Culture and Society,* 1976, *1,* 201-212.

Scaff, A. "The Effect of Commuting on Participation in Community Organizations." *American Sociological Review,* 1952, *17,* 215-220.

Scanzoni, J. H. *Sex Roles, Life Styles, and Childbearing: Changing Patterns in Marriage and the Family.* New York: Free Press, 1975.

Schaffer, A. "A Rural Community at the Urban Fringe." *Rural Sociology,* 1958, *23,* 277-285.

Schick, F. L. *The Paperbound Book in America.* New York: Bowker, 1958.

Schiller, H. *The Mind Managers.* Boston: Beacon Press, 1973.

Schlesinger, A. M. "City in American History." In P. Kramer and F. Holborn (Eds.), *The City in American Life.* New York: Capricorn, 1971.

Schmalenbach, H. "Die Soziologische Kategorie des Bundes." *Die Dioskuren: Jahrbuch fur Geisteswissenschaften,* 1922, *1,* 35-105.

Schmitt, R. C. "Density, Delinquency, and Crime in Honolulu." *Sociology and Social Research,* 1957, *41,* 274-276.

Schmitt, R. C. "Density, Health, and Social Disorganization." *Journal of the American Institute of Planners,* 1966, *32,* 38-40.

Schneider, L., and Dornbusch, S. M. "Inspirational Religious Literature: From Latent to Manifest Functions of Religion." *The American Journal of Sociology,* 1957, *62,* 476-481.

Schnore, L. F. "The Social and Economic Characteristics of American Suburbs." *Sociological Quarterly,* 1963, *4,* 122-134.

Schnore, L. F. "On the Spatial Structure of Cities in the Two Americas." In P. M. Hauser and L. F. Schnore (Eds.), *The Study of Urbanization.* New York: Wiley, 1965a.

Schnore, L. F. *The Urban Scene.* New York: Free Press, 1965b.

Schnore, L. F. *Class and Race in Cities and Suburbs.* Chicago: Markham, 1972.

Schnore, L. F., André, C. D., and Sharp, H. "Black Suburbanization, 1930-1970." In B. Schwartz (Ed.), *The Changing Face of the Suburbs.* Chicago: University of Chicago Press, 1976.

Schnore, L. F., and Jones, J. K. "The Evolution of City-Suburban Types in the Course of a Decade." *Urban Affairs Quarterly,* 1969, *4,* 421-423.

Schorr, A. "The Tasks for Voluntarism in the Next Decade." *Child of Welfare,* 1970, *49,* 425-434.

Schulze, R. O. "Economic Dominants in Community Power

Structure." In R. French (Ed.), *The Community.* Itasca, Ill.: Peacock, 1969.

Schuman, H. "The Religious Factor in Detroit: Review, Replication, and Reanalysis." *American Sociological Review,* 1971, *36,* 30-48.

Schwartz, B. "Images of Suburbia: Some Revisionist Commentary and Conclusions." In B. Schwartz (Ed.), *The Changing Face of the Suburbs.* Chicago: University of Chicago Press, 1976.

Schwarzlose, R. A. "Trends in U.S. Newspapers' Wire Service Resources, 1934-66." *Journalism Quarterly,* 1966, *43,* 627-638.

Schwirian, K. P., and LaGreca, A. J. "An Ecological Analysis of Urban Mortality Rates." *Social Science Quarterly,* 1971, *52,* 574-587.

Scitovsky, T. *The Joyless Economy.* New York: Oxford University Press, 1976.

Scobie, J. R. *Revolution on the Pampas: A Social History of Argentine Wheat, 1860-1910.* Austin: University of Texas Press, 1964.

Scott, M. *American City Planning.* Berkeley: University of California Press, 1971.

Scott, S. "Lessons from the History of American Broadcasting." *Science,* 1972, *178,* 1263-1265.

Seeley, J. R., Sims, R. A., and Loosly, E. W. *Crestwood Heights.* New York: Basic Books, 1956.

Segal, D. R., and Meyer, M. W. "The Social Context of Political Partisanship." In S. Rokkan (Ed.), *Quantitative Ecological Analysis in the Social Sciences.* Cambridge: M.I.T. Press, 1969.

Segal, D. R., and Wildstrom, S. H. "Community Effects on Political Attitudes." *Sociological Quarterly,* 1970, *11,* 67-86.

Seiden, M. H. *Who Controls the Mass Media?* New York: Basic Books, 1974.

Seiler, L. H. "Community Verticalization: On the Interface Between Corporate Influence and Horizontal Leadership." Working Paper RID 74.3. Madison: Center of Applied Sociology, University of Wisconsin, 1973.

Seligson, M. "The Million-Dollar Loneliness of Rod McKuen." *McCall's,* February 1972, pp. 12ff.

Sennett, R. *The Uses of Disorder.* New York: Knopf, 1970.

Seymour-Ure, C. *The Political Impact of Mass Media.* Beverly Hills, Calif.: Sage, 1974.

Shea, J. R., and others. *Dual Careers: A Longitudinal Study of Labor Market Experience of Women.* Columbus: Ohio State University, 1970.

Sheehy, G. *Passages: Predictable Crises of Adult Life.* New York: Dutton, 1976.

Shevky, E., and Bell, W. *Social Area Analysis: Theory, Illustrative Application, and Computational Procedures.* Stanford, Calif.: Stanford University Press, 1955.

Shevky, E., and Williams, M. *The Social Areas of Los Angeles and Berkeley: Analysis and Typology.* Los Angeles and Berkeley: University of California Press, 1949.

Shils, E. A. "Primordial, Personal, Sacred, and Civil Ties." *British Journal of Sociology,* 1957, *8,* 130-145.

Shils, E. A. "Centre and Periphery." In E. A. Shils (Ed.), *The Logic of Personal Knowledge: Essays Presented to Michael Polanyi on His Seventieth Birthday, 11th March 1961.* London: Routledge and Kegan Paul, 1961.

Shils, E. A. "The Theory of the Mass Society." *Diogenes,* 1962, *39,* 45-66.

Shils, E. A. *Center and Periphery: Essays in Macrosociology.* Chicago: University of Chicago Press, 1975.

Shiner, L. "The Concept of Secularization in Empirical Research." *Journal for the Scientific Study of Religion,* 1967, *6,* 207-220.

Shippey, F. A. "The Variety of City Churches." In R. D. Knudten (Ed.), *The Sociology of Religion: An Anthology.* New York: Appleton-Century-Crofts, 1967.

Siegan, B. *Land Use Without Zoning.* Lexington, Mass.: Heath, 1972.

Silberman, M. "Toward a Theory of Criminal Deterrence." *American Sociological Review,* 1976, *41,* 442-461.

Sills, D. "The Environmental Movement and Its Critics." *Human Ecology,* Fall 1975, pp. 1-41.

Sim, J. C. *The Grass Roots Press.* Ames: Iowa State University Press, 1969.

Simmel, G. "Die Grossstadt und das Geistesleben." *Die Grossstadt: Jahrbuch der Gehe-Stiftung,* 1903, *9.*

Simmel, G. "The Metropolis and Mental Life." In *The Sociology of Georg Simmel.* (K. H. Wolff, Trans.) New York: Free Press, 1950.

Simon, W., and Gagnon, J. H. "Decline and Fall of the Small Town." In R. French (Ed.), *The Community.* Itasca, Ill.: Peacock, 1969.

Singelmann, J. "The Sectoral Distribution of the Labour Force in Selected European Countries." Unpublished doctoral dissertation, University of Texas at Austin, 1974.

Sjoberg, G. "The Pre-Industrial City." *American Journal of Sociology*, 1955, *60*, 438-445.

Sjoberg, G. *The Pre-Industrial City, Past and Present.* New York: Free Press, 1960.

Sjoberg, G. "Cities in Developing and in Industrial Societies: A Cross-Cultural Analysis." In P. M. Hansen and L. F. Schnore (Eds.), *The Study of Urbanization.* New York: Wiley, 1965.

Sklar, J. "Marriage Regulation and the California Birth Rate." In K. Davis and F. G. Styles (Eds.), *California's Twenty Million: Research Contributions to Population Policy.* Berkeley: Institute of International Studies, University of California, 1971.

Sklare, M. "Intermarriage and the Jewish Future." *Commentary*, 1964, *37*, 46-52.

Sklare, M. "The Jew in American Sociological Thought." *Ethnicity*, 1974, *1*, 151-173.

Sklare, M., and Greenblum, J. *Jewish Identity on the Suburban Frontier: A Study of Group Survival in the Open Society.* New York: Basic Books, 1967.

Skolnick, J. H. *Justice Without Trial.* (2nd ed.) New York: Wiley, 1975.

Slesinger, D. P. "The Relationship of Fertility to Measures of Metropolitan Dominance: A New Look." *Rural Sociology*, 1974, *39*, 350-361.

Smelser, N. *Theory of Collective Behavior.* New York: Free Press, 1963.

Smith, A. *The Theory of Moral Sentiments.* New York: Garland, 1971. (Originally published 1853.)

Smith, B. L. R. "Independence in the Contract State." In B. L. R. Smith and D. C. Hague (Eds.), *The Dilemma of Accountability in Modern Government: Independence Versus Control.* New York: St. Martin's Press, 1971.

Smith, D. S., and Hindus, M. S. "Premarital Pregnancy in America, 1761-1971." *Journal of Interdisciplinary History*, 1975, *5*, 537-570.

Smith, J., Form, W. H., and Stone, G. "Local Intimacy in a Middle-Sized City." *American Journal of Sociology*, 1954, *60*, 276-384.

Smith, R. *The Wired Nation.* New York: Harper & Row, 1972.

Smith, R. E., and Zeitz, D. *American Social Welfare Institutions.* New York: Wiley, 1975.

Smith, T. L. "Sociocultural Changes in Twelve Midwestern

Communities, 1930-70." *Social Science,* 1974, *49,* 195-207.

Smith, T. W. "Satisfaction with Community." Unpublished paper. Chicago: National Opinion Research Center, 1975a.

Smith, T. W. "Satisfaction with Housing." Unpublished paper. Chicago: National Opinion Research Center, 1975b.

Smith, W., and others. *Future Highways and Urban Growth.* New Haven, Conn.: Yale University Press, 1961.

Soares, G. A. D. "The State in Latin America." Mimeograph. Gainesville: University of Florida, 1976.

Sommer, R. *Personal Space.* Englewood Cliffs, N.J.: Prentice-Hall, 1969.

Sommer, R. *Design Awareness.* San Francisco: Rinehart Press, 1972.

Sorokin, P., and Zimmerman, C. C. *Principles of Rural-Urban Sociology.* New York: Holt, Rinehart and Winston, 1929.

Spady, W. G. "The Authority System of the School and Student Unrest." In C. W. Gordon (Ed.), *Uses of the Sociology of Education.* Chicago: National Society for the Study of Education, 1974.

Spate, O. H. K. "Environmentalism." In D. L. Sills (Ed.), *International Encyclopedia of the Social Sciences.* New York: Macmillan, 1968.

Spilerman, S. "The Cause of Racial Disturbance: A Comparison of Alternative Explanations." *American Sociological Review,* 1970, *35,* 627-649.

Stack, C. B. *All Our Kin: Strategies for Survival in a Black Community.* New York: Harper & Row, 1975.

Stanley, M. "Church Adaptation to Urban Social Change: A Typology of Protestant City Congregations." In R. D. Knudten (Ed.), *The Sociology of Religion: An Anthology.* New York: Appleton-Century-Crofts, 1967.

Stark, R., and Glock, C. Y. "Will Ethics Be the Death of Christianity?" In J. K. Hadden (Ed.), *Religion in Radical Transition.* Chicago: Aldine, 1971.

Starkey, M. L. *The Devil in Massachusetts.* New York: Knopf, 1949.

Stearn, J. "Taylor Caldwell's Incredible Psychic Experience—Could She Possibly Have Known Jesus?" *Ladies Home Journal,* October 1972, p. 86.

Steele, E. H., and Jacobs, J. B. "A Theory of Prison Systems." *Crime and Delinquency,* 1975, *21,* 149-162.

Stein, M. *The Eclipse of Community.* New York: Harper & Row, 1960.

Sterling, C. H. "Trends in Daily Newspaper and Broadcast Ownership, 1922-70." *Journalism Quarterly*, 1975, *52*, 247-256, 320.

Sternlieb, G., and Burchell, R. W. *Residential Abandonment: The Tenement Landlord Revisited*. New Brunswick, N.J.: Center for Urban Policy Research, Rutgers University, 1973.

Stinchcombe, A. L. *Rebellion in a High School*. New York: Quadrangle, 1964.

Stone, G. "City Shoppers and Urban Identification." *American Journal of Sociology*, 1954, *60*, 276-284.

Stone, G. "Urban Identification and the Sociology of Sport." Paper presented at the annual meeting of the American Association for the Advancement of Science, 1968.

Stouffer, S. *Communism, Conformity, and Civil Liberties*. New York: Doubleday, 1955.

Stouffer, S., and others. *The American Soldier*. Princeton, N.J.: Princeton University Press, 1949.

Stout, H. S. "Ethnicity: The Vital Center of Religion in America." *Ethnicity*, 1975, *2*, 204-224.

Street, D. "Public Education and Social Welfare in the Metropolis." In M. Zald (Ed.), *Organizing for Community Welfare*. New York: Quadrangle, 1967.

Street, D. (Ed.). *Innovation in Mass Education*. New York: Wiley, 1969.

Street, W. P. "The Reader's Digest, Educator." Unpublished doctoral dissertation, Northwestern University, Evanston, Ill., 1946.

Summers, A. A., and Wolfe, B. L. *Equality of Educational Opportunity Quantified: A Production Function Approach*. Philadelphia: Department of Research, Federal Reserve Bank of Philadelphia, 1975.

Sussman, M. B., and Burchinal, L. "Kin Family Network: Unheralded Structure in Current Conceptualizations of Family Functioning." *Marriage and Family Living*, 1962, *24*, 231-240.

Suttles, G. D. *The Social Order of the Slum: Ethnicity and Territory in the Inner City*. Chicago: University of Chicago Press, 1968.

Suttles, G. D. *The Social Construction of Communities*. Chicago: University of Chicago Press, 1972.

Suttles, G. D. "Community Design: The Search for Participation in a Metropolitan Society." In A. H. Hawley and V. P. Rock (Eds.), *Metropolitan America in Contemporary Perspectives*. New York: Halsted Press, 1975.

Swados, H. "Less Work—Less Leisure." In E. Larrabee and R.

Meyersohn (Eds.), *Mass Leisure.* New York: Free Press, 1958.

Swanson, G. E. *The Birth of the Gods: The Origin of Primitive Beliefs.* Ann Arbor: University of Michigan Press, 1964.

Swanson, G. E. "Modern Secularity: Its Meaning, Sources, and Interpretation." In D. R. Cutler (Ed.), *The Religious Situation, 1968.* Boston: Beacon Press, 1968.

Sweetser, F. *Neighborhood Acquaintance and Association: A Study of Personal Neighborhoods.* New York: Columbia University Library, 1941.

Switzer, E. "Chicago Settlements, 1972: An Overview." *Social Service Review,* 1973, *47,* 581-593.

Taeuber, C., and Taeuber, I. B. *The Changing Population of the United States.* New York: Wiley, 1958.

Taeuber, I. B. "Growth of the Population of the United States in the Twentieth Century." In C. F. Westoff and R. Park, Jr. (Eds.), *Demographic and Social Aspects of Population Growth.* Vol. 1. Washington, D.C.: U.S. Commission on Population Growth and the American Future, 1972.

Taeuber, K. E. "Cohort Population Redistribution and the Urban Hierarchy." *Milbank Memorial Fund Quarterly,* 1965, *43,* 450-562.

Taeuber, K. E. "Race and the Metropolis: A Demographic Perspective on the 1970s." *Studies in Racial Segregation,* 1975, *3,* 1-30.

Taeuber, K. E., and Taeuber, A. F. *Negroes in Cities: Residential Segregation and Neighborhood Change.* New York: Atheneum, 1965.

Tarver, J. D. "Patterns of Population Change Among Southern Nonmetropolitan Towns, 1950-70." *Rural Sociology,* 1972, *36,* 53-72.

Tarver, J. D., and Beale, C. L. "Relationship of Changes in Employment and Age Composition to the Population Changes of Southern Nonmetropolitan Towns." *Rural Sociology,* 1969, *34,* 16-28.

Taub, R., and others. "Urban Voluntary Associations, Locality Based and Externally Induced." *American Journal of Sociology,* 1977, *83,* 425-442.

Taylor, L., and Jones, A. R. *Rural Life and Urbanized Society.* New York: Oxford University Press, 1964.

Tebbel, J. *The American Magazine: A Compact History.* New York: Hawthorne Books, 1969.

Tebbel, J. *The Media in America.* New York: Crowell, 1974.

Theodorson, G. A. (Ed.). *Studies in Human Ecology.* New York: Harper & Row, 1961.

Thernstrom, S. *Poverty and Progress: Social Mobility in a Nineteenth-Century City.* Cambridge, Mass.: Harvard University Press, 1964.

Thomas, B. *Migration and Economic Growth: A Study of Great Britain and the Atlantic Economy.* Cambridge, England: Cambridge University Press, 1973.

Thomas, W. I. *The Unadjusted Girl.* Chicago: University of Chicago Press, 1927.

Thomas, W. I., and Znaniecki, F. *The Polish Peasant in Europe and America.* New York: Dover, 1958. (Originally published in five volumes, 1918-1920.)

Thomas, W. L. *Man's Role in Changing the Face of the Earth.* Chicago: University of Chicago Press, 1956.

Thompson, E. P. *The Making of the English Working Class.* Middlesex, England: Penguin Books, 1970.

Thrasher, F. M. *The Gang: A Study of 1313 Gangs in Chicago.* Chicago: University of Chicago Press, 1926.

Tichenor, P., Donahue, G., and Olien, C. "Mass Media Flow and Differential Growth in Knowledge." *Public Opinion Quarterly,* 1970, *33,* 197-209.

Tifft, L. L., and Bordua, D. J. "Police Organization and Future Research." *Journal of Research in Crime and Delinquency,* 1969, *6,* 167-176.

Tilley, C. *An Urban World.* Boston: Little, Brown, 1974.

Time. "Digest Suspended." March 7, 1938, p. 55.

Time. "Un-Digest-ed." February 21, 1944, p. 43.

Time. "Dig You Later." December 10, 1945, pp. 58-59.

Time. "To Take the Pressure Off." April 27, 1953, pp. 50-51.

Timms, D. W. G. *The Urban Mosaic: Towards a Theory of Residential Differentiation.* Cambridge, England: Cambridge University Press, 1971.

Titmuss, R. M. *The Gift Relationship.* New York: Pantheon, 1971.

Tobin, G. A. "Suburbanization and the Development of Motor Transportation: Transportation and the Suburbanization Process." In B. Schwartz (Ed.), *The Changing Face of the Suburbs.* Chicago: University of Chicago Press, 1976.

Tomasson, R. F. "Religion is Irrelevant in Sweden." In J. K. Haddon (Ed.), *Religion in Radical Transition.* Chicago: Aldine, 1971.

Tönnies, F. *Community and Society.* (C. P. Loomis, Trans. & Ed.) East Lansing: Michigan State University Press, 1957.

Truman, D. B. *The Governmental Process: Political Interests and Public Opinion.* New York: Knopf, 1951.

Tucker, C. J. "Changing Patterns of Migration Between Metropolitan and Nonmetropolitan Areas in the United States: Recent Evidence." *Demography,* 1976, *13,* 435-44.

Turner, R. H. "Sponsored and Contest Mobility and the School System." *American Sociological Review,* 1960, *25,* 855-867.

Turner, R. H. *The Social Context of Ambition.* Scranton, Pa.: Chandler, 1964.

Uhlenberg, P. "Cohort Variations in Family Life Cycle Experiences of U.S. Females." *Journal of Marriage and the Family,* 1974, *36,* 284-292.

Uniform Crime Reports, 1975. Washington, D.C.: U.S. Government Printing Office, 1976.

United Nations. *Statistical Yearbook, 1963.* New York: Statistical Office of the United Nations, 1964.

United Nations. *Growth of the World's Urban and Rural Population 1920-2000.* Population Studies No. 44. New York: Statistical Office of the United Nations, 1969.

U.S. Bureau of the Census. *Historical Statistics of the United States, Colonial Times to 1957.* Washington, D.C.: U.S. Government Printing Office, 1960.

U.S. Bureau of the Census. *County and City Data Book, 1962.* Washington, D.C.: U.S. Government Printing Office, 1962.

U.S. Bureau of the Census. *Current Population Reports.* Series P-20, No. 221. "Characteristics of the Population by Ethnic Origins." Washington, D.C.: U.S. Government Printing Office, 1969.

U.S. Bureau of the Census. *City Government Finances in 1968-69.* Washington, D.C.: U.S. Government Printing Office, 1970a.

U.S. Bureau of the Census. *Census of Business and Manufacturing, 1970.* Washington, D.C.: U.S. Government Printing Office, 1970b.

U.S. Bureau of the Census. *Current Population Reports.* Series P-20, No. 218. "Household and Family Characteristics: March 1970." Washington, D.C.: U.S. Government Printing Office, 1971a.

U.S. Bureau of the Census. *Mobility of the Population of the United States: March 1969 to March 1970.* Washington, D.C.: U.S. Government Printing Office, 1971b.

U.S. Bureau of the Census. *Current Population Reports.* Series P-23, No. 42. "The Social and Economic Status of the Black Population of the United States." Washington, D.C.: U.S. Government Printing Office, 1972.

U.S. Bureau of the Census. *Census of Governments, 1972.* Vol. 1: *Governmental Organization.* Washington, D.C.: U.S. Government Printing Office, 1973a.

U.S. Bureau of the Census. *County and City Data Book, 1972.* Washington, D.C.: U.S. Government Printing Office, 1973b.

U.S. Bureau of the Census. *Current Population Reports.* Series P-20, No. 271. "Marital Status and Living Arrangements: March 1974." Washington, D.C.: U.S. Government Printing Office, 1974.

U.S. Bureau of the Census. *Mobility of the Population of the United States: March 1970 to March 1975.* Washington, D.C.: U.S. Government Printing Office, 1975a.

U.S. Bureau of the Census. *Current Population Reports.* Series P-23, No. 55. "Social and Economic Characteristics of the Metropolitan and Nonmetropolitan Population: 1974 and 1970." Washington, D.C.: U.S. Government Printing Office, 1975b.

U.S. Bureau of the Census. *Historical Statistics of the United States.* Washington, D.C.: U.S. Government Printing Office, 1975c.

U.S. Bureau of the Census. *Current Population Reports.* Series P-20, No. 276. "Household and Family Characteristics: March 1974." Washington, D.C.: U.S. Government Printing Office, 1975d.

U.S. Bureau of the Census. *Statistical Abstract of the United States.* Washington, D.C.: U.S. Government Printing Office, 1975e.

U.S. Bureau of the Census. *Current Population Reports.* Series P-23, No. 58. "A Statistical Portrait of Women in the United States." Washington, D.C.: U.S. Government Printing Office, 1976.

U.S. Department of Agriculture. *Farm Population Migration to and From Farms, 1920-1954.* Washington, D.C.: U.S. Government Printing Office, 1954.

U.S. Department of Labor. *1975 Handbook on Women Workers.* Washington, D.C.: U.S. Government Printing Office, 1975.

U.S. Senate Committee on Interior and Insular Affairs. *The Recreation Imperative.* Senate Hearing, 2nd session. Washington, D.C.: U.S. Government Printing Office, 1975.

Uyeki, E. S. "Residential Distribution and Stratification, 1950-1960." *American Journal of Sociology*, 1964, *69*, 491-498.

Uzzell, J. D., and Provencher, R. *Urban Anthropology*. Dubuque, Iowa: Brown, 1976.

Vanek, J. "Time Spent in Housework." *Scientific American*, 1974, *231*, 116-120.

Van Howyk, J. "The Bars and Taverns of Times Square." Unpublished Research Report, Cooperative Research Unit. New York: Graduate School, City University of New York, 1977.

Veblen, T. *The Theory of the Leisure Class*. New York: Mentor Books, 1953.

Veevers, J. E. "Factors in the Incidence of Childlessness in Canada: An Analysis of Census Data." *Social Biology*, 1972, *19*, 266-274.

Veevers, J. E. "Voluntarily Childless Wives." *Sociology and Social Research*, 1973, *57*, 356-365.

Venturi, R., Brown, D. S., and Izenour, S. *Learning from Las Vegas*. Cambridge, Mass.: M.I.T. Press, 1973.

Verba, S., and Nie, N. *Participation in America: Political Democracy and Social Equality*. New York: Harper & Row, 1972.

Verbrugge, L. M., and Taylor, R. B. "Consequences of Population Density: Testing New Hypotheses." Working Paper. Baltimore: Center for Metropolitan Planning and Research, Johns Hopkins University, 1976.

Veysey, L. *The Emergence of the American University*. Chicago: University of Chicago Press, 1965.

Vidich, A. J., and Bensman, J. *Small Town in Mass Society*. New York: Doubleday, 1958.

Vidich, A. J., and Bensman, J. "The Springdale Case: Academic Bureaucrats and Sensitive Townspeople." In A. J. Vidich, J. Bensman, and M. Stein (Eds.), *Reflections on Community Studies*. New York: Harper & Row, 1964.

Vidich, A. J., and Bensman, J. *Small Town in Mass Society*. (rev. ed.) Princeton, N.J.: Princeton University Press, 1968.

Vidmar, N., and Rokeach, M. "Archie Bunker's Bigotry: A Study in Selective Perception." *Journal of Communication*, 1974, *24*, 36-47.

Villemez, W. J., and Kasarda, J. D. "Veteran Status and Socioeconomic Attainment." *Armed Forces and Society*, 1976, *2*, 407-420.

Wade, R. "The End of the Self-Sufficient City: New York's

Fiscal Crisis in History." *Urbanism Past and Present,* 1976-1977, pp. 1-4.

Wall Street Journal. "Plummeting PMs." May 25, 1976, pp. 1, 18.

Wallerstein, I. *The Modern World System.* New York: Academic Press, 1974a.

Wallerstein, I. "The Rise and Future Demise of the World Capitalist System: Concepts for Comparative Analysis." *Comparative Studies in Society and History,* 1974b, *16,* 387-415.

Walton, J. "The Vertical Axis of Community Organization and the Structure of Power." In C. Bonjean and others (Eds.), *Community Politics.* New York: Free Press, 1971.

Wallis, W. D. "Environmentalism." *Encyclopedia of the Social Sciences,* 1931, *5,* 561-566.

Ward, D. "The Emergence of Central Immigrant Ghettoes in American Cities: 1840-1920." *Annals of the Association of American Geographers,* 1968, *58,* 343-359.

Ward, D. *Cities and Immigrants: A Geography of Change in Nineteenth-Century America.* New York: Oxford University Press, 1971.

Ward, J., and Gaziano, C. "A New Variety of Urban Press: Neighborhood Public Affairs Publications." *Journalism Quarterly,* 1976, *53,* 61-67, 116.

Ward, S. K. "Methodological Considerations in the Study of Population Density and Social Pathology." *Human Ecology,* 1975, *3,* 275-286.

Warner, W. K. "Rural Society in a Post-Industrial Age." *Rural Sociology,* 1974, *39,* 306-318.

Warner, W. L. *Yankee City.* New Haven, Conn.: Yale University Press, 1963.

Warner, W. L., and Lunt, P. S. *The Social Life of a Modern Community.* New Haven, Conn.: Yale University Press, 1941.

Warner, W. L., and Srole, L. *The Social Systems of American Ethnic Groups.* New Haven, Conn.: Yale University Press, 1945.

Warner, W. L., and others. *Democracy in Jonesville: A Study in Quality and Inequality.* New York: Harper & Row, 1949.

Warren, C. *A History of the American Bar.* New York: Fertig, 1966.

Warren, D. I. *Black Neighborhoods.* Ann Arbor: University of Michigan Press, 1975.

Warren, R. L. *The Community in America.* Chicago: Rand McNally, 1963.

Warren, R. L. "A Note on Walton's Analysis of Power Structure and Vertical Ties." In C. Bonjean and others (eds.), *Community Politics.* New York: Free Press, 1971.

Warren, R. L. *The Community in America.* (2nd ed.) Chicago: Rand McNally, 1972.

Weaver, C. Unpublished Attendance Report. New York: American Museum of Natural History, 1973.

Webber, M. M. "Order in Diversity: Community without Propinquity." In L. Wingo (Ed.), *Cities and Space: The Future Use of Urban Land.* Baltimore: Johns Hopkins University Press, 1963.

Weber, A. F. *The Growth of Cities in the Nineteenth Century.* Ithaca, N.Y.: Cornell University Press, 1963. (Originally published 1899.)

Weber, M. *The City.* (D. Martindale and G. Neuwirth, Trans. and Eds.) New York: Free Press, 1958.

Weber, M. *General Economic History.* (F. H. Knight, Trans.) New York: Collier, 1961.

Weiss, W. "The Effects of the Mass Media of Communication." In G. Lindzey and E. Aronson (Eds.), *Handbook of Social Psychology.* Vol. 5. (2nd ed.) Reading, Mass.: Addison-Wesley, 1969.

Wellman, B. "Urban Connections." Research Paper No. 84. Toronto: Center for Urban and Community Studies, University of Toronto, 1976.

Wertham, F. *Seduction of the Innocent.* New York: Holt, Rinehart and Winston, 1954.

West, J. *Plainville, U.S.A.* New York: Columbia University Press, 1945.

Westoff, C. F. "Differential Fertility in the United States: 1900 to 1952." *American Sociological Review,* 1954, *19,* 549-567.

White, M., and White, L. *The Intellectual Versus the City.* New York: Mentor Books, 1962.

Whyte, W. F. *Street Corner Society.* Chicago: University of Chicago Press, 1943.

Whyte, Jr., W. H. *The Organization Man.* New York: Simon & Schuster, 1956.

Whyte, Jr., W. H. "Urban Sprawl." In *The Exploding Metropolis,* by the editors of *Fortune.* New York: Doubleday, 1958.

Whyte, Jr., W. H. *The Last Landscape.* New York: Doubleday, 1970.

Wicker, A. W. "Attitudes Versus Actions: The Relationship of Verbal and Overt Responses to Attitude Objects." *Journal of Social Issues,* 1969, *25,* 41-78.

Wilburn, Y. *The Withering Away of The City.* Bloomington: Indiana University Press, 1964.

Wilensky, H. L. "Uneven Distribution of Leisure: The Impact of Economic Growth on Free Time." In E. O. Smigel (Ed.), *Work and Leisure.* New Haven, Conn.: College and University Press, 1963.

Wilensky, H. L. "Mass Society and Mass Culture: Interdependence or Independence?" *American Sociological Review,* 1964, *29,* 173-196.

Wilensky, H. L. "The Problems and Prospects of the Welfare State." In H. L. Wilensky and C. N. Lebeaux (Eds.), *Industrial Society and Social Welfare.* New York: Free Press, 1965.

Wilensky, H. L. *The Welfare State and Equality: Structural and Ideological Roots of Public Expenditures.* Berkeley: University of California Press, 1975.

Wiley, N. F. "The Ethnic Mobility Trap and Stratification Theory." *Social Problems,* 1967, *15,* 147-159.

Wilkinson, K. P. "Rural Community Change." In T. Ford (Ed.), *Rural USA: Persistence and Changes.* Ames: Iowa State University Press, in press.

Willets, F. K., Bealer, R. C., and Crider, D. M. "Leveling of Attitudes in Mass Society: Rurality and Traditional Morality in America." *Rural Sociology,* 1973, *38,* 36-45.

Willets, F. K., Bealer, R. C., and Crider, D. M. "The Ecology of Social Traditionalism in a Rural Hinterland." *Rural Sociology,* 1974, *39,* 334-349.

Willhelm, S. M. *Urban Zoning and Land-Use Theory.* New York: Free Press, 1962.

Williams, M. D. *Community in a Black Pentecostal Church: An Anthropological. Study.* Pittsburgh: University of Pittsburgh Press, 1974.

Williams, Jr., R. M. "Race and Ethnic Relations." *Annual Review of Sociology,* 1975, *1,* 125-164.

Williams, T., and Goering, J. "The Black Theatre Alliance: Institutional Analysis and Audience Survey." New York: Department of Sociology, Graduate School, City University of New York, 1977.

Wilner, D. M., and others. *The Housing Environment and Family Life.* Baltimore: Johns Hopkins University Press, 1962.

Wilson, A. B. "Educational Consequences of Segregation in a California Community." In U.S. Commission on Civil Rights, *Racial Isolation in the Public Schools.* Washington, D.C.: U.S. Government Printing Office, 1967.

Wilson, J. Q. (Ed.). *Urban Renewal.* Cambridge, Mass.: M.I.T. Press, 1966.

Wilson, J. Q. "The Urban Unease: Community Versus City." *The Public Interest,* 1968a, *12,* 25-39.

Wilson, J. Q. *Varieties of Police Behavior.* Cambridge, Mass.: Harvard University Press, 1968b.

Winch, R. F., and Greer, S. A. "Urbanism, Ethnicity, and Extended Familism." *Journal of Marriage and Family,* 1968, *30,* 40-45.

Winick, C. "Some Observations on Characteristics of Patrons of Adult Theaters and Bookstores." *Technical Report of the Commission on Obscenity and Pornography.* Vol. 3. Washington, D.C.: U.S. Government Printing Office, 1971.

Winsborough, H. H. *A Comparative Study of Urban Population Densities.* Chicago: University of Chicago Press, 1961.

Winsborough, H. H. "An Ecological Approach to the Theory of Suburbanization." *American Journal of Sociology,* 1963, *68,* 565-570.

Winsborough, H. H. "The Social Consequences of High Population Density." *Law and Contemporary Problems,* 1965, *30,* 120-126.

Winter, G. *The Suburban Captivity of the Churches.* New York: Doubleday, 1961.

Winter, G. "Methodological Reflections on 'The Religious Factor.' " In R. D. Knudten (Ed.), *The Sociology of Religion: An Anthology.* New York: Appleton-Century-Crofts, 1967.

Wirt, F. M. "Alioto and the Politics of Hyperpluralism." *Transaction,* 1970, *7,* 44-55.

Wirt, F. M., and Kirst, M. W. *The Political Webs of American Schools.* Boston: Little, Brown, 1972.

Wirt, F., and others. *On the City's Rim: Politics and Policy in Suburbia.* Lexington, Mass.: Heath, 1972.

Wirth, L. *The Ghetto.* Chicago: University of Chicago Press, 1928.

Wirth, L. "Urbanism as a Way of Life." *American Journal of Sociology,* 1938, *44,* 1-24.

Wirth, L. "Housing as a Field of Sociological Research." *American Sociological Review,* 1947, *12,* 137-143.

Wood, J. P. *Magazines in the United States.* (3rd ed.) New York: Ronald Press, 1971.

Wood, R. C. *Suburbia: Its People and Their Politics.* Boston: Houghton Mifflin, 1958.

Wood, R. C. *Metropolis Against Itself.* New York: Committee for Economic Development, 1959.

Wood, R. C. *1400 Governments.* Cambridge, Mass.: Harvard University Press, 1961.

Woodward, C. V. *The Strange Career of Jim Crow.* (2nd rev. ed.) New York: Oxford University Press, 1966.

Wright, C. *Mass Communication: A Sociological Perspective.* (2nd ed.) New York: Random House, 1975.

Wright, W. *Sixguns and Society.* Berkeley: University of California Press, 1975.

Yancey, W. L. "Architecture, Interaction, and Social Control: The Case of a Large-Scale Public Housing Project." *Environment and Behavior,* 1971, *3,* 3-21.

Yancey, W. L., and others. *Patterns of Leisure in the Inner City.* Nashville: Urban and Regional Development Center of Vanderbilt University, 1971.

Ylvisaker, P. "Diversity and the Public Interest: Two Cases in Metropolitan Decision Making." *American Institute of Planners Journal,* 1961, *27,* 109-113.

Youmans, E. G. "Small Town Life in America." *Small Town,* 1976, *6,* 6-10.

Young, M., and Willmott, P. *Family and Kinship in East London.* New York: Penguin, 1957.

Young, M., and Willmott, P. *The Symmetrical Family.* Middlesex: Penguin, 1977.

Zald, M. N. "The Structure of Society and Social Service Integration." *Social Science Quarterly,* 1969, *50,* 257-267.

Zald, M. N. *Organizational Change: The Political Economy of the YMCA.* Chicago: University of Chicago Press, 1970.

Zald, M. N., and Denton, P. "From Evangelism to General Service: On the Transformation and Character of the YMCA." *Administrative Science Quarterly,* 1963, *8,* 214-234.

Zeigler, L. H., and Jennings, M. K. *Governing American Schools: Political Interaction in Local School Districts.* North Scituate, Mass.: Duxbury Press, 1974.

Zeisel, J. "Symbolic Meaning of Space and the Physical Dimension of Social Relations: A Case Study of Sociological Research as the Basis of Architectural Planning." In J. Walton and D. Carns (Eds.), *Cities in Change: Studies in the Urban Condition.* Boston: Allyn & Bacon, 1973.

Zeisel, J. *Sociology and Architectural Design.* New York: Russell Sage Foundation, 1975.

Zeisel, J., and Griffin, M. *Charlesview Housing: A Diagnostic Evaluation.* Cambridge, Mass.: Graduate School of Design, Architecture Research Office, Harvard University, 1974.

Zimmer, B. G. "The Urban Centrifugal Drift." In A. H. Hawley and V. P. Rock (Eds.), *Metropolitan America in Contemporary Perspective.* New York: Halsted Press, 1975.

Zimmer, B. G. "Suburbanization and Changing Political Structures." In B. Schwartz (Ed.), *The Changing Face of the Suburbs.* Chicago: University of Chicago Press, 1976.

Zimmer, B. G., and Hawley, A. H. *Metropolitan Area Schools.* Beverly Hills, Calif.: Sage, 1968.

Zimmerman, J. "The Patchwork Approach: Adaptive Responses to Increasing Urbanization." In A. H. Hawley and V. P. Rock (Eds.), *Metropolitan America in Contemporary Perspective.* New York: Halsted Press, 1975.

Zlutnick, S., and Altman, I. "Crowding and Human Behavior." In J. F. Wohlwill and D. H. Carson (Eds.), *Behavioral Science and the Problems of Our Environment.* Washington, D.C.: American Psychological Association, 1972.

Zorbaugh, H. W. *The Gold Coast and the Slum.* Chicago: University of Chicago Press, 1929.

Zuckerman, M. "The Social Content of Democracy in Massachusetts." *William and Mary Quarterly,* 1968, *25,* 523-544.

Zuckerman, M. *Peaceable Kingdoms: New England Towns in the Eighteenth Century.* New York: Knopf, 1970.

Zuzanek, J. *Leisure and Social Change.* Unpublished manuscript, Department of Recreation, University of Waterloo, Waterloo, Ontario, 1976.

Name Index

Subject Index

727

728 Subject Index